Programming with MFC
for Windows™ 95

Programming with MFC
for Windows™ 95

Vic Broquard

For book and bookstore information

http://www.prenhall.com

Prentice Hall PTR
Upper Saddle River, NJ 07458

Library of Congress Cataloging-in-Publication Data

```
Broquard, Victor E.
    Programming with MFC for Windows 95 / Vic Broquard.
       p.  cm.
    Includes bibliographical references and index.
    ISBN 0-13-459546-7 (paper)
    1. Microsoft Windows (Computer file). 2. Microsoft foundation
    class library. 3. Operating systems (Computers). I. Title.
    QA76.76.063B743  1996
    005.265—dc20                              96-14786
                                              CIP
```

Editorial/production supervision: *BooksCraft, Inc., Indianapolis, IN*
Cover design director: *Jerry Votta*
Cover design: *Joseph Sengotta*
Acquisitions editor: *Paul Becker*
Manufacturing manager: *Alexis R. Heydt*

© 1996 by Prentice Hall PTR
Prentice-Hall, Inc.
A Simon & Schuster Company
Upper Saddle River, NJ 07458

The publisher offers discounts on this book when ordered in bulk quantities.
For more information, contact:

Corporate Sales Department
Prentice Hall PTR
One Lake Street
Upper Saddle River, NJ 07458
Phone: 800-382-3419   Fax: 201-236-7141
E-mail: corpsales@prenhall.com

Printed in the United States of America

10 9 8 7 6 5 4 3 2 1

ISBN: 0-13-459546-7

Prentice-Hall International (UK) Limited, *London*
Prentice-Hall of Australia Pty. Limited, *Sydney*
Prentice-Hall Canada Inc., *Toronto*
Prentice-Hall Hispanoamericana, S.A., *Mexico*
Prentice-Hall of India Private Limited, *New Delhi*
Prentice-Hall of Japan, Inc., *Tokyo*
Simon & Schuster Asia Pte. Ltd., *Singapore*
Editora Prentice-Hall do Brasil, Ltda., *Rio de Janeiro*

To all of my dedicated, persevering students,
and to L. Ron Hubbard who taught me to "Simplify"

Table of Contents

Introduction

Learning to program Windows applications is most challenging; some call it a "black art." To master the material presented in this book, the industry typically allows a beginner a total of 4 months of 40-hour weeks. Don't panic just yet! This book greatly shortens that learning process! I have been successfully teaching Windows programming at a junior college for some time now and we just do not have that kind of time available in a 16-week semester.

For whom is this book designed? Who can benefit? This book uses Microsoft's Visual C++ and the Microsoft Foundation Class (MFC) library. Although designed for beginners and not-yet master Windows programmers, the book should prove valuable for those who wish to learn how to use some of the new Windows 95 features; for those who must port existing Windows 3.1 applications to the Windows 95 platform; and for those who know other class libraries, such as Borland's Object Windows Library (OWL), and wish to learn or convert applications to the MFC. This book has such a broad appeal because of its approach and the materials covered.

We begin with fundamentals and in a step-by-step, gradient manner develop most of the basic Windows 95 programming techniques. There are often many different ways to accomplish the same task. So as you move from example to example, expect to see many alternative approaches illustrated. Since this is not a reference manual, expect also to see the reasons behind the approaches and techniques. It is my opinion that if you have a feel for what is really going on, you can do a better job of programming and debugging.

I have included many of the features that are new to Windows 95 (not available in Windows 3.1) that can be handled easily at a beginning or intermediate level. These include spin controls, property sheets (tabbed dialogs), splitter windows, and DIB Sections. If you already know some Windows programming, you can extend your abilities with these new controls.

I think you will find the sample programs most useful, because they are designed to provide you with a usable shell or model to follow in your applications. The later chapter examples are not just snippets of coding that illustrate the topic at hand, but rather are more robust, real-world examples. Two chapters illustrate how printing and print preview are done. In chapter 7 you will see how to first create dialog boxes and then how to migrate them into the new property sheet control. One sample program in chapter 9 shows you several methods of displaying on the screen a bmp image and numerous "special effects" to catch your user's attention. In chapter 14 we discuss splash screens and graphical pictures or logos that are visible while the application is launching and initializing itself. Sample programs in chapter 14 show you how to set up animated presentations and how to begin game animation using the blazingly fast DIB Section. In chapter 15 we discuss the complex Document-View architecture in depth. Here we use splitter windows to present a narrow window on the left that contains editable company sales data and on the right, a bar chart plot of that data, which automatically redraws itself as the sales data are changed by the user.

Scattered throughout the book are porting tips for converting Windows 3.1 applications to Windows 95. These are marked by **Windows 3.1 Porting Tip.** In a similar fashion, a number of important application design issues are marked as **Design Rule.** You should consider the significance of both the porting and design guidelines as they apply to your circumstances; they highlight some of the potential traps and pitfalls that await.

Perhaps the biggest barrier to learning Windows 95 programming is the enormous number of identifiers, key values, API and MFC class member functions, and variable names. The name-space pollution exceeds anything that I have ever come across, short of that involved in writing an operating system. This proliferation of must-know names and identifiers is nothing short of bewildering. In fact, I still remember my first session with Windows programming and the untold hours I spent just trying to figure out which names had to be coded exactly as given and which were under my control! One of the *key* features of this book is that our typeface conventions tell you at a glance which names are yours and which are not. All variable names are in lowercase; if it's lowercase, it's yours to name. The two exceptions are #define names which, by programming convention, are always uppercase, and class member function names which are capitalized. All function names that belong to the API and MFC classes are also in bold print to distinguish them from our own member functions. When I derive a class from one of the MFC classes, although capitalized, it will not be in boldface. So, even though you may use any convention you want in your own coding, when you refer to this book, the guesswork has been eliminated.

What do you already need to know to make effective use of this book? My assumption is that you know C and C++ and are comfortable with both. You do not need to be a C++ master. Many introductory books spend several chapters on a "crash course" in C++. I do not. If you feel you need a review of C++ or want to know more about C++ principles, browse through the bibliography. I have provided a brief description of many of the available books on Windows programming.

This book does not use the famous (or infamous) "Application-Class Wizards." Microsoft provides "wizards" that are supposed to enable one to rapidly create an application—button-pushing style. Some swear by them, others swear at them. I am involved in both the teaching and consulting industries, and I have heard both viewpoints. It is my opinion—and the opinion of many of my past students—that the wizards are not the best beginning point for learning to program Windows. Rather, the wizards should be considered an advanced topic, for use by those who already are familiar with Windows programming. There are many books on the market that are devoted to the use of the wizards. When you have completed your study of this book, you will find yourself fully prepared to explore the wizards and be able to make good use of them.

This book will be of great value to programmers who are already using another manufacturer's class library—Borland's OWL in particular. While you may be quite content to know how to program Windows 95 with just one of the class libraries, sooner or later, you will find a need for the other. You may find a magazine article showing how to do the very thing you have always wanted to be able to do, but it uses the "wrong" class library. Many of us in the consulting industry must be able to support both platforms. Perhaps you wish to take a new job, but the new company uses the other class library. Note that I've written, and Prentice-Hall is publishing, a companion book that presents parallel versions of all the examples in this one, using Borland's OWL. With the two, you can easily see how to convert from one library to another.

A word about the copyright of the sample programs: you are free to use the sample programs and any of the coding in any of your applications. No permission is required. However, if you do not substantially alter my coding, it would be nice of you to acknowledge my contribution. Of course, I assume no responsibility for any adverse effects of the sample programs—the old "use at your own risk."

If you have any questions, problems, comments, bugs to report, or just want to chat, I can be reached on CompuServe: member ID: 71641,1203 Vic Broquard or on the Internet as vBroquard@flink.com. (Note: I do not logon every day, so it may be a few days before I get your message, but I always answer my mail.)

Please note that this book is a learner's manual and is not intended to be a reference manual. For reference details, consult the documentation or the "On-Line Books" and help that the manufacturer has provided with your product.

SOFTWARE REQUIREMENTS

The Windows API can be programmed in several ways, including C and C++, for example. For this book, I have used Microsoft's Visual C++ 4.0 (MFC version 4.0). Symantec C++ and others can also be used with minor modifications, mostly to the resources, because they use the MFC as well.

THE SAMPLE PROGRAMS ON THE ATTACHED CD

See the next page for directions on installing and using the CD. It contains both the executable versions of all the sample programs and all of the source files and project files. The main folder is \LearnWin. The executables are located in the \LearnWin\Bin folder, while the \LearnWin\Bmp folder contains several bmp image files used for all of the programs.

The sample programs are collected into folders. The folder naming convention is PgmNNL, where NN is the chapter number and L is a letter differentiating among multiple programs in the chapter. Thus, a folder named Pgm05b, would contain the second sample program from Chapter 5.

SAVE A TREE

Some of the programming samples are quite lengthy. Rather than nearly doubling the size of the book (and increasing your cost and using more trees), I refer you to the source files, which are contained on the CD-ROM. You may print out the needed listings or view them on-screen. I know some of you may read the book while not sitting before your computer and the lack of the full coding may be a problem. So I present as much of the coding sequences as possible. Please remember that you are gaining substantial programming samples to follow and not just a book of snippets.

HOW TO USE THE ENCLOSED CD

No setup is required. You can browse and execute from the CD-ROM, but for faster operation or to obtain editable, compilable copies, you should copy the CD-ROM contents to the hard drive of choice. (Long filenames are not used.) You can copy the entire contents to the hard drive by using XCOPY:

```
C>XCOPY x:*.* d: /s
```

where x is your CD-ROM drive letter and d is the desired hard drive letter.

The main folder is called \LearnWin. Executables are in \LearnWin\Bin as well as in the various project\Debug folders. Bitmap images are in \LearnWin\Bmp.

To copy one program sample to hard disk, you also use XCOPY:

```
C>XCOPY x:\LearnWin\Pgm08a\*.* d:\LearnWin\Pgm08a /s
```

Copy \LearnWin\Bmp and its subdirectories for samples that reference bitmap files.

If you use other folder names, you may need to change some coding references in the cpp and re files. This is particularly true for Pgm09b, Pgm14b, Pgm14c, Pgm14d, Pgm15a, and Pgm15b.

The files on the CD-ROM have the read-only attribute set because a CD-ROM is a read-only device. When you copy files to your hard drive, you must remove these attributes before you can modify the files. Use the DOS ATTRIB command.

Use the following command to remove the read-only attribute for all files in all subdirectories of LearnWin:

```
CD\LearnWin
ATTRIB /s /-r
```

Windows 95 Basics

1.1 INTRODUCTION TO WINDOWS 95 PROGRAMMING

For most of us, our programming background is the text-based DOS system. In text mode, the fundamental I/O unit is a character and perhaps its screen color attribute byte. The screen most frequently has 25 rows of 80 characters, with each discrete position capable of holding one character. The location of a specific character on the screen is given by its column and row number, thought of as the x (column) and y (row) coordinates. Each character position occupies the same number of pixels both horizontally and vertically. Some characters use only a few horizontal pixels (the letter I, for example) while others use a maximum number (the letters w and m). The character nature of the text-based mode makes it relatively easy for a program to display a series of characters. And nearly all business data processing programs follow the programming logic of Input a record, Process the record, Output the record. This is the programming logic style with which non-Windows programmers are familiar and comfortable.

In contrast to the DOS text-based modes, Windows 95 is a graphical operating environment. Graphics modes present new and huge complexities compared to text modes. The fundamental I/O unit is now the single pixel. Access to a pixel is still by x and y coordinates, but with SuperVGA monitors, the resolution available varies widely along with the number of colors that can be simultaneously displayed on the screen. The higher the resolution is, the more pixels per inch, the finer the details, and the better the resultant image is. Commonly, graphics modes may contain 640×480, 800×600, or 1024×768 pixels. The screen may simultaneously display 2, 4, 16, 256, or more colors.

Each color mode has its own unique internal scheme for storing the pixel values. The worst case among the more common modes is that of the 256-color mode, in which one pixel's color is stored in 1 byte. Large amounts of video memory are needed to store one screen image in the 1024×768 256-color mode: 1024×768 or 786,432 bytes! And there are even higher resolution and higher color modes. From the viewpoint of architecture, Windows 95 still runs under DOS (although it is not so obvious); DOS still can handle a maximum of only 65,536 bytes at one time in a segment of memory. Thus every hardware manufacturer of SuperVGA boards has devised its own proprietary schemes for producing graphical images. This yields a nightmare for the programmer who is creating a program that must be able to be run on any system. That is, the program must be able to detect which video board is present and have special coding for that specific board—an enormous and thankless task.

Windows 95 completely removes this programming bottleneck. Windows 95 owns the screen and provides the programmer with a standard method of sending data to the screen, providing device independence for the programmer. (Windows 95 device drivers handle the board dependencies under the hood.)

Output in graphics mode is pixel based. Gone is the simple idea of displaying a single character, let alone a character string! A character is composed of a series of pixels that form a letter. Gone is the standard spacing or size that a text character occupies. The letter I, in some fonts, now needs only a width of three pixels (off-on-off), whereas the letter w has a larger width in pixels. The impact: in text mode, all characters have the same width; in graphics mode, characters have a variable width, unless a nonproportional, or fixed, font is used. The two strings—cat and CAT—have the same length in text mode but completely different widths or lengths in pixels if shown in a variable width font. Therefore, in graphics mode, when displaying text, you must consider the "average character widths"—always an imprecise amount. However, the benefit of this scheme is multiple fonts and letter sizes (measured in "points")—fonts that can be scaled to many print sizes.

Windows 95 has a new *Console Interface* to support the simpler text mode I/O programs. This new interface is supposed to be used for simple, short utility programs. It is somewhat similar to the old "Easy Window" DOS wrap-around facility of Windows 3.1.

Windows 95 supports a multitasking environment (the ability to run more than one program concurrently). It adds support for long filenames, adds some new controls, alters the appearance of the common dialog boxes for file open and saves, and has a new desktop and window styles.

However, for a programmer new to the graphical operating environment, Windows 95 forces a new program design mode—gone is the Input, Process, Output logic. The overall processing design of *every* Windows 95 application *must* be as follows:

```
get a message
while there is another message to process
  process the message
```

```
    get another message
    end the program
```

This cycle of get/process a message is the highest level logic of every Windows 95 program:

Imagine that the user has a WordPad session going, a Paintbrush image under construction, and a Solitaire game in progress, *and* the user has all these nicely tiled on screen and is moving among them. Suppose you are writing the Notepad type of program: you no longer own the screen; you are sharing it with these other applications! Further, the user can resize your editor window at any time, affecting which text in your editor window can be visible.

From time to time, a Windows 95 application is called upon to redraw what is currently visible on the screen. Thus, nearly all Windows 95 applications have a function (called Paint) that, when Windows 95 (not necessarily the application itself) requests it, can at *any* moment redisplay the application's entire screen. Further, although the application can at some logical point display a message, that same message must somehow become available to the Paint function as well. If a dialog box opens over that message, when it closes, the application's Paint must redisplay that message. This is a very different logic approach indeed.

Actually, Windows 95 owns all the devices on the system, including the keyboard! Things are starting to get complicated quickly.

Memory is the next complication. Under DOS your application can potentially use all memory on the computer—there is only one task running. Often under Windows 95, however, many applications are activated concurrently. In the earlier example, suppose that the WordPad document contained 100,000 bytes and the Paintbrush image was for 256-color 1024×768, requiring nearly 800,000 bytes. Now add in the program exe sizes for WordPad, Paintbrush, and Solitaire. Now do not forget to add in the Windows 95 and DOS code sizes. Then add in SMARTDRV and its 1 megabyte cache. Memory is becoming a scarce commodity. Sure, Windows 95 can swap to disk, but what does that do to speed of execution? Now try to launch a memory-hogging application and real troubles occur.

Thus, at all times, well-behaved Windows 95 applications should keep their memory requirements as small as possible. Couple this guideline with the idea that, at any instant, a user might switch to some other task, requiring a totally different procedure for file handling. Under DOS one would open the file, read records, and close the file at the end of the job. Under Windows 95, to be well behaved, when an application needs a record (even just the next sequential record), it opens the file, reads the required record, closes the file, and *then* processes the record. Never leave a file open any longer than is needed to retrieve the required record.

In summary, the programming logic behind a Windows 95 application is totally different from the logic of the DOS-based applications you have likely seen. The Windows 95 application programming interface (API) consists of over 1000 confusing and sometimes overlapping function calls; many, many data structures used to pass the requisite information to these functions: and hundreds of possible messages to which your application could be called upon to respond. Learning to write Windows 95 applications is indeed a very daunting challenge.

1.2 CODING THE WINDOWS 95 API

To a programmer, the Windows 95 API appears to be C-style. That is, the functions and methods are strictly C. (Internally, Windows 95 is object-oriented—written with a combination of C++, C, and Microassembler.) The external world interface is a C interface.

Therefore, programmers learning how Windows 95 works and how to program the functions generally begin by using C. In fact, you could write all of your Windows 95 applications in C alone. Once the application goes beyond a simple window with perhaps a very few dialogs and minimal menu choices, however, the task of writing the application in C becomes a real nightmare. Global variables abound, and 90% of the program is contained in one message processing "switch" statement. In the industry, this message-processing loop in C is often called "the nightmare switch from Hell."

To preserve your sanity, to get applications debugged quickly, and to get applications written quickly, you will find you want to wrap an object-oriented class library around the Windows 95 API, coding in C++ and using class libraries. In fact, once you become comfortable with the C++ interface, you will never want to go back to the C nightmare.

Unfortunately, C++ is not standardized fully yet—although it soon will be so—and the wraparound class libraries are still manufacturer dependent. With the release of Microsoft Visual C++ 4.0 and the accompanying Microsoft Foundation Class (MFC) library 4.0, writing Windows 95 applications has become easier than ever to do. The focus of this book is on the MFC 4.0; therefore any manufacturer who provides access to MFC 4.0 can be used. (The companion book, *Programming with OWL for Windows 95*, shows how these same sample applications can be done using Borland's C++ 5.0.) There are some smaller, independently written class libraries—see the bibliography—that are even simpler to learn and use. In fact, you can write your own class libraries.

In this book I follow this cycle: first, learn some of the API by studying the C-style API functions, structures, and messages; second, examine how to use the MFC class libraries for the same functions; and then back to C and some more API features. You will find that a large portion of the class library member functions are just an encapsulation of the corresponding C-style API functions. Therefore, you need to become somewhat familiar with the rudiments of the C-style API approach.

Normally one would not write the complete program in Microassembler. Quite often, you will find real-world applications written mainly in C++ with some C-style coding (especially in file handling) with limited Microassembler coding at critical speed points.

1.3 CONVERTING A WINDOWS 3.1 APPLICATION TO A WINDOWS 95 APPLICATION

Although I assume that most readers are new to Windows programming, this book is also valuable for those with previous Windows 3.1 programming experience. For those readers who may already have some familiarity writing Windows 3.1 applications,

there are also sections devoted to the Windows 3.1 conversion process. For the beginning applications that this text addresses, those changes are fairly small. But there
are several important stylistic changes. Perhaps the most significant changes include
the use of the flat memory model in place of the DOS segmented models, the extreme
ease of changing what used to be relatively "constant" values such as the video resolution, and the new common dialogs and controls.

1.4 COMMON WINDOWS 95 GRAPHICAL OBJECTS

To begin programming an application in Windows 95, a programmer must be thor-
oughly acquainted with the labels assigned to the many Windows 95 graphical elements. Therefore, we begin our study of Windows 95 programming with a quick
review of the key graphical elements. Note the "official" names of these elements
because they are often referred to in the literature.

All applications run in a *window* of some kind. Often the application has a border around the main window, facilitating window resizing. This is called a *frame window* and the area inside the frame window is known as the *client window*. Figure 1.1
identifies the major elements of the frame and client windows. All windows have a
title bar (1), which contains the descriptive name of the application. Each application
provides a character string to be used as the window's title, which may change while
the application is running. For example, the WordPad program inserts the document
name before the string WordPad. The *active application* or *task* has its title bar highlighted, while all inactive applications are grayed.

Most title bars contain the *system menu icon* (5), which is used to pull down the
system menu (6). The system menu normally contains choices for restoring the appli-

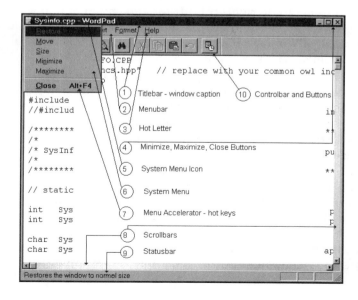

Fig. 1.1 Main Windows 95
Graphical Elements

cation, moving the window, resizing the window, minimizing and maximizing the window, closing the application, and task switching. Many of these are programmer controlled. That is, it is possible to have windows that cannot be resized, that run maximized, and so on. When a menu choice is not available, the menu item is *grayed out*. Windows automatically grays some items for you. If you notify Windows 95 that this window cannot be resized, for example, the Size menu item is grayed. Additionally, you can request Windows 95 to gray other menu items and "ungray" them—recall the operations of the cut and paste options in any editing type sessions.

An application may have one or more *menu accelerators* (7). These are hot keys for specific menu options. Here on the system menu, *Alt+F4* is the menu accelerator or hot key for closing the application. Additionally, and far more commonly, menu items have an underlined letter, the *hot letter* (3). In the system menu, R for restore is underlined; M for move; S for size, and so on. In nonsystem menus, these are programmer defined; when you set up the menu, you can tell Windows 95 which, if any, letter is the hot letter.

Most applications also have a *menu bar* (2). Entries may be added and removed dynamically from the menu bar. Clicking on a menu choice can activate an option or pop up another submenu.

Design Rule 1: **All Windows 95 applications *should* follow the standard Windows 95 look-and- feel design for ease of user operation and speed of user learning.**

To appreciate this rule, play around with the applications in Main and Accessories. Look at the way the various menu bars are constructed. For example, you find that if the application has anything to do with files, then the first menu item on the left is Files. Help is always the last item on the right. If Editing is an option, it follows Files. The hot keys and often the menu accelerators are the same. This common user interface is a major design advantage of Windows 95. Thus, well-behaved applications should follow the normal look-and-feel of Windows 95.

The title bar also may have one or more buttons on the left—the Minimize-Maximize-Normalize buttons and the new Close application or *x* button. These are application controlled; when your program begins execution, it notifies Windows 95 which of these buttons, if any, are allowed. (You can dynamically alter these as well.) If the user activates the Maximize button, for example, Windows sends the application a message telling the application to maximize itself.

With all of the title bar buttons and with the system menu and any user menu bars, all of the details of pushing and releasing, selecting, mouse cursor movement, hot letter pressing, and accelerator keying is done by Windows 95 itself. The application does not have to do anything other than tell Windows 95 which title bar options are needed and how to construct the menu bar. Windows 95 sends the program messages, notifying the application whenever any of these has been activated by the user. In other words, you code only a minuscule amount to get a maximum amount of response!

Scroll bars (8) come in two types and two kinds. There are vertical and horizontal scroll bars; an application may have either or both or none. There can be *system scroll bars,* which are provided and controlled by Windows 95 itself. These scroll bars are always present, unless the application notifies Windows 95 to remove them. Windows 95 sends the application messages when the user is activating them. There are also *user scroll bars*, which the application controls totally. User scroll bars may dynamically appear and disappear as the application chooses. Generally, system scroll bars are easier to program because Windows 95 handles most of the details.

Control bars with buttons (10) are now quite common. Often they are called tool bars or decorations. They are discussed in chapter 11.

Figure 1.2 illustrates the idea of *child windows*. Child windows are any subsequent windows that open over the top of the application's client window; child windows can be regular windows or dialogs.

A *dialog box* is a smaller window that allows the user to enter data and choose options, among other actions. *Modal dialog boxes*, when launched (most often from menu choices), receive the input focus, and the user is limited to completing actions in that dialog box only. The application's normal operations are halted until the user terminates the dialog box in some manner, at which time the dialog box disappears. *Modeless dialog boxes*, in contrast, can remain on the screen, and the user can task switch between the application and the dialog box.

Further, Windows 95 provides a series of standard dialog boxes for easy application use, known as the *common dialogs*. The Open File dialog is one of these. The application merely needs to request this dialog and Windows provides the box, handles all user entry, and returns to the program the filename chosen. There is a common dialog box for sending a document to the printer and one for choosing a font. Unless there is a compelling reason not to, all applications should utilize these common dialogs because the user instantly knows how to make the proper choices.

A dialog box can contain many different graphical elements, known as *controls*. *Push-button controls* permit instant user responses. The differently highlighted button is called the *default push button* (the Open button in Figure 1.2). Push buttons provide choices, such as to OK or Cancel an action or to launch further dialogs or windows. They are usually positioned in the upper left corner or the bottom of the box.

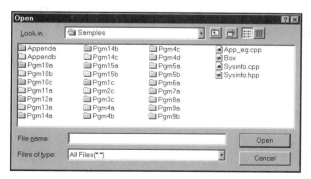

Fig. 1.2 Open Modal Dialog Box

List box controls—the main window area shown in Figure 1.2 with folders and files—display a list of things for the user to see or choose from. When the number of items in the list exceeds the list box size, scroll bars are used.

Combo box controls combine a push button and a dropdown list box. In Figure 1.2 the Files of Type is a combo box. The chosen entry from the list appears in the combo box window when a selection in the dropdown list box portion is made.

An *Edit control*, File name, for example, allows the user to enter text data directly from the keyboard. An application can even install data editing features to edit boxes. While an edit box normally contains one line, they are not limited to that. One could have the entire screen be one giant edit control.

Dialog boxes usually have many titles called *static text controls*. In Figure 1.2, "Look in," "Files of type," and "File name" are static text controls. No user input can be made on these, but the application can change the string being shown as needed.

Figure 1.3 comes from the WordPad application. The Find modeless dialog box remains on screen until you cancel it or close the application that launched it. You can switch back to the original task at any time. This feature makes modeless dialogs useful in the right circumstances. The *Check box controls*, shown in Figure 1.3, are commonly used as toggle switches, enabling or disabling an option. For each check box, the application notifies Windows 95 whether the box should be checkmarked or not; Windows 95 takes care of the details.

Most dialogs have one or more *Group box controls*, which are static boxes that only serve to group items together. Figure 1.4 shows three group boxes. They have a defined border; here, a simple line edge. *Radio button controls*, shown in the Answer mode group in Figure 1.4, allow the user to select one option from a group. Notice the difference between check boxes and radio buttons. Each check box is a separate entity that can be checked or not, while only one radio button in a group can be on at one time.

One of the new Windows 95 controls, the *slider*, controls the speaker volume.

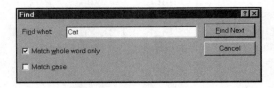

Fig. 1.3 Find Modeless Dialog Box

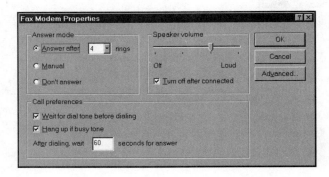

Fig. 1.4 Fax App's Properties with Radio Buttons and Slider

1.5 RESOURCES

These dialogs and windows are composed of a set of graphical elements known collectively as resources. Resources include the following:

icons	cursors
bitmaps	character strings
menus	menu accelerators
fonts	complete dialog boxes
user-defined resources	

An *icon* is a small graphical image used to represent something. Commonly every application has an icon that Windows 95 uses to represent that application when the user minimizes the program.

A *cursor* is a small graphical image that represents the mouse cursor. The default is the standard arrow cursor. There are several other images that a program can use as replacement cursors, such as an hourglass, finger pointer, and so on. Additionally, the application can provide its own cursors.

Bitmaps come in all sizes and can represent nearly anything. Some bitmaps are very small, representing menu commands on the application's tool bar. Others, like the giant ?, are used for informational purposes only. Actually, push buttons are a set of three bitmaps: one for the button not depressed, one for when the button has the focus and is not depressed, and one for the button while it is depressed. Windows alters the display between the three, yielding an action sequence.

Character strings are considered a resource. The static text in the dialogs represents character strings. (Windows 95 applications are often ported to foreign countries and all messages must be converted into the appropriate foreign language. By collecting all text strings in the entire application into one set of resources found in one place, it is an easy task to translate the application.)

Thus, a major design consideration, often neglected for convenience by novice programmers, is to place all character strings into the application's resource file (including all strings normally found, for instance, in printf's!). An additional benefit of placing every string into the resource table is that the strings are removed from the code and data segments of the program, reducing the total memory footprint of the program. Only the strings that are currently needed are loaded into memory; all others are stored on disk.

Menus are a straightforward resource. One enters the text of each item, possibly showing a hot letter to be underlined, and any accelerator hint to be displayed. The *menu accelerator table* is a collection of keyboard hot keys that correspond to specific menu choices, providing a shortcut for the user. While many *display fonts* are available from the Windows 95 system, including all of the myriad add-on font packages, you can provide your own fonts for your application. This is not often done, since so many fonts are readily available. The user can also make up any other type of object and call it a *user-defined resource* and make it available to the application. Finally, complete *dialogs* are considered resources by Windows.

1.5.1 Construction of Resources

Resources are constructed in several ways. The absolute easiest method is to use the provided software, *Resource Editor*. The Resource Editor allows you to design a complete dialog box with any number of features. Additionally, existing resources and dialogs can be altered. All of the resources can be created by hand with nothing more than the simplest text editor. To do so, though, you must know the exact syntax and possible options available for each resource.

All resources are *bound* by the linker program onto the end of the application exe file. When an application needs a resource, Windows 95 loads that resource into memory from the exe file. When the resource is no longer needed, it becomes "discardable." When the memory it is occupying is needed, the resource is removed from memory. Should that resource be needed once again, Windows 95 reloads it from disk. Hence the extreme need for SMARTDRV!

Now you can see the benefit of placing all character strings into the resource table. (Actually, Windows 95 loads into memory groups of 16 strings at one time.)

Further, since all resources are in the exe file, the Resource Editor can be run on the exe file, stripping all or some resources from the application, modifying them, and then replacing the updated resources back on the end of the exe file. All of this is accomplished without recompiling the application or even having the source code!

1.5.2 Resource Styles

The standard Windows 3.1 graphical elements were rather plain. Microsoft next created what has become known as *3-D* replacements for all of the standard elements in an attempt to "dress up" dialogs and controls. When the 3-D replacement package was selected, rather than drab, black and white dialogs, they could have gray backgrounds, bumps and ridges for group box boundaries, and other effects. Under Windows 95, the dialogs and controls have been revised further and the 3-D look is the default. Additionally, you can install replacement elements of your own design, using *owner-draw controls*.

1.6 WINDOWS 95 NEW DATA TYPES AND DEFINES AND THEIR WINDOWS 3.1 COUNTERPARTS

The Windows 95 API has defined many new data types and many new structure tags and classes to be used as data types for defining variables. Some of these differ from the Windows 3.1 API. Several common data types have different sizes depending upon which API is used. Table 1.1 shows the common data types and the applicable Windows API types. When porting Windows 3.1 programs to Windows 95, be alert to these data types. Using the **#define STRICT** option before any other includes allows the compiler to assist you in finding any difficulties in advance.

All of these are defined in the WINDOWS.H header file or other similar header files. They are fully discussed along with hundreds of other structures and other spe-

Table 1.1 Windows 95 Data Types

Item	Windows 95	Windows 3.1
int	32-bit signed number	16-bit signed number
unsigned	32-bit unsigned	16-bit unsigned
long	32-bit signed	32-bit signed
short	16-bit signed	16-bit signed

Item	Identification
BOOL	[a]an int whose values are TRUE or FALSE
HANDLE	[a]unsigned int used as a handle (an index into a table)
LONG	long
LPSTR	pointer to a string
UINT	[a]unsigned int
WORD	unsigned short int
LPARAM	long value passed as a parameter
WPARAM	[a]unsigned int passed as a parameter
BYTE	unsigned char
HINSTANCE	[a]handle to an instance of an application in memory
HWND	[a]handle to a window
HPEN	[a]handle to a colored pen for drawing text and lines
HBRUSH	[a]handle to a brush for coloring areas, such as backgrounds
HCURSOR	[a]handle to a cursor, such as the arrow mouse cursor
HFILE	[a]handle to a file
HGLOBAL	[a]handle to a global memory area
MSG	structure defining the information about a Windows message
PAINTSTRUCT	structure defining the region of the client screen that needs to be updated
POINT	[a]structure defining a point, containing int x and int y
RECT	[a]structure defining a rectangle, containing four ints, called left, right, top, bottom
TEXTMETRIC	structure containing the basic information about a physical font, such as character heights and widths
WNDCLASS	structure containing the window's class attributes, such as the window's style, icon to be used on minimizing, the cursor to be used, the background brush to color or paint the window's background, the main menu to be used

[a]Indicates this data type is different between the two APIs.

cialized data types in *Programmer's Reference, Volume 3: Messages, Structures, and Macro* (Microsoft Press) and in the Visual C++ On-Line documentation, under the SDK choice.

In addition, there are a huge number of numerical constants that identify various key values. For example, **IDC_ARROW** identifies the standard arrow cursor. Such defined items are always in uppercase. Figure 1.5 shows how you can use the On-Line Help to look up these values in the WIN32 SDK.

The defines generally have a compound name, separated by the _ character. The name IDC refers to the *ID*entifier for a *C*ursor. Table 1.2 shows some of the other commonly used identifier prefixes.

There are identifiers for the standard colors, file attributes, error codes and many more. Again, they are located in WINDOWS.H or similar files and described in the *Programmer's Reference* and on-line documentation.

There are identifiers for the standard colors, file attributes, error codes and many more. Again, they are located in WINDOWS.H or similar files and described in the *Programmer's Reference* and on-line documentation.

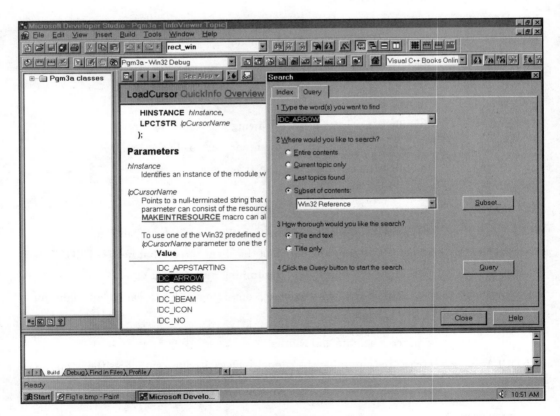

Fig. 1.5 Using On-Line Help to Look Up IDC_ARROW

Table 1.2 Some Common Identifier Prefixes

Prefix	Meaning
IDC	identifier for a cursor
IDI	identifier for an icon
IDS	identifier for a character string
IDM	identifier for a menu
CS	class style
CW	create window
WS	window style
WM	window message

 Windows 3.1 Porting Tip: Watch data types and structure alignment. The data types that you must examine when porting an application to Windows 95 include: **int**, **unsigned int**, **UINT**, **WPARAM**, **POINT**, **RECT**, and all forms of **HANDLE**s. All of these data types used to be 16-bit quantities but now become 32-bit quantities. Compiler warnings about truncation should be carefully followed. If an **int** only needs to be a 16-bit quantity, use a **short int**. Similarly, use an **unsigned short** for a 16-bit UINT. Be extra cautious about assigning a **WPARAM** to a **WORD**.

There are identifiers for the standard colors, file attributes, error codes and many more. Again, they are located in WINDOWS.H or similar files and described in the *Programmer's Reference* and on-line documentation.

1.7 STRUCTURES UNDER WINDOWS 95: SIZE AND ALIGNMENT EFFECTS

Pay close attention to older data files being input under Windows 95 into user data structures. Consider the following Windows 3.1 data structure for cost records

```
struct COSTREC {
   int itemnumber;
   int qty;
   char descr[21];
   double cost;
};
```

The first two fields were originally 16-bit values. If left as is, under Windows 95 both would become 32-bit values, causing input problems. The remedy would be to change the structure to

```
struct COSTREC {
  short int itemnumber;
  short int qty;
  char descr[21];
  double cost;
};
```

In addition, determine the structure data alignment option. Often under Windows 3.1, byte alignment was used. Windows 95 gives the best performance when using the natural alignment of packed data within structures in which each data type is aligned on a boundary that is the size of itself. Consider the following misaligned structure:

```
struct GOOF {
  char food_types[2]; // byte alignment for each byte is "normal"
  long qty;           // misaligned item - should be 32-bit aligned
};
```

Windows 95 inputs the data, but only after a processor fault on the **qty** field occurs and is handled by realigning the data—a significant performance hit. By redesigning the structure and the data file, this degradation can be removed

```
struct FIXED {
  long qty;           // now properly aligned
  char food_types[2]; // still byte aligned and normal
};
```

Alternatively, add filler bytes to force proper alignment

```
struct FIXED2 {
  char food_types[2]; // byte aligned ok
  char dummy[2];      // filler to align the long
  long qty;           // now properly aligned
};
```

If you were to define an array of these structures, only structure FIXED2 would be correct, since the FIXED structure lacks two bytes for the next element's long field.

Design Rule 2: **The 16-bit data types should be aligned on *even* address boundaries; the 32-bit data types, on 32-bit boundaries; doubles, on 64-bit boundaries; and structures, on a boundary of the type corresponding to the largest data type in the structure.**

1.8 HUNGARIAN NOTATION

Because of the critical nature of passing many parameters of the correct type to the Windows 95 API, many programmers opt to use the Hungarian notational scheme when making up variable names. The Windows 95 API, unlike the Windows 3.1 API, now does data type checking of the parameters passed in an attempt to detect bad values in advance of their use. This was not done under Windows 3.1, so that passing the wrong thing could be both devastating and very difficult to locate.

Hungarian notation is named in honor of the Microsoft programmer Charles Simonyi. Simply put, all variable names begin with a lowercase letter or series of letters to represent the data type. The capitalized (if not, it becomes unreadable!) variable name follows. Table 1.3 shows some of the common prefixes.

Thus **lpszCmdParam** is long pointer to a null-terminated string command parameter. **hInstance** would be a handle to this instance of the application in memory; **hPrevInstance** would be a handle to a previous instance or copy of the application in memory.

Similarly, when defining or referencing structures, the structures are often named the same but spelled in lowercase. Often if the name is too long, it is abbreviated. For example:

POINT   point;

RECT   rect;

PAINTSTRUCT   ps;

Table 1.3 Common Hungarian Notation Prefixes

Prefix	Meaning
c	char
by	byte
n	short int—number
i	int
x,y	short int coordinates
cx,	cy count length of x or y distances
b	BOOL
w	UINT or WORD unsigned int or word
l	long
dw	DWORD double word, 32-bit quantity
lp	long pointer or far pointer
lpsz	long pointer to a string of chars
s	string
sz	string null terminated
h	handle

1.9 WINDOWS 95 API FUNCTION NAMES

Windows API function names are all capitalized. For example,

LoadIcon

LoadCursor

LoadString

CreateWindow

1.10 OUR SAMPLE PROGRAM CODING NOTATION

The result of all these new names is total confusion for programmers just learning to program under Windows! As you look over the first few chapters, you may have an even more emphatic statement about all of this. It is not uncommon to be totally confused as to what must be coded exactly as is, what your variable names are, and so on. I still recall my first exposure to Windows programming—it was anything but pleasant! In fact, when you couple all of this complexity with the next layer—object-oriented classes—it becomes exceedingly difficult to decipher what is going on. Therefore, I am going to adopt "Vic's semiunderstandable coding scheme."

In my early examples, when you see an identifier that has one or more capital letters in it, it is the name of a function or structure or message or define and must be coded as is. The exceptions begin occurring when I start to create resources; at that point, I use uppercase defines as well. When we deal with the class libraries in chapter 4, class names and functions are also capitalized and the scheme tends to break down. But by then you should have a good feel for names.

All variables that are user-created names are in lowercase. I dislike Hungarian notation for many reasons. The only exception is that I will use the prefix h for handle fields.

In summary, in the initial examples, if an identifier has one or more capital letters in it, that identifier must be used *as is*; it is a Windows 95-defined key item. If it has no capitals in it, it is a user nameable entity that can be called anything you desire. I hope this will be of great assistance at the beginning, as you try to understand what is being coded.

When the class libraries are presented beginning in chapter 4, I capitalize member function names. Class data members, however, still follow the lowercase style. Thus, from the name and capitalization, you can tell what it is. You may appreciate the wisdom of this by the time that you finish chapter 15. However, this is just a learning crutch. Feel free to use whatever stylistic approach you desire in your coding. I am only trying to simplify the learning process a bit.

1.11 GETTING STARTED: THE SOFTWARE

When I am doing Windows 95 programming, I have my desktop set up as shown in Figure 1.6. I attempt to keep easily accessible those program icons most likely to be needed.

While the Visual C++ group has a number of choices, the fully integrated development platform—the highlighted icon Microsoft Developer Studio—is all that is really needed. Nearly everything beginners require is available from the platform. Hence, I only use this single icon to launch.

1.11.1 Using Folders (Subdirectories) and the Sample Programs

If you load the source files onto a hard disk, a number of subdirectories or folders are created. The base folder is LearnWin which has the Bmp folder containing all of

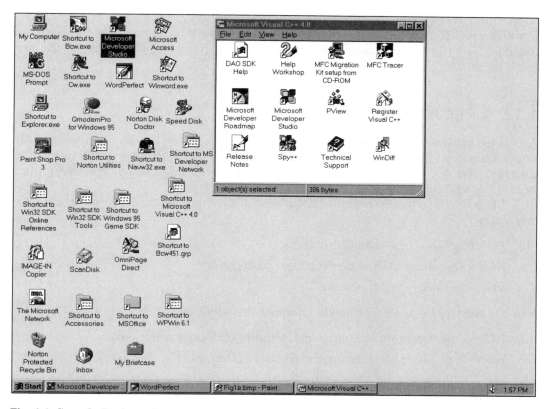

Fig. 1.6 Sample Desktop Screen

the sample bitmap images for our applications and one or more folders identified by program numbers. The naming convention for the program folders is PgmnnA, where nn represents the chapter number and the letter A represents the specific program within that chapter. So for chapter 1, there is a folder called Pgm01a, which contains the sole example for this chapter. For chapter 2, there are folders for Pgm02a and Pgm02b. The actual programs are similarly named.

If you are new to Windows programming, I strongly recommend that you create a separate folder or subdirectory for each program that you write. When you use the class libraries, numerous files are created.

1.11.2 Building the Application: Running the Software

Let's say that you have copied the first sample program I gave you and are ready to build it into an application. How do you do so? (Note that each example program has an exe executable version located on the CD so that you can just run the program when needed from the Explorer.)

There are two methods available: build the application from within the IDE or build the application from a DOS prompt using a MAKE file. For program development, I prefer the IDE approach. Launch the Developer Studio and select File and then Open Workspace. Navigate to the \LearnWin\Pgm01a folder and choose Pgm01a.mdb. If changes are needed to the Visual C++ environment, use Project and Settings. To build the application, select Build and Rebuild All. Then test run the program by choosing Build and either Debug or Execute Pgm01a.

1.12 A PROJECT'S FILES

A C-style application will contain a basic set of files. When the application is built, many additional files will be created. The resultant .exe file is the *sole* file needed for its execution. A C++ style application will contain even more basic files, including a header file and code file for each class.

Let's begin with the normal "Hello World" type program. There are three files originally:

PGM01a.C	the C source file
PGM01a.mdb	the development platform file
PGM01a.mak	the make file

Later, there will be more files needed. Among them will be:

RC	the program's resource file defining dialogs, strings, etc.
RH	a header file defining the resource ID numbers

When the build is done, many additional files will have been created; some of these include

PGM01.EXE	the final product—the executable program
PGM01.OBJ	the object file(s)
PGM01.PCH	Microsoft's precompiled headers file
PGM01.RES	compiled resources in a form to be appended to the exe file

Later, there may be additional files that appear after debugging sessions—to remember your last set of breakpoints, for example. Notice that all of the object files, support files, and the exe file are stored in the Debug folder. If you choose the release form, these files are placed in a Release folder. This conveniently separates source project files from the intermediate and output files.

Windows 3.1 Porting Tip: All Windows 3.1 applications also had a def module definition file. Under Windows 95, def files are no longer needed. For example, the Windows 3.1 def file for Pgm01 used to be as shown in Figure 1.7.

Uppercase predominates. The NAME and DESCRIPTION are used for documentation purposes. The EXETYPE and STUB notify the linker that this is to become a

```
NAMEHELLOWIN
DESCRIPTION'Hello from Windows - C style'
EXETYPEWINDOWS
STUB'WINSTUB.EXE'
CODEPRELOAD MOVEABLE DISCARDABLE
DATAPRELOAD MOVEABLE MULTIPLE
HEAPSIZE1024
STACKSIZE8192
```

Fig. 1.7 Sample Desktop Screen

Windows application and for the linker to include the WINSTUB code. This stub of code will display the message "program must be run under Windows" should it be executed from DOS.

You are able to define the local heap and the stack size. Remember that the data segment (which holds static and global variables), the local heap (which holds the dynamically allocated items), and the stack (which holds the automatic and parameter class variables) together cannot exceed 64K in the medium model. (Even in the large model, the stack cannot exceed 64K.) Please note that the use of automatic storage and parameter class becomes a premium commodity in a large application. Under Windows 3.1 this is perhaps the most compelling reason to place all of your character strings into a resource file and not in the code.

The Code and Data options begin to give one the feel of how Windows 3.1 and Windows 95 handle memory. The PRELOAD option notifies Windows that this segment must be loaded before the application can begin. The MOVEABLE option denotes that the segment of memory can be moved about in real memory; Windows will do so when it attempts to consolidate smaller unused blocks into larger blocks. The DISCARDABLE option notifies Windows that it may remove this segment from memory when that memory is needed, later reloading the segment from the exe file. This ability allows Windows to maintain the smallest memory footprint when many tasks are competing for memory. Only segments that contain constant data may be marked DISCARDABLE. Code segments and any program resources are normally so designated. Data segment contents vary and are instead designated MULTIPLE. Under Windows 3.1, if the user launches three copies of the same application, only one code segment and one set of resources (which are constant) need be loaded, while there will be MULTIPLE data segments, which contain the variable information.

1.13 PRECOMPILED HEADERS

The use of precompiled headers greatly speeds up the compilation phase. The basic idea is that as each module's header files are compiled, you save the header compilation results on disk. Then the next time the module is compiled, if no changes are made to the headers, the compiler merely inputs the precompiled header information, bypassing including and compiling them. This saves a great deal of time on large projects. When using MFC class libraries, the compile time is unbelievably slow without precompiled headers.

However, the price you pay for indiscriminant use of precompiled headers is huge file size. On an 80K MFC program with ten cpp and hpp files, I have seen the pch precompiled header file exceed 10M! Therefore, you must establish some controls when using precompiled headers.

Your own class header files are volatile until you get the application working, so any change to your header will also cause a complete redo of the precompiled header file. Therefore you should include only nonvolatile headers. Instruct the compiler to halt precompiling after the nonvolatile includes, which are various window headers and the MFC class library includes.

Thus, your best method in *every* module (.C, .CPP, .H, .HPP) is to place the nonvolatile headers first, followed by the command to halt precompiling:

```
#pragma hdrstop
```

Further, to minimize the size of the precompiled header file, the *same* set of files should be included in *every* file to be compiled. While this requires planning ahead to include all system header files that will be needed, doing so will drastically reduce the size of your pch file.

I have not done that here in Pgm01a.c since there is only one file to compile. In subsequent sample programs, I will illustrate this optimum method of handling the precompiled headers.

The MFC uses another approach: the stdafx.h header file. Its use is discussed in chapter 4.

1.14 Pgm01a: The Hello World Program

OK. We've put it off long enough (or we've saved the best for last). Let's examine a C-style program that displays a Hello message in a window. Figure 1.8 shows how the program appears when run.

1.14.1 Listing for File: Pgm01a.c

```
/****************************************************************************/
/*                                                                        */
/* PGM1 - Hello in a window shell program by Vic Broquard                 */
/*                                                                        */
/* C style  basic model                                                   */
/*                                                                        */
/****************************************************************************/

#include <windows.h>

/****************************************************************************/
/*                                                                        */
```

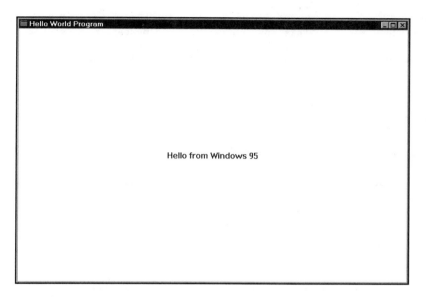

Fig. 1.8 The Hello Program

```
/* structure definitions, external/global data, and function prototypes    */
/*                                                                          */
/****************************************************************************/
LRESULT CALLBACK  winproc (HWND, UINT, WPARAM, LPARAM); // main window proc
                                     // winproc is normally called WinProc
BOOL initapplication (HINSTANCE);    // make and register our window class
BOOL initinstance (HINSTANCE, int);  // construct an instance of our window

char appname[] = "HelloPgm";         // the name of our application

/****************************************************************************/
/*                                                                          */
/* WinMain: windows equivalent to a "main" in C pgms - MUST always be coded*/
/*                                                                          */
/****************************************************************************/
int APIENTRY  WinMain (HANDLE hinstance, HANDLE hprevinstance,
                       LPSTR  cmdline,   int howshow) {
 MSG          msg;

 // under Windows 95 and NT, hprevinstance is now ALWAYS 0, just invoke
 // initapplication to construct the window's class parameters that tell
 // Windows how to build the main window and register the window's class

 if (!initapplication (hinstance)) return FALSE;

 // create an instance of the main window, based upon the way Windows
 // desires the window to be shown - such as launch minimized for example

 if (!initinstance (hinstance, howshow)) return FALSE;
```

```
 // enter the main processing loop consisting of getting the next message
 // that Windows sends to this app, converting its message into standard codes
 // and sending that message to our app's appropriate message handler
 // continue until Windows notifies us that there will never be any further
 // messages, because the app has requested termination

 while ( GetMessage (&msg, NULL, 0, 0)) {
  TranslateMessage (&msg);
  DispatchMessage  (&msg);
 }

 return msg.wParam;  // pass along the generated success/fail return code
}
/****************************************************************************/
/*                                                                        */
/* initapplication: fill in the WNDCLASS structure about how to construct */
/*                  our main window and then register this window with    */
/*                  Windows                                               */
/*                                                                        */
/* Note: better style to call this function InitApplication               */
/*                                                                        */
/****************************************************************************/

BOOL initapplication (HINSTANCE hinstance) {

 WNDCLASS wndclass;
 wndclass.style        = CS_HREDRAW | CS_VREDRAW;
                         // force repaint whenever the window size changes
 wndclass.lpfnWndProc  = winproc;
                         // name of our main window procedure
 wndclass.cbClsExtra   = 0;
                         // advanced feature - reserves extra space
 wndclass.cbWndExtra   = 0;
                         // in windows class and window structures
 wndclass.hInstance    = hinstance;
                         // insert handle to this window's instance
 wndclass.hIcon        = LoadIcon (NULL, IDI_APPLICATION);
                         // load in the icon to be used whenever we are
                         // minimized use system provided default icon
                         // use hinstance if the icon is our own
 wndclass.hCursor      = LoadCursor (NULL, IDC_ARROW);
                         // load the mouse cursor to be used -
                         // the Windows' provided arrow cursor
 wndclass.hbrBackground = GetStockObject (WHITE_BRUSH);
                         // create the background colored brush
 wndclass.lpszMenuName  = NULL;
                         // will eventually id the menu to be displayed
 wndclass.lpszClassName = appname;
                         // the char string name of the application

 return RegisterClass (&wndclass); // registers this window so it can be shown
}

/****************************************************************************/
/*                                                                        */
```

```
/* initinstance: construct an instance of our main window using our just   */
/*               registered class or the previous instance running         */
/*               concurrently                                              */
/*                                                                          */
/* Note: better style to call this function InitInstance                   */
/*                                                                          */
/****************************************************************************/
BOOL initinstance (HINSTANCE hinstance, int howshow) {

 HWND hwnd;

 hwnd = CreateWindow (appname,              // char string ids the app
                      "Hello World Program", // title bar caption
                      WS_OVERLAPPEDWINDOW,  // window style
                      CW_USEDEFAULT,        // window's initial x position
                      CW_USEDEFAULT,        // window's initial y position
                      CW_USEDEFAULT,        // window's initial x size - width
                      CW_USEDEFAULT,        // window's initial y size- height
                      NULL,                 // parent window's handle
                      NULL,                 // handle to window's menu
                      hinstance,            // handle of this instance
                      NULL);                // creation parameters - advanced

 if (!hwnd) return FALSE;                   // window construction failed

 ShowWindow (hwnd, howshow); // creates window on the screen
 UpdateWindow (hwnd);        // paints the client (user area) of the window
 return TRUE;
}

/****************************************************************************/
/*                                                                          */
/* winproc: our main window procedure - normally called WinProc            */
/*                                                                          */
/****************************************************************************/
LRESULT CALLBACK winproc (HWND hwnd, UINT msg, WPARAM wparam, LPARAM lparam) {

 HDC         hdc;
 PAINTSTRUCT ps;
 RECT        rect;

 // our app's message processing section - given a message from Windows,
 // determine if the message is one that we wish to respond to and do so
 // or pass it on down to the Windows provided default message handler
 // to take the appropriate Windows default handling
 // here is the tiniest "Nightmare Switch From Hell"
 // imagine what it will look like when it processes hundreds of messages

 switch (msg) {

  // when a paint message is received, we are being asked to redraw our
  // window - either completely or in part

  case WM_PAINT:

    // acquire a device context upon which to draw
    hdc = BeginPaint (hwnd, &ps);
```

```
    // get the size of the client area that needs to be redrawn - a rectangle
    GetClientRect (hwnd, &rect);

    // printf a hello message
    DrawText (hdc, "Hello from Windows", -1, &rect,
              DT_SINGLELINE | DT_CENTER | DT_VCENTER);

    // notify Windows that we are done redrawing the window
    EndPaint (hwnd, &ps);

    // notify the message processor that we have successfully handled the
    // message
    return 0;

  // the user has selected the "Close Application" menu item - here we
  // must handle any processing needed to terminate the app - for now nothing

  case WM_DESTROY:
    PostQuitMessage (0);   // send ok to quit the app message back to Windows
    return 0;              // notify the message processor that we have handled
  }

  // all unhandled messages are passed on down to the default Windows handler
  return DefWindowProc (hwnd, msg, wparam, lparam);
}
```

1.15 USING COMMENTS

The first thing you should notice is the proliferation of comments. Because this is our first program, I have added many more instruction comments than are usually needed to make the program more understandable for beginners. In your real programs, you should use appropriate instruction comments; target your reader, often one who is somewhat familiar with Windows 95 programming.

Design Rule 3: Use block comments to identify the major sections or functions of the program and instruction comments either just ahead or on the right of the instruction to identify what the instruction is to do.

Why? The three key reasons for the use of comments are:

1. Comments will aid your understanding of both what and why when you look at the code a month later.
2. Comments assist the person who performs program maintenance. If you do not fully document your program, other programmers will continually query you about the program code.
3. Commenting as you code helps you spot errors early before you compile and run.

1.16 THE WINMAIN FUNCTION

In a DOS C/C++ program, the function **main** is automatically invoked by the C start-up code. Similarly, Windows 3.1 and Windows 95 startup code always invokes a function whose name is **WinMain**. (Notice the capitalization.)

Normally, this startup function has minimal coding and the coding is quite standard, program to program. Windows 95 gives **WinMain** four parameters. The LPSTR, or pointer to a string, points to the command line, should you need to pick up values from the launching command line. Notice that the command line is not parsed into a variable number of character strings as in a DOS C/C++ program.

Two handles to program applications are passed. The first handle is the most important one; it is the handle to this instance of the application. Under Windows 95, the second handle—the handle to any previous instance currently running—will always be 0 and is ignored.

 Windows 3.1 Porting Tip: Under Windows 3.1 the previous instance handle would point to any concurrently running instance of the application. If an application did not want to allow a second instance or multiple instances of itself to launch, it could check this previous instance handle. In Windows 95 the previous instance handle will always be 0 because every application is now launched in its own address space. The previous instance handle was retained for backwards compatibility.

The variable names usually assigned to these parameters are **hinstance** and **hprevinstance**; some programmers capitalize these names (and **CmdLine** or **nCmdLine**) for readability. The handle to this instance, **hinstance**, is used frequently in API function calls.

The fourth parameter determines how the application is to be shown on-screen. Usually Windows 95 requests that our application be shown in a visible window or else minimized on start-up. This variable usually has the value SW_SHOWNORMAL.Other often used possibilities include

SW_SHOWNOACTIVE	displays the window as an icon, minimized on start-up
SW_SHOWMAXIMIZED	displays the window in a maximized state

WinMain has three basic actions to perform. First, it must fill in a structure that defines how this application is to be run, its style or class, and then register this definition with Windows 95. While the coding of these actions could be done directly in **WinMain**, I have placed this coding into an **initapplication** function. (Yes, I really want to call it **InitApplication**; it is lowercase here to help you spot which names are yours and which must be coded as-is.) Also, when we begin discussing the class libraries, this function will become a member function. Should the registration API function fail, **WinMain** will terminate. Notice that this registration does not involve a C++ "class" but rather a style and method of window display among other things. (In my opinion, **RegisterClass** is a misnomer.)

Second, it must create an instance of the main window, based on the registered style or class, and show the window on-screen. Here these steps are done in **initin-stance**. Once again, it is more likely to be called **InitInstance**, and it will also become a member function in the class libraries.

Third, it runs the application through the message processing loop. Windows 95 has an MSG structure that defines the hundreds of possible messages that could be sent to your application. Here is the basic message processing code: get a message, translate it, and send it to the appropriate function to handle. The cycle continues until **GetMessage** returns 0, indicating there are no more messages; the application is done.

Windows 95 dispatches messages to our main message processing function, here named **winproc**. In the industry, this function is usually called **WinProc**. It is in **winproc** that most of our application coding will be found. Before we examine the coding details, let's examine the function prototype for **winproc** and the header for **WinMain**

```
LRESULT CALLBACK  winproc (HWND, UINT, WPARAM, LPARAM);
// the main window procedure - note winproc is normally called WinProc
int APIENTRY  WinMain (HANDLE hinstance, HANDLE hprevinstance,
                LPSTR  cmdline,   int howshow) {
```

WinMain returns an integer success code and has an entry type or calling convention of **APIENTRY**. Alternatively you could use **WINAPI** because they are equivalent. By default, C and C++ functions have the C calling convention.

 Windows 3.1 Porting Tip: In Windows 3.1 programs, **WinMain** had the **FAR PASCAL** calling convention. This should be changed to **APIENTRY** or **WINAPI**. There are several types of calling sequences: C, PASCAL, WINAPI. Many languages, except C, pass parameters in what is called the PASCAL style. The parameters are passed on the **stack**, which is a last in-first out (LIFO) save area. So in the PASCAL style, if one invoked a CALC function as

```
CALC (a, b, c);
```

then the stack would contain c, b, a, in that order—last in-first out.

On the other hand, C-style parameter passing stores the parameters in the order of appearance in the function call—here the parameters on the stack would be a, b, c. (C-style places or *pushes* the parameters on to the stack in reverse order and LIFO then makes them appear in the forward order.) There are also some differences on stack cleanup after the function completes, among them, whether the caller or callee removes the parameters from the stack.

In general, the PASCAL style is more efficient, but the C style will handle a variable number of arguments. The WINAPI, among other things, combines the best of both, permitting speedy execution and a variable number of arguments.

The prototype for **winproc** begins **LRESULT CALLBACK winproc**, signifying that it returns a long integer. The option **CALLBACK** indicates that this function will be called from within the Windows 95 API; Windows will call back to this function.

This is a common occurrence: our application calls an API function that then calls back to one of our app's functions. This is parallel to the C **qsort** function, in which **qsort** must call back to our comparison function.

 Windows 3.1 Porting Tip: Callback functions were prototyped by **LONG FAR PASCAL _export**; this should be changed to **LRESULT CALLBACK**.

The **FAR** option says this function is not in the same code segment as the Windows 3.1 system code. Any function in your program that is directly called from Windows 3.1 system code must have the option **FAR PASCAL _export** in it. The reason for this is obscure and highly technical. Perhaps the easiest way to get a feel for this is to say that internally Windows 3.1 code has the segment registers DS and SS pointing to *two* segments of up to 64K each. DS and SS are data and stack segment registers. A register is a high-speed work area, generally 32- or 16-bits (all segment registers are 16-bits). The C and C++ programming languages keep DS and SS pointing to the *same* 64K segment. Here, Windows 3.1 calls directly our **winproc** (**WinProc**) so our application will process its messages. So the **FAR PASCAL _export** option creates a bit of code to correct the DS/SS situation. When the message processor function, **winproc** (**WinProc**), calls other subfunctions to handle specifics relating to the processing of that message, *do not use this option*, since DS/SS are already in agreement.

In a large application with many functions, very few functions must have this special option, **CALLBACK**.

Windows always passes **winproc** (**WinProc**) four parameters: a handle to the window that is receiving the message (yes, you can examine all messages); an **unsigned int** (UINT), representing the message ID number; and a WPARAM and a LPARAM, which contain the various parameter values associated with this specific message. The **winproc** always returns a **long**—TRUE or FALSE, 0 or 1—showing whether we handled the message or not.

The global variable **appname** contains the character string name that we give to Windows 95 to identify our application.

Next, examine the **initapplication** function. Two actions are performed: fill in the WNDCLASS structure and then register that window class with Windows 95. Note that the use of the term "class" is not a true C++ class, rather just our window's style.

The variable **wndclass** is an instance of the structure WNDCLASS. The WNDCLASS structure defines many key elements about our window. The **style** field determines many key features. This field is actually a bit string, whose individual bits represent the on/off status of the available possibilities. Often several options are needed; they are ORed together. Some possibilities include:

CS_DBLCLKS	sends double clicks to the application
CS_HREDRAW	redraws the whole screen if the horizontal size changes
CS_VREDRAW	redraws the whole screen if the vertical size changes

The field **lpfnWndProc** is assigned the name of our message handling procedure, **winproc** (**WinProc**). It is through this field that Windows 95 knows the name of our message processing function.

 Windows 3.1 Porting Tip: A type-cast **(WNDPROC)** is now needed, since the data type of **lpfnWndProc** has been changed from a simple pointer to a function to a typedef of **WNDPROC**.

Similarly, **hinstance** and **appname** are assigned. The pointer to the main menu string is set to a NULL pointer. (Later, menus are added.)

The field **hIcon** is assigned the icon that we wish to use to identify our application. Under Windows 3.1 the icon is used when the application becomes minimized. Under Windows 95, the icon is now used in many places to represent the application. Since we have not yet learned how to create icons, we use a default icon whose ID is **IDI_APPLICATION**. However, that icon must be loaded into memory. The windows function **LoadIcon** is invoked. **LoadIcon** is passed the handle of this instance and the ID number of the resource to load from our exe file. If we were loading our own icon, we might code it as

```
LoadIcon (hinstance, IDI_OUR_ICON);
```

Table 1.4 shows other built-in icons. Since we are loading a Windows 95 supplied icon, we use NULL for the application instance and the predefined identifier of the icon

```
LoadIcon (NULL, IDI_APPLICATION);
```

A similar process sets the field **hCursor** to the desired default mouse cursor. (Note that we can change cursors any time later; this is just the default cursor.) Table 1.5 shows some of the standard cursors. (Look in the Windows folder under the Cursors folder for even more cursors.) The **LoadCursor** function expects parameters similar to the **LoadIcon**. Here we use the standard arrow cursor:

```
LoadCursor (NULL, IDC_ARROW);
```

Finally, Windows 95 requires a colored brush for painting the background of our window. When our window is created or needs to be redrawn, say after an overlapping

Table 1.4 Standard Windows 95 Icons

Icon	Function
IDI_APPLICATION	default application icon
IDI_ASTERISK	information icon
IDI_EXCLAMATION	exclamation point icon
IDI_HAND	hand or stop sign icon
IDI_QUESTION	question mark icon

Table 1.5 Some Standard Windows 95 Cursors

Cursor	Shape or Function
IDC_ARROW	arrow
IDC_CROSS	crosshair
IDC_IBEAM	vertical I-beam
IDC_WAIT	hourglass
IDC_UPARROW	straight-up arrow
IDC_SIZE	used to resize a window
IDC_ICON	drag file icon
IDC_SIZENWSE	upper-left to lower-right two-headed arrow
IDC_SIZENESW	upper-right to lower-left two-headed arrow
IDC_SIZEWE	horizontal two-headed arrow
IDC_SIZENS	vertical two-headed arrow

application is closed or moved, Windows 95 repaints our corrupted background for us. Painting areas is done via *brushes*; painting lines (or text) is done with a *pen*. Makes sense doesn't it? Hence, we must create a colored brush for the background. Brushes either may be created or "borrowed from" several stock, standard brushes provided by Windows 95—default ready-made brushes, if you please:

BLACK_BRUSH

WHITE_BRUSH

LTGRAY_BRUSH

DKGRAY_BRUSH

These are called *stock objects*. Thus we need to get a stock object, namely a colored brush, via the function **GetStockObject**

```
GetStockObject (WHITE_BRUSH);
```

Notice the return values from **LoadIcon, LoadCursor,** and **GetStockObject**; all of them return handles to the appropriate graphical objects.

Once the WNDCLASS structure is filled, we invoke the **RegisterClass** function, which registers our window with Windows 95. Our window is then placed onto the window's queue; no actual window has yet been made.

Function **initinstance** actually constructs our visible window. Three steps are required. First, the actual memory instance of our window is done via the function **CreateWindow**, which then returns a handle to this window in memory. We must save this handle because it will be used in subsequent functions. The **CreateWindow** function has many parameters that define specifically how the window is to be constructed. It returns either a handle to the window or a 0 if the function fails.

The first parameter is the **appname**—the same value used in the WNDCLASS structure before. Next comes the created windows style (note that it is a different style field from the WNDCLASS style field). **CreateWindow**'s style offers many specific features for this window. The documentation gives many different sets of possibilities for this function, including creating buttons, edit boxes, list boxes, and combo boxes, as well as windows. For a main window, the options are prefixed with WS_.

As you examine some of the possibilities of WS_ options in Table 1.6, notice that some imply others. This means that if you specify a certain option, you do not need to mention the other associated options. For example, specifying **WS_CAPTION**, which creates a window with a title bar, automatically implies the **WS_BORDER**, which creates a window with a border.

WS_OVERLAPPEDWINDOW is our choice and it is a common one. The next four parameters are ints defining the starting x and y coordinates of the upper-left corner of the window and the width (x size) and the height (y size) of the window. If you do not care how big or where the window will appear, you can code **CW_USEDEFAULT** to tell Windows to use its best judgment based upon what is currently on-screen.

The next parameters you pass are the handle of the parent window, if this is a child window, and the menu handle. For now, these are NULL. Then comes the handle of this application instance or hinstance. The last argument represents some advanced features and will be NULL.

Based upon these values, Windows 95 creates our window in memory only (the window is not displayed on screen just yet). Two more steps are required. To display

Table 1.6 Some Windows 95 Window WS_ Style Identifiers

Window Option	Appearance
WS_MINIMIZEBOX	has a minimize button on title bar
WS_MAXIMIZEBOX	has a maximize button on the title bar
WS_BORDER	with thin line border, no resizing
WS_CAPTION	has a title bar, implies WS_BORDER
WS_THICKFRAME	has a thick border for resizing
WS_SYSMENU	has a System menu box on the title bar
WS_VSCROLL	has a vertical scroll bar
WS_HSCROLL	has a horizontal scroll bar
WS_OVERLAPPEDWINDOW	main window type, which implies WS_OVERLAPPED (the window can overlap others), WS_CAPTION, WS_SYSMENU, WS_MINIMIZEBOX, WS_MAXIMIZEBOX, and WS_THICKFRAME

our window for the first time, we must call **ShowWindow**, passing both our handle to the window and how we want the window to be displayed. Since this is the first time the window is to appear, the original how-to-show we should use the window parameter passed down to us from Windows 95: the **howshow**. This is because the application may have been launched in the minimized state. Normally, **howshow** will be requesting the window to be active and visible.

Finally, we call **UpdateWindow** passing the handle to our window. **ShowWindow** draws the border, title bar, and similar items. However, Windows 95 does not know how to draw what is inside our window—the client area—so it just paints the background for us. **UpdateWindow** sends our application a message saying that we need to paint our client area. The code to do so will be found in our **winproc** (**WinProc**) and we will examine it shortly.

Now that the window is visible, the application enters the standard Windows 95 processing cycle: get a message and then handle the message, until there are no more messages.

The coding for the **WinMain** function and its supporting functions, except for adjusting the various options for our windows, is the same in every application.

Our message processing function, **winproc** (**WinProc**), while small here, contains the rest of the entire application's processing. In real applications, it gets to be huge with many subfunctions added. Let's examine this minimal **winnproc** that processes Windows 95 messages. It is called from within the Windows 95 shell and is passed the handle of the window receiving the message, the MSG structure containing the message, and two message-specific parameters. Its entire purpose is to process the messages that Windows 95 passes it. A very different way to program indeed!

Examine the overall coding; there is one **switch** statement based upon the passed message number. There are predefined names for all the Windows 95 message numbers (and we can even create our own messages to send). In the simplest case, we are checking for and handling just two messages: WM_PAINT, which is sent anytime the client area of the window needs to be redrawn, and WM_DESTROY, which is sent after the user chooses Close from the system menu.

The response to a WM_PAINT message nearly always begins with a call to the **BeginPaint** function, passing it the handle of the window and a reference to a paint structure. Windows 95 fills the fields of the paint structure with information that we can use in the painting process of the client area. One step of the **BeginPaint** function is to erase the background of the client window. It does this by painting the background using the brush defined in the WNDCLASS passed on into the **RegisterClass** function. It then validates the client area (meaning the area has been successfully erased and painted), and then it returns back a **handle to a device context** (HDC). A device context defines an output device—here the screen—with all of its properties, such as its pen and brush. You must have a handle to a device context to display any graphics or text information on the screen.

When using this HDC, you cannot display anything outside your client window, even if you try to do so. The various functions that will display text, draw graphics, circles, lines, fill solids, and so on, all require a valid HDC, which defines the area of the screen upon which you can paint.

When the client area of the window has been completely painted as you want, the **EndPaint** function is invoked, passing the handle of the window and a reference to the paint structure. Thus, **BeginPaint/EndPaint** functions always occur in pairs; when completed, they validate the client area of the window, which means Windows 95 may consider that the window contains the currently correct information.

Whenever the window is resized, for example, windows will invalidate the client area and send a WM_PAINT message to the application. The **BeginPaint/EndPaint** pair then validates the client area again. Note that we can send ourselves an "Invalidate Window" message to force our paint routines to redraw the window. In fact, this becomes a prime method of operation; the paint code must know how to redraw the entire client area of the window at any time.

Within the paint code, the first step is to acquire the current dimensions of the client area, given in a RECT, **rectangle structure**, which contains the four ints known as: **left**, **top** (x, y coordinates of the upper-left corner) and **right** and **bottom** (the width and height of the client area in pixels). The function **GetClientRect** is used and is passed the handle of the window and a reference to a RECT (rectangle) structure that is to be filled.

There are many ways to display messages. A simple one is to use the function **DrawText**. It is passed the handle to the device context, the character string or message or text to be displayed, a -1 to show the text is a null-terminated string (or the number of bytes to be displayed if not null-terminated), a reference to the client rectangle in which to draw, and finally a series of bit flags that define how to draw the text. Here, we are displaying a single line of text that is to be centered in the client rectangle both horizontally and vertically: DT_SINGLELINE forces the text onto one line, DT_CENTER centers the text horizontally, DT_VCENTER centers the line vertically. Again, we code one function call and gain enormous functionality. Run the application and resize the window; watch how the text remains centered within the window. What happens to the text when the window becomes too narrow to display the whole message? Try it. Consult the On-Line documentation about the **DrawText** function for other possibilities. We will be discussing **DrawText** further in the ensuing chapters.

Finally, the handling required within the WM_DESTROY message is to send Windows 95 an OK to shut the application down. It's done with the **PostQuitMessage** function that places a WM_QUIT message into the message queue. This message is what causes **GetMessage** to return a 0 value and cause the program to terminate.

Note that when each message has been processed, a 0 is returned, indicating our code has successfully handled that message.

All other messages that Windows 95 passes our **winproc (WinProc)** drop out of the switch statement. Our coding returns the results of taking the default Windows 95 standard action by calling **DefWindowProc**, passing the message and the parameters on down to the default handlers. Here is where all of the other messages went, such as maximize, minimize, open the system menu, make a system menu selection, move the window, and so on.

When you run the application, notice all of the things that you can do to the window. Among these are moving, resizing, maximizing, and minimizing the window; activating the system menu; and selecting system menu options. When maximizing, the maximize button on the title bar is replaced with the normalize button. Note that Windows 95 handles all of this functionality; our application needs to respond to a redraw or paint message and to a close message—that's all!

1.17 WHAT TO DO NEXT

Your next step is to build this Pgm01a application and test it. Then review the possible styles for **CreateWindow** and experiment with those. See what the window looks like if there are no thick borders, for example. Examine the possible stock brushes and see what different background brushes look like. Then experiment with opening the window at specific screen coordinates and having a specific width and height. Then write your first program.

1.12 WHAT TO DO NEXT

Outputting Text and Using Scroll Bars

2.1 THE PAINT PROCESS

The *client area* of a window is all the space of the window except that space occupied by the thick borders, title bar, menu bar, and the scroll bars, if present. The dimensions of the client area are not necessarily constant; the user may resize the window at anytime. This gives rise to the following design rule.

> ***Design Rule 4:*** **Your paint routine must be able to accept whatever dimensions the current client area has and display what is appropriate on that client area at that time.**

Besides resizing, many things can temporarily overlay the client area: dialog boxes, pull-down menus, the mouse cursor, other applications. Similarly, when the user activates the scroll bars, whatever is displayed in the client area needs to be adjusted. Whenever your client area needs to be redrawn either completely or in part, Windows 95 sends your application a WM_PAINT message. You can even send yourself a WM_PAINT message when you want to alter what is being displayed.

> ***Design Rule 5:*** **Structure your program so that it accumulates all of the data needed to display the client area and then force a repaint of the client area.**

Part of the paint message is the rectangular dimension of the portion of the window that needs to be updated. Quite often, only a small portion of the entire client area needs to be updated. When dealing with graphical objects, rather than regenerating the whole image, the application can be structured so that it only updates that portion that needs to be repainted. We will do this in chapter 9. When you are displaying text information, however, it is usually more convenient to just go ahead and repaint the whole client area.

The *invalid region* or *update region* or *invalid rectangle* is that portion of the client area that needs to be repainted; it is defined by a rectangle. Thus, the presence of an invalid region in the client area is what prompts Windows 95 to send the WM_PAINT message. WM_PAINT messages are low priority; other messages, such as resize the window, are higher. Higher priority messages are sent first. Often, Windows 95 simply accumulates your not-yet-sent WM_PAINT messages and consolidates them into one WM_PAINT message by adjusting the dimensions of the invalid rectangle.

The function to invalidate your client area is

```
BOOL InvalidateRect (HWND, RECT*, BOOL erase_flag);
```

If the erase_flag is TRUE, Windows 95 erases the background (that is, paints it with the background brush), and then sends the WM_PAINT message. It returns TRUE if successful. If the erase flag is FALSE, the background is not erased. A typical usage is coded

```
InvalidateRect (HWND, &rect, TRUE);
```

Within the paint code, one can get the invalid rectangle either directly from the **BeginPaint** function or by calling

```
BOOL GetUpdateRect (HWND, RECT*, BOOL erase flag);
```

A typical coding could be

```
RECT *ptrrect;
GetUpdateRect (hwnd, ptrrect, TRUE);
```

Since TRUE is passed, Windows 95 sends a WM_ERASEBKGND message, but we normally just pass it on to the default handler that paints the background for us. Alternatively, we can gain access to the invalid portion by referencing member fields of the PAINTSTRUCT structure that are filled in by the **BeginPaint** function. A typical coding is

```
PAINTSTRUCT ps;
hdc = BeginPaint (HWND, &ps);
```

The three fields of the paint structure intended for our use are identified as

ps.hdc   = the device context handle that is returned by **BeginPaint**

ps.fErase   = BOOL - TRUE if Windows has erased the background already

ps.rcPaint   = RECT structure of the invalid portion of client area

The RECT fields are **top, left, bottom, right**—all ints. But what do they contain? They are the coordinates (x, y) in pixels, of the respective corners. But where exactly is the point (0,0)? The origin of the coordinates is the upper-left corner of the client area. How convenient—the Graphical Device Interface (GDI) coordinates with which we must deal are simply our working window area, *not* those of the full screen. Thus we are not forever trying to adjust coordinates. (There are ways of obtaining a handle to the entire screen and displaying there, but if we do so we may overlay other applications.)

Further, with GDI operations, Windows 95 normally *clips* all display operations so that nothing is displayed outside your client area. In fact, you do not even need to be concerned—just display the text and if the message is too long, Windows 95 automatically clips it. Rerun the Pgm01 program and resize the window so that it is much too narrow for the message and watch the clipping occur. (Notice that you can set up a smaller clipping region within your client area and force text/graphics to stay within that clipping rectangle or region.) Most likely, your processing of WM_PAINT messages appears as

```
case WM_PAINT:
  hdc = BeginPaint (hwnd, &ps);
  ... insert your paint code here
  EndPaint (hwnd, &ps);
  return 0;
```

It is important that if you do not process WM_PAINT messages, you pass them on the default handler, which repaints the background. Failure to repaint the background results in a "black hole." The Windows 95 default handler's code would be

```
case WM_PAINT:
  BeginPaint (hwnd, &ps);
  EndPaint (hwnd, &ps);
  return 0;
```

If you want to create an infinite loop and lock up the application, just code

```
case WM_PAINT:
  return 0;      // forces infinite loop
```

Since the **BeginPaint/EndPaint** pair is not called, Windows 95 does not mark the invalid region as now being valid. Instead, Windows 95 immediately sends another WM_PAINT message, and another, and on and on and on.

2.2 PAINTING FROM OTHER PLACES

You can paint the screen in ways other than in response to WM_PAINT messages. However, you must get a handle to a valid device context (DC) to do so. Think of the DC as being the link between Windows 95 and the physical screen. There are several ways to get the DC; perhaps the simplest is to use the function pair

```
HDC  GetDC    (HWND);
     ReleaseDC (HWND, HDC);
```

Our typical coding is

```
HDC hdc;
hdc = GetDC (hwnd);
... insert coding to paint
ReleaseDC (hwnd, hdc);
```

> ***Design Rule 6:*** **While processing a message, whenever you get a GDI object, such as a DC, you must release it before you end processing of that message (or before the automatic storage of the HDC is freed). Failure to do so results in a *memory leak.***

That is, the memory occupied by that GDI object is *never* freed. And more important, there are a finite number of DCs. Your resources just keep getting smaller with each debug run! This applies to nearly everything you allocate under Windows 95, from GDI objects you create, such as brushes and pens, to global memory allocations. Memory leaks often are very hard to locate. Therefore, a tool like NuMega's Bounds Checker for Windows becomes invaluable, since it locates all such leaks. Visual C++, when in debugging mode, also notifies you of memory leaks.

2.3 How to Use the TextOut Function

An alternative function to **DrawText** to display text is **TextOut**, whose prototype appears as

```
BOOL TextOut (HDC hdc, int x, int y, char *ptrstring, int length);
```

TextOut displays a string beginning at the x,y coordinates using the current pen in the DC. If the length is -1 or omitted (the default if not coded is -1), it displays to the null terminator. The upper left corner of the text string rectangle is aligned on the x,y coordinates, which are based upon the client area. Actually there are many coordinate schemes possible (see chapter 11), but the default mapping mode, MM_TEXT, has the upper-left corner as 0,0 and the values increase downward and rightward. The other mapping modes are not often used. All values in MM_TEXT are given in pixels (in some other modes, strange units are used). Notice that you must have a valid DC to display text.

What colors are used? Each time you get a DC, it has a default pen and default background brush: a black pen with a white brush. This is because a common color scheme is black text on a white background. So we have to see how to set up other color schemes. Often at odds with this default DC color scheme, Windows 95 erases the background of the window by painting the window with the background color with which you originally registered the window. This is why I did not use my favorite light gray brush for a background in the sample programs. Chapter 4 addresses how to handle these two effects. If you are curious, consult "What To Do Next" at the end of this chapter.

The DC also provides a default clipping region that is the total size of the available client area. (Again, you could alter this, if desired.) The DC also specifies what font is to be used. The default is identified as SYSTEM_FONT and is the font used in the title bar. Fonts are fully covered in chapters 8 and 10, but, you must fully understand some details right at the start. Many fonts, including the system font, are called *variable-width,* or *proportional, fonts*, because the letter I has a smaller width than an M or W. In a *fixed-width,* or *nonproportional, font*, as used in DOS, all characters have the same width. There is also a SYSTEM_FIXED_FONT available, which emulates a DOS-style font in which all characters have the same dimensions. With variable-width fonts, spacing multiple lines in columnar alignment becomes much more difficult.

2.4 ACQUIRING TEXT MEASUREMENTS

The text metrics or measurements of a font can be found by the function **GetText-Metrics**, which retrieves those values from the passed handle to a DC. In other words, after a font has been selected into a DC (the system font by default), the function fills a structure with the relevant details about that font. The function syntax is

```
BOOL GetTextMetrics (HDC, TEXTMETRICS &);
```

Coding would be similar to

```
TEXTMETRIC tm;
HDC        hdc;
hdc = GetDC (hwnd);
GetTextMetrics (hdc, &tm);
ReleaseDC (hwnd, hdc);
```

Now where would this coding be placed? Not in the WM_PAINT handling! Normally the metrics only need to be determined once, not each time a paint is required. Unless you need to handle font changes, a better place to get these values would be in response to the WM_CREATE, which is a message sent as the window is about to be created. Sample coding to get the text metrics of the default font could be

```
case WM_CREATE:
 hdc = GetDC (hwnd);
 GetTextMetrics (hdc, &tm);
 ... save values into global variables or static variables
 ReleaseDC (hwnd, hdc);
 return 0;
```

What character values are desired? Well, we need to determine the characters' average width and height and the width of capital letters. The field in the TEXTMETRICS structure, **tmAveCharWidth,** contains the width. The height is given by **tmHeight**. However, there must be some whitespace separating lines of text which is given by **tmExternalLeading**. So the total height would be **tmHeight + tmExternalLeading**. (See chapter 10 for a complete discussion of this structure.) Assume that we have defined three global variables to hold the average character dimensions, such as

```
static int avg_char_width;   // average character width
static int avg_char_height;  // average character height
static int avg_caps_width;   // caps average width
```

Cap widths are generally 150% of lowercase widths for variable fonts and are the same width for fixed fonts. Since one does not know in advance what type of font the user may have installed, another textmetrics field is needed to identify which type, fixed or variable, is present. This is the **tmPitchAndFamily**, which is 0 for fixed and 1 for variable fonts. Thus the complete coding to capture these would be

```
case WM_CREATE:
 hdc = GetDC (hwnd);
 GetTextMetrics (hdc, &tm);
 avg_char_width  = tm.tmAveCharWidth;
 avg_char_height = tm.tmHeight + tm.tmExternalLeading;
 avg_caps_width  = (tm.tmPitchAndFamily & 1 ? 3 : 2)*avg_char_width / 2;
 ReleaseDC (hwnd, hdc);
 return 0;
```

2.4.1 Using the Text Measurements

Suppose you are going to display several lines of text. The x coordinate for the start of each line would be at **avg_char_width**, which would leave one character's worth of whitespace between the border of the window and the first letter. The clever part is figuring out the y coordinate. The y coordinate of the *ith* line (*ith* so that you can wrap a loop around the printing process) is given by **(I+1)*avg_char_height**. The +1 allows for one blank line at the top of the window so that the text is not up against the menu or title bar.

Next, how do we replace our familiar **printf**'s? Suppose that the **printf** used to be

```
printf ("Student ID: %71d  Grade: %3d", stud_id[i], grade[i]);
```

where **stud_id** is an array of longs and **grade** is an array of ints. What is needed is a method to convert the entire output of the printf into one string. In C, we learned the trick of using **sprintf**:

```
char msg[70];
sprintf (msg, "Student ID: %71d  Grade: %3d", stud_id[i], grade[i]);
```

Now we can pass **msg** to **TextOut**. But there is an even better method. Windows 95 provides a built-in function to replace **sprintf**. If we use the Windows 95 replacement, **wsprintf**, then the **sprintf** library routine does not have to be included in our program, making a smaller final program. But there is one caveat: **wsprintf** does not support floating-point numbers.

Windows also supplies a replacement function for **strlen** called **lstrlen**. Assuming that the field, **num_students**, contained the total number of students, the following would be try #1 for the paint operation:

```
case WM_PAINT:
 hdc = BeginPaint (hwnd, &ps);
 for (int i=0; i<num_students; i++) {
  wsprintf (msg, "Student ID: %71d  Grade: %3d", stud_id[i], grade[i]);
```

```
    TextOut (hdc, avg_char_width, (i+1)*avg_char_height,msg,lstrlen(msg));
    }
    EndPaint (hwnd, &ps);
    return 0;
```

Suppose there were 100 students and the user maximized the window. How many students will appear? Twenty-five lines, less one for the title bar and less one more for the whitespace at the top, would be shown. The first 23 or so students are displayed; Windows would clip all the rest. (We need Scroll Bars!)

2.5 SETTING THE TEXTOUT ALIGNMENT

The default is to align the top-left corner of the text string rectangle with the x,y coordinates. Other alignments are possible via the function

```
    UINT SetTextAlign (HDC, UINT alignflagbits);
```

The commonly used align bits can be one from each set ORed together. From x-direction:

TA_CENTER	horizontal centering
TA_LEFT	left side—the default
TA_RIGHT	right side

and from y-direction:

TA_BASELINE	baseline or middle
TA_BOTTOM	bottom edge
TA_TOP	top edge—the default

The default would be established if one had coded

```
    SetTextAlign (hdc, TA_LEFT | TA_TOP);
```

The following would right align the subsequent **TextOut**s:

```
    SetTextAlign (hdc, TA_RIGHT | TA_TOP);
```

Be sure to include the length of the text in the x,y coordinates. The function returns the previous align flags if it is successful. For example, suppose that we wished to right align the previous student grade lines. We could code

```
    char msg[70];

    case WM_PAINT:
    hdc = BeginPaint (hwnd, &ps);
    SetTextAlign (hdc, TA_RIGHT | TA_TOP);
    for (int i=0; i<num_students; i++) {
      wsprintf (msg, "Student ID: %7ld  Grade: %3d", stud_id[i], grade[i]);
      TextOut (hdc, avg_char_width*(1+70), (i+1)*avg_char_height, msg,
               lstrlen(msg));
```

```
    }
    EndPaint (hwnd, &ps);
    return 0;
```

Notice that the x coordinate is the max length +1 for the left space at the border multiplied by the average character width.

2.6 OBTAINING THE CURRENT SIZE OF THE CLIENT AREA

Before we can approach scroll bar processing, we must determine the current size of the client area. We would first define a pair of ints to hold the x,y dimensions.

```
    static int width, height;  // current client area size
```

When a window is being formed, both initially and after a resize operation, the application is sent a WM_SIZE message. The two short ints are stored in one long parameter so that it becomes necessary to extract them. This idea of placing two two-byte short ints in one four-byte long is common under Windows 95. Extracting the parameters from the message and placing them into usable fields is known as *message cracking* and is one major advantage of using MFC. Windows 95 provides two macros to extract the two short ints from the long: **LOWORD** and **HIWORD**. The processing would be

```
    case WM_SIZE:
      width  = LOWORD (lparam);
      height = HIWORD (lparam);
      return 0;
```

For any given client area dimensions, we have then the two formulae

    int number_lines = height/avg_char_height;

    int number_chars = width/avg_char_width;

What about division by 0? When **WinMain** calls **CreateWindow**, the application is sent the WM_CREATE message; later during the **ShowWindow** call, the application is passed the WM_SIZE message. Thus it is safe to insert the calculations in the WM_SIZE message processing; the average character dimensions are found in response to WM_CREATE before WM_SIZE is sent.

Be aware that it is possible for the number of lines or chars or both to be 0! A very small window may show only part of a text line. Further, when an application is launched, it is passed a series of WM_SIZE messages, beginning with 0,0 and ending with the final dimensions as the window first appears.

2.7 SCROLL BARS: THEORY OF OPERATION

A scroll bar consists of two endpoint *arrow buttons*, a *thumb bar* that shows the relative position within the document and a *slider track*. When the user clicks on either arrow button, you should scroll one unit. If text lines are shown, one unit would be one line or one column. If a graphical image is shown, usually the image is moved one pixel for smooth scrolling.

The thumb bar can be dragged by the user. Now you have two options. If you can repaint the client area quickly, you can immediately follow thumb bar motions on screen. However, if you cannot keep up, it is better to let the user reposition the thumb bar; when the button is released, repaint the client area.

One game that most users try when scrolling is to see if you can keep up with their fast thumb bar movements. Your users will get an inordinate amount of satisfaction if your application cannot keep up with their actions. In graphics mode, even when you have complex images to reform, there are techniques you can use to give the user the "high" of seeing blazingly fast scrolls, keeping up with his or her motions. This is covered in chapter 9.

Finally, the user may click at some point within the slider area. Again you have two choices. You may scroll one page per click or you may locate to the relative position that that place on the slider represents. I prefer the latter.

A window can have scroll bars placed automatically by Windows 95 by using the **CreateWindow** styles of WS_VSCROLL and WS_HSCROLL. Note that Windows manages these graphical elements and that their dimensions are not included in the client area. They always appear on the right and bottom. (To get scroll bars to appear elsewhere, you must create your own bars as a resource.)

Four functions are used to manage scroll bars; Windows 95 sends your application up to seven messages notifying you of user actions. Every scroll bar has an associated *range of travel* and the *current thumb bar position*. The functions include setting/getting the range and setting/getting the thumb bar position. The default range setting is from 0 to 100, where 0 is the top or left position and 100 represents the bottom or right position and where the ints, **min** and **max,** specify the new range.

```
BOOL SetScrollRange (HWND, SB_VERT or, min, max, BOOL redraw);
or                   SB_HORZ
```

The BOOL **redraw** is TRUE if Windows 95 is to redraw the scroll bar with the new range in effect. The second parameter is one of the two special identifiers. Related functions include:

```
BOOL GetScrollRange (HWND, SB_VERT or, int *min, int *max);
or                   SB_HORZ

BOOL SetScrollPos (HWND, SB_VERT or, int newpos, BOOL redraw);
or                 SB_HORZ

int newpos GetScrollPos (HWND, SB_VERT);
or                       SB_HORZ
```

The **newpos** is a discrete position within the range including the endpoints. Thus if we used a range of 0–100, the thumb bar position could be from 0 to 100.

Windows 95 takes care of handling the mouse actions, reversing video flash on clicks, displaying the ghost box on thumb bar dragging, and sending your application appropriate messages concerning scroll bar events. Your responsibilities include initializing the range, processing the desired scroll bar messages, and updating the thumb bar's current position.

Each mouse action generates two messages—one when the button is pressed and one when it is released. The messages are WM_VSCROLL and WM_HSCROLL. The **LOWORD(wparam)** parameter that accompanies the message indicates what the mouse action was. All the identifiers for these values, as you might have guessed by now, begin with SB_.

SB_LINEUP (pressed) or SB_ENDSCROLL (released)	top or left button
SB_LINEDOWN (pressed) or SB_ENDSCROLL (released)	bottom or right button
SB_PAGEUP (pressed) or SB_ENDSCROLL (released)	slider area top or left
SB_PAGEDOWN (pressed) or SB_ENDSCROLL (released)	slider area bot or right
SB_THUMBTRACK (pressed and dragged) or SB_THUMBPOSITION (released) and HIWORD (wparam) = current position of the thumb bar within the defined range	thumb bar action

Note that if the thumb bar action is ongoing, Windows 95 undoubtedly will be sending the application a barrage of SB_THUMBTRACK messages. If you cannot keep up with them, then act only on the SB_THUMBPOSITION message.

 Windows 3.1 Porting Tip: The WM_VSCROLL and WM_HSCROLL messages are significantly different. Under Windows 3.1 the ID was in **wparam** and the LOWORD of **lparam** contained the current position of the thumb bar. Be sure to look for the ID in **LOWORD(wparam)** and the position in **HIWORD(lparam)**. Under Windows 95 the **lparam** now contains the handle of the scroll bar control.

Under Windows 95 there is a new design consideration for the thumb bar and the page size (the amount to scroll the window when the user clicks in the slider area). The page size should be that amount of the scroll range that can be on-screen at one time. Thus a click in the slider area scrolls up or down one screen's worth of text, in this case. Correspondingly, the thumb bar should be representative of this size as well. The net effect of setting the page size under Windows 95 is widely variable thumb bar heights or widths (if horizontal). In other words, if there are 30 lines of text in the document and the screen can show 25, then the page size would be the size occupied by 25 lines. The scroll range would be 5 lines. The thumb bar height would span nearly the entire length of the scroll bar's slider height!

Personally, I dislike such monster thumb bars, although I appreciate the estimate of the actual amount of text that can be seen by scrolling. Windows 95 provides only one function to set the page size; it also sets the scroll range and thumb bar position. Hence, the preferred (but not by me) method of setting scroll ranges is the new function **SetScrollInfo**

```
SetScrollInfo (hwnd, SB_VERT or SB_HORZ, &scroll_info, TRUE);
```

where the TRUE requests the bar to be repainted with the new settings. The address of a SCROLLINFO structure, which defines all of the information to set the range and page size, is passed. The structure has the following members:

WORD fMask	ORed series specifying which of the following are valid
int nMin	the minimum scroll amount (usually 0)
int nMax	the maximum scroll amount in pixels
int nPage	the number of pixels in a page or screen height
int nPos	the current thumb bar position

The flags for the WORD that specify which are to be used include

SIF_PAGE	use the page amount to set page size
SIF-POS	set the position, use nPos
SIF_RANGE	set the range, use nMin and nMax
SIF_DISABLENOSCROLL	disable the scroll bar

Thus if one defined the scroll information structure as follows, then the page size, scroll range, and thumb bar position are all set by one function call:

```
SCROLLINFO si;
si.nMin = 0;
si.nMax = number_lines_to_scroll * avg_char_height;
si.nPage = height; // the current window height
si.nPos = 0;
SetScrollInfo (hwnd, SB_VERT, &si, TRUE);
```

2.8 STRUCTURING A PROGRAM FOR PAINTING

It is true that you can get a DC to your client area and paint on it nearly anytime. Occasionally, this would be the optimum approach. Another useful approach is to force a repainting by calling **InvalidateRect**, which results in a paint message being sent. Because WM_PAINT messages are low-priority messages, you may force a repainting at once by invoking

```
UpdateWindow (hwnd);
```

However, the nature of Windows 95 dictates that at some point it will be sending the application the WM_PAINT message and, when it does, the application must repaint the whole client area. (Task switching from an overlaying window is one example.) In other words, no matter what logical action your application is doing, the WM_PAINT coding must be able to recreate the whole window.

> ***Design Rule 7:*** **It is best to structure the application so that all of the client area painting is done in response to the WM_PAINT message whenever possible.**

This rule is so different from the normal processing logic with which programmers are comfortable that protests, perhaps even curses, are not uncommon. However, you will find that if you begin painting in multiple places, you will be duplicating code like mad. Let's examine how we might structure the text scrolling process so that the actual painting is done in response to WM_PAINT. We'll concentrate on the vertical scrolling process.

The starting point is the known total possible number of lines that are to be displayed: **TOTAL_LINES**. When we receive the WM_SIZE message, we can retrieve the current size of the client area and save the dimensions in the static fields **width** and **height**. From this, we can calculate the number of lines per client window page as

```
num_lines_per_page = height / avg_char_height;
```

that is, the number of vertical pixels of the client area divided by the average height of a character in pixels.

Now the total lines minus the number of lines per page, plus one for a top blank line for readability, would be the number of lines that are not yet on screen—or the number of lines to scroll. This is the maximum scrolling range. However, if the total lines were fewer than could be shown or the number of lines possible in the client area exceeds the total to be displayed, then the maximum scroll should be 0. Therefore, using the following, we can set the new vertical scroll range:

```
max_scroll_lines = max (0, TOTAL_LINES - num_lines_per_page + 1);
```

MFC provides a built-in pair of macros, **max** and **min**, that are defined as follows:

```
#define min(a,b) (((a) < (b)) ? (a) : (b))
#define max(a,b) (((a) > (b)) ? (a) : (b))
```

The thumb bar's position is really the current line that is at the top of the client window, called **current_top_line**. The thumb position is more complex. Consider the following situation. There are 50 lines to be shown, the client area can show 20, the user has scrolled such that line 10 is at the top of the window, the thumb bar setting would be at line 10, and now the user resizes the window smaller. The **current_top_line** would be 10, and say we calculate a new **max_scroll_lines** as 15. So after coding the following, we would then set the new current thumb position:

```
current_top_line = min (current_top_line, max_scroll_lines);
```

Now we need to establish the number of lines to scroll: **num_lines_to_scroll**. This is handled as we process the WM_VSCROLL message; the **LOWORD(wparam)** parameter is switched into the possible mouse events. For line up/down, we set the number of lines to scroll to -1 for up, +1 for down. For page up/down, we use the number of lines per page, forcing at least 1 line up or 1 line down. For the thumb bar motion, the

HIWORD(wparam) of the message contains the current new position, so the new position minus **current_top_line** yields the amount to scroll.

To guard against variables out of range, we reassign the number of lines to scroll to be the larger of either the current max number of lines we could go up or the requested number of lines to move (the smaller number between the previously calculated number of lines to scroll and the difference between the current max lines and the current top line).

If there are lines to scroll, then four steps are needed: add the number of lines we are scrolling to the current top, yielding the new current top line; force the scroll by calling the **ScrollWindow** function; reset the new thumb position; and call **UpdateWindow** to force the repaint to top priority.

The **ScrollWindow** function handles the scrolling details, like hiding the mouse cursor, sending the paint message, and restoring the cursor. By calling the **UpdateWindow** we cause Windows 95 to repaint the uncovered area at the time of the scroll.

```
BOOL ScrollWindow (hwnd, int amount of horiz scrolling,
                   int amount of vert scrolling, NULL, NULL);
```

The two null parameters are pointers to the client area rectangle and the clipping rectangle. Since we want the whole window, both can be null (otherwise the parameters are both RECT*).

The WM_PAINT processing is now quite simple. We just need to calculate the actual starting and ending line numbers and perform a simple loop displaying those lines. The paint structure's rectangle's top coordinate divided by the **avg_char_height** gives any offset from the current top line, should Windows 95 request only part of the client area be repainted. Thus the start line number would be

```
start_line = max (0, current top - the offset if any -1);
```

Similarly, the ending line number would be

```
end_line - min (TOTAL_LINES, current top + bottom offset);
```

Within the display loop, all lines start at x coordinate **avg_char_width** so there will be some whitespace at the left border. The y coordinate would be **avg_char_height** times the ith line less current top +1, where the +1 allows for the blank first line. OK. So now we need some text to display to try all of this.

2.9 THE SYSTEM METRICS STRUCTURE

The function **GetSystemMetrics** retrieves any of the 40 system values, many that are of keen interest to us as programmers. It contains dimensions of the screen, dimensions of the main window, presence of a mouse, and so on. There are 40 special defined ID numbers to find the system values we might want. The function returns as an **int** the requested system value:

```
int GetSystemMetrics (id_desired);
```

2.10 PGM02a: THE WRONG WAY TO DISPLAY WITH VARIABLE-WIDTH FONTS

I adopt display logic in Pgm02a.c that most of you are familiar with—creating an array of 40 strings that contain the text, including a %5d to be used as a control string. For each system metric value, I use a **wsprintf** to print into the text message both the control string text and the system metric's value. It works perfectly under DOS. Examine the coding in Pgm02a.c. Notice how nicely formatted the strings in **sysmetrics_msg** appear. Notice too that there is an array of the special defined IDs, **sysmetrics_ids**.

Follow through the code and examine the implementation, and then run the application and experiment with the scrolling. Notice that I took the liberty to use capitalization for **WinProc**, **InitApplication**, and **InitInstance** for greater readability. When you see the screen output, you will see why this is the wrong way to handle this. Figure 2.1 below shows how the screen appears when the application is maximized. Can you figure out WHY this has occurred?

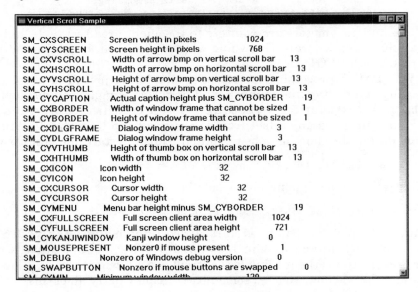

Fig. 2.1 Pgm02a. Poor Display of System Metrics with Scroll Bars

2.10.1 Listing of File Pgm02.c—Excerpts

```
/***********************************************************************/
/*                                                                     */
/* Pgm02a Vertical Scrolling Shell          by Vic Broquard            */
/*                                                                     */
/* C style  basic model                                                */
/*                                                                     */
/***********************************************************************/
```

```
#include <windows.h>

// min and max can be handy macros
#define min(a,b) (((a) < (b)) ? (a) : (b))
#define max(a,b) (((a) > (b)) ? (a) : (b))

/**************************************************************************/
/*                                                                        */
/* structure definitions, external/global data, and function prototypes   */
/*                                                                        */
/**************************************************************************/

LRESULT CALLBACK  WinProc (HWND, UINT, WPARAM, LPARAM); // main window proc
BOOL InitApplication (HINSTANCE);    // make and register our window class
BOOL InitInstance (HINSTANCE, int); // construct an instance of our window

char appname[] = "ScrollPgm";        // the name of our application

// global constants to facilitate processing SYSTEM METRICS display

#define TOTAL_LINES        40
#define TOTAL_CHAR_WIDTH 71          // width of message lines
#define NUM_WIDTH          5          // width of numerical values
#define LEN_CTL_SPEC       3          // length of %5d spec
#define TOTAL_WIDTH        TOTAL_CHAR_WIDTH + NUM_WIDTH - LEN_CTL_SPEC +1

int sysmetrics_ids [TOTAL_LINES] = {
 SM_CXSCREEN,            SM_CYSCREEN,        SM_CXVSCROLL,         SM_CXHSCROLL,
 ...
 SM_MENUDROPALIGNMENT, SM_PENWINDOWS,    SM_CMOUSEBUTTONS,       SM_DBCSENABLED
};

char sysmetrics_msg [TOTAL_LINES] [TOTAL_CHAR_WIDTH] = {
"SM_CXSCREEN            Screen width in pixels                  %5d",
"SM_CYSCREEN            Screen height in pixels                 %5d",
...
"SM_DBCSENABLED         Nonzero if double-byte character set enabled %5d"};

/**************************************************************************/
/*                                                                        */
/* WinMain: windows equivalent to a "main" in C pgms - MUST always be coded*/
/*                                                                        */
/**************************************************************************/

int APIENTRY  WinMain (HANDLE hInstance, HANDLE hPrevInstance,
                       LPSTR cmdline,  int howshow) {
 MSG         msg;

 // fill in WNDCLASS and register the app's window
  if (!InitApplication (hInstance)) return FALSE;

 // create an instance of the main window, show based on howshow
 if (!InitInstance (hInstance, howshow)) return FALSE;

 // enter the main processing loop consisting of get the next message,
 // convert the message into standard codes, send it our app's msg handler
 while ( GetMessage (&msg, NULL, 0, 0)) {
```

```
    TranslateMessage (&msg);
    DispatchMessage  (&msg);
  }

  return msg.wParam;   // pass along the generated success/fail return code
}
/***************************************************************************/
/*                                                                       */
/* InitApplication: fill in the WNDCLASS structure about how to construct */
/*                  our main window and then register this window         */
/*                                                                       */
/***************************************************************************/

BOOL InitApplication (HINSTANCE hInstance) {

  WNDCLASS wndclass;

  wndclass.style         = CS_HREDRAW | CS_VREDRAW; // repaint on size change
  wndclass.lpfnWndProc   = (WNDPROC) WinProc;       // our main win function
  wndclass.cbClsExtra    = 0;                       // reserves no extra space
  wndclass.cbWndExtra    = 0;
  wndclass.hInstance     = hInstance;               // insert our instance
  wndclass.hIcon         = LoadIcon (NULL, IDI_APPLICATION);
  wndclass.hCursor       = LoadCursor (NULL, IDC_ARROW);
  wndclass.hbrBackground = GetStockObject (WHITE_BRUSH);
  wndclass.lpszMenuName  = NULL;                    // no menu yet
  wndclass.lpszClassName = appname;                 // string name of the app

  return RegisterClass (&wndclass); // registers this window so it can be shown
}
/***************************************************************************/
/*                                                                       */
/* InitInstance: construct an instance of our main window using our just  */
/*          registered class or the previous instance running concurrently */
/*                                                                       */
/***************************************************************************/

BOOL InitInstance (HINSTANCE hInstance, int howshow) {

  HWND hwnd;

  hwnd = CreateWindow (appname,                 // char string ids the app
                       "Vertical Scroll Sample", // title bar caption
                       WS_OVERLAPPEDWINDOW,     // window style
                       CW_USEDEFAULT,           // window's initial x position
                       CW_USEDEFAULT,           // window's initial y position
                       CW_USEDEFAULT,           // window's initial x size - width
                       CW_USEDEFAULT,           // window's initial y size- height
                       NULL,                    // parent window's handle
                       NULL,                    // handle to window's menu
                       hInstance,               // handle of this instance
                       NULL);                   // creation parameters - advanced

  if (!hwnd) return FALSE;                      // window construction failed
```

```
  ShowWindow (hwnd, howshow); // creates window on the screen
  UpdateWindow (hwnd);        // paints the client (user area) of the window
  return TRUE;
}
/*************************************************************************/
/*                                                                     */
/* WinProc: our main window message processing function                */
/*                                                                     */
/*************************************************************************/

LRESULT CALLBACK WinProc (HWND hwnd, UINT msg, WPARAM wparam, LPARAM lparam) {

  static int num_lines_per_page;       // current number of lines/page
  static int max_scroll_lines;         // maximum vert scroll range
  static int current_top_line = 0;     // current vert scroll position
  static int num_lines_to_scroll = 0;  // current number of lines to scroll

  static int avg_char_height;          // average character height
  static int avg_char_width;           // average character width
  static int avg_caps_width;           // average capital chars width
  static int height;                   // current client window height
  static int width;                    // current client window width

  HDC          hdc;
  PAINTSTRUCT  ps;
  TEXTMETRIC   tm;
  int          start_line;
  int          end_line;
  int          I, x, y;
  char         textbuffer [TOTAL_WIDTH];

  // our app's message processing section - given a message from Windows,
  // determine if the message is one that we wish to respond to and do so
  // or pass it on down to the Windows provided default message handler
  switch (msg) {

/*************************************************************************/
/*                                                                     */
/* WM_CREATE: window creation processing                               */
/*                                                                     */
/*************************************************************************/

  case WM_CREATE:

    // acquire the system font's characteristics
    hdc = GetDC (hwnd);          // acquire a DC to get textmetrics of system font
    GetTextMetrics (hdc, &tm); // get the information

    // calculate average character parameters
    avg_char_width  = tm.tmAveCharWidth;
    avg_char_height = tm.tmHeight + tm.tmExternalLeading;
    avg_caps_width  = (tm.tmPitchAndFamily & 1 ? 3 : 2) * avg_char_width / 2;

    ReleaseDC (hwnd, hdc);       // free up the DC
    return 0;
```

```
/**************************************************************************/
/*                                                                      */
/* WM_SIZE: resize the window processing                                */
/*                                                                      */
/**************************************************************************/

  case WM_SIZE:

    // get current client window size
    width = LOWORD (lparam);
    height = HIWORD (lparam);

    // calculate new max range based on current size
    num_lines_per_page = height / avg_char_height;
    max_scroll_lines = max (0, TOTAL_LINES - num_lines_per_page +1);
        // note: if there is more screen than actual lines, set to 0

    // adjust thumb line position - could now exceed bottom position
    current_top_line = min (current_top_line, max_scroll_lines);

    // set up scroll range and position of thumb bar
    SetScrollRange (hwnd, SB_VERT, 0, max_scroll_lines, FALSE);
    SetScrollPos   (hwnd, SB_VERT, current_top_line, TRUE);

    return 0;

/**************************************************************************/
/*                                                                      */
/* WM_VSCROLL: process vertical scroll messages                         */
/*                                                                      */
/**************************************************************************/

  case WM_VSCROLL:

    switch (LOWORD(wparam)) { // Win 3.1 used only (wparam) a 16 bit value
      case SB_LINEUP:     // scroll up 1 line
        num_lines_to_scroll = -1; break;

      case SB_LINEDOWN:   // scroll down 1 line
        num_lines_to_scroll = +1; break;

      case SB_PAGEUP:     // scroll one screen up
        num_lines_to_scroll = min (-1, -num_lines_per_page); break;

      case SB_PAGEDOWN:   // scroll one screen down
        num_lines_to_scroll = max ( 1,  num_lines_per_page); break;

      case SB_THUMBTRACK: // follow thumb bar motion
                          // Win 3.1 used LOWORD(lparam)
        num_lines_to_scroll = HIWORD (wparam) - current_top_line; break;

      case SB_TOP:        // goto top
        num_lines_to_scroll = -current_top_line; break;

      case SB_BOTTOM:     // goto bottom
        num_lines_to_scroll = max_scroll_lines - current_top_line; break;

      default:
```

```
        num_lines_to_scroll = 0;
    }

  num_lines_to_scroll = max (-current_top_line,  // this is absolute max up
                        min (num_lines_to_scroll, // this is the requested num lines
                        max_scroll_lines - current_top_line) // is actual max num
                        );

  if (num_lines_to_scroll !=0) { // any lines to really scroll?
   current_top_line += num_lines_to_scroll; // increment thumb position ctr
   ScrollWindow (hwnd, 0, -avg_char_height*num_lines_to_scroll, NULL, NULL);
   SetScrollPos (hwnd, SB_VERT, current_top_line, TRUE); // set new thumb pos
   UpdateWindow (hwnd); // force repaint of client area
   }
   return 0;
/***************************************************************************/
/*                                                                       */
/* WM_PAINT: display text upon the current client window                 */
/*                                                                       */
/***************************************************************************/

  case WM_PAINT:

    hdc = BeginPaint (hwnd, &ps);

    // calculate start and ending lines to be displayed
    // start line num is the larger of 0 and the sum of the current top line
    // plus the number of lines from the top of the window down to the invalid
    // portion to be updated less one for the blank line at the very top
    start_line = max (0, current_top_line + ps.rcPaint.top/avg_char_height -1);

    // end line num is the smaller of the total possible lines and the sum of
    // the current top line + the number of lines that can fit in the

    // invalid rectangle
    end_line = min (TOTAL_LINES,
                    current_top_line + ps.rcPaint.bottom/avg_char_height);
    // display only those lines that can be visible
    for (I=start_line; i<end_line; I++) {
     x = avg_char_width;
     y = avg_char_height * (1 - current_top_line + I);
     TextOut (hdc, x, y, textbuffer,
              wsprintf (textbuffer, sysmetrics_msg[i],
                        GetSystemMetrics (sysmetrics_ids[i])));
    }

    EndPaint (hwnd, &ps);
    return 0;

/***************************************************************************/
/*                                                                       */
/* WM_DESTROY: close down the app processing                             */
/*                                                                       */
/***************************************************************************/
```

```
  case WM_DESTROY:
    PostQuitMessage (0);    // send ok to quit the app message back to Windows
    return 0;               // notify the message processor that we have handled
}
/**************************************************************************/
/*                                                                        */
/* Process all unhandled messages                                         */
/*                                                                        */
/**************************************************************************/

  return DefWindowProc (hwnd, msg, wparam, lparam);
}
```

2.11 PGM02b: THE RIGHT WAY TO DISPLAY WITH VARIABLE-WIDTH FONTS

The reason that the text columns did not align has to do with the variable-width font. Letters have differing widths between themselves and blanks. The first field was in all uppercase and had a varying number of letters; thus the total width of the capital letters' column varied from line to line. The solution is to break the line down into three columns that are to be aligned. Specifically, the "metric id" is the first column; the description becomes the second; the integer value, the third. Further, the first two columns are left aligned while the integer column is right aligned.

Examine the included sysmets.h file, which first defines the sysmetrics structure consisting of the three fields and then allocates and initializes that array.

2.11.1 Listing of File Sysmets.h—Excerpts

```
/**************************************************************************/
/*                                                                        */
/* SysMetrics header to define system metrics arrays for display in paint */
/*                                                                        */
/**************************************************************************/
#define TOTAL_LINES 40
#define COL_FIELD_2 22
#define COL_FIELD_3 46

struct {
 int  index;
 char *label;
 char *desc;
}
SysMetrics [TOTAL_LINES] = {
 {SM_CXSCREEN,    "SM_CXSCREEN",    "Screen width in pixels"},
 {SM_CYSCREEN,    "SM_CYSCREEN",    "Screen height in pixels"},
 ...
 {SM_DBCSENABLED, "SM_DBCSENABLED", "Nonzero if double-byte character set enabled"}
};
```

Next examine the revised Pgm02b.c program. The major changes are contained
in the WM_PAINT section. They consist simply of doing three **TextOut** calls combined
with **SetTextAlign** calls. Notice the calculations for the x coordinates of the second
and third **TextOut** calls. The second display accounts for the width of the first field.
The third display adjusts the x coordinate to the *ending* value of the third column
since the numbers are to be right aligned (Figure 2.2).

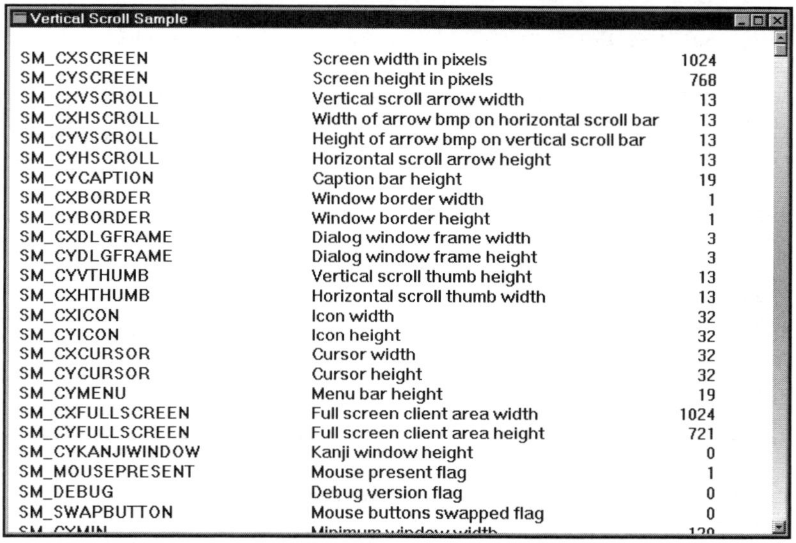

Vertical Scroll Sample		
SM_CXSCREEN	Screen width in pixels	1024
SM_CYSCREEN	Screen height in pixels	768
SM_CXVSCROLL	Vertical scroll arrow width	13
SM_CXHSCROLL	Width of arrow bmp on horizontal scroll bar	13
SM_CYVSCROLL	Height of arrow bmp on vertical scroll bar	13
SM_CYHSCROLL	Horizontal scroll arrow height	13
SM_CYCAPTION	Caption bar height	19
SM_CXBORDER	Window border width	1
SM_CYBORDER	Window border height	1
SM_CXDLGFRAME	Dialog window frame width	3
SM_CYDLGFRAME	Dialog window frame height	3
SM_CYVTHUMB	Vertical scroll thumb height	13
SM_CXHTHUMB	Horizontal scroll thumb width	13
SM_CXICON	Icon width	32
SM_CYICON	Icon height	32
SM_CXCURSOR	Cursor width	32
SM_CYCURSOR	Cursor height	32
SM_CYMENU	Menu bar height	19
SM_CXFULLSCREEN	Full screen client area width	1024
SM_CYFULLSCREEN	Full screen client area height	721
SM_CYKANJIWINDOW	Kanji window height	0
SM_MOUSEPRESENT	Mouse present flag	1
SM_DEBUG	Debug version flag	0
SM_SWAPBUTTON	Mouse buttons swapped flag	0
SM_CXMIN	Minimum window width	120

Fig. 2.2 Pgm02b Revised Display Method

2.11.2 Listing of File Pgm02b.c—Excerpts

```
/**********************************************************************/
/*                                                                    */
/* Pgm02b - Revised Vertical Scrolling Shell        by Vic Broquard   */
/*                                                                    */
/* C style  basic model                                               */
/*                                                                    */
/**********************************************************************/

#include <windows.h>
#pragma hdrstop

#include "sysmets.h"
// min and max can be handy macros
#define min(a,b) (((a) < (b)) ? (a) : (b))
#define max(a,b) (((a) > (b)) ? (a) : (b))
...
/**********************************************************************/
/*                                                                    */
/* WinProc: our main window message processing function               */
```

```
/*                                                                        */
/**************************************************************************/

LRESULT CALLBACK WinProc (HWND hwnd, UINT msg, WPARAM wparam, LPARAM lparam) {

static int num_lines_per_page;        // current number of lines/page
static int max_scroll_lines;          // maximun vert scroll range
static int current_top_line = 0;      // current vert scroll position
static int num_lines_to_scroll = 0;   // current number of lines to scroll

static int avg_char_height;           // average character height
static int avg_char_width;            // average character width
static int avg_caps_width;            // average capital chars width
static int height;                    // current client window height
static int width;                     // current client window width

HDC         hdc;
PAINTSTRUCT ps;
TEXTMETRIC  tm;
int         start_line;
int         end_line;
int         i, x, y;
char        textbuffer [10];

 switch (msg) {
...
/**************************************************************************/
/*                                                                        */
/* WM_PAINT: display text upon the current client window                  */
/*                                                                        */
/**************************************************************************/

  case WM_PAINT:

    hdc = BeginPaint (hwnd, &ps);

    // calculate start and ending lines to be displayed
    // start line num is the larger of 0 and the sum of the currrent top line
    // plus the number of lines from the top of the window down to the invalid
    // portion to be updated less one for the blank line at the very top
    start_line = max (0, current_top_line + ps.rcPaint.top/avg_char_height-1);

    // end line num is the smaller of the total possible lines and the sum of
    // the the current top line + the number of lines that can fit in the
    // invalid rectangle
    end_line = min (TOTAL_LINES,
                    current_top_line + ps.rcPaint.bottom/avg_char_height);

    for (i=start_line; i<end_line; i++) {

      // calculate starting coords of this line
      x = avg_char_width;
      y = avg_char_height * (1 - current_top_line + i);

      // display the capitalized string
      TextOut (hdc, x, y, SysMetrics[i].label,lstrlen(SysMetrics[i].label));
      // display the lowercase string, adjusting x for the length of cap field
      TextOut (hdc, x + COL_FIELD_2 * avg_caps_width, y, SysMetrics[i].desc,
```

```
                lstrlen (SysMetrics[i].desc));

    // set for numbers right aligned
    SetTextAlign (hdc, TA_RIGHT | TA_TOP);

    // get the value, fill the textbuffer, and display text
    // adjusting x start to skip to end of msg column
    TextOut (hdc,
             x + COL_FIELD_2 * avg_caps_width + COL_FIELD_3 * avg_char_width,
             y,
             textbuffer,
             wsprintf (textbuffer, "%5d",
                       GetSystemMetrics (SysMetrics[i].index))
            );

    // reset for normal left justification
    SetTextAlign (hdc, TA_LEFT | TA_TOP);
}

EndPaint (hwnd, &ps);
return 0;
```

2.12 OTHER POSSIBLE METHODS

Another way around the columnar alignment problem would be to switch to the SYSTEM_FIXED_FONT as shown in chapter 3. However, for variable-width fonts, there is a function that calculates the total length of a string in pixels: **GetTextExtentPoint32**

```
    BOOL GetTextExtentPoint32 (HDC, char *, int len, SIZE* sz);
```

Pass the string and its length along with the address of your SIZE structure (see chapter 3), which consists of two longs, **cx** and **cy**. The function calculates the pixel dimensions that the string would need based upon the font that is currently selected into the passed DC.

 Windows 3.1 Porting Tip: The commonly used function **GetTextExtent** is now obsolete and not available under Windows 95. Use the above replacement function. The old **GetTextExtent** function returned a DWORD in which the low order word contained the length in pixels, while the high word contained the height of the string:

```
DWORD GetTextExtent (HDC hdc, LPCSTR string, int length of string);
```

2.13 WHAT TO DO NEXT

Experiment with either of these programs, change the background brush to LTGRAY_BRUSH, and run the program. You will observe the problem of the DC containing only a default black pen and white brush. In chapter 4, we will see two ways of remedying the problem: use of either the function **SetBkMode** or **SetBkColor**. Look up these two API functions and then try each of them by adding one line in the paint section. If you feel creative, examine your documentation and add horizontal scroll bars to Pgm02b.

Handling the Keyboard and the Mouse

3.1 KEYBOARD BASICS

To appreciate a full treatment of the complete handling of the keyboard requires a thorough understanding of DOS keyboard operations and Microassembler language. (For a robust discussion of the keyboard, see the book by Charles Petzold listed in the bibliography.) Fortunately, for most Windows 95 programs, the keystroke processes can be simplified.

The ASCII coding sequence stores a single character in 1 byte; it is an arbitrary encoding scheme developed during the CM/P 8-bit microcomputer era and solidified in the early 1980s. For example, the character A is stored as a hex 0×41 code (decimal 65); a B is 0×42 (66). Commonly displayed special codes, such as !@#$%^&* and (, are included. The control key plus any letter, such as ^Z or ^C, are also stored, along with some CRT control codes, such as carriage return (\r), line feed (\n), form feed (\f), and the ESC key (0×1B). Two hundred fifty-six possibilities exist in any 1 byte. The lower 127 bytes contain all of the above. The upper ASCII sequence holds the foreign language set, text codes that form boxes, and text shading characters. These upper 127 values are seldom used in Windows 95 applications and, when needed, are often entered by the Character Map applet.

The IBM PC.AT introduced the *extended key codes*, including the arrow keys, the function keys, Ins, Del, Home, and End, for example. Since the ASCII sequence was completely filled, the coding got more complex. Special processing is required under DOS to get these extended 101 keystrokes. There are certain keystroke combinations that DOS and BIOS do not interpret, such as shift+right arrow, Alt+Tab, and Alt+Esc. Under DOS, these are ignored, but under Windows 95, some of them have meaning. More complexity is involved when you consider that the keystroke could include the shift, Alt, or control key being held down while another key is pressed—Alt+F4, for example.

Further, the keyboard sends two messages to the CPU: a key has been pressed down and a key is released. The CPU has to decide if the key was held down long enough to cause the auto repeat feature to begin and generate multiple keystrokes. And the final complexity is that the keyboard messages must be sent in real time— when they occur—and not just when an application is requesting a keystroke. Windows 95 allows an application to process keystrokes at any level of complexity desired.

Fortunately, unless your application is going to do exotic things with the keyboard, the process of getting keystrokes is nearly as simple as we are used to in C/C++. You only need to know whether the keystroke desired is a basic character/control code that is in the ASCII sequence or one of the extended 101 special control codes. Bear in mind that *all* keystroke actions are passed along to your application, most of which your application simply passes along to the Windows 95 default handler.

3.2 THE WINDOWS 95 KEYBOARD MESSAGES

Windows 95 sends a series of keyboard messages. Assume that the A key is pressed. The following series of messages are sent:

WM_KEYDOWN	indicates which key is pressed
WM_CHAR	indicates the a key and a repeat count if applicable
WM_KEYUP	indicates the key is released

If your application wishes to input normal characters and the ASCII control codes, only the WM_CHAR message is needed. Assume that the left arrow key is pressed. The following series of messages are sent:

WM_KEYDOWN	indicates which key is pressed: the left arrow
WM_KEYUP	indicates the key is released

Note that no WM_CHAR message is generated. If your application wishes to process any of the 101 extended keys, only the WM_KEYDOWN message is normally needed. If you use the Alt key in conjunction with a key press, then the following is sent:

WM_SYSKEYDOWN	indicates which key is pressed
WM_SYSCHAR	indicates the keystroke with Alt
WM_SYSKEYUP	indicates the keys are released

Windows usually examines the Sys Key messages, looking for menu hot keys, task switch keys, and so on. There are several other possible keyboard messages and more complexity as well, but these are the basics. Looking these messages over, only two are commonly needed by applications: WM_CHAR and WM_KEYDOWN.

Design Rule 8: **The WM_CHAR messages are processed to get normal characters and control codes.**

Design Rule 9: **The WM_KEYDOWN messages are processed for the 101 special key codes.**

With both messages, **wparam** contains the keystroke code. When processing regular characters, filter out (and handle if desired) the control codes. When processing the extended 101 keys (arrow keys, PgUp, function keys, and so on), use the Windows key ID values listed in Table 3.1 or in the WINUSER.H header file or in the Windows reference manuals.

Table 3.1 Windows 95 Virtual Key Identifiers (wparam)

Identifier	Hex value	Key
VK_CANCEL	0×03	Ctrl+Break Ctrl+C
VK_BACK	0×08	Backspace
VK_TAB	0×09	Tab
VK_CLEAR	0×0C	5 on numeric keypad with Numlock Off
VK_RETURN	0×0D	Enter
VK_SHIFT	0×10	Shift
VK_CONTROL	0×11	Ctrl
VK_MENU	0×12	Alt
VK_PAUSE	0×13	Pause or Ctrl+Numlock
VK_CAPITAL	0×14	Caps Lock
VK_ESCAPE	0×1B	Esc
VK_SPACE	0×20	Space Bar
VK_PRIOR	0×21	PgUp
VK_NEXT	0×22	PgDn
VK_END	0×23	End
VK_HOME	0×24	Home
VK_LEFT	0×25	Left Arrow

Table 3.1 Windows 95 Virtual Key Identifiers (wparam) (Continued)

Identifier	Hex value	Key
VK_UP	0×26	Up Arrow
VK_RIGHT	0×27	Right Arrow
VK_DOWN	0×28	Down Arrow
VK_SNAPSHOT	0×2C	Print Screen
VK_INSERT	0×2D	Ins
VK_DELETE	0×2E	Del
VK_0	0×30	ASCII '0'
....	....	
VK_9	0×39	ASCII '9'
VK_A	0×41	ASCII 'A'
....		
VK_Z	0×5A	ASCII 'Z'
With Numlock On		
VK_NUMPAD0	0×60	0
VK_NUMPAD1	0×61	1
VK_NUMPAD2	0×62	2
VK_NUMPAD3	0×63	3
VK_NUMPAD4	0×64	4
VK_NUMPAD5	0×65	5
VK_NUMPAD6	0×66	6
VK_NUMPAD7	0×67	7
VK_NUMPAD8	0×68	8
VK_NUMPAD9	0×69	9
VK_MULTIPLY	0×6A	*
VK_ADD	0×6B	+
VK_SUBTRACT	0×6D	-
VK_DECIMAL	0×6E	.
VK_DIVIDE	0×6F	/
VK_F1	0×70	F1
VK_F2	0×71	F2
VK_F3	0×72	F3

Table 3.1 Windows 95 Virtual Key Identifiers (wparam) (Continued)

Identifier	Hex value	Key
VK_F4	0×73	F4
VK_F5	0×74	F5
VK_F6	0×75	F6
VK_F7	0×76	F7
VK_F8	0×77	F8
VK_F9	0×78	F9
VK_F10	0×79	F10
VK_F11	0×7A	F11
VK_F12	0×7B	F12

3.3 WHO HAS THE INPUT FOCUS?

The keyboard is a shared resource between the Windows 95 system and all applications. When a key is pressed, the application with the *input focus* receives the keystroke messages. The *active window* or *active child window* normally has the input focus. Within a complex dialog box that has many controls, the control that has the input focus is shown by its altered image, often a dotted box around text within the button, for example. An application can trap WM_SETFOCUS and WM_KILLFOCUS messages if needed.

3.4 RESPONDING TO WM_KEYDOWN MESSAGES

As an example of how to process WM_KEYDOWN messages, let us add a keyboard assist to the vertical scrolling sample program from chapter 2. The up and down arrow should scroll one line; PgUp and PgDn should go up or down one client screen line; Home and End go to the very top or very bottom. At first glance, one might decide to code as follows:

```
case WM_KEYDOWN:
  switch (wparam) {
   case VK_HOME:  // same as SB_TOP
    num_lines_to_scroll = -current_top_line; break;

   case VK_END:   // same as SB_BOTTOM
    num_lines_to_scroll = max_scroll_lines - current_top_line; break;

   case VK_UP:    // same as SB_LINEUP
    num_lines_to_scroll = -1; break;

   case VK_DOWN:  // same as SB_LINEDOWN
    num_lines_to_scroll = +1; break;
```

```
  case VK_PRIOR: // same as SB_PAGEUP
   num_lines_to_scroll = min ( -1, -num_lines_per_page); break;

  case VK_NEXT:  // same as SB_PAGEDOWN
   num_lines_to_scroll = max ( 1, num_lines_per_page); break;

  default: break;
  }
 num_lines_to_scroll = max (-current_top_line,
     min (num_lines_to_scroll, max_scroll_lines - current_top_line));

 if (num_lines_to_scroll !=0) {
  current_top_line += num_lines_to_scroll;
  ScrollWindow (hwnd, 0, - avg_char_height * num_lines_to_scroll,
               NULL, NULL);
  SetScrollPos (hwnd, SB_VERT, current_top_line, TRUE);
  UpdateWindow (hwnd);
  }
 return 0;
```

We have just DUPLICATED the scrolling code, however—a very bad practice. If you wanted to change the scrolling code, you would have to alter it in two separate places. The solution, and this is a commonplace solution, is to send us the appropriate scroll message and let the existent scroll coding handle it.

3.5 SENDING A MESSAGE TO YOUR OWN APPLICATION

Messages can be sent by using the **SendMessage** function, whose signature appears as

```
   LRESULT SendMessage (HWND, UINT message, wparam, lparam);
```

where the UINT is the WM_ message ID and **wparam** and **lparam** contain values appropriate for the message. In this instance, the message to send is WM_VSCROLL. The **wparam** contains an appropriate SB_nnnn code in the LOWORD and thumb bar position in the HIWORD. The **lparam** handle of the scroll bar control is not needed. The thumb bar position can also be safely ignored. The keyboard processing now becomes

```
   case WM_KEYDOWN:
     switch (wparam) {
     case VK_HOME:  // same as SB_TOP
       SendMessage (hwnd, WM_VSCROLL, SB_TOP, 0L); break;

     case VK_END:   // same as SB_BOTTOM
       SendMessage (hwnd, WM_VSCROLL, SB_BOTTOM, 0L); break;

     case VK_UP:    // same as SB_LINEUP
       SendMessage (hwnd, WM_VSCROLL, SB_LINEUP, 0L); break;

     case VK_DOWN:  // same as SB_LINEDOWN
       SendMessage (hwnd, WM_VSCROLL, SB_LINEDOWN, 0L); break;

     case VK_PRIOR: // same as SB_PAGEUP
```

```
        SendMessage (hwnd, WM_VSCROLL, SB_PAGEUP, OL); break;

    case VK_NEXT:   // same as SB_PAGEDOWN
        SendMessage (hwnd, WM_VSCROLL, SB_PAGEDOWN, OL); break;

    }
    return 0;
```

3.6 PROCESSING WM_CHAR MESSAGES

When processing WM_CHAR messages, the control codes are usually filtered out of the normal text stream with special actions taken occasionally, such as backspace-rub out. Also, the LOWORD of **lparam** contains the repeat count, if you wish to recognize the auto repeat feature.

Important simplification: when entering text into an edit control, Windows 95 assumes total responsibility for all keystroke actions, returning to the application the final complete string! This is discussed in chapter 7. Thus an application often does not need to trap WM_CHAR messages. The following represents how this may be accomplished:

```
case WM_CHAR:
 if (wparam<32) {  // all control codes are below a blank
  switch (wparam) {
   case '\b':   // backspace code
     ...
   case '\n':   // line feed code
     ...
   case '\r':   // carriage return code
     ...
   case '\f':   // form feed code
     ...
```

or you can use their values

```
    case 0x08:
    case 0x0A:
    case 0x0D:
    case 0x0C:
   }
   else {
    ... save or use character
   }
   return 0;
```

3.7 INPUTTING TEXT LINES: THE CARET

When inputting text characters, the DOS cursor normally marks the current input location. Under Windows 95 terminology has changed: the *cursor* refers only to the mouse cursor, and the *caret* refers only to the text insertion point (the old DOS cursor). The application is responsible for displaying a caret when needed. The main Windows 95 functions for handling the caret include

CreateCaret	constructs a hidden caret	called from WM_SETFOCUS
DestroyCaret	destroys a caret	called from WM_KILLFOCUS
SetCaretPos	sets caret position	called as chars are entered
HideCaret	hides caret	at the start of WM_PAINT
ShowCaret	displays caret	at the end of WM_PAINT

The caret normally appears as a vertical line or a solid rectangle, but it also can be a bitmap image. (I usually use the function **SetCaretBlinkTime** to force the caret to blink at its maximum, because the vertical bar is so hard to see.)

Windows 95 always sends an equal number of WM_SETFOCUS and WM_KILLFOCUS messages; that is, they always occur in pairs. During the processing of these messages, an application should create the caret and destroy the caret, respectively. The WM_SETFOCUS message indicates that the application now has the input focus and is the active task. When the WM_KILLFOCUS message arrives, the application is no longer the active task and should either destroy or hide the caret.

The caret must be hidden before painting the window; if the caret is not hidden, it is painted over. In response to a WM_PAINT message, then, the initial processing step should be to hide the caret and the last step should be to reshow the caret. Similarly, it is up to the application to update the caret after a character has been input and displayed. The different caret functions are coded

```
BOOL CreateCaret (HWND, HBITMAP, int width, int height);
```

If the HBITMAP, a handle to a bitmapped image, is a real bitmap image, the width and height are ignored. If HBITMAP is NULL, the caret is a solid; if it is 1, the caret is gray. The function returns TRUE if successful. For now, the width and height are in pixels. Often the width is one or two pixels, while the height is **avg_char_height**, the average character height for that font. All return a BOOL that is TRUE if the function was successful:

```
DestroyCaret ();                // destroys and removes it from screen
SetCaretPos  (int x, int y);    // moves caret to x,y on screen
HideCaret    (hwnd);            // removes caret from screen
ShowCaret    (hwnd);            // redisplays caret on screen
```

Realistically, unless you are writing some form of text editor, when an application needs to input some user text, an edit text control within a dialog box is most often used, so that Windows 95 handles all of the entry details returning the complete string to the application.

3.8 WRITING A TEXT EDITOR

Consider what steps would be needed to enter a line of text with the caret always pointing to the next point for data entry. If this were a DOS application, one could set the caret to the initial entry column and get a character. After displaying the character, the caret would be advanced one column. Under Windows 95 it becomes much more complex because of variable-width fonts. Yes, you can set the initial entry column and get the first character and display it; but exactly how many pixels do you advance the caret before showing it again?

On a long line, using the average character width can throw you so far off that the caret is several characters behind or ahead of the real insertion point. The easy way out is to use a fixed system font—and that is just what the Notepad editor does. (Ever wondered why no font selection is possible under Notepad, yet font selection is possible in WordPad?) Table 3.2 shows several of the Windows 95 stock fonts that can be selected for use.

All DCs begin with the SYSTEM_FONT installed as the default. If you want a fixed font, the ANSI_FIXED_FONT is recommended or, alternatively, the older SYSTEM_FIXED_FONT. To change fonts, you must have a valid DC. Before we examine dialog boxes, font changes are either done at the beginning of WM_PAINT, in order to install the required font before painting text, or during the processing of WM_CREATE, where the average character dimensions are currently acquired. The function **GetStockObject** retrieves the indicated stock object and the function **SelectObject** installs that new font or object into the DC. The two functions are often combined; the following installs a fixed font:

```
SelectObject (hdc, GetStockObject (ANSI_FIXED_FONT));
```

To restore the system proportional font, as the variable width fonts are known, code

```
SelectObject (hdc, GetStockObject (SYSTEM_FONT));
```

The two functions' prototypes are actually

```
HGDIOBJ SelectObject (HDC, HGDIOBJ);
HGDIOBJ GetStockObject (int object_id);
```

in which HGDIOBJ is a handle to a GDI object, a generic handle that can be used not only for a font, but also for pens, brushes, color palettes, and so on—any GDI object. Note that the function **SelectObject** returns the GDI object that was previously selected into this HDC. Later on, when we begin to create our own GDI objects, such

Table 3.2 Windows 95 Stock Fonts

Font name	Kind
ANSI_FIXED_FONT	Fixed pitch
OEM_FIXED_FONT	OEM defined
SYSTEM_FIXED_FONT	Font used by older versions of Windows
ANSI_VAR_FONT	Variable pitch
DEVICE_DEFAULT_FONT	Default device
DEFAULT_GUI_FONT	Default GUI
SYSTEM_FONT	Font used by Windows 95

as brushes and pens, we will make use of the return values, specifically to delete items no longer needed.

Note that one could repair the Pgm02a.c sample program by switching to a fixed font; the application would then respond with proper columnar alignment as in DOS programs.

WM_SIZE messages are sent not only when the user resizes the window, but also when the application is about to be minimized or maximized. Hence, some care must be taken when processing WM_SIZE messages; some of these messages may force a repositioning of the caret. WM_SIZE caret processing must only occur *if* our application has the input focus. This can be checked by the function

```
HWND GetFocus();  // returns HWND of the window with the input focus
```

The following code illustrates where and how the various functions would be handled in a text processing application:

```
case WM_CREATE:

  hdc = GetDC (hwnd);
  SelectObject (hdc, GetStockObject (ANSI_FIXED_FONT) );
  ... // get average character dimensions
  ReleaseDC (hwnd, hdc);
  return 0;

case WM_SIZE:
  any handling for the size alterations
  if (hwnd == GetFocus()) SetCaretPos (xpos, ypos);
  return 0;

case WM_SETFOCUS:
  // create a block cursor
  CreateCaret (hwnd, NULL, avg_char_width, avg_char_height);
  SetCaretPos (xpos, ypos);
  ShowCaret (hwnd);
  return 0;

case WM_KILLFOCUS:
  HideCaret (hwnd);
  DestroyCaret ();
  return 0;

case WM_KEYDOWN:
  switch (wparam) {
   case VK_DELETE: // handle delete key
   case VK_INSERT: // handle insert key
   ...
  }
  return 0;

case WM_PAINT:
  hdc = BeginPaint (hwnd, &ps);
  SelectObject (hdc, GetStockObject (ANSI_FIXED_FONT) );
  ... display all lines with TextOut
  EndPaint (hwnd, hdc);
  return 0;
```

```
case WM_CHAR:
  for (i=0; i< (int) LOWORD(lparam); i++) { // handle repeat count
    switch (wparam) {
    case '\b':  // handle backspace
    case '\t':  // handle tab
    case '\n':  // handle line feed
    case '\r':  // handle carriage returns
    case 0x1b:  // handle escape key
    default:    // handle actual character - note that some control
                // codes can still be passed here as valid codes
    }
  }
  SetCaretPos (xpos, ypos);
  return 0;
```

Of course the details of how you handle each depends upon the application's needs. You may not want to handle all of the editing keys.

3.9 THE MOUSE INTERFACE

To verify that a mouse is present, use **GetSystemMetrics (SM_MOUSEPRESENT)**, which returns TRUE if a mouse is installed. (This is a trivial point as it is nearly inconceivable that any one seriously runs Windows 95 without a mouse installed.)

The mouse cursor is a small bitmapped graphical image that moves about the screen pointing out things. The *hot spot* is the precise pixel at which the cursor is pointing. The tip of the default arrow, known as IDC_ARROW, is that cursor's hot spot. The center of the hourglass, known as IDC_WAIT, is the hot spot for that cursor. The center of the crosshair, known as IDC_CROSS, is that cursor's hot spot. Later, when we are designing our own cursors, we must notify Windows 95 where our custom cursor's hot spot is located. (See chapter 7.)

To install a cursor to be used as the default cursor for an application, load and assign it to **hCursor** in the WNDCLASS structure

```
wndclass.hCursor = LoadCursor (NULL, IDC_ARROW);
```

Later, we will change cursors when needed. We may want to display the hourglass cursor when the application enters a time-consuming process, for example.

A mouse has one or more buttons; most have two. They are identified as LBUTTON, RBUTTON, and MBUTTON. There are three mouse actions that occur with buttons and additional complexity is introduced by holding the shift or control key down while pressing a button.

single click	press and release a button
double clicking	press and release twice sufficiently fast
dragging	moving the mouse while a button is pressed

While there are many varied mouse messages potentially available, an application usually needs to respond to only a few. There are twenty-four mouse messages;

eleven, the *client messages*, are sent while the mouse is over the client area; thirteen, the *non-client messages*, are sent when it is not. Unlike keystroke messages queued and sent only when the application has the input focus, mouse messages are always sent, even when the application is not active or does not have the input focus. In fact, an application can *capture* all mouse actions whether or not they apply to your application. Normally, though, only those mouse events that occur over the client area are available for processing. In other words, Windows 95 directs the mouse event messages to those applications to which they pertain or to those applications that request to see all events. Usually, an application only wants to see mouse event messages that occur over its client area. Windows 95 processes and handles those events that occur on the frame window (resizing, moving) and the title bar, menus, and buttons.

3.10 CLIENT AREA MOUSE MESSAGES

Perhaps one of the more important messages is the WM_MOUSEMOVE message, which is sent anytime the mouse moves while over the client area. By processing these, you can know exactly where the cursor is within the client area. For example, in a window displaying a map of the world, WM_MOUSEMOVE could be used to continually update a message area that displays the current location—latitude and longitude. The **wparam** message parameter contains the status of whether keys are being held down. You can test whether the control or shift keys are being held down with these identifiers:

MK_CONTROL	for the control key
MK_SHIFT	for the shift key
MK_LBUTTON, MK_MBUTTON, MK_RBUTTON	for the buttons

Coding for the presence of these could be

```
if (MK_SHIFT & wparam)
 if (MK_CONTROL & wparam) // here both are held down while moving
 else // here only the shift key
else if (MK_CONTROL & wparam) // here only the control key is held
else // here none are held down
```

The current client area coordinates are found from **lparam** by extracting the two integer coordinates from the long value.

```
xpos = LOWORD (lparam);
ypos = HIWORD (lparam);
```

Button actions generate three possible messages for each available button on the mouse. For the left button

WM_LBUTTONDOWN	when pressed
WM_LBUTTONUP	when released
WM_LBUTTONDBLCLK	when double clicked

Similar messages are sent for the middle and right buttons for a total of nine different messages. In these messages, **wparam** contains the status of the shift key while the client area coordinates are in **lparam**. If an application is capturing all mouse events, then the coordinates can be full-screen coordinates; if not, they are client window-based coordinates.

However, to receive the **double clicks**, the application must have requested Windows to send double clicks. This is done by adding **CS_DBLCLKS** to the wndclass style

```
wndclass.style = CS_HREDRAW | CS_VREDRAW | CS_DBLCLKS;
```

Conveniently, for these messages, **lparam** contains the x,y coordinate of the hot spot at the time of the mouse action. The LOWORD contains the x coordinate; while HIWORD contains the y coordinate. The **wparam** field contains the status of the buttons and the status of the shift and control keys at the time of the button press.

Processing double clicks can get messy because a series of messages is sent. Assuming that one double clicks the left button over something in the client area, Windows sends the series

```
WM_LBUTTONDOWN, WM_LBUTTONUP, WM_LBUTTONDBLCLK, WM_LBUTTONUP
```

The WM_LBUTTONDBLCLK replaces a second WM_LBUTTONDOWN. Thus if a single click means one thing and a double click means something totally unrelated, the application will commence processing an action when it receives the first click and then it must cancel that action upon detecting that it really is getting a double click! Therefore, we formulate the following rule.

> ***Design Rule 10:*** **Double click messages are easier to handle if the first click of the sequence does the same action as a regular single click would have done. The ensuing double click then does something in addition to the simple single click.**

Recall mouse actions upon filenames within the Explorer's List of Files list box. A single click selects (highlights) the filename. A double click also selects that filename and, in addition, attempts to launch the associated application.

3.11 NONCLIENT AREA MOUSE MESSAGES

When the mouse is outside the client area window but still in the frame window area (such as on the frame border, menu bar, or title bar), Windows 95 sends the same messages as given earlier but with a different message ID. The identifiers are prefixed with NC for nonclient area. Thus, one would have such messages as

```
WM_NCMOUSEMOVE, WM_NCLBUTTONDOWN, WM_NCRBUTTONUP
```

wparam contains a special ID that identifies which portion of the frame window is involved, such as HTCAPTION or HTSYSMENU. **lparam**'s x,y coordinates are total

CRT screen coordinates. Two functions convert between screen coordinates and client area coordinates. Both are passed a pointer to the POINT to be converted. Both convert the points within the structure, replacing the previous point values.

```
ScreenToClient (hwnd, &p);
ClientToScreen (hwnd, &p);
```

The next mouse message is the nonclient area hit message, WM_NCHITTEST. This message precedes and accompanies all other mouse messages. **wparam** is not used while **lparam** has the coordinates. Applications usually pass this message on to the default handler, which then uses it to generate all of the other mouse messages.

If an application has captured the mouse in response to a pressed left button in order to begin drawing a line, for example, a WM_CAPTURECHANGED message is sent when the window is going to loosing mouse capture to another application that is suddenly activating. The WM_MOUSEACTIVATE message is sent when the cursor is in an inactive window and a button is pressed; here Windows 95 default action is to reactivate that inactive application. Finally, a WM_SETCURSOR message is sent to a window when the mouse moves; it then generates the WM_MOUSEMOVE message.

3.12 BUTTON CLICK PAIRING

Usually you would think that if your application gets a button down message then it should get a corresponding button up message later on. But this is not always the case. If you click the left button over an inactive window, Windows 95 changes the status to active and then passes WM_LBUTTONDOWN to the application. Thus your application can safely assume that your window is active when processing WM_LBUTTONDOWN messages. But if the user holds the button down and drags the mouse into another application's window and then releases the button, no WM_LBUTTONUP is sent to your application. Similarly, if your application gets a WM_LBUTTONUP message, there may not have been a WM_LBUTTONDOWN sent—the user presses the mouse button while in one window, but then moves into your window and releases the button.

3.13 MESSAGES SENT UPON CLOSING AN APPLICATION

This is a very general idea found repeatedly in Windows 95 operations. One basic message can beget a host of other messages in turn. This happens when the user attempts to close the application by any of the various methods, for instance. The attempt generates a WM_SYSCOMMAND message into the system with **wparam** set to SC_CLOSE. This generates a WM_CLOSE message. WM_CLOSE then invokes the **DestroyWindow** function, which generates a WM_DESTROY message we have been responding to by invoking **PostQuitMessage(0);**. This then generates the WM_QUIT message that causes **GetMessage** to return 0, which cancels the message processing loop.

Very often, an application traps WM_CLOSE messages. Processing would include asking the user if he or she really wants to quit, asking about unsaved files, and making similar queries. In later chapters, I make heavy use of these WM_CLOSE messages.

3.14 WORKING WITH COORDINATES

Windows provides two structures that greatly aid the communication of coordinates: POINT and RECT. All fields are ints. The POINT fields are **x** and **y**, in that order, while RECT contains **left**, **top**, **right**, and **bottom**, in that order. The SIZE fields are **cx** and **cy**.

Often the **lparam** contains the *x,y* coordinates of some event. Windows provides a macro to convert the **lparam** coordinates into a point structure: **MAKEPOINT**

```
POINT p = MAKEPOINT (lparam);
```

Notice that the RECT structure really is two POINT structures. Thus one can convert from a RECT to POINTs

```
POINT up_left = * (PPOINT) &rect.left;
POINT bot_rt  = * (PPOINT) &rect.right;
```

where PPOINT is a Windows 95–defined pointer to a POINT structure. An array of two points can be transferred into a RECT structure directly

```
POINT p[2];
RECT  r = * (PRECT) p;
```

where PRECT is a type pointer to a RECT.

3.15 HIT TESTING

When the user may select from a series of items, often the application, upon receiving the mouse click message, must determine which, if any, is the indicated item. This is known as *hit testing* or *hit checking*, and it can be done many ways.

One fundamental method is to construct an array of valid object locations. One matches the *x,y* mouse position with each object's location. When the mouse position is within an object's location, the current index into the array is then used to reference the object. The array could contain two points: upper-left corner and bottom-right corner. Or the array could contain one bounding rectangle. From the standpoint of coding ease, points are preferred; from the standpoint of data names, rectangles are preferred.

When dealing with graphical objects, upper-left and lower-right points are used directly. When dealing with text lines, one will either calculate and store actual *x,y* points or convert the mouse *x,y* position into text row and column by dividing the average character heights and widths.

In any event, hit testing can become a bit involved. Child windows can offer an easier approach, as we shall see shortly. Using a special color palette with unique color indices is another method, see chapter 9.

3.16 OTHER MOUSE FUNCTIONS

The mouse cursor can be hidden and reshown by the function **ShowCursor** where **which** is TRUE for showing the cursor and FALSE for hiding the cursor.

```
ShowCursor (BOOL which);
```

The current mouse position can be found from **GetCursorPos** and the mouse position can be set to a specific location by **SetCursorPos**. Both return a BOOL if successful.

```
GetCursorPos (POINT *);
SetCursorPos (int x, int y);
```

3.17 SOME MORE GRAPHICS FUNCTIONS

Once a DC has been obtained, many graphics functions can draw on that canvas or affect the drawing process. Although the default window background brush is selected when registering the class, when we get a default DC, only the black pen on white brush is provided. Before using the drawing functions, we can change from black on white by using the function **SelectObject**, which requires getting the required stock object by again using **GetStockObject**.

```
SelectObject (hdc, GetStockObject (LTGRAY_BRUSH));
```

Rectangles can be drawn using the **Rectangle** function.

```
Rectangle (hdc, left, top, right, bottom);
```

Ellipses and circles can be drawn with the **Ellipse** function.

```
Ellipse (hdc, left, top, right, bottom);
```

We can move the drawing pen to a position with the **MoveToEx** function

```
MoveToEx (hdc, x, y, POINT*oldpt);
```

where **oldpt** is filled with the pen's previous coordinates.

 Windows 3.1 Porting Tip: The function **MoveTo** no longer exists under Windows 95; convert those calls to **MoveToEx**.

We can draw a line from one position to another with the **LineTo** function

```
LineTo (hdc, x, y);
```

We will be discussing many more GDI functions, particularly in chapter 9.

3.18 USING CHILD WINDOWS

The main window often creates child windows to handle additional processing steps. Normally, a child window appears over the top of the parent window's client area. For a child window to be used, it must have been registered with Windows 95 before it can be created. The child window can be registered dynamically just before the application wishes to create it or, perhaps more conveniently, it can be registered in the **WinMain** procedure just after the main window has been registered.

In other words, the construction of child windows parallels completely that of the main window: **wndclass** must be filled and **RegisterClass** called. The child window must have its own message processing function similar to **WinProc**. The child window is created by using the **CreateWindow** function.

If the child window properties are known and not being dynamically determined in some fashion, the child windows most often are registered in **WinMain** just after the main window class is registered. It is very convenient here since often the **wndclass** structure can have a few fields modified and then registered. The **wndclass.lpfnWndProc** must be assigned the name of the child window message processing function. If the child window does not have a frame (and therefore max/min buttons and so on), the **wndclass.hIcon** is set to NULL. Then the **wndclass.lpszClassName** is assigned a new string name of the class.

When it becomes appropriate to create the child windows, the **CreateWindow** function is used. The returned HWND must be saved. The create window style often includes WS_CHILD | WS_VISIBLE.

The tenth parameter to **CreateWindow** is the handle to a menu or the *child window unique identifier*. It is important to note that if you are creating several instances of the same child window, each instance must be given a unique identifier when **CreateWindow** is invoked. Also, the parent's HWND and HINSTANCE are passed to the function.

Four functions can be used to acquire and set values contained in the WND-CLASS structure while the application is running.

```
DWORD GetClassLong (HWND, int id);
DWORD SetClassLong (HWND, int id, long newval);
```

For the **id** value, use the GCL_ values given in Table 3.3 below. These access the WNDCLASS values. The next pair access this window's WNDCLASS values and any extra data allocated. These should use the ID values that begin with GWL_.

```
DWORD GetWindowLong (HWND, int id);
DWORD SetWindowLong (HWND, int id, long newval);
```

 Windows 3.1 Porting Tip: These four functions must be updated. Under Windows 3.1 the WNDCLASS values were 16-bit and the functions used to get or set values are

Table 3.3 The WNDCLASS and WINDOW Special IDs

Windows 3.1	Windows 95	Purpose
GCW_CURSOR	GCL_CURSOR	get/set the cursor in use
GCW_HBRBACKGROUND	GCL_HBRBACKGROUND	get/set the background brush
GCW_HICON	GCL_HICON	get/set the icon in use
GCW_CBCLSEXTRA	GCL_CBCLSEXTRA	get/set extra bytes in WNDCLASS
GCW_CBWNDEXTRA	GCL_CBWNDEXTRA	get/set extra bytes in window
	GCL_MENUNAME	get/set the menu in use
GWW_HINSTANCE	GWL_HINSTANCE	get/set the hinstance
GWW_HWNDPARENT	GWL_HWNDPARENT	get/set the parent window HWND
	GWL_STYLE	get/set the window's style
GWW_ID	GWL_ID	get/set the child window's id
GWW_USERDATA	GWL_USERDATA	get/set any userdata

```
WORD GetClassWord  (HWND, int id);
WORD SetClassWord  (HWND, int id, WORD newval);
WORD GetWindowLong (HWND, int id);
WORD SetWindowLong (HWND, int id, WORD newval);
```

These functions must be updated to the 32-bit version. The ID numbers must also be changed.

The function **GetWindowLong (hwnd, GWL_HINSTANCE);** is used to retrieve the parent's HINSTANCE value. For example, you could create a child window as follows:

```
hwndchild = CreateWindow (child_win_name, NULL, WS_CHILD | WS_VISIBLE,
            0, 0, 0, 0, hwnd, 1, // unique child window id
            (HINSTANCE) GetWindowWord (hwnd, GWL_HINSTANCE), NULL);
```

Now in **WinProc**, the main window message processor, we have access to the defined **hwndchild**; thus it can communicate or send messages to the child window. But how about the child to its parent? Well, one could make the HWND of the parent a global field, but a far better practice would be to have the child call the **GetParent** function

```
hwndparent = GetParent (hwndchild);
```

where **hwndchild** is the HWND passed to the child window's message processing function. Messages, then, can be sent easily using **SendMessage**

```
SendMessage (hwnd of receiver, message id,
            wparam for msg, lparam for msg);
```

With **SendMessage**, the sender does not get control back from the function until the receiver has finished processing the message. An alternative is the **PostMessage** function, in which control is returned to the sender when Windows 95 places the message in its message queue. Both functions have the same syntax and similar purposes.

3.19 WINDOW LONGS: AN ADVANCED FEATURE

When working with child windows, there is frequently a need to have information concerning a child window readily available. Windows 95 provides this capability. When registering the child window class, you can notify Windows 95 to reserve some additional space in the class structure for user-defined fields. This is done with the **windclass.cbWndExtra** field. For example, to reserve a long of storage for our use, we could code

```
wndclass.cbWndExtra   = sizeof (long); // 4 bytes for our use
```

Note that the meaning and use of these extra bytes is *totally* user defined. The memory is within the child window class instance. Next, to access that data, we use the two functions

```
GetWindowLong (hwndchild, offset from the start of the extra longs);
SetWindowLong (hwndchild, offset from the start, new long value);
```

The WindowLong mechanism can be a very handy mechanism to store window instance data. We will do just this in the next sample program.

 Windows 3.1 Porting Tip: Consider using the four new long functions instead of the word functions.

Finally, child windows can be moved by the application (not the user directly) by using the **MoveWindow** function

```
MoveWindow (hwndchild, new x, new y, new width, new height,
        TRUE or FALSE to repaint or not);
```

3.20 PUTTING KEYSTROKES, MOUSE ACTIONS, AND CHILD WINDOWS INTO ACTION: TIC TAC TOE

A Tic-Tac-Toe game illustrates all of the ideas covered here. Figure 3.1 shows our game in progress.

The first implementation detail is how to handle the 3×3 grid of boxes. One approach would be to define a series of rectangles to represent the boxes. Displaying the grid would consist of drawing each box in turn. When a player presses the left button, we would place an X or O in the box. However, we must have smart code in the WM_LBUTTONDOWN message handler. It first has to decide if the mouse cursor is

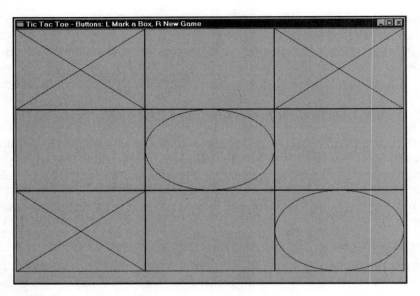

Fig. 3.1 The Tic-Tac-Toe Game in Progress

over any box, decide if the box is empty, and finally cause the X or O to be drawn. WM_PAINT must also be able to display the boxes and their contents. Suddenly, complexity is entering, but there is a simpler method.

Let's have each "box" be a child window. Each child window can then draw its defining box as defined by the size of the child window client rectangle. Now when the left button is pressed, if the cursor is within the client area of a box—the child window—then the child window's message processing function automatically passes the button message to the indicated child window. No coding is needed to decide where the mouse is or to learn which, if any, box is selected.

While a global array could be used to contain the child windows current contents—empty, X, or O—the class instance structure (the window long) easily could be used for this purpose. In other words, by requesting that Windows 95 reserve one long of memory for each child instance, then each child instance contains that instance's contents and is easily accessible.

We can use the **Ellipse** function to draw Os and the pair **MoveTo-LineTo** to draw the Xs—both sizes based upon the current child window's client area dimensions. So the resizing of the main window automatically resizes not only the box outline, but also the contained Xs and Os! We are beginning to have an elegant solution.

How do we control whose turn it is, which controls whether an X or O is drawn? If we have a global field, **whose_turn**, then when a child window accepts and places an X or O, the child window can send the parent window a fake WM_MBUTTONDOWN message. The parent window's WM_MBUTTONDOWN can then toggle **whose_turn** between 1 and 2 for X and O. It also needs to check to see if the game has been won. When **whose_turn** is 0, no game is in progress. All messages can check for this before handling messages to prevent spurious actions. All actual drawing can now be done in the WM_PAINT sections.

What do we do with erroneous user actions, such as attempting to select an occupied box? How do we identify the winner to the user? There are two valuable Windows 95 functions that are very useful for programmers: **MessageBeep** and **MessageBox**.

```
MessageBeep ( type );
```

MessageBeep either plays the sounds of the entries in WIN.INI [sounds] section or a standard beep. The possibilities of the type integer are

0 the standard beep

MB_ICONASTERISK

MB_ICONEXCLAMATION

MB_ICONHAND

MB_ICONQUESTION

MB_OK

The **MessageBox** function fulfills a very important role—how to display something quickly and easily. When invoked, a window opens up over the top of everything, displaying an icon, a title bar message, a text message within the box, and buttons to press. The syntax is

```
MessageBox (hwnd, text string, titlebar string, box style);
```

The text strings can be literal strings or string variables. The box style can be ORed combinations of the following elements (only common ones shown here). Button possibilities include

MB_ABORTRETRYIGNORE	3 push buttons for Abort, Retry, Ignore
MB_OK	1 push button for OK
MB_OKCANCEL	2 push buttons for OK and Cancel
MB_RETRYCANCEL	2 push buttons for Retry and Cancel
MB_YESNO	2 push buttons for Yes and No
MB_YESNOCANCEL	3 push buttons for Yes, No, and Cancel

OR possibilities for informational icons displayed in the left area of the box include

MB_ICONASTERISK

MB_ICONEXCLAMATION

MB_ICONHAND

MB_ICONINFORMATION

MB_ICONQUESTION

MB_ICONSTOP

The **MessageBox** function returns the following ID, depending upon which button was pressed:

> IDABORT
>
> IDCANCEL
>
> IDIGNORE
>
> IDOK
>
> IDNO
>
> IDRETRY
>
> IDYES

You probably can envision many uses for the simple message box. It is very handy. Our use here is to do a **MessageBeep (0)** on any invalid user action and display a **MessageBox** to announce the winner of the game.

So how about a new game? There should be a way the user can request a new game at any point. The winner's message box can ask if a new game is wanted. How can we allow the user to restart whenever he or she wishes? We can pick another unused mouse button, say the right button, which, when pressed, signals the start of a new game. OK, but more than likely, the mouse cursor is not over the main window but over a child window that is receiving the right button down message.

My solution is to use the keystroke CNTR-R (for restart) as the actual message signal for a new game. (So we can practice processing WM_CHAR messages.) Thus, a child window, upon detecting the right button down, can send the parent main window a WM_CHAR message with **wparam** set to the CNTR-R code. If the right button is pressed over the main window, it sends itself the CNTR-R code. This avoids the problems of the cursor being in the child window when the right button is pressed.

Figure 3.1 shows the main window and nine child windows in operation. Figure 3.2 shows the message box. Here is the coding for Pgm03.c.

3.20.1 Listing of File Pgm03.c —Excerpts

```
/********************************************************************************/
/*                                                                            */
/* Pgm03 - Tic Tac Toe With Mouse, Keyboard, and Child Windows        */
/*                                              by Vic Broquard        */
/*                                                                    */
/* C style  basic model                                               */
/*                                                                    */
/********************************************************************************/

#include <windows.h>
#include <string.h>
#pragma hdrstop

#define NUMBOX 3

/********************************************************************************/
```

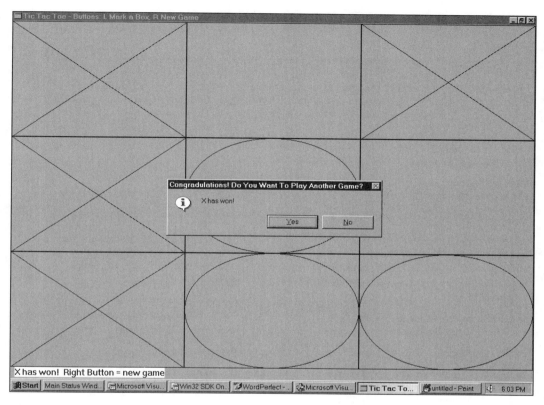

Fig. 3.2 The Tic-Tac-Toe Game Over Display

```
/*                                                                        */
/* structure definitions, external/global data, and function prototypes   */
/*                                                                        */
/*************************************************************************/

LRESULT CALLBACK  WinProc (HWND, UINT, WPARAM, LPARAM); // main window proc
LRESULT CALLBACK  BoxProc (HWND, UINT, WPARAM, LPARAM); // child window proc
BOOL InitApplication (HINSTANCE);    // make and register our window class
BOOL InitInstance (HINSTANCE, int); // construct an instance of our window

int        iswon (void);             // checks on a possible winner
int        whose_turn;               // 0, 1, 2 for none, X's, O's turn
static HWND hwndbox [NUMBOX] [NUMBOX]; // handles to the 9 box child windows
char       box_win_name[] = "box child window"; // child window names
static char appname[] = "TicTacToe";

/*************************************************************************/
/*                                                                        */
/* WinMain: windows equivalent to a "main" in C pgms                       */
/*                                                                        */
/*************************************************************************/
```

```
int APIENTRY  WinMain (HANDLE hInstance, HANDLE hPrevInstance,
                  LPSTR  cmdline,   int howshow) {
...
/****************************************************************************/
/*                                                                        */
/* InitApplication: fill in the WNDCLASS structure about how to construct */
/*                  our main window and then register this window         */
/*                  then alter WNDCLASS for the child windows and register */
/*                                                                        */
/****************************************************************************/

BOOL InitApplication (HINSTANCE hInstance) {

 WNDCLASS wndclass;
 BOOL retcd1, retcd2;

 wndclass.style          = CS_HREDRAW | CS_VREDRAW; // repaint on size change
 wndclass.lpfnWndProc    = (WNDPROC) WinProc;       // our main win function
 wndclass.cbClsExtra     = 0;                       // reserves no extra space
 wndclass.cbWndExtra     = 0;
 wndclass.hInstance      = hInstance;               // insert our instance
 wndclass.hIcon          = LoadIcon (NULL, IDI_APPLICATION);
 wndclass.hCursor        = LoadCursor (NULL, IDC_ARROW);
 wndclass.hbrBackground  = GetStockObject (LTGRAY_BRUSH);
 wndclass.lpszMenuName   = NULL;                    // no menu yet
 wndclass.lpszClassName  = appname;                 // string name of the app

 retcd1 = RegisterClass (&wndclass); // registers main window

 wndclass.lpfnWndProc    = BoxProc; // message processor for child windows
 wndclass.cbWndExtra     = sizeof (long); // 4 bytes for our x-o-empty id
 wndclass.hIcon          = NULL;
 wndclass.lpszClassName  = box_win_name;

 retcd2 = RegisterClass (&wndclass); // registers box window

 return retcd1 & retcd2;
}
...
/****************************************************************************/
/*                                                                        */
/* WinProc: our main window message processing function                   */
/*                                                                        */
/****************************************************************************/

LRESULT CALLBACK WinProc (HWND hwnd, UINT msg, WPARAM wparam, LPARAM lparam) {

 static int   x_box_dim, y_box_dim;  // box x,y dimensions
 static int   y_msg;                 // y coord for win message

 static int   avg_char_height;       // average character height
 static int   avg_char_width;        // average character width
 static int   avg_caps_width;        // average capital chars width
 static int   height;                // current client window height
 static int   width;                 // current client window width

 static int   won;                   // indicates winner 1,2,3 X,O,cat
```

```
int          x, y;
HDC          hdc;
PAINTSTRUCT  ps;
TEXTMETRIC   tm;

char win_msg1[] = " has won!";
char win_msg2[] = "  Right Button = new game";
char players[3][11] = {"The CAT", "X", "O"};
char shortmsg[25];
char textmsg[70];
/**************************************************************************/
/*                                                                      */
/* Message Processing Loop:                                             */
/*                                                                      */
/**************************************************************************/

switch (msg) {

/**************************************************************************/
/*                                                                      */
/* WM_CREATE: window creation processing                                */
/*                                                                      */
/**************************************************************************/

  case WM_CREATE:

    // acquire the system font's characteristics
    hdc = GetDC (hwnd);        // acquire a DC to get textmets of system font
    GetTextMetrics (hdc, &tm); // get the information

    // calculate average character parameters
    avg_char_width = tm.tmAveCharWidth;
    avg_char_height = tm.tmHeight + tm.tmExternalLeading;
    avg_caps_width = (tm.tmPitchAndFamily & 1 ? 3 : 2) * avg_char_width / 2;
    ReleaseDC (hwnd, hdc);

    // construct the child windows - for the 9 boxes - 3 X 3 grid
    for (x = 0; x<NUMBOX; x++)
     for (y = 0; y<NUMBOX; y++)
       hwndbox [x] [y] = CreateWindow (box_win_name, NULL,
                          WS_CHILD | WS_VISIBLE, 0, 0, 0, 0, hwnd,
                          (HMENU) ((y<<8) | x), // unique child window id
                          (HINSTANCE) GetWindowLong (hwnd, GWL_HINSTANCE),
                          (LPVOID) NULL);

    won = 0;          // set no one won
    whose_turn = 1;   // set for start up game
    return 0;

/**************************************************************************/
/*                                                                      */
/* WM_SIZE: resize the window processing                                */
/*                                                                      */
/**************************************************************************/

  case WM_SIZE:

    // get current client window size
```

```
    width  = LOWORD (lparam);
    height = HIWORD (lparam);

    // calculate new box sizes and y coord for win msg based on current size
    y_box_dim = (height - avg_char_height) / NUMBOX;
    x_box_dim = width / NUMBOX;
    y_msg     = y_box_dim * NUMBOX;

    // move child windows to their respective locations
    for (x = 0; x<NUMBOX; x++)
     for (y = 0; y<NUMBOX; y++)
      MoveWindow (hwndbox[x][y], x * x_box_dim, y * y_box_dim,
                  x_box_dim, y_box_dim, TRUE);
    return 0;
/***************************************************************************/
/*                                                                       */
/* WM_LBUTTONDOWN: process main window left button presses = here error   */
/*                                                                       */
/***************************************************************************/
  case WM_LBUTTONDOWN:
   MessageBeep (0);     // sounds the beeper
   return 0;
/***************************************************************************/
/*                                                                       */
/* WM_RBUTTONDOWN: process main window right button = start up new game   */
/*                                                                       */
/***************************************************************************/
  case WM_RBUTTONDOWN:
   SendMessage (hwnd, WM_CHAR, 18, 0L);  // send CNTL-R code signaling new game
   return 0;
/***************************************************************************/
/*                                                                       */
/* WM_CHAR: process normal keystrokes - CNTL-R = start a new game         */
/*                                                                       */
/***************************************************************************/
  case WM_CHAR:
   if (wparam==18) {  // is it CNTL-R?
    won = 0;           // set no winner
    whose_turn = 0;    // set no game yet so child windows can clear all boxes
    for (x=0; x<NUMBOX; x++)                      // for each child window
    for (y=0; y<NUMBOX; y++) {
      SetWindowLong (hwndbox[x][y], 0, 0);       // turn off X/O indicator
      InvalidateRect (hwndbox[x][y], NULL, TRUE); // force box to be cleared
    }
    InvalidateRect (hwnd, NULL, TRUE);           // force clearing of win msg
    }
    whose_turn = 1;                              // activate game
    return 0;
/***************************************************************************/
/*                                                                       */
/* WM_MBUTTONDOWN: process main window middle button presses              */
```

```
/*                                                                      */
/* child boxes signal an X or O was placed                             */
/*                                                                      */
/***********************************************************************/
  case WM_MBUTTONDOWN:
   if (!wparam && !lparam) {               // check for child's signal - both 0
    won = iswon();                         // is there a winner now?
    if (won) InvalidateRect (hwnd, NULL, TRUE); // if so, PAINT will show who
    else whose_turn = whose_turn==1 ? 2 : 1;    // no, so switch players
   }
   else MessageBeep (0);                   // beep on real middle button press
   return 0;

/***********************************************************************/
/*                                                                      */
/* WM_PAINT: if winner, show who - otherwise clear window              */
/*                                                                      */
/***********************************************************************/
   case WM_PAINT:
   hdc = BeginPaint (hwnd, &ps);

   if (won) {                              // any winner yet?
    // construct short msg for message box and long for window bottom
    if (won==3) {                          // is CAT game?
     strcpy (textmsg, players[0]);         // move in CAT winner
     strcpy (shortmsg,players[0]);         // move in CAT winner
    }
    else {                                 // no, is player
     strcpy (textmsg, players[won]);       // move in player winner
     strcpy (shortmsg, players[won]);      // move in player winner
    }
    strcat (textmsg, win_msg1);            // insert has won msg
    strcat (shortmsg, win_msg1);           // insert has won msg
    strcat (textmsg, win_msg2);            // insert prompt on screen

    // show the winner
    TextOut (hdc, avg_char_width, y_msg, textmsg, lstrlen(textmsg));

    // display message box and find out if another game is desired
    // but show congrats message box only once per game
    if (whose_turn) {
     whose_turn = 0;                       // halt game
     if (MessageBox (hwnd, shortmsg,
                "Congratulations! Do You Want To Play Another Game?",
               MB_ICONINFORMATION | MB_YESNO) == IDYES)
     SendMessage (hwnd, WM_CHAR, 18, 0L);  // send start new game
    }
   }

   EndPaint (hwnd, &ps);
   return 0;

/***********************************************************************/
/*                                                                      */
/* WM_DESTROY: close down the app processing                           */
```

```
/*                                                                      */
/**********************************************************************/

  case WM_DESTROY:
   PostQuitMessage (0);  // send ok to quit the app message back to Windows
   return 0;
  }

 return DefWindowProc (hwnd, msg, wparam, lparam); // process unhandled msg
}

/**********************************************************************/
/*                                                                      */
/* BoxProc: child window message processor                              */
/*                                                                      */
/**********************************************************************/

LRESULT CALLBACK BoxProc (HWND hwnd, UINT msg, WPARAM wparam, LPARAM lparam) {

HDC         hdc;
PAINTSTRUCT ps;
RECT        rect;
HWND        hwndparent;

 switch (msg) {

/**********************************************************************/
/*                                                                      */
/* WM_CREATE: window create msg                                         */
/*                                                                      */
/**********************************************************************/

  case WM_CREATE:
   SetWindowLong (hwnd, 0, 0);     // clear x-o flag
   return 0;

/**********************************************************************/
/*                                                                      */
/* WM_RBUTTONDOWN: right button = request for a new game                */
/*                                                                      */
/**********************************************************************/

  case WM_RBUTTONDOWN:
   hwndparent = GetParent (hwnd);
   SendMessage (hwndparent, WM_CHAR, 18, 0L);  // send parent start new game
   return 0;

/**********************************************************************/
/*                                                                      */
/* WM_LBUTTONDOWN: left button = mark this box                          */
/*                                                                      */
/**********************************************************************/

  case WM_LBUTTONDOWN:
   if (GetWindowLong (hwnd, 0)>0) MessageBeep (0); // if already marked, beep
   else if (whose_turn>0) {                        // if X's or O's turn, then
    SetWindowLong (hwnd, 0, whose_turn);           // mark X or O in this box
    InvalidateRect (hwnd, NULL, TRUE);             // signal to paint X or O
    hwndparent = GetParent (hwnd);                 // notify parent a box has
```

```
          SendMessage (hwndparent, WM_MBUTTONDOWN, 0, 0L); // been chosen
          }
        else MessageBeep (0);                          // game not in progress-beep
        return 0;
/**************************************************************************/
/*                                                                      */
/* WM_PAINT: draw box and insert X or O if needed                       */
/*                                                                      */
/**************************************************************************/
      case WM_PAINT:
        hdc = BeginPaint (hwnd, &ps);

        GetClientRect (hwnd, &rect);                   // get size of window
        SelectObject (hdc, GetStockObject (LTGRAY_BRUSH)); // set background color
        Rectangle (hdc, 0, 0, rect.right, rect.bottom);  // outline window

        if (GetWindowLong (hwnd, 0) == 1) {            // draw an X case
          MoveToEx (hdc, 0, 0, NULL);
          LineTo (hdc, rect.right, rect.bottom);
          MoveToEx (hdc, 0, rect.bottom, NULL);
          LineTo (hdc, rect.right, 0);
        }
        else if (GetWindowLong (hwnd, 0) == 2)        // draw an O case
          Ellipse (hdc, rect.left, rect.top, rect.right, rect.bottom);

        EndPaint (hwnd, &ps);
        return 0;
    }
    return DefWindowProc (hwnd, msg, wparam, lparam); // pass on unhandled msg
}

/**************************************************************************/
/*                                                                      */
/* iswon: determines if there is yet a winner                           */
/*                                                                      */
/* returns 0 = no winner, 1 = X, 2 = O, 3 = CAT                         */
/*                                                                      */
/**************************************************************************/
int  iswon (void) {

  int  x, y, I=0, winner = 0;
  int  ans [NUMBOX*NUMBOX];
  BOOL notdone = FALSE;

  for (y=0; y<NUMBOX; y++)                            // copy all box contents to ans
    for (x=0; x<NUMBOX; x++) {                        // for faster access to checking
      ans[i] = GetWindowLong (hwndbox[x][y], 0);
      if (ans[i++]==0) notdone = TRUE;                // if blank boxes remain, then
    }                                                // if no winner, game's not done

  // check for winner
  if (ans[0]==ans[1] && ans[0]==ans[2] && ans[0]>0) winner = ans[0];
  else if (ans[3]==ans[4] && ans[3]==ans[5] && ans[3]>0) winner = ans[3];
  else if (ans[6]==ans[7] && ans[6]==ans[8] && ans[6]>0) winner = ans[6];
  else if (ans[0]==ans[3] && ans[0]==ans[6] && ans[0]>0) winner = ans[0];
```

```
else if (ans[1]==ans[4] && ans[1]==ans[7] && ans[1]>0) winner = ans[1];
else if (ans[2]==ans[5] && ans[2]==ans[8] && ans[2]>0) winner = ans[2];
else if (ans[0]==ans[4] && ans[0]==ans[8] && ans[0]>0) winner = ans[0];
else if (ans[2]==ans[4] && ans[2]==ans[6] && ans[2]>0) winner = ans[2];

if (winner==0 && notdone==FALSE) winner = 3; // no winner and none empty =CAT

return winner;
}
```

The three globals are **whose_turn**, **hwndbox**, which is a 3×3 array to store the nine child windows' HWNDs, and **box_win_name**, which holds the child window's class name string.

In **WinMain**, after the main window class is registered with a light gray background brush, the child window box class is also registered, with **BoxProc** being the name of the child window message handler. Additionally, one extra long is reserved to store the box's contents.

In WM_CREATE, the child windows are created. The unique id becomes a combination of the 3×3 grid row/column index. Specifically, I store the column index in the rightmost byte and the row index in the left byte ($y << 8$). The field **won** is set to 0, for no winner yet, and **whose_turn** is set to 1, for X goes first. Notice the int **id** is cast to HMENU.

The child window sizes are calculated in WM_SIZE, based upon the new main window client area. However, space is left at the bottom of the main window for a winner message. This is in addition to the message box notification, which occurs only once per game. Why? The user selects no new game from the message box; the window then appears as it last was so we need a message showing the winner and stating "press right button to restart." Finally, now that the new dimensions are calculated, all child windows must be resized and/or moved and TRUE notifies the child window to repaint itself.

The main window beeps if the left button is pressed while in the winner message at the very bottom of the window. If the right button is pressed there, a WM_CHAR with CNTR-R code is sent (a decimal 18 or 0×12).

In WM_CHAR, if the character pressed is CNTR-R, we set both no winner and **whose_turn** to 0, saying no game is in progress. Next, all child windows have their window long containing the box contents cleared and the child window cleared. By having no game in progress, a child window only draws its box, with nothing inside it.

The WM_MBUTTONDOWN processes turns. It is invoked by messages sent from child windows after they have responded by placing an X or O in a box. I have used special values of **wparam** and **lparam**—0—to differentiate from middle button presses from someone who actually has three mouse buttons. First, **iswon** is invoked to find out if the game is over or if it is time to switch players. If the game has been won, the main window is forced to be repainted. All painting is done in WM_PAINT.

The main window's paint process does nothing until there is a winner. Remember, all of the main window is hidden behind the nine child windows, except for the results line at the bottom. When the game is won, two messages are constructed—one for the message box and one for the bottom of the window. The **whose_turn** coding keeps the message box from appearing more than once per game. If the user chooses "start new game," paint sends the CNTR-R message.

The child window message processor, **BoxProc**, is fairly short. In WM_CREATE, the reserved Window Words are cleared. In response to WM_RBUTTONDOWN, the handle of the parent window is retrieved so that the WM_CHAR message from CNTR-R can be sent to the parent.

When the user presses the left button, if the window long is not zero, the box is already occupied and a beep results. If it is empty, the window long is set to the player number and the window invalidated so that paint draws the X or O. Finally, the next turn message, WM_MBUTTONDOWN, is sent to the main window. The child WM_PAINT messages are processed by first installing a light gray background brush in the paint DC. Thus, the **Rectangle** function appears to outline the client area. Then, depending on the child window's window long, either an X or O is drawn.

After each turn, the **iswon** function checks to see if there is a winner. If the boxes are all filled and neither X nor O has won, the CAT wins the game. Therefore, **iswon** must get to the window longs of the child windows. This is why I made the array of handles global, so they can be referenced easily here. Perhaps you can come up with a better way to figure out a winner; my solution is rather crude.

3.21 WHAT TO DO NEXT

See if you can construct a main window and then construct a child window that is about one-half the dimensions of the main window. Whenever the mouse is in the child window area, display the cursor's current position in both client and whole screen coordinates. Have a right mouse button press launch the child window. Then have any subsequent mouse button press close the child window.

Controlling Windows 95 From C++ MFC

4.1 INTRODUCTION

Now that you have seen the basic C-style method of controlling Windows 95, you may appreciate using Class Libraries to greatly simplify the programming. MFC offers many benefits over C-style Windows 95 programming. Each window on screen is associated with a single instance of a class. Thus all coding for one class is located in one place, unlike the Tic-Tac-Toe game in chapter 3.

The message processing giant "switch" is replaced with class member function calls. For example, WM_PAINT messages are routed to the MFC **OnPaint** member function of the window involved. The message "switch" logic is totally eliminated. (Actually, it is hidden deep within the class libraries.)

Furthermore, the class library performs *message cracking*. This means that when a member function that is to handle a message is invoked, the MFC environment presents that function with parameters in a usable format. For example, when a window's paint function—the **OnPaint** member function—is invoked, you construct an instance of the **CPaintDC** class, which then encapsulates the invalid rectangle, the paint DC, and so on. If the background also needs to be repainted, when **OnPaint** is invoked, the MFC has already done so for you.

Similarly, when the class libraries invoke the member function that handles WM_MOUSEMOVE, the first parameter is the status of the keys and the second is a point representing the cursor location. In other words, all parameters to the member functions are in a form easily used by that function.

In the Tic-Tac-Toe game, the nine child windows would be controlled by nine instances of the child window class. MFC passes a hidden **this** pointer to the class instance. Additionally, the **this** parameter also simplifies and allows the removal of most static/global fields, since these often can be made class member fields and used only by the specific class instance.

What is the cost of all this simplification? Complexity and a nonstandardized language. It has been said that C is a cryptic language, but in C++ coding effects may become obscure, leaving the programmer with little idea of what is occurring. Also, programs get the "**fats**," that is, the exe file size balloons. To control Windows 95 from MFC effectively, a programmer must be well versed in C++ practices, especially with deriving classes and inheritance.

The payback is high, for it generally takes only a few C++ lines to generate enormous functional capabilities. In chapter 12, I will show you a complete text editor program that can perform full editing capabilities simultaneously on as many files as desired, each of which (complete with fancy tool bar) could be minimized or maximized, cascaded, or tiled—all done with about 100 lines of code!

This text uses Microsoft's MFC version 4.0 class library available with Visual C++ 4.0 and above. (We could also use other vendors that use MFC 4.0 as well, or use the companion book on Borland's OWL.) It is perfectly acceptable to use any other class library; it will be your responsibility to determine how to convert MFC coding into the alternative class library—not a difficult chore.

 Windows 3.1 MFC Porting Tip: If you used the **#define STRICT** option, try simply rebuilding the entire project under the new class library. Only a very few items may not port directly. Because of the class library, porting might be as simple as a recompile.

4.2 BEGINNING ACTIONS

Where do you start? Based upon personal experience, I would strongly encourage you to browse the on-line MFC Help system, which provides an excellent screen topic display for each MFC class. Figures 4.1, 4.2, and 4.3 show screen snapshots of on-line Help displaying information about the first of the class topics—**CWinApp**. Notice that all the MFC classes begin with **C**.

If you do not have a hard copy of the various texts of the class libraries, I would highly recommend that you spend the time and paper required to get a printout of each of the main MFC class headers as they are discussed in this and the following chapters. You will find these help listings extremely handy when programming. If you are an experienced C++ programmer, you may find it valuable to print out each of the MFC header files so you can see all of the member names defined in the class. Be forewarned that this generates a lengthy printout! (By the time you finish this book, you will be ready to read the MFC code to find exact answers to your ques-

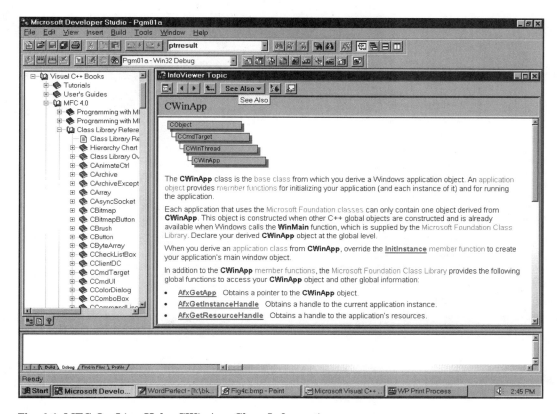

Fig. 4.1 MFC On-Line Help: CWinApp Class Information

tions.) The headers are in \MSDEV\INCLUDE\MFC and the source files are in \MSDEV\SOURCE\MFC.

Design Rule 11: **The first action when creating a new application is to code only the basic shell required for that application and then try to get the shell functioning.**

In my adventures learning windows programming, I have had more trouble getting the appropriate basic shell to compile and successfully display blank windows than nearly anything else! Remember this when you get to the later chapters, especially when we are dealing with the fancy decorations. (You could use the App Wizard to create the basic shell; for beginners, however, using the Wizards often creates more confusion than clarity.)

When you survey the MFC texts and magazine articles, you may encounter a bewildering number of what appear to be totally different basic shells and application code generators. This is a benefit of a good class library. There are numerous ways to

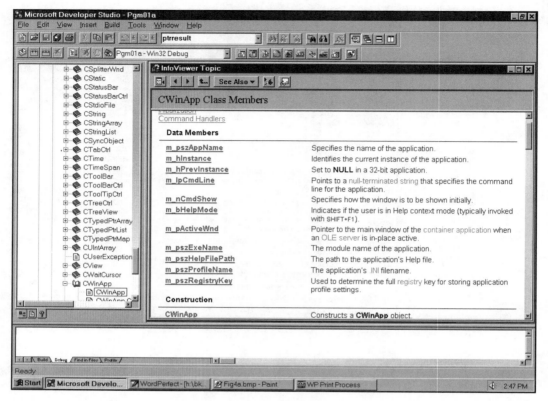

Fig. 4.2 MFC On-Line Help: CWinApp Class Data Members

accomplish the same task. But for very beginners who are even a little shaky on C++ coding and who are not intimate with Window 95 C programming, and who are not yet familiar with the names used and member fields contained within the classes, it can be awfully overwhelming, even to the point where simple shells refuse to compile or crash with weird errors.

A different problem you may encounter is others' use of the App and Class Wizards. Some beginning books use the App Wizard exclusively to construct their applications. Classroom experience has taught me that beginners who do not know the Windows 95 API or the MFC have trouble understanding the coding and knowing what they can change. I highly recommend that you avoid the Wizards until you have some experience programming Windows 95. When you reach the end of this book, you should be ready to master the Wizards.

Further, you may find that the exact sequence of initial function calls upon application and window launching can be both involved and confusing. Which Windows 95 options can be set and where is not as well documented as it might be.

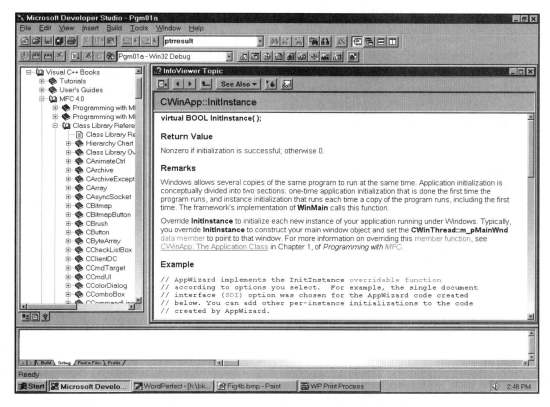

Fig. 4.3 MFC On-Line Help: CWinApp Class InitInstance Member Function

4.3 SOME BASIC PROPERTIES OF THE MFC CLASS LIBRARY

The MFC class library encapsulates the Windows 95 and Windows NT C-style API. Roughly three-quarters of the member functions used by beginning programmers are merely a convenience "wrap-around" of the C-style interface, providing independence from the C-style giant message switch, message cracking, and simplification by use of the **this** parameter. For example, when dealing with a window class, there is no need for the **hwnd** parameter; it is passed with the **this** parameter. Still, you need to study the C-style API that underlies the class libraries.

The MFC is limited to single inheritance. As a result, the MFC closely parallels the C-style API interface, function by function, and C-style methods.

> ***Design Rule 12:*** **Always compile with all messages on to get the best possible chance of having the compiler detect errors.**

You can comment out the variable names in parameter lists to avoid warnings about variables not used in function headers.

```
void  Fun (int /*first_parm*/, char* /*title*/) {
```

> **Design Rule 13: There should be no errors or warnings when compiling any module in the program if the option to report all errors and warnings is enabled. Under MFC use Level 4 warnings.**

To build a new project, first select File | New, then Project Workspace, and enter the path and name of the project in the dialog box. Next, if one or more of the project files already exist, choose Insert | Insert Files Into Project and select those that are to be included. (Omit the header files since they will be automatically found.) Next, choose Build | Settings. In the General property sheet, select Use MFC in a shared DLL and set the Intermediate and Output entries to Debug. Next, select the tab for C++ and set the error level to 4 to catch all possible errors. If you do not yet have any of the project files created, just select File | New and choose Text File. You will still need to set the Build options just mentioned.

4.4 MFC BASIC APPLICATIONS

All MFC programs begin by allocating an instance of their **CWinApp** derived class. **CAppWin** contains the **WinMain** function and provides application-wide activities. Thus, the first action in writing a MFC application is to create an application class derived from **CWinApp**. The public data members of **CWinApp** most often used include

```
CWnd       m_pMainWnd          // pointer to app's main window
LPCSTR     m_lpCmdLine         // the null-terminated command line string
HINSTANCE  m_hInstance;        // handle to this app instance
HINSTANCE  m_hPrevInstance;    // handle to any previous instances
int        m_nCmdShow;         // how to display the window - normal,
                               // minimized, maximized, and so on

LPCSTR     m_pszAppName;       // pointer to the app's string name
```

MFC provides several global functions for convenient access to application-wide information.

```
CWinApp *AfxGetApp ();                 // returns a pointer to the app object
HANDLE   AfxGetInstanceHandle ();  // returns the handle to this instance
HANDLE   AfxGetResourceHandle ();  // get a handle to the app's resources
LPCSTR   AfxGetAppName ();             // get a pointer to the app's name

                                       // - same value as m_pszAppName
```

Key Point: When you are not in your **CWinApp** derived class's member functions where these values are directly available, use these globally available functions to gain access. You'll need the handle to the application's resources in order to load strings and dialogs, for example, into memory for use. A typical **CWinApp** derived class header would appear as follows:

```
class MyApp : public CWinApp {

public:
        MyApp () : CWinApp () {}   // constructor of app
        ~MyApp () {}               // destructor of app
BOOL   InitInstance ();            // create & install main window

DECLARE_MESSAGE_MAP();             // reserve space for any message
                                   // handlers required - currently none
};
```

For beginning applications, the constructor simply invokes the base class constructor; the destructor is only needed if the application allocates items that need to be freed or destroyed (not often the case). All of the action occurs in the required **Init-Instance** member function. Essentially, the **WinMain** framework function calls your **InitInstance** member, which must be provided; then it calls the **Run** function; and finally it calls your **ExitInstance** function, if you have provided one. In **InitInstance**, you will allocate an instance of the main window class at least. Its coding closely parallels the C-style interface; typical coding would be

```
BOOL  MyApp::InitInstance () {

// construct new frame window
ptrframe = new FrameWin (NULL, "Hello From Windows 95 - MFC Style");

// install the frame window as the main window and show that window
m_pMainWnd = ptrframe;
m_pMainWnd->ShowWindow (m_nCmdShow); // show window in style passed
                                     // from Windows 95 command line
m_pMainWnd->UpdateWindow ();         // force window to be displayed
return TRUE;
}
```

To construct an instance of the application and run it, code

```
MyApp myapp;  // constructs the app object and executes it
```

The **CWinApp** class automatically invokes its **Run** member function on myapp. The sequence is different if your window class wants to dynamically create and run a child window. Dynamic launching is addressed in a later chapter. The three fundamental actions you need to do within **InitInstance** are: create (via **new**) an instance of your main window's class and install that instance as the main window of the application, using the data member **m_pMainWnd**; notify the framework how the window is to be displayed by passing along any parameter from the command line, such as a request to be shown maximized (**ShowWindow**); and force the window to be initially displayed or painted (**UpdateWindow**). Notice how closely this parallels the C-Style API interface.

If any clean up actions are required at the application level, you can place such coding in the **ExitInstance** function, as we will soon see.

The **CWinApp** function **UpdateWindow** updates the client area by sending a WM_PAINT message, while **ShowWindow** specifies how the window is to be shown. Their prototypes are

```
void UpdateWindow();
BOOL ShowWindow (int nCmdShow);
```

The parameter **nCmdShow** commonly has one of the following values:

```
SW_HIDE
SW_SHOW
SW_SHOWMAXIMIZED
```

 Windows 3.1 MFC Porting Tip: Under the Windows 95 MFC, 3d controls are now built-in to the operating system, eliminating the need to enable the three dimensional (3d) custom controls DDL, CTL3D.DLL. The function **Enable3dControls** is no longer needed. MFC will automatically handle the 3d controls and will ignore this function if you invoke it.

4.5 THE RELATIONSHIP BETWEEN MFC AND WINDOWS 95

The cycle to get a window displayed on-screen under the MFC closely parallels the C-style interface. As **WinMain** constructs the **CWinApp** object, a specific sequence of **CWinAPP** member functions are invoked. In order, they are

InitApplication: perform application-wide initializations, such as display a splash startup screen

InitInstance: allocate and show the main window class—*always coded*

Run: execute the application (seldom overridden)

ExitInstance: any special termination processing—not often coded

Normally only InitInstance is overridden. In chapter 13 splash screens are displayed from **InitApplication**.

 Windows 3.1 MFC Porting Tip: Assume that you have three instances of your application running, such as three Calculator programs. Under Windows 3.1 the relationship of these three functions has a specific meaning that tends to disappear under Windows 95. **InitApplication** is invoked *once* per application. **InitInstance** and **Run** are invoked once for each instance— here three times. The parameter **hPrevInstance** would be nonzero for the second and third instances. Under Windows 95 each application instance is in its own address space and does not normally know about the other instances. We have seen that **hPrevInstance** is now *always* zero. Under Windows 95 all three functions are executed once per instance.

Run handles the main message processing loop. When temporarily there are no more messages to be processed, **Run** invokes the **OnIdle** function, which we can override to perform idle-time processing. When the application is terminating, **Run** invokes **ExitInstance**.

4.6 DERIVING YOUR MAIN WINDOW CLASS

The basic MFC window class is **CWnd**, from which many specialized window classes are derived. **CWnd** provides for a fully functional window class but is rarely used as a main window. Another window class derived from **CWnd**, **CFrameWnd**, is a far better choice for the main window. **CFrameWnd** provides specialized operations useful for a main window. It conveniently handles borders, title bars, menu bars and choices, scroll bars, and so on. Later, we will want to create decorated frame windows with a control bar, tool bar, and status bar. These fancy items are easily handled through **CFrameWnd**. So for now, although we do not really need a frame window, we will make one. (We are going to be adding menus shortly; at that point we want a frame-type window to encapsulate the menu processing.)

A frame window can also support and manage a client window within its frame. And many fancier programs have a frame window class and a client window class, which is derived from **CWnd**. As we begin our first MFC examples, we do not need any of the specialized member functions or members of the **CFrameWnd** class. Because most items discussed in conjunction with **CFrameWnd** are inherited from the base **CWnd** class, the following discussion applies to both.

Creating windows requires that we understand several interrelated **CWnd** member functions—the constructor, **PreCreateWindow**, **Create**, **OnCreate**, and **OnDestroy**—along with the concept of the *window interface element* versus the *window interface object*. The real window currently displayed on-screen is called a *Windows 95 interface element* while the MFC class instance is known as an *interface object*. There is a specific pathway followed to get from instantiating an object of a class to having it appear on screen. Several steps are involved in the process; you can intervene in many different places in this cycle to tailor the window creation process to your needs. The problem is knowing where and how to intervene to make the change you desire.

An interface object (i.e., the class) provides member functions for creating, initializing, managing, and destroying its associated Windows interface element, automatically handling many Windows 95 details for you. It encapsulates the data needed to handle communications, such as window handles. Thus, the first step is to allocate (usually via **new**) a C++ instance of the class (the interface object). In the C++ constructor, the **CWnd Create** function is called to begin the Windows 95 interface element construction. Then, at the point when the actual window is about to be physically constructed, the **CWnd** member function **OnCreate** is invoked. It is in **OnCreate** that we would acquire those items that depend on the existence of a valid handle to a window, HWND.

If you have both a **CFrameWnd** and a client **CWnd** and if the client window has installed itself as a child window of the parent frame window (the normal case), then when the MFC destroys the application, the **CFrameWnd** must remove the **CWnd** main client window by destroying the windows interface element and the C++ object. The best place for such coding is in the **CFrameWnd** events response function **OnDestroy**, which is invoked to process WM_DESTROY messages. Here the frame window destroys the client child window and deletes the class object. No further actions on your part will be required for proper application termination.

4.6.1 Cycle to Set Up an Interface Object and Its Associated Interface Element

A. **WinMain** calls **InitApplication**, then **InitInstance**, then **Run**, and finally **ExitInstance**.

B. The default **InitApplication** function is not normally overridden, unless splash screens are desired.

C. Your **InitInstance** function does the following steps:

1. Allocates a new frame or window class, which builds the Interface Object.

2. Calls your window's overridden **Create** function, in which you can control all aspects of initialization, or in the class constructor, calls the **Create** function.

3. Calls **ShowWindow**. By altering **nCmdShow**, you can have the application appear minimized, maximized, or shown normally.

4. Calls your window's **SetWindowPos** to determine initial position and dimensions, or determines these in the constructor or **Create** function.

5. Calls **UpdateWindow** to cause a window to become visible.

D. Note that as **Create** is being invoked, the framework first calls your window's **PreCreateWindow** function. Here you also have complete access to the creation styles.

E. The framework, after **Create** is done and before the interface element is constructed, calls your window's **OnCreate** function. After invoking the **OnCreate** base class, the real Windows 95 Interface Element is built. The handle to the window is now valid.

F. While on screen, some items can be altered by **CWnd** member functions. Among these are the title caption, the current mouse cursor, and the window's position (**SetWindowPos** or **MoveWindow**).

Design Rule 14: **With only a few exceptions, always invoke the base class version of the overridden function as your first action in the derived function. Vital Point: If you need the HWND for some initialization steps, invoke the base class's OnCreate function first!**

More disasters of UEs and GP faults occur during program development from this one simple cause: failure to invoke the base class's **OnCreate** function before using the HWND. Be sure that it is the *correct* base class. If your application fails to appear on-screen or crashes before you see your main windows, the first thing to check is **OnCreate** and whether you invoked the correct base class as the very first action.

This sequence provides a great flexibility in application design. For example, the class constructor could directly call the **Create** function dictating how the window is to appear. I took this approach in some of the subsequent sample programs. However, there are circumstances in which the **Create** function must be called outside the constructor. This occurs when creating modeless dialogs and dynamically launching child windows, for example. The **Create** function could itself be overridden to provide special setup processing, if needed. **OnCreate** is commonly overridden to provide for construction of tool bars and to construct needed objects that depend upon the existence of a real HWND, such as obtaining the character size.

4.7 CWND AND CFRAMEWND PUBLIC DATA MEMBERS

CWnd has a vital public data member that is frequently used, HWND, the handle to the real window.

```
HANDLE  m_hWnd; // the handle of this window
```

4.7.1 CFrameWnd and CWnd Constructors

Normally, neither the **CFrameWnd** or the **CWnd** constructor needs parameters. However, since the constructors often invoke the **Create** function and therefore have access to the full WNDCLASS structure, if you wish the application derived class to pass such items as window style and placement, you can do so. With a frame window, for example, you might wish to pass the frame window constructor the caption title to be used and any potential child windows. Additionally, you might pass other application-specific parameters.

If you are constructing a client window **CWnd** as the child window of a frame window, in order to enable automatic destruction of the client window, you must pass a pointer to the parent frame window. The client **CWnd** then invokes the **Create** function, passing along the parent window pointer.

There is a reason that the **CWnd** and **CFrameWnd** constructors take no parameters—serialization. Serialization is a method by which a class can be dynamically constructed at run time from data stored on disk. In other words, a window could save its state (size and on-screen location) to disk; when the application starts, it can reload the window exactly as it was previously. Another term for this is a persistent data object. Nearly all of the entire MFC classes can be dynamically constructed. When you decide to pass a parameter to your class constructors, realize that you are generally going to lose a built-in framework default ability to stream that class to and from disk. For now, this is of no importance, but it will become important when we discuss it in chapter 15.

4.8 CWND MEMBER FUNCTIONS (INHERITED BY CFRAMEWND)

There are an enormous number of member functions in the **CWnd** class. Throughout the ensuing chapters, I will present many that are commonly used. Let's begin with the all-important **Create**. There is a slight difference between the **Create** function in the **CWnd** class and the **CFrameWnd** class. For **CWnd** derived classes, the **Create** function prototype is

```
BOOL Create (LPCSTR classname, LPCSTR title, DWORD style,
             RECT &rect, CWnd *ptrparent, UINT childid);
```

while for **CFrameWnd** derived classes, the **Create** function is invoked as

```
BOOL Create (LPCSTR classname, LPCSTR title, DWORD style,
             RECT &rect, CWnd *ptrparent, LPCSTR menu);
```

The **classname** is the null-terminated string name of a registered WNDCLASS, Windows 95 class. Commonly, we use another global MFC function, **AfxRegisterWnd-Class**, to create a new WNDCLASS structure with our values installed and return the string name for **Create**'s use.

```
LPCSTR AfxRegisterWndClass (UINT winstyle, HCURSOR cursor,
                           HBRUSH brush, HICON icon);
```

Typically, **winstyle** will be CS_VREDRAW | CS_HREDRAW so that the window receives scroll messages. The **style** parameter is often WS_OVERLAPPEDWINDOW. The **rect** contains the initial area to be occupied by the window. The special value, **rectDefault**, permits Windows 95 to position and size the window as it chooses. For client windows, **ptrparent** should be a pointer to the parent frame window. The **menu** parameter is the string name of the menu resource, which is discussed in chapter 6.

Notice in particular that you control the window style and placement and size. Additionally, you can provide the background brush or window background color, the default cursor, and the icon to be associated with the window. Specifically, the background brush is set by using the C API function

```
::GetStockObject (WHITE_BRUSH);
```

The presence of :: before a function is used to denote that the pure Windows 95 API function is being invoked. Many MFC functions have the same names as the C API function. Although the :: is purely optional (MFC determines which is which by the function's parameters), I use the :: in the examples to help you read the code.

In chapter 5, we will see how to install all manner of background colors. The functions to install the cursor and icon depend upon whether or not the object is a Windows 95 default stock object or one of our own creation. For the standard stock objects, use the following functions:

```
AfxGetApp()->LoadStandardCursor (IDC_ARROW);
AfxGetApp()->LoadStandardIcon (IDI_APPLICATION);
```

Notice that these functions belong to the **CWinApp** class and the global function **AfxGetApp** returns a pointer to the application class. Two other **CWinApp** functions can be used to load our own cursors and icons

```
AfxGetApp()->LoadCursor (IDC_OURCURSOR);
AfxGetApp()->LoadIcon (IDI_OURAPP);
```

These will be used in chapter 7 when we learn how to create cursors and icons. Another useful function not only moves the window to another location but can also alter its size

```
BOOL SetWindowPos (CWnd* ptr_insert_after_window, int x, int y,
                   int width, int height, UINT flags);
```

The first parameter is a pointer to the window that will precede this one, and it often is coded as 0 or NULL. (There are other special values this parameter can have, but they are an advanced topic.) The next parameters are the location and dimensions of the window in pixels. The flags commonly used are

```
SWP_HIDEWINDOW  - to hide the window
SWP_SHOWWINDOW  - to display the window
```

The return value will be nonzero if the window was previously visible or zero if it was previously hidden.

To destroy any child windows, the frame window must be able to acquire a pointer to its child. This is done using the **GetDescendantWindow** function whose prototype is

```
CWnd* GetDescendantWindow (int windowID);
```

This handy function returns a pointer to a specific child window. Recall that the child ID number is one parameter to the **Create** function. When a **CFrameWnd** wishes to destroy and delete a child or client **CWnd**, this function is invoked to obtain a pointer to the child window.

Another **CWin** function that sometimes can be used to set up the window's attributes is **PreCreateWindow**, which is called by the framework before the actual **Create** process is launched. Its prototype is

```
BOOL PreCreateWindow (CREATESTRUCT&)
```

Here you have access to the same CREATESTRUCT as in the **Create** function, whose members are

```
LPVOID  lpCreateParams;  // points to data to create the window
HANDLE  hInstance;       // the HINSTANCE of the owner, the exe file
HMENU   hMenu;           // identifies the menu, if any
HWND    hwndParent;      // identifies the parent window, if any
int     cy;              // these four specify the window's position
int     cx;              // and dimensions
int     y;
int     x;
LONG    style;           // the window's style flags
LPCSTR  lpszName;        // window's name string
LPCSTR  lpszClass;       // the WNDCLASS
DWORD   dwExStyle;       // any extended style flags
```

Here one could also set the window's dimensions and initial position as well as any style types.

Functions that respond to events are typically prefixed with **On**. Hence, the MFC member function that responds to WM_PAINT messages is **OnPaint**, which has no parameters. Instead of passing a DC ready for painting operations, the MFC provides another class, **CPaintDC,** to encapsulate the paint DC. The first action upon entering **OnPaint** is often

```
void  MyClass::OnPaint () {
 CPaintDC dc (this);
```

MFC provides several support classes that parallel exactly their Windows 95 counterparts. The **CSize** class encapsulates a two-dimensional quantity such as the height and width of a rectangle.

CPoint   class for POINT with int members: **x** and **y**.

CRect   class for RECT with int members: **top**, **left**, **right**, and **bottom**.

CSize   class for SIZE with int members: **cx** and **cy**.

To display our "Hello World" message centered, we need the size of the whole client area. The **CWnd** function **GetClientRect (&rect)** returns the dimensions of the client area for us. The parameter **rect** must be an instance of the **CRect** class, which also includes member functions for **Height ()** and **Width ()** of the rectangle. The **Get-ClientRect** function is passed a pointer to the **CRect** to be filled; you can view the prototype as either of these

```
void  GetClientRect (CRect*);
void  GetClientRect (LPRECT);
```

Actually, **CPaintDC** is derived from the more general **CDC** class that encapsulates a C-style HDC. The **CDC** class also has numerous functions for drawing and displaying, closely paralleling the HDC. One of the frequently used **CDC** functions sets the text alignment. The text alignment default is left justified but it can be set under MFC by the **CDC** member function

```
SetTextAlign (typedesired);
```

where the **typedesired** could be TA_CENTER. The **TextOut CDC** function is a bit different from the Windows 95 counterpart; it now has four parameters

```
TextOut (x, y, the text, length);
```

Often the length is omitted. If omitted, the default displays the whole null-terminated string. Notice that all of these **CDC** functions require the class instance, **dc**.

```
dc.SetTextAlign (TA_CENTER);
dc.TextOut (x, y, "Hello");
```

Finally, the **OnDestroy** function of **CWnd** is invoked as a window is terminating

```
void OnDestroy ();
```

but for either WM_PAINT and WM_DESTROY messages to be passed to member functions, entries must be made in the events map table

```
ON_WM_DESTROY()
ON_WM_PAINT()
```

4.9 MFC MESSAGE RESPONSE TABLES AND WINDOWS 95 WM_ MESSAGES

The MFC event handler receives all Windows 95 messages and routes each to the corresponding window instance. However, MFC must know which messages your derived windows class wishes to receive and what the member function name is to invoke to handle that message. This is the purpose and contents of the *message response table*. If your derived class does not wish to respond to a message, the MFC framework then checks to see if your base classes wish to do so.

The response table contains a series of specially named functions that will be invoked when the corresponding WM_ messages are received. These specific functions begin with ON_WM_ name of the message such as ON_WM_MOUSEMOVE and the MFC invokes a member function with the name **OnMouseMove**.

> *Design Rule 15:* **To determine the message identifier, take the normal Windows 95 message ID and prefix it with ON_. Thus the MFC response table message identifiers would be**

```
ON_WM_SIZE          for the Windows 95 message WM_SIZE
ON_WM_RBUTTONDOWN for the Windows 95 message WM_RBUTTONDOWN
ON_WM_LBUTTONDOWN for the Windows 95 message WM_LBUTTONDOWN
ON_WM_PAINT         for the Windows 95 message WM_PAINT
```

> *Design Rule 16:* **To determine the event handler member function name remove the WM_ from the Windows 95 message ID; prefix it with On; and convert to a capitalized format.**

So for the above, the member functions would be

```
OnSize
OnRButtonDown
OnLButtonDown
OnPaint
```

If the **CWinApp** or **CWnd** derived class wish to handle messages, the class definition header file must include a placeholder stating that there will be such a table for that derived class. Additionally, the table itself must be defined in the cpp file, rather like a member function would be defined. Somewhere within the class definition must be

```
DECLARE_MESSAGE_MAP();
```

The actual table is defined in the cpp file just like a member function. The basic syntax for an empty table is

```
BEGIN_MESSAGE_MAP(classname, baseclass)
END_MESSAGE_MAP();
```

Since there is normally no multiple inheritance in the MFC, there is usually only one base class. In our simplest examples, we must respond to paint messages. Thus, the message map for a client window might be

```
BEGIN_MESSAGE_MAP(ClientWin, CWnd)
 ON_WM_PAINT()
END_MESSAGE_MAP();
```

Design Rule 17: **Use a prefix of afx_msg to the event handler member function name in the class header, but do not use the prefix in the implementation cpp file.**

In the **ClientWin** header file, the paint function must be declared as

```
afx_msg  void  OnPaint ();
```

The prefix **afx_msg** must be present in the header. However, in the cpp implementation file, you omit the prefix

```
void  ClientWin::OnPaint () {
 CPaintDC dc (this);
 }
```

When you are creating a shell for your application, many functions are defined but you have placed no coding yet in the member functions. For example, you might code

```
void ClientWin::OnMouseMove () {
 }
```

When the shell is operational, you begin adding functional code step by step. This is an excellent approach, except with the **OnPaint** function.

Design Rule 18: **In OnPaint functions, always at least get a CPaintDC. A failure to get a paint dc in the OnPaint function may crash the application!**

4.10 PREDEFINED HEADERS: HOW TO MAKE THEM WORK FOR YOU

The idea behind the use of predefined headers is to speed up the compilation cycle by compiling the headers and storing them on disk. The next time the program is compiled, if those headers have not changed, the compiler simply reads in the results from disk. It sounds simple.

When we get to MFC applications, the header files become huge and compilation time is very, very long, even on fast machines. (Notice how long it takes on your machine to build the first example Pgm04a.) Precompiled headers become a must with MFC. There are several approaches that one can take to effectively utilize precompiled headers. However, here I make the first two of three concessions to the App Wizard (the second occurs in the next chapter with resources). Pragmatically, you may ultimately wish to learn how to use the App and Class Wizards, if only to be able to understand the many sample programs that use them. Also the wizard's solution is quite simple.

Construct a header file called **stdafx.h** and include all of the MFC headers required by the entire application. Second, create a one-liner cpp file called **stdafx.cpp** that includes this header file. Then include stdafx.h in *every* cpp file as the very first header include. (It is not needed in the class header files, just the cpp files.) The compiler creates the PCH precompiled header file once and uses it for all of the other cpp files. For now, the stdafx.h file appears as follows:

4.10.1 Listing for File: StdAfx.h

```
/*********************************************************************/
/*                                                                   */
/* Major Includes For Whole App - done for best use of precompiled headers */
/*                                                                   */
/*********************************************************************/

#ifndef MFCINCLUDES
#define MFCINCLUDES

#include <afxwin.h>    // MFC core and standard components
#include <afxext.h>    // MFC extensions
#include <afxcmn.h>    // MFC support for Windows 95 Common Controls
#endif
```

The size of the precompiled header for the first sample program below is about 2.6M. There is a special define that can be used that reduces the size of the headers by not including rarely used portions from the headers

```
#define VC_EXTRALEAN  // Exclude rarely-used stuff from Windows headers
```

If we use extra lean on the first sample program, the PCH file becomes 2M, for a savings of about 600K.

The second concession I make involves the extension for the class header files. I prefer to use an extension of hpp for C++ header files, reserving h for C-style headers. However, the wizards all use the h extension for everything. So to remain compatible with the wizards, I also use the h extension.

4.11 THE SAMPLE HELLO MFC PROGRAMS: PGM04a, PGM04b, AND PGM04c

If you examine the models shown in texts, magazine articles, and bulletin board samples (BBS), you find a bewildering array of possibilities. That's the benefit of OOP. Which one do we use for our applications? Remember that in texts, magazines, and BBS files, space is at a premium; often the examples are extremely short, just illustrating some idea. Seldom are these examples a real-world application. So while these are nice and compact for brief examples, such an approach can lead to a humongous single source file in a real application.

Good C++ design has probably been forcing you to have an h and a cpp file for each class. This approach has many benefits and is the one that I recommend and follow myself. The only drawback, as far as I am concerned, is the rather large number of files that can be generated.

This series of three versions of the "Hello" program illustrates several approaches. Pgm04a is the most complex—having both frame and client window classes. It is often found in decorated frame window SDI and MDI applications (single and multiple document interface). All classes have their h and cpp files. Pgm04b is the general approach I would recommend for beginning applications. The frame window serves as the main window. All classes have their h and cpp files. Pgm04c is the common shortcut that appears frequently in texts and magazines. It has the benefit of compactness—all is in one file. Figure 4.4 shows what the three versions produce.

All three programs use the same StdAfx.h and StdAfx.cpp files. Pgm04a uses both a **CFrameWnd** and a client **CWnd**. Pgm04b uses only a **CFrameWnd**. Pgm04c places all coding into one header and cpp file. It is recommended that Pgm04b be used as your model for beginning applications. Later on, we will begin to use the more complex model given in Pgm04a.

4.12 THE SAMPLE HELLO PROGRAM PGM04a: WITH SEPARATE CLIENT WINDOW

Let's examine the Pgm04a version first. The Pgm4AApp.h file contains the Pgm4AApp class definition, derived from **CWinApp**. For convenience, it is sometimes helpful to

Fig. 4.4 The Hello Program from Our Three Versions

keep pointers to the frame and client windows as protected data members, allowing fast access to such pointers. They can be ignored in programs that do not need them. But because I wish to save these pointers, the file begins with a forward reference to these classes: FrameWin and ClientWin. If the Pgm4AApp is not going to process any events, the response table can be omitted. In **InitInstance** in this sample, instances of both the frame and client window classes are allocated. Notice that a pointer to the frame class is passed to the constructor of the child client window. This way the client window constructor can call its **Create** function directly, passing the parent pointer so that the client window is installed as a child of the frame window. Alternatively, the constructor would not call **Create** directly; instead, **InitInstance** could call the client window's **Create** function, passing the pointer to the parent frame class.

4.12.1 Listing for File: Pgm4AApp.h from Pgm04a

```
#ifndef PGM4AAPP
#define PGM4AAPP

class FrameWin;    // forward reference to our CFrameWnd derived class
class ClientWin;   // forward reference to our main CWnd derived class

/*****************************************************************************/
/*                                                                         */
/* Pgm4AAPP: Class Definition                                              */
/*                                                                         */
/*****************************************************************************/

class Pgm4AApp : public CWinApp {

/*****************************************************************************/
/*                                                                         */
/* Data Members                                                            */
/*                                                                         */
/*****************************************************************************/

protected:

FrameWin*   ptrframe;    // ptr to the frame window
ClientWin*  ptrclient;   // ptr to the main client window

/*****************************************************************************/
/*                                                                         */
/* Class Functions                                                         */
/*                                                                         */
/*****************************************************************************/

public:

     Pgm4AApp () : CWinApp () {}        // constructor - no actions required
    ~Pgm4AApp () {}                     // destructor - no actions required

BOOL  InitInstance ();                  // constructs instances of frame and
                                        // main windows

/*****************************************************************************/
/*                                                                         */
```

```
/* Events Response Table Place Holder                                     */
/*                                                                        */
/* will be used in advanced applications - until then could be omitted    */
/*                                                                        */
/**************************************************************************/

DECLARE_MESSAGE_MAP();

};
#endif
```

4.12.2 Listing for File: Pgm4AApp.cpp from Pgm04a

```
#include "stdafx.h"

#include "pgm4aapp.h"
#include "framewin.h"
#include "mainwin.h"

/**************************************************************************/
/*                                                                        */
/* Events Response Table - currently none                                 */
/*                                                                        */
/**************************************************************************/

BEGIN_MESSAGE_MAP(Pgm4AApp, CWinApp)
END_MESSAGE_MAP ()

/**************************************************************************/
/*                                                                        */
/* InitInstance: Allocate instances of our frame and main client windows  */
/*                                                                        */
/* Note that a separate client CWnd is NOT required on smaller apps -     */
/* instead, the CFrameWnd class can handle the display actions within its */
/* client portion.                                                        */
/*                                                                        */
/**************************************************************************/

BOOL   Pgm4AApp::InitInstance () {

 // construct new main and frame windows
 ptrframe = new FrameWin (NULL, "Hello From Windows 95 - MFC Style");
 ptrclient = new ClientWin (ptrframe);

 // install the frame window as the main app window and show that window
 m_pMainWnd = ptrframe;              // m_pMainWnd is a public member of CFrameWnd
 m_pMainWnd->ShowWindow (m_nCmdShow);

 // setup an initial position and size for the client CWnd
 CRect rect;
 ptrframe->GetClientRect (&rect);
 ptrclient->SetWindowPos (0, rect.left, rect.top, rect.right, rect.bottom,
                          SWP_SHOWWINDOW);

 // force windows to be painted initially
 m_pMainWnd->UpdateWindow ();
 // Enable3dControls(); -- obsolete: enable 3d controls
```

```
  return TRUE;
}

Pgm4AApp  Pgm4a;  // constructs the app object and executes it
```

4.12.3 Listing for File: FrameWin.h from Pgm04a

```
#ifndef FRAMEWIN
#define FRAMEWIN
/******************************************************************************/
/*                                                                          */
/* FrameWin: Class Definition                                               */
/*                                                                          */
/******************************************************************************/

class FrameWin : public CFrameWnd {

/******************************************************************************/
/*                                                                          */
/* Class Functions                                                          */
/*                                                                          */
/******************************************************************************/

public:
        FrameWin (CWnd* ptrparent, const char* title); // constructor
        ~FrameWin () {}                                 // destructor

protected:

void    OnDestroy ();     // remove the client window

DECLARE_MESSAGE_MAP();
};
#endif
```

4.12.4 Listing for File: FrameWin.cpp from Pgm04a

```
#include "stdafx.h"

#include "framewin.h"

/******************************************************************************/
/*                                                                          */
/* FrameWin's Message Response Table - currently no events                  */
/*                                                                          */
/******************************************************************************/

BEGIN_MESSAGE_MAP(FrameWin, CFrameWnd)
 ON_WM_DESTROY()
END_MESSAGE_MAP();

/******************************************************************************/
/*                                                                          */
/* FrameWin: constructor provides access to wndclass before registration    */
/*                                                                          */
/* set up window's icon, cursor, background color, and the like             */
```

```
/*                                                                        */
/*************************************************************************/

          FrameWin::FrameWin (CWnd* ptrparent, const char* title) {
 CFrameWnd ();  // construct base class

 Create (AfxRegisterWndClass (
              CS_VREDRAW | CS_HREDRAW, // register window style UINT
              AfxGetApp()->LoadStandardCursor (IDC_ARROW), // use arrow cur
              (HBRUSH) ::GetStockObject (WHITE_BRUSH),     // use white bkgnd
              AfxGetApp()->LoadStandardIcon (IDI_APPLICATION)),// set min icon
        title,                  // window caption
        WS_OVERLAPPEDWINDOW,    // wndclass DWORD style => implies several others
        rectDefault,            // CFrameWnd member provides windows default pos
        ptrparent,              // the parent window, here none
        NULL);                  // no main menu
}

/*************************************************************************/
/*                                                                        */
/* OnDestroy: remove the child client window                              */
/*                                                                        */
/*************************************************************************/

void      FrameWin::OnDestroy () {

 ClientWin *ptrmainwin = (ClientWin*) GetDescendantWindow (0);
 if (ptrmainwin) {                 // if there is a client window, then
  ptrmainwin->DestroyWindow (); // destroy the interface element
  delete ptrmainwin;             // delete the object
 }
 CFrameWnd::OnDestroy();
}
```

4.12.5 Listing for File: MainWin.h from Pgm04a

```
#ifndef MAINWIN
#define MAINWIN

/*************************************************************************/
/*                                                                        */
/* ClientWin Class Definition                                             */
/*                                                                        */
/*************************************************************************/

class ClientWin : public CWnd {

/*************************************************************************/
/*                                                                        */
/* Functions:                                                             */
/*                                                                        */
/*************************************************************************/

public:
          ClientWin (CWnd *ptrparent); // constructor
         ~ClientWin () {}               // destructor
```

```
afx_msg void OnPaint ();                    // responds to WM_PAINT messages
DECLARE_MESSAGE_MAP ();

};
#endif
```

4.12.6 Listing for File: MainWin.cpp from Pgm04a

```
#include "stdafx.h"

#include "mainwin.h"

/****************************************************************************/
/*                                                                        */
/* ClientWin's Message Response Table                                     */
/*                                                                        */
/****************************************************************************/
BEGIN_MESSAGE_MAP (ClientWin, CWnd)
 ON_WM_PAINT ()
END_MESSAGE_MAP ();

/****************************************************************************/
/*                                                                        */
/* ClientWin: create the working client window                            */
/*                                                                        */
/****************************************************************************/
         ClientWin::ClientWin (CWnd *ptrparent) {

 CWnd ();            // construct base class
 CRect rect (0);    // real size determined after windows are made

 Create (AfxRegisterWndClass (
            CS_VREDRAW | CS_HREDRAW,
            0,
            (HBRUSH) ::GetStockObject (LTGRAY_BRUSH), // light gray backgrnd
            0),
        0,
        WS_CHILD,    // this is a child window of CFrameWnd
        rect,        // will be later reset when windows are active
        ptrparent,   // points to parent CFrameWnd
        0);          // child ID number
}
/****************************************************************************/
/*                                                                        */
/* OnPaint: paint client window lt. gray and display "Hello" message      */
/*                                                                        */
/****************************************************************************/

void      ClientWin::OnPaint () {

 CPaintDC dc (this);            // create a paint dc
 CRect    rect;
 GetClientRect (&rect);         // get client area size for scaling
```

```
dc.SetTextAlign (TA_CENTER );   // set for centering

dc.TextOut (rect.right/2, rect.bottom/2, "Hello From Windows 95");
}
```

First examine the constructor of the client window. It passes the pointer to the parent frame window class to the **Create** function so that the client window becomes a child window of the frame window. Also, a child window ID number is assigned—here a zero. When the application terminates, it is the frame window's responsibility to destroy the client window. Since we allocated the frame class before the client class, we do not have a pointer to the client window to give the frame window. However, the **CFrameWnd** has a useful function that returns a pointer to any child window which is thus a descendant window.

```
CWnd*  GetDescendantWnd (child id number);
```

A child window has two components: the interface object and the interface element. The interface element, the Windows 95 real window, must be destroyed, and then the C++ object, the interface object, deleted. The function to destroy a window is

```
DestroyWindow ();
```

Observe how the child or client window is destroyed in the member function **OnDestroy**. The child window, ClientWin, was given the ID number of 0 in the ClientWin's constructor call to **Create**; so **GetDescendantWindow** is passed that value and its returned **CWnd** pointer cast back to the ClientWin derived class. If the window exists, then the window's element is destroyed and the object deleted

```
ClientWin *ptrmainwin = (ClientWin*) GetDescendantWindow (0);
if (ptrmainwin) {              // if there is a client window, then
 ptrmainwin->DestroyWindow (); // destroy the interface element
 delete ptrmainwin;            // delete the object
}
CFrameWnd::OnDestroy();
```

OnDestroy of the base class must be invoked LAST. Child windows are destroyed before their parents.

When working with multiple windows, one trick that I often employ is to use a different colored background brush for each so that I can tell the windows apart. Here the frame window uses a white brush, but the client window uses a light gray brush. If the main window fails to appear, I see the unusual white window that provides instant notice of no main window on screen.

4.13 THE SAMPLE HELLO PROGRAM PGM04b: THE FRAME WINDOW ONLY MODEL

Pgm04b is the model I recommend for your first Windows 95 programs. Here just the frame window is used as the main window. Since most of the coding in the Pgm4BApp files is essentially the same as the previous example, only the coding for the **InitInstance** function is shown below.

4.13.1 Listing for File: Pgm4BApp.cpp—Extracts from Pgm04b

```
...
/************************************************************************/
/*                                                                    */
/* InitInstance: Allocate instances of our frame window               */
/*                                                                    */
/************************************************************************/

BOOL   Pgm4BApp::InitInstance () {

 // construct new main and frame windows
 ptrframe = new FrameWin (NULL, "Hello From Windows 95 - MFC Style");

 // install the frame window as the main app window and show that window
 m_pMainWnd = ptrframe;                   // m_pMainWnd- public member of CFrameWnd
 m_pMainWnd->ShowWindow (m_nCmdShow); // install show type, nor, min, maximized
 m_pMainWnd->UpdateWindow ();            // force windows to be painted initially
 // Enable3dControls(); obsolete: enable 3d controls
 return TRUE;
}
...
```

4.13.2 Listing for File: FrameWin.h from Pgm04b

```
#ifndef FRAMEWIN
#define FRAMEWIN

/************************************************************************/
/*                                                                    */
/* FrameWin Class Definition                                          */
/*                                                                    */
/************************************************************************/

class FrameWin : public CFrameWnd {

/************************************************************************/
/*                                                                    */
/* Class Functions:                                                   */
/*                                                                    */
/************************************************************************/
public:
          FrameWin (CWnd* ptrparent, const char* title); // constructor
          ~FrameWin () {}                      // destructor
afx_msg void OnPaint ();                        // paint the window - WM_PAINT msgs

DECLARE_MESSAGE_MAP();

};
#endif
```

4.13.3 Listing for File: FrameWin.cpp from Pgm04b

```cpp
#include "stdafx.h"

#include "framewin.h"
/***********************************************************************/
/*                                                                   */
/* FrameWin Events Response Table                                    */
/*                                                                   */
/***********************************************************************/

BEGIN_MESSAGE_MAP(FrameWin, CFrameWnd)
 ON_WM_PAINT ()
END_MESSAGE_MAP();
/***********************************************************************/
/*                                                                   */
/* FrameWin: constructor provides access to wndclass before registration */
/*                                                                   */
/* set up window's icon, cursor, background color, and the like      */
/*                                                                   */
/***********************************************************************/

        FrameWin::FrameWin (CWnd* ptrparent, const char* title) {

 CFrameWnd ();  // construct base class

 Create (AfxRegisterWndClass (
          CS_VREDRAW | CS_HREDRAW, // register window style UINT
          AfxGetApp()->LoadStandardCursor (IDC_ARROW), // use arrow cur
          (HBRUSH) ::GetStockObject (LTGRAY_BRUSH),    // use lt gray bkgrnd
          AfxGetApp()->LoadStandardIcon (IDI_APPLICATION)),// set min icon
       title,               // window caption
       WS_OVERLAPPEDWINDOW, // wndclass DWORD style => implies several others
       rectDefault,         // CFrameWnd member provides windows default pos
       ptrparent,           // the parent window, here none
       NULL);               // no menu
}
/***********************************************************************/
/*                                                                   */
/* OnPaint: paint client window lt. gray and display "Hello" message */
/*                                                                   */
/***********************************************************************/

void      FrameWin::OnPaint () {

 CPaintDC dc (this);           // create a paint dc
 CRect    rect;
 GetClientRect (&rect);        // get client area size for scaling

 dc.SetTextAlign (TA_CENTER ); // set for centering

 dc.TextOut (rect.right/2, rect.bottom/2, "Hello From Windows 95");
}
```

4.14 THE SAMPLE HELLO PROGRAM PGM04C: THE CONDENSED MODEL

Pgm04c is version B condensed into one h and one cpp file. You could go even farther and put everything into one file as some do. I do not recommend this model for anything but tiny examples.

4.14.1 Listing for File: Pgm4CApp.h from Pgm04c

```
#ifndef PGM4CAPP
#define PGM4CAPP

/****************************************************************************/
/*                                                                          */
/* Framewin Class Definition                                                */
/*                                                                          */
/****************************************************************************/

class FrameWin : public CFrameWnd {

/****************************************************************************/
/*                                                                          */
/* Class Functions                                                          */
/*                                                                          */
/****************************************************************************/

public:
          FrameWin (CWnd* ptrparent, const char* title);
          ~FrameWin () {}                    // destructor no actions
afx_msg void OnPaint ();                      // handle WM_PAINT msgs

DECLARE_MESSAGE_MAP();
};

/****************************************************************************/
/*                                                                          */
/* Pgm4CApp Class definition                                                */
/*                                                                          */
/****************************************************************************/

class Pgm4CApp : public CWinApp {

/****************************************************************************/
/*                                                                          */
/* Data Members                                                             */
/*                                                                          */
/****************************************************************************/

protected:

FrameWin*   ptrframe;  // ptr to this instance of the main frame window

/****************************************************************************/
/*                                                                          */
/* Class Functions                                                          */
/*                                                                          */
```

```
/*************************************************************************/

public:

       Pgm4CApp () : CWinApp () {}           // constructor - no actions required
       ~Pgm4CApp () {}                       // destructor - no actions required

BOOL  InitInstance ();                       // constructs instance of framewindow

DECLARE_MESSAGE_MAP();                       // future message response table
};

#endif
```

4.14.2 Listing for File: Pgm4CApp.cpp from Pgm04c

```
#include "stdafx.h"

#include "pgm4capp.h"

/*************************************************************************/
/*                                                                       */
/* FrameWin Events Response Table                                        */
/*                                                                       */
/*************************************************************************/

BEGIN_MESSAGE_MAP(FrameWin, CFrameWnd)
 ON_WM_PAINT ()
END_MESSAGE_MAP();

/*************************************************************************/
/*                                                                       */
/* FrameWin: constructor provides access to wndclass before registration */
/*                                                                       */
/* set up window's icon, cursor, background color, and the like          */
/*                                                                       */
/*************************************************************************/

         FrameWin::FrameWin (CWnd* ptrparent, const char* title) {

 CFrameWnd ();  // construct base class

 Create (AfxRegisterWndClass (
             CS_VREDRAW | CS_HREDRAW, // register window style UINT
             AfxGetApp()->LoadStandardCursor (IDC_ARROW), // use arrow cur
             (HBRUSH) ::GetStockObject (LTGRAY_BRUSH),    // use lt gray bkgnd
             AfxGetApp()->LoadStandardIcon (IDI_APPLICATION)),// set min icon
        title,               // window caption
        WS_OVERLAPPEDWINDOW, // wndclass DWORD style => implies several others
        rectDefault,         // CFrameWnd member provides windows default pos
        ptrparent,           // the parent window, here none
        NULL);               // no menu
}

/*************************************************************************/
/*                                                                       */
/* OnPaint: paint client window lt. gray and display "Hello" message     */
/*                                                                       */
/*************************************************************************/
```

```
void        FrameWin::OnPaint () {

  CPaintDC dc (this);              // create a paint dc
  CRect    rect;
  GetClientRect (&rect);           // get client area size for scaling

  dc.SetTextAlign (TA_CENTER );  // set for centering

  dc.TextOut (rect.right/2, rect.bottom/2, "Hello From Windows 95");
}
/********************************************************************/
/*                                                                */
/* Events Response Table - currently none, but later on, will respond to  */
/* control bar events                                             */
/*                                                                */
/********************************************************************/

BEGIN_MESSAGE_MAP(Pgm4CApp, CWinApp)
END_MESSAGE_MAP ()
/********************************************************************/
/*                                                                */
/* InitInstance: Allocate instances of our frame window           */
/*                                                                */
/********************************************************************/

BOOL  Pgm4CApp::InitInstance () {

  // construct new main and frame windows
  ptrframe = new FrameWin (NULL, "Hello From Windows 95 - MFC Style");

  // install the frame window as the main app window and show that window
  m_pMainWnd = ptrframe;                    // m_pMainWnd - set to our framewin
  m_pMainWnd->ShowWindow (m_nCmdShow); // use Windows passed show type
  m_pMainWnd->UpdateWindow ();              // force windows to be painted
  // Enable3dControls();  obsolete: enable 3d controls
  return TRUE;
}

Pgm4CApp  Pgm4c;  // constructs the app object and executes it
```

4.15 STYLE GUIDELINES

Notice how readable and easily located the different sections and functions are. In a large application, block comments greatly aid program readability and hence program maintenance. These block comments allow the reader to rapidly find functions, in particular. This will be particularly helpful when you want to read and find items in the more lengthy examples later.

```
/********************************************************************/
/*                                                                */
/*                                                                */
/*                                                                */
/********************************************************************/
```

4.16 HANDLING EVENTS IN PGM04d

Using Pgm04b as a model, let's add some action events to make Pgm04d. A very few Windows 95 messages go immediately and automatically to a member function. **OnPaint** is one such example. Other events or Windows 95 messages have standard member functions invoked if the class message response table indicates that the window wishes to process them. Still other events must be tied to the member functions that are to handle them. You can always override function names and force those events to another member function. And you can even invent your own messages and member functions to process them.

Let's begin with the simpler messages or events: mouse button presses. In addition, let's add many of the MFC functions that correspond to the Windows 95 functions that we have been using through chapter 3. Figure 4.5 shows what Pgm04d looks like when launched and the left button is pressed.

Let's install a light gray background and adjust some of the window creation properties. Further, let's get the window resizing operation to center the text properly by processing WM_SIZE messages. (If you run the previous programs, notice that they do not handle the window resize operation by recentering the text.)

When the left button is pressed, display a message box and set the **data_saved** member to FALSE to simulate a potential file save operation at application-termination time. Normally, if a file has not been saved and a user attempts to close the application, a message box appears, notifying the user of the situation and asking whether the file should be saved. The **OnClose** function responds to the WM_CLOSE messages. If no save is needed, **OnClose** destroys the window. If a save is needed, the application would carry out a save operation and then shut down. Figure 4.6 shows how the message appears on-screen.

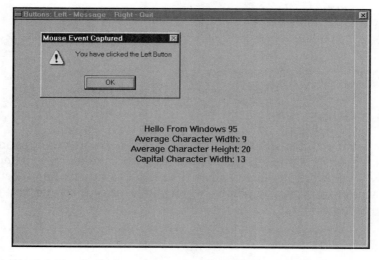

Fig. 4.5 Pgm04d's Appearance After a Left Button Click

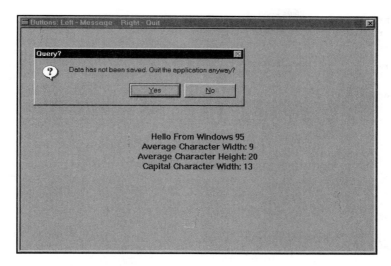

Fig. 4.6 Pgm04d After a Close Request

With an **OnClose** function operational, let's have the right mouse button send an **OnClose** message just to see how to send ourselves a message. Pgm04d implements these actions. There are no significant changes to the Pgm4DApp application class coding from the previous example, Pgm4BApp, and it is therefore not shown. As a general rule, the **CWinApp** class remains unchanged for many chapters. Let's examine the FrameWin class definition in the FrameWin.h file.

4.16.1 Listing for File: FrameWin.h from Pgm04d

```
#ifndef FRAMEWIN
#define FRAMEWIN
/**********************************************************************/
/*                                                                    */
/* FrameWin Class Definition                                          */
/*                                                                    */
/**********************************************************************/

class FrameWin : public CFrameWnd {

/**********************************************************************/
/*                                                                    */
/* Class Data Members                                                 */
/*                                                                    */
/**********************************************************************/

protected:

BOOL data_saved;      // when TRUE, data has been saved - so ok to quit
int  height;          // current client window height in pixels
int  width;           // current client window width in pixels
```

```
int   avg_caps_width;  // average capital letter width
int   avg_char_width;  // average character width
int   avg_char_height; // average character height

/*******************************************************************/
/*                                                               */
/* Class Functions:                                              */
/*                                                               */
/*******************************************************************/

public:

            FrameWin (CWnd* ptrparent, const char* title);
            ~FrameWin () {}                    // destructor - no actions
afx_msg void  OnPaint ();                      // respond to WM_PAINT msgs

protected:

afx_msg int   OnCreate (LPCREATESTRUCT);       // set avg char dimensions
afx_msg void  OnClose ();                      // determines if app can quit
afx_msg void  OnLButtonDown (UINT, CPoint);    // display message on L button
afx_msg void  OnRButtonDown (UINT, CPoint);    // quit message on R button
afx_msg void  OnSize (UINT, int, int);         // resize the window
DECLARE_MESSAGE_MAP();
};
#endif
```

The **data_saved** protected member is TRUE if the data has been saved and the application can safely close. When **data_saved** is FALSE and the user attempts to close the application, we should query the user first. The protected members, **height** and **width**, store the current extent of the client area. The data is extracted from processing WM_SIZE messages. Next come the familiar three average-character dimension fields. *All* member functions are overridden member functions of **CWnd**, the base class of **CFrameWnd**. The constructor, destructor, and **OnPaint** functions are defined exactly as before. What new functions and classes are needed? The following list shows the new MFC functions and classes we need to implement or use:

OnCreate

OnClose

OnLButtonDown

OnRButtonDown

OnSize

DestroyWindow

MessageBox

SendMessage

CClientDC

Let's look at the signatures of these functions and then at their uses. Recall how the message map is constructed. If we wish to respond to the WM_CREATE message, in the message map the ON_ prefix is added and the corresponding member function would be **OnCreate**, constructed by dropping the WM_ and by capitalizing initial letters of the uppercase words. The signature of the overridden **OnCreate** function and the message map macro are

```
afxmsg int OnCreate (LPCREATESTRUCT lp);
ON_WM_CREATE()
```

Remember that you must invoke the base class's **OnCreate** *before* the HWND becomes valid. Once the window element is constructed, the average character dimensions can be acquired by using a TEXTMETRIC structure. However, the **GetTextMetrics** function required a DC. When the handle to the window is valid (the window interface element exists), a device context can be constructed using the **CClientDC** class whose constructor is passed the **this** parameter

```
int retcd = CFrameWnd::OnCreate (lpCS); // pass along to base class
TEXTMETRIC  tm;
CClientDC *ptrdc = new CClientDC (this);   // acquire a DC
ptrdc->GetTextMetrics (&tm);               // get the information
delete ptrdc;                              // delete the dc
// calculate average character parameters
avg_char_width  = tm.tmAveCharWidth;
avg_char_height = tm.tmHeight + tm.tmExternalLeading;
avg_caps_width  = (tm.tmPitchAndFamily & 1 ? 3 : 2)*avg_char_width / 2;
return retcd;
```

The **OnClose** function definition and message map macro are

```
afxmsg void  OnClose ();
ON_WM_CLOSE()
```

In your **OnClose** function, if the data needs to be saved, do so. In this example, I display a message box instead. When the application can terminate, **OnClose** must invoke **DestroyWindow** to complete the termination process. Its definition is

```
void  DestroyWindow();
```

The **OnSize** function responds to WM_SIZE messages; its prototype and message map macro are

```
afxmsg void  OnSize (UINT type, int newwidth, int newheight);
ON_WM_SIZE()
```

The **type** field notifies you if the window is now maximized, minimized, or normal. Commonly used identifiers include SIZE_MAXIMIZED, SIZE_MINIMIZED, and SIZE_RESTORED. There are some other less frequently required choices that we shall explore later on. In response to WM_SIZE messages, the size of the window's client area is acquired and saved in member variables for later use.

The **Invalidate** function forces a paint message to be sent, requesting that the ENTIRE window be repainted. It has one parameter, a BOOL, which when TRUE forces the background to be repainted as well. The BOOL defaults to TRUE. Normal usage is simply

```
Invalidate ();
```

The **InvalidateRect** function can be used when only a portion of the window should be repainted. Its signature is

```
InvalidateRect (LPCRECT ptrrect, BOOL erasebkgrnd = TRUE);
```

WM_PAINT messages are one of the lowest priority messages Windows 95 handles. They are processed and sent to windows only when there are no other higher priority messages in the system's queue. Sometimes an application must have an immediate screen repaint. In such situations, use the **UpdateWindow** function, which forces an immediate repainting of the window. This is precisely what goes on in the **CWinApp**'s **InitInstance** following the call to **ShowWindow**.

The mouse button-down messages are sent via the message map to the functions: **OnLButtonDown**, **OnRButtonDown**, and **OnMButtonDown**

```
afxmsg void  OnLButtonDown (UINT keys, CPoint at);
afxmsg void  OnRButtonDown (UINT keys, CPoint at);
ON_WM_LBUTTONDOWN ()
ON_WM_RBUTTONDOWN ()
```

Here **keys** could be a combination of one or more of the identifiers MK_CONTROL, MK_SHIFT, MK_LBUTTON, MK_MBUTTON, and/or MK_RBUTTON; **at** defines the coordinates of the point where the button was pressed down. Now examine the FrameWin implementation in the cpp listing.

4.16.2 Listing for File: FrameWin.cpp from Pgm04d

```
#include "stdafx.h"

#include "framewin.h"
/*****************************************************************/
/*                                                               */
/* FrameWin Events Response Table                                */
/*                                                               */
/*****************************************************************/

BEGIN_MESSAGE_MAP(FrameWin, CFrameWnd)
 ON_WM_PAINT ()
 ON_WM_LBUTTONDOWN ()
 ON_WM_RBUTTONDOWN ()
 ON_WM_SIZE ()
 ON_WM_CLOSE ()
 ON_WM_CREATE ()
END_MESSAGE_MAP();
/*****************************************************************/
/*                                                               */
/* Framewin: Construct the object                                */
/*                                                               */
/*****************************************************************/
```

```
                FrameWin::FrameWin (CWnd* ptrparent, const char* title) {

 CFrameWnd ();   // construct base class

 DWORD style = WS_OVERLAPPEDWINDOW;                    // set basic window styles
 style &= ~(WS_MINIMIZEBOX | WS_MAXIMIZEBOX); // remove max/min buttons

 CRect rect (100, 100, 500, 300);                     // set init pos and size

 Create (AfxRegisterWndClass (
              CS_VREDRAW | CS_HREDRAW, // register window style UINT
              AfxGetApp()->LoadStandardCursor (IDC_ARROW), // arrow cur
              (HBRUSH) ::GetStockObject (LTGRAY_BRUSH),    // gray bkgnd
              AfxGetApp()->LoadStandardIcon (IDI_APPLICATION)),
         title,                 // window caption
         style,                 // wndclass DWORD style
         rect,                  // set initial window position
         ptrparent,             // the parent window, here none
         NULL);                 // no menu

 data_saved = TRUE;            // initialize control member
}
/**********************************************************************/
/*                                                                  */
/* OnCreate: get average character height and width                 */
/*                                                                  */
/**********************************************************************/
int       FrameWin::OnCreate (LPCREATESTRUCT lpCS) {

 int retcd = CFrameWnd::OnCreate (lpCS); // pass along to base class

 TEXTMETRIC  tm;

 // set the system font's characteristics in tm
 CClientDC *ptrdc = new CClientDC (this);    // acquire a DC
 ptrdc->GetTextMetrics (&tm);                // get the information
 delete ptrdc;                               // delete the dc

 // calculate average character parameters
 avg_char_width  = tm.tmAveCharWidth;
 avg_char_height = tm.tmHeight + tm.tmExternalLeading;
 avg_caps_width  = (tm.tmPitchAndFamily & 1 ? 3 : 2) * avg_char_width / 2;

 return retcd;
}
/**********************************************************************/
/*                                                                  */
/* OnSize: acquire the current dimensions of the client window      */
/*                                                                  */
/**********************************************************************/
void       FrameWin::OnSize (UINT, int, int) {

 CRect rect;
 GetClientRect (&rect);                 // get the size of the client window
 height = rect.Height();                // calc and save current height
 width  = rect.Width();                 // calc and save current width
 Invalidate();                          // force repainting of window
}
```

```
/**************************************************************************/
/*                                                                      */
/* OnPaint: display centered "Hello" message and average character dims*/
/*                                                                      */
/**************************************************************************/

void        FrameWin::OnPaint () {

  CPaintDC dc (this);              // create a paint dc
  CRect    rect;
  GetClientRect (&rect);           // get client area size for scaling
  char msg [80];

  dc.SetTextAlign (TA_CENTER |TA_BASELINE ); // set for centered text
  dc.SetBkMode (TRANSPARENT);                // backgrnd color visible

  dc.TextOut (width/2, height/2, "Hello From Windows 95");

  wsprintf (msg,"Average Character Width: %d", avg_char_width);
  dc.TextOut (width/2, height/2 + avg_char_height, msg);

  wsprintf (msg,"Average Character Height: %d", avg_char_height);
  dc.TextOut (width/2, height/2 + avg_char_height*2, msg);

  wsprintf (msg,"Capital Character Width: %d", avg_caps_width);
  dc.TextOut (width/2, height/2 + avg_char_height*3, msg);
}
/**************************************************************************/
/*                                                                      */
/* OnLButtonDown: display message box showing L Button captured         */
/*                                                                      */
/**************************************************************************/

void        FrameWin::OnLButtonDown (UINT, CPoint) {

  MessageBox ("You have clicked the Left Button", "Mouse Event Captured",
              MB_OK | MB_ICONEXCLAMATION);

  data_saved = FALSE;  // pretend that some data has been altered
}
/**************************************************************************/
/*                                                                      */
/* OnRButtonDown: send close app msg and let CanClose do the work       */
/*                                                                      */
/**************************************************************************/

void        FrameWin::OnRButtonDown (UINT, CPoint) {

  SendMessage (WM_CLOSE); // send close signal
}
/**************************************************************************/
/*                                                                      */
/* OnClose: determine if the app can be shut down                       */
/*                                                                      */
/**************************************************************************/

void        FrameWin::OnClose () {
```

```
if (!data_saved)
  if (MessageBox ("Data has not been saved. Quit the application anyway?",
                 "Query?", MB_YESNO | MB_ICONQUESTION) == IDYES)
  DestroyWindow ();
  else;
 else DestroyWindow ();
}
```

Notice how window style options are added and removed in the constructor. You an use an OR operator to add additional style identifiers and AND the NOT value of an identifier to remove a style. Here, the style WS_OVERLAPPEDWINDOW implies that there are to be both maximize and minimize buttons. To remove them, code

```
DWORD style = WS_OVERLAPPEDWINDOW;            // set basic window styles
style &= ~(WS_MINIMIZEBOX | WS_MAXIMIZEBOX);  // remove max/min buttons
```

Note that we use the bit-wise NOT ~ and not the logical NOT ! operator. Even though there are no resizing buttons, the user can still click on the title bar to maximize the application. (To force a window to specific dimensions, the WM_GETMINMAXINFO message must be processed.) Next, we can force the window to be located initially at x,y coordinates 100,100 and to have an initial size of 400×200 pixels by constructing a rectangle with these values

```
CRect rect (100, 100, 500, 300);             // set init pos and size
```

Both the style and the rectangle are then passed to the **Create** function.

4.17 THE ONSIZE FUNCTION

When a window's dimensions change, Windows 95 and MFC invoke that window's **OnSize** function to notify the application of the change. As the application launches, **OnSize** is invoked with a width and height of 0 pixels. Shortly thereafter, during the construction steps, **OnSize** is called once more with the desired dimensions specified. While the application is running, any time the window is resized, maximized, or minimized, **OnSize** will again be called.

The **OnSize** function is passed the width and height of the basic **CFrameWnd** and not the actual client area. For painting purposes, we really need to know the size of the client area of the frame window. To get this, we use the member function **Get-ClientRect**. Observe that the only parameter needed is the rectangle—another class benefit is an overall reduction in the number of parameters needed. The **this** parameter is used by the class library to pass the "missing" argument.

The **CRect** class has member functions to retrieve the height and width fields from a rectangle class, creating more readable coding: **Height();** and **Width();**

```
GetClientRect (&rect);
height = rect.Height();
width  = rect.Width();
```

Once the current client area dimensions are saved, the client area is forced to be repainted by the **Invalidate** function.

4.18 THE SETBKMODE, SETBKCOLOR, AND SETTEXTCOLOR FUNCTIONS

Examine the **OnPaint** function. I added a new function, **SetBkMode**, which sets the background mode for **TextOut** operations to transparent. Normally, the DC will have a default color scheme for **TextOut** operations—black on white. Did you notice that effect on the first three programs? If not, just run Pgm03 again. We set a window background color to light gray, but the text string was black on white—an interesting effect, but not always desirable. Two approaches may be used to create a more presentable screen.

The first method involves setting both foreground and background colors for **TextOut** operations using the **CDC** functions. (More details on the use of color will be found in chapter 5.)

```
SetBkColor (color);
SetTextColor (color);
```

The second method employs an option that toggles between displaying the actual selected (or default) background color when text is displayed—the **OPAQUE** option—and allowing the window's background color to shine through—the **TRANSPARENT** option. The default is OPAQUE. The option is toggled by using the function **SetBk-Mode**; notice the nice effect this option has on the text output in Pgm04d here.

```
SetBkMode (TRANSPARENT);
```

Since the **OnSize** function now sets the class members, width and height, the "Hello" message is now correctly centered whenever the window size is altered. Additionally, I also displayed the current values of the average character dimensions.

4.19 THE ONLBUTTONDOWN FUNCTION

The mouse event message parameters are "cracked" by MFC and our function is given the unsigned int flags identifying the status of the keys at the time of the button press (exactly as discussed in chapter 3) and a **CPoint** reference of the cursor location. Later as we work with the location of the cursor, having the x,y coordinates in a **CPoint** structure will be a convenient feature.

In response to the left button press, a message box is displayed, notifying the user of the event. Notice that there is one fewer parameter to the **MessageBox** function under MFC:

```
MessageBox (string to be displayed, string on titlebar,
            the flags);
```

Message boxes are extremely handy objects to display information, even DEBUG-GING information. Frequently when I need to see the value of some data, I **wsprintf** the information into a string and display it in a message box. The only requisite item is you must have or find a valid handle to a window. If none is available, use the global macro **AfxMessageBox**, which encapsulates the C-style API **MessageBox** function

```
int  AfxMessageBox (LPCSTR text, UINT type, UINT help = 0);
```

in which the **type** is an ORed series of the normal **MessageBox** types, such as MB_OK. The return value is the button identifier that was pressed.

Just for fun, when the left button is pressed, I set the **data_saved** member to FALSE as if the data were somehow changed. In this manner, we can see the different operations of **OnClose** based on the **data_saved** member.

4.20 SENDING MESSAGES

The user can close the application by pressing ALT-F4 or by choosing Close from the system menu. Additionally, when the right button is pressed, we will attempt to shut down the application. And once more, an all-too-frequent Windows 95 programming design problem surfaces. Can you spot the design problem?

Whether or not it is safe to terminate the application is based upon the status of the **data_saved** BOOL. Now both **OnClose** and **OnRButtonDown** can handle the termination request by interrogating **data_saved**, displaying an appropriate Data Not Yet Saved message, and obtaining the user's response. This is a common design problem: the potential for multiple occurrences of the same coding.

> ***Design Rule 19:*** **Avoid multiple instances of the same coding. Code the action event once; then when similar circumstances arise elsewhere, simply send a fake message to the original event.**

The MFC function is **SendMessage**. The first parameter is the message ID needed and next come the parameters to be sent, based upon the type of message. Here, we wish to send the WM_CLOSE message, a message that requires no parameters. Therefore, code

```
SendMessage (WM_CLOSE);
```

This is all that is required. But what window gets the message? By default, MFC passes the **this** parameter, which will point to this window, **m_hWnd**. To force the message to go, for instance, to the parent window of this window, if one existed (which means that this is a child window as in the Tic-Tac-Toe game), one would use:

```
ptrparent->SendMessage (WM_CLOSE); // child sends to parent
```

Remember that when your application issues a **SendMessage**, processing is halted until that message is processed. Use **PostMessage** for asynchronous operations when it is not important that the message be fully handled before continuing operations.

Finally, notice one other feature in most of these On message response functions—there are no C-style **return 0;** statements. Most On functions have a void return. It is just another convenience of using class libraries.

4.21 THE ONCLOSE FUNCTION

If the **data_saved** indicates that data has been altered and not saved, a message box is displayed, querying the user, who must select Yes or No. Until we learn about file processing, if the user does not want to quit, rather than saving the data and then proceeding with the close operation, we will fail the **OnClose** operation simply by *not invoking* the base class; when the function ends, normal operations continue.

4.22 USING FIXED FONTS

MFC provides an easy switch from SYSTEM_FONT, the default variable-width font, to SYSTEM_FIXED_FONT or ANSI_FIXED_FONT, the fixed-width fonts. In the **OnPaint** function, use the **SelectStockObject** function

```
dc.SelectStockObject (SYSTEM_FIXED_FONT);
```

One advantage of using a fixed font is that all characters have the same width. This can be convenient when handling text operations. In a later chapter, we will examine how to work with variable-width fonts.

We now have quite a bit of functionality in the application. The next step is to add menus to windows and then dialogs and other controls.

4.23 WHAT TO DO NEXT

To solidify the basics, see if you can convert the Tic-Tac-Toe game from chapter 3, Pgm03, into MFC.

Timers, Colors, Brushes, and Resource Files

5.1 TIMERS

Sometimes an application would like to use elapsed time intervals for special processing effects. Windows 3.1 provided a maximum of 32 different interval timers active across the system at one time. Under Windows 95 the number is substantially larger. Each timer that is set needs a unique nonzero identifier that Windows 95 uses when reporting that the designated interval has elapsed.

A timer is basically software wrapped around a hardware clock and is rather involved. (See the Petzold book listed in the bibliography for a complete discussion of timers.) The basic operation is quite simple, and for many normal uses of the timer, only a few details are critical. One sets the interval desired, such as 10 milliseconds (ms). Then, Windows 95 sends the application a WM_TIMER message every 10 ms until the application turns the timer off.

Perhaps the most significant detail is the fact that the WM_TIMER message sent to your application indicating that your indicated amount of time has elapsed is *not* an accurate timing event. Under DOS expiring timer intervals are an *asynchronous* event; they occur in real time, or nearly so, and can be a fairly accurate measure of time. Under Windows 95 the WM_TIMER event is a low-priority message, as is WM_PAINT, and it is only sent and processed when the Windows 95 system is in control. If an application is tying up the CPU cycles, the timer messages are held back until the application releases control to Windows 95. Just like the WM_PAINT messages, several timer "dings" can be stacked up before the application is actually notified of the first timer "ding." There is no way to learn how many "dings" of the timer are represented by that one WM_TIMER message that you receive.

There are two basic functions needed to use timers, **SetTimer** and **KillTimer**, and one message to respond to, WM_TIMER.

The C-style syntax for these is

```
UINT SetTimer (hwnd, UINT uniqueID, UINT interval, NULL);
BOOL KillTimer (hwnd, UINT uniqueID);

case WM_TIMER:  // wparam contains the ID of the expired timer
```

The interval is an unsigned int containing the number of milliseconds (1000 milliseconds are in one second) to count down. Under Windows 3.1 the timer can be set for a maximum of 65,535 milliseconds or about 1 minute. Under Windows 95 it becomes longer. The last parameter is the address of any timer function to be notified, normally 0, in which case the WM_TIMER message is sent to the application.

Crucial note: the **SetTimer** function returns NULL if no more timers are available. An application *always* should check the return value and act appropriately upon the failure to set up a timer.

Once set, the timer keeps on ticking, sending dings whenever the specified interval has elapsed. So, before the application terminates, the timer must be turned off, or "killed." An application therefore requires a balanced number of **SetTimer** / **KillTimer** function calls; if a different interval is needed at some point, kill the existing timer and set a new timer.

When processing the WM_TIMER messages, if the application has set more than one timer, perform a switch on the **wparam**, which contains the timer's ID.

In C-style programming, **SetTimer** is often invoked in the WM_CREATE message processing and killed in the WM_DESTROY message processing of **WinProc**. In MFC-style processing, the timer is often set in the **OnCreate** function and destroyed in the class destructor or in the **OnDestroy** member function. The WM_TIMER event is captured by using the message map event ID of **ON_WM_TIMER** and the corresponding member function that is invoked is **OnTimer**. The functions and message response or map are coded

```
UINT SetTimer (UINT uniqueID, UINT interval, NULL);
BOOL KillTimer (UINT uniqueID);

afx_msg void OnTimer (UINT); // message member function

BEGIN_MESSAGE_MAP(....        // and message map entry
   ON_WM_TIMER ()
END_MESSAGE_MAP();
```

What shall we do with a timer? As you look over the various texts on the market, you will see several interesting timer animation effects, and we will begin to create some animation effects of our own. We'll start with colors. Our animation effect is to cycle through all of the Windows 95 *system colors* (21 in all) contained within the default color scheme you have installed via Control Panel—Set Colors.

5.2 HOW COLORS ARE HANDLED

The topic of colors under Windows 95 is actually quite involved and the complete discussion must wait until chapter 9 devoted to the GDI interface and all of its details. The basic background color is set in the WNDCLASS member, **hbrBackground**. Should you alter the color scheme or even task switch to the Control Panel and use SetColors to change the system color scheme, you will notice an interesting effect. While the color chosen may appear in your window, it does not last long. When Windows 95 sends a WM_PAINT message with erase background set to TRUE, the WNDCLASS default once again determines the background color! Whenever you display text with **TextOut**, the default colors in the acquired DC are always black on white. Both problems can easily be solved.

Windows 95 defines and maintains the *system colors* for painting objects. You can get and change these colors by using **GetSysColor** and **SetSysColor**. These colors can be altered from the Control Panel. The specific identifiers of the system colors are shown in Table 5.1; those used most often are in boldface.

If you wish to have your window's background be the system default for consistency across all applications (though I do not know why any one would want a Neon colored background), use the following C-style approach:

```
wndclass.hbrBackground = COLOR_WINDOW + 1;
```

Windows 95 requires that you add 1 to these identifiers only when using them in the WNDCLASS background; it is done to avoid using a value of 0. Next, whenever you are going to display some text and have acquired a DC, the colors must be inserted into the DC. When displaying text, after the DC is obtained and before any **TextOut**, use

```
SetBkColor    (hdc, GetSysColor (COLOR_WINDOW));
SetTextColor (hdc, GetSysColor (COLOR_WINDOWTEXT));
```

Under MFC the two **CDC** functions, **SetBkColor** and **SetTextColor**, are coded

```
dc.SetBkColor    (::GetSysColor (COLOR_WINDOW) );
dc.SetTextColor (::GetSysColor (COLOR_WINDOWTEXT) );
```

Table 5.1 The System Color Identifiers

COLOR_APPWORKSPACE	**COLOR_BACKGROUND**	COLOR_SCROLLBAR
COLOR_WINDOW	**COLOR_WINDOWTEXT**	COLOR_WINDOWFRAME
COLOR_MENU	COLOR_MENUTEXT	COLOR_ACTIVECAPTION
COLOR_ACTIVEBORDER	COLOR_INACTIVECAPTION	COLOR_INACTIVEBORDER
COLOR_INACTIVECAPTIONTEXT	COLOR_BTNHIGHLIGHT	COLOR_BTNFACE
COLOR_BTNSHADOW	COLOR_BTNTEXT	COLOR_CAPTIONTEXT
COLOR_GRAYTEXT	COLOR_HIGHLIGHTTEXT	COLOR_HIGHLIGHT

To install an initial background brush into the **hbrBackground** of WIND-CLASS, in the **CWnd** constructor's call to **Create** pass to **AfxRegisterWndClass** as the third parameter

```
wndclass.hbrBackGround = ::CreateSolidBrush
    (::GetSysColor(COLOR_WINDOW));
```

Before we launch into brushes and pens, however, let us examine colors further. The earlier procedure is the method to use if you want to utilize the user's choice for the system colors. There is some benefit in so doing, for, if nothing else, it keeps the user happy.

5.3 SETTING COLORS

More often than not, we would like our own choices of color. Windows 95 represents a specific color with the *RGB method*. That is, the color is formed from the combination of the three primary colors—Red, Green, and Blue. The amount of each color is given by a single byte, unsigned char, ranging from 0 to 255, where 0 implies none of that color and 255 represents the maximum of that color. Windows 95 provides a handy macro to create the RGB combined color value

```
RGB ( red amt, blue amt, green amt);
```

To have a wild background, try setting **wndclass.hbrBackground** to

```
::CreateSolidBrush (RGB (255, 0, 0));  // red brush
```

5.4 DYNAMIC ALTERATIONS TO WNDCLASS

Now suppose that you wish to dynamically alter the background brush. **SetClassLong**, which we first saw in chapter 3, is a Windows 95 function that allows access to the WNDCLASS structure while the application is running. (Use **SetClassWord** under Windows 3.1.) *Important detail:* if you wish to install a new background brush, the old brush must be deleted. So, in keeping with cryptic C-style coding and in a generalized format, the background brush alterations could be done as

```
DeleteObject (SetClassLong (hwnd, GCL_HBRBACKGROUND,
        (long) CreateSolidBrush (RGB (color[0], color[1], color[2]))));
```

The third parameter is the new replacement value. The function returns the old value so that you can delete it. Recall that the function **SetClassLong** allows changing

```
GCL_HBRBACKGROUND     GCL_HCURSOR     GCL_HICON     GCL_STYLE
```

Incidentally, this would be the *best* method to dynamically alter the permanent cursor of the application as well. Always remember that if you cannot figure out how to do something within the MFC member functions, you can revert to pure Windows 95 coding at nearly any point. In MFC, unfortunately, the **CWnd** class does not encapsulate the **GetClassLong/SetClassLong** functions. WNDCLASS alterations must be done C-style, using the public member **m_hWnd** for the handle to the window. The RGB macro is supported

```
::DeleteObject ((HBRUSH)::SetClassLong (m_hWnd, GCL_HBRBACKGROUND,
  (long) ::CreateSolidBrush (::GetSysColor (colors[current_color]))));
Invalidate ();
```

or

```
::DeleteObject ((HBRUSH)::SetClassLong (m_hWnd, GCL_HBRBACKGROUND,
  (long) ::CreateSolidBrush (RGB (color[0], color[1], color[2]))));
Invalidate ();
```

The MFC does not have a color class, so we use either RGB values or a COLOR-REF structure, which is basically a 32-bit number whose format in hex is 0x00bbggrr and each color is stored as a byte. The WIN32 macros **GetBValue**, **GetGValue**, and **GetRValue** return the corresponding byte color value.

5.5 CREATING BRUSHES AND PENS

There are several stock brushes available. What is more important, solid color brushes and hatch pattern brushes can be created. The C-style syntax is

```
HBRUSH hbrush = CreateSolidBrush (rgbcolor);
HBRUSH hbrush = CreateHatchBrush (hatch type, rgbcolor);
```

in which hatch type can be one of these IDs

```
HS_HORIZONTAL  HS_VERTICAL  HS_FDIAGONAL  HS_BDIAGONAL  HS_CROSS
    HS_DIAGCROSS
```

Solid brushes are not necessarily a solid, pure color; when Windows 95 selects the brush into a DC, it creates an 8×8 pixel bitmap of dithered colors. With the hatch style, the color you specify is the color of the lines of the pattern. More details are found in chapter 9.

MFC has encapsulated brushes into the class **CBrush** with several different types of constructors

```
CBrush br (RGB(...));
CBrush br (style, RGB(...));
```

For both, the **style** is one of the C-style hatch patterns given above. Alternatively, a **CBrush** member function can be used to create a new brush

```
CBrush br;
br.CreateSolidBrush (RGB(...));
```

or

```
br.CreateSolidBrush (::GetSysColor(...));
```

Pens are similarly created. There are two stock pens (WHITE_PEN and BLACK_PEN), but colored pens are more popular. C-style offers two approaches to pen creation

```
HPEN pen = GetStockObject (WHITE_PEN);
```

or

```
HPEN pen = CreatePen (style, width, rgbcolor);
```

where style is one of

```
PS_SOLID    PS_DASH    PS_DOT    PS_DASHDOT    PS_DASHDOTDOT
```

If the width is 0 or 1, any of these can be chosen as the style. However, if the width is greater than 1 and any style other than solid is chosen, the style is altered to PS_SOLID by Windows 95.

In MFC, pens are similarly encapsulated by **CPen**

```
CPen pen (style, width, RGB(...));
```

Once the pen or brush is created, it must be selected into the DC for use. The C-style function **SelectObject** inserts this pen or brush into the **hdc** and returns the value of the old brush or pen as an HGDIOBJECT, so you can delete it if it is not a stock object

```
HGDIOBJECT SelectObject (hdc, hpen or hbrush);
```

Under MFC a pen must be selected into the **dc** as well. The **CDC** member function **SelectObject** closely resembles the C function

```
CPen*    dc.SelectObject (CPen* ptrpen);
CBrush* dc.SelectObject (CBrush* ptrbrush);
```

This function inserts the pen or brush into the **dc** and returns a pointer to the old object that has been deselected. Note that the returned pointer has been typecast already to the correct GDI object type. If you wanted to insert a new pen for some action, therefore, and then go back to the original pen, you might code

```
CPen *ptroldpen;
CPen *ptrnewpen = ...
ptroldpen = dc.SelectObject (ptrnewpen);
... use it
dc.SelectObject (ptroldpen);
delete ptrnewpen;
```

All pens and brushes are GDI objects and they belong to the GDI itself. When a program terminates, Windows 95 does not automatically delete the GDI objects you have created. You must specifically delete them. To avoid any resource leaks, adhere to three design rules.

Design Rule 20: **Delete all GDI objects that you create.**

> ***Design Rule 21:*** **Do not delete GDI objects while they are selected into a DC!**

> ***Design Rule 22:*** **Do not delete stock objects (Windows 95 ignores such a request).**

Creating pens and brushes does take time. If you find that you are continually creating pens and brushes in your **OnPaint** member, you can take another approach for faster operation: create the pens at the beginning of the application and delete them at the end.

5.6 OTHER MFC TEXT MEMBER FUNCTIONS

Member functions and event responses exist for the other Windows 95 text processing functions that we have covered. All work similar to their Windows 95 counterparts. For MFC the insertion point or text caret is handled by other **CWnd** member functions

```
CreateGrayCaret (int width, int height);
HideCaret ();
SetCaretPos (CPoint);
ShowCaret ();
```

Note that the member function **CreateCaret(CBitmap*)** must have a bitmap image to use as the caret; therefore, you should use **CreateGrayCaret**. There are no member functions for **DestroyCaret** or **SetCaretBlinkTime**; therefore, you should use the C-style versions.

Keyboard keystrokes are handled by the following events:

```
event id         event function

ON_WM_CHAR()     afx_msg void OnChar (UINT key, UINT repcnt, UINT flags);
ON_WM_KEYDOWN()  afx_msg void OnKeyDown(UINT key,UINT repcnt,UINT flags);
```

Now let's put these to use in our first animation application.

5.7 SAMPLE PROGRAM PGM05a

When program Pgm05a begins, it uses the standard system colors for the window's background. **Paint** displays the name of the system color in the client window. Whenever the down arrow key is pressed, the program installs the next system color in the background and displays its name. The up arrow key backs up one color. CTL-A toggles animation effects. When animation is active, the display cycles through all 21 system colors until another CTL-A key halts the animation. Figure 5.1 shows how the window appears.

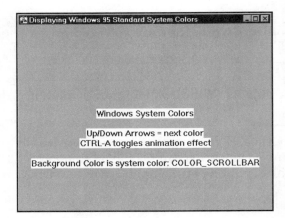

Fig. 5.1 Pgm05a: 21 System Colors

There are no significant changes to the **CWinApp** derived class; all of the changes are in the FrameWin class and members. The FrameWin class definition in the h file contains the toggle switch **animate**, which controls the animation effects. When **animate** is TRUE, the timer is active; WM_TIMER messages cause the next system color to be installed as the background color. The **current_color** member holds the index into the **colors** array that corresponds to the system color in use. New member functions now include the **OnChar**, **OnKeyDown**, and **OnTimer** events. A pair of static data members, **color_msg**, an array of 21 color name strings, and **colors**, an array of the 21 system color IDs, which remove the need of global values. Because these two arrays are members of the class, all functions can access them. Finally, notice that I am now passing the frame window's caption to the constructor, which passes it on to the **Create** function.

In the FrameWin.cpp file, the constructor sets **animate** to off, initializes the **timer_id** field, and sets **current_color** to 3, which is COLOR_WINDOW. The destructor must kill any timer still active. When the constructor invokes the **Create** function, it uses COLOR_WINDOW to install the beginning background brush.

In the **OnPaint** function, please note that the default text mode is OPAQUE which means the color choices for text background overlays any background color. This leaves the foreground text color always visible. For the text foreground and background, I used the normal system colors for window text.

In the **OnKeyDown** function, the extended keys are detected, and only up and down arrows are used. The process consists of incrementing or decrementing the current_color index and forcing it into range should it go too high or too low. Thus it becomes cyclical. The previous background brush is deleted when the new brush is created and installed. Do not forget to **Invalidate** the window to make the changes visible at once. The **OnChar** function processes normal keystrokes; here we want only the CTL-A key—for "animate." If it is pressed, then, depending upon the setting of **animate**, the timer is either killed or set to 1 second (1000 milliseconds). The **OnTimer** coding duplicates the down arrow coding. OK, so I have duplicated code! Can I plead "but it is very small"? Notice that the insertion of a new background brush involves four C-style functions

```
           // install new background color
           ::DeleteObject ((HBRUSH)::SetClassLong (m_hWnd, GCL_HBRBACKGROUND,
             (long) ::CreateSolidBrush (::GetSysColor (colors[current_color]))));
```

5.7.1 Listing for File: FrameWin.h—Pgm05a—Excerpts

```
...
#define MAX_COLORS    21  // 21 system colors
#define MAX_COLOR_LEN 26  // length of color names
/*************************************************************************/
/*                                                                       */
/*  FrameWin Class Definition                                            */
/*                                                                       */
/*************************************************************************/

class FrameWin : public CFrameWnd {

/*************************************************************************/
/*                                                                       */
/*  Class Data Members                                                   */
/*                                                                       */
/*************************************************************************/

protected:

// static members obviate the need for globals
static char color_msgs[MAX_COLORS][MAX_COLOR_LEN]; // 21 system color names
static int  colors[MAX_COLORS];                    // 21 system color IDs

BOOL animate;          // when TRUE, timer changes the background colors
int  current_color;    // current idx of the system color in use
int  timer_id;         // id of the timer
int  height;           // current client window height in pixels
int  width;            // current client window width in pixels

int  avg_caps_width;   // average capital letter width
int  avg_char_width;   // average character width
int  avg_char_height;  // average character height

/*************************************************************************/
/*                                                                       */
/*  Class Functions:                                                     */
/*                                                                       */
/*************************************************************************/

public:

            FrameWin (CWnd*, const char*); // constructor
            ~FrameWin () {}                // destructor
afx_msg void  OnPaint ();                  // paint the window - WM_PAINT

protected:
afx_msg int   OnCreate (LPCREATESTRUCT);   // construct window, avg char dims

afx_msg void  OnClose ();                  // determines if app can quit yet
afx_msg void  OnChar (UINT, UINT, UINT);   // process key characters CTL-A
afx_msg void  OnSize (UINT, int, int);     // process window resize
afx_msg void  OnKeyDown (UINT, UINT, UINT); // process spcl keys up/down arrow
```

```
afx_msg void  OnTimer (UINT);              // process timer interval elapsed
afx_msg void  OnDestroy ();                // remove any active timer

DECLARE_MESSAGE_MAP();
...
```

5.7.2 Listing for File: FrameWin.cpp—Pgm05a—Excerpts

```
...
/***********************************************************************/
/*                                                                     */
/* FrameWin Events Response Table                                      */
/*                                                                     */
/***********************************************************************/
BEGIN_MESSAGE_MAP(FrameWin, CFrameWnd)
 ON_WM_KEYDOWN ()
 ON_WM_CHAR ()
 ON_WM_SIZE ()
 ON_WM_TIMER ()
 ON_WM_PAINT ()
 ON_WM_CREATE ()
 ON_WM_CLOSE ()
 ON_WM_DESTROY ()
END_MESSAGE_MAP();
/***********************************************************************/
/*                                                                     */
/* Colors static arrays                                                */
/*                                                                     */
/***********************************************************************/
char FrameWin::color_msgs[MAX_COLORS][MAX_COLOR_LEN] = {
  "COLOR_APPWORKSPACE", "COLOR_BACKGROUND",
...
  "COLOR_HIGHLIGHT"};

int FrameWin::colors[MAX_COLORS] = {
                COLOR_APPWORKSPACE, COLOR_BACKGROUND, COLOR_SCROLLBAR,
...
                COLOR_HIGHLIGHTTEXT, COLOR_HIGHLIGHT};
/***********************************************************************/
/*                                                                     */
/* Framewin: Construct the window object                               */
/*                                                                     */
/***********************************************************************/
         FrameWin::FrameWin (CWnd* ptrparent, const char* title) {

 CFrameWnd ();  // construct base class

 DWORD style = WS_OVERLAPPEDWINDOW;             // set basic window styles
 style &= !(WS_MINIMIZEBOX | WS_MAXIMIZEBOX);  // remove max/min buttons
 style |= WS_SYSMENU | WS_THICKFRAME;

 CRect rect (50, 100, 500, 300);               // set init pos and size
```

```
  Create (AfxRegisterWndClass (
                CS_VREDRAW | CS_HREDRAW, // register window style UINT
                AfxGetApp()->LoadStandardCursor (IDC_ARROW), // use arrow cur
                ::CreateSolidBrush (::GetSysColor (COLOR_WINDOW)),
                AfxGetApp()->LoadStandardIcon (IDI_APPLICATION)),// set min icon
         title,              // window caption
         style,              // wndclass DWORD style
         rect,               // set initial window position
         ptrparent,          // the parent window, here none
         0,                  // no extended style DWORD
         NULL);              // no CCreateContext
  animate = FALSE;    // set animate feature off
  timer_id = 1;       // assign a unique non-zero id for the timer
  current_color = 3; // set the color idx in use
}
/****************************************************************************/
/*                                                                        */
/* OnDestroy: remove any timer still active                               */
/*                                                                        */
/****************************************************************************/
void        FrameWin::OnDestroy () {

  if (animate) KillTimer (timer_id);
}
/****************************************************************************/
/*                                                                        */
/* OnCreate: get average character height and width                       */
/*                                                                        */
/****************************************************************************/
int        FrameWin::OnCreate (LPCREATESTRUCT lpCS) {

  int retcd = CFrameWnd::OnCreate (lpCS); // pass along to base class

  TEXTMETRIC  tm;

  // set the system font's characteristics in tm
  CClientDC *ptrdc = new CClientDC (this);   // acquire a DC
  ptrdc->GetTextMetrics (&tm);                // get the information
  delete ptrdc;                               // delete the dc

  // calculate average character parameters
  avg_char_width  = tm.tmAveCharWidth;
  avg_char_height = tm.tmHeight + tm.tmExternalLeading;
  avg_caps_width  = (tm.tmPitchAndFamily & 1 ? 3 : 2) * avg_char_width / 2;

  return retcd;
}
/****************************************************************************/
/*                                                                        */
/* OnSize: acquire the current dimensions of the client window            */
/*                                                                        */
/****************************************************************************/
```

```
void       FrameWin::OnSize (UINT, int, int) {

 CRect rect;
 GetClientRect (&rect);              // get the size of the client window
 height = rect.Height();             // calc and save current height
 width  = rect.Width();              // calc and save current width
 Invalidate();                       // force repainting of window
}
/***************************************************************************/
/*                                                                         */
/* OnPaint: displays instructions and the current system color in use      */
/*                                                                         */
/***************************************************************************/
void       FrameWin::OnPaint () {

 CPaintDC dc (this);               // create a paint dc
 char msg [80];

 dc.SetTextAlign (TA_CENTER |TA_BASELINE ); // set for centered text

 // set specific colors - use default mode opaque so msgs always visible
 dc.SetBkColor (::GetSysColor (COLOR_WINDOW));
 dc.SetTextColor (::GetSysColor (COLOR_WINDOWTEXT));

 dc.TextOut (width/2, height/2, "Windows 95 System Colors");
 dc.TextOut (width/2, height/2 + avg_char_height*2,
             "Up/Down Arrows = next color");
 dc.TextOut (width/2, height/2 + avg_char_height*3,
             "CTRL-A toggles animation effect");

 strcpy (msg, "Background Color is system color: ");
 strcat (msg, color_msgs[current_color]);         // insert current color in use
 // display current bkgrnd color message
 dc.TextOut (width/2, height/2+avg_char_height*5, msg);
}
/***************************************************************************/
/*                                                                         */
/* OnKeyDown: process up and down arrows to go to next system color        */
/*                                                                         */
/***************************************************************************/
void       FrameWin::OnKeyDown (UINT key, UINT, UINT) {

 if (!animate) {       // only effective when not in animation mode
  if (key==VK_UP) {    // get previous color
   current_color--;
   if (current_color<0) current_color = MAX_COLORS-1;  // force into range

   // install new background color
   ::DeleteObject ((HBRUSH)::SetClassLong (m_hWnd, GCL_HBRBACKGROUND,
     (long) ::CreateSolidBrush (::GetSysColor (colors[current_color]))));
   Invalidate ();  // force window repaint
  }
  else if (key==VK_DOWN) { // get next color
   current_color++;
   if (current_color>MAX_COLORS-1) current_color = 0;  // force into range
```

```
      // install new background color
      ::DeleteObject ((HBRUSH)::SetClassLong (m_hWnd, GCL_HBRBACKGROUND,
        (long) ::CreateSolidBrush (::GetSysColor (colors[current_color]))));
      Invalidate ();  // force window repaint
    }
  }
}
/*****************************************************************************/
/*                                                                         */
/* OnChar: process CTL-A for animation toggle                              */
/*                                                                         */
/*****************************************************************************/

void      FrameWin::OnChar (UINT key, UINT, UINT) {

  if (key==0x1) {           // use only CTL-A code
    if (animate) {          // if animate is active
      KillTimer (timer_id); // turn off timer
      animate = FALSE;      // reset toggle switch
    }
    else {
      animate = TRUE;       // turn on animation
      SetTimer (timer_id, 1000, 0); // set for 1 second intervals
    }
  }
}

/*****************************************************************************/
/*                                                                         */
/* OnTimer: process timer intervals elapsed - set next system color        */
/*                                                                         */
/*****************************************************************************/

void      FrameWin::OnTimer (UINT) {

  current_color++;  // get next color idx
  if (current_color>MAX_COLORS-1) current_color=0; // force into range

  // install new background color
  ::DeleteObject ((HBRUSH)::SetClassLong (m_hWnd, GCL_HBRBACKGROUND,
      (long) ::CreateSolidBrush (::GetSysColor (colors[current_color]))));
  Invalidate ();  // force repainting of window
}

/*****************************************************************************/
/*                                                                         */
/* OnClose: determine if the app can be shut down                          */
/*                                                                         */
/*****************************************************************************/

void      FrameWin::OnClose () {

  if (MessageBox ("Do you want to quit the application?",
                  "Query?", MB_YESNO | MB_ICONQUESTION) == IDYES )
      DestroyWindow ();
}
```

5.8 RESOURCE FILES: AN INTRODUCTION

Our next step is to begin to include *resource files* with our applications. Resource files have an extension of rc and contain extensive resources for an application. Such resources contain character strings that are loaded when needed: menus; menu accelerators; hexadecimal bitmaps that either represent bitmaps in general or icons, cursors, and the like; references to files that contain the bitmaps, cursors, and icons; dialog box definitions; and the myriad controls that may appear within a dialog box or stand alone.

To be used by an application, these resources must be compiled by the Resource Compiler, the App, into their *binary format*. The binary format of the resource file has the extension res. Once the res file has been made, the linker appends the resource file onto the end of the exe file.

While an application's resources usually are contained on the end of the exe file, they also might be located in another dynamic link library (dll). When the application requires a specific resource, Windows 95 loads it from the exe file. When the application no longer needs that resource, the resource becomes discardable; if Windows 95 needs the memory, it is discarded from memory. Now should the application need that same resource again, Windows 95 can reload it from the exe file. Now you can see why SMARTDRV is needed when running Windows 95. If the programmer is lucky, the entire exe file, or at least the resource portion of it, can remain in the extended memory buffer of SMARTDRV.

Memory is a precious commodity, even when running under the flat memory model. This scheme of discardable resources greatly reduces the total memory requirements of applications. Why waste memory retaining all these resources if they are not needed? Just bring them into memory when and for as long as they are required by an application.

The RC resource file is a simple text file that can be edited by nearly any editor, including the Developer Studio's editor. The resource workshop is quite complex, so before tackling its full operations, let's begin in a simpler fashion.

One of the sections of a resource file contains the character strings, stored one after the other. Here is an excerpt from the string table from my WWII game

```
STRINGTABLE
{
                              // hint messages
      CM_WW2_DSPLYMAP,        "Opens a new Map Window"
      CM_WW2_TOGGLEHINT,      "Toggles tool bar hint mode"
      CM_WW2_TOGGLEBAR,       "Toggles tool bar position"
                              // program messages
      IDS_WW2_NAME,           "World War II Game"
      IDS_WW2_FILE_OPEN_ERR,  "Cannot Open File: %s"
      IDS_WW2_DRIVE_LET,      "C:\\"
      IDS_WW2_MAIN_PATH,      "WAR\\"
      IDS_WW2_MAP_PATH,       "MAPS\\"
      IDS_WW2_RES_PATH,       "RESOURCE\\"
      IDS_WW2_NOT256_ERR,     "WW2 needs a 256 color Windows 95 video driver"
```

```
    IDS_WW2_IGNORE_ERR,     "Ignore this error and try to continue?"
    IDS_WW2_CLOSEAPP,       "Close down the whole game?"
    IDS_WW2_MAPFAILS,       "Map System Initialization Failure - more memory"
    IDS_WW2_MAPERROR,       "Cannot allocate another Map Object - free memory"
  }
```

A string in the table follows this syntax:

```
    unique ID, "string's contents"
```

Usually, string identifiers begin with the prefix IDS_ (for ID for a String). Look at some of these strings. Some look like drive and path specifications, others look like the hint messages that would appear as the cursor passes over the tool bar's icons, others look like portions of error messages, and one even looks like a **printf** control string:

```
    IDS_WW2_FILE_OPEN_ERR, "Cannot Open File: %s."
```

In a complex resource file, the string table is often found near the end of the resource file. The string table is identified by coding a begin-end block (many other sections have their own identifiers and begin-end block markers as well)

```
    STRINGTABLE
    {
    }
```

or by

```
    STRINGTABLE
    BEGIN
    END
```

Design Rule 23: **Any string can be stored in the resource file and loaded into memory when needed.**

With character strings, this rule is valuable for several reasons. First, the overall memory requirements are lowered. Second, an application that has stored all of its character strings in the resource file can be easily converted into another language. (Imagine how difficult it would be to search through a huge application trying to find the strings that need to be converted to German, for instance). Most applications, therefore, that have any possibility of overseas markets will generally have all of their strings in the resource file. Note that the flat memory model has removed another reason they are used under Windows 3.1, since the stack segment is no longer limited to 64K.

5.9 STRING RESOURCES: A HOW TO

Resource files and their header files contain text, and they can be created or updated in one of two ways. If treated as text, both the rc file and its header can be opened with any text editor or with the Developer Studio's text editor. This works well for string tables. However, for graphical resources such dialogs or icons, the resource file is best edited in graphical or visual form using the Developer Studio's Resource Editors. As you might expect, the graphical form is the default that the Developer Studio uses to open a resource file. So if you attempt to open the rc file by double clicking on its name either in the left tabbed dialog box or by using a File I Open, the Developer Studio assumes that you want to launch the automated Developer Studio graphical resource workshop to edit them. To open the resource file as a text file, you must use File I Open and set the bottom combo box to Open As Text.

There are a number of approaches you can take to construct the resource files. However, if you wish to use the Developer Studio graphical resource workshop to create or modify the more complex resources, such as dialogs, you really have only *one* way because resource editing is the most inflexible part of the Visual C++ 4.0 package. Unless you want to do everything by hand, you must do it the graphical Studio way. True, you can import other non-Developer Studio resource files. However, if you save the resource file, Developer Studio completely rewrites the rc file using its own format—the format produced by the App Wizard. It adds far more complexity than is needed, inserts ugly comments (in my opinion), and removes all of your comments. Thus, I have made this my third concession to the Wizards. Since I do not want to edit all of the more complex resources manually, I will have to use the Developer Studio's resource files and methods.

To construct a new resource file, choose File I New I Resource Script, and a new script window opens. Next do a File I Save As and save it as Pgm05b.rc, for example. Automatically, the header file is also saved as resource.h. Close this window and add Pgm05b.rc to the project file. To begin to use the Developer Studio options, click on the tab for resources and expand the rc file. If it is a new file, it displays "no resources." Now choose Insert I Resources I StringTable and away you go. Click in the blue empty row, and enter the string ID and the text or caption in the control. It is that easy.

Be aware that the Developer Studio always places the identifiers into resource.h so we must include it in our cpp files.

For an example, let's take the strings out of Pgm05a.

We find the caption in PGM5AAPP.CPP	"Buttons: Left - Message Right - Quit"
from **OnPaint**	"Windows System Colors"
	"Up/Down Arrows = next color"
	"CTRL-A toggles animation effect"
	"Background Color is system color: "
from **OnClose**	"Do you want to quit the application?"
	"Query?"

Finally, we can further reduce the storage requirements of the application by reworking the **colors_msg** array that occupied 21×26, or 546, bytes. While one could replace it with an array to a series of constant pointers to char, doing so would not

reduce the total storage requirement significantly because the strings are all nearly
the same length. Placing the strings into the string table is again the best answer. To
do so in this case requires the insertion of another int array that contains the corresponding string ID of the message. We cannot use the actual Windows 95 ID names
directly, so we make up names and tie them back to our **current_color** index. As a
result, we replace 546 bytes with 42 bytes for the int array, a good savings. Then in
OnPaint, when a specific color name is required, we load the one string that is needed
into **msg2**.

Next, we make up identifiers for these strings; it is common practice to prefix all
strings in the string table with IDS_ (for ID of a String). Then we add a good descriptive name. We obtain the following resource file (note that I have omitted the clutter
and some repetitious values)

5.9.1 Listing for File: Pgm5b.rc—Pgm05b—Excerpts

```
. . .
#include "afxres.h"
. . .
/////////////////////////////////////////////////////////////////////////////
//
// String Table
//

STRINGTABLE DISCARDABLE
BEGIN
    IDS_MAINTITLE           "Displaying Windows 95 System Colors"
    IDS_WINNAME             "AnimatePgm"
    IDS_HEADER              "Windows System Colors"
    IDS_CMD_MSG1            "Up/Down Arrows = next color"
    IDS_CMD_MSG2            "CTRL-A toggles animation effect"
    IDS_COLOR_MSG           "Background Color is system color: "
    IDS_MSG_QUIT            "Do you want to quit the application?"
    IDS_MSG_QUERY           "Query?"
    IDS_COLOR00             "COLOR_APPWORKSPACE"
    IDS_COLOR01             "COLOR_BACKGROUND"
    IDS_COLOR02             "COLOR_SCROLLBAR"
    IDS_COLOR03             "COLOR_WINDOW"
. . .
    IDS_COLOR20             "COLOR_HIGHLIGHT"
END
. . .
```

5.9.2 Listing for File: resource.h—Pgm05b—Excerpts

```
. . .
#define IDS_MAINTITLE                 2000
#define IDS_WINNAME                   2001
#define IDS_HEADER                    2002
#define IDS_CMD_MSG1                  2003
#define IDS_CMD_MSG2                  2004
#define IDS_COLOR_MSG                 2005
#define IDS_MSG_QUIT                  2006
```

```
#define IDS_MSG_QUERY              2007
#define IDS_COLOR00                2010
#define IDS_COLOR01                2011
#define IDS_COLOR02                2012
#define IDS_COLOR03                2013
...
#define IDS_COLOR20                2030
...
```

The four major coding rules are for string resources are:

1. There can be only one string table per resource file (rc); if we have more than one, the compiler automatically merges them into one for us.
2. Strings can be only one line long with up to 255 characters.
3. Strings cannot contain any C-style escape codes, except the tab code '\t' and '\n'.
4. When retrieving one string, Windows 95 actually loads a set of 16 strings at one time; each string as stored in the string table is 255 bytes long.

When you request that a string be loaded, Windows 95 does not just load in that single string. Windows 95 organizes the string table into units of 16 strings, each of which is 255 bytes long. When a request to load in a string is received, Windows 95 loads in the entire unit of up to 16 strings. As a consequence, you should organize your strings into "use blocks," keeping together those that are likely to be needed together, thereby reducing the number of times units must be loaded from disk. The load and memory options default as follows:

```
STRINGTABLE  LOADONCALL  MOVEABLE  DISCARDABLE
```

Since these are what are normally desired, you usually omit coding them.

Notice the new file resource.h that defines our string IDs; by convention, I have used a relatively large starting number for the string IDs. Icons, bitmaps, menus, and so on are usually given low numbers. For convenience and to avoid using a duplicate number, the assigned numbers are in sequence. (Normally, I would have liked to add a comment after each definition so when the file is viewed, the user can more easily recall the significance of an ID. However, the Developer Studio removes all comments on every save operation.) The resource.h file is also included in other cpp implementation files where the resource IDs are needed.

5.10 RETRIEVING STRINGS AT RUN TIME

To load a string from the resource file C-Style, use the **LoadString** function

```
LoadString (HINSTANCE hInstance, UINT id, char *string, int len);
```

The C-Style **CanClose** function could be rewritten

```
case WM_CLOSE:
 char mboxtitle[7];
```

```
char mboxtext [38];
LoadString (hinst, IDS_MSG_QUERY, mboxtitle, 7);
LoadString (hinst, IDS_MSG_QUIT,  mboxtext, 38);
MessageBox (hwnd, mboxtext, mboxtitle,
                 MB_ICONQUESTION | MB_YESNO);
```

You can load the strings into automatic storage fields that come and go as functions are invoked. Or you can reuse a static set of strings of a maximum length for the largest message to be used, a method that is valuable in larger applications where memory is scarce.

MFC offers two approaches; one is based upon the C-style function and the other uses a member function of the provided string class, **CString**.

The MFC version of **LoadString** is a member function of the **CString** class; also the **CString** class itself is a part of the MFC and has its own internal access to HINSTANCE. Further, all of the MFC functions also expect a **CString** as well as a **char***. Its signature is

```
BOOL LoadString (id);
```

To load in the window title, one would code

```
CString wintitle;
wintitle.LoadString (IDS_WINTITLE);
```

The C-style approach can also be used if a **char*** version is handier. With MFC, the global function **AfxGetApp** is used to retrieve the hinstance value

```
char msg[70];
::LoadString (AfxGetApp()->m_hInstance, IDS_ERRORMSG, msg, sizeof(msg));
```

5.11 THE IMPROVED PGM05b PROGRAM

Rather than printing the entire Pgm05b set of modules, I have printed only the sections that have changed from Pgm05a: the FrameWin files and the new resource files above. Examine these changes.

In Pgm5BApp.cpp, in **InitInstance**, the new FrameWin title string is loaded before the **new** constructor. I have used the **CString** method

```
CString wintitle;
wintitle.LoadString (IDS_MAINTITLE);
ptrframe = new FrameWin (NULL, wintitle);
```

From the FrameWin.h file, the string array of **color_msg** is replaced

```
class FrameWin : public CFrameWnd {
protected:
// these static members obviate the need for any globals
static int colors_msg_idx[MAX_COLORS]; // the resource ids for the string msgs
static int colors[MAX_COLORS];          // correspond to these system color ids
```

Most of the coding changes are in the FrameWin.cpp file. Again the resource.h file is included and the int array **color_msgs** is defined; using **colors[current_color]**

accesses the name of the Windows 95 system color and then using **colors_msg_idx [current_color]** accesses our ID number in the string table.

   OnClose illustrates common coding for getting the strings needed for **Message-Box**es. We simply load in the two strings. If any other manipulation is needed, take those actions and then display the message box.

   The **OnPaint** function uses the familiar char* method

```
::LoadString (AfxGetApp()->m_hInstance, IDS_HEADER, msg, 80);
dc.TextOut (width/2, height/2, msg);
```

5.11.1 Listing for File: Pgm05bApp.cpp—Pgm05b—Excerpts

```
...
/****************************************************************************/
/*                                                                          */
/* InitInstance:    allocate instance of our frame main window              */
/*                                                                          */
/****************************************************************************/

BOOL   Pgm5BApp::InitInstance () {

 // construct new main and frame windows
 CString wintitle;
 wintitle.LoadString (IDS_MAINTITLE); // load the title caption
 ptrframe = new FrameWin (NULL, wintitle); // construct window with this title

 // install the frame window as the main app window and show that window
 m_pMainWnd = ptrframe;                 // m_pMainWnd- public member of CFrameWnd
 m_pMainWnd->ShowWindow (m_nCmdShow); // install show type, nor, min, maximized
 m_pMainWnd->UpdateWindow ();          // force windows to be painted initially

 return TRUE;
}
...
```

5.11.2 Listing for File: FrameWin.cpp—Pgm05b—Excerpts

```
...
#include "pgm5b.rh"
...

/****************************************************************************/
/*                                                                          */
/* Paint: displays instructions and the current system color in use         */
/*                                                                          */
/****************************************************************************/

void       FrameWin::OnPaint () {

 CPaintDC dc (this);          // create a paint dc

 char msg [80];
 char msg2[40];

 dc.SetTextAlign (TA_CENTER |TA_BASELINE ); // set for centered text
```

```
// set specific colors - use default mode opaque so msgs always visible
dc.SetBkColor (::GetSysColor (COLOR_WINDOW));
dc.SetTextColor (::GetSysColor (COLOR_WINDOWTEXT));

::LoadString (AfxGetApp()->m_hInstance, IDS_HEADER, msg, 80);
dc.TextOut (width/2, height/2, msg);
::LoadString (AfxGetApp()->m_hInstance, IDS_CMD_MSG1, msg, 80);
dc.TextOut (width/2, height/2+avg_char_height*2, msg);
::LoadString (AfxGetApp()->m_hInstance, IDS_CMD_MSG2, msg, 80);
dc.TextOut (width/2, height/2+avg_char_height*3, msg);

::LoadString (AfxGetApp()->m_hInstance, IDS_COLOR_MSG, msg, 80);
::LoadString (AfxGetApp()->m_hInstance, colors_msg_idx[current_color], msg2, 40);
strcat (msg, msg2);  // insert current color in use
// display current bkgrnd color message
dc.TextOut (width/2, height/2+avg_char_height*5, msg);
}
...

/******************************************************************************/
/*                                                                            */
/* OnClose: determine if the app can be shut down                             */
/*                                                                            */
/******************************************************************************/
void       FrameWin::OnClose () {
 CString msgtitle;
 CString msgtext;

 msgtext.LoadString (IDS_MSG_QUIT);
 msgtitle.LoadString (IDS_MSG_QUERY);

 if (MessageBox (msgtext, msgtitle, MB_YESNO | MB_ICONQUESTION) == IDYES )
  DestroyWindow ();
}
```

5.12 WHAT TO DO NEXT

Write a "Balloon Busting" application. It should draw a balloon (a circle) on the screen and set the timer. The user has until the timer expires to position the mouse over the balloon and left click. Use **MessageBeep** if the user fails and use the "Ta-Da" sound if the user succeeds. Do it ten times and tally the user's score and display it. You could have the timer interval be user adjustable. Use **GetSystemMetrics** to make the main window as large as possible.

Menus

6.1 MENU SYNTAX

An application may have more than one menu, can have floating menus, and can have dynamically modified menus. A good place to begin is the menu's general syntax

```
menuname MENU
{
 MENUITEM "your text1",   your ID number
}
```

or

```
menuname MENU
BEGIN
 MENUITEM "your text1",   your ID number
END
```

The **menuname** can be either a defined ID number or a string. For example, if you call the menu by MAINMENU, then MAINMENU could be a defined name or used as "MAINMENU"

```
MAINMENU MENU        // will be used as a string: "MAINMENU"

#define MainMenu 100
MainMenu MENU        // will be used as an identifier: MAINMENU
```

When you ask for the menu resource in the first case, you provide the string "MAIN-MENU"; whereas, in the second case, you provide the ID MAINMENU, which is compiled to the resource number 100. In general, I prefer the first case for the name of the complete menu because there is one less ID.

Next come the individual menu entries, which either can be menu items as shown above or a pop-up menu. The **MENUITEM** has a fairly complex full syntax

```
MENUITEM "C&hoice\taccelerator info",  ID number, other options
```

After the keyword **MENUITEM** comes the string that you want to be displayed for this item. If there is an & in the string, the character immediately after it is underlined and is the hot letter the user can press to activate this menu choice. In contrast, keyboard accelerators are hot keys that, when pressed, immediately perform the corresponding menu action even though the menu is not activated. If you use a keyboard accelerator for a menu item, then coding **\tacc** info displays your **acc**erator info after the text of the choice and a tab. If you use **\a**, the text after it is right justified in the column.

For normal menu items, the remaining options are omitted, including

CHECKED	displays a check mark to the left of the menu item
GRAYED	displays an item greyed indicating it's not currently available
INACTIVE	shown normal, but does not do anything if selected
MENUBREAK	the item and the following items appear in a new column
MENUBARBREAK	the item and the following items appear in a new column with a vertical bar separating the columns
MENUITEM SEPARATOR	causes a horizontal line at this point in the list of menu items

The ID numbers are numbers that Windows 95 sends to your application when the item has been selected. These should be unique. By convention, these ID numbers all begin **IDM_** for (ID of a Menu item) for Windows 95 coding. Alternatively, use the prefix **CM_** (for CoMmand). The App Wizard uses simply **ID_**.

In place of MENUITEM, you can have a pop-up menu. The File menu choice is a pop-up menu that, when selected, pulls down another submenu of choices. The syntax for pop-up menu items is

```
POPUP "menu &Choice"
  {
  MENUITEM ... etc
  }
```

> **Design Rule 24:** **Preserve the common look and feel of menus between Windows 95 applications.**

If you are going to have a File menu, it should be the leftmost menu entry. Next to it is the Edit group. Help is always the rightmost menu entry. Further, from application to application, the pop-up File menus have similar submenu items, as do the pop-up Edit menus. If, in response to a menu item, the user must provide more information (typically from a dialog box), use the Windows 95 ellipsis notation (**...**) to so indicate. Another reason for following the common look and feel involves the menu descriptors, which are used to merge a child window's menu modifications into the main menu dynamically when the child is launched.

A menu's relative location on the menu bar is called the **position** or often the **zero position**. The first menu item, most often Files, is said to be identified as position 0. Edit, which is usually next, is position 1, and so on. MFC can make use of the zero position.

Let's examine a common menu definition for an application that would use files in some manner. We will include keyboard accelerator hints for the user.

```
MAINMENU MENU
BEGIN
    POPUP "&File"
    BEGIN
        MENUITEM "&New",                CM_FILENEW
        MENUITEM "&Open...",            CM_FILEOPEN
        MENUITEM "&Close",              CM_FILECLOSE, GRAYED
        MENUITEM SEPARATOR
        MENUITEM "&Save",               CM_FILESAVE, GRAYED
        MENUITEM "Save &As...",         CM_FILESAVEAS, GRAYED
        MENUITEM SEPARATOR
        MENUITEM "&Print...",           CM_FILEPRINT, GRAYED
        MENUITEM "P&rint Setup...",     CM_FILEPRINTERSETUP, GRAYED
        MENUITEM SEPARATOR
        MENUITEM "E&xit\tAlt+F4",       CM_EXIT
    END

    POPUP "&Edit"
    BEGIN
        MENUITEM "&Undo\tAlt+BkSp",     CM_EDITUNDO, GRAYED
        MENUITEM SEPARATOR
        MENUITEM "Cu&t\tShift+Del",     CM_EDITCUT, GRAYED
        MENUITEM "&Copy\tCtrl+Ins",     CM_EDITCOPY, GRAYED
        MENUITEM "&Paste\tShift+Ins",   CM_EDITPASTE, GRAYED
        MENUITEM SEPARATOR
        MENUITEM "Clear &All\tCtrl+Del", CM_EDITCLEAR, GRAYED
        MENUITEM "&Delete\tDel",        CM_EDITDELETE, GRAYED
    END

    POP UP "&Search"
    BEGIN
```

```
        MENUITEM "&Find...",                CM_EDITFIND, GRAYED
        MENUITEM "&Replace...",             CM_EDITREPLACE, GRAYED
        MENUITEM "&Next\aF3",               CM_EDITFINDNEXT, GRAYED
    END

    MENUITEM "&Display Map",                IDM_DISPLAYMAP

    POP UP "&Help"
    BEGIN
        MENUITEM "&About...",               CM_HELPABOUT
    END
END
```

Notice that several choices have the ... included and that most accelerator hints are preceded by **\t**. Note that those menu selections that at first are inactive have been initialized to GRAYED.

6.2 PREDEFINED MFC MENU ID NAMES AND NUMBERS

MFC provides an integrated set of commonly used identifiers and their associated resource items, such as menus, accelerators, tool bar hint strings, and tool bar bitmaps. These identifiers are closely tied to automatic framework commands. They all begin ID_ and they are defined in one file, MFC\INCLUDE\AFXRES.H. The special IDs are not easily used outside of the App Wizard or the Document View architecture. To avoid accidentally triggering framework menu command handlers, you should avoid the use of the ID_ prefix when working outside of the App Wizard. So that it is quite clear, I have used either IDM_ or CM_ for menu items that are not using the MFC built-in command IDs. In chapter 15, we explore the special ID_ values in depth.

Under the MFC, those menu items that have both an ON_COMMAND handler, which responds to that menu selection, and an ON_UPDATE_COMMAND_UI command enabler function, which enables and disables the menu item, are said to be following the MFC command structure. Normally our menu items and commands would follow the MFC command structure. Technically, a user's menu item **ID_** numbers should lie between 0×8000 and 0×DFFF, while the internal MFC **ID_** numbers lie between 0×E000 and 0×EFFF. To assist us, the MFC provides the define WM_USER to be used as the base number for the user IDs. For example, one could code

```
#define CM_MYMENU1     (WM_USER + 1)
#define CM_MYMENU2     (WM_USER + 2)
```

Just remember that when you save the resource file, Developer Studio converts the (WM_USER + 1) into a real number. The menu in Pgm08a follows this scheme. However, small numbers also work fine. In practice, I often use small numbers for my MFC menu command ID numbers.

```
#define CM_MYMENU1     100
#define CM_MYMENU2     101
```

Both schemes work fine. The one thing that you want to avoid when not using the App and Class Wizards is to use the MFC built-in **ID_** names. These reserved IDs and numbers may be processed internally by MFC, yielding different results than you intended when that menu item is selected.

6.3 SAMPLE MENU FOR PGM06a

6.3.1 Listing for File: resource.h—Pgm06a—Excerpts

```
#define CM_DISPLAYMAP          101
#define CM_FILENEW             102
#define CM_FILEOPEN            103
#define CM_FILECLOSE           104
#define CM_FILESAVE            105
#define CM_FILESAVEAS          106
#define CM_FILEPRINT           107
#define CM_FILEPRINTERSETUP    108
#define CM_EXIT                109
#define CM_EDITUNDO            110
#define CM_EDITCUT             111
#define CM_EDITCOPY            112
#define CM_EDITPASTE           113
#define CM_EDITDELETE          114
#define CM_EDITCLEAR           115
#define CM_EDITFIND            116
#define CM_EDITREPLACE         117
#define CM_EDITFINDNEXT        118
#define CM_HELPABOUT           119

#define IDS_MAINTITLE    200
#define IDS_WINNAME      201
#define IDS_MSG_QUIT     202
#define IDS_MSG_QUERY    203
```

6.3.2 Listing for File: Pgm06a.rc—Pgm06a—Excerpts

```
...
MAINMENU MENU DISCARDABLE
BEGIN
    POPUP "&File"
    BEGIN
        MENUITEM "&New",                    CM_FILENEW
        MENUITEM "&Open...",                CM_FILEOPEN
        MENUITEM "&Close",                  CM_FILECLOSE, GRAYED
        MENUITEM SEPARATOR
        MENUITEM "&Save",                   CM_FILESAVE, GRAYED
        MENUITEM "Save &As...",             CM_FILESAVEAS, GRAYED
        MENUITEM SEPARATOR
        MENUITEM "&Print...",               CM_FILEPRINT, GRAYED
        MENUITEM "P&rint Setup...",         CM_FILEPRINTERSETUP, GRAYED
```

```
        MENUITEM SEPARATOR
        MENUITEM "E&xit\tAlt+F4",                 CM_EXIT
    END
    POPUP "&Edit"
    BEGIN
        MENUITEM "&Undo\tAlt+BkSp",               CM_EDITUNDO, GRAYED
        MENUITEM SEPARATOR
        MENUITEM "Cu&t\tShift+Del",               CM_EDITCUT, GRAYED
        MENUITEM "&Copy\tCtrl+Ins",               CM_EDITCOPY, GRAYED
        MENUITEM "&Paste\tShift+Ins",             CM_EDITPASTE, GRAYED
        MENUITEM SEPARATOR
        MENUITEM "Clear &All\tCtrl+Del",          CM_EDITCLEAR, GRAYED
        MENUITEM "&Delete\tDel",                  CM_EDITDELETE, GRAYED
    END
    POPUP "&Search"
    BEGIN
        MENUITEM "&Find...",                      CM_EDITFIND, GRAYED
        MENUITEM "&Replace...",                   CM_EDITREPLACE, GRAYED
        MENUITEM "&Next\aF3",                     CM_EDITFINDNEXT, GRAYED
    END
    MENUITEM "&Display Map",              CM_DISPLAYMAP
    POPUP "&Help"
    BEGIN
        MENUITEM "&About...",                     CM_HELPABOUT
    END
END
...
MAINMENU ACCELERATORS MOVEABLE PURE
BEGIN
    VK_DELETE,        CM_EDITCUT,               VIRTKEY, SHIFT
    VK_INSERT,        CM_EDITCOPY,              VIRTKEY, CONTROL
    VK_INSERT,        CM_EDITPASTE,             VIRTKEY, SHIFT
    VK_DELETE,        CM_EDITCLEAR,             VIRTKEY, CONTROL
    VK_BACK,          CM_EDITUNDO,              VIRTKEY, ALT
    VK_F3,            CM_EDITFINDNEXT,          VIRTKEY
END
...
STRINGTABLE DISCARDABLE
BEGIN
    IDS_MAINTITLE         "Menu Processing Program"
    IDS_WINNAME           "MenuPgm"
    IDS_MSG_QUIT          "Do you want to quit the application?"
    IDS_MSG_QUERY         "Query?"
END
...
```

6.4 INSTALLING A MENU, C-STYLE

We define the name of a menu either as a defined integer or as a string. Thus there are two methods of getting to the resource, either by string name or by ID. Constructing menus can be done several ways.

6.4.1 C Method 1: Assign the Menu in the Window Class Structure

Under Windows 95 C-style, if a string name is used, the main menu is often assigned in the WNDCLASS structure, using the **lpszMenuName** field

```
wndclass.lpszMenuName = "MAINMENU";
```

If the ID format is used, the resource ID number must be converted into a resource using the **MAKEINTRESOURCE** macro

```
wndclass.lpszMenuName = MAKEINTRESOURCE (IDM_MAINMENU);
```

or

```
wndclass.lpszMenuName = "#IDM_MAINMENU";
```

6.4.2 C Method 2: Dynamically Load and Install a Menu

Use the appropriate form

```
HMENU hMenu = LoadMenu (hinstance, "MAINMENU");
HMENU hMenu = LoadMenu (hinstance, MAKEINTRESOURCE (MAINMENU));
```

Then specify **hMenu** as the ninth parameter to **CreateWindow**, if it is to be used at once. If the menu is to be used later, the menu can be installed using

```
SetMenu (hwnd, hMenu);
```

Any menu attached to a window is destroyed when the window is destroyed; all others should be deleted.

6.4.3 C Method 3: Manually Build the Menu from Component Menuitems

By using the **CreateMenu** function followed by many **AppendMenu** functions, you can dynamically create new menus, but it is a tedious business.

```
hMenu = CreateMenu ();
hMenuPopup = CreateMenu();
AppendMenu (hMenuPopup, MF_STRING, IDM_NEW, "&New");
...
```

6.5 INSTALLING A MENU, MFC-STYLE

Under MFC, there are various methods to install a menu as well.

6.5.1 MFC Method 1: Pass the String Name in the Frame Window Class Constructor

In the call to **Create**

```
Create ( AfxRegisterWndClass (
            CS_VREDRAW | CS_HREDRAW,          // register window style UINT
            AfxGetApp()->LoadStandardCursor (IDC_ARROW), // use arrow cur
            (HBRUSH) GetStockObject (LTGRAY_BRUSH),
            AfxGetApp()->LoadStandardIcon (IDI_APPLICATION)),// set min icon
        title,                  // window caption
        style,                  // wndclass DWORD style
        rect,                   // set initial window position
        ptrparent,              // the parent window, here none
        "MAINMENU");            // assign the main menu
```

Note that we could always pass the desired menu ID or name as another parameter to the constructor. The idea is the window class knows how to set up or wants to set up its own menu.

6.5.2 MFC Method 2: Use the C-style Method 2 or 3

Use the member functions **SetMenu**, **GetMenu**, **AppendMenu**, and **Load-Menu** with method 2 or 3 of the C-style.

6.5.3 MFC Method 3: Use a CMenu Class to Construct Menu Objects

We can wrap a **CMenu** object around the menu in use and then use that **CMenu** to perform many actions on that menu object. The key is to construct the menu object. If the application begins with an initial main menu, install it as normal. Then, in the **OnCreate** function, after passing control to the base classes, we can construct instances of the **CMenu** class in many ways, but the common way is from a resource (where **ptrmenu** is likely a protected data member)

```
CMenu menu();
menu.LoadMenu(resource id); // a new menu or use a string name
```

or

```
CMENU *ptrmenu = GetMenu(); // use current window's menu
```

We can now make any number of changes to the menu. Where do we delete the allocated menus? The best place to remove items allocated in **OnCreate** is the **OnDestroy** function, which is invoked just before the class destructor. If **ptrmenu** was really a protected FrameWin class member that was **new**ed in **OnCreate** or even **new**ed at another time during the running of the application, then we would have

```
void  FrameWin::OnDestroy () {
 delete ptrmenu;
 CFrameWnd::OnDestroy();
}
```

Now many fancy actions can be easily done dynamically to this menu object that is the application's current menu. However, before we look at the more exciting effects possible, including floating pop-up menus, let's see how a basic static, nonchanging menu is handled.

6.6 Working with the Menu Choices of the User

6.6.1 C-Style

Once the menu has been installed, Windows 95 takes total control of the menu and user interactions with it. When the user makes a menu selection that is itself a pop-up menu, Windows 95 pops up the submenu. The only action that we must code for is a response for a given menu choice. When the user finally makes a menu selection that is currently enabled and not grayed and not a pop-up menu, Windows 95 sends our program a WM_COMMAND message along with the menu ID number the user selected. (Many messages are sent concerning the menu events, but most are not of interest to the application; normally only the final user choice is wanted.)

Thus, when processing the WM_COMMAND message, we immediately switch on the **wparam** with a case to process each of the menu possibilities. Here is where the message switch coding becomes lengthy, yielding the "nightmare switch from Hell."

6.6.2 MFC-Style

Each possible menu selection that we wish to respond to has both a member function that performs the appropriate processing based upon the menu item selected and a corresponding entry in the Message Map Table. The table contains the ON_COMMAND rahter than the ON_WM_COMMAND you might have expected. ON_COMMAND has the following syntax:

```
ON_COMMAND(menu ID, member function),
```

You supply the menu ID number and the name of the member function that is to be invoked. MFC traps the WM_COMMAND messages, deciphers which menu item is being requested, and then invokes the correct member function to carry out that request. Notice that the member function names are based upon the menu ID number name. Here I have chosen to use the CM_ prefix for all menu items. Above all, make the function member name follow a predictable pattern derived from the CM_ identifier to avoid such confusions as

```
ON_COMMAND(CM_FILENEW, NewProcess),
```

because it is not immediately clear to the reader that **NewProcess** is invoked in response to the user selecting the File | New menu item.

The MFC response table for Pgm06a would appear as

```
BEGIN_MESSAGE_MAP(FrameWin, CFrameWnd)
  ON_WM_SIZE ()
  ON_WM_PAINT ()
  ON_WM_CREATE ()
  ON_WM_CLOSE ()
  ON_WM_DESTROY ()
  ON_WM_RBUTTONDOWN ()
  ON_COMMAND(CM_DISPLAYMAP, CmDisplayMap)
  ON_COMMAND(CM_EXIT, CmExit)
```

```
ON_COMMAND(CM_FILENEW,          CmFileNew)
ON_COMMAND(CM_FILEOPEN,         CmFileOpen)
ON_COMMAND(CM_FILECLOSE,        CmFileClose)
ON_COMMAND(CM_FILESAVE,         CmFileSave)
ON_COMMAND(CM_FILESAVEAS,       CmFileSaveAs)
ON_COMMAND(CM_FILEPRINT,        CmFilePrint)
ON_COMMAND(CM_FILEPRINTERSETUP, CmFilePrinterSetup)
ON_COMMAND(CM_EDITUNDO,         CmEditUndo)
ON_COMMAND(CM_EDITCUT,          CmEditCut)
ON_COMMAND(CM_EDITCOPY,         CmEditCopy)
ON_COMMAND(CM_EDITPASTE,        CmEditPaste)
ON_COMMAND(CM_EDITCLEAR,        CmEditClear)
ON_COMMAND(CM_EDITDELETE,       CmEditDelete)
ON_COMMAND(CM_EDITFIND,         CmEditFind)
ON_COMMAND(CM_EDITFINDNEXT,     CmEditFindNext)
ON_COMMAND(CM_EDITREPLACE,      CmEditReplace)
ON_COMMAND(CM_HELPABOUT,        CmHelpAbout)
END_MESSAGE_MAP()
```

The next coding step would be the implementation of the myriad functions. For now, they all display a message box stating the function is not yet implemented.

6.7 DYNAMICALLY CHECKMARKING, GRAYING/UNGRAYING, ENABLING/DISABLING MENU ITEMS

As you look over the menu items, a number are initialized to GRAYED because they currently have no meaning. Consider the pop-up File menu. File | Save and File | SaveAs are initially grayed because no file is loaded yet. Whenever the user selects File | New or File | Open, there is a file that could be saved. Now we would like to immediately have the menu item UNGRAYED to show that this choice is now available.

Note that the MFC ignores the GRAY options in the menu proper; instead, when the menu is constructed, the class library grays any menu item that has no entry in any window's response table. It searches the frame window, the application class, and the client window (and a number of other classes) looking for one that would potentially respond to that command ID. If it finds one that is going to respond to that command ID, the corresponding menu item is enabled. It grays out all those menu items for which it cannot find a response to that command ID. The search is done using the message response tables and maps.

Now this behavior is perfect for such menu items as Choose Font, Bold, and File | New. It is not at all what we desire for menu items such as File | Save, Edit | Cut, and Edit | Paste; in these cases, if there is no file currently opened nor text selected nor anything on the clipboard to insert, having enabled active menu items is pointless as well as misleading to the user. We must modify this behavior.

Similarly, some menu items, such as BOLD FONT, should be checkmarked when the user selects it, showing that that option is now in effect. Later, should the user select BOLD FONT to turn it off, we would like the CHECKMARK to disappear.

With MFC, these kinds of minor alterations to existing menu items can be done in two entirely different ways: using *command enablers* and using **CMenu** member functions directly. Let's examine the command enablers first.

6.7.1 MFC Command Enablers

For each menu item that is to be controlled, you provide a member function defined as

```
void    your_function_name (CCmdUI *ptrenabler);
```

Usually, the enabler's body is quite short, using the member function **Enable**. If **Enable** is passed TRUE, the menu item is enabled; FALSE disables or grays it. To avoid name-pollution, choose function names that relate to the commands that they are enabling. In the File I Save menu above, we would have

```
void CmEnableFileSave (CCmdUI *ptrenabler) {
 ptrenabler->Enable (haveFile);
}
```

where **haveFile** is likely a BOOL class data member. Two other enabler member functions are

```
SetText (new menu text string);
SetCheck (special id for check or no check);
```

If the string, **menustr**, contained the new text for this menu item, coding the following in the command enabler function would install the new text

```
ptrenabler->SetText (menustr);
```

To use the checkmark, code

```
ptrenabler->SetCheck (1); // 1 shows checkmark, 0 removes checkmark
```

Next, we must tie these enabler functions to the menu command to which they apply. Assume we have an enabler for the File I Save and File I SaveAs menu items. The coding in the response table would be

```
ON_COMMAND(CM_FILESAVE, CmFileSave)
ON_COMMAND(CM_FILESAVEAS, CmFileSaveAs)

ON_UPDATE_COMMAND_UI(CM_FILESAVE, CmEnableFileSave)
ON_UPDATE_COMMAND_UI(CM_FILESAVEAS, CmEnableFileSaveAs)
```

Notice that the menu ID is duplicated! CM_FILESAVE is used in both the ON_COMMAND and ON_UPDATE_COMMAND_UI macros. Again, by convention and for clarity, the enabler member functions use the same name as the actual command processing functions prefixed with **Enable**.

> *Design Rule 25:* **If you are going to both change the menu item's text and set a checkmark, be sure to set the text first because the process overlays any previous checkmark.**

6.8 USING MFC'S CMENU MEMBER FUNCTIONS

In many ways, the easiest method to gain total control of the menu system is by turning the main menu into a **CMenu** object and using the member functions to manipulate the menu. In the **CMenu** member functions (most are parallel to Windows 95 API functions) the flags are a combination from one or more sets. The functions are

```
MF_STRING, MF_BITMAP, MF_OWNERDRAW,
MF_DISABLED, MF_ENABLED, MF_GRAYED
MF_CHECKED, MF_UNCHECKED
MF_MENUBREAK, MF_MENUBARBREAK, MF_SEPARATOR
MF_POPUP
MF_BYCOMMAND (item is an ID number), MF_BYPOSITION (is the items
          zero-based position in the menu, where the leftmost menu
          item is position 0, and so on.
```

The MFC functions include:

```
AppendMenu (flags, ID, "menuchoice");
                     // adds a menu item to the end of the menu
InsertMenu (ID current, flags, ID new, "menuchoice");
                     // adds a menu item after the menu item of id
ModifyMenu (ID current, flags, ID new, "menuchoice");
                     // changes the given menu item.
DeleteMenu (ID current, flags);
                     // removes the menu item, pop up item from a menu
EnableMenuItem (ID current, flags);
                     // enables or disables the menu item,
                     // usually checkmark or grayed
CheckMenuItem (ID current, flag);
                     // checks or unchecks the menu item,
                     // use MF_CHECKED or MF_UNCHECKED
GetMenuState (ID current, flags to check status of);
                     // returns the state of the indicated flags
                     // of the menu item
CWnd member function:
DrawMenuBar ();       // redraws the menu bar after alterations
```

To use these, we need to set up a protected data member, often called a **ptrmenu**, which is a **CMenu***. Under MFC, the **CMenu*** pointer is most often initialized in **OnCreate** and later deleted in **OnDestroy**

```
int FrameWin::OnCreate (LPCREATESTRUCT lp) {
 int retcd = CFrameWnd::OnCreate (lp); // invoke base class first
 ptrmenu = GetMenu ();         // initialize ptrmenu to main menu
 return retcd;
}

void FrameWin::OnDestroy () {
 delete ptrmenu;           // remove the CMenu
 CFrameWnd::OnDestroy(); // invoke base class last
}
```

To add a new menu item to the menu bar, invoke

```
ptrmenu->AppendMenu (MF_STRING, IDM_NEWONE, "&NewItem");
```

When we are processing the File | New or File | Open requests, after successfully creating a new file or opening an existing file, and before terminating the function

```
ptrmenu->EnableMenuItem (CM_FILESAVE, MF_ENABLED);
```

or for a checkmark

```
ptrmenu->CheckMenuItem (CM_FILESAVE, MF_CHECKED);
```

The texts in the bibliography give many examples of adding, modifying, and deleting menu items and pop-up menus.

Remember if you are in a function that is handling a part of the menu selection process, such as adding a new menu item, be sure to invoke **DrawMenuBar** after making the changes. This will immediately reflect the changes on screen. In other functions, such as in the **CmFileNew**, you do not need to redraw the menu bar; it is not active because the user has already made a choice.

6.9 FREE FLOATING POP-UP MENUS

Floating or pop-up menus that appear where the cursor is located give a professional look to applications. Windows 95 makes extensive use of floating pop-up menus triggered by right mouse clicks. Floating menus are easily done under the MFC. Usually the trigger is pressing the right mouse button. First we create a protected **CMenu** class member, called, for instance, **ptrmenu**, that encapsulates the application's main menu. When the right button is pressed in the **OnRButtonDown** function, the floating menu details are handled.

If the floating menu is one of the existent pop-up menus from the menu bar, as often happens, we need to get a handle to it. On the other hand, if the menu is a special one, we may need to load it from the resource file. Or we could painstakingly construct the entire menu from scratch. Let's assume that when the right button is pressed, we would like the Edit pop-up menu to appear. The key is to determine its zero-position number from the main menu bar. File is position 0, Edit is next at position 1. Thus, we would code

```
void      FrameWin::OnRButtonDown (UINT, CPoint point) {
  CMenu *ptrmenu  = GetMenu ();              // point to main menu object
  CMenu *ptrpopup = ptrmenu->GetSubMenu (1); // point to edit pop up menu
  ptrpopup->TrackPopupMenu (0, point.x, point.y, this, 0);
}
```

The first and last parameters of **TrackPopupMenu** are normally 0; the second and third are the x,y coordinates where the menu is to pop up; and the fourth is a handle to this window

```
BOOL TrackPopupMenu (UINT flags, int x, int y, CWnd*, CRect*);
```

The flags can be an ORed value from each of two groups

TPM_CENTERALIGN	centers the pop-up menu on x,y
TPM_LEFTALIGN	positions so left side is aligned on x
TPM_RIGHTALIGN	positions so right side is aligned on x
TPM_LEFTBUTTON	pop up tracks the left button
TPM_RIGHTBUTTON	pop up tracks the right button

The **CRect*** points to a **CRect** that contains the screen coordinates in which the user can click without dismissing the pop-up menu. If NULL, the pop up is dismissed if the user clicks outside the menu. One slight detail arises. The coordinates passed to the **OnRButtonDown** have their origin point at the upper-left edge of the client window. The pop-up function requires full screen coordinates. The function **Client-ToScreen** converts a **CPoint**

```
ClientToScreen (&point);          // convert coordinates
```

Another **CWnd** function does the reverse

```
ScreenToClient (&point);
```

The MFC framework and Windows 95 work together to display the menu, get the user selection, remove the menu, repaint the overlaid windows, and invoke the command handler corresponding to the selected menu item.

6.10 MENU ACCELERATORS

Keyboard menu accelerators are easy to set up. In the resource RC file, add an accelerators section

```
identifier ACCELERATORS
{
}
```

The identifier is often the same name as the main menu. In our case, MAINMENU:

```
MAINMENU ACCELERATORS
BEGIN
END
```

The definition of an accelerator consists of

```
event, idvalue, type ALT SHIFT CONTROL VIRTKEY
```

Consider these possible accelerator keys:

```
  "h", IDM_xxx                       ; the H key alone - DANGEROUS
  "H", IDM_xxx                       ; Shift + H key   - DANGEROUS
 "^H", IDM_xxx                       ; Control + H key
  "H", IDM_xxx, ALT                  ; Alt + H key
VK_F7, IDM_xxx, VIRTKEY             ; F7 key
VK_F7, IDM_xxx, SHIFT, VIRTKEY      ; Shift + F7 key
VK_F7, IDM_xxx, CONTROL, VIRTKEY    ; Control + F7 key
```

```
VK_F7, IDM_xxx, ALT, VIRTKEY          ; Alt + F7 key
VK_F7, IDM_xxx, ALT, SHIFT, VIRTKEY ; Alt + Shift + F7 key
```

Careful! If you use a single letter or a letter and the shift key, these cannot then be entered into a text stream; instead they would trigger the command for which they are a shortcut. For Pgm06a, the accelerator table is

```
MAINMENU ACCELERATORS
BEGIN
  VK_DELETE, CM_EDITCUT,      VIRTKEY, SHIFT
  VK_INSERT, CM_EDITCOPY,     VIRTKEY, CONTROL
  VK_INSERT, CM_EDITPASTE,    VIRTKEY, SHIFT
  VK_DELETE, CM_EDITCLEAR,    VIRTKEY, CONTROL
  VK_BACK,   CM_EDITUNDO,     VIRTKEY, ALT
  VK_F3,     CM_EDITFINDNEXT, VIRTKEY
END
```

The last step is to insert the accelerator table into the FrameWin. Under C-Style you need to add

```
HANDLE haccel = LoadAccelerators (hinstance, "MAINMENU");
```

Then you need to check for these by modifying the Get Message/Translate Message/ Dispatch Message loop

```
while (GetMessage (&msg, NULL, 0)) {
 if (!TranslateAccelerator (hwnd, haccel, &msg)) {
  TranslateMessage (&msg);
  DispatchMessage (&msg);
 }
}
```

Here the **TranslateAccelerator** invokes the correct item if it matches the accelerator table entry.

Under MFC, in the FrameWin constructor, code

```
LoadAccelTable ("MAINMENU"); // install keybd accelerators
```

There are also functions to access the system menu and add, alter, or delete menu items. However, most users will expect the system menu to be similar among all applications, so it is not wise to modify it.

6.11 The Coding for Pgm06a

Figure 6.1 shows what the main menu looks like with the File pop-up group opened. Figure 6.2 shows the floating Edit pop-up menu activated.

Notice that the MFC enables all of the Edit menu choices although they were GRAYED in the resource file. This occurs because MFC has found a corresponding command handler for these items. The command enablers would then provide for their current settings. Follow the **haveFile** and **haveSaved** logic through the various File menu choices. By having indicators such as these, the handling of menu enabling

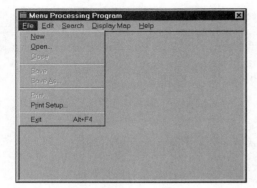

Fig. 6.1 Pgm06a Showing the File Pop-Up Menu Activated

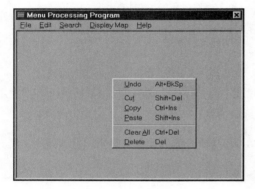

Fig. 6.2 Pgm06a Showing the Edit Pop-Up Menu Activated

is easily done. Try out the floating pop-up edit menu; it is a nice effect. As you examine the coding you'll see I have omitted the **CWinApp** module. Notice too the extensive list of command handler member functions in the header file. Since many of these are stubbed or dummied out, only a representative sample is shown in the cpp file. To save space, I have omitted some repetitive coding.

6.11.1 Listing for File: FrameWin.h—Pgm06a—Excerpts

```
...
/******************************************************************************/
/*                                                                            */
/* FrameWin Class Definition                                                  */
/*                                                                            */
/******************************************************************************/

class FrameWin : public CFrameWnd {

/******************************************************************************/
/*                                                                            */
/* Class Data Members                                                         */
/*                                                                            */
/******************************************************************************/

protected:
```

```
int   height;           // current client window height in pixels
int   width;            // current client window width in pixels

int   avg_caps_width;   // average capital letter width
int   avg_char_width;   // average character width
int   avg_char_height;  // average character height

BOOL  haveFile;         // when TRUE, we have opened or have begun a new file
BOOL  haveSaved;        // when TRUE, we have saved the existent file
/*****************************************************************************/
/*                                                                           */
/* Class Functions:                                                          */
/*                                                                           */
/*****************************************************************************/
public:

                FrameWin (CWnd*, const char*); // constructor
                ~FrameWin () {}                // destructor

protected:

afx_msg void    OnPaint ();                    // paint the window - WM_PAINT
afx_msg int     OnCreate (LPCREATESTRUCT);     // construct window, avg char dims
afx_msg void    OnClose ();                    // determines if app can quit yet
afx_msg void    OnSize (UINT, int, int);       // process window resize
afx_msg void    OnDestroy ();                  // remove allocated menus
afx_msg void    OnRButtonDown (UINT, CPoint);  // popup edit menu

afx_msg void    CmExit ();
afx_msg void    CmDisplayMap ();               // our unique menu item
afx_msg void    CmFileNew ();                  // start a new file
afx_msg void    CmFileOpen ();                 // open existing file
afx_msg void    CmFileClose ();                // close the file
afx_msg void    CmFileSave ();                 // save the file with same name
afx_msg void    CmFileSaveAs ();               // save with new name
afx_msg void    CmFilePrint ();                // print the file
afx_msg void    CmFilePrinterSetup ();         // set up the printer
afx_msg void    CmEditUndo ();                 // undo last change
afx_msg void    CmEditCut ();                  // cut to clipboard
afx_msg void    CmEditCopy ();                 // copy to clipboard
afx_msg void    CmEditPaste ();                // paste from the clipboard
afx_msg void    CmEditDelete ();               // delete text
afx_msg void    CmEditClear ();                // clear text
afx_msg void    CmEditFind ();                 // find text
afx_msg void    CmEditFindNext ();             // find next text
afx_msg void    CmEditReplace ();              // find and replace
afx_msg void    CmHelpAbout ();                // help about our app
afx_msg void    CmEnableFileClose (CCmdUI*);   // enable/disable FileClose
afx_msg void    CmEnableFileSave (CCmdUI*);    // enable/disable FileSave
afx_msg void    CmEnableFileSaveAs (CCmdUI*);  // enable/disable FileSaveAs
afx_msg void    CmEnableFilePrint (CCmdUI*);   // enable/disable FilePrint

DECLARE_MESSAGE_MAP()
...
```

6.11.2 Listing for File: FrameWin.cpp—Pgm06a—Excerpts

```
...
/*************************************************************************/
/*                                                                       */
/* FrameWin Events Response Table                                        */
/*                                                                       */
/*************************************************************************/

BEGIN_MESSAGE_MAP(FrameWin, CFrameWnd)
 ON_WM_SIZE ()
 ON_WM_PAINT ()
 ON_WM_CREATE ()
 ON_WM_CLOSE ()
 ON_WM_DESTROY ()
 ON_WM_RBUTTONDOWN ()
 ON_COMMAND(CM_DISPLAYMAP, CmDisplayMap)
 ON_COMMAND(CM_EXIT, CmExit)
 ON_COMMAND(CM_FILENEW, CmFileNew)
 ON_COMMAND(CM_FILEOPEN, CmFileOpen)
 ON_COMMAND(CM_FILECLOSE, CmFileClose)
 ON_COMMAND(CM_FILESAVE, CmFileSave)
 ON_COMMAND(CM_FILESAVEAS, CmFileSaveAs)
 ON_COMMAND(CM_FILEPRINT, CmFilePrint)
 ON_COMMAND(CM_FILEPRINTERSETUP, CmFilePrinterSetup)
 ON_COMMAND(CM_EDITUNDO, CmEditUndo)
 ON_COMMAND(CM_EDITCUT, CmEditCut)
 ON_COMMAND(CM_EDITCOPY, CmEditCopy)
 ON_COMMAND(CM_EDITPASTE, CmEditPaste)
 ON_COMMAND(CM_EDITCLEAR, CmEditClear)
 ON_COMMAND(CM_EDITDELETE, CmEditDelete)
 ON_COMMAND(CM_EDITFIND, CmEditFind)
 ON_COMMAND(CM_EDITFINDNEXT, CmEditFindNext)
 ON_COMMAND(CM_EDITREPLACE, CmEditReplace)
 ON_COMMAND(CM_HELPABOUT, CmHelpAbout)
 ON_UPDATE_COMMAND_UI(CM_FILECLOSE, CmEnableFileClose)
 ON_UPDATE_COMMAND_UI(CM_FILESAVE, CmEnableFileSave)
 ON_UPDATE_COMMAND_UI(CM_FILESAVEAS, CmEnableFileSaveAs)
 ON_UPDATE_COMMAND_UI(CM_FILEPRINT, CmEnableFilePrint)
END_MESSAGE_MAP()

/*************************************************************************/
/*                                                                       */
/* FrameWin Constructor: setup style, dims, and create window            */
/*                                                                       */
/*************************************************************************/

         FrameWin::FrameWin (CWnd* ptrparent, const char* title)
                  : CFrameWnd () {

DWORD style = WS_OVERLAPPEDWINDOW;              // set basic window styles
style &= !(WS_MINIMIZEBOX | WS_MAXIMIZEBOX); // remove max/min buttons
style |= WS_SYSMENU | WS_THICKFRAME;

CRect rect (50, 50, 500, 400);                 // set init pos and size

LoadAccelTable ("MAINMENU"); // install keybd accelerators
```

```
  Create ( AfxRegisterWndClass (
            CS_VREDRAW | CS_HREDRAW,          // register window style UINT
            AfxGetApp()->LoadStandardCursor (IDC_ARROW), // use arrow cur
            (HBRUSH) GetStockObject (LTGRAY_BRUSH),
            AfxGetApp()->LoadStandardIcon (IDI_APPLICATION)),// set min icon
        title,               // window caption
        style,               // wndclass DWORD style
        rect,                // set initial window position
        ptrparent,           // the parent window, here none
        "MAINMENU");         // assign the main menu
  haveFile  = FALSE;  // indicates no file loaded yet
  haveSaved = FALSE;  // indicates if a file is present, it is not saved
}
/***************************************************************************/
/*                                                                       */
/* OnCreate: get average character height and width                      */
/*                                                                       */
/***************************************************************************/
int      FrameWin::OnCreate (LPCREATESTRUCT lpCS) {

  int retcd = CFrameWnd::OnCreate (lpCS); // pass along to base class

  TEXTMETRIC  tm;

  // set the system font's characteristics in tm
  CClientDC *ptrdc = new CClientDC (this);  // acquire a DC
  ptrdc->GetTextMetrics (&tm);              // get the information
  delete ptrdc;                             // delete the dc

  // calculate average character parameters
  avg_char_width  = tm.tmAveCharWidth;
  avg_char_height = tm.tmHeight + tm.tmExternalLeading;
  avg_caps_width  = (tm.tmPitchAndFamily & 1 ? 3 : 2) * avg_char_width / 2;

  return retcd;
}
/***************************************************************************/
/*                                                                       */
/* OnDestroy: remove any menu objects, here none                         */
/*                                                                       */
/***************************************************************************/
void      FrameWin::OnDestroy () {

  CFrameWnd::OnDestroy();
}
...
/***************************************************************************/
/*                                                                       */
/* OnRButtonDown: popup edit menu as a floating menu                     */
/*                                                                       */
/***************************************************************************/
void      FrameWin::OnRButtonDown (UINT, CPoint point) {
```

```
CMenu *ptrmenu  = GetMenu ();                    // point to main menu object
CMenu *ptrpopup = ptrmenu->GetSubMenu (1);  // point to edit popup menu
ClientToScreen (&point);                         // convert coordinates
ptrpopup->TrackPopupMenu (0, point.x, point.y, this, 0); // get selection
}
/***************************************************************************/
/*                                                                       */
/* CmDisplayMap: display our map                                         */
/*                                                                       */
/***************************************************************************/

void     FrameWin::CmDisplayMap () {

 MessageBox ("DisplayMap is not yet implemented","Display Map",
            MB_ICONINFORMATION | MB_OK);
}
/***************************************************************************/
/*                                                                       */
/* CmExit:   determine if the app can be shut down                       */
/*                                                                       */
/***************************************************************************/

void     FrameWin::CmExit () {

 SendMessage (WM_CLOSE);
}
/***************************************************************************/
/*                                                                       */
/* CmFileNew: open a new file                                            */
/*                                                                       */
/***************************************************************************/

void     FrameWin::CmFileNew () {

 if (haveFile && !haveSaved) SendMessage (WM_COMMAND, ID_FILE_SAVE, 0L);
 MessageBox ("File New is not yet implemented - will pretend have a new file",
            "File New", MB_ICONINFORMATION | MB_OK);
 haveFile  = TRUE;
 haveSaved = FALSE;
}
/***************************************************************************/
/*                                                                       */
/* CmFileOpen: open an existent file                                     */
/*                                                                       */
/***************************************************************************/

void     FrameWin::CmFileOpen () {

 if (haveFile && !haveSaved) SendMessage (WM_COMMAND, ID_FILE_SAVE, 0L);
 MessageBox ("Open not implemented - pretend file is open", "File Open",
            MB_ICONINFORMATION | MB_OK);
 haveFile  = TRUE;
 haveSaved = TRUE;
}
```

```
/***************************************************************************/
/*                                                                         */
/* CmFileClose: close an opened file                                       */
/*                                                                         */
/***************************************************************************/

void       FrameWin::CmFileClose () {

  if (haveFile && !haveSaved) SendMessage (WM_COMMAND, ID_FILE_SAVE, 0L);
  MessageBox ("Close not implemented - pretend file is closed", "File Close",
              MB_ICONINFORMATION | MB_OK);
  haveFile  = FALSE;
  haveSaved = FALSE;
}

/***************************************************************************/
/*                                                                         */
/* CmFileSave: save an existent file                                       */
/*                                                                         */
/***************************************************************************/

void       FrameWin::CmFileSave () {

  MessageBox ("Save not implemented - Pretending file has been saved",
              "File Save", MB_ICONINFORMATION | MB_OK);
  haveSaved = TRUE;
}
...

/***************************************************************************/
/*                                                                         */
/* CmEditUndo: undo last typing error                                      */
/*                                                                         */
/***************************************************************************/

void       FrameWin::CmEditUndo () {

}
...

/***************************************************************************/
/*                                                                         */
/* CmHelpAbout: shows who wrote this app                                    */
/*                                                                         */
/***************************************************************************/

void       FrameWin::CmHelpAbout () {

  MessageBox (
    "Illustrates menu processing - try file menu items and right mouse button",
    "Help About PGM6A", MB_ICONINFORMATION | MB_OK);
}

/***************************************************************************/
/*                                                                         */
/* CmEnableFileClose: enables/disables FileClose menu item                  */
/*                                                                         */
/***************************************************************************/
```

```
void        FrameWin::CmEnableFileClose (CCmdUI *ptrenabler) {
 ptrenabler->Enable (haveFile);
}
...
```

6.12 WHAT TO DO NEXT

Experiment with the Tic-Tac-Toe game program that you converted from the C-style Pgm03a. Add a menu for the game. Under the File pop-up, include New Game, Cancel Game, and Exit. Under the Help pop-up menu, include a Help About that, when selected, displays a simple message box identifying the program's author. You might try to add some real help message boxes defining the controls that operate the game.

Dialogs, Resources, Property Sheets: Their Construction and Use

7.1 INTRODUCTION

The Windows 95 environment offers a wealth of graphical resources. There are simple items such as icons, cursors, and bitmaps. Then there are more complex items such as list boxes, edit boxes, and buttons of all kinds (radio, push button); and several new controls such as the progress control, as well as very complex items such as dialog boxes and property sheets or tabbed dialogs with many control elements. While this wide variety of graphical resources makes Windows 95 visually appealing for a user, it offers a challenge to the Windows 95 programmer.

This portion of Windows 95 is so involved that a text could be written on using the controls, dialogs, and property sheets. As you look over the presentations of Windows 95 resources in the literature, you can easily be overwhelmed by the complexity of resource construction. There are many different approaches to resource construction to say nothing about the mechanical and artistic styles involved. Construction and use of Windows 95 resources in an application range from the tedious bit-by-bit, manual construction from the "ground-up" approach to the almost "one-coding-line" approach using a previously created resource (built in the Workshop).

Resources can be used all by themselves within part of the main window area, such as a push button off to one side in the window. These are known as *child window controls*. Often, the resources are organized into a package presented to the user upon demand—a *dialog box*. An application can even have these resources, especially a dialog box, as its main window (see chapter 14)! Windows 95 provides several *common dialog boxes* to simplify several universal situations: selecting a file to open, choosing a color, choosing a font, and printing a file, for example.

If we were to discuss all aspects of resource creation and usage from the C and MFC styles and the various methods of construction via resource editors, we would consume all the remaining pages of this text. Thus, it is at this point that we must make some restrictions. Our restrictions on coverage include:

1. Whenever possible, we create resources using the Developer Studio.
2. Because of the first restriction, we discuss only the basic syntax involved in manual construction of resources and then only as it applies to using resources already constructed.
3. The major coding discussions illustrate the MFC approach to using resources. We do not cover C-style.
4. This book covers only the basics of how to use these resources. The bibliography contains references to many other sources for additional details. This is likely one area that you will continually be learning new and fancier ways of doing things.

Realize that, in the creation of a real application, a great deal of time is spent designing the optimum visual resources and their intended methods of use. Do not be surprised to discover that you are spending from one-third to one-half of your program development time on this task.

7.2 USING A DEVELOPER STUDIO TO BROWSE EXISTING RESOURCES

Before launching into the Developer Studio and trying your hand at creating fancy resources, look over the Visual C++ User's Guide, chapter 5, "Working with Resources." Explore chapters 6 through 11 as well, for they describe in detail the methods used to construct icons, bitmaps, and dialogs.

An excellent way to begin your study of resources is to examine the resources of known applications. Their resources are stored in their exe files. Bring up the Developer Studio and Choose File | Open; browse for your favorite Windows 95 application and choose Open. The Workshop decompiles the resources and displays the resources in the small window. It also displays a warning that it cannot save changes back into the exe file, of course. Now select the different dialogs, icons, cursors, and so on. Notice that it is possible to extract a resource from an application and copy it into your own resource file. Browse until you get a feel of what different resources look like and are familiar with the various styles and the look and feel of Windows 95 dialogs.

Now begin a new resource project File | New | Resource Script. Then experiment creating some resources.

7.3 CREATION OF ICONS, BITMAPS, AND CURSORS

Let's begin with the simpler resources: icons, cursors, and bitmaps. What does the application require? Normally, one icon represents the application in all of the various locations, not only when it is minimized. If the standard mouse cursors are not sufficient, then perhaps you will need a cursor or two. Bitmaps are often small pictures that represent something. For now, we have almost no use for them; however, when we begin adding tool bars (control bars) and tool boxes to our frame windows in chapter 11, bitmaps play a vital role. When we discuss the graphics interface in chapter 9, bitmaps become crucial.

See if you can create an icon and a cursor. Figure 7.1 shows what the pair that I created for this sample program looks like.
I chose to call these

```
IDI_TREE   ICON     "trees.ico"
IDC_TREE   CURSOR   "tree.cur"
```

Observe the convention: the prefix IDI_ identifies icons; the prefix IDC_ identifies cursors. (It is only a convention.) As with the name of a menu, the identifiers, IDI_TREE and IDC_TREE, can be used as shown—in other words, as string identifiers—or one could define these names in the resource.h file, in which case they become resource ID numbers.

The numbering scheme: Within a dialog, menu, string table, and so on, the ID numbers must be different. However, the same numbers can be reused on different type objects. That is, the first menu, icon, bitmap, and cursor can all have the same number, say 100, and still be independent items.

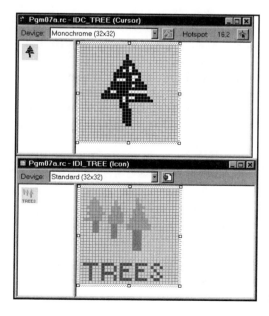

Fig. 7.1 Icon and Cursor

When the resource compiler is run as part of the Build program option, it includes the above two resource files. You can also code a partial or full path; for example, if the files were in a resource subdirectory, one could code

```
IDI_TREE  ICON  "resource\trees.ico"
```

or

```
IDI_TREE  ICON  "d:\learnwin\vc\pgm07a\resource\trees.ico"
```

However, supplying the full path makes the program development nonportable; it now is tied to a specific drive and set of subdirectories. I recommend using only the first method.

7.4 USING ICONS AND CURSORS

We already know how to install the application icon by using the **LoadIcon** function on the assignment to the **wndclass.hIcon** member using the C style approach. Under MFC, the icon would be loaded in the FrameWin constructor's invocation of the **Create** function as the fourth parameter to **AfxRegisterWndClass** as has been done in all examples thus far.

```
AfxGetApp()->LoadIcon (IDI_TREE)),// set min icon
```

After the invocation of **Create**, the cursor can be loaded by using the **LoadCursor** function and installed by using the **SetClassLong** function.

```
hcursor = LoadCursor (AfxGetApp()->m_hInstance,
                      MAKEINTRESOURCE (IDC_TREE));
SetClassLong (m_hWnd, GCL_HCURSOR, (long) hcursor);
```

However, let's examine some possible dynamic uses of a cursor. Assume that the arrow cursor is the default. Whenever an application enters a relatively long processing process, it is common to change the arrow cursor to the hourglass. When the process is finished, the arrow cursor is returned. Since this is so frequently desired, MFC has provided an extremely easy method to perform this switching. The **CWnd** class is derived from the **CCmdTarget** class; it is this base class that provides the wait cursor capabilities. To switch cursors use

BeginWaitCursor ();	installs the hourglass cursor
EndWaitCursor ();	restores the previous cursor
RestoreWaitCursor ();	restores wait cursor after an interruption such as a MessageBox or dialog box operations done during a wait sequence

These functions are best utilized within the processing sequences of a single message. When Windows 95 is allowed to process other messages during the long wait period, the cursor can be altered by other framework actions as we are about to see.

Another common use of changing cursors is to provide a special cursor while within a particular window. For example, in my WWII game, the arrow cursor is the normal cursor; but when the cursor is over a map window, a special location crosshair cursor appears. When the mouse moves out of the map window, the arrow cursor reappears. This behavior comes about because of the default behavior of the **CWnd** message handler **OnSetCursor**. If the mouse is not captured and mouse movement is within a window, the framework calls the window's **OnSetCursor** handler. The default implementation calls the parent window's handler before it calls the child window's handler, and it uses the arrow cursor if the mouse in not in the client area of the window. If the mouse is in the client area, then the registered class cursor is used. Thus, if the application is using a **CFrameWnd** only and has installed a special cursor, then, when the mouse is over the client area, the special cursor is automatically used; when the mouse is over the frame window elements, such as the menu bar, the arrow cursor appears. This behavior is implemented in the sample programs in this chapter. The sample programs install a special cursor for use while within the client area; the arrow cursor appears automatically when the mouse moves outside the client window area. Simply by changing the cursor registered to the **CWnd** class, our applications can make use of this behavior. In case you wish to refine the process further, the signature of the **OnSetCursor** function is

```
afxmsg  BOOL  OnSetCursor (CWnd* ptrwin, UINT hittest, UNIT msg);
```

The **msg** parameter is one of the various mouse messages, while the **hittest** parameter is one of the many mouse hit identifiers, such as HTCLIENT meaning it is within the client area. See the documentation given in **CWnd::OnNcHitTest** for the rather long list of hit codes.

The new cursor must be loaded. If the cursor is not going to change, one can install it directly into the WNDCLASS structure. If the cursor is being loaded once only, it makes sense to install it directly into the WNDCLASS structure as the window is being registered at creation time.

7.4.1 Method 1: The C API Method

The **LoadCursor** function requires the hInstance value and the cursor identifier which can be given in one of two ways depending upon whether the cursor identifier is a string or an ID number. If the identifier is a number, use the macro MAKEINTRESOURCE to convert it into a string.

```
HCURSOR  hcursor;
hcursor = LoadCursor (AfxGetApp()->m_hInstance,
                      MAKEINTRESOURCE (IDC_TREE)); // id is numeric
```

or

```
hcursor = LoadCursor (AfxGetApp()->m_hInstance, IDC_TREE);
```

If you have access to WNDCLASS

```
wndclass.hCursor = hcursor;
```

```
wndclass.hCursor = LoadCursor (AfxGetApp()->m_hInstance,
                              MAKEINTRESOURCE (IDC_TREE));
```

or

```
::SetCursor (hcursor);
```

7.4.2 Method 2: Use the CWinApp Functions to Load the Cursor

```
HCURSOR  LoadCursor (stringid);
HCURSOR  LoadCursor (UINT id);
```

where **stringid** is char* or LPCTSTR. In the above example, one could code

```
wndclass.hCursor = AfxGetApp()->LoadCursor (IDC_TREE);
```

If the cursor is one of the cursors supplied by Windows 95 (there are a lot of them—use Explorer and look in the \WINDOWS\CURSORS folder), then use the following **CWinApp** function:

```
HCURSOR LoadStandardCursor (LPCTSTR lpszCursorName) const;
```

The identifiers are defined in WINDOWS.H and include

IDC_ARROW	Standard arrow cursor
IDC_IBEAM	Standard text-insertion cursor
IDC_WAIT	Hourglass cursor used when Windows performs time-consuming task
IDC_CROSS	Crosshair cursor for selection
IDC_UPARROW	Arrow that points straight up
IDC_SIZE	Cursor to use to resize a window
IDC_ICON	Cursor to use to drag a file
IDC_SIZENWSE	Two-headed arrow with ends at upper left and lower right
IDC_SIZENESW	Two-headed arrow with ends at upper right and lower left
IDC_SIZEWE	Horizontal two-headed arrow
IDC_SIZENS	Vertical two-headed arrow

7.4.3 Method 3: the SetClassLong Method

This is best used when you wish to dynamically alter the cursor while the application is running.

```
SetClassLong (type id, (long) cursor object);
```

The type can be any one of the following:

```
GCL_HCURSOR      - changes cursor
GCL_HICON        - changes the minimize icon
```

```
GCL_HBACKGROUND  - changes the background brush
GCL_STYLE        - changes window styles
```

To permanently alter the cursor, code

```
SetClassLong (GCL_HCURSOR, (long) HCURSOR);
```

These approaches are used in Pgm07a; experiment with the mouse cursor. Notice when it is over the client window area, the tree cursor is visible. When the cursor passes over the menu bar or out of the window altogether, the standard arrow cursor reappears.

7.5 CONTROLS AND DIALOG BOXES

The basic controls that communicate user-entered information include: push buttons, list boxes, edit boxes, check boxes, radio button groups, combo boxes, and scroll bars. Windows 95 adds some new controls: progress bars, spin bars (up/down control), track bars, and tree views. Also, property sheets or tabbed dialog boxes are new. Note that any needed scroll bars within list and combo boxes are automatically handled by Windows 95. We will examine general scroll bars later. For now, we will concentrate on the others.

The basic procedure to install an object under the resource editor is to select an object from the tool bar or from the Insert | Resource menu; position approximately the upper left corner; drag to the bottom right position. The basic shape appears in selected mode—to really see what you have, click in the main blank window. Next, double-click on the item to begin to edit it; insert desired captions, your ID names and numbers, and so on. Then, select the item and move and resize by dragging on the border as you would any window. Click in the blank area to see the results. I find that this involves continuously fiddling around to get it the way I want. If you wish, you can choose Edit as Text and then edit the form that it should be in the rc file. I do this to alter the dialog name. Layout | Guide Settings can be used to superimpose a grid to assist control positioning.

As a suggestion, open the rc file for Pgm07a and browse the dialogs and tinker. Just do not save the project with the same name. Once you are very familiar with the way my dialogs appear visually, then examine the rc file shown below to see the coding representation of those dialogs.

7.6 CONSTRUCTION OF DIALOG BOXES

There are two major dialog types: *modal* and *modeless*. A modal dialog is the most common. When activated, the user is allowed to make entries only in the dialog box. The rest of the application is locked out from receiving any messages until the dialog box has finished operations and disappears. The **MessageBox** is modal, for example.

Modeless dialog boxes appear and stay visible on-screen until the user terminates them. Unlike a modal dialog, a modeless dialog allows the application to continue receiving and processing events. The title bar highlighting notifies the user which window has the input focus or is currently active. The Find-Replace Dialogs are a familiar example. Modeless boxes are commonly used to display some additional information often as information boxes.

When creating a dialog box with resource editors, a modal box is the default. So next you need to select what options are needed. Since a dialog is a form of window, the WNDCLASS style must be chosen. The default includes WS_POPUP | WS_BORDER | WS_SYSMENU, which is often what is wanted. Note that you should get a printout of all the resource constants from the Resource Help system or from the On-Line documentation.

In Figure 7.2 I have opened the Help system and am looking at the Control Styles from the WIN32 SDK contained in CreateWindow. In Figure 7.3 I have moved to Static Control Styles. When using a resource editor, I find that having a printed copy of these styles is invaluable during resource construction.

Note when you double-click on an item in the dialog under construction, you are given a window in which to set all of the various parameters. Experiment.

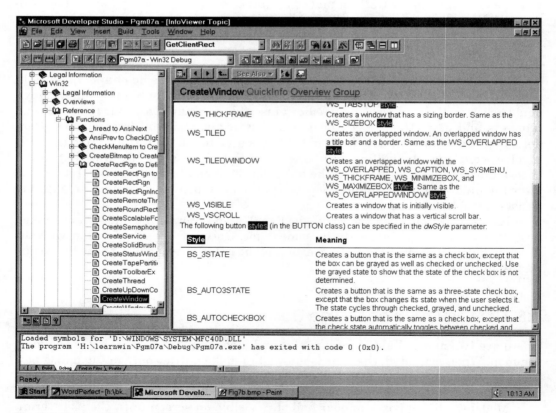

Fig. 7.2 Control Styles—WIN32 SDK—CreateWindow

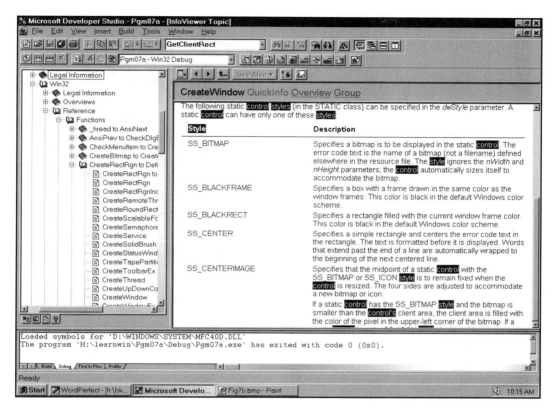

Fig. 7.3 SS Control Styles

 Resource Editor Tip: I usually just let the Workshop create whatever names and ID numbers it wants for all items, concentrating instead upon obtaining the visual appearance that I desire. When this is done, I save the file and open the resource file as "Text" and set up the controls' names and identifiers and their values as I wish, concentrating my full attention at this point on how I am going to refer to the controls and associated programming.

7.7 THE DIALOG BOXES FOR PGM07A

Figure 7.4 shows how the six dialog boxes appear visually. The Help—About dialog box has only an OK button and is nearly indistinguishable from a message box. Figure 7.5 shows the main window after I have selected a cursor, selected a line on which to display the name, and entered a name.

The Cursor Track dialog contains no readily discernible controls for the user to click on. Actually, there are two static text controls that contain the numbers representing the x,y coordinates. These values are to be updated as the mouse moves. This

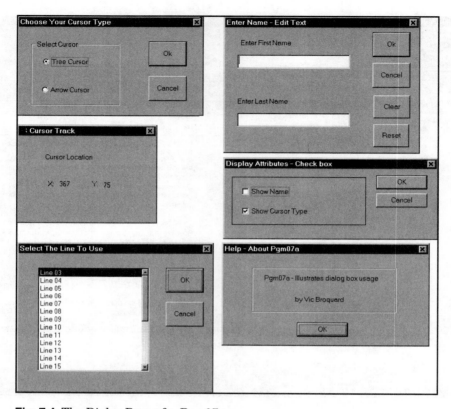

Fig. 7.4 The Dialog Boxes for Pgm07a

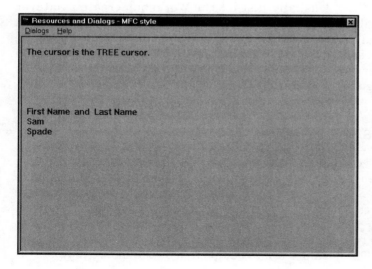

Fig. 7.5 The Main Window
Showing the Name and
Cursor Chosen—Pgm07a

is the only modeless dialog in the set. Once activated by the user, this dialog remains visible until the user closes it from the system menu bar. Unlike the modal dialogs, the user can task switch to any other task and the coordinates are updated as the mouse moves over the client area of the frame window. Thus, in order for this action of displaying the mouse position to be accomplished, the dialog *has* to be modeless. A modal dialog does not allow the user to do anything else in the application until the dialog actions are complete.

The Enter Name dialog has two edit controls, in which the user enters the first and last name, as well as four button controls. The OK and Cancel buttons are the system-default-type buttons (Help has been removed). These buttons provide the standard responses; the OK button is really a default push button. However, two additional buttons have been added: Clear and Reset. Programming-wise, the Clear button provides a fast method for the user to erase all entries in the two edit controls. The Reset button, when pressed, places the original names back into the two edit controls so that the user may undo changes and try again.

The Choose Cursor Type dialog illustrates the handling of radio buttons; only one of the two buttons can be "on." The Display Attributes dialog illustrates the use of check boxes in which each control is a separate independent item with its own on-off state. Additionally, I kept the provided Help button, although no help is provided. No coding is supplied for processing a user click on Help. Thus, although it responds when pressed, no action is taken. The last is the Select Line dialog that uses a list box to allow the user to select the line on which to display the three lines that show the name as entered.

Since the cursor type is displayed on the second line of the window with a blank line above and below it, the top-most position for the name display is fixed on line *three*. On the other hand, the bottom line is a variable number based upon the current window size. That is, as the user shrinks the window in height, there are fewer lines available upon which to display the three name lines. If the window becomes too small, the list box shows at least line three, although it may not be visible in a tiny window. In short, we have a dynamic variable number of items to be shown in the list box.

As you examine the dialog resources for Pgm07a, notice that I often surround the "real" controls—namely list boxes, edit boxes, check boxes, and radio buttons—with some form of grouping box. There are several styles and approaches that create differing illusions. See what you think of these. Here is where creativity enters.

There are some dialog design guidelines that you should follow. Expect to spend some time getting your dialogs just the way you want them to look.

Design Rule 27: **Dialog Box Design Guidelines**

---

1. Group all radio button items that the user is to select from into a visible group box.
2. Buttons are usually on the right or bottom.

3. User entry Edit boxes and other control items should have some form of static text prompt or descriptive label.

4. If there are many entries or groups for the user to enter, the Tab key should proceed in an orderly manner from one to the next—top down, left to right.

5. Follow the industry guidelines for good screen data entry design—if in doubt, consult relevant texts on good screen design layouts or the Microsoft *Windows Interface* listed in the bibliography.

If you discover that the Tab feature is not moving through the controls in a reasonable manner, top down and left to right, you can use a text editor on the dialog in the rc file and cut and paste the controls into the correct order. Even better, use Layout I Tab Order; the Developer Studio identifies the current tab order and you can make changes. The Tab feature generally begins on the first control in the dialog given in the resource file and moves on down the sequence.

7.8 THE TEXT SYNTAX OF DIALOGS AND CONTROLS

Examine Pgm07a.rc and resource.h files. First, note the menu layout. There are two main menu items: Dialogs and Help, both of which are pop-ups. When you select the Dialogs pop-up, you are presented with a choice of five actions, each corresponding to one dialog. The remaining sixth dialog is activated from Help—About.

The dialog box definition syntax is

```
nameID DIALOG [load option] [memory option] x, y, width, height
STYLE    ORed string of WS_ DS_ styles
CLASS    "bordlg"
CAPTION  "caption for the title bar"
FONT     points, "name"
MENU     yes, a dialog box can have a menu!!
BEGIN or {
END or }
```

If CLASS is omitted, Microsoft style is assumed. The load and memory options default to LOADONCALL MOVEABLE DISCARDABLE and are often omitted. One can easily reset the coordinates where the dialog box pops up—the *x,y* values. Caution: resetting the width and style should be done within the resource editor because these affect the general appearance with respect to the other controls in the dialog box. Altering the width may chop off some controls.

I generally adjust the **nameID** ID of the whole dialog to IDD_ followed by a descriptive name. It can be a string or have a defined value in the resource.h file. When I finally get the dialog appearing on-screen, I sometimes alter the *x,y* values and perhaps the caption phrasing. The controls' definitions all lie within the BEGIN—END pair. Each type of control has its own set of style possibilities. The exact syntax varies from control to control, and knowing the syntax is not really important when using the Developer Studio. (It would be vital if one were going to create the control manually within the program.) If you desire more specific details, consult the On-Line documentation or some of the texts listed in the bibliography for further details of specific control syntax.

The default text string to be displayed in the control is contained in " ". The last four numbers represent the *x,y* and width and height of the control. Often, I find it a bit hard to align a series of control items, say along their left edges, from within the resource editor. After getting them approximately aligned, I manually edit the rc file and force all *x* values of the group of controls to be identical.

 Programming Tip: When developing a new application with dialogs and controls, first create a basic shell and construct the shell resource.h and rc file, perhaps with a menu. Get this shell running. Next, construct the dialogs with the Developer Studio and adjust them with a text editor, if needed. Finally, compile the basic shell with the rc file and remove any accidental resource file errors. Only then go on to code the actual usage of the dialogs. Use a building-block approach—it is easier to debug.

7.8.1 Listing for File: resource.h—Pgm07a—Excerpts

```
. . .
// IDs for the menu items

#define CM_CURSOR_DLG         101
#define CM_NAME_DLG           102
#define CM_ITEM_DLG           103
#define CM_LINE_DLG           104
#define CM_LOCATION_DLG       105
#define CM_ABOUT              106

// IDs for the various dialogs

#define IDD_RADIO             501
#define IDD_CHECKBOX          502
#define IDD_MODELESS          503
#define IDD_EDITDLG           504
#define IDD_LISTBOX           505

#define IDC_LISTBOX           201
#define IDC_CHECK_NAME        202
#define IDC_CHECK_CURSOR      203
#define IDC_FIRSTNAME         204
#define IDC_LASTNAME          205
#define IDC_CLEARBUTTON       206
#define IDC_RESETBUTTON       207
#define IDC_RADIOBUTTON_TREE  208
#define IDC_RADIOBUTTON_ARROW 209
#define IDC_CURSOR_X          210
#define IDC_CURSOR_Y          211
#define IDC_GRPBTN            212

// IDs for icon and cursor

#define IDI_TREE              300
```

```
#define IDC_TREE               301

// IDs for strings

#define IDS_MAINTITLE          2000   // frame window's title
#define IDS_WINNAME            2001   // GetClassName's wndclass name
#define IDS_MSG_QUIT           2002   // quit application query msg
#define IDS_MSG_QUERY          2003   // title of quit query messagebox
#define IDS_ISTREE             2004   // msg is tree cursor
#define IDS_ISARROW            2005   // msg is arrow cursor
#define IDS_NAMEID             2006   // header for first and last names
#define IDS_LINEMSG            2007   // msg for line number
...
```

7.8.2 Listing for File: Pgm07a.rc—Pgm07a—Excerpts

```
...
MAINMENU MENU DISCARDABLE
BEGIN
    POPUP "&Dialogs"
    BEGIN
        MENUITEM "Choose &Cursor",           CM_CURSOR_DLG
        MENUITEM "Enter &Name",              CM_NAME_DLG
        MENUITEM "Set &Display Items",       CM_ITEM_DLG
        MENUITEM "Choose Display &Line",     CM_LINE_DLG
        MENUITEM "Show &Location of Cursor", CM_LOCATION_DLG
    END
    POPUP "&Help"
    BEGIN
        MENUITEM "Help &About",              CM_ABOUT
    END
END

IDD_EDITDLG DIALOG  DISCARDABLE 23, 81, 189, 125
STYLE DS_MODALFRAME | WS_POPUP | WS_VISIBLE | WS_CAPTION | WS_SYSMENU
CAPTION "Enter Name - Edit Text"
FONT 8, "MS Sans Serif"
{
    CTEXT          "Enter First Name",-1,12,11,56,10
    EDITTEXT       IDC_FIRSTNAME,12,27,110,14
    LTEXT          "Enter Last Name",-1,12,70,56,10
    EDITTEXT       IDC_LASTNAME,12,86,110,14
    DEFPUSHBUTTON  "OK",IDOK,144,4,37,25
    PUSHBUTTON     "Cancel",IDCANCEL,144,35,37,25
    PUSHBUTTON     "Clear",IDC_CLEARBUTTON,145,68,36,23
    PUSHBUTTON     "Reset",IDC_RESETBUTTON,145,97,35,23
}

IDD_ABOUT DIALOG DISCARDABLE  48, 113, 200, 92
STYLE DS_MODALFRAME | WS_POPUP | WS_VISIBLE | WS_CAPTION | WS_SYSMENU
CAPTION "Help - About Pgm07a"
FONT 8, "MS Sans Serif"
BEGIN
    DEFPUSHBUTTON    "OK",IDOK,72,70,50,14
```

```
      LTEXT              "by Vic Broquard",IDC_STATIC,70,42,57,8
      LTEXT              "Pgm07a - Illustrates dialog box usage
                         ",IDC_STATIC,40,20,128,11
      GROUPBOX           "",IDC_STATIC,28,10,141,50
END

IDD_RADIO DIALOG DISCARDABLE  34, 29, 179, 88
STYLE DS_MODALFRAME | WS_POPUP | WS_CAPTION | WS_SYSMENU | WS_CLIPSIBLINGS
CAPTION "Choose Your Cursor Type"
FONT 8, "MS Sans Serif"
BEGIN
    CONTROL           "Tree Cursor", IDC_RADIOBUTTON_TREE,"BUTTON",
                      WS_GROUP|WS_TABSTOP|BS_AUTORADIOBUTTON,23,30,62,10
    CONTROL           "Arrow Cursor", IDC_RADIOBUTTON_ARROW, "BUTTON",
                      WS_TABSTOP|BS_AUTORADIOBUTTON, 22,56,66,15
    GROUPBOX          "Select Cursor",IDC_GRPBTN, 12,13,87,66, WS_GROUP
    DEFPUSHBUTTON "OK",IDOK,127,14,37,25
    PUSHBUTTON        "Cancel",IDCANCEL,127,49,37,25
END

IDD_CHECKBOX DIALOG DISCARDABLE  32, 94, 207, 69
STYLE DS_MODALFRAME | WS_POPUP | WS_VISIBLE | WS_CAPTION | WS_SYSMENU
CAPTION "Display Attributes - Check box"
FONT 8, "MS Sans Serif"
{
 CONTROL "", -1, "static", SS_BLACKFRAME | WS_CHILD | WS_VISIBLE, 7, 8, 131, 48
 CONTROL "Show Name", IDC_CHECK_NAME, "BUTTON", BS_AUTOCHECKBOX | WS_CHILD |
         WS_VISIBLE | WS_TABSTOP, 17, 16, 61, 14
 CONTROL "Show Cursor Type", IDC_CHECK_CURSOR, "BUTTON", BS_AUTOCHECKBOX |
         WS_CHILD | WS_VISIBLE | WS_TABSTOP, 17, 35, 79, 15
 DEFPUSHBUTTON "OK", IDOK, 148, 6, 50, 14
 PUSHBUTTON        "Cancel", IDCANCEL, 148, 24, 50, 14
 PUSHBUTTON        "Help", ID_HELP, 148, 42, 50, 14
}

IDD_MODELESS DIALOG 34, 51, 134, 86
STYLE WS_POPUP | WS_VISIBLE | WS_CAPTION | WS_SYSMENU
CAPTION "Cursor Track"
FONT 8, "MS Sans Serif"
{
 CONTROL "Cursor Location", -1, "static", SS_SIMPLE | WS_CHILD | WS_VISIBLE, 26,
         17, 56, 9
 CONTROL "X:", -1, "static", SS_LEFT | WS_CHILD | WS_VISIBLE, 29, 44, 9, 9
 CONTROL "640", IDC_CURSOR_X, "static", SS_LEFT | WS_CHILD | WS_VISIBLE, 40, 44,
         25, 9
 CONTROL "Y:", -1, "static", SS_LEFT | WS_CHILD | WS_VISIBLE, 72, 44, 8, 8
 CONTROL "480", IDC_CURSOR_Y, "Static", SS_LEFT | WS_CHILD | WS_VISIBLE, 83, 45,
         16, 8
}

IDD_LISTBOX DIALOG 20, 38, 189, 140
STYLE DS_MODALFRAME | WS_POPUP | WS_VISIBLE | WS_CAPTION | WS_SYSMENU
CAPTION "Select The Line To Use"
FONT 8, "MS Sans Serif"
{
```

```
DEFPUSHBUTTON     "OK",IDOK,144,14,37,25
PUSHBUTTON        "Cancel",IDCANCEL,144,49,37,25
LISTBOX           IDC_LISTBOX,19,14,109,106,LBS_SORT | LBS_NOINTEGRALHEIGHT |
                  WS_VSCROLL | WS_TABSTOP
}

IDI_TREE                  ICON    DISCARDABLE     "TREES.ICO"
IDC_TREE                  CURSOR  DISCARDABLE     "TREE.CUR"
STRINGTABLE DISCARDABLE
BEGIN
     IDS_MAINTITLE            "Resources and Dialogs - MFC style"
     IDS_WINNAME             "ResourcesPgm"
     IDS_MSG_QUIT            "Do you want to quit the application?"
     IDS_MSG_QUERY          "Query?"
     IDS_ISTREE             "The cursor is the TREE cursor."
     IDS_ISARROW            "The cursor is the ARROW cursor."
     IDS_NAMEID             "First Name   and   Last Name"
     IDS_LINEMSG            "Line %02d"
END
```

7.9 CHANGES TO THE IMPLEMENTATION OF THE APPLICATION-DERIVED CLASS

Under MFC, there is only one change required in **InitInstance**. A call is made to the function **SetDialogBkColor** that sets the dialog's background color. The default is gray.

```
BOOL   Pgm7AApp::InitInstance () {
 ...
 m_pMainWnd->UpdateWindow ();
 SetDialogBkColor ();        // set gray dialog boxes and messageboxes
 return TRUE;
}
```

At this point I made a design decision compromise for this book. Each of the dialogs used has its own class derived from **CDialog**. In the real world, I would keep each one of these in its own separate set of h and cpp files. Here, doing so would add a dozen more files to the project! Hence, to keep the number of files more manageable in a book format, I have purposely merged the dialog classes into the FrameWin files. Note that in the header files, the dialog class definitions precede the FrameWin definition for forward reference handling; in the implementation files, the dialog implementation comes after the FrameWin implementation.

7.10 MFC DIALOG IMPLEMENTATION

Begin by examining just the FrameWin class definition portion of the FrameWin.h file. All of the dialog-derived classes are defined ahead of the frame window class.

Skim over the class definitions for all of the dialogs and go to the FrameWin definition proper.

There are several public members—all are used to assist in the transfer of data to and from the dialogs. Since the dialogs are separate classes, if they are to communicate with the FrameWin class, those members must be public. (The alternative is to use friend classes.) The uppercase data types are structures for transferring data between the dialogs and the FrameWin and are defined ahead of the dialogs.

The BOOL public member **track_on** is used to indicate whether WM_MOUSEMOVE messages are to be processed by displaying the current position in the dialog box. We will examine the other public data members shortly. The protected data members include the familiar members for the current client area's dimensions and the font's average character dimensions. In addition, there is a pointer to the background brush. In this example, I dynamically install a new background brush. The member **linenum** represents the current line number on which to display the names. The **ptrlocate_dlg** contains a pointer to locate the modeless dialog, and **real_names_db** contains the real application names database. Here it can contain just one set of data; in reality, it would likely be an array. MFC returns the zero-based index of which radio button in the group is "on" and the status of each check box independent of all other check boxes. The list box must load its strings directly from a transfer array of strings. Therefore, the member **which_cursor** contains which radio button is on; **show_name** and **show_cursor** are to be 1 if checked and 0 if not. The array **line** contains all of the strings to be displayed in the list box.

Now examine the member functions. **OnDestroy** deletes any active modeless dialogs that may yet be running. **OnMouseMove** enables us to find the current mouse position when **track_on** is TRUE. Finally, there are six Cmxxxx members that respond to the menu items being activated.

In the FrameWin.cpp file, the response table shows the expected connections to be made when the menu items are selected plus the events of resizing and mouse move. Commonly, dialog boxes are activated in response to a menu selection.

Now, let's look at the general operation of the main frame window functions, ignoring the instructions for dialog-related actions, and then go back and study the implementation of each dialog box in turn. The FrameWin constructor positions the window and installs the menu as normal. The members **track_on** and **linenum** are initialized to FALSE and line three. The default cursor, which_cursor, is initialized to the tree cursor. Here I have used a public enum to assist in the transfer of data to and from the dialog; we'll examine the enum shortly. Next that cursor is installed by using the **SetClassLong** method.

```
which_cursor = CRadioBtnsDlg::Tree;
hcursor = LoadCursor (AfxGetApp()->m_hInstance, MAKEINTRESOURCE (IDC_TREE));
SetClassLong (m_hWnd, GCL_HCURSOR, (long) hcursor);
```

More actions occur in **OnCreate**. Here we wish to install a new background brush by using the **SetClassLong** method. The basic actions would include creating the new desired background brush, installing the brush, and converting the new HBRUSH to a **long**.

```
        hbkgrndbrush = CreateSolidBrush (RGB (192, 192, 192));
        HBRUSH oldbrush = (HBRUSH) GetClassLong (m_hWnd, GCL_HBRBACKGROUND);
        SetClassLong (m_hWnd, GCL_HBRBACKGROUND, (long) hbkgrndbrush);
        DeleteObject (oldbrush); // failure to delete old brush = memory leak
```

However, if this is all that is done, a **memory leak** results since the original brush
installed in the WNDCLASS structure has not been deleted. While this amount of
memory is small, realize its full effect. The undeleted memory or objects forever
remain unaccessible long after the application has ended. Thus, before replacing
the background brush via **SetClassLong**, we must get the handle to the existing
brush. Then, after installing the new brush, the old brush is deleted. Note that the
framework automatically deletes any objects that are assigned in the WNDCLASS
structure.

7.10.1 Listing for File: FrameWin.h—Pgm07a—Excerpts

```
...
/***************************************************************************/
/*                                                                         */
/* CLocateDlg Class Definition for Track Mouse Cursor Modeless Dialog Box   */
/*            no data transfer - public ShowPos function is called to       */
/*            update controls                                              */
/*                                                                         */
/***************************************************************************/

class CLocateDlg : public CDialog {

public:
        CLocateDlg (CWnd *ptrparent = NULL);

void      ShowPos (CPoint&);        // our member function to update coordinates
BOOL      DestroyWindow ();         // trap close msgs to notify not tracking

protected:

void      OnCancel ();              // must trap and destroy modeless dlg
};

/***************************************************************************/
/*                                                                         */
/* CNamesDlg class definition for Entering first & last names dialog box    */
/*         Use GetParent() to get ptr to xfer buff and OnOk copy to it       */
/*                      and in OnInitDialog copy from it                    */
/*         Using manual methods of data xfer                                */
/*                                                                         */
/***************************************************************************/

#define MAX_NAME_LEN 40    // max length of first and last names allowed

struct  TRANSFER_NAMES {          // edit dialog transfer buffer structure
  char first_name[MAX_NAME_LEN]; // members must be in the same order as
  char last_name[MAX_NAME_LEN];  //  the CEdit controls are created
};

class CNamesDlg : public CDialog {
```

```
protected:

TRANSFER_NAMES original_names;    // saves original names before this edit
TRANSFER_NAMES *ptrparentbuf;     // points to parent's xfer buffer

public:

                CNamesDlg (CWnd *ptrparent = NULL)
                    : CDialog (IDD_EDITDLG, ptrparent) {}   // dialog constructor
afx_msg void    CmCancel () { OnCancel (); }    // process cancel button
afx_msg void    CmOk ()     { OnOK (); }        // process ok button
afx_msg void    CmReset ();                     // resets original passed names
afx_msg void    CmClear ();                     // clears out name fields

afx_msg void    OnOK ();                         // get and save new name
afx_msg void    OnCancel ();                     // pitch new name

protected:

virtual BOOL    OnInitDialog ();                 // setup dialog

DECLARE_MESSAGE_MAP()
};
/****************************************************************************/
/*                                                                        */
/* CRadioBtnsDlg: select which type of cursor is desired                  */
/*              Use automatic DDX xfer method                             */
/*                                                                        */
/****************************************************************************/

class CRadioBtnsDlg :  public CDialog {

public:

        CRadioBtnsDlg (CWnd *ptrparent = NULL)
                : CDialog (CRadioBtnsDlg::IDD, ptrparent) {} // constructor

 // first define the xfer buffer - one buffer int for all the buttons in group
 enum {IDD = IDD_RADIO};    // set the name of the dlg resource to load
 int  which_btn_is_on;      // contains the index of which btn in group is on
                            // will be retrieved by the parent
 enum Order {Tree, Arrow};  // convenience enum to determine which button is on

protected:

virtual void DoDataExchange (CDataExchange*); // xfer data to and from dlg btns
};
/****************************************************************************/
/*                                                                        */
/* CCheckBoxDlg: dialog determines what is to be displayed names or cursor */
/*              Use automatic DDX exchange method                         */
/*                                                                        */
/****************************************************************************/

class CCheckBoxDlg : public CDialog {

public:
```

```
            CCheckBoxDlg (CWnd *ptrparent = NULL)
                    : CDialog (CCheckBoxDlg::IDD, ptrparent) {} // constructor
  //  define the xfer buffers - one buffer int for each check box
  enum {IDD = IDD_CHECKBOX}; // provide resource dlg name
  int  ck_show_name;            // show names when TRUE - accessed by parent
  int  ck_show_cursor;          // show cursor when TRUE - accessed by parent

protected:

virtual void DoDataExchange (CDataExchange*); // xfer data to and from dlg btns
};
/**************************************************************************/
/*                                                                      */
/* CListBoxLinesDLg: dialog list box select which line to display name on  */
/*                   Get a ptr to parent to access xfer information       */
/*                                                                      */
/**************************************************************************/

class CListBoxLinesDlg : public CDialog {

public:

            CListBoxLinesDlg (CWnd *ptrparent = NULL)
                        : CDialog (IDD_LISTBOX, ptrparent) {}

virtual BOOL  OnInitDialog ();  // fill up list box

protected:

afx_msg virtual void  OnOK ();  // trap ok button to send item index num
DECLARE_MESSAGE_MAP()
};
/**************************************************************************/
/*                                                                      */
/* FrameWin Class Definition                                            */
/*                                                                      */
/**************************************************************************/

class FrameWin : public CFrameWnd {

/**************************************************************************/
/*                                                                      */
/* Class Data Members                                                   */
/*                                                                      */
/**************************************************************************/

public:

// transfer areas to/from dialogs - need to be public so they can be accessed
//                                  from dialogs without using globals

// accessed by location dlg directly

BOOL            track_on;    // when true, displays mouse coordinates

// accessed by edit names dlg directly

TRANSFER_NAMES  xfer_edit_names; // edit names transfer buffer
```

```
// place to store current index of which radio btn is on - not accessed by dlg

int  which_cursor; // radio button xfer buffer = index of which btn is on

// place to store current checkbox statuses - not accessed by dlg

int  show_name;   // show names when TRUE - for checkboxes
int  show_cursor; // show cursor when TRUE

// members accessed by listbox dlg

char line[50][10];// lines for listbox
int  linetot;      // total lines in array that are used
int  linenumnew;   // set by CmOk from TListBoxLines
int  linenum;      // current line number to show names on

protected:
int             height;      // current client window height in pixels
int             width;       // current client window width in pixels

int             avg_caps_width;  // average capital letter width
int             avg_char_width;  // average character width
int             avg_char_height; // average character height

HCURSOR         hcursor;         // current cursor in use
HBRUSH          hbkgrndbrush;    // current background brush
CLocateDlg      *ptrlocatedlg;   // ptr to the TLocateDlg modeless dialog
TRANSFER_NAMES  real_names_db;   // real data base - first and last name
/**************************************************************************/
/*                                                                        */
/* Class Functions:                                                       */
/*                                                                        */
/**************************************************************************/

public:
              FrameWin (CWnd*, const char*); // constructor
              ~FrameWin () {}                 // destructor

protected:

afx_msg void  OnPaint ();                  // paint the window - WM_PAINT
afx_msg int   OnCreate (LPCREATESTRUCT);   // set initial class members
afx_msg void  OnDestroy ();                // delete allocated class members
afx_msg void  OnClose ();                  // determines if app can quit yet
afx_msg void  OnSize (UINT, int, int);     // process window resize
afx_msg void  OnMouseMove (UINT, CPoint);  // track current position

afx_msg void  CmCursorDlg ();              // start cursor choice dialog
afx_msg void  CmNameDlg ();                // start enter name dialog
afx_msg void  CmItemDlg ();                // start choose item dialog
afx_msg void  CmLineDlg ();                // start choose line dialog
afx_msg void  CmLocationDlg ();            // start cursor location dialog
afx_msg void  CmAbout ();                  // help about dialog

DECLARE_MESSAGE_MAP()
...
```

7.10.2 Listing for File: FrameWin.cpp—Pgm07a—Excerpts

```
...
/**************************************************************************/
/*                                                                        */
/* FrameWin Events Response Table                                         */
/*                                                                        */
/**************************************************************************/
BEGIN_MESSAGE_MAP(FrameWin, CFrameWnd)
 ON_WM_SIZE ()
 ON_WM_PAINT ()
 ON_WM_CREATE ()
 ON_WM_CLOSE ()
 ON_WM_DESTROY ()
 ON_WM_MOUSEMOVE ()
 ON_COMMAND(CM_CURSOR_DLG,   CmCursorDlg)
 ON_COMMAND(CM_NAME_DLG,     CmNameDlg)
 ON_COMMAND(CM_ITEM_DLG,     CmItemDlg)
 ON_COMMAND(CM_LINE_DLG,     CmLineDlg)
 ON_COMMAND(CM_LOCATION_DLG, CmLocationDlg)
 ON_COMMAND(CM_ABOUT,        CmAbout)
END_MESSAGE_MAP()
/**************************************************************************/
/*                                                                        */
/* Framewin: Construct the window object                                  */
/*                                                                        */
/**************************************************************************/
          FrameWin::FrameWin (CWnd* ptrparent, const char* title)
                  : CFrameWnd () {
...
 ptrlocatedlg = NULL;  // set no TLocateDlg modeless cursor pos yet
 track_on = FALSE;     // indicate mouse position tracking is not on yet

 // clear and set all transfer buffers
 memset (&real_names_db, 0, sizeof(TRANSFER_NAMES)); // initialize names

 which_cursor = CRadioBtnsDlg::Tree; // set our member to default cursor

 // load that cursor
 hcursor = LoadCursor (AfxGetApp()->m_hInstance, MAKEINTRESOURCE (IDC_TREE));
 SetClassLong (m_hWnd, GCL_HCURSOR, (long) hcursor);

 show_name   = FALSE;  // init check box xfer buf
 show_cursor = TRUE;   // show cursor type but not names
 linenum     = 3;      // set default line for showing names on
}
/**************************************************************************/
/*                                                                        */
/* OnCreate:    get average character height and width and initialization */
/*                                                                        */
/**************************************************************************/
int     FrameWin::OnCreate (LPCREATESTRUCT lpCS) {
```

```
    int retcd = CFrameWnd::OnCreate (lpCS); // pass along to base class
... normal acquiring of the average character dimensions
    // the following illustrates how to change the background color AFTER
    // it has been set initially in the wndclass structure
    // you need to get the handle of the original brush so that it can be
    // deleted, if not, you will get a memory leak

    hbkgrndbrush = CreateSolidBrush (RGB (192, 192, 192)); // make new background brush

    // get old brush so we can delete it after installing new brush
    HBRUSH oldbrush = (HBRUSH) GetClassLong (m_hWnd, GCL_HBRBACKGROUND);
    // install new brush
    SetClassLong (m_hWnd, GCL_HBRBACKGROUND, (long) hbkgrndbrush);

    DeleteObject (oldbrush); // failure to delete old brush = memory leak

    return retcd;
}
/**************************************************************************/
/*                                                                        */
/* OnDestroy:      delete inited items                                    */
/*                                                                        */
/**************************************************************************/
void      FrameWin::OnDestroy () {

 if (ptrlocatedlg) delete ptrlocatedlg;     // only delete it if it was newed
 CFrameWnd::OnDestroy ();
}
/**************************************************************************/
/*                                                                        */
/* OnSize: acquire the current dimensions of the client window            */
/*                                                                        */
/**************************************************************************/
void      FrameWin::OnSize (UINT a, int b, int c) {

 CFrameWnd::OnSize (a, b, c);

 CRect rect;
 GetClientRect (&rect);               // get the size of the client window
 height = rect.Height();              // calc and save current height
 width  = rect.Width();               // calc and save current width

 char msg[10];
 int  i, j;

 // now dynamically adjust the number of possible lines upon which the names
 // can be displayed:

 // retrieve printf control string "Line %02d"
 LoadString (AfxGetApp()->m_hInstance, IDS_LINEMSG, msg, sizeof(msg));

 // insert line choices into the list box lines that will be loaded into box
 j = height / avg_char_height - 5; // -3 for the cursor msgs; -2 since 3 nameslines

 if (j<0) j=1;                 // set at least line 3
 linetot = j;
```

```
 for (i=0; i<j; i++) wsprintf (line[i], msg, i+3);

 Invalidate ();                // force repainting of window
}
/******************************************************************/
/*                                                              */
/* OnMouseMove: display current mouse position                  */
/*                                                              */
/******************************************************************/

void      FrameWin::OnMouseMove (UINT, CPoint pt) {

 // if tracking is on, force the modeless dialog to display new position
 if (track_on) ptrlocatedlg->ShowPos (pt);
}
/******************************************************************/
/*                                                              */
/* OnPaint: displays instructions and the current system color in use  */
/*                                                              */
/******************************************************************/

void      FrameWin::OnPaint () {

 CPaintDC dc (this);
 CString msg;
 dc.SetBkMode (TRANSPARENT);

 if (show_cursor) {
  if (which_cursor == CRadioBtnsDlg::Tree) msg.LoadString (IDS_ISTREE);
  else msg.LoadString (IDS_ISARROW);
  dc.TextOut (avg_char_width, avg_char_height, msg);
 }
 if (show_name) {
  msg.LoadString (IDS_NAMEID);
  dc.TextOut (avg_char_width, avg_char_height*(linenum), msg);
  dc.TextOut (avg_char_width, avg_char_height*(linenum+1),
            real_names_db.first_name);
  dc.TextOut (avg_char_width, avg_char_height*(linenum+2),
          real_names_db.last_name);
 }
}
 ...
/******************************************************************/
/*                                                              */
/* CmAbout: Help About dialog                                   */
/*                                                              */
/******************************************************************/

void      FrameWin::CmAbout () {

 // informational modal dialog - create instance of CDialog and execute it
 CDialog aboutdlg ("IDD_ABOUT", this);
 aboutdlg.DoModal ();
}
/******************************************************************/
```

```
/*                                                                          */
/* CmLocationDlg: cursor location modeless dialog activation                */
/*                No data xfer - ShowPos updates the dlg controls           */
/*                                                                          */
/****************************************************************************/

void      FrameWin::CmLocationDlg () {

 // note dialog already exists - simply Create a new instance and show it

 if (!track_on) {                          // avoid multiple instances of the dlg
   ptrlocatedlg = new CLocateDlg (this);
   POINT p;
   GetCursorPos (&p);                      // retrieve current mouse position
   CPoint pt (p);                          // convert to CPoint
   ptrlocatedlg->ShowPos (pt);             // display new position
   ptrlocatedlg->ShowWindow (SW_SHOW);     // make dialog visible
   track_on = TRUE;                        // indicate tracking is active
 }
}

/****************************************************************************/
/*                                                                          */
/* CmNameDlg: enter first name dialog                                       */
/*            Use the manual method to transfer data into and out of ctrls  */
/*                                                                          */
/****************************************************************************/

void      FrameWin::CmNameDlg () {

 // copy into transfer buf the current name in use
 memcpy (&xfer_edit_names, &real_names_db, sizeof (TRANSFER_NAMES));

 CNamesDlg edit (this);          // construct dialog
 if (edit.DoModal () == IDOK) {  // execute dlg, if ok get new name
   memcpy (&real_names_db, &xfer_edit_names, sizeof (TRANSFER_NAMES));
   Invalidate();                 // force new name to be shown
 }
}

/****************************************************************************/
/*                                                                          */
/* CmCursorDlg: choose cursor radio button dialog                           */
/*              Use automatic DDX exchange method                           */
/*                                                                          */
/****************************************************************************/

void      FrameWin::CmCursorDlg () {

 CRadioBtnsDlg radio (this);
 radio.which_btn_is_on = which_cursor;            // xfer current settings into dlg
 if (radio.DoModal () == IDOK) {                  // create & execute dlg
   which_cursor = radio.which_btn_is_on;          // update our members with checks
   if (which_cursor == CRadioBtnsDlg::Tree) {     // install correct cursor
     hcursor = LoadCursor (AfxGetApp()->m_hInstance, MAKEINTRESOURCE (IDC_TREE));
     SetClassLong (m_hWnd, GCL_HCURSOR, (long) hcursor);
   }
   else {
```

```
   hcursor = AfxGetApp()->LoadStandardCursor (IDC_ARROW), // use arrow cur
   SetClassLong (m_hWnd, GCL_HCURSOR, (long) hcursor);
   }
   Invalidate (); // force paint to display msg of new cursor
 }
}
/*****************************************************************************/
/*                                                                       */
/* CmItemDlg: checkmark dialog box - choose item                         */
/*            Use automatic DDX exchange method                          */
/*                                                                       */
/*****************************************************************************/

void       FrameWin::CmItemDlg () {

 CCheckBoxDlg ckbox (this);
 ckbox.ck_show_name   = show_name;      // transfer current settings into dlg
 ckbox.ck_show_cursor = show_cursor;
 if (ckbox.DoModal () == IDOK) {        //  create & execute dlg
  show_name   = ckbox.ck_show_name;     // update our members for next time
  show_cursor = ckbox.ck_show_cursor;
  Invalidate ();
 }
}
/*****************************************************************************/
/*                                                                       */
/* CmLineDlg: list box choose line for display                           */
/*                                                                       */
/*                                                                       */
/*****************************************************************************/

void       FrameWin::CmLineDlg () {

 CListBoxLinesDlg listbox (this);
 if (listbox.DoModal () == IDOK) { //  create & execute dlg
  if (linenumnew >= 0) {           // if OK, set our new line number
   linenum = linenumnew + 3;       // save new line number
   Invalidate();                   // force names to show on this line
  }
 }
}
/*****************************************************************************/
/*                                                                       */
/* ClocateDlg: constructor - create modeless dlg - hidden                */
/*                                                                       */
/*****************************************************************************/

         CLocateDlg::CLocateDlg (CWnd *ptrparent)
                  : CDialog (IDD_MODELESS, ptrparent) {

 Create (IDD_MODELESS, ptrparent); // modeless dlgs must be created
}
/*****************************************************************************/
/*                                                                       */
```

```
/* CLocateDlg::DestroyWindow: activated when user closes modeless dialog  */
/*                                                                        */
/* we need to alter parent's tracking on indicator to false or off        */
/*                                                                        */
/************************************************************************/
BOOL      CLocateDlg::DestroyWindow () {
  // gain access to a pointer to the track_on public member
  // FrameWin *ptrparent = (FrameWin*) AfxGetApp()->m_pMainWnd;
  FrameWin *ptrparent = (FrameWin*) (GetParent ());

  // set parent's public tracking indicator off to cease sending us position msg
  ptrparent-> track_on = FALSE;
  return CDialog::DestroyWindow ();
}

/************************************************************************/
/*                                                                        */
/* CLocateDlg::OnCancel: handle ESC and closing by calling DestroyWindows */
/*                                                                        */
/* because default handler does not delete the modeless dlg box, just hides*/
/*                                                                        */
/************************************************************************/
void      CLocateDlg::OnCancel () {
  DestroyWindow();   // modeless dlgs must be destroyed
}

/************************************************************************/
/*                                                                        */
/* CLocateDlg::ShowPos: updates the static x,y mouse position fields in box*/
/*                                                                        */
/************************************************************************/
void      CLocateDlg::ShowPos (CPoint &pt) {
  char x[5];
  char y[5];
  itoa (pt.x, x, 10);
  itoa (pt.y, y, 10);
  SetDlgItemText (IDC_CURSOR_X, x);
  SetDlgItemText (IDC_CURSOR_Y, y);
}

/************************************************************************/
/*                                                                        */
/* CNamesDlg Response Table for enter names dialog                         */
/*                                                                        */
/************************************************************************/

BEGIN_MESSAGE_MAP(CNamesDlg,      CDialog)
  ON_BN_CLICKED (IDC_CLEARBUTTON, CmClear)
  ON_BN_CLICKED (IDC_RESETBUTTON, CmReset)
  ON_BN_CLICKED (IDCANCEL,        CmCancel)
  ON_BN_CLICKED (IDOK,            CmOk)
  ON_COMMAND    (IDCANCEL,        CmCancel)
  ON_COMMAND    (IDOK,            OnOK)
```

```
END_MESSAGE_MAP()
/***************************************************************************/
/*                                                                         */
/* CNamesDlg::OnInitDialog: loads xfer buffer,save area in case of restore */
/*                          and loads in init values for edit controls     */
/*                                                                         */
/***************************************************************************/

BOOL      CNamesDlg::OnInitDialog () {

 FrameWin *ptrparent = (FrameWin*) (GetParent ()); // get the parent ptr
 ptrparentbuf = &ptrparent->xfer_edit_names; // save the addr of xfer buf

 // copy the original contents of the xfer buffer to dlg's save area
 memcpy (&original_names, ptrparentbuf, sizeof (TRANSFER_NAMES));

 // copy original contents into the dlg controls
 SetDlgItemText (IDC_FIRSTNAME, original_names.first_name);
 SetDlgItemText (IDC_LASTNAME,  original_names.last_name);
 return TRUE;
}
/***************************************************************************/
/*                                                                         */
/* CNamesDlg::CmReset: reinsert the original values into the name fields    */
/*                                                                         */
/***************************************************************************/

void      CNamesDlg::CmReset () {

 // copy saved original values back into the transfer buffer
 memcpy (ptrparentbuf, &original_names, sizeof (TRANSFER_NAMES));

 // copy saved original values back into the edit controls boxes
 SetDlgItemText (IDC_FIRSTNAME, original_names.first_name);
 SetDlgItemText (IDC_LASTNAME,  original_names.last_name);
}
/***************************************************************************/
/*                                                                         */
/* CNamesDlg::OnOk: retrieve new values                                    */
/*                                                                         */
/***************************************************************************/

void      CNamesDlg::OnOK () {

 // retrieve new values from edit controls and store in parent's xfer buffer
 GetDlgItemText (IDC_FIRSTNAME, ptrparentbuf->first_name, MAX_NAME_LEN);
 GetDlgItemText (IDC_LASTNAME,  ptrparentbuf->last_name, MAX_NAME_LEN);
 CDialog::OnOK ();  // now continue the Ok process
}
/***************************************************************************/
/*                                                                         */
/* CNamesDlg::OnCancel: restore the original values into  transfer buffer   */
/*                                                                         */
/***************************************************************************/

void      CNamesDlg::OnCancel () {
```

```
 // restore original values into the parent's transfer buffer
 memcpy (ptrparentbuf, &original_names, sizeof (TRANSFER_NAMES));
 CDialog::OnCancel (); // now continue the cancel process
}

/***************************************************************************/
/*                                                                         */
/* CNamesDlg::CmClear: remove contents of both fields, appears blank       */
/*                                                                         */
/***************************************************************************/

void      CNamesDlg::CmClear () {

 // clear transfer buffer - set to nulls
 memset (ptrparentbuf, 0, sizeof (TRANSFER_NAMES));
 // clear dlg controls
 SetDlgItemText (IDC_FIRSTNAME, ptrparentbuf->first_name);
 SetDlgItemText (IDC_LASTNAME,  ptrparentbuf->last_name);
}

/***************************************************************************/
/*                                                                         */
/* CRadioBtnsDlg::DoDataExchange: transfer data in and out of radio btn dlg*/
/*                                                                         */
/***************************************************************************/

void      CRadioBtnsDlg::DoDataExchange (CDataExchange *ptrdata) {

 CDialog::DoDataExchange (ptrdata);

 // transfers all settings of the series of buttons beginning with the first
 // be sure that only the first radio btn of the group has the WS_GROUP style
 // the value in which_btn_is_on is the index of the button in the group that
 // is on - taken from the order that the btns are defined in the dialog box
 // in the resource file - tree is first with index 0, arrow is second with
 // index 1 and so on - the enum makes it easier to extract which btn is on

 DDX_Radio (ptrdata, IDC_RADIOBUTTON_TREE, which_btn_is_on);
}

/***************************************************************************/
/*                                                                         */
/* CCheckBoxDlg::DoDataExchange: transfer data to/from check box dlg       */
/*                                                                         */
/***************************************************************************/

void      CCheckBoxDlg::DoDataExchange (CDataExchange *ptrdata) {

 CDialog::DoDataExchange (ptrdata);

 // trasnsfers TRUE/FALSE settings of each check box

 DDX_Check (ptrdata, IDC_CHECK_NAME, ck_show_name);
 DDX_Check (ptrdata, IDC_CHECK_CURSOR, ck_show_cursor);
}

/***************************************************************************/
/*                                                                         */
/* CListBoxLinesDlg Response Table                                         */
/*                                                                         */
```

```
/***************************************************************************/
BEGIN_MESSAGE_MAP(CListBoxLinesDlg, CDialog)
 ON_COMMAND(IDOK, OnOK)
END_MESSAGE_MAP()
/***************************************************************************/
/*                                                                       */
/* CListBoxLinesDlg::OnOK: notify parent of the selected index number    */
/*                                                                       */
/***************************************************************************/

void  CListBoxLinesDlg::OnOK () {

 // get a ptr to the listbox control itself
 CListBox *ptrlistbox = (CListBox*) (GetDlgItem (IDC_LISTBOX));

 // get a ptr to the parent
 FrameWin *ptrparent = (FrameWin*) (GetParent ());

 // save the current user selection index
 ptrparent->linenumnew = ptrlistbox->GetCurSel ();

 CDialog::OnOK (); // invoke base class to destroy
 }
/***************************************************************************/
/*                                                                       */
/* CListBoxLinesDlg::OnInitDialog: fill up the list box                  */
/*                                                                       */
/***************************************************************************/

BOOL  CListBoxLinesDlg::OnInitDialog () {

 // obtain a pointer to the existing listbox
 CListBox *ptrlistbox = (CListBox*) (GetDlgItem (IDC_LISTBOX));

 // get a ptr to the parent
 FrameWin *ptrparent = (FrameWin*) (GetParent ());

 // fill up list box from parent's line array
 for (int i=0; i<ptrparent->linetot; i++) {
  ptrlistbox->AddString (ptrparent->line[i]);  // insert lines into dlg
  if (i+3 == ptrparent->linenum) ptrlistbox->SetCurSel (i);
  }
 return TRUE;
 }
```

7.11 MFC BASIC DIALOG IMPLEMENTATION—THE HELP-ABOUT DIALOG

Modal dialog boxes are instantiated by invoking the constructor via **new** or allocated on the stack. The dialog constructors usually are passed at least the dialog resource identifier and the **this** parameter of the parent owning window. They are subsequently executed by use of the member functions **DoModal**. When a dialog box has no controls (other than the default buttons), one simply creates the box as a **CDialog** object, using nothing more than the **CDialog** base class defaults

```
CDialog aboutdlg ("IDD_ABOUT", this);
aboutdlg.DoModal ();
```

Here the **DoModal** function displays the box on screen; gets user actions; and, when OK or Cancel is chosen, destroys the dialog box and returns to the application with its return code representing which button was pressed. You can use the IDs IDOK and IDCANCEL to check the return code. With the About Dialog, the return code is ignored. With modal boxes, when they are executed, all other application actions are halted while the dialog is constructed on-screen, does all of its tasks, and is destroyed, returning the OK or Cancel results.

7.12 MFC MODELESS DIALOGS—THE CLOCATEDLG DIALOG

Modeless dialogs are handled differently from modal boxes. The reason is that, unlike modal dialogs, a modeless dialog can remain active/visible while the user switches back to other actions in the application. Thus, the dialog may remain up and running while other application functions are subsequently begun.

Because of this and because the user may request that particular modeless dialog more than once while the application is running, programmers often create a protected data member to hold one instance of the modeless dialog box. Then, whenever the user requests that dialog, it has only to be shown on-screen. The pointer-protected member must be in existence for other application functions to be able to interact with the modeless dialog. Hence, in the FrameWin class definition, the pointer to the modeless dialog was included

```
CLocateDlg      *ptrlocatedlg;
```

Notice that, with this dialog, we are sending it x,y coordinates to be displayed. Therefore, we need more functionality than a pure **CDialog** class can provide. So we must derive our specialized class from **CDialog**. Examine the CLocateDlg class definition in the above h file.

CLocateDlg is derived from **CDialog** and contains three public member functions. The constructor is obviously needed. **ShowPos** is used to update the current mouse position. **OnCancel** must be overridden because the default handler does not invoke the **DestroyWindow** function, rather it just hides the dialog box. This then suggests an alternative approach: construct the dialog in **OnCreate** and let **CmLocationDlg** simply use **ShowWindow** to first show the dialog and let the default action of **OnCancel** hide it. In many respects, showing and hiding would be a superior implementation. Here **OnCancel** invokes the **DestroyWindow** function.

The member function **DestroyWindow** is overridden. Why? Once **track_on** has been set to TRUE, mouse move positions are sent to the dialog for display. When the dialog is closed, how do we turn tracking off? This is a problem that has many possible solutions. Communication between dialogs and the application is a problem. Since dialogs are child windows, one could have the dialog **send back messages**. A more common solution that you will see in many, many texts and examples is just making the items to be shared **global/external**; then the problem goes away! My attitude toward global *anything*, which is based upon over 30 years of experience in real-world coding, is simply "global equals bad, bad, bad design."

My solution is simple: communication can be done via public data members. In this dialog, the communication item is the setting of **track_on**. Only the CLocateDlg object knows when the user wishes to end tracking, by selection of the Close Menu item off the system menu or the new X button. Thus, my solution is to have the dialog member function that responds to the termination request—**DestroyWindow**—actually set **track_on** back to FALSE. Failure to set it to FALSE results in mouse position messages being sent to the nonexistent dialog! This is the purpose of overriding **DestroyWindow**—to set **track_on** to FALSE.

While gaining access to the public members is straightforward, as we shall see shortly, it does become rather exotic. There are other alternatives. Many are explored in the other dialogs. One other simple method often used is to pass a pointer to the dialog box's owner as another parameter on the dialog box constructor. That parent pointer is saved as a protected member in the dialog object. Then, whenever the dialog needs to reach the public members of the parent, it has a pointer readily available. Or a dynamic cast can be made from the first **CWnd** pointer on up to the FrameWin class, thereby obviating the need for passing the second parameter. Yet another alternative is to pass a pointer directly to the needed data item as another parameter to the dialog box constructor, which then saves the pointer. Whenever the dialog needs to reference the parent's data item, it has direct access to it.

The following illustrates the real distinction between modal and modeless dialogs. Modal dialogs have a sequential operation

```
constructor + DoModal() + return value => point A
```

with no other possible functions invoked. At point A, the dialog box is now totally gone. Modeless dialogs are never executed via **DoModal**! They must be

```
constructor + Create + ShowWindow => point B
at a later point in time, user closes dialog
```

At point B the modeless dialog is visible and active and remains fully operational. The box remains visible and potentially active. Only at some later point in time or even application termination is the box destroyed.

Examine the CLocateDlg constructor; notice that it simply invokes the **CDialog Create** function, passing the dialog ID number and the parent **CWnd**

```
CLocateDlg::CLocateDlg (CWnd *ptrparent)
           : CDialog (IDD_MODELESS, ptrparent) {
  Create (IDD_MODELESS, ptrparent); // modeless dlgs must be created
}
```

Now let's see how **DestroyWindow** can alter its parent's BOOL **track_on**. The main problem is how to dynamically acquire a pointer to the invoker of the dialog. A number of approaches exist, depending upon the flexibility and reuse desired from this dialog box. If the owner of the dialog is the main frame window, then one could code

```
FrameWin *ptrparent = (FrameWin*) AfxGetApp()->m_pMainWnd;
```

If the parent is not necessarily the main window, then use the **GetParent** function

```
FrameWin *ptrparent = (FrameWin*) (GetParent ());

ptrparent-> track_on = FALSE;
return CDialog::DestroyWindow ();
```

Another function of CLocateDlg, **ShowPos**, is our own function that handles the actual displaying of the x,y position in the dialog box itself. Any static text control that has an ID other than -1 (-1 for unchangeable text or true static text) can be altered. The method for updating the contents of a static text control uses the function **Set-DlgItemText.**

```
SetDlgItemText (control id number, new text string);
```

For convenience, I used **itoa** to create the strings to display.

```
char x[5];
char y[5];
itoa (pt.x, x, 10);
itoa (pt.y, y, 10);
SetDlgItemText (IDC_CURSOR_X, x);
SetDlgItemText (IDC_CURSOR_Y, y);
```

Finally, look at the frame window's use of the CLocateDlg. In FrameWin's class definition, the purpose of maintaining the protected member **ptrlocatedlg** is to be able to invoke its **ShowPos** function from **OnMouseMove** when **track_on** is TRUE. When the user selects the menu item for cursor tracking, **CmLocationDlg** is executed. If **track_on** is TRUE, then the dialog is currently up and running. Avoid multiple instances. Next, I allocate a new instance. Here I pass only the parent window via **this**. Notice that I have opted to *not* pass the string or ID number of the dialog as the second parameter in the dialog constructor. This differs somewhat from other texts, which pass the string or ID number as the second parameter in the class constructor. I want to contain as many details of a dialog within that dialog class. Since I do not have several different dialogs that all use the same dialog definition, passing the string or ID number is not necessary. Therefore, my desire for containment of details is feasible. Again, this is purely stylistic.

Notice one subtlety—the modeless dialog must be created. I chose to do this within the constructor by issuing the call to the **CDialog Create** function. If not done here, you must call **Create** directly after constructing the dialog. Again, this is stylistic.

Next, **GetCursorPos** fills a POINT structure with the current position of the mouse. This point is then used as the initial value for **ShowPos**. Once the current x,y values are installed in the controls, the dialog box is then made visible using the familiar **ShowWindow** function:

```
ptrlocatedlg = new CLocateDlg (this);
POINT p;
GetCursorPos (&p);                      // retrieve current mouse position
CPoint pt (p);                          // convert to CPoint
ptrlocatedlg->ShowPos (pt);             // display new position
ptrlocatedlg->ShowWindow (SW_SHOW);     // make dialog visible
track_on = TRUE;                        // indicate tracking is active
```

Using SW_SHOW causes the dialog to be shown, while SW_HIDE hides it.

Now examine **OnMouseMove**. When the mouse moves, the function checks to see if **track_on** is TRUE. If so, it passes the current mouse position to the **ShowPos** function

```
if (track_on) ptrlocate_dlg->ShowPos (pt);
```

And the new position is displayed in the modeless dialog box. Notice that this display occurs even if the modeless box is not the active task. Try it. Click back in the main window area and the focus leaves the modeless dialog and returns to the application. Yet the position is continuously being updated as the mouse moves.

7.13 MANUAL DIALOG DATA TRANSFER—THE ENTER NAMES CNAMESDLG DIALOG

Edit controls present a more involved situation. An edit control may (optionally) display some initial default text and allow user entry of text with full Windows 95 editing capabilities. Somehow we must get the user-entered data back to the launching application. Additionally, data validation can be done simultaneously as the user is entering the data. In the Name dialog, we have to implement two edit controls: first name and last name.

Let's begin by examining the general effects we would like to see occur when the user selects this dialog from the pop-up menu. Normally when entering data, the application has more than one set of data to be entered or somehow used. Only one specific set of data would be edited via the dialog box at a time. Thus, the application maintains the real sets of data. In this example, only one set of data is maintained, and that set of names is the protected FrameWin member **real_names_db**. (In reality, this would likely be an array of names; in Pgm07a, only one name is stored to avoid complexity.)

When the user begins the Edit dialog, we would like to pass into the dialog the current name from **real_names_db**. Within the dialog, the user could then modify those names, making needed corrections, for example. When done, we need to get the modified data. Additional complexity arises from the common technique of providing a *Reset button* that, when pressed, reinserts the original data values that the dialog box displayed when it was initially invoked. The idea is that if users get their changes so messed up, they may wish to start over. It is not an optimum situation to force users to cancel this edit, return to the application, and reselect the Edit dialog again. Instead, they press the Reset button; we must redisplay the original data again. Therefore, we must preserve a copy of the original data values being passed into the Edit dialog. The *Clear button* allows users to wipe or blank the contents of the edit controls. Note that this action would not alter the preserved copy of the original data because the user might next press the Reset button.

MFC provides a simple, effective method of transferring data into dialog boxes and controls and transferring data back out when the dialog is completed. The mechanism is known as the *transfer buffer*. The transfer buffer is a structure whose address is passed to MFC which then handles all of the details. Each control has its starting values stored in a specific manner. With edit controls, the data are character strings, as you would expect. Each control that you wish to transfer data into or out of must be created in the dialog class constructor. There is one major rule to be followed.

Design Rule 28: **The order of the transfer buffer's members must be in the same order that the controls are allocated in the dialog's constructor!**

To see the Edit dialog's transfer buffer, examine the CNamesDlg class definition. I defined the maximum length for either name as 40 characters and then defined the structure as

```
#define MAX_NAME_LEN 40
struct TRANSFER_NAMES {
 char first_name [MAX_NAME_LEN];
 char last_name  [MAX_NAME_LEN];
};
```

Then as a protected member, **original_names** is defined to be an instance of this structure. It holds the original values of the names when the dialog is invoked. When the user requests a reset, these values are transferred back into the edit controls. FrameWin's data member, **real_names_db**, is also an instance of this structure, for convenience only. But where is the real transfer buffer? In FrameWin's public data area, the Edit dialog transfer buffer is **xfer_edit_names**. OK. Confused?

FrameWin has a set of data—**real_names_db**. One set of data is to be transferred to/from a dialog, so the current set of data is copied from **real_names_db** into the transfer buffer, **xfer_edit_names**. In the dialog, this initial record is saved into **original_names** so that, if the user botches the edit, the original values can be restored.

Let's see how the CNamesDlg is invoked and then we will examine the implementation of the dialog. The function **CmNameDlg** responds to the user's request to edit the names. The first step is to copy the current set of data (here, the only set) into the transfer buffer, **xfer_edit_names**.

```
memcpy (&xfer_edit_names, &real_names_db, sizeof (TRANSFER_NAMES));
```

Next, an instance of the dialog is created and executed.

```
CNamesDlg edit (this);        // construct dialog
if (edit.DoModal () == IDOK) { // execute dlg, if ok get new name
```

```
    memcpy (&real_names_db, &xfer_edit_names, sizeof (TRANSFER_NAMES));
    Invalidate();                      // force new name to be shown
}
```

Notice that this time I used the return code so that I can distinguish between OK and Cancel messages. Next, if the OK button was selected, the updated values in the transfer buffer are copied into the application's **real_names_db** area (which could be an array of records, output to a file, and so on). Also, the **Invalidate** function is invoked to display the new values on-screen, if the display names option is currently active. That is all the application must do to gain the enormous functionality of edit controls!

Now let's examine the CNamesDlg class in detail. The **CDialog** function **OnInitDialog** is the place where we are expected to save the original data and initially install the data into the controls. Since we need to respond to two buttons, Reset and Clear, we must have a response table for the dialog and member functions for them: **CmReset** and **CmClear**. As a safety precaution, trap cancel messages and restore the transfer buffer to the original values. (In the processing of **CmNameDlg**, we used the values only if IDOK was sent.)

In this example, the constructor acquires the address of the transfer buffer back in FrameWin and saves it in **ptrparentbuf** for our convenience. Four button response handlers are defined along with two actual member functions to implement the OK and Cancel buttons. Specifically, the **CmCancel** and **CmOk** functions just pass control on down to these two handlers.

Now examine **OnInitDialog**'s implementation in cpp file. The **GetParent** function is used to acquire a pointer to the FrameWin and then to obtain a pointer to the transfer buffer, which is preserved in our protected member for later convenient use.

```
    FrameWin *ptrparent = (FrameWin*) (GetParent ());
    ptrparentbuf = &ptrparent->xfer_edit_names;
    memcpy (&original_names, ptrparentbuf, sizeof (TRANSFER_NAMES));
    SetDlgItemText (IDC_FIRSTNAME, original_names.first_name);
    SetDlgItemText (IDC_LASTNAME,  original_names.last_name);
```

Examine the message map. For dialogs, the button click messages are ON_BN_CLICKED. However, two ON_COMMAND messages are also present. MFC distinguishes between button presses and the system menu/Alt-F4 commands. Hence, both routes of termination must be covered. The other four member functions— **OnOk**, **OnCancel**, **OnClear**, and **OnReset**—work exactly as expected.

7.14 MFC RADIO BUTTONS AND CHECK BOXES AND DYNAMIC DATA EXCHANGE (DDX)—THE CRADIOBTNSDLG AND CCHECKBOXDLG DIALOGS

The handling of radio buttons and check boxes is easy. By using the automatically updated button style, the current state of the buttons is loaded from and saved to a transfer buffer in a manner similar to the **CEdit** controls. For radio buttons, the transfer member is an int containing the 0-based index of which button is on in the group of radio buttons. For check boxes, the buffer is also an int containing usually 0 or 1. However, there are really three values possible: MF_CHECKED, MF_UNCHECKED, MF_GRAYED. The first yields 0 while the second yields 1.

These two dialogs illustrate yet another method for getting the user selections transferred to/from the dialog. The secret is to construct the dialog in automatic storage so that the dialog is *not* destroyed until block exit. Then, if the dialog variables containing the user selections are public, they can be directly accessed from the parent after the dialog terminates but before the dialog is actually destroyed. Additionally, these two dialogs illustrate the automatic transfer of data between the dialog and its controls.

The MFC also provides for a dynamic exchange between the controls and the transfer buffer, automatically installing the initial values and updating the transfer buffer from the controls. The mechanism is called dynamic data exchange (DDX). Its use requires a number of details. The first is in the class definition. Examine the CRadioBtnsDlg definition in the h file above. The base **CDialog** constructor is passed a derived class enum—**CRadioBtnsDlg::IDD**—identifier, which is defined to be the numerical ID of the dialog in the resource file.

The member **which_btn_is_on** is the DDX transfer buffer, which places the burden of copying its contents back into the FrameWin member **which_cursor** squarely on FrameWin. To assist users of this dialog in determining which radio button is on, an enum is defined in the same order as the buttons, **Order**. The only other function that must be defined is the DDX member to actually handle the data transfer—**DoDataExchange**.

Examine the FrameWin **CmCursorDlg** function that launched the dialog. Instead of using **new** to construct an instance, automatic storage is used, which cleverly keeps the derived class in existence after the **DoModal** has destroyed the Windows 95 interface element. The current contents of the FrameWin transfer buffer is copied into the dialog's transfer buffer and the dialog is launched. When it completes with IDOK, the dialog's transfer buffer is copied back into FrameWin's transfer buffer. Then the correct cursor is loaded and installed.

```
CRadioBtnsDlg radio (this);
radio.which_btn_is_on = which_cursor;
if (radio.DoModal () == IDOK) {
 which_cursor = radio.which_btn_is_on;
 if (which_cursor == CRadioBtnsDlg::Tree) {
  hcursor = LoadCursor (AfxGetApp()->m_hInstance,
                        MAKEINTRESOURCE (IDC_TREE));
  SetClassLong (m_hWnd, GCL_HCURSOR, (long) hcursor);
 }
 else {
  hcursor = AfxGetApp()->LoadStandardCursor (IDC_ARROW);
  SetClassLong (m_hWnd, GCL_HCURSOR, (long) hcursor);
 }
 Invalidate ();
}
```

Now, assuming that the invoker of the dialog using DDX is willing to copy its transfer data into and out of the dialog transfer members, then only the DDX member function needs to be coded. Examine the **DoDataExchange** function. The base class is invoked passing along the pointer to the **CDataExchange** object. And then the transfer of the data in the controls to/from the dialog's transfer buffer is done using **DDX_Radio** passing the **CDataExchange** pointer, the ID of the first radio button in the group, and the name of the transfer buffer within the dialog.

```
void CRadioBtnsDlg::DoDataExchange (CDataExchange *ptrdata) {
 CDialog::DoDataExchange (ptrdata);
 DDX_Radio (ptrdata, IDC_RADIOBUTTON_TREE, which_btn_is_on);
}
```

Design Rule 29: It is vitally important that only the first radio button of the group of buttons has the WS_GROUP style attribute in the resource file.

WS_GROUP is used to denote the start of the group for data transfer. The value placed in **which_btn_is_on** is the zero-based index of the button in the group, taken from the order in which the buttons are defined in the dialog box in the resource file. Here, tree is first with index 0, arrow is second with index 1.

The **CCheckBoxDlg** is handled in a manner similar to the radio buttons dialog. The difference comes only in the DDX function. In **DoDataExchange**, the DDX_Check member is invoked for each check box.

```
CDialog::DoDataExchange (ptrdata);
 // transfers TRUE/FALSE settings of each check box
 DDX_Check (ptrdata, IDC_CHECK_NAME, ck_show_name);
 DDX_Check (ptrdata, IDC_CHECK_CURSOR, ck_show_cursor);
}
```

Look back to the FrameWin's menu handlers for the check boxes; notice how the final settings of the check boxes are retrieved and stored.

```
CCheckBoxDlg ckbox (this);
ckbox.ck_show_name   = show_name;
ckbox.ck_show_cursor = show_cursor;
if (ckbox.DoModal () == IDOK) {
 show_name   = ckbox.ck_show_name;
 show_cursor = ckbox.ck_show_cursor;
 Invalidate ();
}
```

Now examine the **OnPaint** function of FrameWin. If the checkmark is TRUE for the **show_cursor** member of the transfer buffer, the correct display message for the current cursor is loaded and shown on-screen. Finally, if the checkmark is TRUE for the **show_names** member of the transfer buffer, a heading message is loaded and displayed, followed by the first and last names shown on the **linenum** line. The list box dialog alters the line number to be used.

```
if (show_cursor) {
 if (which_cursor == CRadioBtnsDlg::Tree) msg.LoadString (IDS_ISTREE);
 else msg.LoadString (IDS_ISARROW);
 dc.TextOut (avg_char_width, avg_char_height, msg);
}
if (show_name) {
 msg.LoadString (IDS_NAMEID);
 dc.TextOut (avg_char_width, avg_char_height*(linenum), msg);
 dc.TextOut (avg_char_width, avg_char_height*(linenum+1),
            real_names_db.first_name);
 dc.TextOut (avg_char_width, avg_char_height*(linenum+2),
            real_names_db.last_name);
}
```

7.15 OTHER DDX FUNCTIONS AND DATA VALIDATORS

What other DDX members are available? MFC provides several collections based on the control's type. Edit text controls are more numerous. For text operations:

```
DDX_Text (CDataExchange* pDX, int nIDC, BYTE& value);
DDX_Text (CDataExchange* pDX, int nIDC, int& value);
DDX_Text (CDataExchange* pDX, int nIDC, UINT& value);
DDX_Text (CDataExchange* pDX, int nIDC, long& value);
DDX_Text (CDataExchange* pDX, int nIDC, DWORD& value);
DDX_Text (CDataExchange* pDX, int nIDC, CString& value);
DDX_Text (CDataExchange* pDX, int nIDC, float& value);
DDX_Text (CDataExchange* pDX, int nIDC, double& value);
```

Special control types include check box, radio button, list, and combo box:

```
DDX_Check (CDataExchange* pDX, int nIDC, int& value);
DDX_Radio (CDataExchange* pDX, int nIDC, int& value);
DDX_LBString (CDataExchange* pDX, int nIDC, CString& value);
DDX_CBString (CDataExchange* pDX, int nIDC, CString& value);
DDX_LBIndex (CDataExchange* pDX, int nIDC, int& index);
DDX_CBIndex (CDataExchange* pDX, int nIDC, int& index);
DDX_LBStringExact (CDataExchange* pDX, int nIDC, CString& value);
DDX_CBStringExact (CDataExchange* pDX, int nIDC, CString& value);
DDX_Scroll (CDataExchange* pDX, int nIDC, int& value);
```

To get a pointer to the actual control's window:

```
DDX_Control (CDataExchange* pDX, int nIDC, CWnd& rControl);
```

7.16 DATA VALIDATION

There are some data validators to help ensure the data being entered into an edit control is valid. Most simply validate numerical ranges, verifying that the number is between **minVal** and **maxVal** inclusive of the endpoints. (If the data type is UINT, DWORD, or one of the floating point types, typecasts are required on **minVal** and **maxVal**.)

> ***Design Rule 30:*** **The Data Validation Dynamic (DDV) function must immediately follow the Dynamic Data Transfer (DDX) function for the same control.**

The validator functions are

```
DDV_MinMaxByte    (CDataExchange* pDX, BYTE value, BYTE minVal, BYTE maxVal);
DDV_MinMaxInt     (CDataExchange* pDX, int value, int minVal, int maxVal);
DDV_MinMaxLong    (CDataExchange* pDX, long value, long minVal, long maxVal);
DDV_MinMaxUInt    (CDataExchange* pDX, UINT value, UINT minVal, UINT maxVal);
DDV_MinMaxDWord   (CDataExchange* pDX, DWORD value, DWORD minVal,
                   DWORD maxVal);
DDV_MinMaxFloat   (CDataExchange* pDX, float const& value, float minVal,
                   float maxVal);
DDV_MinMaxDouble  (CDataExchange* pDX, double const& value, double minVal,
                   double maxVal);
DDV_MaxChars      (CDataExchange* pDX, CString const& value, int nChars);
```

A dialog can also force the DDX operation at times other than on OK button selections. The **CWnd** member function **UpdateData** causes the data to be transferred

```
UpdateData (TRUE);
UpdateData (FALSE);
```

where TRUE causes the transfer of data from the controls to the dialog transfer buffer and FALSE causes the transfer of data to the controls from the dialog transfer buffer. **CDialog::OnOK** calls **UpdateData (TRUE)**, while **CDialog::OnInitDialog** calls **UpdateData (FALSE)**.

7.17 MFC LIST BOX IMPLEMENTATION—THE CLISTBOXLINESDLG DIALOG

A list box requires a series of strings to be displayed. Options control whether the list is alphabetized (sorted) or not and whether multiple selections are allowed. Examine the CListBoxLinesDlg class definition. Notice that the constructor does nothing more than pass the ID of the dialog on down to the base **CDialog** constructor. Only two member functions are overridden. The **OnInitDialog** function loads the list box with strings from the FrameWin line array and the **OnOK** member stores the user's selection—the zero-based index—into FrameWin's **linenumnew**.

The strings to be displayed in the list box are contained in the FrameWin's data members.

```
char line[50][10];// lines for list box
int  linetot;     // total lines in array that are used
int  linenumnew;  // set by CmOk
int  linenum;     // current line number to show names on
```

The strings are given their values in **OnSize** which is called by the framework whenever the window size is changed. The height of the client area determines how many lines are available on which to display the name data. Recall that when Windows 95 is ready to create the window at its actual size and position, it sends a WM_SIZE message. So before the user can ever get a chance to activate the list box dialog, **OnSize** has set up the line strings for transfer.

The current number of lines possible is given by dividing the height by the average character height. Then remove three lines for the cursor line and two more lines since the display of the names requires three lines (header, first name, last name). Then force at least one line to be present. While the offset begins at zero, the corresponding line number to be shown is three. Thus, the loop always adds three to the current counter **i**. The Windows 95 function **wsprintf** installs the **i+3** line number completing the string that reads "Line: 03." The leading 0 is necessary if the list is being alphabetized; otherwise, "Line: 10" appears ahead of "Line: 3." Thus, in **OnSize** the text of the lines is created.

```
char msg[10];
int  i, j;
LoadString (AfxGetApp()->m_hInstance, IDS_LINEMSG, msg, sizeof(msg));
j = height / avg_char_height - 5;
if (j<0) j=1;             // set at least line 3
linetot = j;
for (i=0; i<j; i++) wsprintf (line[i], msg, i+3);
```

Next look over how the dialog is launched in the **CmLineDlg** function. Minimal actions are required. An automatic storage version of the dialog is created and then executed with **DoModal**. If the OK button is pressed, then the **linenum** is updated from the **linenumnew** transfer buffer that holds the zero-based selection index and the window is repainted.

```
CListBoxLinesDlg listbox (this);
if (listbox.DoModal () == IDOK) { //  create & execute dlg
 if (linenumnew >= 0) {           // if OK, set our new line number
  linenum = linenumnew + 3;       // save new line number
  Invalidate();                   // force names to show on this line
 }
}
```

In **OnInitDialog** a pointer to the dialog's list box control is obtained by invoking the **GetDlgItem** member function of **CWnd**. This is a very useful **CWnd** function because a pointer to any control can be retrieved dynamically merely by providing its ID number, assuming the dialog interface element has been created. Then all strings in FrameWin's **line** array are added into the list box by its member function **AddString**, with the current line number in use being highlighted in the list box by **SetCurSel**.

```
BOOL  CListBoxLinesDlg::OnInitDialog () {
 CListBox *ptrlistbox = (CListBox*) (GetDlgItem (IDC_LISTBOX));
 FrameWin *ptrparent = (FrameWin*) (GetParent ());
 for (int i=0; i<ptrparent->linetot; i++) {
  ptrlistbox->AddString (ptrparent->line[i]);
  if (i+3 == ptrparent->linenum) ptrlistbox->SetCurSel (i);
```

```
    }
    return TRUE;
  }
```

Finally, in **OnOK** a pointer is obtained to the list box control once more and a pointer is also obtained to the FrameWin parent. The current user selection, assuming no multiple selections are allowed, is done using **GetCurSel**, and the zero-based index is stored in FrameWin's **linenumnew**. The last step is to invoke the base class to finish the termination process.

```
void  CListBoxLinesDlg::OnOK () {
  CListBox *ptrlistbox = (CListBox*) (GetDlgItem (IDC_LISTBOX));
  FrameWin *ptrparent = (FrameWin*) (GetParent ());
  ptrparent->linenumnew = ptrlistbox->GetCurSel ();
  CDialog::OnOK (); // invoke base class to destroy
}
```

Now you have an introduction to making and using controls and dialog boxes. These are the fundamentals. As you study the other examples in other texts and magazines, you will see many other possibilities for controls and dialogs.

7.18 PROPERTY SHEETS OR TABBED DIALOGS

A property sheet is basically a container for multiple pages, each of which is akin to a separate dialog. In a complex application, provision for setting many options must be made, all too often in a tangled jumble of nested dialogs. Property sheets offer a very convenient wrapper that is exceedingly easy for users to manipulate. So make your users happy—give them property sheets.

Pgm07b represents the simple conversion from a menu of dialogs to a property sheet. Figures 7.6 and 7.7 show how the conversion appears when the property sheet is opened.

There are two subdirectories of resource files provided: CONVT_RC and GOOD_RC. The first folder's rc file represents the simple conversion of Pgm07a dialogs into a property sheet by just placing those original dialogs into a page. The second folder's rc file illustrates better design of those dialogs, a better visual appeal, a better consistency. Figures 7.6 and 7.7 show the good conversion. Figures 7.8 and 7.9 show the "bad" or straight conversion.

Converting a series of dialogs into one property sheet is surprisingly easy to do. Each dialog becomes a property page. An instance of each page is allocated along with one instance of the property sheet. Then each page is added into the sheet and the sheet is then launched. It is that simple.

To convert to property pages, some small changes must be made to the dialogs themselves in the resource file.

1. Remove all OK and Cancel buttons—the property sheet provides these.
2. Set the dialog style attributes to Child, Thin Border, Disabled, and Title bar.

```
STYLE WS_CHILD | WS_VISIBLE | WS_DISABLED | WS_CAPTION
```

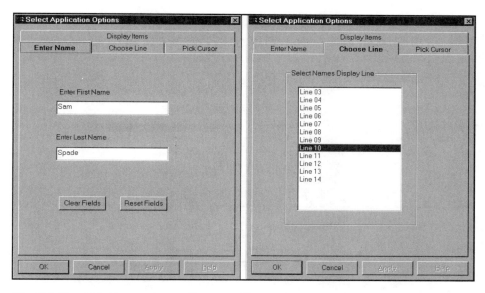

Fig. 7.6 Pgm07b Conversion to Property Sheet—First Two Pages

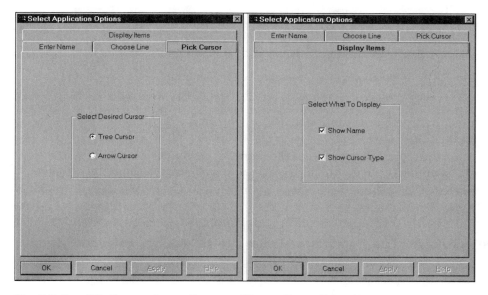

Fig. 7.7 Pgm07b Conversion to Property Sheet—Second Two Pages

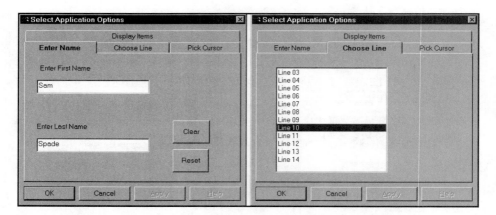

Fig. 7.8 Straight Dialog Box Conversion, Poor Visual Consistency—First Two Pages

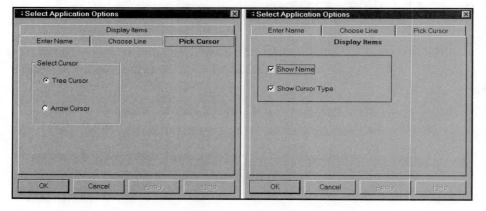

Fig. 7.9 Straight Dialog Box Conversion, Poor Visual Consistency—Second Two Pages

3. Give the title bar or caption a one- or two-word title; remember this title appears on the tab.

4. Alter the menu. Remove all of the menu items for the dialogs that are now a part of the property sheet. Add a new menu item to launch the property sheet.

5. Add another include for afxcmn.h which contains the Windows 95 common controls.

7.18.1 Listing for File: Pgm07b.rc—Better Design Version—Excerpts

```
...
MAINMENU MENU DISCARDABLE
BEGIN
    POPUP "&Dialogs"
```

```
          BEGIN
              MENUITEM "&Set Options",              CM_PROPERTYSHEET
              MENUITEM "Show &Location of Cursor",  CM_LOCATION_DLG
          END
          POPUP "&Help"
          BEGIN
              MENUITEM "Help &About",               CM_ABOUT
          END
  END
  ... modeless locate dialog is unchanged

  IDD_RADIO DIALOG DISCARDABLE  20, 40, 200, 200
  STYLE WS_CHILD | WS_VISIBLE | WS_DISABLED | WS_CAPTION
  CAPTION "Pick Cursor"
  FONT 8, "MS Sans Serif"
  BEGIN
      CONTROL         "Tree Cursor",IDC_RADIOBUTTON_TREE,"Button",
                      BS_AUTORADIOBUTTON | WS_GROUP | WS_TABSTOP,66,78,52,13
      CONTROL         "Arrow Cursor",IDC_RADIOBUTTON_ARROW,"Button",
                      BS_AUTORADIOBUTTON | WS_TABSTOP,66,97,52,13
      GROUPBOX        "Select Desired Cursor",IDC_GRPBTN,49,60,87,66,WS_GROUP
  END

  IDD_CHECKBOX DIALOG DISCARDABLE  20, 40, 200, 200
  STYLE WS_CHILD | WS_VISIBLE | WS_DISABLED | WS_CAPTION
  CAPTION "Display Items"
  FONT 8, "MS Sans Serif"
  BEGIN
      CONTROL         "Show Name",IDC_CHECK_NAME,"Button",BS_AUTOCHECKBOX |
                      WS_TABSTOP,64,70,69,15
      CONTROL         "Show Cursor Type",IDC_CHECK_CURSOR,"Button",
                      BS_AUTOCHECKBOX | WS_TABSTOP,64,97,69,15
      GROUPBOX        "Select What To Display",IDC_STATIC,48,47,96,83
  END

  IDD_LISTBOX DIALOG DISCARDABLE  20, 40, 200, 200
  STYLE WS_CHILD | WS_VISIBLE | WS_DISABLED | WS_CAPTION
  CAPTION "Choose Line"
  FONT 8, "MS Sans Serif"
  BEGIN
      LISTBOX         IDC_LISTBOX,44,33,102,125,LBS_SORT |
                      LBS_NOINTEGRALHEIGHT | WS_VSCROLL | WS_TABSTOP
      GROUPBOX        "Select Names Display Line",IDC_STATIC,32,15,129,158
  END

  IDD_EDITDLG DIALOG DISCARDABLE  20, 40, 200, 200
  STYLE WS_CHILD | WS_VISIBLE | WS_DISABLED | WS_CAPTION
  CAPTION "Enter Name"
  FONT 8, "MS Sans Serif"
  BEGIN
      CTEXT           "Enter First Name",-1,36,35,56,10
      EDITTEXT        IDC_FIRSTNAME,36,48,110,14
      LTEXT           "Enter Last Name",-1,36,80,56,10
      EDITTEXT        IDC_LASTNAME,36,94,110,14
      PUSHBUTTON      "Clear Fields",IDC_CLEARBUTTON,39,144,46,14
```

```
     PUSHBUTTON        "Reset Fields",IDC_RESETBUTTON,99,144,46,14
END

...
```

7.18.2 MFC Property Sheet Conversion—Pgm07b

The new MFC classes are **CPropertySheet** and **CPropertyPage**. After converting the resource file, be sure that your stdafx.h header includes the header file that defines the new Windows 95 common controls.

```
#include <afxcmn.h>    // MFC support for Windows 95 Common Controls
```

Next, modify the message response map to include a property sheet menu item command handler and remove all of the dialog command launchers

```
BEGIN_MESSAGE_MAP(FrameWin, CFrameWnd)
 ON_WM_SIZE ()
 ON_WM_PAINT ()
 ON_WM_CREATE ()
 ON_WM_CLOSE ()
 ON_WM_DESTROY ()
 ON_WM_MOUSEMOVE ()
 ON_COMMAND(CM_PROPERTYSHEET,CmPropertySheet)
 ON_COMMAND(CM_LOCATION_DLG, CmLocationDlg)
 ON_COMMAND(CM_ABOUT,        CmAbout)
END_MESSAGE_MAP()
```

The four dialogs must now be derived from the **CPropertyPage** class. Begin with the simpler cases; CRadioBtnsDlg is altered to CRadioBtnsPP. The base constructor requires the ID of only the dialog in the resource file. Thus, the only changes for the radio button definition were the class name and the constructor.

```
class CRadioBtnsPP :  public CPropertyPage {

public:
       CRadioBtnsPP () : CPropertyPage (CRadioBtnsPP::IDD) {}
 enum {IDD = IDD_RADIO};
 int  which_btn_is_on;
 enum Order {Tree, Arrow};

protected:
 virtual void DoDataExchange (CDataExchange*);
};
```

Similarly, the CCheckBoxDlg class definition becomes CCheckBoxPP with a slight change in its constructor.

```
class CCheckBoxPP : public CPropertyPage {

public:
       CCheckBoxPP () : CPropertyPage (CCheckBoxPP::IDD) {}
 enum {IDD = IDD_CHECKBOX};
 int  ck_show_name;
 int  ck_show_cursor;
```

```
protected:
 virtual void DoDataExchange (CDataExchange*);
};
```

Then convert CListBoxLinesDlg to CListBoxLinesPP. Our first problem now arises. In order to access the FrameWin's public members containing the strings to add and the current line number transfer buffer, **GetParent** was used. Now, however, the parent is the **CPropertySheet** class. One quick solution is to pass a pointer to the FrameWin object itself which can be saved in a protected member and used to access the numerous transfer fields required. The constructor was so modified in-line. The other problem surfaced only during test runs. If a new line was selected and the OK button pressed, the new line selection was passed back properly through the **OnOK** function. However, if after the selection was made a new page was activated and then OK was pressed, the new line selection was not passed back; **OnOK** was not called. When a page loses the focus, the **OnKillActive** function is invoked, so I simply saved the current selection here as well.

```
class CListBoxLinesPP : public CPropertyPage {

protected:

FrameWin *ptrframe;

public:
      CListBoxLinesPP (FrameWin* ptrfrm)
    : CPropertyPage (IDD_LISTBOX) {
       ptrframe = ptrfrm;
    }

virtual BOOL  OnInitDialog ();

protected:

afx_msg virtual void  OnOK ();
afx_msg virtual BOOL  OnKillActive ();
DECLARE_MESSAGE_MAP()
};
```

Finally, the CNamesDlg was modified to CPropertyPage. The unneeded button response handlers were removed and **OnKillActive** added for the same reason as before with the list box. To avoid the **GetParent** problem, a pointer to the transfer buffer is passed to the constructor and saved in the in-line constructor.

```
class CNamesPP : public CPropertyPage {
protected:
TRANSFER_NAMES original_names;
TRANSFER_NAMES *ptrparentbuf;

public:
      CNamesPP (TRANSFER_NAMES *ptrnam)
    : CPropertyPage (IDD_EDITDLG) {
       ptrparentbuf = ptrnam;
     }
afx_msg void   CmReset ();
afx_msg void   CmClear ();
```

```
afx_msg void    OnOK ();
afx_msg void    OnCancel ();
afx_msg BOOL    OnKillActive ();

protected:
virtual BOOL    OnInitDialog ();
DECLARE_MESSAGE_MAP()
};
```

Next examine the implementation of the **CmPropertySheet** function that launches the action. First an automatic storage instance is allocated for each page and the transfer buffers filled by using the same coding that is removed from the corresponding dialog launchers. Then allocate one instance of the **CPropertySheet** class. Normally, the base class provides all the services required. The property sheet constructor is passed a string ID for the main title bar. Next, each page is added into the sheet using the **AddPage** function.

Caution: when converting existing dialogs, be sure that the largest-size dialog is added first. The size of the sheet is determined by the size of the first page. Thus, if the largest page is not first, when it is activated, portions may be clipped.

DoModal creates and executes the entire process, returning only when OK or Cancel buttons are pressed. If IDOK is returned, then all the values must be recovered and implemented. The only other changes required to the FrameWin implementation are the alteration of the few enum references.

```
void        FrameWin::CmPropertySheet () {
 CRadioBtnsPP radio;                    // allocate radio buttons page
 radio.which_btn_is_on = which_cursor; // xfer current settings to dlg
 CCheckBoxPP ckbox;                     // allocate check box page
 ckbox.ck_show_name   = show_name;      // transfer current settings
 ckbox.ck_show_cursor = show_cursor;
 CListBoxLinesPP listbox (this);        // allocate listbox page
 CNamesPP edit (&xfer_edit_names);      // allocate names page
 memcpy (&xfer_edit_names, &real_names_db, sizeof (TRANSFER_NAMES));
 CPropertySheet tabdlg (IDS_TAB_TITLE); // allocate one sheet for all
 tabdlg.AddPage (&listbox);
 tabdlg.AddPage (&radio);
 tabdlg.AddPage (&ckbox);

 if (tabdlg.DoModal () == IDOK) {       // create & execute dlg
  which_cursor = radio.which_btn_is_on; // update our members' checks
  show_name    = ckbox.ck_show_name;     // update members for nexttime
  show_cursor = ckbox.ck_show_cursor;
  memcpy (&real_names_db, &xfer_edit_names, sizeof (TRANSFER_NAMES));
  if (linenumnew >= 0)                  // if OK, set our new line num
   linenum = linenumnew + 3;            // save new line number
  if (which_cursor == CRadioBtnsPP::Tree) { // install correct cursor
   hcursor = LoadCursor (AfxGetApp()->m_hInstance,
                        MAKEINTRESOURCE(IDC_TREE));
   SetClassLong (m_hWnd, GCL_HCURSOR, (long) hcursor);
  }
  else {
   hcursor = AfxGetApp()->LoadStandardCursor (IDC_ARROW), // use arrow
   SetClassLong (m_hWnd, GCL_HCURSOR, (long) hcursor);
```

```
  }
  Invalidate (); // force paint to display msg of new cursor
 }
}
```

In the CRadioBtnsPP and CCheckBoxPP implementations the only change in
the base class is the invocation for DDX.

```
void      CRadioBtnsPP::DoDataExchange (CDataExchange *ptrdata) {
CPropertyPage::DoDataExchange (ptrdata);
DDX_Radio (ptrdata, IDC_RADIOBUTTON_TREE, which_btn_is_on);
}

void      CCheckBoxPP::DoDataExchange (CDataExchange *ptrdata) {
CPropertyPage::DoDataExchange (ptrdata);
DDX_Check (ptrdata, IDC_CHECK_NAME, ck_show_name);
DDX_Check (ptrdata, IDC_CHECK_CURSOR, ck_show_cursor);
}
```

Next, examine the CListBoxLinesPP implementation. The saved pointer to
FrameWin is used to access the transfer members, and the base class becomes
CPropertyPage.

```
BEGIN_MESSAGE_MAP(CListBoxLinesPP, CPropertyPage)
 ON_COMMAND(IDOK, OnOK)
END_MESSAGE_MAP()

void  CListBoxLinesPP::OnOK () {
 CListBox *ptrlistbox = (CListBox*) (GetDlgItem (IDC_LISTBOX));
 ptrframe->linenumnew = ptrlistbox->GetCurSel ();
 CPropertyPage::OnOK ();
}

BOOL  CListBoxLinesPP::OnKillActive () {
 CListBox *ptrlistbox = (CListBox*) (GetDlgItem (IDC_LISTBOX));
 ptrframe->linenumnew = ptrlistbox->GetCurSel ();
 return CPropertyPage::OnKillActive ();
}

BOOL  CListBoxLinesPP::OnInitDialog () {
 CListBox *ptrlistbox = (CListBox*) (GetDlgItem (IDC_LISTBOX));
 for (int I=0; i<ptrframe->linetot; i++) {
  ptrlistbox->AddString (ptrframe->line[i]);  // insert lines
  if (i+3 == ptrframe->linenum) ptrlistbox->SetCurSel (i);
 }
 return TRUE;
}
```

Finally, the CNamesPP implementation shows the removal of several button
message processing functions. The message map becomes much smaller; only our two
additional buttons are required. The base class becomes **CPropertyPage**, and the
saved pointer to the transfer buffer replaces the **GetParent** approach.

```
BEGIN_MESSAGE_MAP(CNamesPP, CPropertyPage)
 ON_BN_CLICKED (IDC_CLEARBUTTON, CmClear)
 ON_BN_CLICKED (IDC_RESETBUTTON, CmReset)
END_MESSAGE_MAP()
```

```
BOOL       CNamesPP::OnInitDialog () {
 memcpy (&original_names, ptrparentbuf, sizeof (TRANSFER_NAMES));
 SetDlgItemText (IDC_FIRSTNAME, original_names.first_name);
 SetDlgItemText (IDC_LASTNAME,  original_names.last_name);
 return TRUE;
}

void       CNamesPP::CmReset () {
 memcpy (ptrparentbuf, &original_names, sizeof (TRANSFER_NAMES));
 SetDlgItemText (IDC_FIRSTNAME, original_names.first_name);
 SetDlgItemText (IDC_LASTNAME,  original_names.last_name);
}

void       CNamesPP::OnOK () {
 GetDlgItemText (IDC_FIRSTNAME, ptrparentbuf->first_name,
                 MAX_NAME_LEN);
 GetDlgItemText (IDC_LASTNAME,  ptrparentbuf->last_name,
                 MAX_NAME_LEN);
 CPropertyPage::OnOK ();  // now continue the OK process
}

BOOL       CNamesPP::OnKillActive () {
 GetDlgItemText (IDC_FIRSTNAME, ptrparentbuf->first_name,
                 MAX_NAME_LEN);
 GetDlgItemText (IDC_LASTNAME,  ptrparentbuf->last_name,
                 MAX_NAME_LEN);
 return CPropertyPage::OnKillActive ();  // now continue OK work
}

void       CNamesPP::OnCancel () {
 memcpy (ptrparentbuf, &original_names, sizeof (TRANSFER_NAMES));
 CPropertyPage::OnCancel ();  // now continue the cancel process
}

void       CNamesPP::CmClear () {
 memset (ptrparentbuf, 0, sizeof (TRANSFER_NAMES));
 SetDlgItemText (IDC_FIRSTNAME, ptrparentbuf->first_name);
 SetDlgItemText (IDC_LASTNAME,  ptrparentbuf->last_name);
}
```

7.19 SOME NEW WINDOWS 95 CONTROLS: SLIDER (TRACK BAR) AND SPIN (UP/DOWN) CONTROLS

Windows 95 provides several new controls. The slider or track bar is a smaller-sized variation of the scroll bar giving clearer view of the position. The spin or up/down (which can also be left/right) control allows for fast digital incrementing. Spin controls often have a corresponding edit control in which the numerical position is recorded or manually set by the user. This "buddy" edit window is coupled to the up/down arrows. Actually, the spin control appends itself onto the side of the edit control window. Any time the spin buttons are pressed, the spin control converts the integer position into a string and displays it in the edit control.

Sliders send scroll messages and are identified with the track bar prefix TB_ and have numerically the same values as the corresponding SB_ scroll bar messages. Spin controls with buddy edit controls are accessed via the edit control's **CWnd** base class—**GetWindowText**.

In Pgm07c, a slider control appears at the top right of the main window area and can be used as an alternative method of setting the line number on which the names are displayed. The spin and edit controls appear just below the slider control and provide yet another method to set the display line number. The three independent methods of adjusting the display line number have to be coordinated with each other. Figure 7.10 shows how our main window now appears after some data has been entered.

7.19.1 MFC Implementation of Sliders and Spin Control Buttons

To use any of the new controls, be sure that stdafx.h includes

```
#include <afxcmn.h>   // the common new controls
```

Sliders are implemented by the **CSliderCtrl** class, spin buttons by **CSpinButtonCtrl**. The edit control would be the normal **CEdit** class. Since these controls are going to be placed directly in our window and not in a dialog, they have to be constructed using the manual method instead of using the resource editor. Three control IDs are defined in the resource.h file.

```
#define IDC_SLIDER        213
#define IDC_SPINEDIT      214
#define IDC_SPINCTL       215
```

Next, the FrameWin class must define three members that are used to instantiate these controls.

```
CSliderCtrl     slider;  // slider control to adjust display
CEdit           editctl; // buddy edit box for the spin control
CSpinButtonCtrl spinctl; // up/down spin button
```

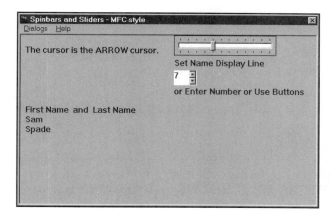

Fig. 7.10 Pgm07c with Slider and Spin Control

In the FrameWin's **OnCreate** function, after the base class has been constructed, instances of the three controls are created.

```
int      FrameWin::OnCreate (LPCREATESTRUCT lpCS) {
 int retcd = CFrameWnd::OnCreate (lpCS); // pass to base class
 ...
 // construct the slider/trackbar control
 CRect r (300,0,500,40);
 slider.Create (TBS_HORZ | TBS_AUTOTICKS | TBS_BOTH |
             TBS_ENABLESELRANGE | WS_CHILD | WS_VISIBLE |
             WS_BORDER, r, this, IDC_SLIDER);
 slider.SetRange (3, linetot + 2, TRUE); // force into range
 slider.SetLineSize(1);     // set amt a click/arrow key reports
 slider.SetPageSize(1);     // set amount one PgXX reports
 slider.SetPos(3);          // set initial position
 // create the edit control for the spin control's buddy window
 CRect er (300,70,345,100);
 editctl.Create (WS_CHILD | WS_VISIBLE, er, this, IDC_SPINEDIT);
 // create the spin or up/down control
 CRect sr (300,70,365,100);
 spinctl.Create (UDS_ARROWKEYS | UDS_SETBUDDYINT | UDS_ALIGNRIGHT
              | WS_CHILD | WS_BORDER | WS_VISIBLE,
              sr, this, IDC_SPINCTL);
 spinctl.SetBuddy (&editctl); // set edit ctrl as buddy window
 spinctl.SetRange (3, linetot + 2); // set range of the spin ctrl
 spinctl.SetPos (3);              // set its initial position
 return retcd;
}
```

Examine the **Create** for the slider. The first parameter is the window style for the control. Notice the new style options.

TBS_HORZ	default horizontal orientation
TBS_VERT	make slider vertical
TBS_AUTOTICKS	create tick marks for each unit in the range
TBS_NOTICKS	display no tick marks
TBS_BOTTOM	place tick marks on bottom only
TBS_TOP	place tick marks on top only
TBS_RIGHT	place tick marks on right only
TBS_LEFT	place tick marks on left only
TBS_BOTH	place tick marks on both sides
TBS_ENABLESELRANGE	place triangles on each endpoint

Design Rule 31: **Since the control is being manually constructed, you must add in the WS_CHILD, WS_VISIBLE, and WS_BORDER options or the control will not be visible.**

The **CRect r** defines the initial placement of the slider as well as its dimensions. For all of these new controls, I have used absolute numbers so that you can quickly see their exact values and use.

Next, the initial range of slider motion is set using **SetRange**, giving the minimum and then maximum line numbers. The third parameter, when True, forces a redrawing of the control with this new range, including the tick marks. Next, the **SetLineSize** and **SetPageSize** are used to set the integer number of scroll units to be reported for the scrolling events. I use a value of one for both in this example because the range is so small. Finally, the slider's thumb bar position is set to the initial position of line 3 by using **SetPos**. From now on, slider events send normal scrolling messages. Hence, WM_HSCROLL messages must be monitored.

To construct a spin control with its buddy edit window, the edit control is created first and then the spin control is created. The spin control also has some new style identifiers including:

UDS_HORZ	arrow buttons are left/right; note that default is up/down
UDS_WRAP	causes the position to wrap around the limits so an increment beyond max val gives min val
UDS_ARROWKEYS	allows the arrow keys to activate the buttons
UDS_SETBUDDYINT	sets the text in a buddy window on any change
UDS_NOTHOUSANDS	do not insert commas every three decimal places
UDS_AUTOBUDDY	automatically selects the previous window as the buddy window—*use with care*
UDS_ALIGNRIGHT	positions spin ctrl to the right of the buddy
UDS_ALIGNLEFT	positions spin ctrl to the left of the buddy; note that spin ctrl size is forced to fit the buddy window

Again, you MUST add in the WS_CHILD, WS_VISIBLE, and WS_BORDER options or the control is not visible. Next, the buddy edit control window is attached as the spin control's buddy window by using the **SetBuddy** function which is passed the address of the base class **CWnd**. The range is set by **SetRange** providing the minimum and then the maximum values. Finally, the spin control's initial position is set with **SetPos**. Notice that the spin control subsequently sends the edit control a string version of its initial position—here, line 3.

Now examine what steps are required when the user changes the main window's size, **OnSize**. The maximum number of lines is altered by the window's size. Thus, a new range of line number values must be installed using both the slider's and spin's **SetRange** functions. As a precaution, the current position is also reset.

```
void    FrameWin::OnSize (UINT a, int b, int c) {
CFrameWnd::OnSize (a, b, c);
CRect rect;
GetClientRect (&rect);
```

```
   ...
   // set new slider and spin controls' range based on window size
   // and set their current position
   slider.SetRange (3, linetot + 2, TRUE);
   slider.SetPos (linenum);
   spinctl.SetRange (3, linetot + 2);
   spinctl.SetPos (linenum);
   Invalidate();          // force repainting of window
   }
```

In **OnPaint**, two messages are displayed to provide instructions for the user. **OnPaint** repaints the whole main window, which then forces the two controls to repaint themselves, yielding screen flicker. But for a simple example, let's live with this.

```
void        FrameWin::OnPaint () {
  CPaintDC dc (this);
  CString msg;
  dc.SetBkMode (TRANSPARENT);
  // display heading for the slider and spin controls
  msg.LoadString (IDS_SLIDER);
  dc.TextOut (300, 45, msg);
  msg.LoadString (IDS_SPINEDIT);
  dc.TextOut (300, 102, msg);
  ...
  }
```

Examine the small changes in the **CmPropertySheet** menu item function that launches the property sheet dialog. Since the user can change the line number from a property page, when the property sheet terminates with IDOK, the current positions of the slider and spin controls must be updated.

```
void        FrameWin::CmPropertySheet () {
  ...
  if (tabdlg.DoModal () == IDOK) {        // create & execute dlg
   which_cursor = radio.which_btn_is_on;  // update with check
   show_name    = ckbox.ck_show_name;
   show_cursor = ckbox.ck_show_cursor;
   memcpy (&real_names_db, &xfer_edit_names,
          sizeof (TRANSFER_NAMES));
   if (linenumnew >= 0) {          // if OK, set our new line number
    linenum = linenumnew + 3;      // save new line number
    slider.SetPos (linenum);        // update slider's position
    spinctl.SetPos (linenum);       // update spin control's pos
   }
  ...
  }
```

Now for the dynamic interactions with the controls. First let's see how the slider interacts. Whenever a slider motion occurs, whether by mouse or keyboard event, the slider sends its parent window a WM_HSCROLL message, using TB_ identifiers that parallel and actually have the same numerical values as the corresponding WM_HSCROLL messages. The message map table has two new entries—one each for the WM_HSCROLL slider messages and EN_CHANGE edit control messages. The edit control sends its message after it has altered the text in its small window. The message map appears.

```
BEGIN_MESSAGE_MAP(FrameWin, CFrameWnd)
 ON_WM_HSCROLL()                      // trap slider/track bar events
 ON_EN_CHANGE (IDC_SPINEDIT, OnSpinChange) // trap spin changes
 ...
END_MESSAGE_MAP()
```

The coding of the **OnHScroll** member function closely resembles a normal horizontal scroll bar event handler.

```
void FrameWin::OnHScroll (UINT type, UINT pos, CScrollBar*) {
 switch (type) {
  case TB_BOTTOM:         // slider to min value
   linenum = 3; break;
  case TB_LINEDOWN:       // right/down arrow
  case TB_PAGEDOWN:       // pgdn key or mouse click before slider
   linenum++; break;
  case TB_LINEUP:         // left/up arrow
  case TB_PAGEUP:         // pgup key or mouse click after slider
   linenum--; break;
  case TB_THUMBPOSITION:  // slider moved using the mouse to pos
  case TB_THUMBTRACK:     // slider dragged using the mouse to pos
   linenum = pos; break;
  case TB_TOP:            // slider to max position
   linenum = linetot + 2; break;
 };
 // force into the current range
 if (linenum <3) linenum = 3;
 if (linenum > linetot + 2) linenum = linetot + 2;
 // update all ctrls to new settings - both slider, spin and edit
 slider.SetPos (linenum);
 spinctl.SetPos (linenum);
 Invalidate();     // repaint to display at the new line number
}
```

Notice that, after assigning a proposed new line number, the edit control is then forced back into range once more, and the current positions of both controls are updated. In the **OnSpinChange** function, the current text is retrieved using the **CWnd** member function **GetWindowText**, converted into an integer, and forced back into range. Notice that only the slider's position is then reset. If we also attempted to reset the edit control, we would preclude the user entering a two-digit number. Every time the user entered 1 for 13, we would reject it converting it back into a 3, the minimum number. While the display and slider are immediately reset and shown at line 3, the edit control still says 1, ready for the user to enter the second digit, 3, at which point all is adjusted to line 13.

```
void FrameWin::OnSpinChange () {
 CString msg;
 editctl.GetWindowText (msg); // get edit ctrl's new text
 linenum = atoi (msg);        // convert into line number
```

```
    // force into range
    if (linenum <3) linenum = 3;
    if (linenum > linetot + 2) linenum = linetot + 2;
    slider.SetPos (linenum);   // set corresponding slider position
    Invalidate();              // show name on new line number
}
```

Notice how easy it is to add sliders and spin controls. Their use enhances the user interface. In the next chapter we explore the new Windows 95 common controls.

Memory, Files, Common Dialog Boxes, Scroll Bars

8.1 INTRODUCTION

A benefit of Windows 95 is the common look and feel shared by all applications. To achieve this characteristic appearance, Windows 95 provides several *common dialog boxes* that applications should use to handle those basic actions most applications need to do, such as selecting a file to open or choosing a font. The common dialogs include dialogs for file open, file save, search and replace, choose colors, choose fonts, and print. (C style: these are in the COMMDLG.H header file.) MFC encapsulates these into classes. But before examining the common dialog specifics, we must understand how Windows 95 uses memory and the new file system with long filenames.

8.2 WINDOWS 3.1 AND WINDOWS 95 MEMORY MANAGEMENT

To code a real application under Windows 3.1, programmers had to understand the basics of memory management. Since C/C++ was used to create the applications, one also had to understand how C/C++ handled memory. DOS segmented architecture is indeed a labyrinth. If one had a grounding in Microassembler Programming, one probably well understood the idea of memory segmentation. But the impacts upon C/C++ may not have been understood.

Under Windows 95, nearly all complexities of memory management have been eliminated! Virtually all of the methods for allocating memory are acceptable, and there is really only one potential pitfall for which to be alert. Since porting of Windows 3.1 applications will be a frequent task in the immediate future, let's briefly examine how Windows 3.1 utilized memory and then see how memory can be used under Windows 95.

8.2.1 Windows 3.1 Memory Usage

When running under DOS memory is used in up to 64K segments. The reason behind the 64K segments lay with the high-speed work areas, called *registers*, which originally were only 16 bits or 2 bytes in size. If an address was to be stored and manipulated by the registers, then the maximum address would be 0×FFFF or 65535. That is, a memory location could range from 0 to 65,535 for a total of 64K. When PCs were created, the designers dreamed up a scheme that would allow access to 1M of memory by breaking the memory address, called a *linear* or *flat address*, down into two components: a *segment* and an *offset address*, together known as a *vector address*. Basically, the segment address points to which a chunk of 64K is being referenced, and the offset address points to the offset from the start of that 64K chunk to where the item can be found.

Of course the problem is that to address 1M requires not a 16-bit address but a 20-bit address. The designers got around this problem by defining a *paragraph boundary* as any linear or flat address that is evenly divisible by 16 or 0×10. This way, all segment addresses must begin on a paragraph boundary. For example, if we wanted to address the last 64K segment in the 1M of memory, its real address would be in hex 0×FFFF0, which is still too large to fit in a word register. Notice that all segment addresses end with a 0 hex digit by virtue of being on the paragraph boundary. Thus, if you shift the segment address to the right 4 bits or 1 hex digit, you end with 0×FFFF in this case. And the result now fits in the 16-bit registers! All that is then required is a special internal address register that is 20 bits long. Whenever a memory location is accessed, the program specifies a segment and an offset address. The CPU inserts the segment address into the large register, shifts it 4 bits to the left, and adds the offset address, yielding the real linear or flat address! Thus, the nightmare of segmented architecture was born!

Generally most all programs define a minimum of three different segments: the code segment, the data segment, and the stack segment. C\C++ combines the data segment and the stack segments into one 64K segment. The Linker places all of the actual instructions in the code segment; similarly for the data and stack segments. The stack is a last in first out (LIFO) memory area, ideal for automatic storage items. In C/C++, the code is placed into the code segment. All automatic data and all parameter class data are placed in the stack segment. The data segment holds first all global/external and static class items. All remaining storage in the segment becomes the *local heap*. The local heap is used to handle dynamic **malloc** or **new** operations. Since, in C\C++, the data and the stack segments are combined, all these data must fit within one 64K segment.

Next, the designers created six different memory models to accommodate small to large programs. Specifically, the general differences are

Tiny	only 1 64K segment into which all code, data, and stack reside often used for .COM programs
Small	1 64K code and 1 64K combined data and stack seg
Medium	multiple 64K code seg and 1 64K combined data and stack seg
Compact	1 64K code seg and multiple data seg and 1 64K stack seg
Large	multiple 64K code segs and multiple 64K data segs but only 1 64K stack seg
Huge	nearly anything, including 1M for stack

The pointer size is based upon the memory model

Tiny–Small	pointer is 2 bytes—offset address only
Medium	pointer is 2 bytes for data; 4 bytes seg:offset for code
Compact	pointer is 4-bytes seg:offset for data, 2-byte offset for code
Large	pointers are all 4-bytes seg:offset for code and data
Huge	pointers are 6-bytes seg:32 bit offset

where 2-byte pointers are near, 4-byte pointers are far, and 6-byte pointers are huge. There is even more complexity than this, but this is the basic idea.

Unfortunately, almost no library functions of either C/C++ or Windows 95 accept huge pointers. So that model is almost never used. The impact on C/C++ programming is severe. Usually, C/C++ forces the data segment and the stack segment to be the same 64K segment. The stack can never be larger than 64K for the entire program, which severely limits automatic storage. The local heap for **new** and **malloc** is limited to 64K minus the amount of global/external and static memory and automatic storage required. All remaining memory is classified as the far heap. It is accessed with **faralloc**, but is limited to chunks of 64K per allocation. Additionally, static and global data can be defined with the **far** option, and the linker places those data into segments other than the combined DS/SS segment.

Under early Windows releases, the medium model was used. By version 3.1, nearly all machines ran Windows in 386-Enhanced mode, and the large model became widely adopted. The redeeming quality for large programs was to use a modular design with many functions that define far static and global data instead of automatic data. In this way, the static and global data were spread across several 64K segments, up to 1M worth (but no single data item exceeding 64K). Thus, for real-world, larger C/C++ programs, the compact or large model was very often used. In math and engineering programs where the code becomes equally large, the large model was nearly always used.

DOS, with this segmented architecture, is running in what is called *real mode* where a segment register points to which 64K chunk of memory is needed. Windows runs in *protected mode* where a segment register now contains a 16-bit *selector address* that points to potentially up to 4 gigabytes (G) of memory. The memory model is called the *flat* model because all addresses are 32 bits, and code, data, and stack are all in the same potential 1G segment of memory.

Windows 3.1 on the other hand had to run under DOS with this segmented architecture but also had to use all the memory on the machine—the extended memory. To do so, Windows 3.1 used an extended memory manager and continually managed the memory layout in use. This huge chunk of memory that was not in use by DOS was called Windows *global memory* (then and now).

When Windows (then and now) loads an application, it loads in the code segment and the data segment and makes the registers for the data segment and stack segment contain the same segment address. (Internally within many Windows 3.1 API functions, the data and stack segments are different. The coding to split or join these two is called a *thunk*.) As the application runs, resources are loaded into global memory as needed.

After many applications run, load, and free various segments of memory, the memory space becomes quite fragmented into smaller free pieces. If left alone, eventually the system would run out of memory. No single chunk of memory would now be large enough for the current request, but, taken together, all of the freed bits would be more than ample. Therefore, the Windows Memory Manager (then and now) attempts to move blocks or segments around in an attempt to merge all freed areas into one large chunk.

But under Windows 3.1, if Windows moved your needed data segment, what happened to the addresses your application was currently using? They would become completely invalid! To avoid this fiasco, Windows 3.1 maintained its own internal tables of where the block of memory really was and where it told you it was—the segment address.

Under Windows 95 with the flat model, the segment registers contain the selector address that points to an internal table of where the memory is really located. Thus, Windows can alter this internal table to adjust memory, combining smaller chunks into one larger area of memory independent of your program.

Every segment that Windows 3.1 loads is marked as "fixed" or "moveable." Obviously, avoid fixed segments at all costs, because they cannot ever be moved by Windows 3.1 when it needs to adjust memory to group unused chunks into large units.

When the program needs to actually reference that moveable chunk, the program requests that Windows (then and now) *lock* the memory. At this point, Windows (then and now) decides where it really wants the segment to be and creates a *locked far pointer* to that data (far is omitted under Windows 95). It is up to the program, via an *unlock* request, to notify Windows when the program no longer needs to use that segment. With the severe memory limitations of early Windows releases, programmers were advised to keep no memory locked longer than needed. These early Windows applications would lock memory upon entry to the processing of *one* message and unlock it when done processing that same message. These programs were filled with numerous lock/unlock instructions. Later, when Windows 3.1 commonly was run in 386-Enhanced mode, Windows could adjust the selector addresses independent of the application. So common coding practice became: lock the global memory immediately after it is allocated and unlock it one time just before it is freed.

The discardable attribute has further aided all versions of Windows—when memory is becoming tight, all discardable resources that are not currently locked and therefore in active use can be immediately discarded from memory. Should the application need that discarded resource, all versions of Windows can later reload it. Obviously, the discardable attribute can be used only upon resources that are read-only. A data segment, whose contents change, could not be discardable. The code segment, on the other hand, could be, since good programming practices dictate that an application should never modify its own code while running.

So what was the impact on writing Windows 3.1 applications? First, the use of **malloc** and **new** and the Windows function **LocalAlloc** (which used its own 64K segment) were avoided because they allocated in the local heap or stack that was limited to the one 64K segment. Instead, extensive use was made of the Windows API functions to dynamically allocate global memory—**GlobalAlloc**, for example. Windows 3.1 defined *local memory* as the unused portion of the one 64K combined data and stack segment of the application and *global memory* as all remaining memory on the machine that was not used by DOS. Since local memory was in extremely short supply (all automatic, parameter, new storage items), larger applications avoided as much automatic and new storage as possible, relying extensively on global memory.

Design Rule 32: **When using the Windows 95 API memory allocation functions, lock the memory one time and unlock it just before freeing it.**

If you are converting an older application with numerous lock/unlock instructions, replace these with just one pair. Caution: be sure that the locked pointer is not altered. It was common practice to obtain a locked pointer to the memory area and then increment the pointer through the memory as it was used. The next time that memory was needed, a new locked pointer was obtained. If such occurs in the application, just create a working copy of the locked pointer to increment.

Design Rule 33: **Usually all forms of data allocation are equivalent and acceptable, since all memory comes from the one address space.**

You may use automatic allocation on the stack at block entry, **malloc**, **new**, or the Windows API functions **LocalAlloc** and **GlobalAlloc** and other functions interchangeably as you desire and as they fit the application design.

Design Rule 34: **If the application dynamically allocates thousands of memory objects, then consider allocating one sufficiently large chunk from Windows 95 and handling your own suballocations independently of Windows 95.**

Otherwise, when the application terminates, the user may be forced to wait many seconds for the thousands of objects to be freed! (I find applications that do this annoying.)

There are also some MFC debugging memory functions that can be used to assist in tracking down memory overruns and memory resource leaks. In this chapter, I will concentrate on the Windows 95 global memory allocation routines, primarily to assist you in converting from Windows 3.1 code which likely made extensive use of global memory.

8.3 WINDOWS 95 GLOBAL MEMORY API FUNCTIONS

Let us examine the API functions to get Windows 95 global memory. Although all memory allocation methods can be used to allocate megabytes under Windows 95, I am concentrating here on the global method because this procedure is still used when interfacing with some Windows 95 functions such as the clipboard. Remember that there is no such thing as a far pointer any longer; all pointers are near, within the 1G memory. When a block of memory is requested, Windows 95 provides a *handle* to the global memory. Only when that memory is locked does Windows 95 provide a pointer to the block. For example, let's say that you needed two large arrays that potentially were to be defined as

```
char    buffer[40000];
TPoint vertices[10000];
```

Under Windows 95, both could be allocated as shown as automatic storage. Let's allocate them on the global heap. First, in the class definition, include handles to the requests.

```
HANDLE  hbuffer;    // handle to global memory for char buffer array
HANDLE  hvertices; // handle to global memory for TPoint vertices
```

Next, in the class constructor, request global memory from Windows 95 using the **GlobalAlloc** function.

```
HANDLE   GlobalAlloc (type ID, long amount of memory requested);
```

The type ID is usually GMEM_MOVEABLE for global memory moveable. One could OR in GMEM_ZEROINIT if you wish Windows 95 to initialize the memory to zeros. Other seldom used options would include asking for fixed memory (which defeats the whole purpose) or discardable memory (for read-only items), along with a few others even less likely to be needed. Assuming the following defines, the constructor coding would then be

```
#define  BUFFER_SIZE  40000
#define  MAX_POINTS   10000

hbuffer = GlobalAlloc (GMEM_MOVEABLE, BUFFER_SIZE);
hvertices = GlobalAlloc (GMEM_MOVEABLE, MAX_POINTS);
```

If the handle is NULL, then Windows 95 is completely out of memory. Protect your application—test the return code.

```
if (hbuffer == NULL || hvertices == NULL) {
  MessageBox ("Try Closing Outstanding Applications",
              "Out of Memory", MB_OK);
}
```

What actions should occur if the allocation should fail is application dependent. For example, if the application cannot proceed if the allocation fails, then post a quit message. (This is done in Pgm08a here.) Whenever the application needs to use these global memory blocks, they must be locked or tied to a specific real address. The syntax for the function is

```
char* GlobalLock (handle of global memory block);
```

Generally, typecasting is done to the return value to get the pointer into the correct type. So if the handles are not NULL, both handles should be locked to real memory, most likely into protected class members.

```
char   *ptrbuffer;    // will be used as *ptrbuffer or ptrbuffer++
CPoint *vertices;     // will be used as vertices[j]
ptrbuffer = (char*) GlobalLock (hbuffer);
vertices  = (CPoint*) GlobalLock (hvertices);
```

From now on until the destructor or the memory is freed, access the memory normally, such as:

```
*ptrbuffer = 'A';
vertices[i] = point;
```

Before the application terminates, often in the destructor or **OnDestroy**, unlock the memory and free it. The function syntax is

```
GlobalUnlock (handle of global memory);
GlobalFree (handle of global memory);
```

Here the sequence would be

```
GlobalUnlock (hbuffer);
GlobalUnlock (hvertices);
GlobalFree   (hbuffer);
GlobalFree   (hvertices);
```

That is all you need to do to use megabytes of extended memory under Windows 95. The key is to identify the program's larger data items and then to methodically allocate and use them.

8.4 WINDOWS 95 NEW HEAP MEMORY FUNCTIONS

The new heap memory management functions in Windows 95 allow the creation of a private heap that can be used to eliminate lengthy termination actions of countless delete operations. The new private heap can grow dynamically and allow you to define working sets of data to reduce swapping of virtual memory and to simplify the deallocation process. Additionally, in multiple document interface (MDI) applications (chapter 12), each new document could have its own separate heap, tending to group memory references to one localized portion of the gigabyte address space, thereby improving efficiency.

The basic function to allocate a private heap is **HeapCreate**.

```
HANDLE  heap = HeapCreate (DWORD flags, DWORD initsize,
                           DWORD maxsize);
```

The flags can be:

HEAP_NO_SERIALIZE	for single thread apps to prevent the overhead of exclusion locks from other threads
HEAP_GENERATE_EXCEPTIONS	to have error exceptions thrown
HEAP_ZERO_MEMORY	to zero the memory

The initial size determines the heap's initial size. Use a maximum size of 0 for a heap that can grow or code an upper limit if desired. Save the handle for use in all of the other functions. To destroy the private heap, use

```
HeapDestroy (handle);
```

To allocate memory from the private heap, use **HeapAlloc**.

```
void* HeapAlloc (HANDLE heaphandle, DWORD flags, DWORD numbytes);
```

The flags often would include HEAP_ZERO_MEMORY to have the memory cleared upon allocation. For example, to allocate the char buffer from the above example on the private heap, code

```
ptrbuffer = (char*) HeapAlloc (heap, HEAP_ZERO_MEMORY, 40000);
```

To remove an item from the private heap, use **HeapFree**.

```
HeapFree (HANDLE heap, DWORD flags, LPVOID memory_item);
```

At any time, the validity of the private heap can be checked. Either the entire contents can be validated, or a specific allocation on the heap can be validated.

```
BOOL HeapValidate (HANDLE heap, DWORD flags, LPVOID mem);
```

If the LPVOID memory item is NULL, then the whole private heap is validated. If it points to an item that is allocated in the heap, then that one item is validated. The function returns TRUE if all is OK and FALSE if the heap contains errors. This could be a useful debugging aid. There are many more uses and functions that can assist debugging.

Perhaps the easiest way to begin to use private heaps is to allocate specific non-class items in a private heap, such as a bitmap. Class instances can also be allocated on the private heap, but the new and delete functions for that class would have to be overridden. (See the bibliography for some related texts.)

8.5 FILE HANDLING UNDER WINDOWS 95—LONG FILENAMES

Handling files has become more complex. Under Windows 95 there are several possible file-handling systems available, including the older DOS file allocation table (DOS FAT) system used if Windows 95 is booted as DOS in real mode, the protected-mode FAT system (the default often called VFAT for virtual FAT), and the NTFS for Windows NT. Obviously, there is a world of difference between the filenames and paths between these systems.

The first time that a file function accesses a hard disk or volume and whenever a disk is placed in a floppy disk drive, Windows 95 examines the volume to determine which file system is appropriate for that volume. The Windows 95 file system can then access files independently of the underlying file system in use. Thus, the best approach is to ask Windows 95 which system is in use by calling the **GetVolumeInformation** function.

```
BOOL GetVolumeInformation (
         LPCSTR   rootpath,        LPSTR    volumelabel,
         DWORD    lenvolumelabel,  LPDWORD  volsernum,
         LPDWORD  maxcomplen,      LPDWORD  sysflags,
         LPSTR    filesysname,     DWORD    lenfilesysname);
```

Here, **rootpath** is a string containing the root directory of the volume to be described by this function. If Null is passed, the root directory of the current volume is used. Upon return, the **volumelabel** string contains the specified volume's label, where **lenvolumelabel** contains the defined length of our **volumelabel** string. The DWORD pointed to by **volsernum** contains the DOS volume serial number; if Null is passed, no volume serial number is returned. Upon return, the DWORD pointed to by **maxcomplen** contains the maximum component length. This is defined to be the length of the name between backslashes that form the path. Under Windows 95 and NT, filenames can be up to 255 bytes long with a full path including the filename of 260 bytes. The pointer to the DWORD **sysflags** could likely be a combination of one of the following:

FS_CASE_IS_PRESERVED	system will preserve the filename case
FS_CASE_SENSITIVE	system supports case-sensitive filenames
FS_FILE_COMPRESSION	system supports file-based compression
FS_VOL_IS_COMPRESSED	this volume is a compressed volume

Note the last two compression flags are mutually exclusive. On return the string **filesysname** contains the name of the type of file system, FAT, NTFS, and so on. Protected-mode FAT and the DOS FAT are not distinguished. If the pointer is Null, the name is not returned. The DWORD **lenfilesysname** contains the length of our passed **filesysname** string. Note that, if one of the strings passed is Null, the function ignores the DWORD length field. Typical coding to obtain which file system is being used on the current disk drive is

```
DWORD complen, flags;
char systypename[10];
GetVolumeInformation (NULL, NULL, 0, NULL, &complen, &flags,
                      systypename, sizeof(systypename));
```

If the protected-mode FAT system is in use, which is the Windows 95 default, the return values are "FAT" and 255 for long names. Actually, one byte must be added to store the null terminator, so the long filename could be 256 bytes. In the protected-mode FAT system, the full file specification including drive letter, colon, backslash, path, filename.extension, and the null terminator is 260 bytes. A path specification excluding the filename and extension but including the drive letter, colon, and backslash can be 246 characters, leaving room for the standard 8.3 filename and extension.

When an application creates a file or directory that has a long filename, Windows 95 creates an *alias* for the filename that is in the standard DOS 8.3 format. Note that a blank or 0×20 is a possible character in the 8.3 shortened version. (A blank has been a valid DOS 8.3 character, but many programs do not recognize a blank in the filename.) For example, if a WordPad user enters the document-long filename of "Memo to Bill Jones on 19 April 1995," Windows 95 attempts to create an alias of MEMOTO~1.DOC. If this alias is in use, the system tries ~2 and so on. A DIR command at the DOS prompt shows that the filename DOS must use is MEMOTO~1.DOC, while within Windows 95 the case-sensitive long filename is used.

Considering that the application might be connected to a network volume, the **GetVolumeInformation** function should be used to determine which file system is in use on that drive; allocate the length of filenames and paths accordingly. If dynamic allocation of filename strings cannot be done, then use 256-byte strings for the names and 260 bytes for the full path file specification.

Alternatively, use the defined **MAX_PATH** number of characters in the path as I have done in all of my sample programs here.

Design Rule 35: **Do not assume that a filename and extension are 8 + 3 bytes long. Extensions do not have to contain a maximum of only three characters. Use MAX_PATH.**

Design Rule 36: **Do not assume that there are no blanks in the filename nor that there is only one period. If you need to parse a filename, work from the end of the string backward looking for the first period. If present, it is the separator for name and extension.**

8.5.1 Which File Processing Functions Should We Use?

Since long filenames are likely to be in use under Windows 95, avoid the older Windows 3.1 file processing functions. Instead use the Windows 95 C-style functions that work with long filenames and provide full support for input/output (I/O), asynchronous I/O, find file operations, delete, copy/move, and more.

Once more, since you may need to convert Windows 3.1 applications, let's review how files were often handled under Windows 3.1. The best approach to file handling under Windows 3.1 was to use the Windows 3.1-supplied C-style file-handling functions. These functions were fully capable of using far and huge pointers to global memory. Note that the standard C file functions such as **fread** and **fwrite** all require near pointers that preclude their easy use with global memory addresses. About the only way they could be used would be to input via a local buffer and copy each portion into the global memory buffer. The earlier versions of the C++ iostreams could work with far pointers, but they tended to be slow in execution and had some problems inputting files of about 28K or larger. Hence, frequently applications would use the Windows 3.1 file I/O replacement functions.

```
_lcreat, _lopen, _lclose, _lread, _lwrite, and _llseek
```

Each used a file handle that is an int or HFILE, not a FILE*. The **_lopen** flags are OF_READ, OF_WRITE, OF_READWRITE, or READ, WRITE, and READWRITE. The **_lcreat** flag is normally 0. The **_llseek** flags are SEEK_SET, SEEK_CUR, and SEEK_END. With **_lopen**, the file must exist. With **_lcreat**, if the file exists, it is opened and previous contents are lost; if it does not exist, it is created. Failure to open returns a -1 or HFILE_ERROR.

Under Windows 3.1 when dealing with files 64K or less, it is common to input the entire file with one read. For files larger than 64K, data is often read/written in large blocks, say 32K at a time. Typical coding that must be converted to Windows 95 would be

```
HANDLE      hbuffer;      // class member handle to file buffer
char        filename[81]; // class member filename from open dlg
// local function members
char far *ptrbuffer;      // locked pointer to the file buffer
int         hfile;        // handle to the file
long        filesize;     // file size

hfile = _lopen (filename, OF_READ); // attempt the file open
if (hfile==-1) {                     // open fails
  // display error message
}
else {                               // open successful
  filesize = _llseek (hfile, 0L, SEEK_END); // get file size
  _llseek (hfile, 0L, SEEK_SET);           // set back to start
  // allocate and lock a global buffer area
  hbuffer = GlobalAlloc (GMEM_MOVEABLE, filesize);
  ptrbuffer = GlobalLock (hbuffer);
  _lread (hfile, ptrbuffer, filesize);  // input whole file
  _lclose (hfile);                      // and close file
  GlobalUnlock (hbuffer);               // unlock global buf
}
```

The output function syntax is

```
_lwrite (hfile, ptrbuffer, number of bytes);
```

Both **_lread** and **_lwrite** return the number of bytes entered or written. A return value of 0 from **_lread** indicates the end of file (EOF). A return value *from* **_lwrite** that is different from the number of bytes it was *to* write says the disk is full. There are several file-handling principles that are just as valid under Windows 95.

> ***Design Rule 37:*** **Never open a file in one member function and leave it open for later functions.**

That is, in response to one Windows 95 message, do not open a file and leave it open once processing of that message is complete. Doing so makes it much more difficult for applications to share master files. Should the application crash, not only is the file corrupted, but also memory leaks can result.

> ***Design Rule 38:*** **If the application must work on an individual record basis, the processing cycle should be: open file, seek to the desired record, input/output that record, close the file—all done in one concise series within one member function that responds to one Windows 95 message.**

> ***Design Rule 39:*** **If the entire file should be input into a global memory buffer, then input the file in one read operation.**

The trick of fast-file I/O is to I/O the entire file with one read or write command. Under Windows 3.1, the 64K barrier forced I/O of larger files into an input loop I/Oing large chunks, often 32K, at one time. Under Windows 95, the 64K barrier is gone; input the whole file with one read. This becomes particularly important when inputting large bmp files as we'll do in the next chapter.

 Windows 3.1 Porting Tip: When working with larger buffers of data, the far version of the string and memory functions were used.

     _fstrnnn where nnn are any of the numerous string functions such as:
     _fmemcpy, _fmemchr, _fmemcmp, _fmemicmp, _fmemset

These should be replaced by the normal versions, that is, remove the _f prefix.

8.6 WORKING WITH THE WINDOWS 95 FILE FUNCTIONS

Your practical choices for Windows 95 file operations are to use the new C-style Windows 95 file functions or the MFC **CFile** class or iostreams. (These last two methods are used in chapter 15.) The Windows 95 file functions are ideal and fast for handling binary files. However, if you need the facilities of **fgetchar** or **fgets**, you have to write your own functions or use the file iostreams. In this book, I use the new Windows 95 file functions.

The basic Windows 95 file functions (all of which handle long filenames) include **CreateFile**, **CloseHandle**, **SetFilePointer**, **ReadFile**, and **WriteFile**. Let's examine these one by one. The syntax for **CreateFile** is

```
HANDLE CreateFile (LPCSTR filename, DWORD access, DWORD share,
                   LPSECURITY_ATTRIBUTES security,
                   DWORD create_flags, DWORD attribs,
                   HANDLE filetemplate);
```

This versatile function opens or creates a file, pipe, communications resource, console, or other disk device. If successful, the file handle is returned. If it fails, INVALID_HANDLE_VALUE is returned.

The DWORD **access** identifies the access mode which can include ORed values.

GENERIC_READ   allows read access and sets file pointer

GENERIC_WRITE   allows write access and sets file pointer

The **share** DWORD specifies file-sharing options.

0   prevents file from being shared

FILE_SHARE_READ   other open operations for read can be done

FILE_SHARE_WRITE   other open operations for write can be done

The LPSECURITY_ATTRIBUTES points to the security options. If there are no security options, pass NULL. (This option can be used on Windows NT.)

The **create_flags** DWORD is an important parameter specifying creation details that include

CREATE_NEW   creates a new file; fails if file exists

CREATE_ALWAYS   creates a new file; overwrites existing file

OPEN_EXISTING   opens existing file; fails if file does not exist

OPEN_ALWAYS   opens a file; if it does not exist, creates it

TRUNCATE_EXISTING   opens existing file; resets to contain 0 bytes—must be used with GENERIC_WRITE; fails if file does not exist

The **attribs** DWORD specifies file attributes and includes any combination (all others override the NORMAL attribute).

FILE_ATTRIBUTE_NORMAL   no attributes; only if no others are used

FILE_ATTRIBUTE_ARCHIVE   file has the archive bit on

FILE_ATTRIBUTE_HIDDEN   file has the hidden attribute

FILE_ATTRIBUTE_READONLY   file has the read only attribute

FILE_ATTRIBUTE_SYSTEM   file has the system attribute

The file template option is an advanced option; use NULL for simple applications. For example, suppose that **filename** contains the long filename retrieved from the Open common dialog box. The following would open the file for read operations.

```
HANDLE hfile;
hfile = CreateFile (filename, GENERIC_READ, FILE_SHARE_READ,
                    NULL, OPEN_EXISTING, 0, NULL);
if (hfile == INVALID_HANDLE_VALUE) {
  // display error
}
else {
 // read data
}
```

The following would open the existing file, but, if the file did not exist, a new one would be created with 0 bytes.

```
HANDLE hfile;
hfile = CreateFile (filename, GENERIC_READ, FILE_SHARE_READ,
                    NULL, OPEN_ALWAYS, 0, NULL);
```

Compared to similar older-style coding, this streamlines the operation. The file close operation is done by **CloseHandle**.

```
CloseHandle (hfile);
```

where **hfile** is a HANDLE. The read operation is done with the **ReadFile** function.

```
BOOL ReadFile (HANDLE hfile, LPVOID buffer, DWORD numbytes,
               LPDWORD ptractualbytes, LPOVERLAPPED ol);
```

The HANDLE **hfile** specifies which file is to be read, and it must have been opened with the GENERIC_READ option; **buffer** points to the input area; **numbytes** contains the requested number of bytes to input; **ptractualbytes** points to the DWORD that contains the actual number of bytes that was input. The LPOVERLAPPED is an advanced option and is often NULL. The function returns TRUE on success. However, TRUE is also returned along with 0 bytes read if the file pointer is beyond the current EOF at the time of the read operation—this *is* the normal EOF condition for which we must test. If FALSE is returned, then **GetLastError** returns the cause of the error

```
DWORD GetLastError();
```

where the return value is one of many possibilities. Consult the documentation if you wish to check and display appropriate error messages. For example, if inventory records were being read in one at a time, then the following C-style processing would handle the EOF condition.

```
INV_REC inv_rec[MAX_LIMIT];
int rec_count;
DWORD act_size;
...
rec_count = 0;
while (rec_count < MAX_LIMIT &&
       ReadFile (hfile, &inv_rec[count], sizeof (INV_REC),
```

```
                    &act_size, NULL) && act_size != 0) rec_count++;
if (rec_count == MAX_LIMIT) {
 // too many records
}
```

Using one read to input the entire file would improve performance. To do so, the **SetFilePointer** function is required, and its syntax is somewhat unusual.

```
DWORD SetFilePointer (HANDLE hfile,
                      LONG low_order_num_bytes_to_move,
                      LONG *high_order_num_bytes_to_move,
                      DWORD method_flags);
```

The potential number of bytes to move could be a 64-bit quantity less 2 bytes. This huge number is broken into two long halves, similar to the way two 16-bit values could be placed into one long. Notice that the high-order DWORD is passed by address. This high word serves a dual purpose. Upon invocation, the high DWORD contains the high-order portion of the requested offset. If the function is successful, the high DWORD contains the high-order portion of the current file offset, also a 64-bit quantity, and the DWORD return value contains the low-order part. Note that, if this high-order DWORD pointer is NULL, then the function assumes that the file offset cannot exceed a length of 32-bit less 2 bytes. This would be the most likely case for many applications. The method flag is one of these possibilities.

FILE_BEGIN   the offset is from the file's beginning

FILE_CURRENT   the offset is from the current file position

FILE_END   the offset is from the end of the file

Should the function fail, the return value is 0×FFFFFFFF, which accounts for the "less 2 bytes" in maximum file offsets. Thus, to input the inventory array as fast as possible, use the following sequence:

```
INV_REC *inv_rec;
HANDLE  hinv_rec;
int     rec_count;
DWORD   actsize;
...
// set to 0 bytes from the end of the file, returning the file size
DWORD filesize = SetFilePointer (hfile, 0, NULL, FILE_END);
SetFilePointer (hfile, 0, NULL, FILE_BEGIN);
hinv_rec = GlobalAlloc (GMEM_MOVEABLE, filesize);
if (hinv_rec == 0) {
 // out of memory
}
inv_rec = (INV_REC*) GlobalLock (hinv_rec);
ReadFile (hfile, inv_rec, filesize, &act_size, NULL);
CloseHandle (hfile);
rec_count = (int) (filesize / sizeof (INV_REC));
```

This approach is often used, particularly in the next chapter when bit mapped image files are loaded. One could also encapsulate these operations in a C++ class if desired.

The function to write to a file is coded

```
BOOL WriteFile (HANDLE hfile, LPVOID buffer, DWORD num_bytes,
                LPDWORD act_bytes, LPOVERLAPPED lp);
```

The file must have been opened with the GENERIC_WRITE option; buffer points to the data to be written; **num_bytes** are to be written; and, upon a successful return (TRUE), the DWORD pointed to by **act_bytes** contains the number of bytes actually written. If the value does not equal the requested number of bytes, then it's likely that the floppy disk contains no more space. (The overlapped option is an advanced feature and should be NULL for our use.)

Some other useful functions include setting the EOF marker and flushing internal buffers. **SetEndOfFile** either truncates or extends a file by marking EOF at the current file pointer position. **FlushFileBuffers** commits any internal buffers by writing them to the file.

```
SetEndOfFile (HANDLE hfile);
FlushFileBuffers (Handle hfile);
```

If there is a chance that the file(s) could be shared, the specific records or bytes that are currently in use can be locked and unlocked when the application is finished with them. A 64-bit offset and 64-bit number of bytes to lock are required.

```
LockFile (HANDLE hfile, DWORD offsetlow, DWORD offhigh,
          DWORD num_bytes_low, DWORD num_bytes_high);

UnlockFile (HANDLE hfile, DWORD offsetlow, DWORD offhigh,
          DWORD num_bytes_low, DWORD num_bytes_high);
```

Functions exist to handle directory/folder operations and to find, delete, and rename files. Consult the documentation for these.

8.7 SIMPLE REPLACEMENT FUNCTIONS FOR FGETS AND FPUTS

A more immediate problem exists. I wish to input and process lines for a very simple text editor to illustrate the common dialogs, global memory, and the file system. So let's examine a **FileGetLine** function that emulates **fgets**, which inputs a line into a null terminated string. Assume that the function is passed an opened file (HFILE) and a pointer to an array of strings of length MAX_LEN. The basic operation is to input single bytes via **ReadFile** until either EOF or a carriage return and line feed is encountered. The <CRLF> codes are nearly always found in pairs. A null terminator is to be inserted upon entering the <CR> code. All line feed codes are ignored or bypassed. Finally, what do I do should I encounter a line that exceeds MAX_LINE? Here, I have chosen to store only the first 132 characters positioning the file at the carriage return or EOF point.

The following is an implementation of **FileGetLine** that returns the original string's address if all is OK or the NULL pointer for EOF.

```
char*  FileGetLine (HANDLE hfile, char *ptrline) {
```

```
   DWORD asize;
   char *start = ptrline;        // save return value
   int I = 0;                    // I = number characters inputted
   while (ReadFile (hfile, ptrline, 1, &asize, NULL) && asize != 0) {
    if (*ptrline == 0x0D) {      // if this char is <CR>
     *ptrline = 0;               // then insert null terminator
     return start;               // and return the line
    }
    if (*ptrline != 0x0A) {      // <LF> linefeeds are ignored
     ptrline++;                  // insert char - point to next slot
     i++;                        // and inc char count
     if (i>=MAX_LEN) i--;        // fix up for lines that exceed max
    }                            // len => ignore rest of the chars
   }
   if (ptrline==start) return NULL;  // unable to get a byte, so send EOF
   *ptrline = 0;                 // EOF but have at least 1 char, so
   return start;                 // insert terminator,return the line
  }
```

Next, we need a version of **fputs** to write out a line inserting the <CRLF> codes for the null terminators. **FilePutLine** is passed the same two parameters, the opened file HANDLE and the address of the string. Upon encountering the null terminator, it inserts the 2-byte codes representing the <CRLF>. The only complexity arises from the possibility of a full disk error. Thus, successful writes return the original string pointer and NULL for an error situation.

```
  char* FilePutLine (HANDLE hfile, char *ptrline) {
   DWORD asize;
   char *start = ptrline;        // save return value
   char cr = 0x0D;               // value to insert for <CR>
   char lf = 0x0A;               // value to insert for <LF>
   while (*ptrline!=0) {         // loop for all actual chars in the line
    // write the byte, but if I/O fails, return error signal
    if (!WriteFile (hfile, ptrline, 1, &asize, NULL) || asize==0)
     return NULL;
    ptrline++;                   // point to next char
   }
   // insert the carriage return/line feed pair
   if (!WriteFile (hfile, &cr, 1, &asize, NULL) || asize==0) return NULL;
   if (!WriteFile (hfile, &lf, 1, &asize, NULL) || asize==0) return NULL;
   return start;                 // all ok, so return good write
  }
```

8.8 MFC ENCAPSULATION OF THE WINDOWS 95 COMMON DIALOGS

Under MFC, **CFileDialog** encapsulates both the File|Open and File|SaveAs dialogs. Similarly, the MFC has **CPrintDialog**, **CFontDialog**, **CColorDialog**, and **CFind-ReplaceDialog**. To make use of the Windows 95 versions of the common dialogs, add two includes to the precompiled headers file stdafx.h; for the dialogs add afxdlgs.h and also add afxcmn.h for the new common controls. Let's begin with the **CFileDialog** class.

8.8.1 The CFileDialog Class

The file open action is frequently done and is found in nearly every application. It involves many interrelated actions and many dialog controls. Figure 8.1 shows the File Open dialog box.

Before coding the dialog constructor, you should understand several key parameters since these are used to define the actions we require of the common dialog box. One parameter is the desired *flags*; among the more frequently used flags are

OFN_ALLOWMULTISELECT	allows multiple selections in FileName list box
OFN_FILEMUSTEXIST	only allows entry of file names that exist
OFN_LONGNAMES	allows long file names
OFN_PATHMUSTEXIST	only allows path entries that exist
OFN_OVERWRITEPROMPT	save—prompt if overwriting a file

The *file filter* is a string that defines one or more pairs of filters. They appear in the lower-left combo box. Each filter contains a text description followed by the DOS pattern, which when selected provides the files in the left list box. The two are separated by a "|" character. For example, "All Text Files (*.TXT)|*.*" would describe all text files and provide the DOS filter of *.TXT. Multiple pairs can be coded

```
All Files (*.*)|*.*|All Text Files (*.TXT)|*.TXT|All PCX Files (*.PCX)|*.PCX
```

The *custom filter* is normally null or 0. The *initial directory string* can specify the drive and path to use when the dialog opens; otherwise the dialog uses the current subdirectory. Remember to include a double \\ in the strings: "\\DOS" for example.

To use the **CFileDialog**, an automatic storage instance of the class is allocated by the constructor.

```
CFileDialog (BOOL open_or_save, // TRUE for Open, FALSE for SaveAs
             LPSTR default_extension,
             LPSTR initial_filename,
             DWORD flags,
             LPSTR filter,
             CWnd *ptrparent);
```

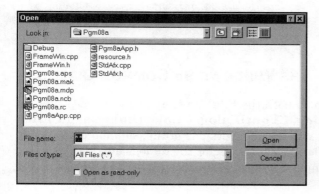

Fig. 8.1 The Windows 95 File Open Common Dialog Box

The BOOL determines whether the Open (TRUE) or SaveAs (FALSE) version is used. The **default_extension** string is appended to user entries when the user omits entering one. The **initial_filename** string, if present, appears in the Filename edit box upon dialog launching. Note that, if either is NULL, then no extensions are added or no string appears when the dialog begins. The **flags** ORed identifiers are important and differ between Open and SaveAs. For Open, we commonly use

```
OFN_FILEMUSTEXIST | OFN_PATHMUSTEXIST | OFN_LONGNAMES
```

which indicates that the file and path must exist and that the new long filenames are desired if the device supports them. For SaveAs, we commonly use

```
OFN_HIDEREADONLY | OFN_OVERWRITEPROMPT | OFN_LONGNAMES
```

which indicates that no read-only files can be altered, that the Over Write Prompt is desired, and that the new long filenames are desired, if the device supports them.

The filter is often a long string of pairs of file type descriptions for the user and Dir extensions to retrieve them. The two items are separated by a vertical bar (|), and two successive bars (||) indicate the end of the pairs. The following example uses a filter that shows the following in the File Types combo box.

```
All Files (*.*)
CPP Files (*.CPP)
C Files (*.C)
Header Files (*.H*)
```

Assume that **filename** is a protected class member; the coding to select a file is as follows:

```
char filename[MAX_PATH];

CFileDialog filedlg (
        TRUE,    // use Open dialog
            "*.CPP", // default extension
            "*.*",   // current file name
        OFN_FILEMUSTEXIST | OFN_PATHMUSTEXIST | OFN_LONGNAMES,
        "All Files (*.*)|*.*|CPP Files (*.CPP)|*.CPP|C Files"
        " (*.C)|*.C|Header Files (*.H*)|*.H*||",
        this);
if (filedlg.DoModal () == IDOK) {  // user has chosen a file, so
 strcpy (filename, filedlg.GetPathName ()); // extract its filename
// attempt to open the file
HANDLE hfile = CreateFile (filename, GENERIC_READ, FILE_SHARE_READ,
             NULL,OPEN_EXISTING, FILE_ATTRIBUTE_NORMAL, NULL);
if (hfile==INVALID_HANDLE_VALUE) { // open failed,display error msg
 DisplayMsg (IDS_MSG_ERROR, IDS_MSG_FILEOPEN, MB_OK | MB_ICONSTOP);
 havefile = FALSE;                 // indicate no file
 return;
}
```

The dialog is executed using **DoModal** and, if IDOK is returned, a successful choice has been made. Several member functions exist to acquire that portion of the user entry we desire; all return a **CString** and the comments indicate what

portion of the user entry is returned. Assume that the user has entered
D:\PGMS\PROBLEM1.CPP.

```
CString GetPathName  (); // returns D:\PGMS\PROBLEM1.CPP
CString GetFileName  (); // returns PROBLEM1
CString GetFileExt   (); // returns CPP
CString GetFileTitle (); // returns PROBLEM1.CPP
```

In the above example, the full path with filename is copied into a data member **file-name** so that user changes can be later saved.

8.8.2 The CFontDialog

Allowing the user to change fonts introduces another layer of complexity to text displays in the **OnPaint** function. Figure 8.2 shows the Windows 95 choose font common dialog box.

Until now, when the application begins, the average character dimensions were found and used to control text displays. Since no font changes were allowed, these could be retrieved once and left alone. If you are going to allow font changes, then we must take a more dynamic approach. We can still set up the application normally as before, assuming the initial font as the standard system font. However, if the user is allowed to change fonts, we need to add two new members to the class; in the constructor, these would be initialized. Construction of a font in paint and similar functions requires two basic items: the font color as a COLORREF or RGB-style structure and a copy of the Windows 95 LOGFONT data structure that contains all of the basic information from which a font can be constructed. Both items are supplied by the common dialog, and our copies are defined as protected members.

```
LOGFONT  *ptrlogfont;    // user selected font
COLORREF fontcolor;      // the font's color
```

There are numerous fields in the LOGFONT structure, and in chapter 10 they are examined in some detail. For normal display usage, we need not be concerned with what information the structure contains, merely that it defines the user's font choice.

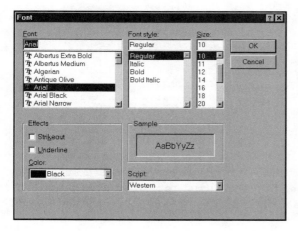

Fig. 8.2 Windows 95 Choose Font Common Dialog Box

The **CFontDialog** is often allocated in the heap using **new**. The constructor of the common dialog appears as

```
CFontDialog (LPLOGFONT ptrinitial_logfont, DWORD flags,
             CDC *ptrprinterdc, CWnd *ptrparent);
```

The first time the application responds to a font change menu command, the default font is likely in use. By passing NULL the first time, no default font is selected in the dialog. On subsequent requests the current font in use can be passed as the first parameter, and that font becomes the initial selected font in the dialog. The flags are important and determine what broad categories of fonts are to be available in the dialog box. For fonts that are going to be used for display purposes, the flags should be set to a combination of the following:

CF_FORCEFONTEXIST   gives an error if user selects a nonexistent font

CF_SCREENFONTS   lists only screen fonts (not printer)

CF_TTONLY   TrueType fonts

CF_EFFECTS   permits underline, etc.

These flags identify the category of fonts (screen as opposed to printer fonts) and that the requested font must exist. The **ptrprinterdc** should be NULL for screen display fonts. Once the dialog is allocated, the internal **m_cf** structure containing the values for the dialog controls is instantiated. The member field **rgbColors** contains the current color in use. **GetColor** retrieves the color selected by the user, while **m_lf** contains the pointer to the LOGFONT structure of the selected font. Initially, it would be black; should the user select yellow, we should initialize the dialog with yellow. The following shows how we respond to the menu item Choose Font depending upon whether this is the first selection or all subsequent selections.

```
CfontDialog  *ptrdlg;
if (ptrlogfont) ptrdlg = new CFontDialog (ptrlogfont,
    CF_EFFECTS | CF_SCREENFONTS | CF_FORCEFONTEXIST, NULL, this);
else ptrdlg = new CFontDialog (NULL,
    CF_EFFECTS | CF_SCREENFONTS | CF_FORCEFONTEXIST, NULL, this);
ptrdlg->m_cf.rgbColors = fontcolor;   // install current color
if (ptrdlg->DoModal () == IDOK) {      // get user font choice
 // if this is the first selection, allocate a new LOGFONT
 if (!ptrlogfont) ptrlogfont = new LOGFONT;
 // in all cases, copy the user's selection
 memcpy (ptrlogfont, &(ptrdlg->m_lf), sizeof (LOGFONT));
 fontcolor = ptrdlg->GetColor ();      // save color choice
 GetAvgCharDims ();                     // get new average char dims
 ...
}
delete ptrdlg;
```

Important note: Our helper function **GetAvgCharDims** must be reinvoked to acquire the altered character dimensions. Next, in the **OnPaint** function or any other time that a DC is obtained, the font must be selected into that DC. The following illustrates how a font is created and installed in **GetAvgCharDims** using the **CFont** class and its member function **CreateFontIndirect** which builds the font from a LOGFONT structure.

```
void        FrameWin::GetAvgCharDims () {
  TEXTMETRIC  tm;  // set the system font's characteristics in tm
  CClientDC *ptrdc = new CClientDC (this);  // acquire a DC
  CFont      *ptroldfont;
  CFont      *ptrfont;
  if (ptrlogfont) {                        // install any user font
   ptrfont = new CFont ();
   ptrfont->CreateFontIndirect (ptrlogfont);
   // install new font and save old font
   ptroldfont = ptrdc->SelectObject (ptrfont);
  }
  ptrdc->GetTextMetrics (&tm);             // get the font information
  if (ptrlogfont) {
   ptrdc->SelectObject (ptroldfont);     // reinstall old font
   delete ptrfont;                       // delete new font
  }
  delete ptrdc;                            // delete the dc
  // calculate average character parameters
  avg_char_width = tm.tmAveCharWidth;
  avg_char_height = tm.tmHeight + tm.tmExternalLeading;
  avg_caps_width = (tm.tmPitchAndFamily & 1?3:2)*avg_char_width / 2;
}
```

Similarly, in **OnPaint**, the font and its color must be installed.

```
void        FrameWin::OnPaint () {
  CPaintDC  dc(this);
  CFont     *ptroldfont;                   // place to save old font
  CFont     *ptrfont;                      // our new font
  if (ptrlogfont) {                        // install any user font
   ptrfont = new CFont ();
   // create the font from LOGFONT
   ptrfont->CreateFontIndirect (ptrlogfont);
  // install new font and save old font
   ptroldfont = dc.SelectObject (ptrfont);
  }
  dc.SetTextColor (fontcolor);             // install font color
  dc.SetBkMode (TRANSPARENT);              // set so background color shows
  ...
  if (ptrlogfont) {                        // deselect and delete user font
   dc.SelectObject (ptroldfont);
   delete ptrfont;
  }
}
```

If the application expects to need to reconstruct the same font frequently, make the **CFont**'s instance, **ptrfont**, be a protected member. The font would be created one time in **GetAvgCharDims** which must be invoked anyway right after a successful user font change. This would make font handling a more efficient process.

I have left the **CColorDialog** as an exercise for you.

8.8.3 The CFindReplaceDialog

The **CFindReplaceDialog** is more complex, encapsulating Find, Find Next, and Replace operations into one dialog class. This is a modeless dialog requiring some form of ongoing communication between the dialog and the parent class. Figure 8.3 shows the Windows 95 Find and Replace common dialogs.

The dialog issues registered messages to notify the parent of Find/Replace requests of the user. **ON_REGISTERED_MESSAGE** is added to the parent's message response map table. This chapter presents the basic mechanics of the dialog construction and communication. In a later chapter, we shall see how to actually perform the Find and Replace operations.

In the parent class, here FrameWin, define three static members. **ptrfind-replacedlg** is a pointer to the modeless Find/Replace dialog that is initialized to NULL. In response to the menu command request for a Find/Replace operation, if this pointer is not NULL, the dialog is on-screen and no action is required. If not, allocate an instance of the common dialog and launch it. The static member **bIsReplaceDialog** identifies whether the Find/Replace dialog is currently active. Finally, the last static member, **nFindMsg**, is a UINT representing our unique message ID provided by Windows 95 for communication between the common dialog and our frame class. Thus, in the FrameWin class definition, define these three as

```
static UINT nFindMsg;
static        CFindReplaceDialog *ptrfindreplacedlg;
static        bIsReplaceDialog;
```

Next, in the cpp file, the three static members must be defined and initialized. The key to obtaining a registered message is the Windows 95 API function **Register-WindowMessage** and the MFC identifier FINDMSGSTRING.

```
UINT FrameWin::nFindMsg = ::RegisterWindowMessage (FINDMSGSTRING);
CFindReplaceDialog *FrameWin::ptrfindreplacedlg = NULL;
BOOL FrameWin::bIsReplaceDialog = FALSE;
```

The message map must include the **ON_REGISTERED_MESSAGE** indicating which registered message goes to which member function.

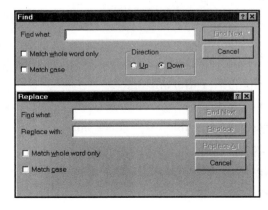

Fig. 8.3 Windows 95 Find and Replace Common Dialogs

```
BEGIN_MESSAGE_MAP(FrameWin, CframeWnd)
...
ON_REGISTERED_MESSAGE(nFindMsg, CmFindReplaceHelper)
...
END_MESSAGE_MAP()
```

And the prototype for a registered message response function is of the form

```
afx_msg LONG  CmFindReplaceHelper (UINT, LONG);
```

To launch the Find common dialog, after allocating a new instance of the common dialog, invoke its **Create** function. To activate this instance, send the dialog the WM_INITDIALOG message and it is then operational.

```
void        FrameWin::CmEditFind () {
 if (ptrfindreplacedlg) return;        // avoids having both on screen
 ptrfindreplacedlg = new CFindReplaceDialog (); // allocate new dlg
 bIsReplaceDialog = FALSE;
 ptrfindreplacedlg->Create (TRUE,    // find box only
                            NULL,    // string = what to find
                            NULL,    // string = replace with this
                            FR_DOWN, // find dlg flags
                            this);
 ptrfindreplacedlg->SendMessage (WM_INITDIALOG); // show modeless dlg
 }
```

The first parameter to **Create** is used to separate a Find request from a Replace operation. For simple initializations, pass NULL to the next two parameters which are the initial string to Find and a Replace With string, which obviously is not needed for a Find. You could get fancy and pick up any used selection in your display and pass that as the initial Find string. But obtaining user selections is involved directly with Cut/Paste operations and is discussed in chapter 13. The flag is usually FR_DOWN, but other possibilities include

FR_DOWN	search down—default is to search up
FR_WHOLEWORD	match whole word is checked
FR_MATCHCASE	search is case sensitive
FR_NOMATCHCASE	search is case insensitive
FR_HIDEMATCHCASE	hides the match case check box
FR_HIDEWHOLEWORD	hides the whole word only check box
FR_HIDEUPDOWN	hides the up/down radio buttons
FR_NOUPDOWN	disables the up/down radio buttons
FR_NOWHOLEWORD	disables the match whole word check box
FR_FINDNEXT	finds next occurrence of string lpstrFindWhat
FR_REPLACE	replaces lpstrFindWhat with lpstrReplaceWith
FR_REPLACEALL	replaces all occurrences

Since the user could terminate the application while the dialog is activated, we must send the dialog notification that it is to terminate. This is accomplished by sending it the IDCANCEL message as if the user had pressed the Cancel button.

```
void        FrameWin::OnDestroy () {
 CframeWnd::OnDestroy();
 ...
 if (ptrfindreplacedlg)
  ptrfindreplacedlg->SendMessage (WM_COMMAND, IDCANCEL, OL);
 ...
}
```

Before examining how the Find request is processed, let's examine how the dialog is launched in response to a Replace and Find Next menu choice. For the Replace operation, the only change is the first parameter to the **Create** function; it is now FALSE.

```
void        FrameWin::CmEditReplace () {
 if (ptrfindreplacedlg) return;        // avoids having both on screen
 ptrfindreplacedlg = new CFindReplaceDialog ();
 bIsReplaceDialog = TRUE;
 ptrfindreplacedlg->Create (FALSE,    // find and replace box
                            NULL,     // string = what to find
                            NULL,     // string = replace with this
                            FR_DOWN,  // find dlg flags
                            this);
 ptrfindreplacedlg->SendMessage (WM_INITDIALOG); // show modeless dlg
}
```

For Find Next requests, if the dialog is active, the dialog's **FindNext** function must be invoked.

```
void        FrameWin::CmEditFindNext () {
 if (ptrfindreplacedlg && bIsReplaceDialog) return; // replace in force
 if (!ptrfindreplacedlg) {       // if find dialog is not active, then
  ptrfindreplacedlg = new CFindReplaceDialog (); // allocate new dlg
  bIsReplaceDialog = FALSE;
  ptrfindreplacedlg->Create (TRUE,    // find box only
                             NULL,     // string = what to find
                             NULL,     // string = replace with this
                             FR_DOWN,  // find dlg flags
                             this);
  ptrfindreplacedlg->SendMessage (WM_INITDIALOG); // show modeless dlg
 }
 // if is active, invoke its find next operation
 else ptrfindreplacedlg->FindNext ();
}
```

Whenever the user makes a choice and clicks on a button, the common dialog sends a registered message to the FrameWin—the parent. The first action in the message handler must be to get a pointer to the current Find/Replace dialog box so we can access its member functions and public data areas. This is done using **GetNotifier**, passing it the **lparam** value received by the registered message. Three member functions return TRUE indicating if that option is the active one: **FindNext**, **Replace-Current**, and **ReplaceAll**. Finally, when the dialog is about to terminate, the registered message handler once again is invoked, sending FrameWin a notification of termination message; member function **IsTerminating** returns TRUE if the dialog is ending. If the dialog is about to terminate, we can then delete the dialog and reset our main pointer to the modeless dialog back to NULL.

```
LONG      FrameWin::CmFindReplaceHelper (UINT wparam, LONG lparam) {
  CFindReplaceDialog  *ptrdlg = CFindReplaceDialog::GetNotifier (lparam);
  if (ptrdlg->FindNext ()) {
   // use member functions to handle find process
  }
  else if (ptrdlg->ReplaceCurrent ()) {
   // use member functions to handle replace this one
  }
  else if (ptrdlg->ReplaceAll ()) {
   // use member functions to replace all occurrences
  }
  else if (ptrdlg->IsTerminating ()) { // is dialog box closing?
   delete ptrfindreplacedlg;          // delete this instance
   ptrfindreplacedlg = NULL;          // and set to none in use
   }
  return 0;
}
```

There are several member functions that assist us in implementing the Find/Replace request. These are discussed in a later chapter. Here, only the shell is implemented.

8.9 PGM08a: HANDLING ALL OF THE FILE MENU CHOICES

We are now in a position to handle all of the File menu choices (New, Open, Close, Save, SaveAs) dummied out in the previous menus chapter (chapter 6) (printing is handled in chapters 10 and 15). First, we need a global memory buffer area in which to enter the text file. Ideally, one would design a scheme by which the file size to be entered is limited only by the total amount of global memory available. However, such schemes are not the easiest for a beginning example. Therefore, I place some severe restrictions on the algorithm that makes the general operation quite easy to follow. Once you have the basics down, feel free to expand the approach to a relatively unlimited one. Figure 8.4 shows Pgm08a in action.

The restrictions are as follows:

1. For convenience in handling the display in the **OnPaint** function, I use a line as the basic unit of input. Since some lines are longer than 80 characters, I assign an arbitrary upper line length limit of 132 characters. Any line longer will be truncated.

2. The lines will be stored in one array in global memory. However, I limit the total amount of memory for the array at less than 64K.

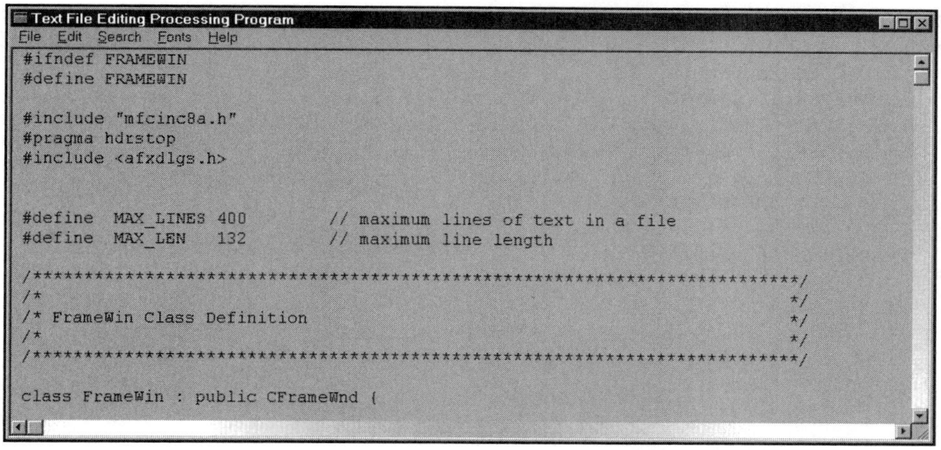

Fig. 8.4 Pgm08a with Header File Opened in a Courier New Fixed Font

3. As a combined result of 1 and 2, an enormous amount of memory is wasted, since most lines will be close to 132 characters. However, the simplification aids us in understanding how to process the **OnPaint** and later the scroll bars.

Thus, the two defines:

```
#define   MAX_LINES 400          // maximum lines of text in a file
#define   MAX_LEN   132          // maximum line length
```

The resource file looks much as it did in chapter 6. There is an accelerator table for the Edit menu items. And in the resource.h file, I used the (WM_USER + n) method for the menu ID numbers, just for variety.

8.9.1 Listing for File: Pgm08a.rc—Excerpts

```
...
MAINMENU MENU DISCARDABLE
BEGIN
    POPUP "&File"
    BEGIN
        MENUITEM "&New",                    CM_FILENEW
        MENUITEM "&Open...",                CM_FILEOPEN
        MENUITEM "&Close",                  CM_FILECLOSE, GRAYED
        MENUITEM SEPARATOR
        MENUITEM "&Save",                   CM_FILESAVE, GRAYED
        MENUITEM "Save &As...",             CM_FILESAVEAS, GRAYED
        MENUITEM SEPARATOR
        MENUITEM "&Print...",               CM_FILEPRINT, GRAYED
        MENUITEM "P&rint Setup...",         CM_FILEPRINTERSETUP, GRAYED
        MENUITEM SEPARATOR
        MENUITEM "E&xit\tAlt+F4",           CM_EXIT
    END
```

```
    POPUP "&Edit"
    BEGIN
        MENUITEM "&Undo\tAlt+BkSp",              CM_EDITUNDO, GRAYED
        MENUITEM SEPARATOR
        MENUITEM "Cu&t\tShift+Del",              CM_EDITCUT, GRAYED
        MENUITEM "&Copy\tCtrl+Ins",              CM_EDITCOPY, GRAYED
        MENUITEM "&Paste\tShift+Ins",            CM_EDITPASTE, GRAYED
        MENUITEM SEPARATOR
        MENUITEM "Clear &All\tCtrl+Del",         CM_EDITCLEAR, GRAYED
        MENUITEM "&Delete\tDel",                 CM_EDITDELETE, GRAYED
    END
    POPUP "&Search"
    BEGIN
        MENUITEM "&Find...",                     CM_EDITFIND, GRAYED
        MENUITEM "&Replace...",                  CM_EDITREPLACE, GRAYED
        MENUITEM "&Next\aF3",                    CM_EDITFINDNEXT, GRAYED
    END
    POPUP "&Fonts"
    BEGIN
        MENUITEM "&Font Change",                 CM_FONTCHANGE
    END
    POPUP "&Help"
    BEGIN
        MENUITEM "&About...",                    CM_HELPABOUT
    END
END

MAINMENU ACCELERATORS MOVEABLE PURE
BEGIN
    VK_DELETE,        CM_EDITCUT,               VIRTKEY, SHIFT
    VK_INSERT,        CM_EDITCOPY,              VIRTKEY, CONTROL
    VK_INSERT,        CM_EDITPASTE,             VIRTKEY, SHIFT
    VK_DELETE,        CM_EDITCLEAR,             VIRTKEY, CONTROL
    VK_BACK,          CM_EDITUNDO,              VIRTKEY, ALT
    VK_F3,            CM_EDITFINDNEXT,          VIRTKEY
END

IDD_ABOUT DIALOG DISCARDABLE  48, 113, 200, 92
STYLE DS_MODALFRAME | WS_POPUP | WS_VISIBLE | WS_CAPTION | WS_SYSMENU
CAPTION "Help - About Pgm08a"
FONT 8, "MS Sans Serif"
BEGIN
    DEFPUSHBUTTON     "OK",IDOK,72,70,50,14
    LTEXT             "by Vic Broquard",IDC_STATIC,70,42,57,8
    LTEXT             "Pgm08a - Common Dialogs, Memory, Files",IDC_STATIC,33,
                      20,228,11
    GROUPBOX          "",IDC_STATIC,28,10,141,50
END

STRINGTABLE DISCARDABLE
BEGIN
    IDS_MAINTITLE       "Text File Editing Processing Program"
    IDS_WINNAME         "EditPgm"
    IDS_INITFONT        "System Font"
    IDS_MSG_NOTSAVE     "File has not been saved. Save File now?"
```

```
        IDS_MSG_QUIT          "Do you want to quit the application?"
        IDS_MSG_QUERY         "Query?"
        IDS_MSG_ERROR         "Edit Program - Error Message"
        IDS_MSG_NOMEM         "Out of memory. Close app. Free some memory. Try again."
        IDS_MSG_FILEERR       "File Save Error. Try File Save As with valid filename."
        IDS_MSG_FILEOPEN      "File Open Error. Try again with valid filename."
        IDS_MSG_NOBAR         "No memory for scrollbars. Free some memory and try again."
        IDS_MSG_FILEWRT       "File Save Error. Output failed - disk full. Try new disk."
END
...
```

8.9.2 Listing for File: resource.h—Excerpts

```
...
#define CM_FILENEW            (WM_USER + 102)
#define CM_FILEOPEN           (WM_USER + 103)
#define CM_FILECLOSE          (WM_USER + 104)
#define CM_FILESAVE           (WM_USER + 105)
#define CM_FILESAVEAS         (WM_USER + 106)
#define CM_FILEPRINT          (WM_USER + 107)
#define CM_FILEPRINTERSETUP   (WM_USER + 108)
#define CM_EXIT               (WM_USER + 109)
#define CM_EDITUNDO           (WM_USER + 110)
#define CM_EDITCUT            (WM_USER + 111)
#define CM_EDITCOPY           (WM_USER + 112)
#define CM_EDITPASTE          (WM_USER + 113)
#define CM_EDITDELETE         (WM_USER + 114)
#define CM_EDITCLEAR          (WM_USER + 115)
#define CM_EDITFIND           (WM_USER + 116)
#define CM_EDITREPLACE        (WM_USER + 117)
#define CM_EDITFINDNEXT       (WM_USER + 118)
#define CM_HELPABOUT          (WM_USER + 119)
#define CM_FONTCHANGE         (WM_USER + 120)

#define IDS_MAINTITLE     2000   // frame window's title
#define IDS_WINNAME       2001   // GetClassName's wndclass name
#define IDS_INITFONT      2002   // name system font
#define IDS_MSG_NOTSAVE   2003   // file not saved msg
#define IDS_MSG_QUIT      2004   // quit application query msg
#define IDS_MSG_QUERY     2005   // title of quit query messagebox
#define IDS_MSG_ERROR     2006   // error has occurred
#define IDS_MSG_NOMEM     2007   // out of memory
#define IDS_MSG_FILEERR   2008   // file save error
#define IDS_MSG_FILEOPEN  2009   // file open error
#define IDS_MSG_NOBAR     2010   // no scroll bars error
#define IDS_MSG_FILEWRT   2011   // file save error - I/O fail
...
```

8.9.3 Listing for File: FrameWin.h—Excerpts

```
...
#define   MAX_LINES 400         // maximum lines of text in a file
#define   MAX_LEN   132         // maximum line length
```

```
/*******************************************************************************/
/*                                                                          */
/* FrameWin Class Definition                                                */
/*                                                                          */
/*******************************************************************************/

class FrameWin : public CFrameWnd {

/*******************************************************************************/
/*                                                                          */
/* Class Data Members                                                       */
/*                                                                          */
/*******************************************************************************/

protected:

int     height;          // current client window height in pixels
int     width;           // current client window width in pixels

int     avg_caps_width;  // average capital letter width
int     avg_char_width;  // average character width
int     avg_char_height; // average character height

BOOL    havefile;        // when TRUE, we have opened or have begun a new file
BOOL    havesaved;       // when TRUE, we have saved the existent file
char    filename[260];   // name of the file

HANDLE  hbuffer;         // handle to global memory lines array buffer
int     numlines;        // number of lines in the file

LOGFONT  *ptrlogfont;    // user selected font
COLORREF fontcolor;      // the font's color

protected:

int     num_lines_per_page; // used for scrolling
int     max_vscroll_lines;
int     current_top_line;
int     num_lines_to_scroll;
int     num_chars_per_line;
int     max_hscroll_chars;
int     current_start_col;
int     num_chars_to_scroll;

static UINT nFindMsg;
static     CFindReplaceDialog *ptrfindreplacedlg;
static     bIsReplaceDialog;

/*******************************************************************************/
/*                                                                          */
/* Class Functions:                                                         */
/*                                                                          */
/*******************************************************************************/

public:
            FrameWin (CWnd*, const char*); // constructor
            ~FrameWin () {}                 // destructor

protected:
```

```
        int    DisplayMsg (UINT, UINT, UINT);  // loads and displays MessageBox
afx_msg void   OnPaint ();                      // paint the window - WM_PAINT
afx_msg int    OnCreate (LPCREATESTRUCT);       // construct window, avg char dims

afx_msg void   OnClose ();                      // determines if app can quit yet
afx_msg void   OnSize (UINT, int, int);         // process window resize
afx_msg void   OnDestroy ();                    // remove allocated menus
afx_msg void   OnRButtonDown (UINT, CPoint);    // pop up edit menu
afx_msg void   OnKeyDown (UINT, UINT, UINT);    // keybd scroller interface
afx_msg void   OnHScroll (UINT, UINT, CScrollBar*); // handle scrolling
afx_msg void   OnVScroll (UINT, UINT, CScrollBar*);

// utility functions
void           SaveCheck ();                    // query user about saving file
void           GetAvgCharDims ();               // get average char dims for font
char*          FileGetLine (HANDLE, char*);     // file input lines
char*          FilePutLine (HANDLE, char*);     // file output lines
void           SaveFile ();                     // save the file
void           SetOurScrollRange ();            // set scroll bar ranges

// command processors
afx_msg void   CmExit ();
afx_msg void   CmFontChange ();                 // get new font
afx_msg void   CmFileNew ();                    // start a new file
afx_msg void   CmFileOpen ();                   // open existing file
afx_msg void   CmFileClose ();                  // close the file
afx_msg void   CmFileSave ();                   // save the file with same name
afx_msg void   CmFileSaveAs ();                 // save with new name
afx_msg void   CmFilePrint ();                  // print the file
afx_msg void   CmFilePrinterSetup ();           // set up the printer
afx_msg void   CmEditUndo ();                   // undo last change
...
// command enablers
afx_msg void   CmEnableFileClose (CCmdUI*);     // enable/disable FileClose
...
afx_msg void   CmEnableEditFindNext (CCmdUI*);// enable/disable FindNext
// process find/replace acts
afx_msg LONG   CmFindReplaceHelper (UINT, LONG);
...
```

Rather than reproduce the entire FrameWin.cpp file which is now quite lengthy, let's examine the main sequences. In the constructor, we need to initialize various members and allocate the global memory.

```
ptrlogfont = NULL;             // set no font loaded
fontcolor = RGB (0, 0, 0);     // set default font color black
... create the window
havefile  = FALSE;             // indicates no file loaded yet
havesaved = FALSE;             // indicates file not saved
numlines = 0;                  // set total lines in file to none
// allocate a file input buffer
hbuffer   = GlobalAlloc (GMEM_MOVEABLE, (long)(MAX_LINES)*MAX_LEN);
if (hbuffer==NULL) {  // error, not enough memory for buffer
  DisplayMsg (IDS_MSG_ERROR, IDS_MSG_NOMEM, MB_OK | MB_ICONSTOP);
  SendMessage (WM_CLOSE);
```

```
}
```

Check **hbuffer** for NULL to see if the request failed or not. One annoying action is coding the numerous message boxes that display the various messages. For convenience, I have defined a helper function called **DisplayMsg** that is passed the two message IDs and the ORed flags; it loads the strings and returns the return value from the **MessageBox** function.

```
int      FrameWin::DisplayMsg (UINT id1, UINT id2, UINT flags) {
  CString msg1;
  CString msg2;
  msg1.LoadString (id1);
  msg2.LoadString (id2);
  return MessageBox (msg2, msg1, flags);
}
```

If you do not like mine, feel free to use MFC's **AfxMessageBox** function.

Next, the member function that responds to the File I New menu selection would need to set **numlines** to 0 and set the **filename** to a null string.

```
void     CmFileNew () {
 // if file not saved, ask user&handle
 if (havefile && !havesaved) SaveCheck();
 strcpy (filename, "");              // set no filename
 numlines = 0;                       // set no lines yet
 havefile  = TRUE;                   // set have a new file
 havesaved = FALSE;                  // that has not been saved
 ... // ignore scrolling for now
 Invalidate();                       // and clear screen

}
```

Notice that no provision whatsoever is made to actually enter any data or modify any data. The member function that responds to the File I Open menu selection is more complex. The common Open File dialog box is executed to obtain the new filename. If the user clicks OK, then we can retrieve the filename and go on to open the file and enter the lines. In this example, several filters are provided for *.C, *.CPP, and all types of header files *.H*.

```
void     CmFileOpen () {
 // if file not saved, ask user&handle
 if (havefile && !havesaved) SaveCheck();
 ... open dialog box coding just as previously shown goes here
 // file is open, so input file into the buffer
 char *ptrlines;
 ptrlines = (char*) GlobalLock (hbuffer); // lock global buffer addr
 int i = 0;                               // count lines inputted
 // input lines until hit max number in buffer or EOF
 while (i<MAX_LINES && FileGetLine (hfile, ptrlines) != NULL) {
  i++;
  ptrlines += MAX_LEN;   // point to next line in buffer
 }
 numlines = i;           // set number of lines in the file
 CloseHandle (hfile);    // close file
```

```
GlobalUnlock (hbuffer);    // unlock global memory
havefile = TRUE;           // set have a file
havesaved = FALSE;         // set file not yet saved
... // ignore scrolling for a while longer

Invalidate ();             // and display new file
```

In processing the file, we lock global memory and go on to read in the file using the **FileGetLine** function, halting further entry if an attempt is made to enter more lines than our array can hold. When done, **numlines** contains the total number of lines in the array. In case there is a file already opened that has not been saved, the **SaveCheck** function is invoked. Its purpose is to ask the user whether the file is to be saved. If it is to be saved, then, if the file was a new one (i.e., no filename yet), send the **FileSaveAs** message. Otherwise send the **FileSave** message.

```
void       FrameWin::SaveCheck () {
 // based on user request and if the file has a name, send save msgs
 if (DisplayMsg (IDS_MSG_QUERY, IDS_MSG_NOTSAVE, MB_YESNO |
                MB_ICONQUESTION) == IDYES) {
  if (strcmp (filename, "")==0)
     SendMessage (WM_COMMAND, CM_FILESAVEAS, 0L);
  else
     SendMessage (WM_COMMAND, CM_FILESAVE, 0L);
 }
}
```

Now, since the File Save operation can be requested from several places, I create one **SaveFile** utility function. Again, lock the pointer to the global memory buffer and use **FilePutLine** to actually write all of the lines in the array.

```
void       FrameWin::SaveFile () {
 HANDLE hfile = CreateFile (filename, GENERIC_WRITE, 0, NULL,
                    CREATE_ALWAYS, FILE_ATTRIBUTE_NORMAL, NULL);
 if (hfile==INVALID_HANDLE_VALUE) { // file create failed, dsplay error
  DisplayMsg (IDS_MSG_ERROR, IDS_MSG_FILEERR, MB_OK | MB_ICONSTOP);
  return;
 }
 char *ptrlines; // ptr to locked buffer
 // get locked ptr to glbl buffer
 ptrlines = (char*) GlobalLock (hbuffer);
 for (int i=0; i<numlines; i++) {          // for every line in the file,
 // write line, if error, display error message
  if (FilePutLine (hfile, ptrlines) == NULL) {
   DisplayMsg (IDS_MSG_ERROR, IDS_MSG_FILEWRT, MB_OK | MB_ICONSTOP);
   return;
  }
  ptrlines += MAX_LEN;       // good write,point to next line
 }
 CloseHandle (hfile);        // close file and
 GlobalUnlock (hbuffer);     // unlock buffer
}
```

The remaining File menu functions become straightforward. The **Close** function simply invokes **SaveCheck** and resets the **numlines** to 0.

```
void      CmFileClose () {
// if file not saved, ask user&handle
if (havefile && !havesaved) SaveCheck();
numlines  = 0;          // set no lines in file
havefile  = FALSE;      // set no file
havesaved = FALSE;      // set not saved
Invalidate ();          // clear screen
}
```

The **FileSave** function either invokes **SaveFile** or sends a **FileSaveAs** message if the file has no name yet.

```
void      FrameWin::CmFileSave () {
// if there is a file, either save it or if no filename, use saveas
if (havefile)
 if (strcmp (filename, "")==0)
    SendMessage (WM_COMMAND, CM_FILESAVEAS, 0L);
 else
    SaveFile();
 havesaved = TRUE;  // indicate file has been saved
}
```

The function for **FileSaveAs** must invoke the common File | SaveAs dialog. **CFileDialog** contains a member, **m_ofn**, that contains the C-style open file dialog information. One member, **lpstrFile**, contains the initial file name to be shown in the dialog. Using these, the SaveAs function is coded

```
void      FrameWin::CmFileSaveAs () {
 if (havefile) {
 // set up transfer buffer
 CFileDialog filedlg (FALSE,    // use SaveAs dialog
              "*.CPP", // default extension
              "*.*",   // current file name
               OFN_HIDEREADONLY | OFN_OVERWRITEPROMPT | OFN_LONGNAMES,
              "All Files (*.*)|*.*|CPP Files (*.CPP)|*.CPP|C Files"
              " (*.C)|*.C|Header Files (*.H*)|*.H*||",
              this);
  strcpy (filedlg.m_ofn.lpstrFile, filename);// install current name
  if (filedlg.DoModal () == IDOK) {          // user has chosen a file
   strcpy (filename, filedlg.GetPathName ());// extract its filename
   SaveFile ();                              // save the file
   havesaved = TRUE;                         // indicate file is saved
  }
 }
}
```

Now we finally have the File menu operational, except for printing which is a chapter unto itself and an actual implementation of Find/Replace strings. All that remains is the **OnPaint** function. In the simplest case, considering also that the user can choose the desired font, **OnPaint** could just display all the lines in the buffer and let Windows 95 clip those that extend beyond the current screen.

```
char *ptrlines;                            // ptr to the buffer
ptrlines = (char*) GlobalLock (hbuffer);   // lock ptr to buffer
```

```
if (ptrlogfont) {                                  // install font in use
  ptrfont = new Cfont ();
  ptrfont->CreateFontIndirect (ptrlogfont);        // create the font
  ptroldfont = dc.SelectObject (ptrfont);          // install font
}
dc.SetTextColor (fontcolor);                        // install font color
dc.SetBkMode (TRANSPARENT);                         // use background color

for (int i=0; i<numlines; i++) {                    // for all lines
  dc.TextOut (cxChar, cyChar*i, ptrlines);          // display it
  ptrlines += MAX_LEN;                              // point to next line
if (ptrfont) dc.RestoreFont ();                     // restore default font
GlobalUnlock (hbuffer);                             // unlock global buffer
}
```

This is a pretty simple **Paint** function that leaves much to be desired. Perhaps its biggest failing is that only the first few lines of the file that can fit within the current screen height is visible. We finally desperately need a scrolling ability.

8.10 USING MFC'S CSCROLLBAR TO SCROLL A TEXT WINDOW

Our use of scroll bars is complicated by two factors that affect the current range needed. Perhaps the largest factor is the total number of lines in the file. Assume that 20 lines can be shown on the screen. If a file contains 100 lines, the vertical scroll bar should have a range of 0 to 80. (If you allow a range from 0 to 100, you would get that peculiar effect of scrolling to the bottom only to find that the last line is now just off the top of the screen. By limiting the range to total lines minus the number on-screen at one time, when you scroll to the bottom, the last line of the file will be at the bottom of the screen.)

Notice also that the number of possible lines per current screen size also depends on the font that is in use as well as the current client window size. Different fonts have differing average character dimensions, particularly in regard to the font point size. The other factor that affects the range of scroll bars is the current size or dimension of the window.

In the constructor, the range in use is set to zero, since there is no file in use. If we have a utility function **SetOurScrollRange** that calculates the current range needed for both horizontal and vertical scroll bars, then that utility would need to be invoked from three places.

1. In our **WM_SIZE** message processing function, reset the scroll bar's current range in response to changing window dimensions.
2. Whenever the user changes fonts, recalculate the scroll bar's range, based upon the new average font character dimensions.
3. Whenever File | Open or File | New is requested, adjust the scroll bar's range based upon the number of lines in the file.

Under MFC a **CWnd** automatically installs scroll bars if the window is created with a WNDCLASS style that includes the WS_VSCROLL and/or WS_HSCROLL. The **CWnd** class contains the key scrolling functions, particularly the **GetScrollPos**, **SetScrollPos**, **SetScrollRange**, and **ScrollWindow**. The scroll bar range must be recalculated whenever there is a font change, a window size change, or a file New or Open request. Therefore, **SetOurScrollRange** is invoked from **OnSize**, **CmFontChange**, **CmFileOpen**, and **CmFileNew**, and it determines the range of both horizontal and vertical scroll bars. The vertical range is the number of lines in the file less the number of lines per screen or page. By using the expression

```
vertical range expression = max (0, numlines - num_lines_per_page)
```

the situation where all lines fit on one screen (that is a negative value) is handled. Whenever a range goes from zero to zero, the scroll bar disappears automatically. Do not forget to reset the thumb bar position whenever the range is reset; failure to do so results in a "jumping" thumb bar when the user attempts the next scroll operation. Recall that MFC has defined a pair of macros to aid us.

```
#define min(a,b) (((a) < (b)) ? (a) : (b))
#define max(a,b) (((a) > (b)) ? (a) : (b))
```

The **SetOurScrollRange** function is coded

```
void        FrameWin::SetOurScrollRange () {
 // if there is a file, adjust scroll range
 if (havefile && numlines>0) {
  num_lines_per_page = height/avg_char_height; // calc num lines / page
  max_vscroll_lines = max (0, numlines - num_lines_per_page );
  current_top_line = min (current_top_line, max_vscroll_lines);
  SetScrollRange (SB_VERT, 0, max_vscroll_lines, FALSE);
  SetScrollPos (SB_VERT, current_top_line, TRUE);
  num_chars_per_line = width/avg_char_width;
  max_hscroll_chars = max (0, 132 - num_chars_per_line);
  current_start_col = min (current_start_col, max_hscroll_chars);
  SetScrollRange (SB_HORZ, 0, max_hscroll_chars, FALSE);
  SetScrollPos (SB_HORZ, current_start_col, TRUE);
 }
}
```

To avoid unnecessary scroll bar flickering, if both the range and position of the thumb bar are going to be adjusted in quick succession as we have done here, set the BOOL for repainting to FALSE on the first function and then TRUE on the last. In this manner, the scroll bar is redrawn only one time. Under MFC, our applications must process and handle scroll bar messages just as they did in the early C-style chapters 2 and 3. The message map entries are **OnVScroll** and **OnHScroll**.

```
BEGIN_MESSAGE_MAP(FrameWin, CFrameWnd)
 ...
 ON_WM_VSCROLL ()
 ON_WM_HSCROLL ()
 ...
END_MESSAGE_MAP()
```

The prototypes for these two messages in the class header would be

```
afx_msg void  OnHScroll (UINT type, UINT pos, CScrollBar*);
afx_msg void  OnVScroll (UINT type, UINT pos, CScrollBar*);
```

where the scroll type is one of the standard SB_ scroll message IDs and the position is that of the thumb bar. The vertical scrolling function first sets the number of lines to scroll based upon the SB_ scroll message ID—one line for up/down one line, the number of lines per page for page up/down, and the relative number of lines from the current top to the thumb bar position when tracking the thumb bar. This potential amount is then forced into range based upon the current top line position in the file and the maximum amount of scrolling possible. Finally, if there really are lines to scroll, the new top line is calculated and the **CWnd** function **ScrollWindow** is invoked. This function requires the amount to reposition the window in both x and y dimensions. For vertical scrolling, the zero is passed for the x dimension. The y dimension is passed the *negative* of the number of lines to scroll multiplied by the average character height. The last two NULL parameters are the address of a rectangular area of the client area to be scrolled and the address of any clipping rectangle. The complete function **OnVScroll** is shown below (**OnHScroll** is similar).

```
void        FrameWin::OnVScroll (UINT type, UINT pos, CScrollBar*) {
  switch (type) {
  case SB_LINEUP:      // scroll up 1 line
   num_lines_to_scroll = -1; break;
  case SB_LINEDOWN:    // scroll 1 line down
   num_lines_to_scroll = 1; break;
  case SB_PAGEUP:      // scroll 1 page up
   num_lines_to_scroll = min (-1, -num_lines_per_page); break;
  case SB_PAGEDOWN:    // scroll 1 page down
   num_lines_to_scroll = max (1, num_lines_per_page); break;
  case SB_THUMBTRACK: // follow thumbbar
   num_lines_to_scroll = pos - current_top_line; break;
  default:
   num_lines_to_scroll = 0;
  }
  num_lines_to_scroll = max (-current_top_line,
                      min (num_lines_to_scroll,
                           max_vscroll_lines - current_top_line));
  // avoid flicker by only scrolling when there are lines to scroll
  if (num_lines_to_scroll !=0) {
   current_top_line +=num_lines_to_scroll;
   ScrollWindow (0, -avg_char_height*num_lines_to_scroll, NULL, NULL);
   SetScrollPos (SB_VERT, current_top_line, TRUE);
   UpdateWindow ();
  }
}
```

Exactly what happens when the **ScrollWindow** is executed? Suppose that 25 lines were painted on the screen. Assume the user scrolls down one line. It does not make sense for Windows 95 to invalidate the whole screen; actually, 24 lines are really visible, and only one line must be new. Hence, Windows 95, based upon the area of the screen to be scrolled, does a **BitBlt** (bit block transfer—see chapter 9) or a graphics copy of that portion of the screen that contains the still-needed 24 lines, copying that block up one line or average character height, overlaying the existing image. Thus, the first 24 lines are now just where they should be for the scrolled effect. Windows 95 now issues a paint message for the only remaining invalid rectangle, that occupied by the bottom line. Smart paint routines *could* take advantage of this and display only that one needed line, creating a very smooth text scroll.

The problem with this approach is that it places a great deal of extra coding into the paint routine just to determine which line or series of lines in the entire file need to be displayed at what portion on the screen. Therefore, almost as good a solution to scrolling is to repaint the entire screen, but paint only those lines that are on-screen. This is the approach that I have taken in the examples in this book. (The very poorest solution would be to repaint the entire text file, letting Windows 95 clip all of those lines that are beyond the current screen position and size. This is a viable option only with very small text files.)

One should also provide a keyboard interface for the scrolling process in response to key down messages. The coding is quite similar to the C style from chapter 2—send ourselves WM_VSCROLL messages based upon which arrow key is pressed. Notice that I used two Page keys to signal page up/down vertical scrolling and used Home-End keys for horizontal page messages.

```
void        FrameWin::OnKeyDown (UINT key, UINT, UINT) {

 // check for and handle any possible keyboard scroll request
 switch (key) {
  case VK_UP:     // requests scroll up 1 line
   SendMessage (WM_VSCROLL, SB_LINEUP, 0L); break;
  case VK_DOWN:   // requests scroll down 1 line
   SendMessage (WM_VSCROLL, SB_LINEDOWN, 0L); break;
  case VK_LEFT:   // requests scroll left 1 col
   SendMessage (WM_HSCROLL, SB_LINEUP, 0L); break;
  case VK_RIGHT:  // requests scroll right 1 col
   SendMessage (WM_HSCROLL, SB_LINEDOWN, 0L); break;
  case VK_PRIOR:  // request scroll 1 page up
   SendMessage (WM_VSCROLL, SB_PAGEUP, 0L); break;
  case VK_NEXT:   // request scroll 1 page down
   SendMessage (WM_VSCROLL, SB_PAGEDOWN, 0L); break;
  case VK_END:    // request goto the bottom
   SendMessage (WM_HSCROLL, SB_PAGEDOWN, 0L); break;
  case VK_HOME:   // request goto the top
   SendMessage (WM_HSCROLL, SB_PAGEUP, 0L);  break;
 }

}
```

Finally, we must revisit the **OnPaint** function to see how it now handles the current scroll position. It is quite easy. The line spacing is simply the average character height times the quantity *i* minus the **current_line_top**.

```
CPaintDC  dc(this);
...
for (int i=0; i<numlines; i++) {
```

```
dc.TextOut (avg_char_width*(1-current_start_col),
            avg_char_height*(i-current_top_line), ptrlines);
ptrlines +=MAX_LEN;
}
...
```

8.11 MFC INITIAL SEQUENCE IN FRAME WINDOW CONSTRUCTORS

Since many actions are going to occur in our overridden functions of **Create** and **OnCreate**, such as obtaining the average character dimensions based upon the current font, it is vital that any data members that are referenced in these overridden functions be assigned their initial values *before* invoking the **Create** function. In Pgm08a the average character dimensions are to be calculated based on the current installed user-selected font. It is crucial that the member **ptrlogfont** be given its initial value of NULL before **Create** is invoked or in **GetAvgCharDims** a garbage font is constructed based upon the uninitialized garbage in the pointer! Those data members that are not referenced in the creation sequence can safely be assigned their initial values after the call to **Create** as shown.

```
FrameWin::FrameWin (CWnd* ptrparent, const char* title)
              : CFrameWnd () {
...
ptrlogfont = NULL;          // set no font loaded
fontcolor = RGB (0, 0, 0);  // set default font color black
Create ( AfxRegisterWndClass (
...
havefile  = FALSE;          // indicates no file loaded yet
havesaved = FALSE;          // if a file is present, it is not saved
numlines = 0;               // set total lines in file to none
// allocate a file input buffer
hbuffer   = GlobalAlloc (GMEM_MOVEABLE, (long)(MAX_LINES)*MAX_LEN);
if (hbuffer==NULL) {  // error, not enough memory for buffer
 DisplayMsg (IDS_MSG_ERROR, IDS_MSG_NOMEM, MB_OK | MB_ICONSTOP);
 SendMessage (WM_CLOSE);
 }
}
```

8.12 THE NEW SETSCROLLINFO METHOD

As we said in chapter 2, the new Windows 95 function **SetScrollInfo** not only can be used to set the scroll range and thumb bar position, but also it provides the only method to set the page size and thereby the size of the thumb bar itself. Under the class libraries, this function is encapsulated by

```
SetScrollInfo (SB_VERT or SB_HORZ, &si, TRUE);
```

where **si** is an instance of the SCROLLINFO structure.

WORD	fMask	ORed series specifying which of the following are valid
int	nMin	the minimum scroll amount—usually 0
int	nMax	the maximum scroll amount in pixels
int	nPage	the number of pixels in a page or screen height
int	nPos	the current thumb bar position

The flags for the WORD that specify which are to be used include

SIF_PAGE	uses the page amount to set page size
SIF_POS	sets the position; use nPos
SIF_RANGE	sets the range; use nMin and nMax
SIF_DISABLENOSCROLL	disables the scroll bar

Note that this function would replace the pair **SetScrollRange** followed by **SetScrollPos**.

8.13 ADDITIONAL CONSIDERATIONS

When you run the application, pay attention to the severe limitations: that of file size, for example. Also, we have not yet discussed coding, which enables us to enter text, change text, or even find and locate text; it is coming in chapter 10. The clipboard functions are implemented in chapter 13. For a real application, we need to implement the processing of the lines in a more memory-efficient manner. There are several possibilities, each offering different benefits and disadvantages.

As you consider how you might actually handle the editing actions, a solution that retains the individual lines and their possible space looms large. If we retain the maximum line length for every line, then it is a fairly easy task to insert and delete text and to cut/paste to/from the clipboard, but memory requirements become large unless we dynamically allocate each line. Yet dynamically allocating and freeing each line is a time-consuming operation. This would be an excellent application for the new Windows 95 private heap functions. Allocate a large, expandable private heap. Derive our own string class (**CString** or any other model) and overload the **new** and **delete** operators to use the new private heap functions. When the entire collection needs to be deleted upon File | Close, File | New, File | Open, or application termination, simply delete the private heap—this will not invoke every string's destructor. You might see if you can adapt Pgm08a to use a private heap.

Another approach is to utilize the class library's array container classes to store the strings. In Pgm15a this is done to show you how to use the array containers.

On the other hand, you could just read in the text file AS-IS, perhaps removing the <CRLF> codes and inserting null terminators. Thus, memory requirements would be reduced to the minimum. But finding the next or a specific line would become trickier, since any given line would be variable in length from 0 bytes (a line with only a

<CRLF>) to the longest line in the file; there would be no line length any longer. The null terminator would signal end of line. With this scheme, the coding for inserting and deleting and displaying text would become much more involved, since variable line lengths are involved.

There are many more possibilities. You could utilize the container classes to store the arrays of lines, for example.

But there is an even simpler way. MFC has some additional ways to fully automate text file processing. Using the **CEdit** control for text file editing is examined in Chapter 10.

8.14 ELIMINATION OF REPETITIVE CODING SEQUENCES

In Pgm08a, many not-yet-implemented command handlers such as that for Edit | Cut were shelled. One constructs larger applications a function at a time. When setting up menus and their corresponding handlers and enabler functions, it is common practice to code shell dummies as done here in Pgm08a. Later on when the basic application is working, a programmer then begins to add the actual code to these shelled functions.

Another shell approach that reduces the amount of initial coding is to make only *one* shell function. Via the events response table or map, point all not-yet-implemented commands to this one dummy. Of course, there is more work to do when you come back to implement one of these shelled functions. To reduce initial coding in Pgm08a, I could have set up the response map as follows:

```
BEGIN_MESSAGE_MAP(FrameWin, CFrameWnd)
 ON_COMMAND(CM_FILEPRINT,        CmNotDoneYet)
 ... lots more of them
 ON_COMMAND(CM_EDITDELETE,       CmNotDoneYet)
 ...
END_MESSAGE_MAP()
void      FrameWin::CmNotDoneYet () {
 MessageBox ("This function is not yet implemented",
           "Notice:", MB_ICONINFORMATION | MB_OK);
}
```

In a similar manner, the repetitious command enabler coding could have been reduced. Notice that all enablers had the same coding. You can write one common enabler function and then use it for all menu items that are enabled by that formula. In Pgm08a, all of the command enablers could have been merged into one as follows:

```
BEGIN_MESSAGE_MAP(FrameWin, CFrameWnd)
 ...
 ON_UPDATE_COMMAND_UI(CM_FILECLOSE,    CmEnableHaveFile)
 ... lots more of them
 ON_UPDATE_COMMAND_UI(CM_EDITFINDNEXT, CmEnableHaveFile)
END_MESSAGE_MAP()

void      FrameWin::CmEnableHaveFile (CCmdUI *ptrenabler) {
 ptrenabler->Enable (havefile);
}
```

CHAPTER 9

Graphics—The GDI Package

9.1 Introduction

The Graphical Device Interface (GDI) is one of the more powerful features of Windows 95. There is an exceedingly large number of complex graphics operations that can be done. Therefore, I have chosen to limit the function coverage to the basic drawing set while still discussing the power features.

Graphics construction at the hardware level is not only a complex undertaking but a highly device-dependent one. The many SuperVGA cards all have significant differences and capabilities. Recall the Tic-Tac-Toe game. From a programming point of view, we merely wanted an "O" drawn and invoked the **Ellipse** function. Windows 95 isolates our program from the specific hardware, handling the ellipse construction. If the graphics coprocessor can draw an ellipse, Windows 95 instructs it to do so. On the other hand, if the hardware cannot, Windows 95 proceeds to calculate the individual points of the ellipse and has the hardware plot the resultant points. The visual effect is the same—the ellipse is drawn.

Windows 95 manages this separation by device-independent graphics, insulating programmer from the board-dependent specifics. The fundamental building block that enables Windows 95 to perform this separation is the device driver, the drv files. Driver files access the hardware of the video display. We know that SuperVGA monitors are capable of several very different graphics modes with differing numbers of

273

colors present (2, 4, 16, and 256) and differing screen resolutions (640×480, 800×600, and 1024×768). Normally, you can choose which color mode and resolution you want your display to operate in. This is done via the Windows 95 Control Panel application. What is new with Windows 95 is that the display resolution and colors can be dynamically altered without closing down all applications and restarting Windows! Now a new complexity has entered, namely all Windows 95 applications should be able to handle display changes in a dynamic fashion. Not only can the resolution and number of colors be affected but also the average character dimensions can be affected because the fonts can be altered based on the display driver. Pgm09a responds to this new Windows 95 message, WM_DISPLAYCHANGE, adjusting for all three factors.

> *Design Rule 40:* **All Windows 95 applications that are in any way affected by dynamic alterations to the screen resolution or number of colors or fonts must respond to the WM_DISPLAYCHANGE message and be able to dynamically adjust for such changes, including the potential impact upon fonts.**

Since I have been using a **GetAvgCharDims** function to acquire font dimensions in the sample programs, it is very easy to respond. In response to the WM_DISPLAYCHANGE message, I can call **GetAvgCharDims** and then **Invalidate** to update the screen.

Graphics are composed of two differing points of view: *raster* and *vector* graphics. Raster graphics is concerned with drawing individual pixel points; most PC displays are raster devices. Vector graphics is concerned with drawing lines; most plotters are vector devices. Windows 95, by virtue of being device independent, allows an application to access the hardware from both points of view. In other words, although the video display plots only points, your application can direct that a line from point A to point B be drawn; Windows 95 handles the details. If the device can handle vector graphics, Windows 95 has little to do except pass along the line request to the device. If the device can handle only raster graphics, Windows 95 proceeds to calculate the individual pixels that need to be shown and requests the series of pixels that represent the line be shown.

9.2 THE DEVICE CONTEXT

The programming key to this independence is the device context (DC). Whenever you want to display anything, you must obtain a handle to a DC first. In doing so, Windows 95 inserts into that DC many current attributes that determine how the GDI functions are to be handled on the specific display device. In addition to the items we have seen so far, such as the pen and brush, these attributes also include such items as the display resolution and the color mode. These attributes allow an application to call a GDI function and pass it the least number of parameters to define that action. (You do not have to pass the drawing color and the background color, for example.)

There are several methods of getting the handle to a DC. The most common method is in response to WM_PAINT messages. In C-style:

```
hdc = BeginPaint (hwnd, &ps);
...
EndPaint (hwnd, &ps);
```

In MFC:

```
void OnPaint () {
 CPaintDC dc(this);
 ...
}
```

Here you can draw only in the invalid client rectangle area. At other times, you can get a handle to the whole client area by using, for C-style:

```
hdc = GetDC (hwnd);
...
ReleaseDC (hwnd, hdc);
```

For MFC:

```
CClientDC dc (m_hWnd);
```

The client DC allows drawing anywhere within the client area of the application. You can gain access to the entire area owned by the window (in other words, the frame window and its client window), including the border, title bar, menu bar, and so on, by using a window DC. In C-style:

```
hdc = GetWindowDC (hwnd);
...
ReleaseDC (hwnd, hdc);
```

In MFC:

```
CWindowDC dc (m_hWnd);
```

You can access or draw anywhere within the entire window of the application. Of course, if you draw over the menu bar, Windows 95 immediately sends your frame window a paint message to redraw the menu bar. In C-style access to the entire screen is provided by

```
      hdc = CreateDC ("DISPLAY", NULL, NULL, NULL);
or    hdc = CreateDC (0);
...
DeleteDC (hdc);
```

In MFC:

```
CDC dc;
dc.CreateDC("Display", NULL, NULL, NULL);
...
dc.DeleteDC();
```

You can now paint anywhere on the screen. It is impolite to do so, for then all other windows are sent subsequent "repaint themselves" messages.

Finally, there is a very powerful DC type known as a *memory DC*. Memory DCs contain all of the information that would normally be displayed on the screen, rather like a memory image of the screen image. A memory DC is the key to fancy graphics operations. For example, suppose that it takes several seconds for your application to draw the current complex image in the client area. Do you really want the user to "watch the buildup" as the bits and pieces are slowly drawn on the screen DC? And what about scrolling? Suppose that your final image is larger than the client area and you have installed scroll bars. Do you want the user to wait several seconds whenever he/she scrolls? Memory DCs solve all these problems.

You draw to the memory DC just as if it were a normal DC, but nothing appears on screen. When you have finished drawing the image, you then copy that portion of the memory DC onto the screen DC. Instantly, the correct portion of the final image appears. Now when a scroll is requested, you merely copy the new correct portion of the memory image onto the screen DC. The copy operation is called a **BitBlt** or bit block transfer and is one of the power features of the GDI.

Using memory DCs adds a professional touch to your graphics application. The only drawback is that the memory DC can take up a significant amount of memory, depending upon the color mode and resolution. For example, a memory DC for an image that is to be in 256 colors at 1024×768 resolution occupies more than 780K! Later in this chapter I demonstrate how to use a memory DC.

One important note: for every DC that you request, be sure that you **ReleaseDC** or **delete** the pointer to the **new**ed DC. Under Windows 3.1, there was only a total of five real device contexts with which to serve all running applications as well as Windows itself. Thus, if you failed to give back a DC repeatedly, Windows 3.1 crashed. While Windows 95 has improved the DC count, avoid failures to give back real DCs. On the other hand, the number of memory DCs is limited only by available memory.

9.3 OBTAINING THE DEVICE CAPABILITIES

The function **GetDeviceCaps** provides access to all of the device capabilities. In C:

```
int value = GetDeviceCaps (hdc, index);
```

In MFC:

```
int value = dc.GetDeviceCaps (index);
```

There are 28 index identifiers with many subidentifiers. Consult your documentation for a full discussion of all of the capabilities and their identifiers. In normal use, only a few are really needed by those applications that require specific knowledge of the color mode or resolution currently in use.

HORZRES	width of the display in pixels
VERTRES	height of the display in pixels
BITSPIXEL	number of color bits per pixel
PLANES	number of color planes

Detecting the color mode requires specific knowledge of the different architectures. For now some generalities: if the color bits per pixel is 8 and the number of color planes is 1, you are in 256-color mode. If the number of planes is 4 and the color bits per pixel is 4, you are in the 16-color mode.

9.4 SAVING DCs

Before using a DC, say, in **OnPaint**, normally one installs several items. So far, we have installed our own brushes and pens and fonts and have set the various aspects for drawing text. Every time **OnPaint** is invoked, we must reselect all these back into the paint DC. These actions take a bit of time. If you were to save that DC all set up properly once, then, whenever **OnPaint** was invoked, all you would need to do is restore that DC and paint.

By setting in **wndclass.Style** the CS_OWNDC attribute, each window class you create from this registered class has its own private DC that exists until the window is destroyed. Initialization of the owned DC is normally done during WM_CREATE message processing—that is during **OnCreate**. Whenever you request a paint DC or a **GetDC** operation, it is the owned DC that is returned. (It is not the DC returned for the system-type DCs, of course.) The cost of having your own permanent DC is about 800 bytes of memory permanently assigned to the DC.

You must still **ReleaseDC** whenever exiting a function, such as **OnPaint**.

Another even broader approach is to use the **Style** CS_CLASSDC. Here all windows, even in another instance of the application that is running, share the same DC. The first instance begun sets up the DC, that it and all other launched instances share. Of course, when you change, say, the text color in one window, suddenly the text color changes in all other instances. Sometimes this is desirable; other times it's a disaster.

9.5 MAPPING MODES AND VIEWPORT VERSUS WINDOW COORDINATES

The DC mapping mode represents the fundamental method of drawing graphics. The basic parameters consist of a mapping unit (often the pixel), the x,y values given in mapping units, and the origin of the x,y coordinate system. Windows 95 supports eight different mapping modes; the default and the most frequently encountered mode is **MM_TEXT**. These are shown in Table 9-1.

In the MM_TEXT mapping mode, the logical unit is the pixel; x,y values are interpreted to be in pixels. The coordinate system's origin is the upper-left corner of the screen. Increasing positive x values go to the right; negative, to the left. Increasing positive y values go down; negative y values go up. Notice that this is the reverse of most math graphs that have the positive y axis going up. It takes a bit of getting used to. In the other mapping modes, the unit of measurement varies among .1 millimeter (mm), .01 mm, .01 inch, .001 inch, and 1/1440 inch. In many of these, the positive y axis goes upward as expected.

Whole window coordinates, such as those used when using a **GetWindowDC** function, are based on (0,0) being the upper-left corner of the sizing or frame window. *Client area coordinates*, which we have used predominately to this point, have (0,0) at the upper-left corner of the client window. *Full screen coordinates* use (0,0) as the upper-left corner of the screen.

The mapping mode determines how Windows 95 converts or maps logical coordinates specified in the GDI functions into specific device coordinates. In other words, the mapping mode determines how the **window** or **logical coordinates** are converted into **viewport** or **device coordinates**.

Here we have a clash of nomenclature. In most graphics packages, the term "viewport" refers to the clipping region. However, in Windows 95, the **viewport coordinates** are in pixels and are usually given in terms of the client area or window, unless we are using a window or screen DC. The **window** or **logical coordinates** are specified in the logical unit of the mapping mode with the origin and direction of the axis appropriate to the mode. There are many Window functions to convert from one scheme into another. Often, scaling can be done to make images "fit."

Table 9.1 lists the mapping modes. Note that a *twip* means a twentieth of a point, and a point is a printer's unit of measurement equal to 1/72 of an inch. Since these more exotic mapping modes are so seldom used, I examine only the common MM_TEXT mode in this chapter. In the next chapter on printing, I examine the two isotropic and twips modes. The odd units of measurement are used only in GDI functions—those that require some form of a **CDC**, or hdc object.

In MM_TEXT mode, the origin point (0,0) can be changed, but the scaling factor or "extent" is fixed at 1 to 1. That is, 1 pixel in window or logical coordinates (either x or y) is 1 pixel in the viewport or device coordinates. Thus, to convert from window or logical coordinates to the viewport or device coordinates, use the following:

Table 9.1 The Mapping Modes

Mapping Mode Identifiers	Logical Unit	Increasing Coordinate Values	
		X-axis	Y-axis
MM_TEXT	Pixel	Right	Down
MM_ANISOTROPIC	Arbitrary x!=y	Selectable	Selectable
MM_ISOTROPIC	Arbitrary x==y	Selectable	Selectable
MM_TWIPS	1/1440 inch	Right	Up
MM_LOMETRIC	.1 mm	Right	Up
MM_HIMETRIC	.01mm	Right	Up
MM_LOENGLISH	.01 inch	Right	Up
MM_HIENGLISH	.001 inch	Right	Up

```
x viewport = x window - x window origin + x viewport origin;
y viewport = y window - y window origin + y viewport origin;
```

Under Windows 95, the origin points can be adjusted via the functions

```
CPoint SetViewportOrg (int x, int y);
CPoint SetViewportOrg (CPoint pt);
CPoint GetViewportOrg ();
CPoint SetWindowOrg   (int x, int y);
CPoint SetWindowOrg   (CPoint pt);
CPoint GetWindowOrg   ();
```

 Windows 3.1 C-Style Porting Tip: These usual Windows 3.1 functions are now obsolete. For each of these—**SetViewportOrg, GetViewportOrg, GetWindowOrg, SetWindowOrg**—use the "Ex" Windows 95 version such as **SetViewPortOrgEx**. The class libraries invoke the correct API function based upon the platform. So you may still call these above functions, and the class library will invoke the correct version.

These functions have the effect of altering where the origin (0,0) is found. Use one of the two, but *not* both, on the same window. Either set the viewport origin or the window origin. Suppose that you wished to display a graph that included equal ranges along the axis +x and -x and +y and -y values, such as a graph of a trigonometric function. If you used the default setup, only the positive values would be displayed and then they would be upside down—only the positive quadrant of the full graphical image. The remedy is to move the viewport origin to the center of the client window area with positive y going up. By invoking **SetViewportOrgEx**, the window's logical point (0,0) is displayed in the center of the client area. Now all four quadrants of the trig plot are visible. In C-style:

```
SetViewportOrgEx (hdc, width/2, height/2, NULL);
```

In MFC:

```
CPoint pt, oldpt;
pt.x = width/2;
pt.y = height/2;
oldpt = dc.SetViewportOrg (pt);
oldpt = dc.SetViewportOrg (width/2, height/2);
```

That is, the logical coordinates range from -width/2 to +width/2 and from -height/2 to +height/2. If you want to display a title at the top of the client window, in C-style use:

```
TextOut (hdc, -width/2, -height/2, "Graph Title", -1);
```

In MFC:

```
dc.TextOut (-width/2, -height/2, "Graph Title");
```

To use the **SetWindowOrg**, use negative values to achieve the same effect.

```
SetWindowOrgEx (hdc, -width/2, -height/2, NULL);
```

Shifting viewport origins is one method of responding to a scroll request with graphical images. The drawback to this approach is that the entire image must be redrawn or all text displayed, letting Windows 95 handle all of the clipping. Using a memory DC provides a better scheme. Only in the two scalable isotropic modes can the viewport or window extent be changed; in all other modes, the scale factor is always 1:1. The two isotropic modes are very useful in chapter 10 when scaling the screen onto a printed page. The extent can be altered via the following functions.

```
CSize SetViewportExt (CSize new);
CSize SetViewportExt (int cx, int cy);
CSize GetViewportExt ();
CSize SetWindowExt   (CSize new);
CSize SetWindowExt   (int cx, int cy);
CSize GetWindowExt   ();
```

9.6 GDI OBJECTS—RULES OF USE

Recall the earlier design rules concerning GDI objects:

1. Delete all GDI objects that you create.
2. Do not delete GDI objects while they are selected in a valid DC.
3. Do not delete stock objects; if you do, Windows 95 will ignore it.

Often, one must save the old object when a new object is created and selected into a DC. Later, just before the DC is to be destroyed, the old object or the original object is selected back into the DC, the new object deleted, and the DC destroyed.

If many objects are selected into a DC, it can be annoying to have to save all of the corresponding original objects and then later reselect the old one back into the DC. The **CDC**-based classes provide a pair of functions for quick restoration.

```
int  SaveDC ();
BOOL RestoreDC (int saveid);
```

When the DC is saved onto the stack, a save ID number is returned for later use in the restore function. DCs can be saved as frequently as desired. However, since they are saved on the stack, there should be a matching number of restores. All GDI objects and the mapping mode are saved and restored.

9.7 PENS AND BRUSHES

9.7.1 Pens

When you invoke many drawing functions, those functions utilize the currently selected pen and brush. Let's examine their creation more fully. Windows 95 provides the stock pens WHITE_PEN and BLACK_PEN. (There is a NULL_PEN that does not draw.) Again, stock objects do not need to be deleted. In C:

```
HPEN hpen = GetStockObject (WHITE_PEN);
SelectObject (hcd, hpen);
```

or

```
SelectObject (hdc, GetStockObject (WHITE_PEN));
```

or

```
HPEN oldhpen = SelectObject (hdc, GetStockObject (WHITE_PEN));
```

When you create your own pens, three parameters are required: the color, the width, and the style. The width is in pixels. The style is one of the following identifiers:

PS_SOLID	solid pen
PS_DASH	only with width 1
PS_DOT	only with width 1
PS_DASHDOT	only with width 1
PS_DASHDOTDOT	only with width 1
PS_NULL - null pen	only with width 1
PS_INSIDEFRAME	a solid pen used in drawing bounding rectangles whose dimensions will be shrunk to fit within the bounding rectangle

The following create pens in C-style and MFC. In C:

```
HPEN pen = CreatePen(PS_SOLID, 1, RGB (255, 0, 0); // solid red pen
```

In MFC:

```
CPen pen (PS_SOLID, 1, RGB (255, 0, 0)); // solid red pen
CPen pen;
pen.CreatePen (PS_SOLID, 1, RGB (255, 0, 0)); // solid red pen
```

Under all methods, the sequence of use is as follows:

Create the logical pen.

SelectObject the pen into the DC.

Draw with the DC.

Select in another or restore the original pen.

When **ReleaseDC** or when a new pen is selected, **delete** the pen.

What appears between the dots and dashes on the fancier pens? The color depends upon the background mode. If it is opaque, Windows 95 fills the spaces with the background color. If it is transparent, Windows 95 does not fill at all, so whatever color is there is still there. The default background color is white, so very often we use the **SetBkColor** function with **SetBkMode** as we have done in previous **OnPaint** functions.

9.7.2 Brushes

A brush is an 8×8 pixel bitmap used repeatedly to cover an area. For a pure black brush, the bit patterns are all 0s; for a white brush, the patterns are all 1s. Windows 95 also creates dithered colored or gray patterns. In black-and-white mode, alternating 0s and 1s in the pattern would yield a visual effect of medium gray. More 1s than 0s would produce a lighter gray; more 0s than 1s, a darker gray. This dithering effect is a result of the eye's inability to differentiate the colors of individual pixels when they are so tiny.

When using colors, the effects are much more difficult to predict unless you have a background in art, specifically in additive color mixing. Although Windows 95 normally uses only 16 solid colors (in the 16-color mode), many more than 16 colors may be produced, or simulated, by dithering. Suppose that you alternated red and green in the 8×8 pixel brush pattern. The visual effect would be an entirely different color— yellow—unless you took a magnifying glass to the screen. Thus, although you may have created a solid brush, if Windows 95 cannot display that color because it is not one of the basic 16 colors, it attempts to create a dithered pattern that closely approximates your request.

There are also a series of hatch patterns that can be used in brush creation. The hatch brush identifiers include

HS_HORIZONTAL	horizontal lines
HS_VERTICAL	vertical lines
HS_FDIAGONAL	forward slanting diagonal lines \\\
HS_BDIAGONAL	backward slanting diagonal lines ///
HS_CROSS	cross hatch pattern rather like +++
HS_DIAGCROSS	diagonal cross pattern rather like xxxx

Brushes are normally created C-style by

```
HBRUSH hbrush = CreateSolidBrush(RGB (255, 0, 255); // yellow brush
```

or

```
HBRUSH hbrush = CreateHatchBrush(HS_HORIZONTAL, RGB (255, 0, 255));
```

Or, if you want, you can create your own bitmap 8×8 to be used as a brush.

```
HBITMAP hbitmap; // to be loaded from the resource file
hbitmap = LoadBitmap (hinstance, "name of bitmap"); // or ID number
HBRUSH  hbrush = CreatePatternBrush (hbitmap);
```

Under MFC use

```
CBrush brush (RGB (255, 255, 0)); // create a yellow brush
CBrush brush (HS_HORIZONTAL, RGB (255, 255, 0)); // hatch yellow
CBrush brush (CBitmap *object); // where a pointer is passed to the
                        // brush bitmap is loaded from the resource file
CBrush brush;
```

```
brush.CreateSolidBrush (RGB (255, 255, 0));
brush.CreateHatchBrush (HS_HORIZONTAL, RGB (255, 255, 0));
brush.CreatePatternBrush (CBitmap *object);
```

9.8 DRAWING GRAPHICAL IMAGES

The number of possible functions used to draw objects is quite extensive. Let's cursorily examine several of these.

 Windows 3.1 C-Style Porting Tip: Substitute **MoveToEx** for the obsolete **MoveTo**.

The C-style pair

```
MoveToEx (hdc, x1, y1, NULL);
LineTo   (hdc, x2, y2);
```

may be used to draw a line from $(x1,y1)$ to $(x2,y2)$. Specifically, **MoveToEx** is used to position the pen to a point without drawing; **LineTo** draws the line with the current pen.

Under MFC, both **MoveTo** and **LineTo** can take either a pair on x,y integer values or a **CPoint**.

```
dc.MoveTo (x, y);
dc.LineTo (point);
```

Therefore, when storing lines, often arrays of **CPoint** or **POINT** structures are used. However, there is a much better method for drawing lines—the **Polyline** function. This function draws a series of connected lines from an array of points. Here the number of points is an integer. In C:

```
POINT    linearray[MAX_POINTS];
Polyline (hdc, linearray, number_of_points);
```

In MFC:

```
CPoint     linearray[MAX_POINTS];
dc.Polyline (linearray, number_of_points);
```

Another workhorse is the **Polygon** function. This function is passed an array of points that, when connected, form a multisided object. Additionally, a line is drawn from the last point back to the first point if they are not the same point. The interior is filled with the current background color.

```
dc.Polygon (arraypoints, number_of_points);
```

where the array is an array of **CPoint** objects. Windows 95 clips as usual. Windows 95 has other functions to draw: **Arc, AngleArc, Chord, Ellipse, FillRect, FrameRect, InvertRect, Pie, Rectangle, RoundRect, SetPixel**, and others—all are encapsulated in the **CDC** classes.

Windows 3.1 Porting Tip: Under Windows 3.1, all coordinates and numbers of points were 16-bit quantities. Under Windows 95, all coordinates and numbers of points are 32-bit integers. That is, the world x,y coordinates can range from -2,147,483,648 to 2,147,483,647. Unfortunately, the GDI is still 16 bits at heart; it *truncates* the 32-bit values to 16 bits! But at least one can now pass more than 16,000 points (64K) to **Polygon**, **Polyline**, and similar functions. This helps my cartography applications.

9.8.1 The Drawing Modes or ROPS and Clipping Regions

Windows 95 provides a set of *drawing modes* that specify how the drawing pen is to interact with the canvas or background underneath the pen. The default is **R2_COPYPEN** in which the pen's color is copied directly onto the screen overlaying all colors beneath it. Actually, what Windows 95 does to plot a pixel from the pen at a specific x,y point is to perform a bitwise Boolean operation on the pen's color and the screen's pixel color. This process is known as a *binary raster operation (ROP)*. There are 16 ROPS possible shown in Table 9.2, and the ROP to use is set using the **SetROP2** function

```
int dc.SetROP2 (id_value); // returns old ROP2 mode
```

Normally, the default of copying the pen's color onto the screen is what is wanted. Perhaps the next frequently used ROP is R2_XORPEN, where the pen's color is exclusively ORed with the background pixel's color. This is frequently used in animation because the XOR logic has a peculiar property: if the same pixel is plotted the same way a second time, the drawn object disappears and the original background reappears. This technique is often used to display a moving cursor. XOR plots the cursor at position 1. When it is to move, replot the same cursor at point 1, and the background that was overlaid by the cursor appears. (See the palette discussion below for the meaning of color inversion.)

What do we mean by the "inverse color"? In black-and-white mode, black inverts to white and vice versa. However, when color enters the picture, it becomes more complex. If the video is in 4-color mode (unlikely) or 16-color mode, the ROPS apply to each of the color planes (4 in the case of 16-color mode). The results can be specifically calculated. However, when in the 256-color mode, the bits that define the colors can be user defined. Windows 95 defines a set of 21 system colors (chapter 5). These colors are in the 256-color color palette as well, unless the application has replaced them. Generally, the colors are grouped into a dark set of 10 and a light set of 10. To invert, switch from one set to the other—a dark blue might invert to a lighter blue, for example. Here the best guidance is to experiment.

Other features of the GDI include establishing clipping regions. The default is the client area and, during an **OnPaint** request, the invalid portion of the client region. However, you can establish other particular regions for clipping within the client area. Once set up and selected into the DC, Windows 95 automatically clips any drawing activities within that region as well.

Table 9.2 The 16 ROPS

ID	Action
R2_COPYPEN	pixel is the pen's color
R2_NOTCOPYPEN	pixel is the inverse of the pen's color
R2_BLACK	pixel is always binary 0, usually black
R2_WHITE	pixel is always binary 1, usually white
R2_XORPEN	pixel = pen XOR screen pixel—colors that are in the pen and screen pixel but not in both
R2_NOTXORPEN	pixel = NOT (pen XOR screen pixel)—the inverse of the colors of an XOR
R2_MASKNOTPEN	pixel = (NOT pen) AND screen pixel—combination of colors common to both the screen and the inverse of the pen
R2_MASKPEN	pixel = pen AND screen pixel—combination of the colors common to both pen and screen pixels
R2_MASKPENNOT	pixel = pen AND (NOT screen pixel)—combination of colors common to the pen and inverse of screen
R2_NOTMASKPEN	pixel = NOT (pen AND screen)—inverse of the R2_MASKPEN color
R2_MERGEPEN	pixel = pen OR screen pixel—combination of both the pen and screen color
R2_MERGENOTPEN	pixel = (NOT pen) OR screen—combination of screen and the inverse of the pen
R2_MERGEPENNOT	pixel = NOT (screen) AND pen—combination of colors common to both the pen and the inverse of the screen
R2_NOTMERGEPEN	pixel = NOT (pen OR screen)—the inverse of R2_MERGEPEN
R2_NOP	pixel is unchanged
R2_NOT	pixel is the inverse of the screen color

9.8.2 BitBlts

BitBlt stands for a bit block transfer, which is an exceedingly fast method of copying all or part of a bitmap onto a canvas, retaining the original dimensions or stretching them in some manner. BitBlts simply copy bitmap bits extraordinarily quickly. Another form of the ROP is used with BitBlts because there are now three items that could combine to form the final colors: the source image, the selected brush, and the background screen or canvas being painted. This tertiary ROP has 256 possibilities, most of which do not even have a name or ID. Only a few are really used: PAT-COPY, SRCCOPY, BLACKNESS, and WHITENESS.

There are several versions of the BitBlt. The first is **PatBlt**—a pattern block transfer. It is used to set a rectangular area to a constant value. The background brush is used along with another ROP method of combining the colors. Since **PatBlt** uses only a destination DC and a brush, only a subset of 16 of the 256 ROPS is valid. Most often, PATCOPY is used when only the brush color is wanted. Other useful ones include BLACKNESS and WHITENESS. In C:

```
PatBlt (hdc, x, y, width, height, PATCOPY);
```

In MFC:

```
dc.PatBlt (x, y, width, height, PATCOPY);
```

The **BitBlt** function operates like the **PatBlt** but introduces a second DC and its coordinates.
In C:

```
BitBlt (desthdc,x,y,width,height,sourcehcd,srcex, srcey, ROP);
```

In MFC:

```
dc.BitBlt (x, y, width, height, sourcehcd, srcex, srcey, ROP);
```

Although all 256 ROP possibilities exist, the most frequently used ROP is SRC-COPY—copy the source unaltered to the destination. **BitBlt** has many uses. You can copy objects from one place in the client area to another area. You can copy objects from another DC to the client area DC. You can copy to/from a memory DC. The only limiting factor is that the dimensions must be the same. In other words no stretching—expansion or contraction—can be done.

StretchBlt is used when you need to alter the resultant dimensions. You can also flip the image vertically or horizontally. Also, when there is a **color mode** difference between the image bitmap and the actual display DC (say from a 256-color bitmap onto a 16-color display), **StretchBlt** can be used, although the performance is very poor.
In C:

```
StretchBlt (hcd, x, y, width, height, sourcehcd, srcex, srcey,
            srcewidth, srceheight, ROP);
```

In MFC:

```
dc.StretchBlt (x, y, width, height, sourcehcd, srcex, srcey,
                  srcewidth, srceheight, ROP);
```

When shrinking a bitmap, **StretchBlt** must combine two or more rows or columns of pixels into one. Three possible methods exist and are set by using **SetStretchBlt**.
In C:

```
SetStretchBlt (hcd, mode);
```

In MFC:

```
dc.SetStretchBltMode (mode);
```

where the mode is

BLACKONWHITE	the default, if two or more pixels have to be combined, a logical AND is performed on the pixels—black pixels tend to dominate
WHITEONBLACK	uses a logical OR on the pixels—white pixels tend to dominate
COLORONCOLOR	eliminates pixels, so whatever one is used has its original color—best for color bitmaps as it avoids color distortion

9.9 CREATING MEMORY DCs

To create a memory DC, two items are needed: a model DC to emulate and a bitmap work area with the desired dimensions. Most often, the memory DC or portions of it will at some point be copied to the real client window DC. Therefore, it is vital that the memory DC parallel exactly the DC upon which it will ultimately be displayed. Windows 95 API provides functions for just this purpose.

```
HDC     dc     = CreateDC ("DISPLAY", NULL, NULL, NULL);
HDC     memdc  = CreateCompatibleDC (dc);
HBITMAP membmp = CreateCompatibleBitmap (dc, int width,
                                         int height);
DeleteDC (dc);
HBITMAP oldbmp = SelectObject (memdc, membmp);
```

CreateDC is used to construct a DC for a specific device, most often for a printer. However, when the keyword string DISPLAY is used as the device, a DC is constructed based upon the current display driver and display settings, such as resolution and color type. This DC is then used as the model DC to be emulated by the memory DC. **CreateCompatibleDC** constructs a memory DC based upon the real display DC. The canvas of the memory DC now has a bitmap consisting of just one pixel. So a bitmap canvas on which to paint must be constructed with the dimensions we want. The bitmap also must match the display color type and resolution. **CreateCompatibleBitmap** does just that, modeling itself upon the model DC and using our provided dimensions. The new bitmap must be selected into the memory DC, while saving the old bitmap. Later on when the memory DC and bitmap are to be destroyed, the old bitmap must be selected back into the memory DC; then both the memory DC and bitmap can be deleted. When DCs are created, they must be deleted. Note this subtly: with **GetDC,** use **ReleaseDC** to remove it, but with **CreateDC** use **DeleteDC** to remove it.

With the memory DC constructed, any function that uses an hdc can draw on it. Pens and brushes can be selected into the memory DC. Rectangles can be drawn, polygons painted, and so on. Of course, nothing appears on the screen; it is all in the memory DC and its bitmap. In the paint processing, the memory DC or portions of it are **BitBlt**ed onto the screen in whatever location you want.

Windows 95 through the Control Panel | Display permits the user to change the display resolution and colors and font sizes without closing all applications and restarting Windows. Now suddenly all running applications must adapt to the new display. Windows 95 sends all applications two WM_DISPLAYCHANGE messages. The **wparam** is zero on the first message indicating that the display characteristics are going to be changed. The second WM_DISPLAYCHANGE message has **wparam** set to one, indicating that the display has now been changed. Windows 95 applications should respond to this message if for no other reason than to reacquire the average character dimensions or screen paints can be garbled. However, if the application is using a memory DC modeled on the screen, that entire model is now invalid. The memory DC and its bitmap must be destroyed, and a new pair must be constructed modeled on the new display characteristics.

Under MFC, the **CDC** encapsulates the memory DC. Where can this creation be done? At any point where a DC can be constructed that is similar to what is needed. The process can be done one time only in the **OnPaint** function, not in the **OnCreate** function as you might suppose. If the memory DC is allocated in the **OnCreate** function, when the **OnCreate** function terminates, the pointer to the memory DC is reset back to NULL; I do not know why. If the pointer to the memory DC is initialized to NULL in the constructor, then, in the **OnPaint** routine, if the pointer is NULL, execute the following sequence:

```
CClientDC dc (this);          // get a dc to model
ptrmemdc = new CDC ();
ptrmemdc->CreateCompatibleDC (&dc);
ptrmembitmap = new CBitmap ();
ptrmembitmap->CreateCompatibleBitmap (&dc, int width, int height);
ptrmemdc->SelectObject(ptrmembitmap);
```

It is important to note the following:

1. Normally, the **ptrmemdc** and the **ptrmembitmap** variables are class members. In the class destructor or in **DestroyWindow** function, the objects are deleted.

   ```
   delete ptrmemdc;
   delete ptrmembitmap;
   ```

2. As with the C-style, after the DC is created, it has an installed bitmap of 1 pixel. We must allocate a bitmap of the proper size and one that is compatible with the current display. There is no sense in having a 256-color bitmap when you are running in 16-color mode. Later in this chapter when we discuss the display of bmp files, I show how one could display with mixed modes.

3. Lastly, it is a good idea to install a clipping region so that Windows 95 can automatically clip while drawing on this memory DC.

   ```
   // install clipping region if desired
   CRgn ptrregn = new CRgn();
   CRect rec (0, 0, width, height);
   ptrregn->CreateRectRgnIndirect (&rec);
   ptrmemdc->SelectClipRgn (ptrregn);
   ```

Notice that the **CRgn** class encapsulates a region object that can be constructed from a **CRect** object by using the **CreateRectRgnIndirect**. **SelectClipRgn** is then used to select it into the memory DC. And now, when any drawing is done on the memory DC, Windows 95 provides proper clipping.

Since the memory DC and its associated bitmap may occupy considerable memory, especially with large bitmaps on a 256-color display, some thought should be given to the lifetime of the DC. If the application needs only to display the image, one might take the approach of constructing the memory DC, performing the drawing operations on it, **BitBlt**ing it to the screen, and then deleting the memory DC. On the other hand, if the application needs to scroll the image or otherwise needs to keep the memory DC available because of frequent usage, then use protected members to store the pointers to the DC and its bitmap; allocate it once and delete it in the destructor.

9.10 Pgm09a: Graphics Scrolling, Memory DCs, and Handling Display Changes

Pgm09a illustrates how to perform smooth scrolling on a graphics window by the use of a memory DC. All drawing is done on the memory DC. Then the portion that can fit in the client area is **BitBlt**ed onto the client area. Whenever the user scrolls, the current thumb bar position is used to **BitBlt** the corresponding rectangle from the memory DC. If a scrolling unit is a single pixel, a very smooth scroll results. The **BitBlt** blazes so that the user can drag the thumb bar and we can keep up! Figure 9.1 shows what the program looks like on-screen.

This program also responds to display mode changes made dynamically by the user through the Control Panel|Display dialog. The new average character dimensions are acquired and the memory DC is deleted and reallocated modeled on the new display mode.

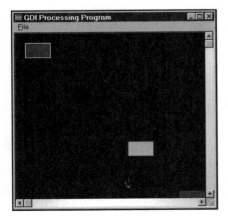

Fig. 9.1 Pgm09a—Using a Memory DC for Smooth Graphics Scrolling

9.11 SETTING UP AN APPLICATIONWIDE INFORMATION CLASS

In larger applications, some data may be needed throughout many different window classes. Such items as the full screen dimensions, the display color mode, and the presence or absence of a mouse are commonly needed data. Rather than maintaining duplicate copies of these items as members of the different window classes or continually using the API functions to retrieve them, it makes sense to make these items broadly available. Often, such fields are made global/external in nature. However, with C++ there is a better alternative for indiscriminate use of global data: static public members that are initialized by static functions.

Try to organize such broadly needed information into meaningful groups. The above-type screen fields might be classed as "system information" while the fields required to maintain a 256-color palette might be in another group. Here, I created a **SysInfo** class to encapsulate the system information. **SysInfo** contains six static public data members, including **screen_width** and **screen_height** that hold the full screen dimensions, **mouse** which is TRUE when a mouse is present, and three fields to contain the color mode information. These system values are gathered by a static member function **InitSysInfo** which is invoked from the **CWinApp**-derived class and also from the function responding to WM_DISPLAYCHANGE messages.

Now suppose that in a non-Windows class function, say **DateTime**, a message must be displayed and that class **DateTime** does not have access to **CWnd** or **CWin-App** member functions or data. Hence, there are no message box actions. The MFC provides for just such eventualities with the global macros.

```
CWinApp *AfxGetApp ();              // returns a pointer to the app object
HANDLE   AfxGetInstanceHandle (); // returns the handle to this instance
HANDLE   AfxGetResourceHandle (); // gets a handle to the app's resources
```

Even though no actual instances of this class will be allocated, a dummy constructor must be provided. The class has one static function, **InitSysInfo**, whose purpose is to initialize the static system data. Although I used C-style to create the DC, it could have been done using a **CDC** class.

```
CDC dc ();
dc.CreateDC ("DISPLAY", NULL, NULL, NULL);
screen_width = dc.GetDeviceCaps (HORZRES);
...
```

9.11.1 Listing for File: SysInfo.h—Pgm09a—Excerpts

```
...
/********************************************************************/
/*                                                                  */
/* SysInfo Class Definition: system wide objects                    */
/*                                                                  */
/********************************************************************/

class SysInfo {

/********************************************************************/
/*                                                                  */
/* Static and Public Access Data Members:                           */
```

```
/*                                                                        */
/************************************************************************/

public:

  static BOOL mouse;              // TRUE = mouse present
  static int  screen_width;       // screen x dimension in pels
  static int  screen_height;      // screen y dimension in pels
  static int  screen_bits_pixel;  // screen bits per pixel
  static int  screen_num_planes;  // screen number of bit planes
  static int  screen_palette;     // screen number of colors

/************************************************************************/
/*                                                                        */
/* Functions:                                                             */
/*                                                                        */
/************************************************************************/

public:
              SysInfo () {}         // dummy constructor
  static BOOL InitSysInfo ();       // initialize the static data
  ...
```

9.11.2 Listing for File: SysInfo.cpp—Pgm09a—Excerpts

```
...
// static members:

BOOL SysInfo::mouse;             // TRUE = mouse present
int  SysInfo::screen_width;      // screen x dimension in pels
int  SysInfo::screen_height;     // screen y dimension in pels
int  SysInfo::screen_bits_pixel; // screen bits per pixel
int  SysInfo::screen_num_planes; // screen number of bit planes
int  SysInfo::screen_palette;    // screen number of colors

/************************************************************************/
/* Static Member Function: replaces the normal constructor              */
/*                                                                        */
/* InitSysInfo: init static values - returns TRUE if init is successful  */
/*                                                                        */
/************************************************************************/

BOOL     SysInfo::InitSysInfo () {

  // get system-wide mouse and screen settings
  mouse = GetSystemMetrics(SM_MOUSEPRESENT)? TRUE: FALSE;

  HDC hdc = CreateDC ("DISPLAY", NULL, NULL, NULL);

  screen_width      = GetDeviceCaps (hdc, HORZRES);
  screen_height     = GetDeviceCaps (hdc, VERTRES);
  screen_bits_pixel = GetDeviceCaps (hdc, BITSPIXEL);
  screen_num_planes = GetDeviceCaps (hdc, PLANES);
  screen_palette    = GetDeviceCaps (hdc, SIZEPALETTE);

  DeleteDC (hdc);

  return TRUE; // successful
}
```

9.12 PGM09a IMPLEMENTATION

The member **mapsize** represents the maximum size of the graphics display area. For scrolling and displaying, the canvas extends from 0 to 400 pixels, square. Since this value could be set in various ways, I also inserted some code to force the map size to not exceed the current screen capabilities, so a maximize operation reveals the entire map with no scroll bars.

Next, the main title is loaded and the **FrameWin** is allocated and passed a special parameter needed by FrameWin to properly construct itself—the desired map size. By doing so, the FrameWin class becomes independent of the map size.

Notice how the **SysInfo** static class members are initialized.

9.12.1 Listing for File: Pgm09aApp.cpp—Pgm09a—Excerpts

```
/**************************************************************************/
/*                                                                        */
/* InitInstance:    allocate instance of our frame main window            */
/*                                                                        */
/**************************************************************************/
BOOL  Pgm9AApp::InitInstance () {

// get system-wide mouse and screen settings
SysInfo::InitSysInfo ();

mapsize = 400;  // set default map size
// guarantee dimension does not exceed screen capacity in current mode
mapsize = SysInfo::screen_height<mapsize? SysInfo::screen_height: mapsize;

char wintitle[70];

LoadString (m_hInstance, IDS_MAINTITLE, wintitle, sizeof(wintitle));
ptrframe = new FrameWin (NULL, wintitle, mapsize);

// install the frame window as the main app window and show that window
m_pMainWnd = ptrframe;                   // m_pMainWnd- public member of CFrameWnd
m_pMainWnd->ShowWindow (m_nCmdShow); // install show type, nor, min, maximized
m_pMainWnd->UpdateWindow ();          // force windows to be painted initially

return TRUE;
}
...
```

Now examine the FrameWin class definition. I defined several pens and brushes. This is also a common technique used in larger applications. If the application needs to create pens and brushes frequently and repeatedly, doing so once saves time and coding. Also, if one is going to do much real drawing, an array of points is needed. Although I really do not need to do so here, I have allocated space for a large array of points from global memory to illustrate using global memory allocations with the GDI functions. The member **hlparray** is the handle to the global memory array, and the member **lp** is the locked pointer. Note that I did not name it **ptrlp** because its main use is in the array style: **lp[i].x**. Next, the pointers to the memory DC and memory bitmap are defined. The vital BOOL member, **bitmap_created**, triggers the drawing process. Whenever **bitmap_created** is FALSE, the drawing must be completely redone, or updated. When it is TRUE, only BitBlts are needed to paint the screen.

The number of member functions is few, and one-half of them center around the memory DC and display change actions. **ConstructMemDC** creates the compatible memory DC; **RemoveMemDC** deletes the memory DC; **DrawMemDC** performs the actual GDI drawing operations on the memory DC. **OnCreate** invokes **GetAvgCharDims** and **ConstructMemDC**. Should the display mode be dynamically altered, **RemoveDC** is called followed by **GetAvgCharDims** and **ConstructMemDC** again. **OnSize** resets any scroll bar's range based on the current child window dimensions.

9.12.2 Listing for File: FrameWin.h—Pgm09a—Excerpts

```
...
class FrameWin : public CFrameWnd {
/******************************************************************************/
/*                                                                          */
/* Data Members                                                             */
/*                                                                          */
/******************************************************************************/

protected:

CPen        *ptrpenwhite;          // a set of pens
...
CBrush      *ptrbrushgray;

HANDLE       hlparray;             // handle of global lp array for points
CPoint      *lp;                   // locked ptr of lp array of x,y points

CDC         *ptrmemdc;             // memory device context for drawing
CBitmap     *ptrmembitmap;         // memory bitmap of drawing
BOOL         bitmap_created;       // TRUE when map has been drawn & is current
CRgn        *ptrregn;              // clipping region

CRect        full_window;          // max sized window
CRect        display_window;       // current display window onto full window
CPoint       scroll_position;      // offset from full window to 0,0 of
                                   // paint's display window

int          current_vpel;         // current vertical scroll offset
int          current_hpel;         // current horizontal scroll offset
int          num_vpels_to_scroll;
int          num_hpels_to_scroll;
int          max_vscroll_pels;     // max num pels vertical to scroll
int          max_hscroll_pels;     // max num pels horizontal to scroll

int          avg_char_width;       // average character width
int          avg_char_height;      // average character height
int          avg_caps_width;       // average capital's width
/******************************************************************************/
/*                                                                          */
/* Class Functions:                                                         */
```

```
/*                                                                      */
/*********************************************************************/
public:
            FrameWin (CWnd*, const char*, int mapsize = 400);
            ~FrameWin ();                        // destructor

protected:
        void  GetAvgCharDims ();              // get the average character dims
        void  RemoveMemDC ();                 // delete memory DC objects
        void  ConstructMemDC ();              // construct new memory DC
        void  DrawMemDC ();                   // draw objects on memory DC
afx_msg void  OnPaint ();                     // paint the window - WM_PAINT
afx_msg int   OnCreate (LPCREATESTRUCT);      // construct window
afx_msg void  OnSize (UINT, int, int);        // process window resize
afx_msg void  OnKeyDown (UINT, UINT, UINT);   // keybd scroller interface
afx_msg void  OnHScroll (UINT, UINT, CScrollBar*); // handle scrolling
afx_msg void  OnVScroll (UINT, UINT, CScrollBar*);
afx_msg void  CmExit ();

//user has changed display settings, so need to rebuild
afx_msg LRESULT OnDisplayChange (WPARAM, LPARAM);
...
```

Notice in particular how the function that responds to the WM_DISPLAYCHANGE message is defined. It returns 0 if it handles the message; **wparam** contains 0 or 1 indicating the display mode is going to be changed and then that it has now changed. Normally, I pass along the "is going to change" message and actually respond when the display has actually changed.

Now examine the FrameWin class implementation. In the constructor, all of the various pens and brushes are created. The **full_window** represents the maximum size rectangle of the graphics area, while **display_window** represents the current client area rectangle whose dimensions are altered in **OnSize** processing. Scroll bars are added just as they were when processing text. The actual range is set in **OnSize**, based upon the current client area dimensions.

The global points array is allocated with room for 1000 points; I need five points! The **bitmap_created** member is set to FALSE to force initial drawing. Any time later when another member decides it is time to redraw a new image, just set **bitmap_created** to FALSE and **Invalidate** the window. In **OnSize**, the current client area dimensions are retrieved and stored in **display_window**. Should the user resize the window so that the display area exceeds the graphic image mapsize, the **display_window** rectangle is forced to not exceed the **mapsize**. Then, the scroll bar ranges are set based on the number of pixel differences between the actual map size (**full_window**) and the current size (**display_window**).

ConstructMemDC allocates the memory DC exactly as discussed above. A compatible DC is created based upon the client DC. A compatible bitmap is created based upon the full screen dimensions. After the bitmap is selected into the memory DC, a clipping region is defined and installed. Now the memory DC is ready for use.

DrawMemDC does the actual drawing. The global memory line points array, **lp**, is locked and filled with a series of points that trace the map size dimensions. **Fill-**

Rect clears out the previous drawing and sets our background color of black. To show how to use Windows 95's globally allocated memory with GDI functions, **Polyline** uses the **lp** array to draw a red line around the border of the graphics area. I used the **lp** array so that you could see how one might handle drawing actions with large amounts of data. Next a series of colored rectangles are drawn.

OnPaint now becomes simple. If **bitmap_created** is FALSE, **DrawMemDC** is invoked to redraw the image. The last line of code, the **BitBlt**, is always executed when **OnPaint** is invoked. When you experiment with this application, notice how fast and smooth the graphics scroll actually is. With a small amount of effort, your graphics handling can be quite professional.

To keep the example shorter, I did not check and display error messages should some of the allocations fail.

9.12.3 Listing for File: FrameWin.cpp—Pgm09a—Excerpts

```
...
BEGIN_MESSAGE_MAP(FrameWin, CFrameWnd)
 ON_WM_CREATE()
 ON_WM_KEYDOWN()
 ON_WM_VSCROLL ()
 ON_WM_HSCROLL ()
 ON_WM_SIZE ()
 ON_WM_PAINT ()
 ON_MESSAGE(WM_DISPLAYCHANGE, OnDisplayChange)
 ON_COMMAND(CM_EXIT, CmExit)
END_MESSAGE_MAP()
/*****************************************************************************/
/*                                                                         */
/* Framewin: Construct the window object                                   */
/*                                                                         */
/*****************************************************************************/
        FrameWin::FrameWin (CWnd* ptrparent, const char* title, int mapsize)
                : CFrameWnd () {

DWORD style = WS_OVERLAPPEDWINDOW | WS_VSCROLL | WS_HSCROLL; // set window styles
CRect rect (0, 0, mapsize, mapsize);  // set init pos and size

Create ( AfxRegisterWndClass (
                CS_VREDRAW | CS_HREDRAW,
                AfxGetApp()->LoadStandardCursor (IDC_ARROW),
                (HBRUSH) GetStockObject (BLACK_BRUSH),
                AfxGetApp()->LoadStandardIcon (IDI_APPLICATION)),
        title,              // window caption
        style,              // wndclass DWORD style
        rect,               // set initial window position
        ptrparent,          // the parent window, here none
        "MAINMENU");        // assign the main menu
ptrpenwhite = new CPen (PS_SOLID, 1, RGB ( 255, 255, 255 )); // make white pen
...
ptrbrushgray  = new CBrush (RGB (192, 192, 192)); // make gray brush
```

```
  full_window.top      = full_window.left      = 0; // set full window rectangle
  full_window.right    = full_window.bottom    = mapsize; // to be mapsize
  display_window.top   = display_window.bottom = 0; // set display rectangle to
  display_window.left  = display_window.right   = 0; // indicate none

  hlparray = GlobalAlloc (GMEM_MOVEABLE, 4000);    // allocate global lp array

  bitmap_created = FALSE; // no bitmap image yet created
  ptrmemdc      = NULL;
  ptrmembitmap = NULL;
  ptrregn       = NULL;
  current_vpel = 0;
  current_hpel = 0;
}
...
/*****************************************************************************/
/*                                                                         */
/* OnDisplayChange: user has changed the display settings, must update      */
/*                                                                         */
/*****************************************************************************/

LRESULT    FrameWin::OnDisplayChange (WPARAM which, LPARAM lp) {

  LRESULT retcd = CFrameWnd::OnDisplayChange (which, lp);

  if (which == 1) {
   SysInfo::InitSysInfo (); // reinitialize system information about the display
   GetAvgCharDims ();       // reacquire the average character dimensions
   RemoveMemDC ();          // delete old memory DC
   ConstructMemDC ();       // build new memory DC compatible with new display
  }
  return retcd;
}
/*****************************************************************************/
/*                                                                         */
/* RemoveMemDC: delete all memory DC items and reset to NULL                */
/*                                                                         */
/*****************************************************************************/

void       FrameWin::RemoveMemDC () {

  if (ptrmemdc)      delete ptrmemdc;
  if (ptrmembitmap)  delete ptrmembitmap;
  if (ptrregn)       delete ptrregn;
  ptrmemdc = NULL;
  ptrmembitmap = NULL;
  ptrregn = NULL;
}
/*****************************************************************************/
/*                                                                         */
/* ConstructMemDC: constructs compatible memory DC and bitmap for drawing   */
/*                                                                         */
/*****************************************************************************/

void       FrameWin::ConstructMemDC () {
```

```
        CClientDC dc (this);
        ptrmemdc = new CDC ();
        ptrmemdc->CreateCompatibleDC (&dc);        // create the memory dc
        ptrmembitmap = new CBitmap ();             // create the bitmap for memdc
        ptrmembitmap->CreateCompatibleBitmap (&dc, SysInfo::screen_width,
                                        SysInfo::screen_height); // a large one
        ptrmemdc->SelectObject(ptrmembitmap);      // install bitmap into memDC
        // install clipping region if desired, not needed in this example
        ptrregn = new CRgn();
        CRect rec (0, 0, SysInfo::screen_width, SysInfo::screen_height);
        ptrregn->CreateRectRgnIndirect (&rec);   // define a region of max size
        ptrmemdc->SelectClipRgn (ptrregn);         // and set up a clipping region
        bitmap_created = FALSE;                    // indicate no image in memory
}
/***************************************************************************/
/*                                                                         */
/* DrawMemDC: draws graphical images into the memory DC                    */
/*                                                                         */
/***************************************************************************/
void        FrameWin::DrawMemDC () {

 lp = (CPoint*) GlobalLock(hlparray);  // lock down mem addr

  // clear out whole previous image
  CRect rec (0, 0, SysInfo::screen_width, SysInfo::screen_height);
  ptrmemdc->FillRect (&rec, ptrbrushblack);

  // draw a red line around full window area - a Rectangle() is easier
  // using the global array to illustrate using global memory use
  ptrmemdc->SelectObject (ptrpenred);  // install red pen to draw box
  lp[0].x=0;                    lp[0].y=0;
  lp[1].x=0;                    lp[1].y=full_window.right-1;
  lp[2].x=full_window.right-1; lp[2].y=full_window.right-1;
  lp[3].x=full_window.right-1; lp[3].y=0;
  lp[4].x=0;                    lp[4].y=0;
  ptrmemdc->Polyline (lp, 5); // draw red line around edge

  // draw a series of rectangles the easy way
  ptrmemdc->SelectObject (ptrpenwhite);
  ptrmemdc->SelectObject(ptrbrushblue);
  ptrmemdc->Rectangle (20, 20, 70, 50);       // white around blue center

  ptrmemdc->SelectObject (ptrpenred);
  ptrmemdc->Rectangle (320, 320, 370, 350); // red around blue center

  ptrmemdc->SelectObject (ptrbrushgray);
  ptrmemdc->Rectangle (220, 220, 270, 250); // red around gray center

  GlobalUnlock(hlparray); // unlock global memory lp array
  bitmap_created = TRUE;  // signal whole image is drawn
}
/***************************************************************************/
/*                                                                         */
/* OnPaint: draw once - then scroll the memDC                              */
/*                                                                         */
```

```
/**************************************************************************/

void        FrameWin::OnPaint () {

 CPaintDC   dc(this);

 if (!ptrmemdc) ConstructMemDC (); // if memory dc is not created, do so

 // whenever bitmap_created is FALSE, redraw whole graphic image
 if (!bitmap_created) DrawMemDC ();

 // display the memDC onto that portion of the display window
 // bitblt copy from memory to the client area dc
 dc.BitBlt (display_window.left, display_window.top,
            display_window.right - display_window.left,
            display_window.bottom - display_window.top, ptrmemdc,
            current_hpel, current_vpel, SRCCOPY);
}
/**************************************************************************/
/*                                                                      */
/* OnSize: get new size and adjust scroll bars                          */
/*                                                                      */
/**************************************************************************/

void        FrameWin::OnSize (UINT a, int b, int c) {

 CFrameWnd::OnSize (a, b, c);

 GetClientRect (&display_window); // get new window size
 // force new display size not to exceed full map window size
 if (display_window.bottom>full_window.bottom)
     display_window.bottom=full_window.bottom;

 if (display_window.right>full_window.right)
     display_window.right=full_window.right;

 // based on size of current display and max full window map size,
 // set scroll range
 max_vscroll_pels = full_window.bottom - display_window.bottom;
 max_hscroll_pels = full_window.right  - display_window.right;
 current_vpel = min (current_vpel, max_vscroll_pels);
 current_hpel = min (current_hpel, max_hscroll_pels);

 SetScrollRange (SB_VERT, 0, max_vscroll_pels, FALSE);
 SetScrollPos (SB_VERT, current_vpel, TRUE);
 SetScrollRange (SB_HORZ, 0, max_hscroll_pels, FALSE);
 SetScrollPos (SB_HORZ, current_hpel, TRUE);
}
/**************************************************************************/
/*                                                                      */
/* OnKeyDown: provide a keyboard scroller interface                     */
/*                                                                      */
/**************************************************************************/

... same coding as in previous examples

/**************************************************************************/
/*                                                                      */
```

```
/* OnVScroll: scroll window vertically                                   */
/*                                                                       */
/*************************************************************************/
void        FrameWin::OnVScroll (UINT type, UINT pos, CScrollBar*) {

 switch (type) {

  case SB_LINEUP:       // scroll up 1 line
    num_vpels_to_scroll = -1; break;

  case SB_LINEDOWN:    // scroll 1 line down
    num_vpels_to_scroll = 1; break;

  case SB_PAGEUP:      // scroll 1 page up
    num_vpels_to_scroll = -8; break;

  case SB_PAGEDOWN:    // scroll 1 page down
    num_vpels_to_scroll = 8; break;

  case SB_THUMBTRACK: // follow thumbbar
    num_vpels_to_scroll = pos - current_vpel; break;

  default:
    num_vpels_to_scroll = 0;
 }
 num_vpels_to_scroll = max (-current_vpel,
                       min (num_vpels_to_scroll,
                          max_vscroll_pels - current_vpel));
 if (num_vpels_to_scroll !=0) {
  current_vpel +=num_vpels_to_scroll;
  ScrollWindow (0, -num_vpels_to_scroll, NULL, NULL);
  SetScrollPos (SB_VERT, current_vpel, TRUE);
  UpdateWindow ();
 }
}
... horizontal coding is similar
```

9.13 DIBs AND COLOR PALETTES

Next, let's get even fancier and add the ability to load and display bitmap images. However, let's extend the simple "show it on the screen" to include some "hot" display methods designed to generate user interest.

The bitmaps that we have used so far and those from **CreateBitmap** and **Load-Bitmap** are stored in a Windows 95 *device-dependent bitmap* (**DDB**) under the control of the GDI and must be compatible with the video display (or printer).

The outside world—i.e., files—can also store bitmaps. They are saved as *device-independent bitmap* (**DIB**) format. The DIB stores all of the pixels in a manner that is not dependent upon the actual device and specifically the color mode. Special consideration must be given to the color palette. The actual method of storing the palette and the method of storing the pixel's color varies totally between the different color modes. The DIB stores this information in a common uniform format that is totally independent of the color mode.

When saved on disk, a DIB has the extension bmp although some applications save DIBs with a dib extension; both are equivalent. DIBs are not GDI objects under Windows 95; therefore normal GDI drawing functions cannot be performed on them. Under MFC, there is no DIB class, so we must create one ourselves.

Windows 95 provides a method to convert DIBs into DDBs. When converted, the color palette is adjusted to fit the real color mode in use, such as a 16-color or 256-color mode. The layout of the DIB file is a bit awkward. A BITMAPFILEHEADER structure is the first item in the bmp file and contains the characters "BM" in the first two bytes in **byType**; the long **bfSize** member contains the file size; the long **bfOffBits** contains the offset to the actual bitmap bits from the beginning of the file. Next comes the BITMAPINFOHEADER structure that provides the details of this bitmap's organization, including the width and height and color mode and so on; it is variable in size. If the color palette is present, it comes next. Last come the actual bits that make up the image.

Remember that these bmp files are often quite large—hundreds of K—and are usually read into global memory areas. A high-resolution, 256-color, full-screen image has 786,432 bytes of pixels! Under Windows 3.1, a huge pointer is required to work with bits within the actual bitmap, but Windows 95 and the flat memory model do simplify this. When read into memory, these DIBs are often referred to as *packed DIB memory format*. As such, they consist of BITMAPINFOHEADER, color table if present, and the bits themselves; the file header is discarded. A bmp file or DIB contains the BITMAPFILEHEADER structure first and is shown in Table 9.3.

Following the file header structure comes a BITMAPINFO structure that contains information about the dimensions and color format of a DIB. Its layout is shown in Table 9.4. Note that the first member is an instance of the BITMAPINFOHEADER structure, which is shown in Table 9.4b.

Table 9.3 The BITMAPINFO Structore

Data Type	Name	Meaning
WORD	bfType	must be BM
DWORD	bfSize	size of file in bytes
WORD	bfReserved1	must be 0
WORD	bfReserved2	must be 0
DWORD	bfOffBits	byte offset from file start to the bits array

Table 9.4a The BITMAPINFO Structure

Data Type	Name	Meaning
BITMAPINFOHEADER	bmiHeader	the info header structure
RGBQUAD	bmiColors[1]	the first element of the color table array

Table 9.4b The BITMAPINFOHEADER Structure

Data Type	Name	Meaning
DWORD	biSize	size of this structure in bytes
LONG	biWidth	bitmap width in pixels
LONG	biHeight	bitmap height in pixels
WORD	biPlanes	target device's number of planes—must be set to 1
WORD	biBitCount	number of bits per pixel: 1, 4, 8, or 24; fields below here may not be present or they may be all 0—they are seldom used
DWORD	biCompression	indicates a compressed bitmap; very rare
DWORD	biSizeImage	size in bytes of the image; not usually set
LONG	biXPelsPerMeter	horizontal resolution in pels per meter of target
LONG	biYPelsPerMeter	vertical resolution in pels per meter of target
DWORD	biClrUsed	number of color indexes actually used
DWORD	biClrImportant	number of colors that are important to render this bitmap
RGBQUAD	bmiColors[1]	the first RGBQUAD color structure

Note that the fields below the **biBitCount** may all be zero or even omitted. Use the **biSize** member to determine the structure's exact length. When creating a bmp file, it is wise to include all of these fields, setting those below **biBitCount** to zeros. While run-length encoding for data compression is possible, I have never seen one that is compressed.

Next comes the color table which defines the precise colors to be used in this DIB. Generally a color value is specified by an RGBQUAD structure as shown in Table 9.5.

The color table setup is a bit unusual because it can hold a variable number of RGBQUAD color structures, depending upon the number of unique colors in the bitmap image. The official color table structure begins at the end of the BITMAPINFO and is defined as containing only the first element in the color table. The remainder of

Table 9.5 The RGBQUAD Structure

Data Type	Name	Meaning
BYTE	rgbBlue	blue intensity
BYTE	rgbGreen	green intensity
BYTE	rgbRed	red intensity
BYTE	rgbReserved	always 0

the variable number of color RGBQUAD structures come immediately after this first RGBQUAD structure in the BITMAPINFO structure.

The color table is followed immediately by the actual bitmap bits, as an array of BYTE data (unsigned char). The best method to unravel the color table is to add **biSize** to the location of the BITMAPINFOHEADER, yielding the possible start of the color table. Then compare that location to the **bfOffBits** member. If they are equal, there is *no* color table present. The difference between the two locations divided by the size of the RGBQUAD structure (4 bytes) yields the number of color table entries actually stored. Alternatively, if the **biClrUsed** is actually present and nonzero, its value can be used. In Pgm09b, I check for this field's presence and use its value if nonzero.

Using DIBs requires solving several problems, including how to input the file in a usable form, how the color palette operates, how to construct and install a proper color palette for the DIB, and how to get the image onto the screen. Let's examine these issues one by one. Under C-style and MFC, the first challenge is to actually input the DIB into a dynamically allocated memory area.

There are other input considerations. I am ignoring OS2 Presentation Manager-style bitmaps which have a slightly different set of headers. The bitmap bits that contain the individual pixel colors can be a very large array. Often some form of data compression can be used to reduce that volume of data. Run Length Encoding (RLE) is one of the most common techniques used to compress images. Operating upon one scan line (one row of pixels) at a time, the basic idea is to replace a series of identical color values with a count of the number of duplicate color values and that color value—10 consecutive blue bits would be replaced by 10 x blue. While RLE is the basis of the PCX file format, it is infrequently used in bmp files. Hence, I am ignoring image compression here.

First, let's examine how the DIBs are input, then how the color palettes are handled, and last how to work with DIBs in memory DCs. Under MFC, we must write our own CDib class. I have purposely kept the class extremely simple so that the basic principles can easily be seen. (Note: the actual CDib class as used in these examples has some alterations added for the game DIB version of **CreateDIBSection**. We will discuss it later.) Examine the class header file.

9.13.1 Listing for File: CDib.h—Pgm09b—Excerpts

```
...
/******************************************************************************/
/*                                                                          */
/* CDib Class Definition                                                    */
/*                                                                          */
/******************************************************************************/

class CDib {

/******************************************************************************/
/*                                                                          */
/* Class Data Members                                                       */
/*                                                                          */
/******************************************************************************/
```

```
protected:

HANDLE   hdib;                    // handle for the DIB in memory
BYTE    *ptrdib;                  // locked ptr to the DIB
/*********************************************************************/
/*                                                                   */
/* Class Functions:                                                  */
/*                                                                   */
/*********************************************************************/
public:

        CDib (char*);            // construct a memory DIB from a .BMP file
        ~CDib ();                // removed the DIB

BOOL    IsValid ();              // returns TRUE if DIB is loaded and ready
void    MakePalette (CPalette*); // constructs a color palette from DIB
BYTE*   GetDibBitsAddr ();       // returns a pointer to the DIB data bits
int     GetDibWidth ();          // returns the width of the DIB in pixels
int     GetDibHeight ();         // returns the height of the DIB in pixels
LPBITMAPINFO GetBitmapInfo ();   // returns ptr to the BITMAPINFO section
protected:

void    ReadDibFile (char*);     // input the DIB file, constructing DIB object
...
```

The DIB is stored in a global memory block, **hdib,** and the locked pointer to the DIB is **ptrdib.** The member function **IsValid** attempts to get around the problem that a constructor cannot return a value. There are functions to return the key information: the width and height of the DIB plus the addresses of the actual color bytes and the BITMAPINFO structure. I also chose to make the palette construction a member function. Let's examine the implementation of the CDib class.

9.13.2 Listing for File: CDib.cpp—Pgm09b—Excerpts

```
...
/*********************************************************************/
/*                                                                   */
/* CDib: Load the DIB into a memory CDib object                      */
/*                                                                   */
/*********************************************************************/

        CDib::CDib (char *filename) {

ReadDibFile (filename); // attempt the loading of the DIB file
}
/*********************************************************************/
/*                                                                   */
/* ~CDib: Delete the CDib object                                     */
/*                                                                   */
/*********************************************************************/

        CDib::~CDib () {

if (ptrdib) {
```

```
  GlobalUnlock (hdib);   // remove allocated objects
  GlobalFree (hdib);
 }
 ptrdib = NULL;              // and set the dib pointer to none loaded
}
/********************************************************************************/
/*                                                                            */
/* IsValid: returns TRUE if DIB is loaded properly                            */
/*                                                                            */
/********************************************************************************/
BOOL      CDib::IsValid () {

 return (ptrdib) ? TRUE : FALSE;
}
/********************************************************************************/
/*                                                                            */
/* ReadDibFile: loads a .BMP file into a dib                                  */
/*                                                                            */
/********************************************************************************/
void      CDib::ReadDibFile (char *filename) {

 BITMAPFILEHEADER bmfh;
 DWORD            dwDibSize;
 DWORD            actsz;

 // open the file .BMP
 HANDLE hfile = CreateFile (filename, GENERIC_READ, FILE_SHARE_READ, NULL,
                            OPEN_EXISTING, 0, NULL);
 if (hfile == INVALID_HANDLE_VALUE) {
  ptrdib = NULL;
  return;
 }
 // input the BITMAPFILEHEADER structure
 ReadFile (hfile, (LPSTR) &bmfh, sizeof (BITMAPFILEHEADER), &actsz, NULL);
 if (actsz != sizeof (BITMAPFILEHEADER)) {
  CloseHandle (hfile);
  ptrdib = NULL;
  return;
 }
 // verify it is a .BMP file
 if (bmfh.bfType != * (WORD *) "BM") {
  CloseHandle (hfile);
  ptrdib = NULL;
  return;
 }
 // calculate the size of the file less the file header and allocate memory for the dib
 dwDibSize = bmfh.bfSize - sizeof (BITMAPFILEHEADER);
 hdib = GlobalAlloc (GMEM_MOVEABLE, dwDibSize);
 ptrdib = (BYTE*) GlobalLock (hdib);
 if (ptrdib == NULL) {
  CloseHandle (hfile);
  return;
 }
```

```
// read in the rest of the DIB - could be huge amount of bytes for a large .BMP file
ReadFile (hfile, (LPSTR) ptrdib, dwDibSize, &actsz, NULL);
CloseHandle (hfile);
if (actsz != dwDibSize) {
  GlobalUnlock (hdib);
  GlobalFree (hdib);
  ptrdib = NULL;
  return;
 }
// check the validity of the size of the info header - fail OS2 bitmaps
if ((((BITMAPINFOHEADER*) ptrdib)->biSize <= sizeof(BITMAPCOREHEADER)) {
 GlobalUnlock (hdib);
 GlobalFree (hdib);
 ptrdib = NULL;
 }
 else {
  // now determine the number of colors in the color palette
  WORD bitcount = ((BITMAPINFOHEADER*) ptrdib)->biBitCount; // get the bitcount

  // there may be a possibility that the biClrUsed field is really there
  // assume biClrUsed is not present and fill it if so
  numcolors = ((BITMAPINFOHEADER*) ptrdib)->biClrUsed;
  // since biClrUsed itself may be 0, as it often is, determine from bit count
  if (numcolors == 0 && bitcount != 24) numcolors = 1L << bitcount;
  // we are not handling the 24-color modes
  if (numcolors == 0) { // no color table is present, so I consider this DIB
                        // to be invalid - you could modify the palette
                        // construction to permit the DIB to be shown using
                        // the default palette, if desired
  GlobalUnlock (hdib);
  GlobalFree (hdib);
  ptrdib = NULL;
  }
 }
}

/*****************************************************************************/
/*                                                                         */
/* GetDibWidth: returns pixel width of image                               */
/*                                                                         */
/*****************************************************************************/
int      CDib::GetDibWidth () {

 return (!IsValid ()) ? 0 : ((BITMAPINFOHEADER*) ptrdib)->biWidth;
}

/*****************************************************************************/
/*                                                                         */
/* GetDibHeight: returns pixel height of image                             */
/*                                                                         */
/*****************************************************************************/
int      CDib::GetDibHeight () {

 return (!IsValid ()) ? 0 : ((BITMAPINFOHEADER*) ptrdib)->biHeight;
}
```

```
/***************************************************************************/
/*                                                                         */
/* GetDibBitsAddr: returns the addr of the color bits of the image         */
/*                                                                         */
/***************************************************************************/

BYTE*   CDib::GetDibBitsAddr () {
 DWORD numcolors, colortablesize;
 WORD  bitcount;

 if (!IsValid ()) return NULL;

 // calculate the offset from the info header over the color table
 colortablesize = numcolors * sizeof (RGBQUAD);
 // and return the address of the bits portion
 return ptrdib + ((BITMAPINFOHEADER*) ptrdib)->biSize + colortablesize;
}
/***************************************************************************/
/*                                                                         */
/* GetBitmapInfo:  returns the addr of the BITMAPINFO data                 */
/*                                                                         */
/***************************************************************************/

LPBITMAPINFO CDib::GetBitmapInfo () {

 return (!IsValid ()) ? NULL : (LPBITMAPINFO) ptrdib;
}
/***************************************************************************/
/*                                                                         */
/* MakePalette: constructs logical color palette                           */
/*                                                                         */
/***************************************************************************/

void     CDib::MakePalette (CPalette *ptrpalette) {

 LPLOGPALETTE ptrpal;
 HANDLE       hpal;                     // handle for the palette in memory
 if (!IsValid ()) return;

 // allocate a LOGPALETTE for the # of colors in use such as 16-color,256-color
 hpal = GlobalAlloc (GHND, sizeof (LOGPALETTE) +
                     numcolors * sizeof (PALETTEENTRY));
 ptrpal = (LPLOGPALETTE) GlobalLock (hpal);
 if (!ptrpal) return;

 // fill up the LOGPALETTE structure by copying from the dib color array
 ptrpal->palNumEntries = (unsigned short) numcolors;
 ptrpal->palVersion = 0x300;

 LPBITMAPINFO ptrinfo = (LPBITMAPINFO) ptrdib;
 for (int i=0; i<(int)numcolors; i++) {
  ptrpal->palPalEntry[i].peRed = ptrinfo->bmiColors[i].rgbRed;
  ptrpal->palPalEntry[i].peGreen = ptrinfo->bmiColors[i].rgbGreen;
  ptrpal->palPalEntry[i].peBlue = ptrinfo->bmiColors[i].rgbBlue;
  ptrpal->palPalEntry[i].peFlags = 0;
 }
```

```
// fill in the caller's palette by creating the palette from LOGPALETTE
ptrpalette->CreatePalette (ptrpal);

// now delete the LOGPALETTE which is no longer needed
GlobalUnlock (hpal);
GlobalFree (hpal);
}
```

The constructor invokes **ReadDibFile** to actually input the DIB. The new API **CreateFile** attempts to open the file for GENERIC_READ operations. If successful, the BITMAPFILEHEADER structure is read into an automatic storage copy of the structure. Verification of the first two bytes is done to ensure that they contain a DIB signature—BM. Next the actual size of the DIB is found by subtracting the size of the file header structure from the **bfSize**, the total file size. Based upon the DIB size, global memory is allocated to hold the DIB and **ptrdib** is locked to point to that memory. One **ReadFile** operation is requested to input the rest of the entire bmp file! Remember that this could be requesting several hundred thousand bytes. This is one very convenient property of the flat memory model. Under Windows 3.1, this input operation would involve a loop reading in, say, 32K chunks at a time. One other validity check is then performed on the BITMAPINFOHEADER portion to verify that **biSize** is at least 16 bytes or more.

Next, the number of colors present in the color table is calculated. If the **biClrUsed** field is present and is nonzero, I use its value. Most often, it is present but is zero. Thus, the number of colors is determined from the **biBitCount** member, eliminating the more complex 24-color mode. Typical values of the bit count are 1, 4, or 8; shifting a 1B left by the bit count amount yields 2 colors, 16 colors, or 256 colors. For all possible errors, the global memory is unlocked and freed and the pointer to the DIB is set to NULL. No error messages are produced. It is up to the user to invoke **IsValid** to determine the success of the load operation. The informational functions simply return the appropriate values extracted from the DIB. Ignore the palette construction function until we discuss palettes next.

9.14 HANDLING COLOR—THE PALETTES

The original color system was the RGB triplet stored in an unsigned long called a COLORREF type. Red intensity is stored in the byte that is farthest to the right. Moving leftward brings us to the green intensity byte, then the blue. The leftmost byte contains the type that could be one of three possibilities, as follows:

```
type = 0 => an explicit RGB color value in the other three bytes
       1 => a logical color palette index number
       2 => an RGB value from a color palette stored elsewhere
```

How does an RGB triplet actually define the color that appears on screen? To understand exactly how Windows 95 handles color palettes, we must examine briefly how the hardware handles color in the 256-color mode. Examine Figure 9.2 for an overview of this complex process.

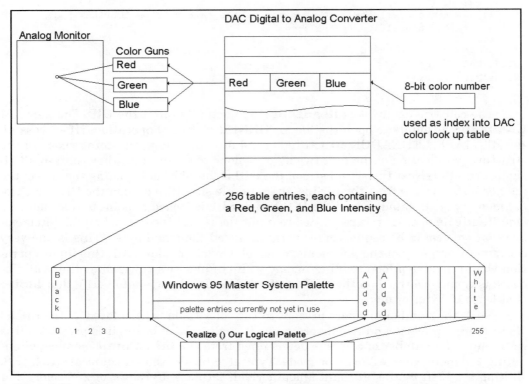

Fig. 9.2 How Colors Are Displayed Using the System Palette and Logical Palette

A pixel's color is created on an analog monitor by the combined intensities from the red, green, and blue guns. The intensity for each color gun comes from an 18-bit value (RGB) stored in the VGA's DAC or digital-to-analog converter. The DAC holds an array of 256 RGB table entries referenced by a byte color number ranging from 0 to 255. This byte can be the color byte coming from the bitmap data bits or DIB; if so, the method is said to be using DAC **index** numbers. When specifying an index, we get whatever color is currently loaded into that DAC color table entry. More frequently, we wish to specify a specific RGB color. (With DIBs we can choose to use RGB or color index methods.)

DOS programs are used to direct DAC manipulation, for it is extremely easy to insert whatever color values are desired. In fact, DOS programs often **animate** the palette by inserting a specific set of colors, for example, for a daytime color scene and then periodically reducing the DAC color values by 10 units or so every few seconds. When the DAC values change on the next CRT refresh cycle, the entire image is now redisplayed using the slightly darker colors. This gives the appearance of sunset. This is called **Palette Animation** and can be done under Windows as well. The only problem is that, under Windows, an application never has direct access to the DAC.

Instead, to enable device-independent programming, Windows 95 maintains *one* master color palette with the DAC colors in it. Windows 95 handles the transfer of the master palette colors into the DAC. The master palette has 256 entries in it corresponding to those of the DAC itself. The master palette index 0 is always black, and index 255 is always white. These two colors can never be changed. Windows 95 also has its 21 system colors loaded into the first 10 and last 10 palette entries, with the middle 235 available for application use. (Specifically indices 0–9 and 246–55 are used.) By using the API functions **GetSysColor** and **SetSysColor**, an application can get the current system colors in use and set them to other colors. Note that these 21 colors are user adjustable from the control panel applet by choosing ready-made schemes such as Arizona or by custom design.

Note that we can now understand the raster operations that invert colors. If a pixel is currently using DAC index 0×00, then its inverse is DAC index 0×FF; if it was using index 0×0F, the inverse is DAC index 0×F0. While the inverse is defined for black and white, it is not defined for colors. This is why Windows uses the first 10 and last 10—they are inverses of each other. If inverse raster operations are important to your 256-color application, then lay out your color scheme accordingly.

When you request a pen or brush using RGB values, Windows 95 tries to match your request with an entry currently in the master palette, adding new entries if needed. However, if your application needs the use of a color palette, as we now need to display a DIB in its proper colors, an application-private **logical color palette** must be used. (There is no method to access Windows 95's master palette directly.) After an application has constructed its desired logical palette, it must instruct Windows 95 to insert or **map** the logical palette onto its master palette. This mapping is quite a complex operation, but the basic idea is to determine a sort of cross index so that, when the application requests color 5 from its logical palette, Windows 95 substitutes the correct entry from the master table. This mapping process is done in response to the **RealizePalette** API function.

Now consider what could happen if several application windows are on-screen concurrently, each requesting its own logical palette to be mapped onto the master palette. We launch our application requesting its palette be mapped and suddenly there is no more room in the master palette! Windows 95 handles this by performing the best match possible, which, if many different colors are currently available, can result in a satisfactory dithered color. On the other hand, suppose that the first launched application has replaced all the system colors (except black and white, of course) and filled all 236 other slots with 254 different shades of red. When we launch our application and request our logical palette be mapped with **RealizePalette**, only reds, black, and white are available—our application is likely to look quite bizarre! In fact, the entire desktop appears bizarre as well. It is not polite to replace the 21 system colors unless the application is running and *only* running full screen (so no one can see the bizarre effect).

In this case—a full master palette—since our application has the input focus, Windows 95 provides another option, that being to replace the colors in its master table. This is done by first invoking **UnrealizePalette** before attempting to realize our logical palette. (Under Windows 95 the **UnrealizePallette** is now obsolete and is maintained for backwards compatibility. Under MFC the corresponding obsolete function is **UnrealizeObject**.) Once done, the application with the 254 shades of red now looks bizarre, but it does not have the input focus. Should you task switch to the red application, it now regains the input focus, and Windows 95 permits it to reset the master palette once more to 254 shades of red; our application now looks strange. The messages to which a palette-using application should consider responding are WM_QUERYNEWPALETTE, which is sent when our application regains the input focus, and WM_PALETTECHANGED, which is sent after another application has changed the palette, allowing us to re-realize our palette for the best appearance under the circumstances.

Windows 95 maps each color to this extended system palette as follows:

1. If a color in the user's logical palette matches a color already in the master system palette, that color is mapped to the existing system palette index or offset from the start of the 256 colors. Index 0 points to the first color in the 256-color palette.

2. If a color in the user's logical palette does not match, then that color is added to the extended system palette, if there is still room for it (236 possibilities).

3. When the extended system logical palette is full, the user's color is matched to the nearest or closest matching color that is already in the 256 extended system palette.

4. When there are several applications with logical palettes, Windows 95 maps the logical palette of the topmost window into the extended system palette.

A logical palette is similar to a hardware palette—it is a table of RGB colors, with the number of entries corresponding to the color mode. If you are using the 256-color mode, the logical palette contains 256 RGB values. The COLORREF item as stored in a logical palette is called the PALETTEENTRY structure, and the logical palette is the LOGPALETTE structure that also contains 1 PALETTEENTRY (unusual coding). The **CPalette** class maintains the logical palette, encapsulating the LOGPALETTE structure. The members of the LOGPALETTE structure are shown in Table 9.6.

Provision is made for an array of palette entries. Only the first is actually defined in the structure. Thus, when allocating a LOGPALETTE structure, allocate memory for two WORDs plus the number of colors to be in the palette times the size of a PALETTEENTRY structure. The PALETTEENTRY structure is defined in Table 9.7. where the flags can be one of the following:

Table 9.6 The LOGPALETTE Structure

Data Type	Name	Meaning
WORD	palVersion	usually 0×0300
WORD	palNumEntries	number of colors in the palette
PALETTEENTRY	palPalEntry[1]	an array of color entries

Table 9.7 The PALETTEENTRY Structure

Data Type	Name
BYTE	peRed
BYTE	peGreen
BYTE	peBlue
BYTE	peFlags

0	for a normal color palette entry of RGB values
PC_EXPLICIT	treats low word as an index into hardware palette
PC_NOCOLLAPSE	does not map this entry to any existing color
PC_RESERVED	reserved for animation effect and is to be altered often

These flags are very important. Normally we use a flag of zero for RGB palette values. However, if the color bits are to be used as a direct index reference into the DAC (assuming the correct colors are already there via the master palette), use PC_EXPLICIT. If dithered and nearest matching colors are not desired, use PC_NOCOLLAPSE. For palette animation special effects, use PC_RESERVED. When Windows 95 encounters either of these latter types, it *must* make a palette entry slot available for that color. The following standard coding determines whether or not the current display driver supports logical palettes.

```
if ( (dc.GetDeviceCaps (RASTERCAPS) & RC_PALETTE) &&
    (dc.GetDeviceCaps (DRIVERVERSION) >= 0x0300) )
{ does support log palettes}
else { does not}
```

To create a logical 256-color palette, for example, one would define

```
#define NUMCOLOR 256
LOGPALETTE  *ptrlogpal;
ptrlogpal = (LOGPALETTE *) new char[sizeof (LOGPALETTE) +
        (NUMCOLOR - 1) * sizeof (PALETTEENTRY) ];
// -1 because logpalette has 1 paletteentry within it
ptrlogpal->palVersion = 0x0300;
ptrlogpal->palNumEntries = NUMCOLOR;
```

Next, you need to install the color RGB values. There are many ways to give these palette entries their color RGB values. You could load in a palette saved on disk. You could initialize them as

```
for (int I = 0; i<NUMCOLOR; i++) {
 ptrlogpal->palPalEntry[i].peRed = i;
 ptrlogpal->palPalEntry[i].peGreen = 0;
 ptrlogpal->palPalEntry[i].peBlue = 0;
 ptrlogpal->palPalEntry[i].peFlags = 0; // for true RGB values
}
```

Next, the palette is ready for implementation. Construct the logical palette object and then realize it.

```
CPalette *ptrpalette = new CPalette ();
dc.CreatePalette (ptrlogpal);
dc.SelectPalette (ptrpalette, 0); // insert the dib's color palette
// where 0 = foreground palette, 1 = background palette
dc.RealizePalette();
```

Here the logical palette is merged into the system extended logical palette. The palette messages sent by Windows 95 that an application using logical palettes should respond to are:

```
DEFINE_RESPONSE_TABLE....
 ON_WM_QUERYNEWPALETTE, // install our own colors, we are active
 ON_WM_PALETTECHANGED,  // not us, so realize onto their pallette
END_RESPONSE_TABLE;

afx_msg void OnPaletteChanged (CWnd *ptr_win_that_changed_the_palette);
afx_msg void OnQueryNewPalette ();
```

Whenever your application gains the input focus or becomes the active task, Windows 95 first gives your application an opportunity to install its own colors in the system logical palette before the window is displayed and activated. Thus, in **OnQueryNewPalette**, you should at least do the following:

```
BOOL      MainWin::OnQueryNewPalette () {
 CDC *ptrdc = GetDC ();
 CPalette *ptroldpal = ptrdc->SelectPalette (ptrpalette, FALSE);
 UINT i = ptrdc->RealizePalette ();
 ReleaseDC (ptrdc);
 if (i)InvalidateRect(NULL, TRUE);
 return TRUE;
}
```

When another window changes the palette, all other windows are sent the palette changed message. If you want your application, when it is not active, to have the best possible colors in the new color scheme, you would respond to these messages with similar coding as given in the query processing.

```
void      MainWin::OnPaletteChanged (CWnd *ptrwin) {
 if (ptrwin != this) OnQueryNewPalette ();
}
```

There are many other Windows 95 API and MFC functions for manipulating palettes. Consult the documentation as the need arises.

Under MFC, we must first construct the LOGPAL 256-color logical palette from the DIB's color table by copying each of the **RGB** values from the DIB into the LOGPAL. Then we create the palette from the LOGPAL. Once the **CPalette** is constructed, the LOGPAL can be deleted. Review the previous coding above for the CDib class and the **MakePalette** function. C-style coding would closely parallel the MFC version.

9.15 METHODS TO DISPLAY THE DIB IMAGE

Next comes the problem of how to display the image. There are a number of approaches to actually getting the DIB image on-screen. They vary according to the application's needs. The number of times the image is to be displayed, the speed required, and game animation are the major factors.

9.15.1 The SetDIBitsToDevice Method

If the image is to be painted one time only, the image could be displayed directly from the CDib class using the C function **SetDIBitsToDevice**.

```
SetDIBitsToDevice (dc.m_hDC, 0, 0, dibrect.right, dibrect.bottom,
                current_hpel, -current_vpel, 0, dibrect.bottom,
                ptrdib-> GetDibBitsAddr (), ptrdib->GetBitmapInfo (),
                DIB_RGB_COLORS);
```

> ***Design Rule 41:*** **The DIB origin (0,0) is at the lower-left corner of the DIB bits array, not the upper-left corner!**

Yes, DIBs are indeed upside down. Thus, if you are using scroll bars similar to the earlier presentations, then the *y* scroll distance must be negated when using **SetDIBitsToDevice.**

The **SetDIBitsToDevice** approach has two drawbacks: a speed versus the color palette hindrance and the inability to draw upon the DIB using GDI functions. If the color mode of the image in the DIB and the color mode of the video driver are the same, there is no problem. However, if these two are different, then, every time the bits are set, the color palette must be adjusted, realizing colors. Specifically, Windows 95 takes each color in the DIB and attempts to find the nearest matching color that the current video display is capable of producing. Sometimes, this is exceedingly slow (when converting 24-bit color DIBs to 16-color mode, for example).

When using **SetDIBitsToDevice** there is one very important consideration: whether to use the DIB's color palette or not. If the DIB's color palette is not installed prior to setting the bitmap bits *and* if that DIB uses some colors that are not matchable on the current palette in use, the resultant display has very weird colors, rather like a "solarized" photograph. On the other hand, if the colors are matchable, the image appears with its expected colors. In Pgm09b, you can experiment with this effect. In the paint routine, I attempt to construct the DIB's color palette, install it, and realize it before the **SetDIBitsToDevice** invocation. If the palette cannot be constructed, I display a message box. Simply comment out the palette construction and subsequent destruction lines and rebuild and open one of the photographic bmp files. You can see how displaying DIBs without their correct color palette appears.

9.15.2 The Two Memory DC Methods

The next approach of getting the image on-screen uses a memory DC. In other words, converting the DIB into a DDB, done once, results in a significant speed boost plus the ability to use GDI functions directly on the memory DC and its bitmap. **BitBlt**s can then be used to display all or parts of the image. If you are going to allow scrolling or other actions that may require a total redisplay of the DIB, it is faster to go ahead and perform these color conversion activities one time. That is, go ahead and convert the DIB image into a normal **memory DC** and **bitmap**. This could be done by constructing a memory DC as we have done previously. Run Pgm09b and load in a larger image using both menu load options. Try dragging the thumb bar and performing a fast scroll. You will notice the memory DC implementation is significantly better.

However, if you simply construct a compatible bitmap and copy the DIB bits into the DDB bitmap, you will lose the color palette information! Thus, there are two methods for constructing the memory copy—one that loses color palette information and one that preserves the DIB color palette. Which method is used depends upon the actual colors used in the DIB and the colors in the normal application palette.

9.15.2.1 Memory DC Method 1: Converting DIBs into DDBs with Possible Color Loss Using SetDIBits

```
CClientDC dc (this);                  // dc to copy
ptrmemdc = new CDC();                 // the memory dc
ptrmemdc->CreateCompatibleDC (&dc); // copy client dc
ptrbitmap = new CBitmap ();           // create the bitmap for memdc
ptrbitmap->CreateCompatibleBitmap (&dc, dibrect.Width(),
                                        dibrect.Height());
ptrmemdc->SelectObject (ptrbitmap); // insert bitmap into memdc
// one time conversion of the DIB color bits to the compatible DC
// display
SetDIBits (ptrmemdc->m_hDC, HBITMAP (ptrbitmap->m_hObject), 0,
        dibrect.Height(), ptrdib->GetDibBitsAddr (),
        ptrdib->GetBitmapInfo (),
        DIB_RGB_COLORS);               // copy dib bits into bitmap
dc.BitBlt (actrect.left, actrect.top, actrect.Width(), actrect.Height(),
              ptrmemdc, current_hpel, current_vpel, SRCCOPY);
```

These actions would be done once. Then, in the **Paint** routine, the new palette is installed and a **BitBlt** makes the transfer, assuming scroll bars are present. Notice that the y scroll position is now **not** negated, since we are now using a real DDB in memory. The new palette must be selected into the paint DC. The realization of the palette installs the colors. The **BitBlt** uses the client area rectangle as before.

9.15.2.2 Memory DC Method 2: Converting DIBs into DDBs with No Color Loss Using CreateDIBitmap

Obviously a color palette must be constructed. Another API function is needed, one that will take each DIB color bit and convert it into a matching color in the selected palette as well as construct the DDB bitmap. This is the **CreateDIBitmap** function that, if successful, returns an HBITMAP that can then be selected into the memory DC. This function is not encapsulated in MFC; we must use the C-style function whose syntax is as follows:

```
HBITMAP CreateDIBitmap (HDC dc, BITMAPINFOHEADER* ptrheader,
                        CBM_INIT, BYTE* ptrbmbits,
                        BITMAPINFO* ptrinfo, DIB_RGB_COLORS);
```

The flag CBM_INIT causes the actual conversion and copying of the bitmap bits. Normally, the DIB_RGB_COLORS flag is used, indicating that the color palette contains RGB values. The alternative is DIB_PAL_COLORS, which indicates the color palette contains actual DAC palette index numbers.

Under MFC, the sequence for memory DC construction prior to **BitBlt**ing in the **Paint** function is as follows:

```
CClientDC dc (this);
ptrpalette = new CPalette ();
ptrdib->MakePalette (ptrpalette);
if (ptrpalette) {
 ptrmemdc = new CDC();
 ptrmemdc->CreateCompatibleDC (&dc);
 ptrmemdc->SelectPalette (ptrpalette, FALSE);
 dc.SelectPalette (ptrpalette, FALSE);
 dc.RealizePalette ();
 hbmp = CreateDIBitmap    (dc.m_hDC,
                    (BITMAPINFOHEADER*)(ptrdib->GetBitmapInfo()),
                    CBM_INIT, ptrdib->GetDibBitsAddr(),
                    ptrdib->GetBitmapInfo (), DIB_RGB_COLORS);
 if (hbmp != 0) SelectObject (ptrmemdc->m_hDC,hbmp);
}
```

9.15.3 Method for Constructing Blazing Memory DCs for Game Animation

The last approach yields the maximum performance needed for fast-action games. What is needed is a memory DC that can be drawn upon directly using the GDI functions, one that can be **BitBlt**ed directly to the screen as fast as DOS games and one in which the application has nearly complete control over the color palette. Enter the **CreateDIBSection** function and an **identity palette**. Under Windows 95 and Windows NT, the **CreateDIBSection** function creates a very special HBITMAP that is tied nearly directly to the hardware. When a **BitBlt** is done, there is *no* palette translation. The bits within the bitmap are assumed to be palette indices mapped directly to Windows' master palette. The **BitBlt** simply copies the bits directly onto the screen, resulting in the absolute fastest **BitBlt**ing in Windows! Additionally, the application has direct access to the bitmap bits for any desired manipulation as well as the ability to use normal GDI drawing functions on the bitmap. Indeed, this is a very special bitmap.

Using a DC model (usually a screen or window DC) that has installed an identity palette and using a BITMAPINFO structure that defines the dimensions and color table, if any, to be used, the function constructs the bitmap. (There are other advanced options that are ignored here.)

```
BYTE *ptrbits; // returned addr of DIBs bitmap bits for direct access
HBITMAP = CreateDIBSection (HDC dc, BITMAPINFO* ptrbm, DIB_RGB_COLORS,
                           (void**) &ptrbits, NULL, 0);
```

If direct manipulation of the bits is desired, save the returned address of the bits—**ptrbits**.

What is an **identity palette**? It is a logical palette that precisely matches the current master palette. Thus, when the identity palette is selected into a DC and realized, it is a duplicate of the master palette. When actions are done, no color table look up or color matching must be done as each entry in the user's logical palette corresponds to the same entry in the master palette. Drawing and bliting can bypass all palette mapping actions and can simply use the palette indices. Instead of taking an RGB value and finding it in the logical palette, matching it to the corresponding entry in the master palette, and then using that corresponding master palette index number as the entry into the hardware DAC, it uses the logical palette's index number for that RGB value as the hardware DAC entry. Ignoring DIBs, the basic method of identity palette construction is as follows:

1. Construct the application's desired logical palette.
2. Force the master palette to be reset to remap itself completely to accommodate the logical palette.
3. Realize the logical palette, setting up a new master palette.
4. Replace the application's logical palette with a copy of the master palette that has our colors flagged with the PC_NOCOLLAPSE option so they do not get remapped when the logical palette is once again realized.

If a DIB is to be converted into a DIB Section, additional steps are needed.

1. The initial logical palette comes from the DIB's color table.
2. After the identity palette is constructed, each entry in the DIB's color RGB table must match to the nearest matching color in the new identity palette.
3. Each bit in the bitmap (which contains an index into the DIB's color table) must be updated to point to the new corresponding identity palette entry.
4. Since the DIB Section is created from the BITMAPINFO and its following color table, the DIB's color table must be replaced with the new identity palette.

The DIB Section's bitmap can then be selected into a normal memory DC and used as any normal memory DC would be, only with much faster operation. Assuming that ptrpalette is an instance of **CPalette**, ptrdib, **CDib**, and ptrmemdc, **CDC**, the sequence is

```
CClientDC dc (this);                    // dc to copy
ptrpalette = new CPalette ();           // construct a color palette
ptrdib->MakeIdentityPalette (ptrpalette); // make identity palette from DIB
if (ptrpalette) {
  ptrmemdc = new CDC ();                // the memory dc
  ptrmemdc->CreateCompatibleDC (&dc);   // copy client dc
  dc.SelectPalette (ptrpalette, FALSE); // into the real DC
```

```
dc.RealizePalette ();                    // realize the palette
// construct a DIB Section from the DIB using the realized identity palette
BYTE *ptrbits;
hbmp = CreateDIBSection (dc.m_hDC, ptrdib->GetBitmapInfo(),DIB_RGB_COLORS,
                         (void**) &ptrbits, NULL, 0);
// if successful, install DIB Section bitmap into the memory DC
if (hbmp) {
 SelectObject (ptrmemdc->m_hDC,hbmp);
 // copy all DIB bits directly into the DIB Section bitmap
 memcpy (ptrbits, ptrdib->GetDibBitsAddr(), ptrdib->GetDibHeight() *
         ptrdib->GetDibWidth ());
}
}
if (!ptrmemdc || !hbmp || !ptrpalette) {
 MessageBox("Cannot create DIB Section Memory DC",
            "Error In Conversion of Dib", MB_OK);
 RemoveObject (); // if not all created, delete all objects
 return;
}
```

In the **OnPaint** function, to display the DIB, use

```
dc.SelectPalette (ptrpalette, 0); // insert the dib's color palette
dc.RealizePalette();               // cause palette to be set up & ready
// copy the memory image to the screen adjusted by scroll bar
dc.BitBlt (actrect.left, actrect.top, actrect.Width(), actrect.Height(),
           ptrmemdc, current_hpel, current_vpel, SRCCOPY);
```

The **MakeIdentityPalette** function is involved. First, I abort the process if the device is not a palettized one with 256 colors.

```
LOGPALETTE   *ptrpal;
CPalette     *ptroldpal;
CDC          dc;
// get access to a screen DC - verify it is a palette device
if (!dc.CreateDC ("DISPLAY", NULL, NULL, NULL)) return FALSE;
else if (!dc.GetDeviceCaps (RASTERCAPS) & RC_PALETTE) {
 dc.DeleteDC ();
 return FALSE;
}
// check that screen is in 256 color mode
int num_syscolors = dc.GetDeviceCaps (NUMCOLORS);
if (num_syscolors > 256) {
 dc.DeleteDC ();
 return FALSE;
}
// retrieve the number of palette entries
int num_palette_entries = dc.GetDeviceCaps (SIZEPALETTE);
```

Now force the Palette Manager to reset the master color table so that the next palette that is realized gets its colors inserted into the master palette. Then construct the logical palette and fill it with the DIB's current color table of RGB values, and then create the palette from the logical palette.

```
// force Palette Manager to reset the master color table
```

```
// so the next palette that is realized gets its colors
// mapped into the order of use in the logical palette
SetSystemPaletteUse (dc.GetSafeHdc (), SYSPAL_NOSTATIC);
SetSystemPaletteUse (dc.GetSafeHdc (), SYSPAL_STATIC);

// allocate a LOGPALETTE for the # of colors in use - be here 256-color
ptrpal = (LOGPALETTE*) malloc (sizeof (LOGPALETTE) +
                                numcolors * sizeof (PALETTEENTRY));
if (!ptrpal) {
 dc.DeleteDC ();
 return FALSE;
}

// construct the basic DIB logical palette
// fill up the LOGPALETTE structure by copying from the dib color array
ptrpal->palNumEntries = (unsigned short) numcolors;
ptrpal->palVersion = 0x300;
int i;
LPBITMAPINFO ptrinfo = (LPBITMAPINFO) ptrdib;
// copy the DIB's RGB colors into the logical palette
for (i=0; i<(int)numcolors; i++) {
 ptrpal->palPalEntry[i].peRed   = ptrinfo->bmiColors[i].rgbRed;
 ptrpal->palPalEntry[i].peGreen = ptrinfo->bmiColors[i].rgbGreen;
 ptrpal->palPalEntry[i].peBlue  = ptrinfo->bmiColors[i].rgbBlue;
 ptrpal->palPalEntry[i].peFlags = 0;
}

// fill in the caller's palette by creating the palette from LOGPALETTE
ptrpalette->CreatePalette (ptrpal);
if (!ptrpalette) {
 dc.DeleteDC ();
 free (ptrpal);
 return FALSE;
}
```

Obtain a copy of the master palette and insert PC_NOCOLLAPSE into the nonsystem colors and replace our logical palette with the identity palette.

```
// install our new palette, realize it to map the logical palette
// into the master palette, then remove the palette from the DC
ptroldpal = dc.SelectPalette (ptrpalette, FALSE);
dc.RealizePalette ();
dc.SelectPalette (ptroldpal, FALSE);

// now construct a copy of the altered, mapped real palette
// by getting all 256 entries
PALETTEENTRY pe[256];
GetSystemPaletteEntries (dc.GetSafeHdc (), 0, num_palette_entries, pe);

// alter the 20 system colors' flags to normal
// (the first 10 and last 10 entries)
// and set our needed colors's flags (the remaining 236) to no collapse
// so that those slots will remain asis and not get remapped to a
// possible duplicate, earlier palette entry
for (i=0; i<num_syscolors/2; i++) pe[i].peFlags = 0;
for (; i< num_palette_entries - num_syscolors/2; i++)
```

```
   pe[i].peFlags =  PC_NOCOLLAPSE;
   for (; i< num_palette_entries; i++) pe[i].peFlags = 0;

   // handle any possible resizing of the palette
   ptrpalette->ResizePalette (num_palette_entries);
   // copy the identity palette in pe into our palette
   ptrpalette->SetPaletteEntries (0, num_palette_entries, pe);
```

Construct the conversion table from the original DIB's RGB colors to the new identity palette's RGB colors.

```
   // next, alter the DIB's color table to match the logical id. palette
   // get a pointer to the DIB's color table
   RGBQUAD *ptrcolortab = (LPRGBQUAD)(ptrdib + sizeof(BITMAPINFOHEADER));
   RGBQUAD *ptrsave = ptrcolortab;
   // for each of the colors in the original DIB color table, find its
   // matching palette index in the identity palette
   BYTE map[256];
   for (i=0; i<256; i++, ptrcolortab++)
    map[i] = (BYTE) ptrpalette->GetNearestPaletteIndex (
     RGB(ptrcolortab->rgbRed, ptrcolortab->rgbGreen, ptrcolortab->rgbBlue));
   ptrcolortab = ptrsave;
```

Replace each DIB bitmap pixel's color index byte with the corresponding mapped color index.

```
   // replace each color byte (for each pixel) in the DIB with the
   // corresponding mapped color index
   BYTE *ptrb = GetDibBitsAddr();
   i = GetDibHeight () * GetDibWidth ();
   while (i--) {
    *ptrb = map[*ptrb];
    ptrb++;
   }
```

Finally, alter the DIB's color table to match the logical identity palette because later on the **CreateDIBSection** uses the DIB's color table to construct the DIB Section bitmap.

```
   // and rewrite the DIB's color table so that it agrees with the identity
   // palette
   ptrpalette->GetPaletteEntries (0, 256, pe);
   for (i=0; i<256; i++) {
    ptrcolortab->rgbRed   = pe[i].peRed;
    ptrcolortab->rgbGreen = pe[i].peGreen;
    ptrcolortab->rgbBlue  = pe[i].peBlue;
    ptrcolortab++;
   }

   dc.DeleteDC ();
   free (ptrpal);
   return TRUE;
```

This is the key to fast games. On this memory DC, you can then perform all of the usual operations for animation effects. These are discussed in chapter 14.

9.16 BITMAP SPECIAL EFFECTS DISPLAYS

While most applications merely display the images and go on, for a more professional and "catchy" look, bitmap images can be displayed using several special effects. Generally, these effects are used once as the original graphic image is first displayed. If you wish to use special effects, then the second approach—converting all the way into a DDB in a memory DC—is needed. Among the easier effects to implement are the following:

The **Vertical Crush** effect begins by showing only the left and right edges and then successively displays the remaining lines until the center is reached.

The **Horizontal Crush** effect displays the top and bottom lines and then the other lines moving toward the center are displayed last.

The **Diagonal** effect begins the display in the upper-left corner and slowly displays the image along a diagonal line until the bottom-right corner is reached.

The **Spiral In** effect begins at the outer edges and displays successive areas in a spiral-inward motion until the center is reached.

The **Spiral Out** effect begins at the center of the image and displays successive areas in a circular, spiral manner outward to all edges (my second favorite).

The **Skip Horizontal** effect alternates drawing vertical columns moving from the left to right and right to left. Each set skips over the next adjacent column, leaving a hole. When one pass is done, it repeats in a similar manner displaying those that were skipped on the first pass.

The **Skip Vertical** effect operates similarly, drawing pairs of rows from the top down and bottom up, each time skipping the next adjacent row, leaving a hole every other row. The next pass displays these missing rows.

The **Skip Diagonal Squares** displays the image diagonally in small squares, omitting every other square, creating a checkerboard appearance. The second pass then fills in these missing squares.

The **Skip Rectangles** effect draws a thin rectangle at the maximum dimensions of the image, then moves inward skipping over the would-be next rectangle, creating a rectangular hole. On the last pass the missing rectangles are displayed. (This is my favorite effect.)

There are many more possibilities than these few I have listed. An excellent reference on how to create these and other special effects in C-style, including how to input the bmp file, is a series of articles by Charles Mirho.[*] I have used three of his C-style routines, adapting them for MFC use. Additionally, I have adapted four routines from a set of C-style effects in an article by Saurabh Dixit; the article has some additional effects.[†]

---

[*] *Window/DOS Developer's Journal*, February, March, May 1994, Vol 5, nos. 2, 3, 5.

[†] "Creating Special-Effect Bitmaps," *Dr. Dobb's Sourcebook*, March/April 1995.

9.16.1 Pgm09b: DIB (bmp) File Display with Fancy Effects

Sample program Pgm09b displays DIBs (bmp files) with scroll bars as needed in either of the two display formats just discussed. Then the image can be displayed using any of the special effects. Once that image has been displayed using the effect, should you scroll the image or resize the window, the bitmap is redrawn normally.

Pgm09b permits the bmp file to be loaded and shown in three ways, including the fast DIB Section with identity palette approach. The loading method is controlled via the menu. You can test loading the bitmap as a DIB and by converting it into a memory DC. All special effects require the memory DC, so, if it has not been converted from a DIB, the choice of any special effect forces the conversion process. Each special effect can be chosen from the menu. However, since there are so many, I have added an Animation Sequence menu item, which is enabled after any bitmap has been loaded. If animation is selected, I display in sequence all of the animation effects, one by one, rapid fire. Figure 9.3 shows Pgm09b after I have loaded ACME.BMP.

In the \LearnWin\Bmp subdirectory there are several bmp files for display. (Yes, I took those photos.) The File Open dialog uses this as the initial directory to display. If the user selects a different subdirectory, then the next time the File Open dialog is launched, that different subdirectory is used as the initial directory.

Examine the resource.h and Pgm09b.rc files. The identifiers (CM_CRUSH_VERT and others) are used both as a menu item's identifier and the effect type ID for painting. The Load File menu allows you to load in the bmp file and display from the DIB or from a fully converted memory DC. The default effect is to display the image normally. Note that, if you have loaded from a DIB and not the memory DC option and then have chosen a special effect, the program must convert to the memory DC before it can show the effect.

This example also shows how to update the title bar. When a new file is opened, its filename is concatenated with the normal window's title. Then the new title is inserted into the title bar. The frame window provides access to the title bar through the more general **CWnd SetWindowText** function

```
SetWindowText (newtitle);     // install new concatenated title
```

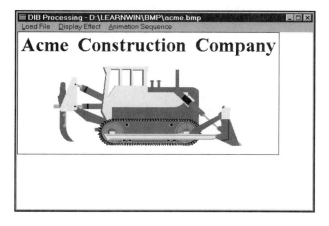

Fig. 9.3 Pgm09b with ACME.BMP Loaded

9.16.2 Listing for File: resource.h—Pgm09b—Excerpts

```
...
#define CM_LOAD_FROM_DIB          (WM_USER + 100)    // normal dib file load
#define CM_LOAD_GAME_MEMORYDC     (WM_USER + 101)    // special dib game load
#define CM_LOAD_FROM_MEMORYDC     (WM_USER + 102)    // normal dib file load mem dc
#define CM_CRUSH_VERT             (WM_USER + 103)    // display crush effect vert
#define CM_CRUSH_HORZ             (WM_USER + 104)    // display crush effect horiz
#define CM_DIAGONAL               (WM_USER + 105)    // display diagonal effect
#define CM_NORMAL                 (WM_USER + 106)    // display normally
#define CM_SPIRAL_IN              (WM_USER + 107)    // display spiral in
#define CM_SPIRAL_OUT             (WM_USER + 108)    // display spiral out
#define CM_SKIPHORIZ              (WM_USER + 109)    // display skip horizontal
#define CM_SKIPVERT               (WM_USER + 110)    // display skip vertical
#define CM_SKIPDIAGSQR            (WM_USER + 111)    // display skip diagonal squares
#define CM_SKIPRECTANGLES         (WM_USER + 112)    // display skip rectangles effect
#define CM_ANIMATE                (WM_USER + 113)    // animate series command
#define CM_EXIT                   (WM_USER + 114)    // exit

#define IDS_FRAMETITLE            2002
...
```

MFC menu numbers can also use the WM_USER base number to guarantee that menu numbers do not conflict with the MFC environment.

9.16.3 Listing for File: Pgm09b.rc—Pgm09b—Excerpts

```
...
MAINMENU MENU
BEGIN
    POPUP "&Load File"
    BEGIN
      MENUITEM "Load and Display from a &DIB",          CM_LOAD_FROM_DIB
      MENUITEM "Load and Display from a &Memory DC",    CM_LOAD_FROM_MEMORYDC
      MENUITEM "Load and Display from a DIB Section (Games)", CM_LOAD_GAME_MEMORYDC
      MENUITEM SEPARATOR
      MENUITEM "E&xit\tAlt+F4",                         CM_EXIT
    END
    POPUP "&Display Effect"
    BEGIN
      MENUITEM "Normal Display",          CM_NORMAL
      MENUITEM "Crush - Vertical",        CM_CRUSH_VERT
      MENUITEM "Crush - Horizontal",      CM_CRUSH_HORZ
      MENUITEM "Diagonal",                CM_DIAGONAL
      MENUITEM "Spiral In",               CM_SPIRAL_IN
      MENUITEM "Spiral Out",              CM_SPIRAL_OUT
      MENUITEM "Skip Horizontal",         CM_SKIPHORIZ
      MENUITEM "Skip Vertical",           CM_SKIPVERT
      MENUITEM "Skip Diagonal Squares",   CM_SKIPDIAGSQR
      MENUITEM "Skip Rectangles",         CM_SKIPRECTANGLES
    END
    MENUITEM    "&Animation Sequence",    CM_ANIMATE
END
```

```
STRINGTABLE  // our apps
{
  IDS_FRAMETITLE, "DIB Processing"
}
...
```

9.16.4 Listing for File: FrameWin.h—Pgm09b—Excerpts

```
...
class FrameWin : public CFrameWnd {
...
protected:

char          filename[MAX_PATH];    // filename of .BMP file
char          init_dir[MAX_PATH];    // open dlg initial dir to show

CDib          *ptrdib;               // pointer a DIB in memory
CDC           *ptrmemdc;             // a memory DC for the .BMP file
HBITMAP       hbmp;                  // a bitmap for the memory DC
CPalette      *ptrpalette;           // the palette for the memory dc

int           effecttype;            // type of effect, 0 = normal
CRect         dibrect;               // dimensions of dib
CRect         actrect;               // dimensions of client area

CRect         full_window;           // max sized window
CRect         display_window;        // current display window onto full window

int           current_vpel;          // current vertical scroll offset
int           current_hpel;          // current horizontal scroll offset
int           num_vpels_to_scroll;
int           num_hpels_to_scroll;
int           max_vscroll_pels;      // max num pels vertical to scroll
int           max_hscroll_pels;      // max num pels horizontal to scroll

BOOL          animate;               // TRUE when going thru effects automatically
...

public:
              FrameWin (CWnd*, const char*); // constructor
              ~FrameWin ();                  // destructor

protected:

afx_msg void  CmLoadFromDib ();        // display .BMP normally from a dib
afx_msg void  CmLoadFromMemoryDC ();   // display .BMP normally from a memdc
afx_msg void  CmLoadFromDIBSection (); // display .BMP from a DIB Section memory DC
afx_msg void  CmCrushVert ();          // display crush effect vertical
afx_msg void  CmCrushHorz ();          // display crush effect horizontal
afx_msg void  CmDiagonal ();           // display diagonal effect
afx_msg void  CmNormal ();             // display normally
afx_msg void  CmSpiralIn ();           // display spiral in effect
afx_msg void  CmSpiralOut ();          // display spiral out effect
afx_msg void  CmSkipHoriz ();          // display skip horizontal effect
afx_msg void  CmSkipVert ();           // display skip vertical effect
afx_msg void  CmSkipDiagSquares ();    // display skip diagonal squares effect
afx_msg void  CmSkipRectangles ();     // display skip rectangles effect
```

```
afx_msg void   CmAnimate ();                // launch animation sequence
afx_msg void   CmEnableAnimate (CCmdUI*);   // enable animate effects
afx_msg void   CmExit ();                    // quit

afx_msg void   OnPaint ();                          // paint the window - WM_PAINT
afx_msg void   OnSize (UINT, int, int);            // process window resize
afx_msg void   OnKeyDown (UINT, UINT, UINT);       // keybd scroller interface
afx_msg void   OnHScroll (UINT, UINT, CScrollBar*); // handle scrolling
afx_msg void   OnVScroll (UINT, UINT, CScrollBar*);

afx_msg LRESULT OnDisplayChange (WPARAM, LPARAM); // handle display changes

void       EffectDiagonal(CDC &);          // perform diagonal effect
void       EffectCrush (CDC &);            // perform crush effect
void       EffectSpiral (CDC &);           // perform spiral effect
void       EffectSkipHoriz (CDC &);        // perform skip horizontal
void       EffectSkipVert (CDC &);         // perform skip vertical
void       EffectSkipDiagSquares (CDC &);// perform skip diagonal squares
void       EffectSkipRectangles (CDC &);  // perform skip rectangles

void       UpdateCaption ();               // include BMP filename in title
void       AdjustScroller ();              // adjust scroll range
void       RemoveObject ();                // deletes all dib objects
void       ConvertToMemoryDC ();           // convert dib to memory DC
void       ConvertToGameDC ();             // convert dib to DIB Section DC

void       LoadBMPFile ();                 // loads a .BMP file into a dib
...
```

All of the work is done in the FrameWin class with support from the CDib class. Examine the class definition; notice the series of four GDI objects. The member **filename** stores the full path and name of the loaded file; further, the filename is appended to the main window's caption on the title bar, just as you would see in Paintbrush. The **effecttype** member contains the effect identifiers, which are the same identifiers as used in the menu item IDs.

Because of the rather lengthy source listing, the FrameWin class implementation, FrameWin.cpp, is not shown. It is on the CD-ROM in the \learnwin\pgm09b directory. You should either print your own listing or open a view window to this file to study how the operations are coded. Save a tree.

The constructor initializes the four object pointers to null: **ptrdib, ptrmemdc, hbmp,** and **ptrpalette**. The default **effecttype** is CM_NORMAL. It is **RemoveObject**'s duty to delete any of these four objects so that the class destructor only needs to remove any scroller. The **OnSize** member acquires the current client area rectangle, **actrect**, and then invokes the **AdjustScroller** function to reset the scroll bar ranges. In **AdjustScroller**, the unit is again 1 pixel and the *x,y* ranges are the differences between the DIB's actual dimensions and those of the current client area rectangle.

The **LoadBMPFile** function follows the general form discussed above. The **ConvertToMemoryDC** function handles the remaining conversions, as needed.

The **UpdateCaption** function illustrates how to append to the main window's title bar. Often, when a window is maximized, the caption is modified. "DIB Processing" is the normal caption. Whenever a file is loaded, the full path/filename is appended. I retrieve the caption string from the resource file, append a " — " and the filename to it. Then the caption is changed.

```
SetWindowText (newtitle);    // install new concatenated title
```

Bmp files are loaded in response to one of two load menu items. The normal DIB request invokes **LoadBMPFile**. Then, if special effects are turned on, it invokes **ConvertToMemoryDC** just as if the user had chosen the second "load into memory." After a successful file load, both these functions then call **AdjustScroller** and **UpdateCaption** before **Invalidate** forces the image to be painted. The various menu item responses for the special effects simply set the **effecttype** to the correct effect ID, complete the conversion to a memory DC if required, and **Invalidate** to cause the image to be displayed with that effect.

The **OnPaint** function does nothing if there is no file loaded. The **effecttype** is cased. For all of the special effects cases, the palette is first realized and then the appropriate effects function is invoked. For the normal display, the coding is as discussed earlier. Remember that, when using **SetDIBitsToDevice**, any scroll y offsets must be negated due to the reversal of the y axis. Notice again that, after the display is complete, the last thing **OnPaint** does is set the **effecttype** back to CM_NORMAL so that the user can scroll and use the image normally.

I will leave it up to you to study the special effects coding—study the code and my comments. The basic idea is to construct small square blocks of dimensions **numpels** and **BitBlt** them to the paint DC. Following Mirho's examples, I have not included special handling for the bitmaps whose dimensions are not an even multiple of the **numpels** block size. The results are less than satisfactory for those cases. To see the effect, try using "arches.bmp" which has an odd width. The odd dimension effect can be greatly minimized by setting **numpels** smaller. Try using 1 pel. Speed of display is also a consideration. The larger the **numpels**, the faster the effect. The diagonal effect goes very slowly with numpels = 1. If wanted, you could add code to pause a bit between loops. In the Paint function, after the special effect is completed, the less-than-satisfactory display can be removed by performing a normal **BitBlt** of the full image.

Study the implementations of Pgm09b on the CD-ROM and experiment with the program. If you do not like the "white streak" effect produced when bitmaps of an odd size are displayed with the special effects, try adding a final complete image **BitBlt** after the effect has finished. Find a large bitmap or make one and experiment with the speed of scrolling and display using the various memory DC forms. See just how much faster the DIB Section method really is.

Using the Printer and Fonts

10.1 Introduction

Ever had a programming nightmare? Well, printing documents under Windows 95 is bad—really bad—but it could be a lot worse. MFC does help speed the process. Perhaps the most significant problem facing the programmer is the vast number of different printers, each with its own printing protocol. Consider the task of writing a DOS application that prints a document that includes both text and graphics. How do you handle the printing process? Windows 95 attempts to solve this nasty situation by providing device-independent printing. Still, it remains a tricky, confusing arena.

10.2 The Design of Printing Operations

The File pop-up menu often offers four menu items for the user: File | Print, File | Page Setup, File | Preview, and File | Print Setup. The File | Preview operation is discussed in depth in chapter 15. The printer setup operation displays the Windows 95 common Printer Setup dialog box in which the user can select the current printer to be used, set the current default printer, and set some printer options such as landscape mode. When File | Print is chosen, the Windows 95 common Print dialog box is displayed. From this dialog, the user selects the specific details for this print run, including portrait/landscape, image dithering, which pages, and how many copies, for example.

Once the user selects OK, the printing process begins and an Abort Printing Process dialog box appears for the duration of the printing process. Should the user select the Abort button, the print is canceled. Under MFC, the programmer must supply the Abort dialog when printing outside of the Document-View architecture.

MFC is designed around a high-level Document-View architecture, which is covered in detail in chapter 15. In the Document-View scheme, the document class encapsulates the actual application data while one or more view classes encapsulate the on-screen images of that data. For example, a document class could hold the data of a spreadsheet, while one view class could display the table form and another view class could display the data in a graphical format. This scheme is complex, adds considerable overhead to the application, and, based upon my experience teaching programmers new to Windows programming, is extremely difficult to understand until the basics of Windows 95 programming are known. While the doc-view approach can simplify somewhat the basic printing process for the programmer, let's ignore this approach initially and examine several direct printing methods because not every application is a doc-view scheme.

10.2.1 Printing Method 1: Printing a Mixed Page of Text and Graphics from the Screen Paint Function

Suppose that one has a screen containing a mixture of text and graphical images to be printed. The paint function is already rendering the page on the screen by drawing upon the passed screen DC. A common approach to printing such a page is to present the paint function with a printer DC and have that same code render the page on the printer. The paint function does not even know that it is actually printing! It simply draws on the presented DC. The big benefit is avoidance of duplicated coding. The disadvantage is that this method works well when only the on-screen information is to be printed. It becomes quite awkward when such things as headings, column headings, footnotes, and page numbers are required.

10.2.2 Printing Method 2: Printing Multiple-Page Documents or Reports

Normally, the phrase "multiple-page document" suggests a letter, memo, or chapter in a book. However, it can also represent a spreadsheet, database, mailing labels, or custom-designed invoices. In other words, a multiple-page document is the *norm*. The printed pages representing mailing labels or custom-designed forms may never even have an equivalent on-screen display. Database systems and spreadsheets, to a lesser extent, often generate various types of printed reports. Under MFC, report-specific functions can be used to actually render reports on the printer.

10.3 SCALING THE PAGE

There is a major difference in scale between the screen image and the printed page; screen images have a different scale than the printer. For example, a square occupying one-fourth of the client area is drawn on the screen; when this is drawn directly on a printer, the printed square is not proportionately the same. Screen resolution is often 640×480 or 1024×768 pixels covering from about 10 inches (14-inch monitor) to 12.5 inches (17-inch monitor). Each printer has a specific resolution given in dots per inch (dpi) with a constant page size of 8 1/2 by 11 inches. Dot-matrix printers typically have a resolution of about 120 dpi, while laser printers may have 300 dpi to 600 dpi. Consider a line 120 pixels long drawn on a 14-inch monitor in VGA resolution (640×480) that appears to be about 1.5 inches long; that same line is rendered about 1 inch long on a dot-matrix printer at 120 dpi and about one-third or one-sixth inch long on a laser printer (120/300 or 120/600). Thus, when drawing graphical images, the two relative scales must be considered.

Normally, the print functions use the MM_TEXT mapping mode where one logical unit, the pixel, is one physical unit, the pixel. This one-to-one correspondence is what is causing the scaling difficulties. The mapping mode best suited for printers is MM_ANISOTROPIC (or possibly MM_ISOTROPIC) because, in this mode, the program can specify its own units, that is scale one axis or both.

10.4 USING FONTS

The font used to render the page plays a critical role in the printing process. The chosen font affects the actual speed that the printer can print the page (particularly true for dot-matrix printers), and it affects the scaling process. Consider the dismal speed of a dot-matrix printer displaying a graphical image—it may take minutes to display even one page. Yet if only printer built-in fonts are used, a dot-matrix printer can print text as fast as it does under DOS. On the other hand, since Windows 3.1, the use of TrueType fonts in documents has become widespread. These fonts are completely scalable, offering the user many point sizes. However, when printing scalable fonts, especially on a laser printer, they must be properly scaled to fit the printer resolution. If they are not, you may see your page rendered in microscopic letters! Note that True-Type fonts sent to a dot-matrix printer are considered bitmapped graphical images and are printed as slowly as a paintbrush image. On dot-matrix printers, only those built-in fonts print at text speeds.

You might think that the solution would be to decide what **printer** font you are going to use and then install that font as the **screen** font. However, this approach does not work because many printer fonts are small; if displayed directly on the screen, they would be illegible. Why? The screen is often viewed from a distance of about 24 inches from the eye, while the printed page is often viewed from a distance of 10–12 inches from the eye. Thus, magnification becomes a problem. When Windows 95 renders a font, it considers the display surface. For example, if the user specifies an 8-point font, when Windows 95 constructs the font for a screen display, it scales the font to become legible. Yet, when that same font is constructed for a printer display, Windows 95 uses the correct point size. If Windows did not do this scaling, many printer fonts would be illegible on the screen. Hence, some form of scaling must be done when printing.

10.5 THE PRINT SPOOLING PROCESS

Windows 95 implements a GDI interface, **Escape**, to handle printing. (Most printers use an escape sequence to enable/disable various special effects and options.) Several crucial subfunctions include **StartDoc**, **EndDoc**, and **NewFrame** that begin a document, stop printing a document, and begin a new page by ending the last page with the issuance of the form feed code to the printer. C-style coding directly accesses these **Escape** functions. The MFC in the Document-View approach completely encapsulates these low-level operations, but does not do so outside of doc-view. For MFC printing in such circumstances, I utilize these **Escape** functions.

The printing process is a complex interaction between the GDI, the printer device driver (drv module) for the specific printer, and the Print Manager program. The complex chain of events begins with the print request. The GDI first builds a temporary disk file containing all of the GDI commands required to construct the printout. These commands are constructed from our functions that display the text and graphical images on the printer DC. Then, this metafile of GDI commands for the entire document is read back and, together with the printer driver, Windows 95 creates another temporary disk file of the specific printer commands needed to render the pages. When this is complete (**EndDoc**), the Print Manager can then begin the process all over with another job that is ready to be printed. Meanwhile, the Print Manager then inputs the temporary rendered file and spools it to the actual printer. These two temporary files can become quite large—many megabytes. If at any point the disk becomes full, an error is raised.

A process called *banding* can reduce the overhead of these temporary files and speed up the process. The idea is to divide a page into a series of printing bands or rectangles and process each directly, creating only the actual file that is to be passed to the Print Manager to be spooled directly to the printer. Often the application just redisplays the whole page, letting the clipping process dictated by the banding rectangle handle what is really to be printed within that band. (The alternative is to have a "band-smart" printing function, which is vastly more complex.) Although the page is completely displayed for each band, there is still an increase in speed from not having to create and read back the GDI metafile for the page. Also the required disk space may be as much as halved. (See the Petzold book in the bibliography for details.)

10.6 PGM10a: PRINTING METHOD 1—USING A DUAL-PURPOSE RENDER FUNCTION

Figure 10.1 shows Pgm10a in operation. The screen display is what is going to be printed, properly scaled to be proportionately the same. There is a sample text message and a rectangle graphic. When you run the program, notice carefully the proportions of the rectangle versus the screen size. The printout should be similar, scaling the rectangle accordingly. Resize the window and reprint.

One method of creating printed output for a page in a device-independent manner is rather clever, if not confusing. The window that owns the page to be printed has

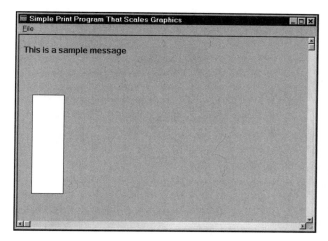

Fig. 10.1 Pgm10a—Printing the Screen with Proportional Scaling

an **OnPaint** function that normally creates that page on the client area via constructing a **CPaintDC** device context and rendering the text and graphics data. When printing, the application constructs a printing DC and renders the same data to it. Both **OnPaint** and the printing function must display the same information in the same manner. Therefore, we write *one* generalized **Render** function that is passed the **CDC** to use and display the data on to that DC. When we get to the document view, we shall see that this is precisely what the MFC actually does, only **Render** becomes **OnDraw**.

When not running under the MFC's doc-view, printing operations more closely parallel the C-style API. Examine the Pgm10a.rc and resource.h files; notice that an Abort Printing dialog box must be created. The Abort Printing dialog appears at the start of the printing process and is removed when the document is finished printing. While the dialog is active, the user can press the Cancel button, terminating the printing process.

10.6.1 Listing for File: resource.h—Pgm10a—Excerpts

```
. . .
#define CM_FILEPRINT        (WM_USER + 100)
#define CM_FILEPRINTERSETUP (WM_USER + 101)
#define CM_FONTCHANGE       (WM_USER + 102)
#define CM_EXIT             (WM_USER + 103)
. . .
```

10.6.2 Listing for File: Pgm10a.rc—Pgm10a—Excerpts

```
. . .
MAINMENU MENU
BEGIN
    POPUP "&File"
    BEGIN
        MENUITEM "&Choose Font",        CM_FONTCHANGE
```

```
            MENUITEM SEPARATOR
            MENUITEM "&Print...",              CM_FILEPRINT, GRAYED
            MENUITEM "P&rint Setup...",        CM_FILEPRINTERSETUP, GRAYED
            MENUITEM SEPARATOR
            MENUITEM "E&xit\tAlt+F4",          CM_EXIT
    END
END

PRINTINGDLG DIALOG 40, 40, 120, 40
STYLE WS_POPUP | WS_CAPTION | WS_SYSMENU | WS_VISIBLE
CAPTION "Printer Routine"
{
 CTEXT           "Printing Document", -1, 4, 6, 120, 12
 DEFPUSHBUTTON   "Cancel", IDCANCEL, 44,22,32,14, WS_GROUP
}
...
```

Implementation of the Abort dialog presents several interesting aspects. Our application is performing its printing operations. Simultaneously, the Abort dialog must have the input focus and be able to process a button press. In order for two independent processes to receive Windows 95 messages, both processes must be polled in the API message-processing loop. Thus, the Abort dialog must provide a temporary hook into the normal API message loop, peeking into the message queue looking for messages to itself. So, if the Abort dialog has established a hook into the message queue, it cannot allow the user to terminate the dialog from its System | Close menu item or Alt-F4 because it is not in the message processing loop.

How can the System menu be changed to gray Close? Access to the System menu is provided by a **CWnd** member function, **GetSystemMenu**, which is passed a BOOL. When the BOOL is FALSE, a copy of the current System menu is provided upon which modifications can be made. When TRUE, the default System menu is reinstalled. Here, we wish to gray or disable the Close menu item whose ID is SC_CLOSE.

```
    GetSystemMenu (FALSE) ->EnablemMenuItem (SC_CLOSE, MF_GRAYED);
```

Next, consider what must occur if the user does press the Cancel button. A BOOL flag, here called **userabort**, must be set. Additionally, the actual C-style message-peeking function must have access to this BOOL to avoid sending the Abort dialog messages after the Cancel button is pressed. Therefore, this BOOL must be external in scope. Finally, since the Abort dialog has the input focus, when the Cancel button is pressed, focus must be returned to the application itself. This is done by the **EnableWindow** member function of **CWnd**.

```
    GetParent () -> EnableWindow (TRUE);
```

Here TRUE enables the window and FALSE disables it. Examine the **PrintingDlg** class definition and implementation for the Abort dialog.

10.6.3 Listing for File: PrintDlg.h—Pgm10a—Excerpts

```
...
/*************************************************************************/
```

```
/*                                                                      */
/* PrintingDlg Class Definition - Display Modeless "Cancel Printing" dlgbox*/
/*                                                                      */
/************************************************************************/

class PrintingDlg : public CDialog {

public:

           PrintingDlg ();    // constructor of modeless dlg
BOOL       OnInitDialog ();   // disable "system "Close" menuitem
void       OnCancel ();       // re-enable main window
...
```

10.6.4 Listing for File: PrintDlg.cpp—Pgm10a—Excerpts

```
...
BEGIN_MESSAGE_MAP(PrintingDlg, CDialog)
  ON_COMMAND (IDCANCEL, OnCancel)
END_MESSAGE_MAP()

/************************************************************************/
/*                                                                    */
/* PrintingDlg: construct the dialog                                  */
/*                                                                    */
/************************************************************************/

           PrintingDlg::PrintingDlg () {

 Create ("PRINTINGDLG");
}

/************************************************************************/
/*                                                                    */
/* OnInitDialog: disable system menuitem: Close                       */
/*                                                                    */
/************************************************************************/

BOOL       PrintingDlg::OnInitDialog () {

 GetSystemMenu (FALSE)-> EnableMenuItem (SC_CLOSE, MF_GRAYED);
 return TRUE;
}

/************************************************************************/
/*                                                                    */
/* OnCancel: re-enable main window to cancel printing operation       */
/*                                                                    */
/************************************************************************/

void       PrintingDlg::OnCancel () {

 extern BOOL userabort; // provide access to "C" style abort indicator
 userabort = TRUE;      // signal abort to the replaced message processor
 GetParent ()->EnableWindow (TRUE); // re-activate parent window
 CDialog::OnCancel (); // new
}
```

When the dialog is being constructed, normally, transfer buffers and perhaps controls are initialized in **OnInitDialog**. Here, the System menu's Close menu item is grayed. The dialog has one message in its message map—**OnCancel**. When the Cancel button is pressed, the notification flag, **userabort**, is set and the parent window is once again given the input focus. The dialog is then terminated by invoking the **CDialog** base class member function **OnCancel**. In normal circumstances, the Abort Printing dialog box is destroyed by using **DestroyWindow** as the successful printing process terminates. Another useful function is **EndDialog** which posts a message to close the dialog and can be used *anywhere* in the entire dialog processing system to terminate a dialog.

```
EndDialog (int returncode);
```

Next, examine the FrameWin class definition and implementation to see the Abort dialog's message-peeking function.

10.6.5 Listing for File: FrameWin.h—Pgm10a—Excerpts

```
...
/*********************************************************************/
/*                                                                 */
/* FrameWin Class Definition                                       */
/*                                                                 */
/*********************************************************************/

class FrameWin : public CFrameWnd {

/*********************************************************************/
/*                                                                 */
/* Class Data Members                                              */
/*                                                                 */
/*********************************************************************/

protected:

int       avg_caps_width;   // average capital letter width
int       avg_char_width;   // average character width
int       avg_char_height;  // average character height
LOGFONT*  ptrlogfont;       // user selected font
COLORREF  fontcolor;        // the font's color

/*********************************************************************/
/*                                                                 */
/* Class Functions:                                                */
/*                                                                 */
/*********************************************************************/

public:
          FrameWin (CWnd*, const char*); // constructor
          ~FrameWin ();                  // destructor

protected:

afx_msg int   OnCreate (LPCREATESTRUCT);  // construct window, avg char dims
afx_msg void  OnPaint ();                 // paint the window - WM_PAINT
```

```
afx_msg void   CmFontChange ();              // get new font from user choice
afx_msg void   CmFilePrint ();               // print the file
afx_msg void   CmFilePrinterSetup ();        // set up the printer
afx_msg void   CmExit ();                     // shut down

void           GetAvgCharDims ();            // acquire average character dims
BOOL           HandlePrinting (CPrintDialog*);// do the actual printing
void           Render (CDC*);                // either paint or print screen
...
```

10.6.6 Listing for File: FrameWin.cpp—Pgm10a—Excerpts

```
...
/****************************************************************************/
/*                                                                        */
/* Externals: for the printing dialog box and substitute msg handler      */
/*                                                                        */
/****************************************************************************/

static HWND   hprintdlg;  // for the msg handler
BOOL          userabort;  // abort when TRUE

/****************************************************************************/
/*                                                                        */
/* AbortProc: replacement msg handler for printing abort dialog box       */
/*                                                                        */
/****************************************************************************/

// While printing, the Printing dialog box is displayed with a Cancel button
// This routine replaces the normal message-handling mechanism, until printing
// is done or the Cancel button is pressed

int APIENTRY  AbortProc(HDC, int) {

 MSG msg;
 while (!userabort && PeekMessage (&msg, NULL, 0, 0, PM_REMOVE)) {
  if (!hprintdlg || !IsDialogMessage(hprintdlg, &msg)) {
   TranslateMessage(&msg);
   DispatchMessage(&msg);
  }
 }
 return !userabort;
}

/****************************************************************************/
/*                                                                        */
/* FrameWin Events Response Table                                         */
/*                                                                        */
/****************************************************************************/

BEGIN_MESSAGE_MAP(FrameWin, CFrameWnd)
...
 ON_COMMAND(CM_FONTCHANGE,       CmFontChange)
 ON_COMMAND(CM_FILEPRINT,        CmFilePrint)
 ON_COMMAND(CM_FILEPRINTERSETUP, CmFilePrinterSetup)
END_MESSAGE_MAP()
```

```
/***********************************************************************/
/*                                                                     */
/* Framewin: Construct the window object                               */
/*                                                                     */
/***********************************************************************/

         FrameWin::FrameWin (CWnd* ptrparent, const char* title)
                 : CFrameWnd () {
...
 ptrlogfont = NULL;                               // set no font loaded
 fontcolor = RGB (0, 0, 0);                       // set default font color black
...
}
...

/***********************************************************************/
/*                                                                     */
/* OnPaint: displays instructions and the current system color in use  */
/*                                                                     */
/***********************************************************************/

void      FrameWin::OnPaint () {

 CPaintDC  dc(this);
 Render (&dc);
}

/***********************************************************************/
/*                                                                     */
/* Render: display screen on device or on the printer                  */
/*                                                                     */
/***********************************************************************/

void      FrameWin::Render (CDC *ptrdc) {

 CFont     *ptroldfont;                           // place to save old font
 CFont     *ptrfont;                              // our new font

 if (ptrlogfont) {                                // install any user font
  ptrfont = new CFont ();
  ptrfont->CreateFontIndirect (ptrlogfont);       // create the font from LOGFONT
  ptroldfont = ptrdc->SelectObject (ptrfont);     // install font in use, save old
 }
 ptrdc->SetTextColor (fontcolor);                 // install font color
 ptrdc->SetBkMode (TRANSPARENT);                  // set so background color shows

 ptrdc->TextOut (avg_char_width, avg_char_height, "This is a sample message");
 ptrdc->Rectangle (avg_char_width*3, avg_char_height*6, avg_char_width*10,
                   avg_char_height*16);

 if (ptrlogfont) {                                // deselect and delete user font
  ptrdc->SelectObject (ptroldfont);
  delete ptrfont;
 }
}

/***********************************************************************/
/*                                                                     */
/* CmFontChange: get users font request and implement it               */
/*                                                                     */
```

```
/***************************************************************************/
void        FrameWin::CmFontChange () {

 CFontDialog  *ptrdlg;

 if (ptrlogfont) ptrdlg = new CFontDialog (ptrlogfont, CF_EFFECTS |
                          CF_SCREENFONTS | CF_FORCEFONTEXIST, NULL, this);
 else ptrdlg = new CFontDialog (NULL, CF_EFFECTS |
                          CF_SCREENFONTS | CF_FORCEFONTEXIST, NULL, this);

 ptrdlg->m_cf.rgbColors = fontcolor;    // install current color
 if (ptrdlg->DoModal () == IDOK) {      // get user font choice
  if (!ptrlogfont) ptrlogfont = new LOGFONT; // 1st time, create LOGFONT
  memcpy (ptrlogfont, &(ptrdlg->m_lf), sizeof (LOGFONT)); // copy user choice
  fontcolor = ptrdlg->GetColor ();      // save color choice
  GetAvgCharDims ();                     // get new average char dims
  Invalidate();                          // on new dims, and reshow
 }
 delete ptrdlg;
}

/***************************************************************************/
/*                                                                         */
/* CmFilePrint: print an existing file                                     */
/*                                                                         */
/***************************************************************************/
void        FrameWin::CmFilePrint () {

 CPrintDialog printdlg (FALSE, PD_USEDEVMODECOPIES, this);

 printdlg.m_pd.nMinPage = 1;
 printdlg.m_pd.nMaxPage = 1;
 printdlg.m_pd.nFromPage = 1;
 printdlg.m_pd.nToPage = 1;
 printdlg.m_pd.nCopies = 1;

 if (printdlg.DoModal () == IDCANCEL) return; // if cancel, quit

 if (!HandlePrinting (&printdlg)) MessageBox ("Unable to print the document",
                          "Printer Section", MB_OK | MB_ICONEXCLAMATION);
}

/***************************************************************************/
/*                                                                         */
/* HandlePrinting: print the document                                      */
/*                                                                         */
/***************************************************************************/
BOOL        FrameWin::HandlePrinting (CPrintDialog *ptrprintdlg) {

 BOOL printerror = FALSE;
 userabort = FALSE;

 // setup a printer DC
 CDC  *ptrprinterDC = new CDC;
 ptrprinterDC->Attach (ptrprintdlg->GetPrinterDC () ); // acquire print DC
 // setup a printing cancel dialog box
 PrintingDlg  *ptrprintingdlg = new PrintingDlg ();
```

```
hprintdlg = ptrprintingdlg->m_hWnd;    // set the external hwnd for abort proc

// attempt to install the abort procedure
if (ptrprinterDC->SetAbortProc (AbortProc) < 0) {
 delete ptrprintingdlg;                              // failed, so clean up
 delete ptrprinterDC;
 return FALSE;
}

// print the document
DOCINFO doc;                                         // used by Windows for msg
doc.cbSize = sizeof(DOCINFO);
doc.lpszDocName = "Printing the screen";
doc.lpszOutput = NULL;
doc.lpszDatatype = NULL;
doc.fwType = 0;

// setup scaling factors
CSize oldwinext, oldprintext;
int   oldmode;
CRect clrect;
GetClientRect(clrect);          // get the size of the display window
CSize clsize = clrect.Size();   // will hold the size of the printed page
CSize pagesize (ptrprinterDC->GetDeviceCaps (HORZRES),
               ptrprinterDC->GetDeviceCaps (VERTRES));

// the main print processing loop
if (::StartDoc (ptrprinterDC->m_hDC, &doc) >0) { // start the document
 if (::StartPage (ptrprinterDC->m_hDC) >0) {     // set for begin page
  // install current scaling - Windows 95 resets the DC in StartPage
  // so we must install our scaling for each page
  oldmode   = ptrprinterDC->SetMapMode (MM_ISOTROPIC);
  oldwinext = ptrprinterDC->SetWindowExt (clsize);
  oldprintext = ptrprinterDC->SetViewportExt (pagesize);
  // actually go print the page
  Render (ptrprinterDC);
  // replace the original DC values
  ptrprinterDC->SetWindowExt (oldwinext);
  ptrprinterDC->SetViewportExt (oldprintext);
  ptrprinterDC->SetMapMode (oldmode);
  // signal end of page and check for errors
  if (::EndPage (ptrprinterDC->m_hDC) >=0)         // set for end page
   ::EndDoc (ptrprinterDC->m_hDC);                 // set for end document
  else printerror = TRUE;
 }
 else printerror = TRUE;
}
else printerror = TRUE;

// if abort pressed, set focus back to our window
if (!userabort) EnableWindow (TRUE);                 // restore main window action
ptrprintingdlg->DestroyWindow ();
delete ptrprinterDC;                                 // clean up
delete ptrprintingdlg;
return !printerror && !userabort;                    // return success code
}
```

```
/*****************************************************************************/
/*                                                                           */
/* CmFilePrinterSetup: set up the printer parameters                         */
/*                                                                           */
/*****************************************************************************/
void        FrameWin::CmFilePrinterSetup () {
 CPrintDialog printdlg (TRUE, PD_USEDEVMODECOPIES, this);
 printdlg.DoModal ();
}
 ...
```

The **AbortProc** is given the **APIENTRY** designation replacing the Windows 3.1 far PASCAL _export. The external variable **userabort** is external so that the C-style **AbortProc** message handler for the Abort dialog can access it, preventing messages from being sent to a closed dialog. The **AbortProc** is a very simple function that must have access to the HWND of the Abort dialog, here also external—**hprintdlg**. Normal message processing loops invoke **GetMessage** and then **TranslateMessage** and **DispatchMessage**. However, all we wish to do is see if there is one for us and then pass it along. The API function **PeekMessage** does just that—it examines the Windows 95 message queue to see if there are any messages. The loop should continue as long as **userabort** is FALSE (indicating the user has not yet pressed the Cancel button) and as long as the dialog is still active and not being destroyed and removed from the system. When a window is being removed, a PM_REMOVE message is sent. Therefore, the loop should continue as long as the PM_REMOVE message has not been sent. Next, the Abort dialog messages must be filtered out from all other application messages and processed. Hence, if the handle to the dialog box is not set to the Abort dialog, pass the message along. Further, if that message is not destined for the Abort dialog, pass the message along. The Windows 95 API function, **IsDialogMessage**, determines if the message is destined for the dialog or specified by the passed HWND; if so, it actually processes the dialog's message. Thus, the **AbortProc** appears as

```
int APIENTRY  AbortProc(HDC, int) {
 MSG msg;
 while (!userabort && PeekMessage (&msg, NULL, 0, 0, PM_REMOVE)) {
  if (!hprintdlg || !IsDialogMessage(hprintdlg, &msg)) {
   TranslateMessage(&msg);
   DispatchMessage(&msg);
  }
 }
 return !userabort;
}
```

Let's look at the FrameWin class to see how printing occurs. In the definition file, the user's selected font is kept in a LOGFONT structure that is copied from the common Choose Font dialog. The user color selection is also used, although not when printing. In the implementation file, the constructor initializes these to no font and black. The now familiar member functions have no real changes from previous coding until the **OnPaint** member. **OnPaint** acquires the paint DC and then invokes the

Render function. Under MFC, a **CPaintDC** must be constructed. In order for one function to render the image on both display surfaces—the screen and the printer—that function must be passed the DC, hence the **Render** function. All of the normal paint coding has been moved into **Render**; install any user font and color, display the text, draw the rectangle, and restore all original objects back into the DC.

Next, examine the **CmFilePrinterSetup** function that responds to the File | Print Setup menu item. An instance of the Windows 95 common Print dialog is allocated on the stack. The first parameter is TRUE, indicating Printer Setup is to be invoked. If FALSE, then Print is invoked. The flags include

PD_ALLPAGES	indicates all pages button is selected
PD_USEDEVMODECOPIES	if the printer supports multiple copies, enable the Copies control; if it does not, disable it
PD_NOPAGENUMS	disables the Pages button
PD_HIDEPRINTTOFILE	hides the print to file option
PD_NOSELECTION	disables the page selection controls

Consult the documentation for the numerous other lesser-used IDs. Here, PD_USEDEVMODECOPIES is used, letting Windows 95 make the determination of whether or not to enable the Copies control based upon the specific printer chosen. Handling Printer Setup is then a simple matter of two lines of coding.

```
CPrintDialog printdlg (TRUE, PD_USEDEVMODECOPIES, this);
printdlg.DoModal ();
```

Unfortunately, handing File | Print is much more complex. Similar to Printer Setup, the first action is to allocate an automatic storage instance of the Windows 95 common Print dialog, but passing FALSE this time.

```
CPrintDialog printdlg (FALSE, PD_USEDEVMODECOPIES, this);
```

Next, the initial pages for user selection are set. The member **m_pd** contains the common Print dialog structure members that define the initial pages for user selection. Since only the screen is to be printed, all page limits are set to 1 as is the number of copies. Next, the common Print dialog is launched as normal with **DoModal**. If Cancel is selected, the print function is terminated. Notice that, should the user select the Setup button, Windows 95 automatically changes to the Printer Setup dialog and then returns back to the Print dialog. If the user selects OK, then the printing process commences. Our member function **HandlePrinting** handles the entire printing process. Notice that, if the process fails for any reason, I display a simple message box informing the user.

HandlePrinting performs the many sequences necessary to getting the file printed. First, it must initialize the external **userabort** flag and our own **printerror** flag which is used to signal any error in the printing process. Next, the printer DC must be acquired. Conveniently, the **CPrintDialog** member function **GetPrinterDC** returns the handle of the currently selected printer DC from the Windows 95 common

Print dialog. A **CDC** object can be constructed on that HDC by encapsulating the real DC using the **Attach** member function.

```
CDC *ptrprinterDC = new CDC;
ptrprinterDC->Attach (ptrprintdlg->GetPrinterDC ());
```

Next, an instance of our Abort dialog box is constructed and its handle saved in the external **hprintdlg** field for use in the **AbortProc**. Then our **AbortProc** function must be installed in the message processing loop. This is done by the **CDC** member function **SetAbortProc**.

```
if (ptrprinterDC->SetAbortProc (AbortProc) < 0) {
```

which takes a pointer to the function, which is the data type of a function's name. Should the process fail, cleanup actions are done and the printing process aborted.

Windows 95 requires a DOCINFO structure to control the printing process. This structure has changed under Windows 95 by the addition of the last two fields.

```
The DOCINFO Structure:

int     cbSize;        // size of the DOCINFO structure
LPCSTR  lpszDocName;   // name of document to print - 32 chars including the NULL
LPCSTR  lpszOutput;    // name of file to print to - also 32 chars max
LPCSTR  lpszDatatype;  // specifies the type of data used to record the print job
DWORD   fwType;        // 0 or DI_APPBANDING if the application will use banding
```

Our use might be

```
DOCINFO doc;
doc.cbSize = sizeof(DOCINFO);
doc.lpszDocName = "Printing the screen";
doc.lpszOutput = NULL;
doc.lpszDatatype = NULL; // new in Windows 95
doc.fwType = 0;          // new in Windows 95
```

The document name is used by Print Manager to identify this print job during the spooling process. Windows 95 uses the last two fields to handle print banding.

 Windows 3.1 Porting Tip: A failure to set these last two fields, even though NULL, results in *no* printout!

Design Rule 42: **Many of the newer structures begin with a member field that stores the size of the structure; in the DOCINFO structure, it is the cbSize member. When creating an instance of such a structure, always initialize the size member! Failure can yield application crashes. In this example, I coded**

```
doc.cbSize = sizeof(DOCINFO);
```

Note that, in this case, the MFC actually fills in the size just in case you forget to do so; do not count on this action for all such structures!

Next, scaling values must be determined. The scale factor to be used represents the ratio of the actual client window size versus the printed page size in pixels. Here I fill the **CSize clrect** with the client window size; similarly **pagesize** contains the dimensions of the printed page obtained from **GetDeviceCaps**.

```
CRect clrect;
GetClientRect(clrect);              // get the size of the display window
CSize clsize = clrect.Size();  // will hold the size of the printed page
CSize pagesize (ptrprinterDC->GetDeviceCaps (HORZRES),
                ptrprinterDC->GetDeviceCaps (VERTRES));
```

Finally, the actual printing cycle can begin, following the C-style Escape sequences: **StartDoc, StartPage, EndPage, EndDoc. StartDoc** is passed the HDC of the printer and a reference to the document structure for Print Manager. If all is OK, then **StartPage** is invoked for the sole page to be printed. Note that, for multiple pages, a loop must be placed around the **StartPage/EndPage** functions. (See the next example program.)

 Windows 3.1 Porting Tip: Under Windows 3.1, the printer DC was reset during the **EndPage** sequence. Now it's done during **StartPage**. The class library handles this subtle difference.

Design Rule 43: **Upon every entry to Render, the printer DC must be reset to the proper circumstances for this particular page, including brushes, pens, fonts, palettes, and—most important—scaling.**

Notice that **Render** is surrounded by the scaling code. Because Windows 95 resets the DC for each page, before we can **Render**, we must set the scale and restore the original values when the page is complete.

```
// the main print processing loop
if (::StartDoc (ptrprinterDC->m_hDC, &doc) >0) { // start the document
 if (::StartPage (ptrprinterDC->m_hDC) >0) {      // set for begin page
  // install current scaling - Windows 95 resets the DC in StartPage
  // so we must install our scaling for each page
  oldmode  = ptrprinterDC->SetMapMode (MM_ISOTROPIC);
  oldwinext = ptrprinterDC->SetWindowExt (clsize);
  oldprintext = ptrprinterDC->SetViewportExt (pagesize);
  // actually go print the page
  Render (ptrprinterDC);
  // replace the original DC values
  ptrprinterDC->SetWindowExt (oldwinext);
  ptrprinterDC->SetViewportExt (oldprintext);
  ptrprinterDC->SetMapMode (oldmode);
  // signal end of page and check for errors
  if (::EndPage (ptrprinterDC->m_hDC) >=0)         // set for end page
   ::EndDoc (ptrprinterDC->m_hDC);                 // set for end document
  else printerror = TRUE;
 }
```

```
    else printerror = TRUE;
}
else printerror = TRUE;
```

The scaling is done using the MM_ANISOTROPIC or MM_ISOTROPIC mode using the **CDC** member function **SetMapMode**.

```
int    ptrdc->SetMapMode (MM_ANISOTROPIC);
```

where the old mode is returned. Remember that all objects and settings in any DC must be reset to their original objects; the old mode is saved. Scaling in one (isotropic) or two dimensions (anisotropic) is done by setting a combination of window and viewport extents. In this case, I wish to have both dimensions properly scaled so the page resembles the screen. The window's extents or dimensions are set to the actual client screen's dimensions (the logical coordinates), while the viewport is set to the printer's page size (the device or physical coordinates).

```
oldwinext = ptrprinterDC->SetWindowExt (clsize);
oldprintext = ptrprinterDC->SetViewportExt (pagesize);
```

The window extent is then set using **SetWindowExt**, which returns the original window extent. The viewport to the printer is set using the **SetViewportExt** function, which also returns the old viewport extent. Both values must be saved for later restoration.

It is important to note that the window extent must be set before setting the viewport, because Windows 95 must know about the window extent as it sets up the viewport extent. The scaling works this way. Assume that the window rectangle is 300 pixels wide and the page is 2400 dots wide, or 8 times larger. Therefore, when the GDI plots 1 pixel, it must plot 8 pixels on the paper. If the rectangle being displayed is one-half of the client area wide, or 150 pixels, then the page size would be 1200 pixels wide for it to be in proportion.

You should run the program as is and then experiment. Comment out the mode and extent changes and rerun the program to see the effect of scaling. Try resizing the window both small and large. What effect does this have if the printer is not scaled. Then adjust the mode to MM_ISOTROPIC and repeat the experiment. What effect does the mode have?

In chapter 15, covering the document view, we see that the on-screen view has a member function of **OnDraw** that is called by both **OnPaint** and by **PrintPage** similar to the way the function **Render** is done in this example.

10.7 MODIFYING DATA IN THE PRINT DIALOG BOX

CPrintDialog provides the means to alter the various values in the Print dialog and, when the user has finished making selections, to retrieve the user's choices. The Windows 95 common Print dialog is shown in Figure 10.2. These options should be set to reflect the document to be printed.

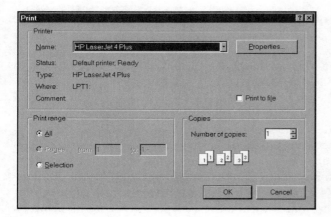

Fig. 10.2 Windows 95 Common Print
Dialog Box

While this seemingly simple task should be an easy one to implement, in reality, setting the correct page range can be so complex that it is often ignored. First, consider the actual document. The initial total number of lines as well as the known page width are usually easily determined. But what is to be done with lines that are too wide for the current page width? Truncation is often a poor choice because of the loss of information. It is a better practice to line wrap, which, of course, adds lines and may impact the number of pages! Line wrapping would occur only when actually rendering that line to the printer, *long* after the dialog box is used. If user fonts are supported, line wrapping can become a serious factor with larger font sizes. Additionally, if a document contains user-forced page breaks by the use of the form feed code, obviously the page total determined from the number of lines is wrong if just based upon the number of lines. Often the only accurate method to determine the page range is to actually go through the complete print rendering of the document before presenting the user with the Print dialog box in a sort of preview, skipping the actual printing itself. On larger documents, this can be time-consuming. And even then, after all your efforts to get the accurate page range displayed in the common Print dialog box, the user can switch printers from the Print File dialog itself, likely invalidating the page range!

This is why so often the page selection is grayed, leaving printing all of the document as the only option. Should you desire to implement the page range, carefully consider all the possibilities.

10.8 THE PRINTING SEQUENCE FOR MFC

Now let's examine more closely the exact sequence followed after launching the Printer Abort modeless dialog box to actually print the document. Here I use a **Print-Page** function to handle the printing process for one page.

```
// BeginPrinting:
if (::StartDoc (ptrdc->m_hDC, &doc) >0) {
  // BeginDocument:
```

```
      while (not at the document end and !printerror) {
       if (::StartPage (ptrdc->m_hDC) >0) {
        ptrdc->SelectObject (ptrfont);    // install font
        PrintPage ();                     // actually print the page
        if (::EndPage (ptrdc->m_hDC) <0) printerror = TRUE;
       }
      }
      ::EndDoc (ptrdc->m_hDC);            // end the doc
      // EndDocument:
     }
     else printerror = TRUE;             // indicate error occurred
     // EndPrinting:
```

At point BeginPrinting any required GDI objects could be constructed, such as brushes and pens; they would be deleted at point EndPrinting. And once only printed titles could be done at point BeginDocument, along with resetting the starting page number and other needed values, because this function is called at the start of every copy should multiple copies be selected by the user. At point EndDocument, print a FormFeed.

Design Rule 44: **If the document uses selectable fonts and therefore line wrap for lines that are too long or has imbedded form feeds, then do not rely on any data member "number_of_line" to know when the last page has been printed. In these situations, only the actual function that is rendering the document, line by line, really knows when the end of the document is reached. It is better to have a BOOL member that the render function PrintPage sets to TRUE when the physical end is reached. The while loop would test this member to detect when the printing is finished.**

10.9 PRINTING DIRECTLY WITHIN MFC'S PRINTPAGE

Thus far, our documents have been quite simple. If there was a font change, it applied to the entire document. Now consider a more practical document. It should support various fonts on-screen at any time via some kind of control codes indicating begin font and end font. Some provisions must be present for bold and underlining (perhaps italics), for printing both page numbers and headers at the top of the page, for centering, and so on. Soon, you'll have your own word processor or a Rich Text Edit document.

Or perhaps the image on-screen is not at all the way you want the image to be on the printed page. On-screen you present data in various **CEdit** controls and so on; yet on the printed page another layout would better express the information. This is often true for mailing labels and printed invoices and reports. In these situations, the best method is to render each page directly within **PrintPage**, never invoking the screen **OnPaint** function.

However, when fonts are mentioned, you need to exercise caution in the printing process. Some fonts cannot be rendered directly by the specific device. Often, to control exactly how the output appears, you must create your own special printer font, especially altering the character dimensions to fit the required scale. Until now, we used the Choose Font dialog to view font possibilities and to select them, ignoring the enormous complexities involved when dealing with fonts. Now let's examine fonts in greater detail.

10.10 FONT DETAILS

Windows 95 provides six stock fonts, shown in Table 10.1, which define a particular typeface and size. Use the following to select them:

```
dc.SelectStockObject (font ID);
```

Fonts fall into two broad categories—*GDI fonts* and *device fonts*—and are stored on disk. Often they have the file extension FON while the newer TrueType fonts are stored in two files with extensions of TTF and FOT. The GDI fonts are those that are to be displayed on the screen and come in three broad kinds: **raster fonts**, **stoke fonts**, and **TrueType fonts**.

Raster fonts are stored as a bitmap pixel pattern representing the character. Each raster font is designed for a specific size. Some slight scaling can be done in integer multiples of the original size by duplicating the pixels, but generally the results look poor. Thus, raster fonts are normally used in specifically available sizes and are often referred to as nonscalable fonts. They have two slight advantages: they display faster since they are just a bitmap to **BitBlt**, and they have been hand tuned to present the best legibility.

Stroke fonts are created by drawing lines and are used only with plotter devices.

Table 10.1 The Windows 95 Stock Fonts

Font Identifier	Description
SYSTEM_FONT	a proportional ANSI character set used in menus, dialog boxes, message boxes, and title bars
SYSTEM_FIXED_FONT	fixed-pitch ANSI font compatible with earlier than version 3.1 of Windows—all chars have the same width
OEM_FIXED_FONT	often called the terminal font, used for windowed DOS apps using text character based modes
ANSI_FIXED_FONT	a Courier font smaller than the system of terminal fonts
ANSI_VAR_FONT	either a Helvetica or Times Roman variable width font usually smaller than the system font
DEVICE_DEFAULT_FONT	a built-in or most suitable font for a specific device—for a CRT there is none usually, so it uses the system font; for printers, such as a dot-matrix, it is often the default text mode font

TrueType fonts are completely scalable. They are stored as a set of curves and lines, with hints for scaling effects. Once a specific height and width are set, Windows 95 "rasterizes" the font into the proper bitmap for display; then it is ready for use. This rasterizing process takes a bit of time, but needs to be done only once. The font is stored in memory. TrueType fonts are almost as legible or "good" as the raster fonts, but offer complete scalability.

If you are trying to match the printer's fonts so that you are displaying in the "what you see is what you get" (WYSIWYG) manner, you need TrueType fonts. As we shall see shortly, the procedure would be to decide which real printer's font is to be used and then to select a TrueType font that most closely matches what will actually be printed. (Remember that an exact match may not be possible because the "real" size of printer fonts may be too small to be legible and because of the magnification effect between the screen and printer.)

A font is a collection of characters in a particular typeface and size. The term *typeface* denotes only the style. (Note that, in the printing world, typeface includes the style, bold, underlining, and size—a complete package.) There are many styles, but the most common are Courier, Helvetica, and Times Roman. (The typeface names listed here are copyrighted. Therefore, Windows 95 modifies the font ever so slightly and assigns another similar name to that font.) The Windows 95 family of typefaces includes Modern, Roman, Swiss, Script, and Decorative.

The differences between typefaces lie in several areas: **stroke width**, **type of pitch**, and **use of serifs**. Stroke widths that make up the characters can be fixed or variable. Pitch can be fixed (all characters have the same width) or variable (different widths for the characters). Therefore, if a font has a fixed stroke width, it usually also has a fixed pitch. A *serif* is a small extra line that finishes off character strokes yielding a different look to the character. The term *sans serif* means without any serifs. Table 10.2 illustrates the Windows 95 font identifiers, and representative samples are given.

Which exact font is available depends upon the video display driver, what fonts you've loaded, what printer driver is installed, what font add-on packages are installed, and which changes you have made to the default settings in the WIN.INI file.

Table 10.2 Windows 95 Fonts and Samples

ID names	Pitch	Serifs	Typefaces
FF_MODERN	fixed	yes	Courier, Elite, Pica
FF_SWISS	variable	no	Helvetica
FF_ROMAN	variable	yes	Times Roman
FF_SCRIPT	variable	no	*Cursive Shelley Volante*
FF_DECORATIVE	variable	yes	Wingdings ☐▤▦
FF_DONTCARE	-	-	any

The size of a character font refers to the height of the character and is given in units of *points* that are about 1/72 inch. A size of 10 points means that the character's height is 10/72 of an inch. Windows 95 defines another term, a *twip*, which is 1/20 of a point or 1/1440 inch. In the raster fonts, each pixel is an integral number of logical twips in size.

You cannot use the point size to accurately determine the size on the display screen because of the internal aspect ratio of the specific monitor being used. If you choose a font size of 24 points, then those characters are formed 24 pixels high. However, those characters will appear as 24 real points high *only* on a monitor that displays 72 pixels per physical inch. Often the scale factor for the monitors is about 40% larger than 1 inch to account for the magnification needed so that the monitor can be viewed from about 2 feet away. However, when the characters are displayed on the printer, they are exactly 24 points or 24/72 of an inch high. The printer canvas contains real inches.

There is a mapping mode MM_TWIPS in which you would get an accurate rendering—the characters would actually be 24/72 of an inch high. But this mode is seldom used because most common printer fonts would be rendered too small to be read easily. Instead, the MM_ANISOTROPIC or MM_ISTROPIC modes are used. The anisotropic mode can have different scales in the x and y directions, while the isotropic mode has the same scale in both directions. If you wish to approach WYSIWYG, the screen display should be MM_ANISOTROPIC.

10.11 THE LOGFONT STRUCTURE

Fonts are described by a LOGFONT structure. To create a font, you create an instance of the LOGFONT structure and initialize the fields to your desired requirements. When you execute the Create Font functions, Windows 95 attempts to match your requested font with the best available matching font—the one that comes closest to your criteria in the LOGFONT object. Once the real font is created, Windows 95 inserts the real characteristics of that font back into the LOGFONT structure for your use. When we use the common Font dialog, the results are returned in a LOGFONT structure.

> **Design Rule 45:** Note that the closest matching process occurs only at the point the font is actually inserted into the DC (dc.SelectObject), not on font creation!

Normally, for choosing font-type actions, you would use the common Font dialog. It is much easier than doing those actions by hand. However, you may need to create the printer fonts and even a matching display font if you are attempting WYSIWYG. Here is the Windows 95 definition of the LOGFONT.

```
#define LF_FACESIZE        32

struct LOGFONT {
    int      lfHeight;     // height in logical units, a negative value means the
```

```
                            // units are in points
    int     lfWidth;        // the avg width in logical units
    int     lfEscapement;   // 0 normally
    int     lfOrientation;  // 0 normally
    int     lfWeight;       // FW_NORMAL (400) or FW_BOLD (700)
    BYTE    lfItalic;       // italics font if nonzero
    BYTE    lfUnderline;    // underline font if nonzero
    BYTE    lfStrikeOut;    // strikeout font if nonzero
    BYTE    lfCharSet;      // ANSI_CHARSET (0), DEFAULT_CHARSET (1),
                            // SYMBOL_CHARSET (2), OEM_CHARSET (255)
    BYTE    lfOutPrecision; // OUT_DEFAULT_PRECIS output match precision
    BYTE    lfClipPrecision;// CLIP_DEFAULT_PRECIS clip match precision
    BYTE    lfQuality;      // DRAFT_QUALITY or PROOF_QUALITY
    BYTE    lfPitchAndFamily;// combined values for pitch and family:
                            // FF_DONTCARE, FF_MODERN, FF_ROMAN
                            // FF_SWISS, FF_SCRIPT, FF_DECORATIVE
                            // ORed with one of these:
                            // DEFAULT_PITCH, FIXED_PITCH, VARIABLE_PITCH
    char lfFaceName[LF_FACESIZE]; // typeface name of the font
    };
```

When you insert your choices, Windows 95 attempts the best matching font. Here are some guidelines to help you make intelligent choices. For lfCharSet, ANSI_CHARSET gives raster or TrueType; OEM-CHARSET gives only the terminal; and SYMBOL_CHARSET gives Wingdings. Specifying FIXED_PITCH gives only fixed-width fonts. If lfFaceName is NULL, then the family becomes an important factor. If a raster font is requested, the lfHeight is matched, even if a smaller height has to be increased. If a raster font is requested with PROOF_QUALITY, height is less important than quality.

Very often, the width is 0, letting the height determine the font. After the font is created and selected into a DC, the textmetrics structure contains the current information on the font. Table 10.3 shows the TEXTMETRIC structure.

The pitch portion of the byte field **tmPitchAndFamily** is different from the corresponding LOGFONT member. The low nibble contains one or more pitch identifiers stored differently than in the LOGFONT member. Mask the pitch nibble (AND) with the identifier TMPF_FIXED_PITCH; if the bit is ON, it is a variable font; otherwise it's a fixed font. Similarly mask and test for TMPF_VECTOR (ON means a vector font), TMPF_DEVICE (ON means a device font), and TMPF_TRUETYPE (ON means TrueType).

The point size is reflected in the **tmHeight** member. In other words, the point size does not include the spacing between lines which is known as *line spacing*. While a typographer determines the shape and size of a character for a given point size, the typesetter actually determines the line spacing, which can be based upon the point size, font color, line length, maximum character size, and so on. Windows provides a suggested or reasonable value for the line spacing in the member **tmExternalLeading**. Thus, the vertical spacing between lines from a programming point of view would be the sum of **tmHeight** and **tmExternalLeading**.

Most fields parallel the LOGFONT. Additionally, the **GetDeviceCaps** function returns similar information. See Figure 10.3 for the basic values for a Panasonic 1124 dot-matrix printer and Figure 10.4 for a Hewlett Packard LaserJet 4 Plus. Notice that both printers have an equal number of dots per inch vertically and horizontally as shown in the LOGPIXELSX and LOGPIXELSY entries. HORZRES and VERTRES provide the page size in pixels.

Table 10.3 The TEXTMETRIC Structure

Structure Member	Meaning
int tmHeight	height of the character cell and is equal to the sum of the tmAscent and tmDescent
int tmAscent	height of the character cell measured from the baseline
int tmDescent	height of the cell measured from the baseline to the bottom of the cell
int tmInternalLeading	the amount of internal leading—equal to the cell height (tmHeight) minus the maximum height of any character in the font but not including the height of accent marks
int tmExternalLeading	recommended amount of leading for this font and is the whitespace above all characters and accent marks
int tmAveCharWidth	average width of characters in the font roughly the width of the letter "X"
int tmMaxCharWidth	the max width of any character in the font
int tmWeight	the weight of the font
BYTE tmItalic	nonzero indicates an italic font
BYTE tmUnderlined	nonzero indicates an underlined font
BYTE tmStruckOut	nonzero indicates struck through font
BYTE tmFirstChar	value of the first character in the set
BYTE tmLastChar	value of the last character in the set
BYTE tmDefaultChar	character to be substituted for characters that are not in the font
BYTE tmBreakChar	character that is used to separate words
BYTE tmPitchAndFamily	identifies the font pitch and its family
BYTE tmCharSet	identifies the character set: ANSI_CHARSET, SYMBOL_CHARSET, OEM_CHARSET
int tmOverhang	nonzero if the driver simulates bold or italics; represents any additional width of the character
int tmDigitizedAspectX	horizontal aspect ratio for which this font was designed
int tmDigitizedAspectY	vertical aspect ratio for which this font was designed

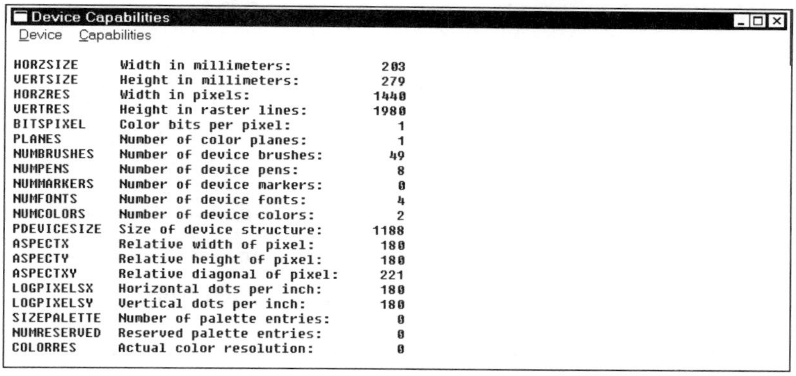

Fig. 10.3 Device Capabilities of a Panasonic 1124 Printer

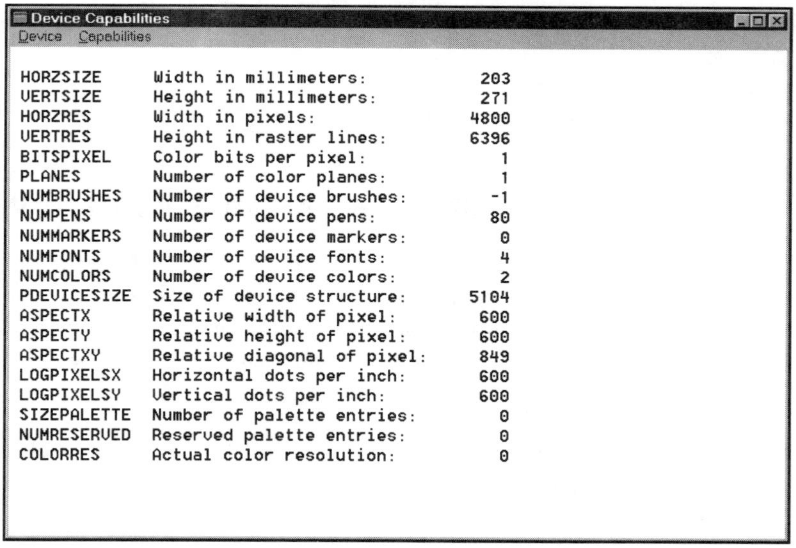

Fig. 10.4 Device Capabilities of a Hewlett Packard LaserJet 4 Plus

If you are attempting WYSIWYG, then, when handling the Choose Font dialog, you can restrict the user's selections by using key flags. Under MFC you can set the **Flags** to an ORed combination of the following:

CF_ANSIONLY	allows ANSI sets only
CF_FIXEDPITCHONLY	allows only fixed pitch sets
CF_SCALABLEONLY	allows scalable fonts only
CF_TTONLY	allows TrueType fonts only

CF_PRINTERFONTS	allows printer fonts only
CF_SCREENFONTS	allows screen fonts only
CF_BOTH	allows both printer fonts and display fonts
CF_WYSIWYG	allows only fonts that are available on both printer and screen
CF_EFFECTS	allows color, underline, and strike through
CF_FORCEFONTEXIST	error of the user selects a nonexistent font
CF_INITLOGFONTSTRUCT	sets dialog controls from a LOGFONT

These IDs can be ORed and passed to the **CFontDialog** constructor.

```
ptrdlg = new CFontDialog (NULL,
        CF_EFFECTS | CF_PRINTERFONTS | CF_FORCEFONTEXIST,
        ptrprinterDC, this);
```

Under MFC, we have

```
LOGFONT logfont;
CFont font;
font.CreateFontIndirect (&logfont);
```

10.12 TEXT OUTPUT FUNCTIONS FOR VARIABLE-WIDTH FONTS

Until now, we have favored the fixed fonts because columns and caret positioning were greatly simplified. But, when printing, we must understand how to process variable-width fonts. Let's review the text outputting functions as they apply to handling the printer and introduce some new ones. The most common function to display a string is

```
dc.TextOut (xstart, ystart, string, length);
```

For null-terminated strings, the length may be omitted. The string is displayed beginning at the logical x,y coordinates given. The meaning of the x,y coordinates is modified by the use of the function

```
dc.SetTextAlign (flag);
```

The groups of flags consist of

```
TA_LEFT,        TA_RIGHT,    TA_CENTER
TA_BOTTOM,      TA_TOP,      TA_BASELINE
TA_NOUPDATECP,  TA_UPDATECP
```

When the Update Current Position flag is enabled (**TA_UPDATECP**), the starting x,y values are ignored. Instead the current position of the last **MoveTo** or **LineTo** function is used and the current position is reset. This represents an alternative method of printing successive fields. If **TA_RIGHT I TA_UPDATECP** is in force, then subsequent **TextOut** requests appear successively after each other.

In chapter 5, we created columnar alignment by printing columns separately.

Another method of solving the problem of creating columnar alignment is to use the **TabbedTextOut** function.

```
CSize dc.TabbedTextOut (x, y, string, length, int numtabpositions,
                        int tabpositions[], int taborigin);
```

The function returns a **CSize** containing the resultant dimensions.

If the string has imbedded tabs ('\t'), then they are expanded in one of two ways based on the three tab parameters. The **tabpositions** array specifies each tab position in device units with **numtabpositions** showing the array bounds. Note that, if both **numtabpositions** and **tabpositions** are 0, then all tabs are expanded to successive eight times the average character width units. If **numtabpositions** is 1, all tabs are expanded **tabpositions[0]** apart. **taborigin** specifies the x logical units from which the tab expansion occurs; most often it is the same value as the x coordinate of the starting point. The function is also modified by **SetTextAlign** values. Using this slightly more complex function, columnar alignment can also be achieved.

DrawText is a higher-level display function.

```
dc.DrawText (string, length, &rectangle, format);
```

If the length is -1, then the null-terminated length is used. The text is displayed in the rectangle (**CRect**) according to the format flags. Multiple lines can be displayed, using the carriage return line feed combination as the signal for a new line or using blanks between words. Special effect: if the flag is **DT_CALCRECT**, no text is displayed; rather the rectangle's width and height are determined such that the text would fit according to the other flags.

When the **format** is 0, Windows 95 interprets the string as a series of lines and begins displaying at the upper-left corner of the rectangle. When a carriage return <CR> is encountered, a new line is begun, spaced one character height below the previous line. Any characters that exceed the rectangle dimensions, either too long a line or too many lines, are clipped. **DT_LEFT**, **DT_RIGHT**, and **DT_CENTER** operate as expected. **DT_SINGLELINE** ignores <CR> codes. **DT_TOP**, **DT_BOTTOM**, **DT_VCENTER** also work as expected. Using **DT_WORDBREAK** specifies that line breaks occur whenever a line exceeds the rectangle's width. Windows 95 backs up and moves the offending words onto the next line—a line wrap, if you please. **DT_NOCLIP** draws without clipping. **DT_EXPANDTABS** expands tabs using a default of 8 characters.

Other necessary functions to properly display text include

```
dc.SetTextColor (TColor color); // to set the text color
dc.SetBkMode (TRANSPARENT or OPAQUE);
dc.SetBkColor (TColor color); // the color to appear with OPAQUE
dc.SetTextCharacterExtra (extra spacing in logical units);
```

This last item converts the extra spacing in logical units into pixels and then adds that extra amount of spacing between each character to be displayed. Normal value is 0.

Perhaps the most useful function for processing variable-width fonts is the **GetTextExtent**.

```
CSize size = dc.GetTextExtent (string, length);
```

This highly useful function calculates the total dimensions the string requires if it were to be displayed using the current font and DC setup. When working with variable-pitched fonts, this function is a workhorse. In text entry situations, after a character is input and appended onto the line string, **GetTextExtent** returns the length that is used to position the caret at the correct position. In printing situations, the function is used to detect line wrap, as we shall see in the next program.

10.13 FORMATTING TEXT

If you have created or chosen a font and selected it into the DC and the average character dimensions have been determined, text formatting can begin. The formatting would include left justifying a string; right justifying a string (often called *flush right* in word processing); and proportional spacing or justifying both the left and right ends of the string and adding extra whitespace between the words of the string. When working with only one-line strings, the process is simple. Assume that a string is to begin at x,y and that the margin coordinates are given by **xleft** and **xright**. First, will the line fit between x and the right margin?

```
int maxlinelen = xright - xleft;
TSize sz = dc.GetTextExtent (string);
if (sz > (xright-x) )                   // error too long, now what?
else dc.TextOut (x, y, string);                  // left justified
```

or

```
else dc.TextOut (xright - sz.width, y, string); // right justified
```

or

```
else dc.TextOut (x+(xright -x -sz.width)/2, y, string); // centered
```

Alternatively, assume that we are at y row and wish to display the string given no x offset into the line.

```
int maxlinelen = xright - xleft;
TSize sz = dc.GetTextExtent (string);
if (sz > (maxlinelen) )                 // error too long, now what?
else dc.TextOut (xleft, y, string);     // left justified
```

or

```
else dc.TextOut (xright - sz.width, y, string); // right justified
```

or

```
else dc.TextOut ((xleft+xright-sz.width)/2, y, string); // centered
```

For proportional spacing or justifying both ends of the string

```
dc.SetTextJustification (xright-xleft-sz.width, numblanks);
dc.TextOut (xleft, y, string);
dc.SetTextJustification (0, 0);
```

The tricky item is finding out the number of blanks in the line. And what about color? While colors should be allowed on-screen, the printed copy should be black only, unless the printer allows the use of color and you want to print in color.

When dealing with word processing, the basic unit of manipulation is the paragraph. When the user entry exceeds the right margin, the offending word is placed on the next line. When the font is changed, the paragraph may need to be reformed. Similarly the paragraph may need to be reformed when margins are adjusted or when text is inserted, and so on. Additional complications arise from user font requests within a document. A word processor should allow as many fonts as desired. A paragraph could potentially have several font changes, including point size, bold, and underlining.

10.14 CREATING A PROGRAM EDITOR WITH PRINT SUPPORT— PGM10b

For this chapter's major application, let's construct a program editor with full printing capabilities. Specifically, the editor should be able to create new programs as well as edit existing files. The file should be displayed in a user-determined font selected from printer-only fonts along with the usual screen fonts. Forced page breaks should be supported and a title (the name of the file) placed at the top of the first page. Further, there should be margins at the top and bottom, avoiding the usual 66-lines-per-page mess. Additionally, with some fonts, even 80-character lines cannot be shown without clipping. Therefore, we provide any needed line wrapping whenever a line is too long for the given font.

My idea behind this program is twofold. First, we really do need a simple editor with editing features. Second, this approach to printing can easily be adapted to printing a spreadsheet, database reports, mailing labels, and other similar record-oriented files.

The Program Editor requires a main window that can fully input text with full editing capabilities, including insert/type over, delete, backspace, maintain the caret, and scroll. The **CEdit** control provides just such support, providing the multiline flag is enabled. Figure 10.5 shows Pgm10b in operation after I have opened a file. Notice the effect of the variable-width font.

10.14.1 The Use of the CEdit Control as a Main Window

In a dialog box, the **CEdit** control provides all the services listed in the previous paragraph. In fact, the **CEdit** control can be designated a multiline control so that many separate lines could be shown. One trick often used in Windows 95 is to make a control or dialog box become the client window! Once we install a **CEdit** control as the client window, all of the powerful features are readily available.

One major consideration is that the **CEdit** control cannot handle more than 64K worth of text; often, it handles considerably less. MFC has a static UINT **nMaxSize** set to 64K-2 bytes—unrealistically high. In practice, do not expect to get more than

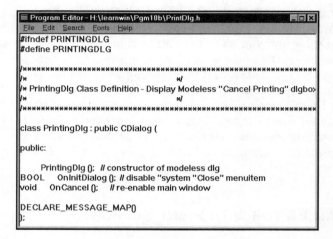

Fig. 10.5 Pgm10b—Program Editor in Operation

about 32K into a **CEdit** control. If we can live with this shortcoming, we gain enormous functionality from **CEdit** and other derived classes.

Because of the many communications between the frame window and the **CEdit** window, it is convenient to have a member pointer to the **CEdit** window—**ptreditwin** in this case. The **CEdit** control is usually allocated in the **OnCreate** function of the frame window.

```
CRect rect;
GetClientRect (&rect);

ptreditwin = new CEdit;
ptreditwin->Create (WS_CHILD | WS_VISIBLE | ES_AUTOHSCROLL |
                    ES_AUTOVSCROLL | ES_MULTILINE | ES_WANTRETURN,
                    rect, this, EDITWINDOW);
```

The EDITWINDOW is a made-up ID used to identify the edit control (in case of multiple **CEdit** controls). The rectangle provides the location and, most important, the dimensions of the control, often set to the client window size. The style IDs are crucial. For a multiline control, use ES_MULTILINE. If ES_AUTOVSCROLL is added, the control automatically handles all scrolling operations!

There are several **CEdit** member functions and several from their base **CWnd** class that are crucial when the control acts as a main window. The first function provides a method to force the dimensions of the control to conform to the size of the frame window's client area. When the frame window responds to WM_SIZE messages, it requests the **CEdit** control to resize itself to fill the client area

```
ptreditwin->MoveWindow (0, 0, width, height, TRUE);
```

where the BOOL indicates the window is to be repainted and the two zero parameters are the x and y coordinates. The **CEdit** control, when in multiline mode, provides automatic support for both horizontal and vertical scroll bars.

Text must be transferred into and out of the edit control during File New, Open, Save, SaveAs, and Print. The member functions for the text transfer are provided from base classes. Under MFC, the **CEdit** class is derived from **CScrollbar** and from **CWnd** and it uses the **CWnd** member functions **GetWindowText** and **SetWindow-Text**

```
ptreditwin->GetWindowText (ptrbuffer,numberbytes);
ptreditwin->SetWindowText (ptrbuffer);
```

where **ptrbuffer** is a char *.

The **CWnd** member function **GetWindowTextLength** returns the number of bytes. Often the two are combined to retrieve the text.

```
ptreditwin->GetWindowText (ptrbuf, ptreditwin->GetWindowTextLength ());
```

These two functions can also be used to assist in enabling/graying the File Save, SaveAs, Print, and other Edit menu items returning an indication of whether there is any text in the control. If the length is zero, there is nothing to print and nothing upon which to perform find/replace operations.

For File Save/SaveAs operations, we need to know if the data in the control has been modified since it was placed into the control. The MFC function **GetModify** returns TRUE if the data has been altered. Typically, in response to File Save, code

```
// if not saved, ask user & handle
if (ptreditwin->GetModify()) SaveCheck();
```

After a save operation and when the text is first transferred into the edit control, any previous setting of the control's modify flag must be cleared.

```
ptreditwin->SetModify (FALSE);  // set CEdit not modified yet
```

The edit control maintains an undo buffer to facilitate removal of the last change. Again, when text is first loaded into the edit control, any previous contents of the edit control must be removed.

```
ptreditwin->EmptyUndoBuffer (); // clear CEdit's undo buffer
```

The edit control can also report on the current number of lines in the text of the control.

```
int totlines = ptreditwin->GetLineCount ();
```

Finally, when the user changes fonts, the edit control must be notified of the font change and a request made to use the new font. Communication is handled through the **SendMessage** function passing the WM_SETFONT message to the edit control. The message passes a handle to the font as the **wparam** parameter and zero for the **lparam**.

```
hfont = CreateFontIndirect (ptrlogfont);
ptreditwin->SendMessage (WM_SETFONT, (UINT) hfont, 0L);
DeleteObject (hfont);
```

Given these member functions, an edit control can easily be installed as a main window providing quite acceptable text editing capabilities. Again the main restriction is the Windows 95 limit of 30K to 64K.

10.14.2 Editing Features Provided by CEdit Controls Implemented in Pgm10b

The **CEdit** class provides automatic support for clipboard operations including Cut, Copy, and Paste along with Undo. These operations are automatically handled by **CEdit** members *if* the menu command handlers invoke the **CEdit** functions for Copy/ Cut/Paste and so on.

The **CEdit** control provides the following member functions that handle the Edit pop-up menu operations. We need only to invoke them.

Edit Undo: `if (ptreditwin->CanUndo ()) ptreditwin->Undo ();`

Edit Cut: `ptreditwin->Cut ();`

Edit Copy: `ptreditwin->Copy ();`

Edit Paste: `ptreditwin->Paste ();`

Edit Clear: `ptreditwin->Clear ();`

Examine the Pgm10b.rc and resource.h files to see the menu structure to implement.

10.14.3 Listing for File: Pgm10b.rc—Pgm10b—Excerpts

```
...
MAINMENU MENU
BEGIN
    POPUP "&File"
    BEGIN
        MENUITEM "&New",                CM_FILENEW
        MENUITEM "&Open...",            CM_FILEOPEN
        MENUITEM "&Save",               CM_FILESAVE, GRAYED
        MENUITEM "Save &As...",         CM_FILESAVEAS, GRAYED
        MENUITEM SEPARATOR
        MENUITEM "&Print...",           CM_FILEPRINT, GRAYED
        MENUITEM "P&rint Setup...",     CM_FILEPRINTERSETUP, GRAYED
        MENUITEM SEPARATOR
        MENUITEM "E&xit\tAlt+F4",       CM_EXIT
    END

    POPUP "&Edit"
    BEGIN
        MENUITEM "&Undo\tAlt+BkSp",     CM_EDITUNDO
        MENUITEM SEPARATOR
        MENUITEM "Cu&t\tShift+Del",     CM_EDITCUT
        MENUITEM "&Copy\tCtrl+Ins",     CM_EDITCOPY
        MENUITEM "&Paste\tShift+Ins",   CM_EDITPASTE
        MENUITEM SEPARATOR
        MENUITEM "Clear &All\tCtrl+Del", CM_EDITCLEAR
    END

    POPUP "&Search"
    BEGIN
```

```
            MENUITEM "&Find...",                 CM_EDITFIND, GRAYED
            MENUITEM "&Replace...",              CM_EDITREPLACE, GRAYED
            MENUITEM "&Next\aF3",                CM_EDITFINDNEXT, GRAYED
        END

        POPUP "&Fonts"
        BEGIN
            MENUITEM "&Font Change",             CM_FONTCHANGE
        END

        POPUP "&Help"
        BEGIN
            MENUITEM "&About...",                CM_HELPABOUT
        END

END

MAINMENU ACCELERATORS
{
  VK_DELETE, ID_EDIT_CUT,       VIRTKEY, SHIFT
  VK_INSERT, ID_EDIT_COPY,      VIRTKEY, CONTROL
  VK_INSERT, ID_EDIT_PASTE,     VIRTKEY, SHIFT
  VK_DELETE, ID_EDIT_CLEAR,     VIRTKEY, CONTROL
  VK_BACK,   ID_EDIT_UNDO,      VIRTKEY, ALT
  VK_F3,     CM_EDITFINDNEXT,   VIRTKEY
}

IDD_ABOUT DIALOG DISCARDABLE  48, 113, 200, 92
STYLE DS_MODALFRAME | WS_POPUP | WS_VISIBLE | WS_CAPTION | WS_SYSMENU
CAPTION "Help - About Pgm10b"
FONT 8, "MS Sans Serif"
BEGIN
    DEFPUSHBUTTON   "OK",IDOK,72,70,50,14
    LTEXT           "by Vic Broquard",IDC_STATIC,70,42,57,8
    LTEXT           "Illustrates CEdit Window and Printing",IDC_STATIC,33,20,228,11
    GROUPBOX        "",IDC_STATIC,28,10,141,50
END

PRINTINGDLG DIALOG 40, 40, 120, 40
STYLE WS_POPUP | WS_CAPTION | WS_SYSMENU | WS_VISIBLE
CAPTION "Printer Routine"
{
 CTEXT           "Printing Document", -1, 4, 6, 120, 12
 DEFPUSHBUTTON   "Cancel", IDCANCEL, 44,22,32,14, WS_GROUP
}

STRINGTABLE  // our apps
{
 IDS_MAINTITLE,    "Program Editor"
 IDS_WINNAME,      "EditPgm"
 IDS_INITFONT,     "System"
 IDS_MSG_QUIT,     "Do you want to quit the application?"
 IDS_MSG_QUERY,    "Query?"
 IDS_MSG_NOTSAVE,  "File has not been saved. Save File now?"
 IDS_MSG_ERROR,    "Edit Program - Error Message"
 IDS_MSG_NOMEM,    "Out of memory. Close app. Free some memory. Try again."
 IDS_MSG_FILEERR,  "File Save Error. Try File Save As with valid filename."
```

```
IDS_MSG_FILEOPEN, "File Open Error. Try again with valid filename."
IDS_MSG_FILEREAD, "File Open Error. Unable to input the file."
IDS_MSG_NOBAR,    "No memory for scrollbars. Free some memory and try again."
IDS_MSG_FILEWRT,  "File Save Error. Output failed - disk full. Try new disk."
IDS_MSG_FILEBIG,  "We can only handle files up to about 64K bytes."
IDS_MSG_FINDREP,  "Find & Replace Error"
IDS_MSG_CANNOTPRT,"Unable to print the document"
IDS_ERR_PRINT,    "Printer Section"
IDS_UNTITLED,     " - (untitled)"
}
...
```

10.14.4 Listing for File: resource.h—Pgm10b—Excerpts

```
...
#define EDITWINDOW            100

#define CM_FILENEW            (WM_USER + 102)
#define CM_FILEOPEN           (WM_USER + 103)
#define CM_FILESAVE           (WM_USER + 105)
#define CM_FILESAVEAS         (WM_USER + 106)
#define CM_FILEPRINT          (WM_USER + 107)
#define CM_FILEPRINTERSETUP   (WM_USER + 108)
#define CM_EXIT               (WM_USER + 109)
#define CM_EDITUNDO           (WM_USER + 110)
#define CM_EDITCUT            (WM_USER + 111)
#define CM_EDITCOPY           (WM_USER + 112)
#define CM_EDITPASTE          (WM_USER + 113)
#define CM_EDITCLEAR          (WM_USER + 114)
#define CM_EDITFIND           (WM_USER + 115)
#define CM_EDITREPLACE        (WM_USER + 116)
#define CM_EDITFINDNEXT       (WM_USER + 117)
#define CM_HELPABOUT          (WM_USER + 118)
#define CM_FONTCHANGE         (WM_USER + 119)

#define IDS_MAINTITLE     2000  // frame window's title
#define IDS_WINNAME       2001  // GetClassName's wndclass name
#define IDS_INITFONT      2002  // name system font
#define IDS_MSG_NOTSAVE   2003  // file not saved msg
#define IDS_MSG_QUIT      2004  // quit application query msg
#define IDS_MSG_QUERY     2005  // title of quit query messagebox
#define IDS_MSG_ERROR     2006  // error has occurred
#define IDS_MSG_NOMEM     2007  // out of memory
#define IDS_MSG_FILEERR   2008  // file save error
#define IDS_MSG_FILEOPEN  2009  // file open error
#define IDS_MSG_NOBAR     2010  // no scroll bars error
#define IDS_MSG_FILEWRT   2011  // file save error - I/O fail
#define IDS_MSG_FILEREAD  2012  // file read error
#define IDS_MSG_FILEBIG   2013  // file size too large
#define IDS_MSG_FINDREP   2014  // find replace error heading
#define IDS_MSG_CANNOTPRT 2015  // cannot print the file
#define IDS_ERR_PRINT     2016  // print error header
#define IDS_UNTITLED      2017  // untitled file message
...
```

One simplification I make is to omit command enablers for the Edit pop-up menu items. As a result, the menu items are not grayed when there is no text, for example. In chapter 13 when the clipboard functions are implemented, I then install command enablers for this pop-up group. However, the Find/Replace pop-up group does have command enablers, and the trio of operations are partially implemented. The commands and messages are processed down to the point where the search operation begins. Unfortunately, **CEdit** does not provide a Search or Insert Member function. These would have to be implemented manually. Such coding becomes rather lengthy if all possibilities are included. Instead, I refer you to the Document-View system that does implement these. Look at the coding in the \MSDEV\MFC\SRC\VIEWEDIT.CPP file for complete details on how to process Find/Replace messages.

First examine the FrameWin header file. For brevity, I have not shown those functions that have not changed from earlier programs. Notice that I have created one common command enabler function to avoid repetitious coding of identical command enablers.

10.14.5 Listing for File: FrameWin.h—Pgm10b—Excerpts

```
...
/****************************************************************************/
/*                                                                        */
/* FrameWin Class Definition                                              */
/*                                                                        */
/****************************************************************************/

class FrameWin : public CFrameWnd {

/****************************************************************************/
/*                                                                        */
/* Class Data Members                                                     */
/*                                                                        */
/****************************************************************************/
protected:
CEdit*     ptreditwin;        // pointer to our CEdit main window

int        height;            // current client window height in pixels
int        width;             // current client window width in pixels

int        avg_caps_width;    // average capital letter width - printer
int        avg_char_width;    // average character width - printer
int        avg_char_height;   // average character height - printer

char       filename[MAX_PATH]; // full path file spec
char       sfilename[14];      // filename.extension

HANDLE     hbuffer;           // handle to global memory file buffer
char*      ptrbuf;            // locked ptr to file buffer
int        totallines;        // total lines at time of printing

// for printing
CDC*       ptrdc;             // passed printer DC
```

```
char*        ptrend;          // locked ptr to file buffer end line work area
int          linesperpage;    // number of lines per page
int          dotsperline;     // number of printer dots per line
long         offset;          // current offset into file
long         maxoff;          // maximum offset into file
BOOL         docdone;         // TRUE when at EOF
BOOL         showtitle;       // TRUE at the start when we need to print a title
char         reporttitle[81]; // header

LOGFONT*     ptrlogfont;      // user selected font for printing
COLORREF     fontcolor;       // the font's color for display
HFONT        hfont;           // font for the CEdit window

static UINT nFindMsg;         // find or replace
static       CFindReplaceDialog *ptrfindreplacedlg; // the modeless dialog
static       bIsReplaceDialog;

/***************************************************************************/
/*                                                                       */
/* Class Functions:                                                      */
/*                                                                       */
/***************************************************************************/
public:
             FrameWin (CWnd*, const char*); // constructor
             ~FrameWin () {}                 // destructor

protected:

afx_msg int  OnCreate (LPCREATESTRUCT);     // construct window, avg char dims
afx_msg void OnPaint ();                     // paint the window - WM_PAINT
afx_msg void OnClose ();                     // determines if app can quit yet
afx_msg void OnSize (UINT, int, int);        // process window resize
afx_msg void OnDestroy ();                   // remove allocated menus
afx_msg void OnRButtonDown (UINT, CPoint);   // pop up edit menu

// utility functions
BOOL         HandlePrinting (CPrintDialog*);// do the actual printing
void         SaveCheck ();                   // query user about saving file
void         GetAvgCharDims ();              // get average char dims for font
void         SaveFile ();                    // save the file
void         UpdateCaption ();               // put filename into title bar
int          DisplayMsg (int, int, UINT);    // displays a message box
void         PrintPage ();                   // prints one page
int          GetNextLine ();                 // retrieves one line of text

// command processors
afx_msg void CmExit ();
afx_msg void CmFontChange ();                // get new font
afx_msg void CmFileNew ();                   // start a new file
afx_msg void CmFileOpen ();                  // open existing file
afx_msg void CmFileSave ();                  // save the file with same name
afx_msg void CmFileSaveAs ();                // save with new name
afx_msg void CmFilePrint ();                 // print the file
afx_msg void CmFilePrinterSetup ();          // set up the printer
afx_msg void CmEditUndo ();                  // undo last change
afx_msg void CmEditCut ();                   // cut to clipboard
```

```
afx_msg void   CmEditCopy ();               // copy to clipboard
afx_msg void   CmEditPaste ();              // paste from the clipboard
afx_msg void   CmEditClear ();              // clear text
afx_msg void   CmEditFind ();               // find text
afx_msg void   CmEditFindNext ();           // find next text
afx_msg void   CmEditReplace ();            // find and replace
afx_msg void   CmHelpAbout ();              // help about our app
afx_msg void   CmEnableHaveFile (CCmdUI*);  // common enabler for menus

afx_msg LRESULT OnDisplayChange (WPARAM, LPARAM); // handle display changes
afx_msg LONG   CmFindReplaceHelper (UINT, LONG);  // process find/replace acts
...
```

Examine the FrameWin class header to familiarize yourself with the data member names and the overall class functions. Many should be familiar to you at this point. Then look over the implementation of the frame window, skipping the actual printing process for now. Some of the functions are unchanged from earlier examples and are not reproduced in this listing. Check the CD for the complete file. Notice that I have included only one command enabler function, **CmEnableHaveFile**, to service all six enable operations because the enable coding is identical in all these cases.

The FrameWin.cpp listing is just too lengthy to be included here; consult the CD-ROM in the Pgm10b folder for the full listing.

10.14.6 Listing for File: FrameWin.cpp—Pgm10b—Excerpts

```
...
BEGIN_MESSAGE_MAP(FrameWin, CFrameWnd)
 ON_WM_KEYDOWN()
 ON_WM_SIZE ()
 ON_WM_CREATE ()
 ON_WM_CLOSE ()
 ON_WM_DESTROY ()
 ON_WM_RBUTTONDOWN ()
 ON_MESSAGE(WM_DISPLAYCHANGE,     OnDisplayChange)
 ON_COMMAND(CM_FONTCHANGE,        CmFontChange)
 ON_COMMAND(CM_EXIT,              CmExit)
 ON_COMMAND(CM_FILENEW,           CmFileNew)
...
 ON_COMMAND(CM_FILEPRINTERSETUP,  CmFilePrinterSetup)
 ON_COMMAND(CM_EDITUNDO,          CmEditUndo)
...
 ON_COMMAND(CM_EDITFIND,          CmEditFind)
 ON_COMMAND(CM_EDITFINDNEXT,      CmEditFindNext)
 ON_COMMAND(CM_EDITREPLACE,       CmEditReplace)
 ON_COMMAND(CM_HELPABOUT,         CmHelpAbout)
 ON_UPDATE_COMMAND_UI(CM_FILESAVE,      CmEnableHaveFile)
...
 ON_UPDATE_COMMAND_UI(CM_EDITFINDNEXT, CmEnableHaveFile)
 ON_REGISTERED_MESSAGE(nFindMsg,       CmFindReplaceHelper)
END_MESSAGE_MAP()

/*****************************************************************************/
/*                                                                         */
```

```
/* Framewin: Construct the window object                                */
/*                                                                      */
/************************************************************************/

         FrameWin::FrameWin (CWnd* ptrparent, const char* title)
                  : CFrameWnd () {

 DWORD style = WS_OVERLAPPEDWINDOW;   // set window styles
 CRect rect (10, 10, 600, 450);      // set init pos and size
 LoadAccelTable ("MAINMENU");        // install keybd accelerators
 ptrlogfont = NULL;                  // set no font loaded
 fontcolor = RGB (0, 0, 0);          // set default font color black
 hbuffer = 0;                        // set no file in memory
 hfont = 0;                          // set no CEdit's font
 ptrbuf = NULL;

 Create ( AfxRegisterWndClass ( ...
 ...
 }

/************************************************************************/
/*                                                                      */
/* OnCreate: get average character height and width                     */
/*                                                                      */
/************************************************************************/

int      FrameWin::OnCreate (LPCREATESTRUCT lpCS) {

 int retcd = CFrameWnd::OnCreate (lpCS); // pass along to base class

 CRect rect;
 GetClientRect (&rect);

 // allocate a CEdit control as a client window to handle the file editing
 // key factor is style ES_MULTILINE
 ptreditwin = new CEdit;
 ptreditwin->Create (WS_CHILD | WS_VISIBLE | ES_AUTOHSCROLL | ES_AUTOVSCROLL |
                     ES_MULTILINE | ES_WANTRETURN, rect, this, EDITWINDOW);

 GetAvgCharDims ();              // set average character dimensions
 return retcd;
 }

/************************************************************************/
/*                                                                      */
/* OnDestroy: remove any menu objects, here none                        */
/*                                                                      */
/************************************************************************/

void      FrameWin::OnDestroy () {

 CFrameWnd::OnDestroy();
 if (ptreditwin) delete ptreditwin; // delete the CEdit control
 if (ptrlogfont) delete ptrlogfont; // delete any user font;
 if (ptrfindreplacedlg)             // delete any find/replace dialog
    ptrfindreplacedlg->SendMessage (WM_COMMAND, IDCANCEL, 0L);
 }

/************************************************************************/
```

```
/*                                                                      */
/* CmExit:  determine if the app can be shut down                       */
/*                                                                      */
/************************************************************************/

void       FrameWin::CmExit () {

  PostMessage (WM_CLOSE);
}

/************************************************************************/
/*                                                                      */
/* OnClose: determine if the app can be shut down                       */
/*                                                                      */
/************************************************************************/

void       FrameWin::OnClose () {

  if (ptreditwin->GetModify ()) SaveCheck (); //save file if needed

  if (DisplayMsg (IDS_MSG_QUERY, IDS_MSG_QUIT, MB_YESNO | MB_ICONQUESTION) ==
     IDYES) CFrameWnd::OnClose ();
}

/************************************************************************/
/*                                                                      */
/* OnSize: acquire the current dimensions of the client window          */
/*                                                                      */
/************************************************************************/

void       FrameWin::OnSize (UINT flags, int width, int height) {
  CFrameWnd::OnSize    (flags, width, height);

  // force the CEdit client to resize itself to our new size
  ptreditwin->MoveWindow (0, 0, width, height, TRUE);
}
...

/************************************************************************/
/*                                                                      */
/* GetAvgCharDims: retrieve current font's average dimensions           */
/*                                                                      */
/************************************************************************/

void       FrameWin::GetAvgCharDims () {

  TEXTMETRIC  tm;  // set the system font's characteristics in tm

  CFont *ptroldfont;
  CFont *ptrfont;
  ptrdc = new CClientDC (this);                  // acquire a DC

  if (ptrlogfont) {                              // install any user font
   ptrfont = new CFont ();
   ptrfont->CreateFontIndirect (ptrlogfont);  // construct the nearest font
   ptroldfont = ptrdc->SelectObject (ptrfont);// install any font, save old one
  }
  ptrdc->GetTextMetrics (&tm);                   // get the font information
  if (ptrlogfont) {
```

```
 ptrdc->SelectObject (ptroldfont);            // reinstall old font
 delete ptrfont;                              // delete new font
 }
delete ptrdc;                                 // delete the dc
// calculate average character parameters
avg_char_width  = tm.tmAveCharWidth;
avg_char_height = tm.tmHeight + tm.tmExternalLeading;
avg_caps_width  = (tm.tmPitchAndFamily & 1 ? 3 : 2) * avg_char_width / 2;
}
...
/***********************************************************************/
/*                                                                   */
/* CmFileNew: open a new file                                        */
/*                                                                   */
/***********************************************************************/

void       FrameWin::CmFileNew () {

 if (ptreditwin->GetModify()) SaveCheck();   // if not saved, ask user & handle
 filename[0] = 0;                            // set no filename
 sfilename[0] = 0;                           // set no filename
 ptreditwin->SetWindowText (NULL);           // send new text to CEdit window
 ptreditwin->SetModify (FALSE);              // set CEdit not modified yet
 ptreditwin->EmptyUndoBuffer ();             // clear CEdit's undo buffer
 UpdateCaption ();                           // insert untitled into caption
 }
/***********************************************************************/
/*                                                                   */
/* CmFileOpen: open an existent file                                 */
/*                                                                   */
/***********************************************************************/

void       FrameWin::CmFileOpen () {

 if (ptreditwin->GetModify()) SaveCheck(); // if changed, ask user & handle
 // create new transfer buffer
 CFileDialog filedlg (TRUE,      // use Open dialog
 ... open and input the file
  ptrbuf [filesize] = 0;                    // insert null terminator for CEdit
  ptreditwin->SetWindowText (ptrbuf);       // set CEdit to new text
  GlobalUnlock (hbuffer);                   // unlock file buffer
  GlobalFree   (hbuffer);                   // and free global memory
  ptreditwin->SetModify (FALSE);            // set CEdit to unmodified
  ptreditwin->EmptyUndoBuffer ();           // clear CEdit's undo buffer
  UpdateCaption ();                         // install filename in title bar
 }
 }
...
/***********************************************************************/
/*                                                                   */
/* SaveFile: write the file                                          */
/*                                                                   */
/***********************************************************************/
```

```
void        FrameWin::SaveFile () {

 // allocate a file buffer based upon current size in the CEdit control
 long filesize = ptreditwin->GetWindowTextLength ();
 hbuffer = GlobalAlloc (GMEM_MOVEABLE, filesize);
 if (hbuffer==NULL) {    // error, not enough memory for buffer
  DisplayMsg (IDS_MSG_ERROR, IDS_MSG_NOMEM, MB_OK | MB_ICONSTOP);
  return;
 }
 ptrbuf = (char*) GlobalLock (hbuffer);  // get locked ptr to global buffer

 // transfer the updated text from CEdit control into global memory
 ptreditwin->GetWindowText (ptrbuf, ptreditwin->GetWindowTextLength ());
 // open the file, replacing any existing file
 ... output the file
}
...

/******************************************************************************/
/*                                                                          */
/* CmEditFind: find text requested dialog box                               */
/*                                                                          */
/******************************************************************************/

void        FrameWin::CmEditFind () {

 if (ptrfindreplacedlg) return;        // avoids having both on screen
 ptrfindreplacedlg = new CFindReplaceDialog (); // allocate new dlg
 bIsReplaceDialog = FALSE;
 ptrfindreplacedlg->Create (TRUE,      // find box only
                            NULL,      // string = what to find
                            NULL,      // string = replace with this
                            FR_DOWN,   // find dlg flags
                            this);
 ptrfindreplacedlg->SendMessage (WM_INITDIALOG); // show the modeless dlg
}

/******************************************************************************/
/*                                                                          */
/* CmEditReplace: replace text dialog box requested                         */
/*                                                                          */
/******************************************************************************/

void        FrameWin::CmEditReplace () {

 if (ptrfindreplacedlg) return;        // avoids having both on screen
 ptrfindreplacedlg = new CFindReplaceDialog ();
 bIsReplaceDialog = TRUE;
 ptrfindreplacedlg->Create (FALSE,     // find and replace box
                            NULL,      // string = what to find
                            NULL,      // string = replace with this
                            FR_DOWN,   // find dlg flags
                            this);
 ptrfindreplacedlg->SendMessage (WM_INITDIALOG); // show the modeless dlg
}

/******************************************************************************/
```

```
/*                                                                        */
/* CmEditFindNext: find next item requested                              */
/*                                                                        */
/************************************************************************/

void        FrameWin::CmEditFindNext () {

  if (ptrfindreplacedlg && bIsReplaceDialog) return; // replace in force
  if (!ptrfindreplacedlg) {                          // if find dialog is active
   ptrfindreplacedlg = new CFindReplaceDialog (); // allocate new dlg
   bIsReplaceDialog = FALSE;
   ptrfindreplacedlg->Create (TRUE,      // find box only
                              NULL,      // string = what to find
                              NULL,      // string = replace with this
                              FR_DOWN,   // find dlg flags
                              this);
   ptrfindreplacedlg->SendMessage (WM_INITDIALOG); // show the modeless dlg
  }
  else ptrfindreplacedlg->FindNext ();
}

/************************************************************************/
/*                                                                        */
/* CmFindReplaceHelper: handle a find or replace operation               */
/*                                                                        */
/************************************************************************/

LONG        FrameWin::CmFindReplaceHelper (UINT /*wparam*/, LONG lparam) {

  CFindReplaceDialog *ptrdlg = CFindReplaceDialog::GetNotifier (lparam);

  if (ptrdlg->FindNext () || ptrdlg->ReplaceCurrent () || ptrdlg->ReplaceAll ()) {
   // for each case: find, find next, replace, replace all, first attempt to
   // find the FindWhat item; Search returns >=0 if found
   // not implemented here - too complex in complete generality
   // see msvc20\mfc\src\viewedit.cpp for complete details
  }
  else if (ptrdlg->IsTerminating ()) { // is dialog box closing?
   delete ptrfindreplacedlg;           // delete this instance
   ptrfindreplacedlg = NULL;           // and set to none in use

  }
  return 0;
}

/************************************************************************/
/*                                                                        */
/* CmFontChange: get users font request and implement it                 */
/*                                                                        */
/************************************************************************/

void        FrameWin::CmFontChange () {

  CFontDialog   *ptrdlg;
  static char   printer[80];
  char          *device, *driver, *output;
  CDC           *ptrprinterDC = new CDC;
```

```
// get access to a printer DC from the ini file installed printer
GetProfileString ("windows", "device", "...", printer, 80);
if (NULL != (device = strtok (printer, ",")) &&
    NULL != (driver = strtok (NULL,    ",")) &&
    NULL != (output = strtok (NULL,    ","))) {
  // a default printer exists, so get a DC for it
  ptrprinterDC->CreateDC (driver, device, output, NULL);
  // if the user has already chosen a font, use that one as the initial font
  if (ptrlogfont) ptrdlg = new CFontDialog (ptrlogfont, CF_EFFECTS |
                   CF_PRINTERFONTS | CF_FORCEFONTEXIST, ptrprinterDC, this);
  else ptrdlg = new CFontDialog (NULL, CF_EFFECTS |
                   CF_PRINTERFONTS | CF_FORCEFONTEXIST, ptrprinterDC, this);
}
else {
  // cannot find the default printer, so use printer only fonts instead, if
  // user has already chosen a font, use it as the initial font in the dialog
  if (ptrlogfont) ptrdlg = new CFontDialog (ptrlogfont, CF_EFFECTS |
                   CF_PRINTERFONTS | CF_FORCEFONTEXIST, NULL, this);
  else ptrdlg = new CFontDialog (NULL, CF_EFFECTS |
                   CF_PRINTERFONTS | CF_FORCEFONTEXIST, NULL, this);
}

ptrdlg->m_cf.rgbColors = fontcolor;   // install current color

if (ptrdlg->DoModal () == IDOK) {     // get user font choice
  if (!ptrlogfont) ptrlogfont = new LOGFONT; // 1st time, create LOGFONT
  memcpy (ptrlogfont, &(ptrdlg->m_lf), sizeof (LOGFONT)); // copy user choice
  fontcolor = ptrdlg->GetColor ();    // save color choice
  GetAvgCharDims ();                  // get new average char dims
  Invalidate();                       // on new dims, and reshow

  hfont = CreateFontIndirect (ptrlogfont);
  // force the CEdit window to use new font
  ptreditwin->SendMessage (WM_SETFONT, (UINT) hfont, 0L);
  DeleteObject (hfont);
}
delete ptrprinterDC;
delete ptrdlg;
}
/*****************************************************************************/
/*                                                                         */
/* CmFilePrint: print an existing file                                     */
/*                                                                         */
/*****************************************************************************/

void      FrameWin::CmFilePrint () {

totallines = ptreditwin->GetLineCount (); // get the total lines from CEdit
if (totallines == 0) return;              // nothing to print, quit

CPrintDialog printdlg (FALSE, PD_USEDEVMODECOPIES, this);

// make a rough guess at the number of pages - could go ahead and
// create a default printerDC and select the current font into it
// then determine the page size and the number of pages
// here I approximate - but will print all the pages
```

```
    int numpages = totallines / 50;
    printdlg.m_pd.nMinPage = 1;
    printdlg.m_pd.nMaxPage = 1;//numpages;
    printdlg.m_pd.nFromPage = 1;
    printdlg.m_pd.nToPage = 1;
    printdlg.m_pd.nCopies = 1;

    // display print dialog box for user selections
    if (printdlg.DoModal () == IDCANCEL) return; // if cancel, quit

    // go handle the printing, displaying error msg if it fails
    if (!HandlePrinting (&printdlg)) DisplayMsg (IDS_MSG_CANNOTPRT, IDS_ERR_PRINT,
                                         MB_OK | MB_ICONEXCLAMATION);
}
/***************************************************************************/
/*                                                                         */
/* HandlePrinting: print the document                                      */
/*                                                                         */
/***************************************************************************/

#define   TopLines 4      // number of lines for top margin
#define   BotLines 2      // number of lines for bottom margin
#define   FF       0x0c   // formfeed - new page code
#define   CR       0x0d   // carriage return code
#define   LF       0x0a   // line feed code

/***************************************************************************/
/*                                                                         */
/* Prints all pages of a document                                          */
/*                                                                         */
/* Uses TopLines as a margin, printing a filename as the title within the  */
/*      top margin area on the first page only                             */
/*                                                                         */
/* Recognizes FF codes:                                                    */
/*  if FF is the first code, does FF and places the title on next page     */
/*  if FF occurs exactly at the bottom of a page, it is ignored since      */
/*      TPrinter correctly does the FF                                     */
/*                                                                         */
/* Handles linewrap on lines that exceed width based on font and printer   */
/*                                                                         */
/***************************************************************************/

BOOL      FrameWin::HandlePrinting (CPrintDialog *ptrprintdlg) {

    // get updated text
    // allocate a file buffer based upon current size in the CEdit control
    long filesize = ptreditwin->GetWindowTextLength ();
    hbuffer = GlobalAlloc (GMEM_MOVEABLE, filesize);
    if (hbuffer==NULL) {     // error, not enough memory for buffer
     DisplayMsg (IDS_MSG_ERROR, IDS_MSG_NOMEM, MB_OK | MB_ICONSTOP);
     return FALSE;
    }
    ptrbuf = (char*) GlobalLock (hbuffer);  // get locked ptr to global buffer

    // transfer the updated text from CEdit control into global memory
    ptreditwin->GetWindowText (ptrbuf, ptreditwin->GetWindowTextLength ());
```

```
maxoff = filesize;        // save filesize
GlobalUnlock (hbuffer); // unlock buffer

// construct print title for system use: "filename"
// and make a report title of the full filename
if (filename[0] == 0) {
 char untitled[14];
 LoadString (AfxGetApp()->m_hInstance, IDS_UNTITLED, untitled,
           sizeof(untitled));
 strcpy (reporttitle, &untitled[3]); // skip over  "- " part
}
else strcpy (reporttitle, filename);

// set clear all error flags
BOOL printerror = FALSE;
userabort = FALSE;

// setup a printer DC from the print dialog's results - attach its hdc
ptrdc = new CDC;
ptrdc->Attach (ptrprintdlg->GetPrinterDC () ); // acquire print DC

// setup a printing cancel dialog box
PrintingDlg  *ptrprintingdlg = new PrintingDlg ();
hprintdlg = ptrprintingdlg->m_hWnd;   // set the external hwnd for abort proc

// attempt to install the abort procedure
if (ptrdc->SetAbortProc (AbortProc) < 0) { // setup failed, so abort print
 ptrprintingdlg->DestroyWindow (); // remove printing dialog box
 delete ptrprintingdlg;                // and remove the dialog object

 delete ptrdc;
 GlobalFree (hbuffer);
 return FALSE;
}

// load font and scale TrueType fonts
LOGFONT  *ptrprlogfont;      // printer version of user selected font
CFont    *ptroldfont;                       // place to save old font
CFont    *ptrfont;                          // our new font

if (ptrlogfont) {                           // install any user font
 // copy the real LOGFONT because we will scale the font height and width
 ptrprlogfont = (LOGFONT*) malloc (sizeof (LOGFONT));
 memcpy (ptrprlogfont, ptrlogfont, sizeof(LOGFONT));
 ptrfont = new CFont ();
 HDC hdc = CreateDC ("DISPLAY",NULL,NULL,NULL); // get a screen DC for scaling
 // calculate both x and y scale dimensions between the screen and the printer
 float xscale = ptrdc->GetDeviceCaps (LOGPIXELSX) /
              (float) GetDeviceCaps(hdc, LOGPIXELSX);
 float yscale = ptrdc->GetDeviceCaps (LOGPIXELSY) /
              (float) GetDeviceCaps(hdc, LOGPIXELSY);
 DeleteDC (hdc);
 // install scaled dimensions
 ptrprlogfont->lfHeight = (long) (ptrprlogfont->lfHeight * yscale);
 ptrprlogfont->lfWidth = (long) (ptrprlogfont->lfWidth * xscale);
 ptrfont->CreateFontIndirect (ptrprlogfont);  // create the font from LOGFONT
 ptroldfont = ptrdc->SelectObject (ptrfont);  // install font, save old
```

```
  free (ptrprlogfont);                               // removed copied LOGFONT
}

// determine real character dims on the printer and total pages
TEXTMETRIC tm;
GetTextMetrics (ptrdc->m_hDC, &tm);

// calculate average character parameters
avg_char_width  = tm.tmAveCharWidth;
avg_char_height = tm.tmHeight + tm.tmExternalLeading;
avg_caps_width  = (tm.tmPitchAndFamily & 1 ? 3 : 2) * avg_char_width / 2;

// calculate pagination data
dotsperline  = GetDeviceCaps (ptrdc->m_hDC, HORZRES);
int charsperline = dotsperline / avg_char_width;
linesperpage = GetDeviceCaps (ptrdc->m_hDC, VERTRES) / avg_char_height;
// if we are removing BotLines, must account for printing at least 1 line
if (linesperpage < (TopLines + BotLines + 1) )
 linesperpage = 1 +BotLines +TopLines; // rounds up to nearest number of pages
int numpages = (totallines + linesperpage - BotLines - TopLines -1) /
            (linesperpage - BotLines - TopLines);

// print the document
DOCINFO doc;                        // used by Windows for msg
doc.cbSize = sizeof(DOCINFO);       // install doc size
doc.lpszDocName = filename;         // install filename
doc.lpszOutput = NULL;
doc.lpszDatatype = NULL;            // Windows 95 new values
doc.fwType = 0;                     // for print banding

offset = 0;                         // set to the beginning of the file
docdone = FALSE;                    // will be set TRUE when doc is done
showtitle = TRUE;                   // indicate title yet to be printed

// main document printing loop - if copies >1 are desired, wrap a copies
// loop around this loop
if (::StartDoc (ptrdc->m_hDC, &doc) >0) { // start the document
 while (offset < maxoff && !printerror && !docdone) {
  if (::StartPage (ptrdc->m_hDC) >0) {    // set for begin page
   // note that Windows 95 resets the DC each time, so we must reselect font
   ptrdc->SelectObject (ptrfont);         // install font
   PrintPage ();                          // actually print the page
   if (::EndPage (ptrdc->m_hDC) <0) printerror = TRUE; // end the page
  }
 }
::EndDoc (ptrdc->m_hDC);            // end the doc
}
else printerror = TRUE;            // indicate printer error occurred

// remove any user selected font in use
if (ptrlogfont) {                  // deselect and delete user font
 ptrdc->SelectObject (ptroldfont);
 delete ptrfont;
}

if (!userabort) EnableWindow (TRUE);   // restore main window action
delete ptrdc;                          // clean up
ptrprintingdlg->DestroyWindow ();      // remove printing dialog box
```

```
 delete ptrprintingdlg;              // remove printing dialog object
 GlobalFree (hbuffer);               // remove the text buffer
 return !printerror && !userabort;   // return success code
}
/****************************************************************************/
/*                                                                        */
/* PrintPage: actually prints the page                                    */
/*                                                                        */
/****************************************************************************/
void      FrameWin::PrintPage () {

 int  line = 0;              // current lines on the page
 int  dif;                   // current chars to print
 BOOL ok;                    // loop controller

 ptrbuf = (char*) GlobalLock (hbuffer); // get locked ptr to global buffer
 ptrbuf += offset;              // set ptrbuf to next char to process

 if (showtitle) {               // print doc title on first page
  if (*ptrbuf == FF) {          // formfeed is first code
   offset++;                    // so skip over it
   ok = FALSE;                  // and do not print title
  }
  else {                        // no formfeed, so print title
   ptrdc->TextOut (0, avg_char_height * 2, reporttitle); // display title line
   showtitle = FALSE;           // signal title has been printed
   ok = TRUE;                   // signal ok to continue this page
  }
 }
 else ok = TRUE;                // show title done, so continue this page
 line += TopLines;              // leave TopLines blank on other pages

 while (ok) {                   // continue until full page or eof breaks out
  dif = GetNextLine ();         // get a line to display
  if (dif > 0)                  // positive dif means chars to display
   ptrdc->TextOut (0, avg_char_height * line++, ptrbuf, dif); // display line
  else if (dif == 0) line++;    // 0 dif means solitary <CR>, skip line
  else if (dif == -1) {         // -1 = eof and no line
   docdone = TRUE;              // signal end of doc
   break;                       // and quit this page
  }
  else { // dif == -2           // -2 = newpage and no line
   if (*ptrend == 0) docdone = TRUE; // avoid double new page if next is eof
   break;                       // and quit this page
  }
  if (line >= linesperpage - BotLines) {  // do we have a full page?
   if (*ptrend == FF) offset++;           // avoid FF as next char
   else if (*ptrend == 0) docdone = TRUE; // avoid double FF at doc end
   break;                                 // and leave
  }
  ptrbuf = ptrend;             // reset for start of next line
 }
 GlobalUnlock (hbuffer);       // unlock file buffer
}
```

```
/***************************************************************************/
/*                                                                         */
/* GetNextLine: returns the length of the next line                        */
/* -1 = end of file - no line to print - ptrend->the '\0' byte             */
/* -2 = new page - no line to print - ptrend->next byte                    */
/*  0 = <CRLF> on line with no characters to print - ptrend-> next byte    */
/*                                                                         */
/* offset is updated for correct number of bytes analyzed                  */
/* Formfeeds, <CRLF>, and linewrap are handled                             */
/*                                                                         */
/***************************************************************************/
int        FrameWin::GetNextLine () {
 CSize sz;
 long  dif = 0;
 ptrend = ptrbuf;

 while (TRUE) {
  if (*ptrend == 0) {         // is this byte EOF?
   offset += dif;             // update offset
   if (dif == 0) dif = -1;    // set EOF and no line
   break;                     // and leave with dif set and ptrend -> '\0'
  }
  else if (*ptrend == FF) {   // is this byte a formfeed for a new page?
   if (dif > 0) {             // any preceding chars?
    offset += dif + 1;        // yes, so return those - update offset
    break;                    // and leave with dif set and ptrend -> FF byte
   }
   ptrend++;                  // no, so point to next char
   dif = -2;                  // and set newpage
   offset++;                  // account for the ff code
   break;                     // and leave signaling FF with no lines
  }
  else if (*ptrend == CR) {   // is this byte a carriage return?
   ptrend++;                  // point to next byte
   if (*ptrend == LF) {       // is next byte the line feed?
    offset += dif + 2;        // yes, update offset for both codes
    ptrend++;                 // point to next byte after the LF
   }
   else {                     // next char is not the LF
    offset += dif +1;         // update offset allowing for the CR
   }
   break;                     // and leave with dif set and ptrend -> next char
  }
  else {                      // this byte is valid
   ptrend++;                  // point to next byte
   dif++;                     // add one to the total len of this line so far
   sz = ptrdc->GetTextExtent (ptrbuf, dif); // check for linewrap
   if (sz.cx > dotsperline) { // if line length exceeds page width
    ptrend--;                 // attempt to back up a character
    dif--;                    // and remove 1 from total line length
    if (dif == 0) {           // avoid problem of even 1 char being too large
     ptrend++;                // force only 1 char to print
     dif = 1;                 // and set dif to the 1 char
```

```
    }
    offset += dif;                  // update offset
    break;                          // and leave with dif set and ptrend -> next char
    }
  }                                 // here line len is ok, so go do another char
 }
 return dif;
}
/*********************************************************************/
/*                                                                   */
/* CmFilePrinterSetup: set up the printer parameters                 */
/*                                                                   */
/*********************************************************************/
void      FrameWin::CmFilePrinterSetup () {

 CPrintDialog printdlg (TRUE, PD_USEDEVMODECOPIES, this);
 printdlg.DoModal ();
}
...

/*********************************************************************/
/*                                                                   */
/* CmEnableHaveFile: enabler for all menus that require existent file */
/*                                                                   */
/*********************************************************************/
void      FrameWin::CmEnableHaveFile (CCmdUI *ptrenabler) {

 ptrenabler->Enable (ptreditwin->GetWindowTextLength () > 0 ? 1 : 0);
}

/*********************************************************************/
/*                                                                   */
/* CmEditUndo: undo last change                                      */
/*                                                                   */
/*********************************************************************/
void      FrameWin::CmEditUndo () {

 if (ptreditwin->CanUndo ()) ptreditwin->Undo ();
}
... others similar
```

The constructor initializes the font variable to no font in use. In **OnCreate** the **CEdit** main window is allocated. In **OnDestroy** the main window and user font are deleted. If the modeless Find/Replace dialog is running, it is sent the cancel message to force it to close.

```
    if (ptrfindreplacedlg)             // delete any find/replace dialog
       ptrfindreplacedlg->SendMessage (WM_COMMAND, IDCANCEL, 0L);
```

In **OnSize** the **CEdit** window is forced to become the size of the current client window by use of the **MoveWindow** function.

```
    ptreditwin->MoveWindow (0, 0, width, height, TRUE);
```

In **CmFileNew**, if any existing file has been modified, the user is queried. Then an empty file is created by passing a NULL pointer to the **CEdit** control. In **CmFile-Open**, although not shown above, I limited the maximum file size to the MFC value of 64K. Although there is no guarantee that a file of even 30,000 bytes can be transferred into any given **CEdit** control, I arbitrarily chose 64K as the limit because MFC uses this value. Experiment with various file sizes; you may wish to lower that upper threshold. For fast I/O, the entire file is then read into a global memory buffer. The global buffer is then transferred into the **CEdit** control and the control's undo buffer is cleared along with its modified flag. And the frame window's caption is updated with the current filename. Under Windows 95, with long filenames, you may wish to append only the actual filename less the full path or perhaps less the extension.

The command enablers use the number of bytes currently in the **CEdit** control to enable/disable the menu items, graying them out when there are no bytes in the control.

```
void       FrameWin::CmEnableHaveFile (CCmdUI *ptrenabler) {
 ptrenabler->Enable (ptreditwin->GetWindowTextLength () > 0 ? 1 : 0);
 }
```

The Edit pop-up menu items' control handlers simply invoke the corresponding **CEdit** member functions as discussed before.

There are a few changes to the sequences in the **CmFontChange** function. Since we wish to allow only printer-only and other supported fonts displayable on a printer, the DC we get must be for the currently selected printer. To simplify matters until chapter 15, I have chosen to use the default printer installed in the WIN.INI file by using **GetProfileString** and then using the C function **strtok** to separate the values that are separated by commas.

```
static char    printer[80];
char           *device, *driver, * output;
CDC            *ptrprinterDC = new CDC;

// get access to a printer DC from the ini file installed printer
GetProfileString ("windows", "device", "...", printer, 80);
if (NULL != (device = strtok (printer, ",")) &&
    NULL != (driver = strtok (NULL,    ",")) &&
    NULL != (output = strtok (NULL,    ","))) {
 // a default printer exists, so get a DC for it
 ptrprinterDC->CreateDC (driver, device, output, NULL);
 // if the user has already chosen a font, use that one as the initial font
 if (ptrlogfont) ptrdlg = new CFontDialog (ptrlogfont, CF_EFFECTS |
                 CF_PRINTERFONTS | CF_FORCEFONTEXIST, ptrprinterDC, this);
 else ptrdlg = new CFontDialog (NULL, CF_EFFECTS |
                 CF_PRINTERFONTS | CF_FORCEFONTEXIST, ptrprinterDC, this);
 }
else {
 // cannot find the default printer, so use printer only fonts instead, if
 // user has already chosen a font, use it as the initial font in the dialog
 if (ptrlogfont) ptrdlg = new CFontDialog (ptrlogfont, CF_EFFECTS |
                   CF_PRINTERFONTS | CF_FORCEFONTEXIST, NULL, this);
```

```
    else ptrdlg = new CFontDialog (NULL, CF_EFFECTS |
                     CF_PRINTERFONTS | CF_FORCEFONTEXIST, NULL, this);
    }
```

Now when the Choose Fonts dialog box is executed, you can see many fonts in the list box that have a little image of a printer to the left of the font name. These are the printer-only fonts. Those that do not have the printer icon are supported fonts that can be displayed graphically via a bitmap on the printer. The TrueType fonts have a "TT" icon before their names. Notice that, when a printer-only font is selected, a message appears by the Sample Example of that font. Windows 95 is notifying you that it is doing a reasonable fit when attempting to render that font on-screen. Namely, the size is sufficiently increased so that you can read it. Remember, most printer fonts if rendered true size would be unreadable on-screen. Once the font is selected, we again send the **CEdit** window the WM_SETFONT message to immediately implement that font on-screen. As you select and try out the various printer-only fonts, remember that most choices within the **same** family can be rendered **identical** on screen. They are rendered correctly when sent to the printer.

In **CmEditFind** if the dialog is already active, the request is ignored to avoid having multiple dialogs on-screen. A new instance of the **CFindReplaceDialog** class is constructed and the **bIsReplaceDialog** is set to FALSE. Notice, as I create the modeless Find dialog, I passed FR_DOWN and then sent the dialog the WM_INITDIALOG to begin its execution.

```
    if (ptrfindreplacedlg) return;     // avoids having both on screen
    ptrfindreplacedlg = new CFindReplaceDialog (); // allocate new dlg
    bIsReplaceDialog = FALSE;
    ptrfindreplacedlg->Create (TRUE,    // find box only
                    NULL,    // string = what to find
                    NULL,    // string = replace with this
                    FR_DOWN, // find dlg flags
                    this);
    ptrfindreplacedlg->SendMessage (WM_INITDIALOG); // show the modeless dlg
```

CmEditReplace follows the same pattern except the flag is set to TRUE, indicating a replace operation. In **CmFindNext**, if there is a replace dialog on-screen, the command is ignored. If no dialog is active, a new Find dialog is launched as before. But if there is a Find dialog on-screen, the **CFindReplaceDialog** has a member function to completely handle a Find Next request—**FindNext**.

```
    ptrfindreplacedlg->FindNext ();
```

All three dialog operations send messages to the common **CmFindReplace-Helper** function which separates the different actions. The first action must be to obtain a pointer to the dialog that sent this message; the static function **GetNotifier** when passed the LPARAM of this helper message returns a pointer to the sending dialog:

```
    CFindReplaceDialog  *ptrdlg =
                    CFindReplaceDialog::GetNotifier (lparam);
```

Next, there are three member functions that return TRUE if the corresponding operation is in effect.

FindNext   a find next operation is requested

ReplaceCurrent   a single replace operation is requested

ReplaceAll   replace all occurrences operation is requested

Again, for each of these activities, a **Search** function would be the first step. Set up a DoUntil loop, performing the common **Search** operation for all cases and repeating only if the Replace All operation is requested. Thus, one would code the following to isolate these three cases:

```
if (ptrdlg->FindNext () || ptrdlg->ReplaceCurrent ()
    || ptrdlg->ReplaceAll ()) {
  // for each case: find, find next, replace, replace all,
  // first attempt to find the FindWhat item by coding a
  // Search function which returns >=0 if found
  // and use a DoUntil
}
else if (ptrdlg->IsTerminating ()) { // is dialog box closing?
 delete ptrfindreplacedlg;              // delete this instance
 ptrfindreplacedlg = NULL;              // and set to none in use
 }
return 0;
```

Unfortunately, **CEdit** does not have the **Search** or **Insert** member functions. However, the Document-View members do. You should examine the file MSDEV\MFC\SRC\VIEWEDIT.CPP for a way to implement the Search and Insert operations, extracting the code as needed. Since this coding is rather extensive, I have not done so here.

The File | Print coding closely follows Pgm10a in many respects. We must install the Abort dialog and run the Print dialog—all are unchanged from the earlier version. Let's examine the sequence required to handle the printing operation. In **Handle-Printing**, the number of bytes currently in the **CEdit** control is retrieved and a global memory area allocated to receive the text via the **CWnd** function **GetWindowText**.

```
long filesize = ptreditwin->GetWindowTextLength ();
hbuffer = GlobalAlloc (GMEM_MOVEABLE, filesize);
ptrbuf = (char*) GlobalLock (hbuffer);
ptreditwin->GetWindowText (ptrbuf,
          ptreditwin->GetWindowTextLength ());
```

One could return if there are no lines to print. The two titles are constructed, one for the report heading and one for the Print Manager. The two error flags are then cleared, and the actual printer HDC constructed by the Print dialog is borrowed for our printer **CDC**.

```
BOOL printerror = FALSE;
userabort = FALSE;
ptrdc = new CDC;
ptrdc->Attach (ptrprintdlg->GetPrinterDC () );
```

Then the Abort Printing dialog and its message hook are installed as in Pgm10a. Next, the user font is copied, installed, and scaled.

```
if (ptrlogfont) {
 ptrprlogfont = (LOGFONT*) malloc (sizeof (LOGFONT));
 memcpy (ptrprlogfont, ptrlogfont, sizeof(LOGFONT));
 ptrfont = new CFont ();
 HDC hdc = CreateDC ("DISPLAY", NULL, NULL, NULL);
 float xscale = ptrdc->GetDeviceCaps (LOGPIXELSX) /
                (float) GetDeviceCaps(hdc, LOGPIXELSX);
 float yscale = ptrdc->GetDeviceCaps (LOGPIXELSY) /
                (float) GetDeviceCaps(hdc, LOGPIXELSY);
 DeleteDC (hdc);
 ptrprlogfont->lfHeight = (long) (ptrprlogfont->lfHeight * yscale);
 ptrprlogfont->lfWidth = (long) (ptrprlogfont->lfWidth * xscale);
 ptrfont->CreateFontIndirect (ptrprlogfont);
 ptroldfont = ptrdc->SelectObject (ptrfont);
 free (ptrprlogfont);
}
```

The average character dimensions on the printer DC are calculated and then the pagination members are calculated.

```
dotsperline  = GetDeviceCaps (ptrdc->m_hDC, HORZRES);
int charsperline = dotsperline / avg_char_width;
linesperpage =GetDeviceCaps(ptrdc->m_hDC, VERTRES)/avg_char_height;
if (linesperpage < (TopLines + BotLines + 1) )
   linesperpage = 1 +BotLines +TopLines;
int numpages = (totallines + linesperpage - BotLines -TopLines-1)/
               (linesperpage - BotLines - TopLines);
```

The DOCINFO structure is filled and the main printing loop is entered. The main printing loop controlling field is **docdone**.

```
if (::StartDoc (ptrdc->m_hDC, &doc) >0) {
 while (offset < maxoff && !printerror && !docdone) {
  if (::StartPage (ptrdc->m_hDC) >0) {
   // note that Windows 95 resets the DC each time
   ptrdc->SelectObject (ptrfont);
   PrintPage ();
   if (::EndPage (ptrdc->m_hDC) <0) printerror = TRUE;
  }
 }
 ::EndDoc (ptrdc->m_hDC);
}
else printerror = TRUE;
```

All of the work is done in **PrintPage**. This includes printing headings, all the text that can fit on the page, any footnotes, and page numbers. Allowance should be made for top and bottom margins. Some form of line counting should be employed, displaying text at **avg_char_height * line**. Blank lines are emulated simply by adding to **line** so that the next **TextOut** occurs at **avg_char_height * line**. As you might expect, the logic for printing a page with many options can become involved. It must be able to handle imbedded form feeds, user printer fonts, top and bottom margins, line wrapping, and placement of a title (the filename) on the very first line.

The **offset** member contains the offset from the beginning of the file of data to the current page. Thus, every time **PrintPage** is invoked and we lock down the global memory area for the file, we can adjust the pointer to where we last were within the file. The member **docdone** is set to TRUE when **PrintPage** detects EOF. This approach guarantees that all pages are printed. Remember that—because of large-point-size fonts, line wrapping, and imbedded form feed codes—an accurate count of the total pages to print cannot be determined without completely previewing the document performing all of the actions except actual printing.

We must provide the margins at the top and bottom. I used two defines for these—**TopLines** and **BotLines**—which are currently set to 4 and 2 respectively. I intend to display the title on line 2 of the four top lines on the first page only; on all other pages the four top lines are blank.

While you are examining the defines, notice that there are defines for the three DOS codes for which we are scanning while printing a page: the form feed (FF) or new page code, the carriage return (CR) code, and the line feed (LF) code. Normally, DOS generates a CR code followed by an LF code. However, in some unusual cases, I have seen only the CR code with no LF code. Also I force at least one line to be printed per page should some monster font be selected onto a small space. Note this value can still be invalid due to imbedded form feeds and line wraps as yet undetected.

All of the major activity of printing variable-width fonts occurs in the **PrintPage** function. When it begins, the current line on which to display and that line's length, **dif**, is set to 0. The user print font is selected into the printer DC, and the **ptrbuf** pointer is locked on to the global memory area containing the document. Since this may not be the first page, **offset** is added to **ptrbuf** to set **ptrbuf** to the first byte we need to examine on this page.

Next, the initial title situation is handled. It is complicated by the fact that sometimes a form feed is the first character in the file. We do not want to print the title and then simulate a page eject. Rather, if that is the situation, do the page eject and then print the title on the next page. Thus, if we are to show the title, then if the first character is the FF code, the offset is incremented and the BOOL **ok** is set to FALSE, preventing the main processing loop from executing. This effectively leaves the **PrintPage** routine, which then does the form feed automatically. On the other hand, when the first byte is not the FF, the title is displayed on line 2, **showtitle** is set to FALSE, and **ok** is set to TRUE to cause the actual main processing loop to be run. The line counter is incremented by the number of **TopLines** we want for the top margin.

The main processing loop invokes **GetNextLine** to get the next line; it returns the length of that line or a special value indicating that the EOF condition or a form feed was encountered. If **dif** or the length of the line is above 0, the line is displayed and the line number is incremented. If a length of 0 is found, indicating only a CRLF or blank line, only the line number is incremented. If **dif** is -1, indicating EOF and no line at all, **docdone** is set to TRUE, which is used to terminate the printing process. Here, the break terminates the loop, leaving **PrintPage**. If **dif** is -2, indicating a form feed was encountered and no line at all, then I check further to see if the next byte is EOF so we can avoid a needless double-page eject. Anyway, the break ends the loop because of the form feed. Finally, the full-page condition is checked. If we now have a full page, less the **BotLines**, I again check the next character for a form feed to avoid double form feeds and check for the EOF code. In any event, the break ends the loop again. If all is normal, **ptrbuf** is set to **ptrend**, ready for the next byte. The member **ptrend** is set by **GetNextLine** and points to the next byte to process. Upon leaving, the original font is restored and the global memory unlocked.

GetNextLine must parse the document handling the different circumstances. The logic is straightforward through the checking for EOF, form feed, and CRLF. If the current byte is none of those, then the potential for line wrap must be examined. First, I assume that all is fine and increment both **ptrend** and **dif**. Then the **GetTextExtent** function is invoked to figure out the total width of the line to this point.

```
sz = DC->GetTextExtent (ptrbuf, dif);
```

Then, if the **sz.cx** length exceeds the dots per line, Windows 95 would clip part or all of the last character. So we fake a CRLF by backing up one byte, which means decrementing **ptrend** and **dif**. However, I force at least one character to be printed in the case of huge fonts and tiny display areas. Note that the general philosophy was to return all good text up to the special code.

There is no escaping the fact that printing is complex. When we examine the Document-View architecture in chapter 15, some simplifications result. But now it's time for the fun stuff—the fancy tool bars and other decorations.

Decorations: Control Bars, Status Bars, Tool Boxes, and Child Client Windows

11.1 INTRODUCTION

Now that we have the basics down, it's time for the fancier effects that can turn a plain application window into a dynamic display. The MFC class library provides support for easily adding many convenience features to your Windows 95 application. They include *message bars*, *status bars*, *control bars* or *tool bars*, and *tool boxes* which may be fixed or floating on the screen.

Message bars and status bars normally appear at the bottom of the window and display program messages as well as hint messages for the buttons on control bars. Status bars also may contain smaller display windows for the status of special keys such as the Scroll Lock, Cap Lock, and Num Lock keys. Message and status bars are useful for displaying key information, such as the page number, line number, and column number of the caret in a text processing application. Because of the smaller, variable-width font used to display messages, more than 80-character messages can be displayed.

Control bars, also known as tool bars, often contain small bitmap buttons that represent menu items providing a shortcut or a fast method of making selections. Usually there are buttons for File | New, File | Open, and so on. Because the function or purpose of a button may not be obvious to a user, *flyover hints* and *dragover hints* can be provided. Many bitmaps do not readily express to beginners (or old timers for that matter) what they are to do. When the mouse cursor is over a button (or when a menu item is highlighted), the corresponding hint string appears in either the message bar or the status bar at the bottom of the screen; these are flyover hints. When using the earlier Microsoft version, the flyover hints are more like dragover hints. When the cursor is over the button, nothing appears. When the left button is pressed and held, the hint appears. If it is not what you want, move the cursor off the button and release. In addition, under Windows 95 a one- or two-word *tool tip* can appear just beside the button if the user keeps the mouse cursor over the button for about a second.

Finally, tool boxes provide a convenient wrapper for any number of additional buttons (but not buttons exclusively), such as providing a selection of pen widths and brush colors. Paintbrush, for example, has a tool box of color selections, drawing pen widths, and bitmapped buttons representing the current mode of operation such as Cut, Text, Line Drawing, and Rectangle Drawing. The simplest tool boxes are fixed in location. However, for any professional application, the user ought to be able to move the tool box to any wanted screen location and hide and reshow the tool box; this is called a floating tool box. Floating tool boxes are often the best choice, since they permit the user to place them wherever desired.

Under Windows 95, MFC now provides control bar docking abilities. The control bar can be docked at one of the four sides or can be "torn off" or floating and placed anywhere the user desires. When torn off, the control bar appears like a floating tool box.

MFC 4.0 now provides direct support for floating tool boxes. (Note to those familiar with older MFC versions: the CToolBar class is now derived from the Windows 95 CToolBarCtrl class providing far superior tool bar control operations.) Figure 11.1 shows the MFC control bar docked at the very top of the window just below the menu bar. A tool box is also docked just below the control bar. The mouse cursor (not shown) is pointing to the second line width button. The corresponding flyover hint appears on the status bar at the bottom of the window. The tool tip is shown just below the line width button. Both the control bar and tool box can be undocked and placed anywhere by the user.

In Figure 11.2 both the control bar and tool box have been dragged from their original locations and placed in new locations. Notice that, when not docked, both appear rather like a modeless dialog box. On the status bar's far right are three small windows for displaying the state of the Caps Lock, Scroll Lock, and Num Lock keys. Notice the flyover hint on the status bar. To the left is a floating tool box with four drawing pen widths and six brush colors. Notice that the upper-left width and color buttons are shown pressed down, like a checkmark indicating these are the current width and color in use.

All of these items are often referred to as as decorations. We cover all of the basic decorations in this chapter. Again, there are many variations possible, including placing text edit windows, list boxes, and combo boxes into control bars. Once you are comfortable with the basics, you can experiment with even fancier decorations. Additionally, we cover several new features in this chapter, including dynamically launching child or main windows and additional methods for handling command messages.

Simpler applications may have just one client window, such as **CEdit** or one for drawing graphical images. However, more complex applications may need to alternate between several client windows. Since each client window has its own special menu item needs, as the client window is dynamically launched, it makes appropriate modi-

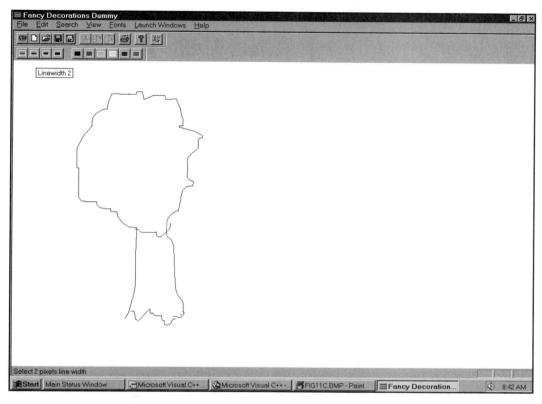

Fig. 11.1 Draw Program with Fancy Decorations

fications to the control bar and the main menu. Our client is an elementary, nonuseful drawing window that allows the user to draw squiggly lines. Nothing is done with the lines—no Save, Erase, or even Paint functions are implemented. I wish to concentrate solely on how to handle the decorations. However, with any drawing operation, the user needs a tool box containing a color palette and line widths as a bare-bones minimum. The tool box will float and can be hidden and reshown where it was last located.

11.2 THE MFC IMPLEMENTATION OF DECORATIONS

The basic **CFrameWnd** class also handles all the decorations. The basic classes for control and status bars are **CToolBar** and **CStatusBar**. A tool box can also be constructed from **CToolBar**. The **CToolBar** class provides support for flyover hints as well as the new tool tips. Instead of menu commands to reposition the control bar or tool boxes, **CToolBar** utilizes user dragging. If a control bar initially located at the top of the window is dragged, the control bar becomes a floating window. If it is dragged sufficiently close to any side, it is then "docked" on that side. Hence the term dockable

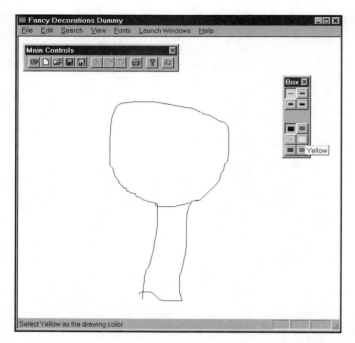

Fig. 11.2 Tool Bar and Tool Box Undocked

tool bars. The MFC framework handles all of this functionality. The only restriction is that **CToolBar** must be a child of a **CFrameWnd** and not a **CWnd** for tool tips and flyover hints to operate automatically. This restriction forces an alteration of our design for Pgm11a—the dynamically launched main window (**CWnd**) cannot allocate the tool box that it uses. In this MFC example, the frame window allocates a main tool bar and also the tool box for the child window. We can just ignore any tool box selections made before the Draw child window is launched (or pass those toolbox choices on to the Draw window constructor making them the initial line width and color choice). Note that MFC **CToolBar** class now uses the Windows 95 **CToolBarCtrl** class to provide this control bar support. (In the next chapter on the multiple document interface [MDI], the ownership of the tool box is transferred to the Draw child who then becomes an MDI child frame window capable of supporting its own controls.)

A control bar generally contains many bitmap buttons that represent menu items. Further, MFC provides many standard bitmaps to be used with the common File, Edit, and Search menu items, such as Open, New, Print, Cut, Paste, and Find. I provide some others, especially one for Quit the application. Another object frequently used in the control bar is a *separator gadget* that adds a gap between the buttons, simulating a group effect. The separator gadget requires a parameter that is the number of pixels of gap to leave. Six pixels or layout units are often used.

There is only one bmp file that contains all of the button images to be found on the control bar or tool box. It is a long strip of adjacent images. In this form, while file proliferation has been completely reduced, tool bar/box image construction and modification are incredibly awkward. There are numerous control bar strips of images avail-

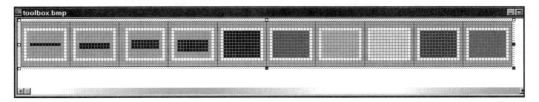

Fig. 11.3 The TOOLBOX.BMP Resource

able for use in the many sample applications under the MFC\SAMPLES folder. Figure 11.3 shows what the tool box strip for the floating tool box looks like when edited with the Developer Studio. Notice that any separators are not contained in the bitmap; they are supplied dynamically when the tool bar/box is constructed.

Let's begin the examination of Pgm11a with the resource file and its header. Notice that, since the Draw child window does not own or create the tool box, there is no need for any other resource files. Look over the Pgm11a.rc and resource.h files. Notice that the View pop-up menu contains three checkmarked items to hide and show the control bar, status bar, and tool box. I have used two of the framework built-in command IDs, **ID_VIEW_TOOLBAR** and **ID_VIEW_STATUS_BAR**. These two IDs permit the framework to hide and show the control bar and status bar automatically, providing there are menu items that can be checkmarked. For other additional tool bars and tool boxes, if the menu item ID is that of the bmp resource, the framework also can handle the hide/show process and the checkmark. Here, I used the identifier of the bitmap tool box resource, **IDB_TOOLBOX**, as the command ID for the hide/show menu item.

The hints themselves are in the Stringtable. The MFC matches the control's command ID number with a similar entry in the Stringtable. Tool Tips are appended to the end of the normal hint message preceded by an '\n' new-line code. For example, for a button representing the File | New command, the string for flyover hint and tool tip might be

```
CM_FILENEW,      "Creates a new document\nFile New"
```

Each button has a command ID associated with it. There is one special framework hint you can include that appears when the user moves off of any button—the idle message. Its identifier is defined in the framework, so just code

```
AFX_IDS_IDLEMESSAGE    "Ready\nReady"
```

11.2.1 Listing for File: resource.h—Pgm11a—Excerpts

```
...
#define IDB_MAINFRAME              2     // the control bar bitmap
#define IDB_TOOLBOX                3     // the tool box bitmap
...
#define CM_LINECHANGE       (WM_USER + 118)
#define CM_COLORCHANGE      (WM_USER + 119)
```

```
#define CM_LINE1            (WM_USER + 121)
#define CM_LINE2            (WM_USER + 122)
#define CM_LINE3            (WM_USER + 123)
#define CM_LINE4            (WM_USER + 124)
#define CM_COLORA           (WM_USER + 125)
#define CM_COLORB           (WM_USER + 126)
#define CM_COLORC           (WM_USER + 127)
#define CM_COLORD           (WM_USER + 128)
#define CM_COLORE           (WM_USER + 129)
#define CM_COLORF           (WM_USER + 130)
...
```

11.2.2 Listing for File: Pgm11a.rc—Pgm11a—Excerpts

```
..
MAINMENU MENU DISCARDABLE
BEGIN
    POPUP "&File"
    BEGIN
        MENUITEM "&New",                        CM_FILENEW
        MENUITEM "&Open...",                    CM_FILEOPEN
...
    END
    POPUP "&Edit"
    BEGIN
...
    END
    POPUP "&Search"
    BEGIN
...
    END
    POPUP "&View"
    BEGIN
        MENUITEM "&Toolbar",                    ID_VIEW_TOOLBAR
        MENUITEM "&Status Bar",                 ID_VIEW_STATUS_BAR
        MENUITEM "Tool &Box",                   IDB_TOOLBOX
    END
    POPUP "&Fonts"
    BEGIN
        MENUITEM "&Font Change",                CM_FONTCHANGE
    END
    POPUP "&Launch Windows"
    BEGIN
        MENUITEM "&Launch Draw",                CM_DRAW
    END
    POPUP "&Help"
    BEGIN
        MENUITEM "&About...",                   CM_HELPABOUT
    END
END
...
IDB_MAINFRAME       BITMAP  MOVEABLE PURE  "TOOLBAR.BMP"
IDB_TOOLBOX         BITMAP  MOVEABLE PURE  "TOOLBOX.BMP"
```

```
...
STRINGTABLE DISCARDABLE
BEGIN
    ID_INDICATOR_EXT        "EXT"
    ID_INDICATOR_CAPS       "CAP"
    ID_INDICATOR_NUM        "NUM"
    ID_INDICATOR_SCRL       "SCRL"
    ID_INDICATOR_OVR        "OVR"
    ID_INDICATOR_REC        "REC"
END
...
STRINGTABLE DISCARDABLE
BEGIN
    CM_DRAW                 "Launch Draw Window\nBegin Draw"
    CM_FONTCHANGE           "Select new font\nFont Change"
    CM_HELPABOUT            "About the Fancy Dialog application\nHelp About"
    CM_FILENEW              "Creates a new document\nNew File"
    CM_FILEOPEN             "Opens an existing document\nOpen File"
...
    CM_LINE1                "Select 1 pixel line width\nLinewidth 1"
...
    CM_LINE4                "Select 4 pixels line width\nLinewidth 4"
    CM_COLORA               "Select Black as the drawing color\nBlack"
...
    CM_COLORF               "Select Purple as the drawing color\nPurple"
    IDB_TOOLBOX             "Hide or Show Tool Box\bHide/Show Tool Box"
    AFX_IDS_IDLEMESSAGE     "Ready\nReady"
END
```

Let's begin by examining the construction and use of the normal main tool bar and status bars. When we have the basics down, we'll look at the tool box construction. Let's examine the FrameWin class definition. Since the main Draw window is to be dynamically allocated, a pointer to it is kept in **ptrmainwin.** Next, the three decoration objects are defined. The control bar is an instance of the **CToolBar** class, while the tool box is from CToolBox, derived from **CToolBar.** Since the frame window is the owner of the tool box, it provides the responses for tool box button presses, saving the current line width and brush color in **linesel** and **colorsel.** When these values are modified, appropriate messages are sent to the Draw window, as we shall see shortly. Member function **CmDraw** launches the client window while the command enabler function **CmEnableDraw** disables the menu item and control bar button once one Draw window is launched. **OnDestroy** destroys any Draw client window. Notice that there are not 10 member functions to respond to the tool box buttons; yet those button IDs are defined in the resource header file above, resource.h. Instead, only two are present: **CmLines** and **CmColors**.

11.2.3 Listing for File: FrameWin.h—Pgm11a—Excerpts

```
...
class FrameWin : public CFrameWnd {
...
protected:
```

```
MainWin    *ptrmainwin;   // pointer to our drawing main window with tool box

CStatusBar statusbar;     // our statusbar - try caps - scroll - num LOCKS
CToolBar   toolbar;       // our control bar
CToolBox   toolbox;       // client window's tool box

int        height;        // frame window's client window's dimensions
int        width;

int        linesel;       // current line width selection
int        colorsel;      // current color selection
...
public:
           FrameWin (CWnd*, const char*); // constructor
          ~FrameWin () {}                 // destructor

protected:

afx_msg int    OnCreate(LPCREATESTRUCT lpCreateStruct);
afx_msg void   OnDestroy ();               // remove allocated menus
afx_msg void   OnClose ();                 // determines if app can quit yet
afx_msg void   OnSize (UINT, int, int);    // readjust sizes
        int    DisplayMsg (int, int, UINT); // displays a message box

//             command processors
afx_msg void   CmDraw ();                             // launch the draw client window
afx_msg void   CmEnableDraw (CCmdUI*);                // enable/disable Draw menu item
afx_msg void   CmHelpAbout ();                        // help about our app
afx_msg void   CmExit ();                             // see if can terminate
afx_msg void   OnUpdateViewToolBox (CCmdUI*);         // checkmark tool box menu item
afx_msg void   CmLines (UINT);                        // process all line width btns
afx_msg void   CmColors (UINT);                       // process all color btns presses
afx_msg void   OnUpdateToolBoxLines (CCmdUI*);        // set selected width button down
afx_msg void   OnUpdateToolBoxColors (CCmdUI*);       // set selected color button down

//             dummy command processors
afx_msg void   CmFontChange ();                       // get new font
...
```

11.3 CONTROL BAR AND STATUS BAR CONSTRUCTION

Begin by constructing the control bar bitmap consisting of all of the button images wanted. Typically the buttons are all 16 pixels wide and 15 pixels high. The framework adds a frame border to each, yielding a final button size of about 20 pixels on the control bar that is 24×22 pixels. Carefully note the exact order of the buttons. Next in the cpp file, create a global static UINT BASED_CODE buttons array that is initialized to the command IDs in the order of the buttons on the control bar bitmap.

```
static UINT BASED_CODE buttons[] = {
  CM_EXIT,
  ...
}
```

(BASED_CODE in a 16-bit application places the data in the code segment; under Windows 95, it is ignored and does nothing, except provide backward compatibility.) Where desired, separator gadgets can be inserted using the special ID of ID_SEPARATOR. Do *not* leave space for these separators in the actual control bar bitmap. The framework constructs the spacing internally for the separators.

For status bars, construct a similar array using any of the special IDs for the keys such as Caps Lock. Here I have included one of every type in the order Microsoft recommends for the common look-and-feel.

```
static UINT BASED_CODE indicators[] = {
  ID_SEPARATOR,        // separator from message section
  ID_INDICATOR_EXT,    // extended selection
  ID_INDICATOR_CAPS,   // caps lock
  ID_INDICATOR_NUM,    // num lock
  ID_INDICATOR_SCRL,   // scroll lock
  ID_INDICATOR_OVR,    // overstrike
  ID_INDICATOR_REC     // macro recording
};
```

The controls are constructed in the frame window's **OnCreate** function *after* the call to the base class constructs the windows interface element. The base class's return value should be saved and returned at the end of the function if all goes well. Construction involves three successive steps, each undertaken only if the previous steps were successful. The **Create** function builds the object; then the bitmap representing the control bar images is loaded from the exe file via **LoadBitmap** which is passed the bmp resource ID; finally the connection between the zero-based offset of the bitmap images and the corresponding command IDs is made using the **SetButtons** function, which is passed the global static array of IDs along with the number of buttons in that array. For the control bar, you would code

```
if (toolbar.Create (this) && toolbar.LoadBitmap (IDB_MAINFRAME) &&
    toolbar.SetButtons (buttons, sizeof(buttons)/sizeof(UINT)))
```

For the status bar, there is no bitmap to be loaded, and the **SetIndicators** function is used to define which, if any, and in what order the status indicators are built.

```
if (statusbar.Create (this) && statusbar.SetIndicators (indicators,
    sizeof(indicators)/sizeof(UINT)))
```

Typical coding in **OnCreate** to create these three bars and return failure if warranted is

```
int      FrameWin::OnCreate (LPCREATESTRUCT lpCS) {
 int retcd;
 if ((retcd = CFrameWnd::OnCreate (lpCS)) == 0)
  if (toolbar.Create (this) && toolbar.LoadBitmap (IDB_MAINFRAME) &&
      toolbar.SetButtons (buttons, sizeof(buttons)/sizeof(UINT)))
   if (statusbar.Create (this) && statusbar.SetIndicators (indicators,
                          sizeof(indicators)/sizeof(UINT)))
   else return -1;
  else return -1;
```

The remaining steps are optional and install docking and flyover hints or tool tips. For those controls for which the hints are desired, the **CToolBar** style must contain ORed values consisting of

CBRS_TOOLTIPS	displays tool tips
CBRS_FLYBY	displays flyby hints
CBRS_ALIGN_ANY	allows control to be docked on any side
CBRS_ALIGN_TOP	allows control to be docked at top of frame
CBRS_ALIGN_BOTTOM	allows control to be docked on bottom of frame
CBRS_ALIGN_LEFT	allows control to be docked on left of frame
CBRS_ALIGN_RIGHT	allows control to be docked on right of frame
CBRS_BORDER_TOP	draws a top border around control
CBRS_BORDER_BOTTOM	draws a bottom border around control
CBRS_BORDER_LEFT	draws a left border around control
CBRS_BORDER_RIGHT	draws a right border around control

Typical use would be to add in any appropriate values to the existing style, which can be retrieved using the **GetBarStyle** function. The coding for **GetBarStyle** and **SetBarStyle** would be

```
toolbar.SetBarStyle (toolbar.GetBarStyle() | CBRS_TOOLTIPS |
                                             CBRS_FLYBY);
```

Next, the control bar must be told that it can be docked using the **EnableDocking** function and what types of docking are allowed.

```
toolbar.EnableDocking (CBRS_ALIGN_ANY);
```

The frame window must be prepared to process docking of controls by use of the **CFrameWnd** function **EnableDocking** along with what types of docking to permit.

```
EnableDocking (CBRS_ALIGN_ANY);
```

The last step is to actually dock the controls at the position where they first become visible using the **CFrameWnd** function **DockControlBar**.

```
DockControlBar (&toolbar, AFX_IDW_DOCKBAR_TOP);
```

The UINT parameter can be one of the following:

```
AFX_IDW_DOCBAR_TOP,  AFX_IDW_DOCBAR_BOTTOM
AFX_IDW_DOCBAR_LEFT, AFX_IDW_DOCBAR_RIGHT
```

A third parameter, an LPCRECT that defaults to NULL, can be used to specify in-screen coordinates where the control bar will be docked in the frame window.

Finally, if and when the user undocks the main tool bar, a floating tool bar appears with a caption and an "X" close button. We can set the text that is shown in such an eventuality by coding

```
toolbar.SetWindowText(_T("Main Controls"));
```

The _T is one of several data-type mappings, defined in TCHAR.H, which provide for proper encoding of data independent of the encoding platform. While we normally use the default generic encoding scheme, some applications may wish to use the UNI-CODE form. By defining your constant data using the data-type mappings and defining or undefining the constant _UNICODE and recompiling, you can switch between encoding schemes. The data-type mappings for the default-generic text types consist of the following:

```
_TCHAR          char
_TINT           int
_TSCHAR         signed char
_TUCHAR         unsigned char
_TXCHAR         char
_T or _TEXT     No effect (removed by preprocessor)
```

If you examine MFC code, you will see these various data-type mappings in action.

From now on, the framework handles all of the docking and hint actions. When the cursor is over a button for about a second, tool tips are displayed. The instant the cursor is over the button, flyover hints appear. How are the hints found? From a string resource that has the same string ID as the button ID. A tool tip comes after the flyover hint separated by a new-line code, \n. For example, the hint string for File | Open might be

```
CM_FILEOPEN, "Opens an existing file\nOpen"
```

Remember that tool tips should be only one or two words while flyover hints can be quite lengthy. If there is a button for application termination, CM_EXIT in this example, code a **PostMessage**, not a **SendMessage**.

```
PostMessage (WM_CLOSE);
```

Why? Because the application and control bar are destroyed by the time the mouse is released and off the button. The framework is then attempting to find the ID of the button which no longer exists.

11.4 THE TOOL BOX CONTROL

This is all that must be done to handle a main tool bar and status bar. Now let us extend this discussion to a more complex case, that of a tool box. The key design factor is the columnar arrangement of the buttons. Specifically, in this example, the tool box should always appear with two columns consisting of four pen widths and six pen colors with separators between. While each of the 10 objects look like buttons, they should operate as if they were two sets of radio buttons with the current selections remaining in the depressed state. Each of the buttons must have the TBBS_CHECKBOX style added to it when the button is created. Thus, to easily constrain the box to two columns and initialize the buttons' style, I have derived a CTool-Box class from **CToolBar**.

11.4.1 Listing for File: CToolBox.h—Pgm11a—Excerpts

```
...
class CToolBox : public CToolBar {

protected:

UINT    m_nColumns;                 // number of columns

public:

        CToolBox ();                // constructor
virtual ~CToolBox ();               // destructor
void    SetColumns (UINT nColumns); // set the number of columns
UINT    GetColumns ();              // get the number of columns
...
```

The constructor can save the requested number of columns. More importantly, the constructor can initialize the four margin widths of the base **CToolBar** class. I find using only 1 pixel yields a pleasing border, while 4 pixels seems too great a space for my tastes. **GetColumns** returns the current number of columns. All the real work is done in **SetColumns** which must actually lay out the buttons into the indicated number of columns.

11.4.2 Listing for File: CToolBox.cpp—Pgm11a—Excerpts

```
...
/****************************************************************************/
/*                                                                          */
/* CToolBox Constructor                                                     */
/*                                                                          */
/****************************************************************************/
        CToolBox::CToolBox () {

 m_nColumns      = 2; // set for two columns
 m_cxLeftBorder  = 1; // set 5 pels as a margin
 m_cxRightBorder = 1; // these fields belong to the base CToolBar class
 m_cyTopBorder   = 1;
 m_cyBottomBorder = 1;
}
...

/****************************************************************************/
/*                                                                          */
/* SetColumns: install number of columns along with radio btn style         */
/*                                                                          */
/****************************************************************************/
void    CToolBox::SetColumns (UINT numcols) {

 m_nColumns = numcols;

 int numbtns = GetToolBarCtrl ().GetButtonCount (); // get total number btns

 // for each button, install checkbox style
 // for each button that begins a new row, install wrapped style
 for (int i=0; i<numbtns; i++) {
```

```
   UINT style = GetButtonStyle (i);           // get current button style
   BOOL wrap = (((i + 1) % numcols) == 0);    // set wrap mod num columns
   if (wrap) style |= TBBS_WRAPPED;           // enable wrapped on this one
   else style &= ~TBBS_WRAPPED;               // or disable wrapped
   style |= TBBS_CHECKBOX;                     // add in the check box style
   SetButtonStyle (i, style);                  // and save as its new style
   }

Invalidate ();
GetParentFrame ()->RecalcLayout ();           // force toolbar to use new layout
}
```

The function **GetToolBarCtrl** retrieves a pointer to the base class of the **CTool-Bar**, the Windows 95 **CToolBarCtrl**. **GetButtonCount** retrieves the number of buttons currently installed so we can iterate through all buttons, at least adding in the TBBS_CHECKBOX style. Each button's style is retrieved by the **GetButtonStyle** function and is reset by **SetButtonStyle**. Since the buttons are in order, a simple MOD operation can tell us when to add the TBBS_WRAPPED style. Since you potentially might want to have more or fewer columns, the code dynamically removes and adds the wrapped style.

The last step in the sequence forces the parent to redisplay the tool box using the new layout and the **RecalcLayout** function. All other actions involving the tool box can be done at a higher level.

To create the tool box, in the frame window after constructing the main tool bar and status bar, add the following:

```
if (toolbox.Create (this, WS_CHILD | WS_VISIBLE | CBRS_SIZE_FIXED |
                    CBRS_TOP | CBRS_TOOLTIPS | CBRS_FLYBY, IDB_TOOLBOX)
    && toolbox.LoadBitmap (IDB_TOOLBOX)
    && toolbox.SetButtons (buttons_box, sizeof(buttons_box)/sizeof(UINT)));
else return -1;

toolbox.SetColumns (2); // set the tool box to 2 columns

// now install flyover hints and the tool tips for the tool box
toolbox.SetBarStyle (toolbox.GetBarStyle() | CBRS_TOOLTIPS | CBRS_FLYBY);

// now notify control to accept any form of docking
toolbox.EnableDocking (CBRS_ALIGN_ANY);

// and dock tool box on the right side
DockControlBar (&toolbox, AFX_IDW_DOCKBAR_RIGHT);

// insert captions to be shown when the tool box is floating
toolbox.SetWindowText(_T("Box"));
```

Now the tool box is constructed. Next, we must provide support for responding to all of the buttons and to hiding and showing the tool box. Just for your information, the button styles include the following button types:

TBBS_BUTTON	defines a push button
TBBS_SEPARATOR	defines a separator button
TBBS_CHECKBOX	defines a pushbutton that acts like a checkmark

The button states include

TBBS_PRESSED	show in the pressed state
TBBS_CHECKED	show in the checked state
TBBS_ENABLED	enable the button

Also, the Windows 95 control bar—**CToolBarCtrl**—from which **CToolBar** is derived uses the very same actual tool box bitmap strip of button images. However, much more information is required than just the command ID that corresponds to a button. A new structure, TBBUTTON, has the following members that more completely define a button.

```
The TBUTTON Structure:

int iBitmap;     // zero-based index of button image
int idCommand;   // command ID sent when button is pressed
BYTE fsState;    // button state
BYTE fsStyle;    // button style
DWORD dwData;    // application defined value
int iString;     // zero-based index of label string, if any
```

The button state flags are an ORed combination of one or more of the following:

TBSTYLE_ENABLED	button is enabled; normal active state
TBSTYLE_CHECKED	button is displayed as pressed or checked
TBSTYLE_PRESSED	button is being pressed right now
TBSTYLE_WRAP	a line break follows this button
TBSTYLE_HIDDEN	button is not visible (for separators)
TBSTYLE_INDETERMINATE	button is grayed

The button style is an ORed combination of one or more of the following:

TBSTYLE_BUTTON	a standard pushbutton
TBSTYLE_CHECK	toggles between checked and unchecked; serves both radio buttons and checkbox styles
TBSTYLE_CHECKGROUP	creates a check button in a group that stays pressed until another button in that group is pressed
TBSTYLE_GROUP	similar to check group
TBSTYLE_SEP	creates a separator control; not visible

Other style options include

TBSTYLE_TOOLTIPS	causes tool tips to be used
TBSTYLE_WRAPABLE	control can have multiple lines of buttons

If the button displays text, an index into an array of strings must be provided so the control can find the text to display. There is no **CWnd** style set text type of function. The 10 buttons and 2 separators could then be defined as follows:

```
TBBUTTON buttons_box[] = {
   {0, CM_LINE1,   TBSTATE_ENABLED, TBSTYLE_CHECKGROUP, 0, NULL },
   {1, CM_LINE2,   TBSTATE_ENABLED, TBSTYLE_CHECKGROUP, 0, NULL },
   {2, CM_LINE3,   TBSTATE_ENABLED, TBSTYLE_CHECKGROUP, 0, NULL },
   {3, CM_LINE4,   TBSTATE_ENABLED, TBSTYLE_CHECKGROUP, 0, NULL },
   {0, 0,          TBSTATE_ENABLED, TBSTYLE_SEP,        0, NULL},
   {0, 0,          TBSTATE_ENABLED, TBSTYLE_SEP,        0, NULL},
   {4, CM_COLORA,  TBSTATE_ENABLED, TBSTYLE_CHECKGROUP, 0, NULL },
   {5, CM_COLORB,  TBSTATE_ENABLED, TBSTYLE_CHECKGROUP, 0, NULL },
   {6, CM_COLORC,  TBSTATE_ENABLED, TBSTYLE_CHECKGROUP, 0, NULL },
   {7, CM_COLORD,  TBSTATE_ENABLED, TBSTYLE_CHECKGROUP, 0, NULL },
   {8, CM_COLORE,  TBSTATE_ENABLED, TBSTYLE_CHECKGROUP, 0, NULL },
   {9, CM_COLORF,  TBSTATE_ENABLED, TBSTYLE_CHECKGROUP, 0, NULL }
};
```

11.5 MFC MESSAGE MAP RESPONSE ENTRIES FOR A CONSECUTIVE RANGE OF COMMAND IDs

The MFC message map macros offer two ranges of ID commands, one for a consecutive series of commands and one for the corresponding command enabler functions: ON_COMMAND_RANGE and ON_UPDATE_COMMAND_UI_RANGE. These message macros take three operands instead of the normal two. The first operand is the beginning command ID of the range of messages; the second is the last ID in the consecutive range; the third is the member function to be invoked. That is why I have used successive command ID numbers in the resource header file for CM_LINE1 through CM_LINE4 and for CM_COLORA through CM_COLORF. The FrameWin message map to respond to the 10 buttons becomes simply

```
BEGIN_MESSAGE_MAP(FrameWin, CFrameWnd)
 ON_COMMAND_RANGE(CM_LINE1, CM_LINE4, CmLines)
 ON_COMMAND_RANGE(CM_COLORA, CM_COLORF, CmColors)
END_MESSAGE_MAP()
```

When the two member functions are invoked, the actual command ID number that was pressed is passed as a UNIT, unlike a normal command handler which has no parameters. Thus, the function prototypes appear in the class header file as

```
afx_msg void  CmLines (UINT);
afx_msg void  CmColors (UINT);
```

It becomes a simple matter to calculate the line width and color index numbers from command IDs. Once the new line width or color index is known, then a WM_MESSAGE or a user message is sent to the Draw window. With user messages, **WPARAM** and **LPARAM** are used to pass additional user-defined information. Here, **wparam** contains either the line width or the color index. For **CmLines**, we have the following:

```
void        FrameWin::CmLines (UINT cmd) {
  linesel = cmd - CM_LINE1 + 1;
  if (ptrmainwin) ptrmainwin->SendMessage (CM_LINECHANGE, linesel, 0L);
}
```

Notice that the change notification is sent only *if* the Draw main window has been launched. If not, the user tool box selection is accepted and stored. The line width and color index are passed to the Draw window's constructor in the **CmDraw** function. The prototype for a user-defined message and its message macro are

```
afx_msg LRESULT  CmColorChange (WPARAM, LPARAM);

ON_MESSAGE(CM_COLORCHANGE, CmColorChange);
```

11.6 HIDING AND SHOWING TOOL BOXES

If the ID of the menu item to hide/show the tool box is the bmp resource ID number, the framework can handle hiding and showing our tool box with only a small effort on our part. To the message map, add two entries

```
ON_UPDATE_COMMAND_UI(IDB_TOOLBOX, OnUpdateViewToolBox)
ON_COMMAND_EX(IDB_TOOLBOX, OnBarCheck)
```

The command enabler actually handles the checkmark. If the box is currently visible, the enabler passes TRUE to the **SetCheck** enabler function. If not, FALSE is passed and no checkmark is displayed.

```
    ptrui->SetCheck ((toolbox.GetStyle() & WS_VISIBLE) != 0);
```

The second entry is lifted from MFC framework coding and handles the work of actually hiding or reshowing the tool box as if it were any other normal tool bar. The undocumented ON_COMMAND_EX macro works similarly to the usual ON_COMMAND except that it passes control to internal framework command targets. Specifically in this case, the framework function **OnBarCheck** handles the desired hide/show operations for us. If we use this magic, then we do not have to do any coding to hide or reshow our tool box.

11.6.1 Listing for File: FrameWin.cpp—Pgm11a—Excerpts

```
...
/****************************************************************************/
/*                                                                        */
/* Control bar buttons and Status bar buttons                             */
/*                                                                        */
/* control bar buttons - IDs are command buttons                          */
/* same order as in the bitmap 'toolbar.bmp'                              */
/*                                                                        */
/****************************************************************************/

static UINT BASED_CODE buttons[] = {

  CM_EXIT,
```

```
    CM_FILENEW,
    CM_FILEOPEN,
    CM_FILESAVE,
    CM_FILESAVEAS,
    ID_SEPARATOR,
    CM_EDITCUT,
    CM_EDITCOPY,
    CM_EDITPASTE,
    ID_SEPARATOR,
    CM_FILEPRINT,
    ID_SEPARATOR,
    CM_HELPABOUT,
    ID_SEPARATOR,
    CM_DRAW,
};

static UINT BASED_CODE buttons_box[] = {

    CM_LINE1,
    CM_LINE2,
    CM_LINE3,
    CM_LINE4,
    ID_SEPARATOR,
    ID_SEPARATOR,
    CM_COLORA,
    CM_COLORB,
    CM_COLORC,
    CM_COLORD,
    CM_COLORE,
    CM_COLORF,
};

static UINT BASED_CODE indicators[] = {

    ID_SEPARATOR,            // status line indicator
    ID_INDICATOR_CAPS,
    ID_INDICATOR_NUM,
    ID_INDICATOR_SCRL,
};

/**************************************************************************/
/*                                                                        */
/* FrameWin Events Response Table                                         */
/*                                                                        */
/**************************************************************************/

BEGIN_MESSAGE_MAP(FrameWin, CFrameWnd)
 ON_WM_SIZE ()
 ON_WM_CREATE ()
 ON_WM_CLOSE ()
 ON_WM_DESTROY ()
 ON_COMMAND(CM_FONTCHANGE, CmFontChange)
 ON_COMMAND(CM_EXIT, CmExit)
 ON_COMMAND(CM_FILENEW, CmFileNew)
 ON_COMMAND(CM_FILEOPEN, CmFileOpen)
 ON_COMMAND(CM_FILESAVE, CmFileSave)
```

```
ON_COMMAND(CM_FILESAVEAS, CmFileSaveAs)
ON_COMMAND(CM_FILEPRINT, CmFilePrint)
ON_COMMAND(CM_FILEPRINTERSETUP, CmFilePrinterSetup)
ON_COMMAND(CM_DRAW, CmDraw)
ON_COMMAND(CM_HELPABOUT, CmHelpAbout)
ON_UPDATE_COMMAND_UI(CM_DRAW, CmEnableDraw)
    ON_UPDATE_COMMAND_UI(IDB_TOOLBOX, OnUpdateViewToolBox)
    ON_COMMAND_EX(IDB_TOOLBOX, OnBarCheck)
ON_COMMAND_RANGE(CM_LINE1, CM_LINE4, CmLines)
ON_COMMAND_RANGE(CM_COLORA, CM_COLORF, CmColors)
ON_UPDATE_COMMAND_UI_RANGE(CM_LINE1, CM_LINE4,  OnUpdateToolBoxLines)
ON_UPDATE_COMMAND_UI_RANGE(CM_COLORA, CM_COLORF, OnUpdateToolBoxColors)
END_MESSAGE_MAP()
/*****************************************************************************/
/*                                                                         */
/* Framewin: Construct the window object                                   */
/*                                                                         */
/*****************************************************************************/

        FrameWin::FrameWin (CWnd* ptrparent, const char *title)
                : CFrameWnd () {

...
ptrmainwin = NULL;  // set no draw window active
linesel = 1;        // set initial pen width
colorsel = 0;       // set initial black color
}

/*****************************************************************************/
/*                                                                         */
/* OnCreate: construct status and control bars                             */
/*                                                                         */
/*****************************************************************************/

int     FrameWin::OnCreate (LPCREATESTRUCT lpCS) {

 int retcd;
 if ((retcd = CFrameWnd::OnCreate (lpCS)) == 0) // pass along to base class
  // if successful, create the control bar & then if all ok, create status bar
  // then create the tool box - for each, Create constructs the object
  // and if successful, the corresponding bitmap of buttons is loaded
  // and if successful, the buttons are initialized
  if (toolbar.Create (this) && toolbar.LoadBitmap (IDB_MAINFRAME) &&
      toolbar.SetButtons (buttons, sizeof(buttons)/sizeof(UINT)))
   if (statusbar.Create (this) &&
       statusbar.SetIndicators (indicators, sizeof(indicators)/sizeof(UINT)))
    if (toolbox.Create (this, WS_CHILD | WS_VISIBLE | CBRS_SIZE_FIXED |
                    CBRS_TOP | CBRS_TOOLTIPS | CBRS_FLYBY, IDB_TOOLBOX)
        && toolbox.LoadBitmap (IDB_TOOLBOX)
        && toolbox.SetButtons (buttons_box, sizeof(buttons_box)/sizeof(UINT)));
    else return -1;
   else return -1;
  else return -1;

 toolbox.SetColumns (2); // set the tool box to 2 columns
```

```
    // now install flyover hints and the tool tips for both controlbar & tool box
    toolbar.SetBarStyle (toolbar.GetBarStyle() | CBRS_TOOLTIPS | CBRS_FLYBY);
    toolbox.SetBarStyle (toolbox.GetBarStyle() | CBRS_TOOLTIPS | CBRS_FLYBY);

    // now notify control to accept any form of docking
    toolbar.EnableDocking (CBRS_ALIGN_ANY);
    toolbox.EnableDocking (CBRS_ALIGN_ANY);

    // notify the framewindow of docking requirements
    EnableDocking (CBRS_ALIGN_ANY);

    // and dock tool bar at the top and the tool box on the right
    DockControlBar (&toolbar, AFX_IDW_DOCKBAR_TOP);
    DockControlBar (&toolbox, AFX_IDW_DOCKBAR_RIGHT);

    // insert captions to be shown when the tool bars are floating
    toolbar.SetWindowText(_T("Main Controls"));
    toolbox.SetWindowText(_T("Box"));

    return retcd;
}
/**************************************************************************/
/*                                                                        */
/* OnUpdateViewToolBox: command enabler for check mark on menu item       */
/*                                                                        */
/**************************************************************************/
void      FrameWin::OnUpdateViewToolBox (CCmdUI *ptrui) {

    // place check mark on menu item if tool box is now visible
    ptrui->SetCheck ((toolbox.GetStyle() & WS_VISIBLE) != 0);
}

/**************************************************************************/
/*                                                                        */
/* CmLines: handle any of the line button presses - route to child window */
/*                                                                        */
/**************************************************************************/
void      FrameWin::CmLines (UINT cmd) {

    linesel = cmd - CM_LINE1 + 1;
    // the line width is the command ID less the command ID of line 1 + 1
    // send the new line width to the child window using a private message
    if (ptrmainwin) ptrmainwin->SendMessage (CM_LINECHANGE, linesel, 0L);
}

/**************************************************************************/
/*                                                                        */
/* CmColors: handle any of the color button presses - route to child window*/
/*                                                                        */
/**************************************************************************/
void      FrameWin::CmColors (UINT cmd) {

    colorsel = cmd - CM_COLORA;
    // the color number is the command number less the command ID of first color
    // send the color number to the child window using a private message
```

```
 if (ptrmainwin) ptrmainwin->SendMessage (CM_COLORCHANGE, colorsel, OL);
}
/*****************************************************************************/
/*                                                                         */
/* OnUpdateToolBoxLines: set pressed state for current line width button   */
/*                                                                         */
/*****************************************************************************/
void       FrameWin::OnUpdateToolBoxLines (CCmdUI *ptrui) {
 ptrui->SetRadio ((UINT) (linesel + CM_LINE1 -1) == ptrui->m_nID ? 1 : 0);
}
/*****************************************************************************/
/*                                                                         */
/* OnUpdateToolBoxColors: set pressed state for current brush color button */
/*                                                                         */
/*****************************************************************************/
void       FrameWin::OnUpdateToolBoxColors (CCmdUI *ptrui) {
 ptrui->SetRadio ((UINT)(colorsel + CM_COLORA) == ptrui->m_nID ? 1 : 0);
}
/*****************************************************************************/
/*                                                                         */
/* OnSize: acquire the current dimensions of the client window             */
/*                                                                         */
/*****************************************************************************/
void       FrameWin::OnSize (UINT a, int w, int h) {
 CFrameWnd::OnSize (a, w, h);

 CRect rect;
 GetClientRect (&rect);
 height = h;              //  save current height
 width  = w;             //   save current width
 // if any draw window, resize MainWin
 if (ptrmainwin) ptrmainwin->MoveWindow(&rect, TRUE);
 Invalidate();           // force repainting of window
}
/*****************************************************************************/
/*                                                                         */
/* CmDraw: Launch a new client window for drawing, with its tool box       */
/*                                                                         */
/*****************************************************************************/
void       FrameWin::CmDraw () {
 if (!ptrmainwin) {                            // avoid duplicate launching
  ptrmainwin = new MainWin (this, 0, linesel, colorsel); // allocate child
  ptrmainwin->Create ("MainWin", (CWnd*) (this));
 }
}
/*****************************************************************************/
/*                                                                         */
```

```
/* CmEnableDraw: enables/disables Draw menu item                         */
/*                                                                       */
/***********************************************************************/

void        FrameWin::CmEnableDraw (CCmdUI *ptrenabler) {

 ptrenabler->Enable (ptrmainwin!=0 ? 0 : 1);
}

/***********************************************************************/
/*                                                                     */
/* OnDestroy: remove any menu objects, here none                       */
/*                                                                     */
/***********************************************************************/

void        FrameWin::OnDestroy () {

 if (ptrmainwin) {                      // if there is a client window, then
   ptrmainwin->DestroyWindow (); // destroy the interface element
   delete ptrmainwin;                   // delete the object
 }
 CFrameWnd::OnDestroy();
}
...

/***********************************************************************/
/*                                                                     */
/* CmExit:   determine if the app can be shut down                     */
/*                                                                     */
/***********************************************************************/

void        FrameWin::CmExit () {

 PostMessage (WM_CLOSE); // Post not Send in case user presses button
}

/***********************************************************************/
/*                                                                     */
/* A Series of dummy command handlers so that all buttons are not grayed */
/*                                                                     */
/***********************************************************************/

void        FrameWin::CmFileNew () {

 MessageBox ("File New is not yet implemented",
            "File New", MB_ICONINFORMATION | MB_OK);
}
...
```

11.7 How to Have a Frame Window Dynamically Launch Client Windows

Until now, the frame window allocated the sole instance of the client window, such as the **CEdit** window. We can achieve a far greater potential by dynamically launching the client windows. This is especially true when using a control bar because a bitmap button can be used to launch the desired client instantly. In Pgm11a, our client is a rudimentary Draw window in which the user can draw lines. Initially, the frame window appears with no client window. Whenever the user presses the Draw button on the control bar or selects Draw from the menu, the frame window launches the Draw client window. Of course, we want only one instance of the client, so, after launching Draw, we should gray out both the menu item and the bitmap button. We do this by using a command enabler on the Draw menu item.

The key data member is the **ptrmainwin**, which is the Draw client window pointer, initially set to 0 in the FrameWin constructor. If you have made a bitmap for the Draw button, then the ID CM_DRAW is assigned to the Launch Draw menu item, the corresponding string hint, and the BITMAP resource. Member functions **CmDraw** and **CmEnableDraw** handle launching the Draw client and disabling the menu item and button. To streamline the program so that we can concentrate solely on these new ideas, the other member functions, such as File | Open, are dummied and do nothing.

Dynamically launched child windows are much like modeless dialogs. They must be allocated and created. To launch a child window in response to a button press, invoke the constructor via **new** and then invoke the **Create** function.

```
if (!ptrmainwin) { // avoid duplicate launching
 ptrmainwin = new MainWin (this, 0, linesel, colorsel);
 ptrmainwin->Create ("MainWin", (CWnd*) (this));
}
```

Cleanup upon application termination must be manually done. The interface element is first destroyed and then the C++ object deleted. A reasonable point to do these operations is in the FrameWin's **OnDestroy** function *before* invoking the base class which destroys the frame window itself.

```
void        FrameWin::OnDestroy () {
 if (ptrmainwin) {
  ptrmainwin->DestroyWindow ();
  delete ptrmainwin;
 }
 CFrameWnd::OnDestroy();
}
```

The main Draw window coding is straightforward. The constructor stores the initial values of the line width and color index. Other data members include the current pen and **CDC** upon which to draw while the Left button is down.

11.7.1 Listing for File: MainWin.h—Pgm11a—Excerpts

```
...
class MainWin : public CWnd {
...
protected:

COLORREF        colors[6];      // the possible colors array
COLORREF        linecolor;      // current drawing pen color
int             colnum;         // current pen color array index
```

```
int             linewidth;      // current pen width
BOOL            buttondown;     // TRUE when left button is down for drawing
CPen            *ptrpen;        // the current drawing pen
CClientDC       *ptrdc;         // the current drawing DC
...
public:
                MainWin (CWnd*, const char*, int, int); // constructor
                ~MainWin () {}              // destructor
        BOOL    Create (LPSTR, CWnd*);      // create the window
afx_msg void    OnPaint ();                 // paint backgrd white

protected:
afx_msg int     OnCreate(LPCREATESTRUCT);   // show msg on status bar
afx_msg void    OnLButtonDown (UINT, CPoint); // begin drawing
afx_msg void    OnLButtonUp (UINT, CPoint);  // end drawing
afx_msg void    OnMouseMove (UINT, CPoint);  // continue drawing
        void    UpdateStatusBar ();          // display current selection

afx_msg LRESULT  CmLineChange (WPARAM, LPARAM); // receive line width
afx_msg LRESULT  CmColorChange (WPARAM, LPARAM);// receive color change
...
```

11.8 DISPLAYING MESSAGES ON THE STATUS BAR

I have included coding to display messages on the status bar. Access to the status bar is gained by obtaining a pointer to the main frame window's status bar child window. The global function **AfxGetApp** returns a pointer to the **CWinApp** whose data member **m_pMainWnd** points to the main frame window. A pointer to any child window, which includes the Draw window, tool box, control bar, and, in this case, the status bar, can be obtained by passing that window's ID to the **GetDescendantWindow** function. What is not so obvious is that the internal ID for the status bar is AFX_IDW_STATUS_BAR.

```
CStatusBar *ptrbar = (CStatusBar*) AfxGetApp()->m_pMainWnd->
                GetDescendantWindow (AFX_IDW_STATUS_BAR);
char msg[80]; // construct a message for the status bar
sprintf (msg,"Draw: line width: %d - Color: %s", linewidth, col[colnum]);
ptrbar->SetPaneText (0, msg, TRUE); // and display the message
```

Once the pointer is obtained, text is displayed using the **SetPaneText** function of **CStatusBar**. The **CStatusBar** is passed the offset index of which section is to be set, the null-terminated message, and TRUE to force an **Invalidate** message to actually repaint the control. For our user messages, the offset is normally 0; other index values would refer to the subsections for the key indicators.

11.9 THE DRAWING PROCESS—CAPTURING THE MOUSE

When drawing, capturing the mouse is often required. When the user presses the Left button, we draw a line from where the cursor is currently located to all of the subsequent positions the mouse is moved to while the button remains held down. While that button is pressed, we cannot allow any other mouse events to be passed to any other window or control. Therefore we capture all mouse events for the duration of the drawing cycle. The complicating factor is that drawing involves three separate mouse events and therefore three separate events functions: **OnLButtonDown**, **OnMouse-Move**, and **OnLButtonUp**. The member **buttondown** is used to communicate between these three functions.

When the Left button is pressed, **OnLButtonDown** does nothing if **buttondown** is TRUE, avoiding double-click problems. If not, then a new pen is created using the current selections of line width and color, and a **CClientDC** is gotten upon which to draw. The mouse actions are captured. The pen is positioned to the position where the Left button was pressed and **buttondown** set to TRUE:

```
if (!buttondown) {                  // avoid multiple invocations by dblclick
  buttondown = TRUE;                // signal drawing
  ptrdc  = new CClientDC (this);    // get new draw DC
  linecolor = colors[colnum];
  ptrpen = new CPen (PS_SOLID, linewidth, linecolor); // create the pen
  ptrdc->SelectObject (ptrpen);     // install pen in DC
  SetCapture ();                    // capture all mouse movements for draw
  ptrdc->MoveTo (point);            // set pen to starting point for draw
}
```

Whenever the user moves the mouse, a line is drawn from the current pen position to the new mouse position.

```
if (buttondown) ptrdc->LineTo (point); // draw line to here, point
```

Finally, when the user releases the button, drawing halts. It is vital that the mouse be released for obvious reasons.

```
if (buttondown) {
  if (ptrdc) delete ptrdc;    // stop drawing, so remove GDI objects
  if (ptrpen) delete ptrpen;  // if flurry of clicks, avoids GP fault
  buttondown = FALSE;         // signal not drawing
  ReleaseCapture ();          // and release mouse
}
```

We need some way to store the lines being created so that **OnPaint** could reproduce the lines when required and the drawing could be saved either as a series of lines or as a DIB in a bmp file. See the Scribble MFC sample program for details on how this could be done.

11.9.1 Listing for File: MainWin.cpp—Pgm11a—Excerpts

```
...
/**********************************************************************/
/*                                                                    */
/* MainWin Events Response Table                                      */
/*                                                                    */
/**********************************************************************/
```

```
BEGIN_MESSAGE_MAP (MainWin, CWnd)
 ON_WM_CREATE ()
 ON_WM_PAINT ()
 ON_WM_LBUTTONDOWN ()
 ON_WM_LBUTTONUP ()
 ON_WM_MOUSEMOVE ()
 ON_MESSAGE (CM_LINECHANGE, CmLineChange)
 ON_MESSAGE (CM_COLORCHANGE, CmColorChange)
END_MESSAGE_MAP ()

// convenient msgs to display on the status bar
char col[6][7] = {"Black","Red","Green","Yellow","Blue","Purple"};

/****************************************************************************/
/*                                                                        */
/* Mainwin: Construct the window object                                   */
/*                                                                        */
/****************************************************************************/

         MainWin::MainWin (CWnd* /* ptrparent */, const char* /* title */,
                          int line, int colr) : CWnd () {

 buttondown = FALSE;                     // signal not drawing now
 ptrpen     = NULL;                      // set no current pen
 ptrdc      = NULL;                      // or DC for drawing

 // initialize possible colors
 colors[0]  = RGB (0,0,0);       // Black
 ...
 colors[5]  = RGB (255, 0,255); // LtMagenta
 linecolor  = colors[colr];      // set beginning pen color
 colnum     = colr;              // set initial pen color index number
 linewidth  = line;              // set initial pen width
}

/****************************************************************************/
/*                                                                        */
/* Create: construct the MainWin object                                   */
/*                                                                        */
/****************************************************************************/

BOOL    MainWin::Create (LPSTR title, CWnd *ptrparent) {
 CRect r (0, 0, 1024, 768); // picked random size - MoveWindow of Frame adjusts
 return CWnd::Create (AfxRegisterWndClass (CS_VREDRAW | CS_HREDRAW, NULL,
           (HBRUSH) GetStockObject (WHITE_BRUSH), NULL),
             title, WS_CHILD|WS_VISIBLE|WS_CLIPSIBLINGS,r,ptrparent,1,NULL);
}

/****************************************************************************/
/*                                                                        */
/* OnCreate: display initial pen width and color on status bar            */
/*                                                                        */
/****************************************************************************/

int     MainWin::OnCreate (LPCREATESTRUCT lpCS) {

 int retcd = CWnd::OnCreate (lpCS); // pass along to base class
 UpdateStatusBar (); // display initial pen color and width on the status bar
```

```
   return retcd;
}
/****************************************************************************/
/*                                                                        */
/* UpdateStatusBar: place message on the status bar - line width and color */
/*                                                                        */
/****************************************************************************/

void      MainWin::UpdateStatusBar () {

 // this display will be temporary only - it will be overlaid by next hints
 // this code is just to show you how to put info on the bar
 // first get a pointer to status bar
 CStatusBar *ptrbar = (CStatusBar*) AfxGetApp()->m_pMainWnd->
                   GetDescendantWindow (AFX_IDW_STATUS_BAR);
 char msg[80]; // construct a message for the status bar
 sprintf (msg,"Draw: line width: %d - Color: %s", linewidth, col[colnum]);
 ptrbar->SetPaneText (0, msg, TRUE); // and display the message

}
/****************************************************************************/
/*                                                                        */
/* OnLButtonDown: begin drawing                                           */
/*                                                                        */
/****************************************************************************/

void      MainWin::OnLButtonDown (UINT, CPoint point) {

 if (!buttondown) {                    // avoid multiple invocations by dblclick
  buttondown = TRUE;                   // signal drawing
  ptrdc  = new CClientDC (this);       // get new draw DC
  linecolor = colors[colnum];
  ptrpen = new CPen (PS_SOLID, linewidth, linecolor); // create the pen
  ptrdc->SelectObject (ptrpen);        // install pen in DC
  SetCapture ();                       // capture all mouse movements for draw
  ptrdc->MoveTo (point);               // set pen to starting point for draw
 }
}
/****************************************************************************/
/*                                                                        */
/* OnLButtonUp: stop drawing the line                                     */
/*                                                                        */
/****************************************************************************/

void      MainWin::OnLButtonUp (UINT, CPoint) {

 if (buttondown) {
  if (ptrdc) delete ptrdc;   // stop drawing, so remove GDI objects
  if (ptrpen) delete ptrpen; // if flurry of clicks, avoids GP fault
  buttondown = FALSE;        // signal not drawing
  ReleaseCapture ();         // and release mouse
 }
}

/****************************************************************************/
```

```
/*                                                                      */
/* OnMouseMove: draw a line to mouse position                           */
/*                                                                      */
/*********************************************************************/

void       MainWin::OnMouseMove (UINT, CPoint point) {

  if (buttondown) ptrdc->LineTo (point); // draw line to here, point
}

/*********************************************************************/
/*                                                                      */
/* CmLineChange: receives a new line width from tool box via parent window */
/*                                                                      */
/*********************************************************************/

LRESULT   MainWin::CmLineChange (WPARAM line, LPARAM) {

  linewidth = line;
  UpdateStatusBar ();
  return 0;
}

/*********************************************************************/
/*                                                                      */
/* CmColorChange: receives a new color from tool box via parent window  */
/*                                                                      */
/*********************************************************************/

LRESULT   MainWin::CmColorChange (WPARAM color, LPARAM) {

  colnum = color;
  UpdateStatusBar ();
  return 0;
}
...
```

11.10 COMMAND ROUTING NOTES

Finally, in case you are considering launching **CWnd**-derived children and wish those children to have control over their own control bars and the like, there is a way. Specifically, the problem you are facing is a non-normal command routing scheme. The normal routing of commands by the main frame window is to any attached documents and associated views; this is covered in chapter 15. The MFC does not expect anyone to design an application outside the Document-View architecture! It is fairly easy to provide a hook into the normal command routing mechanism.

The main Draw window is launched exactly as above. The only other actions of the Draw client window that the frame window must handle is providing a "hook" into the framework message processing queue. The MFC command routing mechanism is quite complex and cannot be discussed in depth here. (See the bibliography for suggested reading.) Specifically, **OnCommand** messages and command handlers are routed in a different method than most all other window messages. Specifically, they are routed only to the active view (when using the Document-View architecture, chapter 15), the frame window, and the application class. Here, a child **CWnd** owns and creates and has the command enablers for its tool box. As it stands, there is never a way for the main Draw window to have its command enablers enable anything on the main menu or control bar! We must manually hook into the framework's routing to give our main Draw window a chance for its command enablers to do their work. The "hook" is overriding the internal **OnCmdMsg** function that is responsible for the message routing and adding our main window to the checking process. Without getting into the details of what is really being passed or why, or what any function is to do with the parameters, the **OnCmdMsg** function in FrameWin is coded as follows:

```
BOOL      FrameWin::OnCmdMsg (UINT id, int code, void *ptrextra,
                             AFX_CMDHANDLERINFO *ptrinfo) {
 if (CFrameWnd::OnCmdMsg (id, code, ptrextra, ptrinfo)) return TRUE;
 if (ptrmainwin)
  return ptrmainwin->OnCmdMsg (id, code, ptrextra, ptrinfo);
 else return FALSE;
 }
```

First, it passes control to the normal channels that begin with the frame window itself, going from there throughout the normal channels for processing. If any command handler for the specific request handles this message, it returns TRUE, indicating it has responded and no further checking is required. So if anyone else handles this request, we are done; return TRUE. If not, it could very well be one of our tool box enablers. However, since the main Draw window is going to be dynamically launched and not created as the frame window comes up, we can proceed only if the **ptrmainwin** exists, indicating that the main window is up and running. If it is, then we simply pass the message as is on to our class.

In the next chapter these examples are going to be converted into the MDI system.

The Multiple Document Interface

12.1 INTRODUCTION

Windows 95 provides two generalized interfaces designed to simplify the handling of one or more documents, where a document is usually thought of as a text file, but can be any window application. These two interfaces are the single document interface (SDI) and the multiple document interface (MDI). The major difference between the two is that the MDI can maintain many documents on-screen while SDI can handle only one. The MDI provides the programmer and user with the tools with which to work and manage many documents concurrently.

Figure 12.1 shows our first MDI sample program—Pgm12a—in operation. The fancy decorations have been brought forward. Notice that two previous applications have been converted into MDI child windows: the graphics GDI scroll program from chapter 9 and the draw program from chapter 11 complete with tool boxes. Two separate instances of each document have been opened.

The MDI framework installs and maintains a new pop-up menu called "Windows," which has been pulled down in Figure 12.2. The MDI framework handles completely all of the Windows menu items without any coding from us. The multiple document windows can be cascaded or tiled (we have used tiled in these figures). When several documents are iconized, the MDI framework arranges them for you. In Figure 12.3 I launched another three documents and then minimized three documents of the seven. We can switch to a different document by clicking anywhere in that document.

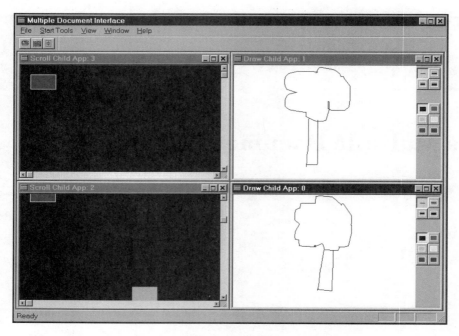

Fig. 12.1 Pgm12a—MDI Application with Four Child Windows Open

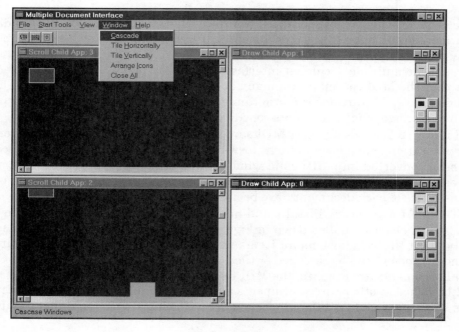

Fig. 12.2 Pgm12a with Window Menu Pulled Down

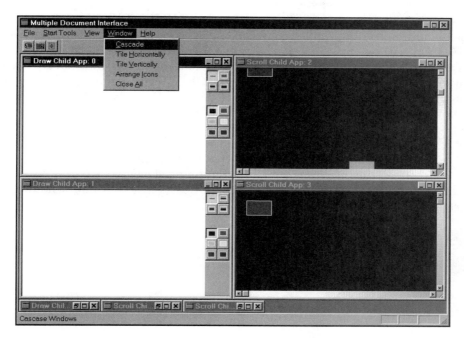

Fig. 12.3 Pgm12a with Window Menu with Seven Child Windows

Each document window normally has its own system caption or title bar with a control bar and Min/Max buttons. Thus, each window has the full use of a normal system menu with Close and Move along with the ability to minimize itself and, most important, to maximize itself just as if that one document were the only one running.

The MDI framework has another even more powerful feature: the canvas area upon which the document views are being displayed, known as the *client window,* is not limited to the size of the screen. Rather the client window is a virtual canvas with world coordinates of ±32,767 pixels wide. The MDI framework creates a minidesktop to organize windows objects or documents. The Windows 3.1 Program and File Managers are both MDI programs as is Microsoft Works, the System Configuration Editor SYSEDIT, and the Developer Studio we have been using.

12.2 MDI TERMINOLOGY

The main window is now derived from **CMDIFrameWnd** that provides the desktop area but no conventional window on which to display documents.

The desktop-like window is managed by an invisible instance of the **MDIClient** window that provides the processing of all document windows, handles the Windows menu, and allocates new instances of documents. There is only one **MDIClient** window that manages all of the other document windows. It normally is not encapsulated in a C++ class; we just use the default.

Each separate document is an instance of a **CMDIChildWnd** window. There can be nearly unlimited child windows opened, subject only to system resources. Note that the **CMDIChildWnd** class is derived from a **CFrameWnd**, *not* a **CWnd**.

The **CMDIFrameWnd** window always has a menu bar that should have at a minimum the Windows pop-up menu. **CMDIChildWnd** windows have *no* menus. Rather they receive menu commands passed down to them from the MDI frame window. They can and very often do merge some of their own needed pop-up menus onto the main menu bar.

When a document window is minimized, its icon is displayed at the bottom of the frame window. If no special icon is provided by the **CMDIChildWnd**, as for the Graphics Scroll, MDI substitutes a standard minimized icon.

When a document is maximized, it takes over the entire frame window area; its controls merge with the frame window as shown in Figure 12.4.

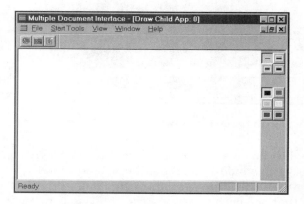

Fig. 12.4 Pgm12a with Draw Child Maximized

The **MDIClient** window, *not* the frame window as one might expect, serves as the *parent window* for all of the MDI children. Since the client window can be huge in size, children can be placed far off-screen and gotten to by scrolling. Or the client can be reduced in size, restricting the area in which the children can be displayed. This restriction or sizing constraint is exactly what is occurring with the control bars and status bars. The MFC implementation, as expected, is a fairly simple encapsulation of the Windows 95 MDI framework.

12.3 Pgm12a: Overview

Unlimited (except by resources) numbers of two different types of MDI child windows can be launched: Draw and Scroll Window. In general, any application that we have coded up to this point could become a MDI child application. Notice that the MDI child window is derived from a frame window class. So the starting point for conversion to MDI is to change the base class to **CMDIChildWnd**. For the Scroll Window application, this conversion process is very simple. For the Draw window, the process is immensely more complex because of the tool box. In the program in chapter 11, there is only one instance of Draw and only one tool box. Now there can be numerous instances of Draw and the tool box as well. How does this affect our design?

First, the main menu should have the familiar Hide/Show Tool Box menu item located under the View pop-up menu. I shall take advantage of the ability of a child MDI window to install its own menu additions *while* it is the active child. So, when Scroll Window is reactivated, Hide/Show Tool Boxes menu is grayed. The ability of the MDI to manage child menus becomes vital. In this version, the tool box's status is determined dynamically using **CWnd** member functions to inquire whether the tool box is currently visible.

Minimization becomes a problem. Since the icon is within the client window, if a tool box is present, then the tool box would be appended to the icon representing the window. It certainly looks funny to see an icon with a tool box appended to it! Thus, we must be able to detect when our Draw window is about to become minimized so that we can hide the tool box. Conversely, we must be able to detect when that window is about to be restored so that we can make the tool box visible once more.

As we examine how to code for the MDI, you will see why we have been coding in so general a manner, dividing the workload among the application, frame, and window classes. It was done for easy insertion into the MDI framework.

12.4 THE MFC IMPLEMENTATION OF MDI—PGM12a

From a design viewpoint, separating each MDI child class from the overall MDI frame window offers great benefits. No longer does the frame window class have to directly manage objects for its child windows, such as the tool box palette in Pgm11a. Now each separate MDI child class has its own source and header files. Since MDI child classes are derived from a frame window, they can have and maintain their own tool boxes, control bars, and so on. But what about their own resources? It would be very practical for each MDI child class to have its own resource files as well.

However, by now you should have realized that the Developer Studio expects one resource file and saves the identifiers in one file—resource.h. Further, have you yet observed what happens if you save a resource file that has some #define macros in it? If not, look back at Pgm11a's resource.h file. For menu IDs I used (WM_USER + 1) for example. Open the resource editor on this file and double-click to add a new string table entry. Then save. Now open resource.h and see what happens to the #defines. They are replaced by the absolute numerical values! I did exactly this in this program. I had used (WM_USER + n) for all of the menu command IDs and then resaved the resource files; notice that all were replaced by their absolute values.

How can we prevent the clobbering of #defines, and how can we have multiple resource files?

12.4.1 How to Have Multiple Resource Files and Read-Only Headers

We keep the main resource file as Pgm12a.rc with resource.h as its header. To construct another resource file for say DrawWin, choose File | New | Resource Script. If this is all we do, when it is saved, the real resource.h for Pgm12a.rc will be overlain!

Instead, we must force the use of a different name. Choose View | Resource Includes. A property sheet opens. In the space for Symbol Header File, enter a new name, such as DrawWin.rh. This replaces resource.h as the header file. When you save, DrawWin.rc and DrawWin.rh are created.

This same property page also has entries for Read-Only Header files, usually only that for afxres.h. If you have some carefully crafted #defines that you do not wish clobbered, place them in a separate header file and enter the #include for it in this Read-Only area after that for afxres.h.

One crucial problem remains. How do we include these two new resource files, DrawWin.rc and ScrolWin.rc, into the main resource file, Pgm12a.rc? *Do not* just add a couple of #includes for these two files, say at the end of the Pgm12a string table. Yes, they will be correctly included. However, if you ever use Developer Studio to edit the main Pgm12a.rc file and save it, the Resource Editor copies all of the data from the included files into the main Pgm12a.rc file and drops the two #includes!

To include our new pair of resource files into the main Pgm12a.rc file, open the main resource file and again use View | Resource Includes. Notice the bottom window labeled Compile Time Directives. In this window enter the two #includes for the pair of additional resource files. Now they are included only during the actual resource compilation phase. When you use Developer Studio on Pgm12a, you cannot edit any of the data in the child window's resource files. However, you can just as easily open DrawWin.rc or ScrolWin.rc and edit them with Developer Studio.

Review the resource file excerpts for Pgm12a now. (For more details, consult MFC Technical Note #35.) The other two resource files are grouped with their respective classes below. The Pgm12a.rc file shows the basic frame menu, consisting of the File pop-up group, the Start Tools group which launches the child windows or documents, the View group to handle the decorations, the new Window group for MDI, and the Help group.

12.4.2 Listing for File: Pgm12a.rc—Pgm12a—Excerpts

```
...
MAINMENU MENU DISCARDABLE
BEGIN
    POPUP "&File"
    BEGIN
        MENUITEM "E&xit\tAlt+F4",              CM_EXIT
    END
    POPUP "&Start Tools"
    BEGIN
        MENUITEM "&Draw",                      CM_DRAW
        MENUITEM "&Scroll",                    CM_SCROLL
    END
    POPUP "&View"
    BEGIN
        MENUITEM "&Toolbar",                   ID_VIEW_TOOLBAR
        MENUITEM "&Status Bar",                ID_VIEW_STATUS_BAR
        MENUITEM SEPARATOR
    END
```

```
    POPUP "&Window"
    BEGIN
        MENUITEM "&Cascade",                    CM_CASCADECHILDREN, GRAYED
        MENUITEM "Tile &Horizontally",          CM_TILECHILDRENH, GRAYED
        MENUITEM "Tile &Vertically",            CM_TILECHILDRENV, GRAYED
        MENUITEM "Arrange &Icons",              CM_ARRANGEICONS, GRAYED
        MENUITEM "Close &All",                  CM_CLOSECHILDREN, GRAYED
    END
    POPUP "&Help"
    BEGIN
        MENUITEM "&About...",                   CM_HELPABOUT
    END
END

IDD_ABOUT DIALOG DISCARDABLE  48, 113, 200, 92
STYLE DS_MODALFRAME | WS_POPUP | WS_VISIBLE | WS_CAPTION | WS_SYSMENU
CAPTION "Help - About PGM12A"
FONT 8, "MS Sans Serif"
BEGIN
    DEFPUSHBUTTON    "OK",IDOK,72,70,50,14
    LTEXT            "by Vic Broquard",IDC_STATIC,70,42,57,8
    LTEXT            "Illustrates Multiple Doc Interface",IDC_STATIC,33,20,
                     228,11
    GROUPBOX         "",IDC_STATIC,28,10,141,50
END

IDB_MAINFRAME             BITMAP  MOVEABLE PURE    "TOOLBAR.BMP"

STRINGTABLE DISCARDABLE
BEGIN
    ID_INDICATOR_EXT      "EXT"
    ID_INDICATOR_CAPS     "CAP"
    ID_INDICATOR_NUM      "NUM"
    ID_INDICATOR_SCRL     "SCRL"
    ID_INDICATOR_OVR      "OVR"
    ID_INDICATOR_REC      "REC"
END

STRINGTABLE DISCARDABLE
BEGIN
    CM_DRAW               "Launch Draw Window\nStart Draw"
    CM_SCROLL             "Launch Scroll Window\nStart Scroll"
    CM_HELPABOUT          "About the MDI application"
    CM_EXIT               "Quit, prompt to save the documents\nQuit App"
    CM_CASCADECHILDREN    "Cascase Windows"
    CM_TILECHILDRENH      "Tile Windows - Horizontally"
    CM_TILECHILDRENV      "Tile Windows - Vertically"
    CM_ARRANGEICONS       "Arrange Icons"
    CM_CLOSECHILDREN      "Close All Windows"
END

STRINGTABLE DISCARDABLE
BEGIN
    ID_VIEW_TOOLBAR       "Hide/Show Tool Bar"
    ID_VIEW_STATUS_BAR    "Hide/Show Status Bar"
END
```

```
STRINGTABLE DISCARDABLE
BEGIN
    AFX_IDS_IDLEMESSAGE        "Ready"
END

STRINGTABLE DISCARDABLE
BEGIN
    IDS_MAINTITLE              "Multiple Document Interface"
    IDS_MSG_QUIT               "Do you want to quit the application?"
    IDS_MSG_QUERY              "Query?"
    IDS_DRAW                   "Draw Child App: "
    IDS_SCROLL                 "Scroll Child App: "
END
. . .
```

12.4.3 Listing for File: resource.h—Pgm12a—Excerpts

```
. . .
#define  IDB_MAINFRAME            2
#define  CM_DRAW                  1124
#define  CM_SCROLL                1125
#define  CM_HELPABOUT             1126
#define  CM_EXIT                  1127
#define  CM_CASCADECHILDREN       1128
#define  CM_TILECHILDRENH         1129
#define  CM_TILECHILDRENV         1130
#define  CM_ARRANGEICONS          1131
#define  CM_CLOSECHILDREN         1132
#define  IDS_MAINTITLE            2000
#define  IDS_MSG_QUIT             2001
#define  IDS_MSG_QUERY            2002
#define  IDS_DRAW                 2003
#define  IDS_SCROLL               2004
. . .
```

The MFC implementation is merely a cover wrapper over the Windows 95 C-style MDI framework. (Note that the Document-View architecture provides much better support for MDI.) The MFC framework has some built-in command IDs for processing the Windows menu items such as Cascade, Tile, and so on. These are

Built-in IDs	Description	CMDIFrameWin function invoked
ID_WINDOW_TILE_VERT	vertically	MDITile (MDITILE_VERTICAL);
ID_WINDOW_TILE_HORZ	horizontally	MDITile (MDITILE_HORIZONTAL);
ID_WINDOW_CASCADE	cascade	MDICascade ();
ID_WINDOW_ARRANGE	icon arrange	MDIIconArrange ();

If you do not use these predefined IDs, then, in the command response function, invoke the **CMDIFrameWnd** functions indicated earlier. In Pgm12a, the usual CM_xxx-style identifiers are used and you can see these functions being invoked to handle the Windows menu actions.

There are no real changes to the application class. Look first to the main frame window class, FrameWin, which in the MFC MDI implementation is derived from **CMDIFrameWnd**. The **CMDIFrameWnd** must create an instance of the Windows 95 default MDI client window. Launch and maintenance of child windows is done by the **CMDIFrameWnd**. Remember that the **CMDIFrameWnd** is also responsible for the tool bar and status bar—it becomes a busy class.

Since frame windows own the decorations, the tool bar and status bar are defined here. To facilitate closing all of the MDI children at one time without forcing the user to respond to numerous can close queries, the public BOOL **fastclose** is defined. It is public so that the MDI child windows can access it. The member **numchildren** is used to count the current number of MDI children as well as to be appended to the children's titles.

The Windows 95 API provides two functions that have been encapsulated in **CMDIFrameWnd** that assist in moving between MDI child windows: **MDIGetActive** and **MDINext**.

```
CMDIChildWnd *  MDIGetActive (BOOL ptrismaximized);
void            MDINext ();
```

MDIGetActive returns a pointer to the currently active MDI child window. It sets the BOOL that is pointed to by **ptrismaximized** to TRUE if that MDI child is currently maximized. The function **MDINext** deactivates the current MDI child and makes the MDI child window immediately behind the now-active MDI child. Thus, one could envision a loop such as:

```
CMDIChild *ptrchild = MDIGetActive (NULL);
while (ptrchild != NULL) {
 ...
 MDINext ();
 ptrchild = MDIGetActive (NULL);
}
```

The Windows 95 implementation of **MDINext** always returns a pointer to the next window. So if there are two children, the function returns a pointer to the other one endlessly and the above code can present an infinite loop. Further, if MDI children are iconized, they are not in the loop and seem to be bypassed. But there is a fail-safe way to determine if there are no more MDI children of a specific type—have the MDI frame window who launched them keep a tally.

Examine the FrameWin definition file noting the new MDI functions. Specifically, observe that I used in-line functions for the Cascade, Tile, and Arrange Icon functions. Each invokes the corresponding **CMDIFrameWnd** function. For Tile, I used both options for tiling vertically or horizontally.

```
afx_msg void  CmCascadeChildren () {MDICascade ();}
afx_msg void  CmTileChildrenH () {MDITile (MDITILE_HORIZONTAL);}
afx_msg void  CmTileChildrenV () {MDITile (MDITILE_VERTICAL);}
afx_msg void  CmTileChildren () {MDITile ();}
afx_msg void  CmArrangeIcons () {MDIIconArrange ();}
```

As you would expect, we must handle the Close All Child Windows ourselves in

```
        afx_msg void  CmCloseChildren ();
```

I also added another in-line function to return the number of children—the field that is used to append to child window titles. It is not an accurate count of the true number of MDI children, however. Suppose six MDI children are launched and then children numbered 1 and 2 are deleted. The number of children cannot be set to four because, if another MDI child were launched, it would then be given the number 4 to append to its title. Now there would be two child windows numbered 4!

```
        int    GetChildCount () {return numchildren;}
```

12.4.4 Listing for File: FrameWin.h—Pgm12a—Excerpts

```
...
class FrameWin : public CMDIFrameWnd {
/***************************************************************************/
/*                                                                       */
/* Class Data Members                                                    */
/*                                                                       */
/***************************************************************************/

public:

BOOL        fastclose;   // avoid lots of query prompts when TRUE

protected:

int         numchildren; // count of children
int         numdraw;     // number of draw children
int         numscroll;   // number of scroll children
CStatusBar  statusbar;   // our status bar - try caps - scroll - num LOCKS
CToolBar    toolbar;     // our control bar
/***************************************************************************/
/*                                                                       */
/* Class Functions:                                                      */
/*                                                                       */
/***************************************************************************/

public:

            FrameWin (const char*);    // init child win counts
            ~FrameWin () {}            // destructor - do nothing

protected:

afx_msg int   OnCreate(LPCREATESTRUCT);    // construct tool bar and status bar
afx_msg void  OnClose ();                  // determines if app can quit yet
int           DisplayMsg (int, int, UINT); // displays a message box

//            command processors
afx_msg void  CmExit ();                   // shut app down - close all children
afx_msg void  CmDraw ();                   // launch the draw client window
afx_msg void  CmScroll ();                 // launch the scroll client
afx_msg void  CmHelpAbout ();              // help about our app

//            MDI Children Functions
```

```
afx_msg void  CmCascadeChildren () {MDICascade ();}  // do cascade
afx_msg void  CmTileChildrenH () {MDITile (MDITILE_HORIZONTAL);} // tile horiz
afx_msg void  CmTileChildrenV () {MDITile (MDITILE_VERTICAL);}   // tile vert
afx_msg void  CmArrangeIcons () {MDIIconArrange ();} // do arrange
afx_msg void  CmCloseChildren ();                    // close all
       int    GetChildCount () {return numchildren;} // get child total windows
...
```

The FrameWin MDI implementation begins in the constructor by creating the MDI frame window and initializing the child count to zero. As usual **OnCreate** constructs the tool bar and status bar exactly as in any other frame window. The first MDI changes occur in the command response handlers that are to launch the MDI children.

12.4.5 Launching a MDI Child

There are several ways to launch child windows. If the child is a Text Editor, for example, you could use the File | New and File | Open menu items to launch the editor with that file. I show how this can be done in chapter 13. Here I provide a button and menu item for each type of child. When either the menu selection or the button to launch the child window—Draw or Scroll—is pressed, the command CM_DRAW or CM_SCROLL is sent to the MDI client for handling in either the **CmDraw** or **CmScroll** function. The two functions differ only in the actual allocation of the new child window itself. The Scroll constructor accepts the desired **mapsize**.

Notice that each instance of either the Draw document or the Scroll object has a *unique* title that helps identify which is which. Since it is the frame window's responsibility to launch another child document, it also should provide a method to help that child in uniquely identifying itself in that child's title bar. Very often a number is appended to the name of the document title. If you are using an actual file new or open, the filename can serve as the unique identifier.

The general procedure for launching child MDI windows begins with creating a string from the current **numberchildren** count that is subsequently passed to the child constructor. In **CmDraw** the child's title is loaded from the resource file, and the current number of children is appended to the end of the title. A new instance of the DrawWin class is allocated and its **Create** function invoked. If the creation was successful, the number of children is incremented and the new child window made visible.

```
LoadString (AfxGetApp()->m_hInstance, IDS_DRAW, title, sizeof(title));
itoa (numchildren, msg, 10);
strcat (title, msg);
// allocate a draw MDI child window
DrawWin *ptrwin = new DrawWin ();
// now create the draw MDI child window
if (!ptrwin->Create (NULL, title, WS_CHILD | WS_VISIBLE |
                     WS_OVERLAPPEDWINDOW | WS_CLIPCHILDREN)) {
 delete ptrwin;
 return;
}
```

```
numchildren++;
ptrwin->ShowWindow (SW_SHOW); // and make child visible
```

CmScroll is exactly parallel. However, notice the wndclass style to the **Create** function.

```
WS_CHILD | WS_VISIBLE | WS_OVERLAPPEDWINDOW | WS_CLIPCHILDREN
```

The first three are the default MDI child window flags. However, for the Draw window, we must also ask it to clip its children. If not, then the user can draw all over the tool box!

When the user requests that a specific window or document be closed, that class provides its own **OnClose** function to decide if work needs to be saved and so on. However, in MDI the user can have a dozen documents active and then select Close the Application or from Window—Close All Windows. Here, the frame window's **OnClose** invokes what it sees as the only client window—MDI Client's **OnClose**—which in turn, one by one, invokes each of the dozen documents' **OnClose** functions. Pity the poor user, who at this point must respond to a dozen "Do you want to close this window?" queries.

The solution is to implement a "fast close" operation that notifies each child window's **OnClose** function that the user is shutting down all applications and therefore not to display a query unless necessary to save work. Now many programmers simply make the BOOL **fastclose** or **expressclose** a global item, but you know how I feel about global anythings! A better solution is to define a public static member—**fastclose**; all child windows can easily access it. So whenever the user requests all windows to be closed, the **fastclose** is set to TRUE. All child windows' **OnClose** functions merely have to check **fastclose** to decide whether to display the "do you want to quit this window" message if work does not have to be saved.

The **CmCloseChildren** function is called whenever all windows are going to be shut down, either from the frame window (Alt-F4, for example) or from the Window | Close All. Incidentally, the **OnClose** MDI client function is called after all children have responded, and this is where you would place the "want to close this application" style message. So in **CmCloseChildren** the BOOL **fastclose** is set to TRUE so that all of the closing MDI child windows can check it to avoid displaying unneeded can close messages. Remember that the children *can* still display a message if file contents need to be saved. Next comes the loop that cycles through all MDI children. We just looked at this very loop earlier. Notice that each MDI child is destroyed before invoking **MDINext;** a NULL pointer is returned after the last child is destroyed.

```
CMDIChildWnd *ptrwin = MDIGetActive ();
while (ptrwin) {
 ptrwin->MDIDestroy ();
 MDINext();
 ptrwin = MDIGetActive ();
}
```

All children counters are reset to zero, and **fastclose** becomes FALSE once more. More children could now be launched.

12.4.6 Listing for File: FrameWin.cpp—Pgm12a—Excerpts

```
...
/******************************************************************************/
/*                                                                            */
/* Control bar buttons and Status bar buttons                                 */
/*                                                                            */
/* control bar buttons - IDs are command buttons                              */
/* same order as in the bitmap 'toolbar.bmp'                                  */
/*                                                                            */
/******************************************************************************/

static UINT BASED_CODE buttons[] = {

  CM_EXIT,
  CM_DRAW,
  CM_SCROLL,
};
...

/******************************************************************************/
/*                                                                            */
/* FrameWin Events Response Table                                             */
/*                                                                            */
/******************************************************************************/

BEGIN_MESSAGE_MAP(FrameWin, CMDIFrameWnd)
 ON_WM_CREATE ()
 ON_WM_CLOSE ()
 ON_COMMAND(CM_EXIT,            CmExit)
 ON_COMMAND(CM_DRAW,            CmDraw)
 ON_COMMAND(CM_SCROLL,          CmScroll)
 ON_COMMAND(CM_HELPABOUT,       CmHelpAbout)
 ON_COMMAND(CM_CASCADECHILDREN, CmCascadeChildren)
 ON_COMMAND(CM_TILECHILDRENH,   CmTileChildrenH)
 ON_COMMAND(CM_TILECHILDRENV,   CmTileChildrenV)
 ON_COMMAND(CM_ARRANGEICONS,    CmArrangeIcons)
 ON_COMMAND(CM_CLOSECHILDREN,   CmCloseChildren)
 ON_MESSAGE(WM_CHILDDESTROY,    OnChildDestroy)
END_MESSAGE_MAP()

/******************************************************************************/
/*                                                                            */
/* Framewin: Construct the window object                                      */
/*                                                                            */
/******************************************************************************/

          FrameWin::FrameWin (const char *title) {

// create the MDI frame window
Create (NULL, title, WS_OVERLAPPEDWINDOW, rectDefault, NULL, "MAINMENU");
fastclose   = FALSE; // set no express close in operation
numchildren = 0;     // set number of children to 0 for title additions
}

/******************************************************************************/
/*                                                                            */
/* OnCreate: construct MDI Client win plus the status and control bars        */
```

```
/*                                                                      */
/************************************************************************/

int     FrameWin::OnCreate (LPCREATESTRUCT lpCS) {

// construct from resource file the main menu to be used
CMenu *ptrmenu;
ptrmenu = new CMenu ();
ptrmenu->LoadMenu ("MAINMENU");

// and construct the MDI hidden client window using the main menu
CreateClient (lpCS, ptrmenu->GetSubMenu(0));
delete ptrmenu;

// attempt to build control bar and status bar
if (toolbar.Create (this) && toolbar.LoadBitmap (IDB_MAINFRAME) &&
    toolbar.SetButtons (buttons, sizeof(buttons)/sizeof(UINT))) // make control bar
 if (statusbar.Create (this) &&                            // make status bar
     statusbar.SetIndicators (indicators, sizeof(indicators)/sizeof(UINT)));
 else return -1;
else return -1;
// all ok, so set for hints and tool tips wanted
toolbar.SetBarStyle (toolbar.GetBarStyle() | CBRS_TOOLTIPS | CBRS_FLYBY);
// now notify control to accept any form of docking
toolbar.EnableDocking (CBRS_ALIGN_ANY);
// notify the framewindow of docking requirements
EnableDocking (CBRS_ALIGN_ANY);
// and dock control bar at top
DockControlBar (&toolbar);

return 0;
}
/************************************************************************/
/*                                                                      */
/* CmDraw: Launch a new client window for drawing, with its tool box    */
/*                                                                      */
/************************************************************************/

void     FrameWin::CmDraw () {

char title[80];
char msg[10];
// construct modified window title appending id number to title
LoadString (AfxGetApp()->m_hInstance, IDS_DRAW, title, sizeof(title));
itoa (numchildren, msg, 10);
strcat (title, msg);
// allocate a draw MDI child window
DrawWin *ptrwin = new DrawWin ();
// now create the draw MDI child window
if (!ptrwin->Create (NULL, title, WS_CHILD | WS_VISIBLE |
                     WS_OVERLAPPEDWINDOW | WS_CLIPCHILDREN)) {
 delete ptrwin;
 return;
}
numchildren++;
ptrwin->ShowWindow (SW_SHOW); // and make child visible
}
```

```
/******************************************************************************/
/*                                                                          */
/* CmScroll: Launch a new client window for scrolling                       */
/*                                                                          */
/******************************************************************************/
void       FrameWin::CmScroll () {
 char title[80];
 char msg[10];
 // construct modified window title appending id number to title
 LoadString (AfxGetApp()->m_hInstance, IDS_SCROLL, title, sizeof(title));
 itoa (numchildren, msg, 10);
 strcat (title, msg);
 // allocate new scroll window with a map size of 400 pixels then create it
 ScrolWin *ptrwin = new ScrolWin (400);
 if (!ptrwin->Create (title)) {
  delete ptrwin;
  return;
 }
 numchildren++;
 ptrwin->ShowWindow (SW_SHOW);            // make child visible

 CMDIChildWnd *ptrcurwin = MDIGetActive ();
 if (ptrcurwin)
  if (ptrcurwin->GetStyle() & WS_MAXIMIZE)
   ptrwin->MDIMaximize();
}
/******************************************************************************/
/*                                                                          */
/* CmCloseChildren: close all children with no child close prompts          */
/*                                                                          */
/******************************************************************************/
void       FrameWin::CmCloseChildren () {
 fastclose = TRUE;                              // turn on express close option
 CMDIChildWnd *ptrwin = MDIGetActive (); // find the current active child
 while (ptrwin) {                               // for all MDI children:
  ptrwin->MDIDestroy ();                        // destroy the child window
  MDINext();                                    // make the next child active
  ptrwin = MDIGetActive ();                     // and get a ptr to next active one
 }
 fastclose = FALSE;                             // turn off express close option
 numchildren = numdraw = numscroll = 0;  // set all child win counts to 0
}
...
```

12.5 CONVERTING SCROLWIN FROM PGM09a INTO A CMDICHILDWND

Now we must convert the scrolling window from Pgm09a into a **CMDIChildWnd**, ScrolWin. First, construct the resource files.

12.5.1 Listing for File: ScrolWin.rc—Pgm12a—Excerpts

```
. . .
STRINGTABLE DISCARDABLE
BEGIN
    IDS_SCROLLQUERY          "Ok to close this scroll window?"
    IDS_MSG_QUERYSCROLL      "Query"
    IDS_SCROLLTITLE          "Graphics Scroll Window"
END
. . .
```

12.5.2 Listing for File: ScrolWin.rh—Pgm12a—Excerpts

```
. . .
#define IDS_SCROLLQUERY                  2101
#define IDS_MSG_QUERYSCROLL              2102
#define IDS_SCROLLTITLE                  2103
. . .
```

I have removed the SysInfo class from the implementation of the first MDI child, ScrolWin, substituting **screen_x_pels** and **screen_y_pels** for the screen dimensions. ScrolWin is now derived from **CMDIChildWnd**. To accommodate MDI, the **CmExit** functionality is moved to **OnClose**, and functions **Create** and **OnDestroy** are added to install the modified title and notify the MDI frame of ScrolWin termination.

12.5.3 Listing for File: ScrolWin.h—Pgm12a—Excerpts

```
. . .
/****************************************************************************/
/*                                                                          */
/* ScrolWin Class Definition: Display a Graphic Scroll Window              */
/*                                                                          */
/****************************************************************************/

class ScrolWin : public CMDIChildWnd {

/****************************************************************************/
/*                                                                          */
/* Data Members                                                             */
/*                                                                          */
/****************************************************************************/

. . .
int       screen_x_pels;        // full screen coords
int       screen_y_pels;
. . .

/****************************************************************************/
/*                                                                          */
/* Functions:                                                               */
/*                                                                          */
/****************************************************************************/

public:

          ScrolWin (int mapsize = 400);  // constructor
```

```
                ~ScrolWin ();                    // destructor
BOOL             Create (LPSTR);                 // MDI create

protected:

        int     DisplayMsg (int, int, UINT);     // display a message
afx_msg void    OnClose ();                       // can close this draw window
afx_msg void    OnDestroy ();                     // destroy all objects
        void    RemoveMemDC ();                   // delete memory DC objects
        void    ConstructMemDC ();                // construct new memory DC
        void    DrawMemDC ();                     // draw objects on memory DC
afx_msg void    OnPaint ();                       // paint the window - WM_PAINT
afx_msg int     OnCreate (LPCREATESTRUCT);        // construct window
afx_msg void    OnSize (UINT, int, int);          // process window resize
afx_msg void    OnKeyDown (UINT, UINT, UINT);     // keybd scroller interface
afx_msg void    OnHScroll (UINT, UINT, CScrollBar*); // handle scrolling
afx_msg void    OnVScroll (UINT, UINT, CScrollBar*);

//user has changed display settings, so need to rebuild
afx_msg LRESULT OnDisplayChange (WPARAM, LPARAM);
...
```

In the ScrolWin implementation the constructor now performs only initialization duties, allocating pens and brushes, defining the window and scrolling rectangles, and similar actions. In **Create** the modified title is passed on to the real **Create** function of **CMDIChildWnd**. In **OnCreate**, once the window element is constructed, the full screen dimensions are acquired. This replaces the SysInfo class which before had maintained the screen dimensions.

In **OnClose**, which is invoked when the user attempts to close this window, the MDI frame's **fastclose** member must be checked to determine if a Close All is currently in effect. The **CWnd** function **GetParentFrame** is used to obtain a pointer to the **CMDIFrameWnd**. It must be cast back into a FrameWin pointer so that **fastclose** can be accessed.

```
FrameWin *ptrparent = (FrameWin*) (GetParentFrame());
if (ptrparent->fastclose == FALSE)
```

OnDestroy does not need to be overridden. I included it just for the model. In many cases, only these few changes must be made to convert a frame window class into a MDI child as part of a larger application. Menu modifications and MDI child tool boxes present a slightly more complex conversion process.

12.5.4 Listing for File: ScrolWin.cpp—Pgm12a—Excerpts

```
...
/******************************************************************************/
/*                                                                          */
/* Response Table:                                                          */
/*                                                                          */
/******************************************************************************/

BEGIN_MESSAGE_MAP(ScrolWin, CMDIChildWnd)
 ON_WM_CREATE()
 ON_WM_DESTROY()
```

```
 ON_WM_CLOSE()
 ...
 ON_MESSAGE(WM_DISPLAYCHANGE, OnDisplayChange)
END_MESSAGE_MAP()
/*************************************************************************/
/*                                                                     */
/* ScrolWin: construct class, get pens, brushes, and setup scroller    */
/*                                                                     */
/*************************************************************************/

       ScrolWin::ScrolWin (int mapsize) {

 ptrpenwhite = new CPen (PS_SOLID, 1, RGB ( 255, 255, 255 )); // make white pen
 ...
 ptrbrushgray  = new CBrush (RGB (192, 192, 192)); // make gray brush

 full_window.top      = full_window.left      = 0; // set full window rectangle
 full_window.right    = full_window.bottom    = mapsize; // to be mapsize
 .. same as before
 }
/*************************************************************************/
/*                                                                     */
/* Create: construct the object                                        */
/*                                                                     */
/*************************************************************************/

BOOL      ScrolWin::Create (LPSTR title) {

 return CMDIChildWnd::Create (NULL, title);
 }
/*************************************************************************/
/*                                                                     */
/* OnCreate: get screen max dimensions                                 */
/*                                                                     */
/*************************************************************************/

int       ScrolWin::OnCreate (LPCREATESTRUCT lpCS) {

 int retcd = CMDIChildWnd::OnCreate (lpCS); // pass along to base class

 CClientDC dc (this);
 screen_x_pels = dc.GetDeviceCaps (HORZRES);
 screen_y_pels = dc.GetDeviceCaps (VERTRES);
 return retcd;
 }
 ...

/*************************************************************************/
/*                                                                     */
/* OnDisplayChange: user has changed the display settings, must update */
/*                                                                     */
/*************************************************************************/

LRESULT   ScrolWin::OnDisplayChange (WPARAM which, LPARAM lp) {

 LRESULT retcd = CMDIChildWnd::OnDisplayChange (which, lp);

 if (which == 1) {
```

```
    CClientDC dc (this);
    screen_x_pels = dc.GetDeviceCaps (HORZRES);
    screen_y_pels = dc.GetDeviceCaps (VERTRES);
    RemoveMemDC ();            // delete old memory DC
    ConstructMemDC ();         // build new memory DC compatible with new display
  }
  return retcd;
}

/**************************************************************************/
/*                                                                        */
/* OnClose:  query user if we can terminate this drawing                   */
/*                                                                        */
/**************************************************************************/
void      ScrolWin::OnClose () {
  FrameWin *ptrparent = (FrameWin*) (GetParentFrame());
  if (ptrparent->fastclose == FALSE)
   if (DisplayMsg (IDS_MSG_QUERYSCROLL, IDS_SCROLLQUERY,
      MB_YESNO | MB_ICONQUESTION) == IDYES) MDIDestroy ();
}
...
```

12.6 Converting Pgm11a's DrawWin to a CMDIChildWnd

Converting chapter 11's DrawWin into a MDI child is more difficult for three reasons.
The Hide/Show menu and tool box are more complex, and the original frame window
and main window classes must be merged back into one MDI child window. First, it
now has its own resource file.

12.6.1 Listing for File: DrawWin.rc—Pgm12a—Excerpts

```
...
IDB_TOOLBOX              BITMAP  MOVEABLE PURE   "TOOLBOX.BMP"
...
STRINGTABLE DISCARDABLE
BEGIN
    CM_LINE1            "Select 1 pixel line width\nLinewidth 1"
    CM_LINE2            "Select 2 pixels line width\nLinewidth 2"
    CM_LINE3            "Select 3 pixels line width\nLinewidth 3"
    CM_LINE4            "Select 4 pixels line width\nLinewidth 4"
    CM_COLORA           "Select Black as the drawing color\nBlack"
    CM_COLORB           "Select Red as the drawing color\nRed"
    CM_COLORC           "Select Green as the drawing color\nGreen"
END

STRINGTABLE DISCARDABLE
BEGIN
    CM_COLORD           "Select Yellow as the drawing color\nYellow"
    CM_COLORE           "Select Blue as the drawing color\nBlue"
    CM_COLORF           "Select Purple as the drawing color\nPurple"
END

STRINGTABLE DISCARDABLE
```

```
BEGIN
    IDB_TOOLBOX              "Hide/Show Tool &Box"
END

STRINGTABLE DISCARDABLE
BEGIN
    IDS_DRAWQUIT             "Ok to close this drawing?"
    IDS_DRAWTITLE            "Make a Drawing"
END
```

12.6.2 Listing for File: DrawWin.rh—Pgm12a—Excerpts

```
#define IDB_TOOLBOX                 3
#define CM_LINE1                    1145
#define CM_LINE2                    1146
#define CM_LINE3                    1147
#define CM_LINE4                    1148
#define CM_COLORA                   1149
#define CM_COLORB                   1150
#define CM_COLORC                   1151
#define CM_COLORD                   1152
#define CM_COLORE                   1153
#define CM_COLORF                   1154
#define IDS_DRAWQUIT                2200
#define IDS_DRAWTITLE               2201
```

Notice specifically that the pop-up menu for Hide/Show the Tool Box is removed and a single menu item for Hide/Show Tool Box is inserted. In this case, the Hide/Show Tool Box menu item logically should be in the View pop-up menu.

How do we intend to implement the Hide/Show Tool Box menu item? In the Draw MDI child class, maintain a static count of the number of launched instances. When the first instance of the Draw MDI child is launched, it can gain access to the main menu and the View pop-up group. If the new menu item is not yet on the menu (which would be the case when the first Draw child is launched), the Draw child can append the Hide/Show menu item. Subsequent Draw children can check the instance count and, if nonzero, the Hide/Show menu item is already installed, avoiding numerous Hide/Show menu items in the View pop-up menu. To remove that menu item, when the Draw child is destroyed it can check the instance count and, if it is now zero, it can remove the menu item.

Look over the DrawWin class header file and notice that there are very few changes needed. Let's examine the implementation step by step, omitting those portions that are unchanged from chapter 11's version. The CToolBox class is exactly the same as it was in chapter 11.

12.6.3 Listing for File: DrawWin.h—Pgm12a—Excerpts

```
...
/****************************************************************************/
/*                                                                          */
/* DrawWin Class Definition                                             */
```

```
/*                                                                              */
/******************************************************************************/

class DrawWin : public CMDIChildWnd {

/******************************************************************************/
/*                                                                              */
/* Class Data Members                                                          */
/*                                                                              */
/******************************************************************************/

protected:

static int       numdraw;        // total number of draw children now active
CToolBox         toolbox;        // client window's tool box

... rest is the same

/******************************************************************************/
/*                                                                              */
/* Class Functions:                                                            */
/*                                                                              */
/******************************************************************************/

...
protected:

afx_msg void   OnSize (UINT, int, int);     // remove tool box when minimized
afx_msg BOOL   OnQueryOpen ();              // reshow tool box when restoring
afx_msg void   OnMove (int, int);           // reposition tool box as win moves
afx_msg void   OnClose ();                  // check if can close
afx_msg int    OnCreate(LPCREATESTRUCT);    // construct tool box
afx_msg void   OnDestroy ();                // remove allocated menus & child
...
```

The first-time-only positioning of the tool box does not need to be done because the MDI child is now a frame window. The tool box is initially placed on the right side of the Draw window. Next, the handling of whether or not to install our Hide/Show menu item is controlled by the static **numdraw**, initially zero.

The pop-up menu layout is vital not only for proper handling of MDI menus but also for object linking and embedding (OLE) operations. The genesis of the menu description is OLE. There had to be a common way for child windows to modify the main menu even when that child had absolutely no idea of what was in the main menu. OLE's big problem is how to link or embed a paintbrush image in a text document, for example; the menu structures appear totally different.

The solution is to generalize the *significance* of the various pop-up menus that appear on the menu bar. OLE defines six logical groups in the order they appear on the menu bar.

1. File group
2. Edit group
3. Container group
4. Object group

5. Window group

6. Help group

Each group may contain 0, 1, or more pop-up menus. Normally, the file group contains only the File menu that we have been using throughout all of our examples. The Edit group often contains two pop-ups—one for Edit (Cut and Paste) and one for Search (Find and Replace). The Windows and Help groups each usually contain one pop-up menu; the Windows pop-up is nearly always the MDI group, perhaps with additions. The Container group often contains a pop-up menu that enables the user to control the various decorations. Finally, the Object group provides one document-specific set of pop-up menus. For example, in Write, the Character, Paragraph, and Document pop-up menus are object-group-specific menus.

Notice that this is a *logical* grouping of pop-up menus. On the menu bar, they all appear one after the other. For example, in Write

```
File Edit Find Character Paragraph Document Help
```

appear. The number of pop-up menus within the six-group scheme is: 1 2 0 3 0 1, or 1 in File, 2 in Edit, none in Container, 3 in Object, none in Window, and 1 in Help.

When dealing with OLE, it is precisely this line of integers that is being provided to the **OleSetMenuDescr** function, which notifies the Menu Manager how to group the pop-up menus. Reexamine the RC file and find the menu layout. We asked for the following pop-up menus:

```
File  Start Tools  View  Window  Help
```

Following the OLE scheme, the File group has one pop-up; Edit group has none; the Container group has one—the Start Tools; the Object group has none (no child windows yet); the Windows group has two—View and Window; the Help group has one. Once we have set up this logical scheme, it becomes very easy for all child windows to modify the main menu at will. Child windows can then add and delete both groups and menu items. Looking over the categories, most frequently a child window would like to add an Object group for those pop-up menus that are unique to it. OK, so this isn't a text on OLE, but you should still consider which is the best group in which to place your menu items.

The installation of the menu item is done in **OnCreate**. If there are no instances yet, access is made to the main menu by dynamically obtaining a pointer to the main **CMDIFrameWnd** and using the member function **GetMenu** which returns a pointer to the main menu, an instance of **CMenu**. This pointer is then used to get a further pointer to the View pop-up menu at offset 2, using **GetSubMenu** which also returns a **CMenu** pointer.

```
CMenu *ptrmenu = AfxGetApp()->m_pMainWnd->GetMenu ();
CMenu *ptrsmenu = ptrmenu->GetSubMenu (2);
```

Then I check to see if the View pop-up menu already contains the Hide/Show Tool Box menu item by using the **CMenu** function **GetMenuState** and passing it the command ID of the menu item and the ID MF_BYCOMMAND, which tells the function to look for this specific command ID in the pop-up menu. If the menu item is not found, the function returns a -1. If the Hide/Show menu item is not yet installed, then I load the menu item from the resource file and use the **CMenu** function **AppendMenu** to install it.

```
if (ptrsmenu->GetMenuState (IDB_TOOLBOX, MF_BYCOMMAND) == -1) {
  char menuitem[40];
  LoadString (AfxGetApp()->m_hInstance, IDB_TOOLBOX, menuitem,
          sizeof(menuitem));
  ptrsmenu->AppendMenu (MF_ENABLED | MF_STRING, IDB_TOOLBOX,
                  menuitem);
}
```

Next, in **OnCreate,** the tool box is constructed exactly as was done in chapter 11; no changes are required.

Conversely, in **OnDestroy**, if this is the last DrawWin child, the menu item must be removed. If **numdraw** is now zero, obtain a pointer first to the main menu and then to the View pop-up menu. Then use the **DeleteMenu** function to remove the Hide/Show Tool Box menu item by passing it the command ID and the MF_BYCOMMAND identifier.

```
numdraw--;
if (numdraw==0) {
  CMenu *ptrmenu = AfxGetApp()->m_pMainWnd->GetMenu ();
  CMenu *ptrsmenu = ptrmenu->GetSubMenu (2);
  ptrsmenu->DeleteMenu (IDB_TOOLBOX, MF_BYCOMMAND);
}
// now continue destroying this MDI child
CMDIChildWnd::OnDestroy ();
```

Similarly there are no significant changes to **UpdateStatusBar**, **OnLButtonDown**, **OnMouseMove**, or **OnLButtonUp**.

The tool box requires more action on our part only when it becomes floating; while docked, the **CMDIFrameWnd** handles it. Therefore, we must be able to detect when Draw is about to be minimized and hide the tool bar before iconization. Later, when the icon is about to be restored, we must reshow the tool box. (We could create another BOOL member to keep track of whether the window was hidden by the user before the minimization request and, upon restoration, preserve that setting. Here, upon restoration, the tool box always reappears.)

 Windows 3.1 Porting Tip: Under Windows 3.1, when a window is about to become minimized, the WM_SYSCOMMAND is sent with the SC_MINIMIZE flag enabled.

As a result, the **OnSysCommand** function was often used to check for minimization. Be careful using this message handler. When the user pressed the left mouse button on the title bar, a WM_SYSCOMMAND message is sent, but the flags have nearly all possibilities set! This occurs because the user could next begin dragging the window (a Move) or could double-click (Maximize/Restore), for example. So here again is the "single-click, drag, or double-click on an object" problem we examined much earlier. Since Windows 95 does not know for certain the exact meaning of the first Left Button Down on the title bar just yet, many of the flags are set. Windows 95 then begins a potential Move Window operation, but quickly alters it to a Maximize or Restore operation. The end result is that, if you check only the flags for SC_MINIMIZED, you may respond to a nonexistent request as the user is actually moving the window.

In this application, only the fact that the application is now minimized is needed so that we can hide the tool box. A far safer place to check for this occurrence is in **OnSize**. A WM_SIZE message is also sent to the window after it has been minimized notifying the window that it is now iconized. The flags are set to the identifier SIZE_MINIMIZED. Thus, in **OnSize** check for iconization and, if iconization has taken place, hide the tool box. Next, whenever an iconized window is about to be restored, Windows sends that window a WM_QUERYOPEN message to see if it wishes to restore. If it does, it returns TRUE. Therefore, respond to **OnQueryOpen** messages to restore the tool box.

Finally, the **SetFocus** function makes the MDI child window that was moved the active window. Failure to invoke **SetFocus** would result in *no* window or the tool box being active. In this manner, when the window is moved, the focus is still the Draw window itself, which avoids making the user reselect the Draw window to make it the active window.

In **OnSize**, if the MDI child has become iconized and if the tool box is visible, I send the Hide message.

```
if (flags & SIZE_MINIMIZED)
 if (toolbox.GetStyle() & WS_VISIBLE)
  SendMessage (WM_COMMAND, IDB_TOOLBOX, OL);
```

In **OnMove**, which is invoked whenever the MDI child window is moved, if the tool box is visible, it is also repositioned by converting the upper-left coordinates of the MDI window (0,0) into full-screen coordinates and invoking **SetWindowPos**, specifying not to change its size, only its position.

```
CMDIChildWnd::OnMove (x, y);
if (toolbox.GetStyle() & WS_VISIBLE) {
 CPoint pt (0,0);
 ClientToScreen (&pt);
 toolbox.SetWindowPos (NULL, pt.x, pt.y, 0, 0,
                       SWP_NOSIZE | SWP_NOZORDER);
 SetFocus();
}
```

In **OnQueryOpen**, when the MDI window is about to be restored, I send the Reshow Tool Box message.

```
SendMessage (WM_COMMAND, IDB_TOOLBOX, OL);
return CMDIChildWnd::OnQueryOpen ();
```

Finally, in **OnClose**, the MDI frame's **fastclose** member is checked to determine if the Express Close is in effect, thereby bypassing normal Can Close messages. The coding is exactly the same as that of ScrolWin.

So, with a minimal effort, both ScrolWin and DrawWin have been converted into MDI children. The next step is to examine how to install Text Editors as MDI children and then how to conduct cut and paste operations—in other words, using the clipboard.

12.6.4 Listing for File: DrawWin.cpp—Pgm12a—Excerpts

```
...
/******************************************************************/
/*                                                              */
/* DrawWin Events Response Table                                */
/*                                                              */
/******************************************************************/
BEGIN_MESSAGE_MAP(DrawWin, CMDIChildWnd)
...
 ON_WM_DESTROY ()
 ON_WM_CLOSE()
 ON_WM_SIZE()
 ON_WM_MOVE()
 ON_WM_QUERYOPEN()
...
END_MESSAGE_MAP()

int    DrawWin::numdraw = 0;   // number of DrawWin - controls hide/show menu item
...

/******************************************************************/
/*                                                              */
/* OnDestroy: destroy child window and possibly remove the hide show menu   */
/*                                                              */
/******************************************************************/
void     DrawWin::OnDestroy () {
 numdraw--;           // dec number of draw children
 if (numdraw==0) { // must remove our menu item for hide/show tool box
  // get access to menu and remove hide/show menu item
  CMenu *ptrmenu = AfxGetApp()->m_pMainWnd->GetMenu ();
  CMenu *ptrsmenu = ptrmenu->GetSubMenu (2);
  ptrsmenu->DeleteMenu (IDB_TOOLBOX, MF_BYCOMMAND);
 }
 // now continue destroying this MDI child
 CMDIChildWnd::OnDestroy ();
}

/******************************************************************/
/*                                                              */
/* OnCreate: construct our tool box                             */
/*                                                              */
/******************************************************************/
int      DrawWin::OnCreate (LPCREATESTRUCT lpCS) {
 int retcd;
 if ((retcd = CMDIChildWnd::OnCreate (lpCS)) !=0) return -1;
```

```
if (numdraw==0) { // this is the first, so install hide/show tool box menu item
  // acquire the main menu and then the offset 3 (4th) pop up menu
  // so that we can append the hide/show tool box item if needed
  CMenu *ptrmenu = AfxGetApp()->m_pMainWnd->GetMenu ();
  CMenu *ptrsmenu = ptrmenu->GetSubMenu (2);
  // so load in a new menu item and install in View menu
  char menuitem[40];
  LoadString (AfxGetApp()->m_hInstance, IDB_TOOLBOX, menuitem,
                                         sizeof(menuitem));
  ptrsmenu->AppendMenu (MF_ENABLED | MF_STRING, IDB_TOOLBOX, menuitem);
}
numdraw++;

// construct the tool box: create, load its bitmap, assign its command IDs
if (toolbox.Create (this, WS_CHILD | WS_VISIBLE | CBRS_SIZE_FIXED |
                          CBRS_TOP | CBRS_TOOLTIPS | CBRS_FLYBY, IDB_TOOLBOX)
    && toolbox.LoadBitmap (IDB_TOOLBOX)
    && toolbox.SetButtons (buttons_box, sizeof(buttons_box)/sizeof(UINT)));
else return -1;

toolbox.SetColumns (2); // set the tool box to 2 columns

// now install flyover hints and the tool tips for both controlbar & tool box
toolbox.SetBarStyle (toolbox.GetBarStyle() | CBRS_TOOLTIPS | CBRS_FLYBY);

// now notify control to accept any form of docking
toolbox.EnableDocking (CBRS_ALIGN_ANY);

// notify the framewindow of docking requirements
EnableDocking (CBRS_ALIGN_ANY);

// and dock both control bar and tool box at top
DockControlBar (&toolbox, AFX_IDW_DOCKBAR_RIGHT);

// insert captions to be shown when the tool bars are floating
    toolbox.SetWindowText(_T("Box"));

UpdateStatusBar (); // display initial pen color and width on the status bar
return retcd;
}
...

/*****************************************************************************/
/*                                                                          */
/* OnSize: on going minimized, hide any visible tool box                    */
/*                                                                          */
/*****************************************************************************/

void      DrawWin::OnSize (UINT flags, int width, int height) {

CMDIChildWnd::OnSize (flags, width, height);

if (flags & SIZE_MINIMIZED)                // check if we are now minimized
  if (toolbox.GetStyle() & WS_VISIBLE)  // yes, so is tool box visible now
    SendMessage (WM_COMMAND, IDB_TOOLBOX, 0L); // yes, so hide it
}

/*****************************************************************************/
/*                                                                          */
```

```
/* OnMove: force tool box to reposition when parent move position        */
/*                                                                       */
/***********************************************************************/
void        DrawWin::OnMove (int x, int y) {

 CMDIChildWnd::OnMove (x, y);

 if (toolbox.GetStyle() & WS_VISIBLE)  // if tool box visible now, yes move it
   toolbox.SetWindowPos (NULL, 0, 0, 0, 0, SWP_NOSIZE | SWP_NOZORDER);
 }

/***********************************************************************/
/*                                                                     */
/* EvQueryOpen: when restoring from icon, reshow tool box              */
/*                                                                     */
/***********************************************************************/
BOOL        DrawWin::OnQueryOpen () {
 SendMessage (WM_COMMAND, IDB_TOOLBOX, 0L); // force show tool box
 return CMDIChildWnd::OnQueryOpen ();           // and continue the Restore
 }
 ...

/***********************************************************************/
/*                                                                     */
/* OnClose:  query user if we can terminate this drawing               */
/*                                                                     */
/***********************************************************************/
void        DrawWin::OnClose () {
 if (((FrameWin*) GetParentFrame())->fastclose == FALSE)
   if (DisplayMsg(IDS_MSG_QUERY, IDS_DRAWQUIT, MB_YESNO | MB_ICONQUESTION) ==
      IDYES) MDIDestroy ();
 }
 ...
```

With fairly minimal additional coding, MDI now allows a very complex application environment. If you always develop your projects with the division of labor as we have been doing in the preceding chapters, only minor changes are required to install that application into a MDI larger application. Next, let's implement the Cut/Paste operations.

Using the Clipboard

13.1 INTRODUCTION

Accessing the clipboard to exchange data between applications or to provide Cut and Paste operations is extremely easy to do. Built-in support for the clipboard is provided by MFC. In fact, **CEdit** controls provide the support automatically with no user coding required. Data can be stored on the clipboard in several formats. Table 13.1 shows the more common clipboard formats.

Table 13.1 Common Clipboard Format

Identifier	Meaning
CF_TEXT	null-terminated ASCI text with <CRLF>
CF_BITMAP	device-dependent bitmaps
CF_DIB	device-independent bitmaps
CF_PALETTE	color palette, usually with dibs
CF_WAVE	.WAV sound data
CF_PRIVATEFIRST	the first type of totally program-defined data
CF_PRIVATELAST	the highest user-defined clipboard format type

An application can cut and paste nearly anything desired such as database records, spreadsheet information, and so on merely by using a clipboard type within the range of the last two identifiers. In this chapter I examine the two most commonly encountered formats—CF_TEXT and CF_BITMAP. The general cycle of action to be followed when using the clipboard is a simple one.

For pastes:

      If the clipboard contains type of data desired

         Open the clipboard

         Copy the clipboard data into your own data member

         Close the clipboard

For cut and copy:

      If there is a selection made

         Open the clipboard

         Create a copy of your data

         Give that copy permanently to the clipboard

         Close the clipboard

The Close operation is vital. During the entire time that your application has the clipboard opened, *no* other applications can access the clipboard.

Design Rule 46: **Always close the clipboard when finished copying, cutting, or pasting.**

When copying to the clipboard, the application provides a *copy* of the data. Windows 95 takes over complete ownership of that data. Do not attempt to reference that data after giving it to the clipboard.

Design Rule 47: **When giving an object to the clipboard, Windows 95 takes complete ownership of that object. Do not attempt to use or reference that object after giving it to the clipboard. If you need to reference that object, make a global memory copy and give Windows 95 that copy.**

The only complicating factor to clipboard access is the requisite **selection** of the data to be cut/copied. If the data is text, for simplicity, I let the **CEdit** control handle the selection process internally. But for graphics, I must implement the selection process. The method I use here emulates the method of graphics selection in the Paintbrush application. Let's begin with the simpler of the two types—text.

13.2 Handling Text with the Clipboard

For Cut/Copy actions in functions **CmEditCut** and **CmEditCopy,** by using some functionality of the **CEdit** control, I do not have to perform the text selection actions. Instead, I call the member function **GetSel**

```
int startpos, endpos;
ptreditwin->GetSel startpos, endpos);
```

where the pointer is assumed to be that of a **CEdit** control. The two positions are passed by reference and contain the offsets of the selected text within the edit buffer of the control. If **endpos** is 0, none is selected.

With MFC the Cut/Copy process is simplified by using the **CEdit** provided functions **Cut** and **Copy**.

```
ptreditwin->Copy ();
ptreditwin->Cut ();
```

These two **CEdit** functions perform the sequence of opening, clearing, copying the data, and closing the clipboard for us. The Paste operation of **CmEditPaste** is equally simple to perform. The first step is to verify that text is available. This is done using the **IsClipboardFormatAvailable** function, which does not require the clipboard to be opened.

```
BOOL IsClipboardFormatAvailable (CF_TEXT);
```

Here, the function is passed an ORed series of acceptable clipboard formats that the application can handle. The **CEdit** function **Paste** handles all of the work for us, and typical coding becomes simply

```
if (IsClipboardFormatAvailable (CF_TEXT))
  ptreditwin->Paste (); // paste from clipboard
```

13.3 Pgm13a: MDI Sample Clipboard Action Program

Pgm13a illustrates both types of clipboard objects—text and graphics. It is a MDI program that can launch three different children. The Draw example from the previous chapter provides an elementary graphics window. From the File menu, two different Text Editors can be launched. Choosing File | New or Open launches the EditWin MDI child that uses a **CEdit** control as its client window. EditWin implements the Cut and Paste operations discussed above.

Begin by studying the resource file excerpts to see the menu setup. Observe that about the only significant change was the addition of the standard Edit pop-up menu. (ScrollWin was removed.) Figure 13.1 illustrates the application running with one child of the three types, tiled vertically.

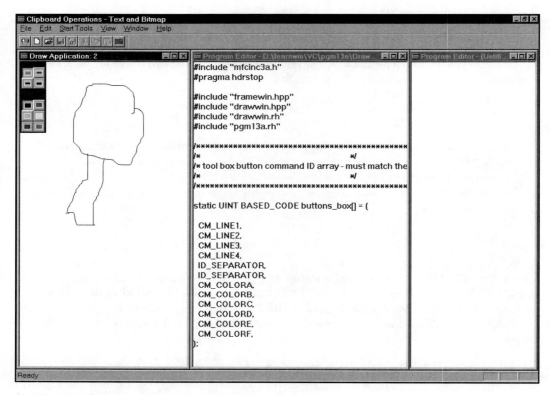

Fig. 13.1 Pgm13a with Three Child Windows Tiled

13.3.1 Listing for File: Pgm13a.rc—Pgm13a—Excerpts

```
...
IDB_MAINFRAME     BITMAP   MOVEABLE PURE      "TOOLBAR.BMP"

MAINMENU MENU
BEGIN
    POPUP "&File"
    BEGIN
        MENUITEM "&New",                CM_FILENEW
        MENUITEM "&Open...",            CM_FILEOPEN
        MENUITEM "&Save",               CM_FILESAVE, GRAYED
        MENUITEM "Save &As...",         CM_FILESAVEAS, GRAYED
        MENUITEM SEPARATOR
        MENUITEM "E&xit\tAlt+F4",       CM_EXIT
    END

    POPUP "&Edit"
    BEGIN
        MENUITEM "&Undo\tAlt+BkSp",     CM_EDITUNDO, GRAYED
```

```
                MENUITEM SEPARATOR
                MENUITEM "Cu&t\tShift+Del",          CM_EDITCUT, GRAYED
                MENUITEM "&Copy\tCtrl+Ins",          CM_EDITCOPY, GRAYED
                MENUITEM "&Paste\tShift+Ins",        CM_EDITPASTE, GRAYED
        END

        POPUP "&Start Tools"
        BEGIN
                MENUITEM "&Draw" ,                   CM_DRAW
        END

        POPUP "&View"
        BEGIN
                MENUITEM "&Toolbar",                 ID_VIEW_TOOLBAR
                MENUITEM "&Status Bar",              ID_VIEW_STATUS_BAR
                MENUITEM SEPARATOR
        END

        POPUP "&Window"
        BEGIN
            MENUITEM "&Cascade",                CM_CASCADECHILDREN,  GRAYED
            MENUITEM "Tile &Horizontally",      CM_TILECHILDRENH,    GRAYED
            MENUITEM "Tile &Vertically",        CM_TILECHILDRENV,    GRAYED
            MENUITEM "Arrange &Icons",          CM_ARRANGEICONS,     GRAYED
            MENUITEM "C&lose All",              CM_CLOSECHILDREN,    GRAYED
        END

        POPUP "&Help"
        BEGIN
                MENUITEM "&About...",                CM_HELPABOUT
        END

END
...
STRINGTABLE DISCARDABLE // hints
BEGIN
        CM_FILENEW      "Creates a new document\nNew Document"
        CM_FILEOPEN     "Opens an existing document\nOpen Document"
...
        CM_HELPABOUT         "About the Fancy Dialog application"
        AFX_IDS_IDLEMESSAGE "Ready"
END
...
```

13.3.2 Listing for File: Resource.h—Pgm13a—Excerpts

```
...
#define IDB_MAINFRAME                      2  // id of main menu

#define CM_DRAW                 (WM_USER + 100) // launch draw window
#define CM_SCROLL               (WM_USER + 101) // launch scroll window
#define CM_HELPABOUT            (WM_USER + 102)
#define CM_EXIT                 (WM_USER + 103)
#define CM_CASCADECHILDREN      (WM_USER + 104)
#define CM_TILECHILDRENH        (WM_USER + 105)
#define CM_TILECHILDRENV        (WM_USER + 106)
```

```
#define CM_ARRANGEICONS       (WM_USER + 107)
#define CM_CLOSECHILDREN      (WM_USER + 108)
#define WM_CHILDDESTROY       (WM_USER + 109)
#define CM_FILENEW            (WM_USER + 110)
#define CM_FILEOPEN           (WM_USER + 111)
#define CM_FILESAVE           (WM_USER + 112)
#define CM_FILESAVEAS         (WM_USER + 113)
#define CM_EDITUNDO           (WM_USER + 114)
#define CM_EDITCUT            (WM_USER + 115)
#define CM_EDITCOPY           (WM_USER + 116)
#define CM_EDITPASTE          (WM_USER + 117)
...
```

13.3.3 Listing for File: DrawWin.rc—Pgm13a—Excerpts

```
...
IDB_TOOLBOX   BITMAP   MOVEABLE PURE    "TOOLBOX.BMP"

STRINGTABLE   // new menu item strings for tool box
{
  CM_LINE1          "Select 1 pixel line width\nLinewidth 1"
  CM_LINE2          "Select 2 pixels line width\nLinewidth 2"
  CM_LINE3          "Select 3 pixels line width\nLinewidth 3"
  CM_LINE4          "Select 4 pixels line width\nLinewidth 4"
  CM_COLORA         "Select Black as the drawing color\nBlack"
  CM_COLORB         "Select Red as the drawing color\nRed"
  CM_COLORC         "Select Green as the drawing color\nGreen"
  CM_COLORD         "Select Yellow as the drawing color\nYellow"
  CM_COLORE         "Select Blue as the drawing color\nBlue"
  CM_COLORF         "Select Purple as the drawing color\nPurple"

  IDS_DRAWQUIT      "Ok to close this drawing?"
  IDS_DRAWTITLE     "Make a Drawing"
  IDB_TOOLBOX       "Hide/Show Tool Box"
  IDS_DRAW          "Draw Application: "
}
...
```

13.3.4 Listing for File: DrawWin.rh—Pgm13a—Excerpts

```
...
#define IDB_TOOLBOX                    3       // the tool box bitmap

#define CM_LINE1          (WM_USER + 121)     // tool box buttons
#define CM_LINE2          (WM_USER + 122)
#define CM_LINE3          (WM_USER + 123)
#define CM_LINE4          (WM_USER + 124)
#define CM_COLORA         (WM_USER + 125)
#define CM_COLORB         (WM_USER + 126)
#define CM_COLORC         (WM_USER + 127)
#define CM_COLORD         (WM_USER + 128)
#define CM_COLORE         (WM_USER + 129)
#define CM_COLORF         (WM_USER + 130)

#define IDS_DRAWQUIT           2200            // quit this drawing query
```

```
#define IDS_DRAWTITLE            2201        // title of draw window
#define IDS_DRAW                 2202        // app title
...
```

13.3.5 Listing for File: EditWin.rc—Pgm13a—Excerpts

```
STRINGTABLE   // our apps
{
 IDS_EDIT,          "Program Editor - "
 IDS_MSG_NOTSAVE,   "File has not been saved. Save File now?"
 IDS_MSG_ERROR,     "Edit Program - Error Message"
 IDS_MSG_NOMEM,     "Out of memory. Close app. Free some memory. Try again."
 IDS_MSG_FILEERR,   "File Save Error. Try File Save As with valid filename."
 IDS_MSG_FILEOPEN,  "File Open Error. Try again with valid filename."
 IDS_MSG_FILEREAD,  "File Open Error. Unable to input the file."
 IDS_MSG_FILEWRT,   "File Save Error. Output failed - disk full. Try new disk."
 IDS_MSG_FILEBIG,   "We can only handle files up to 65,535 bytes long."
 IDS_MSG_EDIT,      "Program Editor - Quit Query"
 IDS_MSG_EDITQUIT,  "Do you want to quit editing this file?"
}
```

13.3.6 Listing for File: EditWin.rh—Pgm13a—Excerpts

```
...
#define EDITWINDOW          100    // id of CEdit control

#define IDS_MSG_ERROR       2050   // error header
#define IDS_MSG_NOMEM       2051   // out of memory
#define IDS_MSG_FILEOPEN    2052   // cannot open file
#define IDS_MSG_FILEBIG     2053   // file too large to edit
#define IDS_MSG_FILEREAD    2054   // read io error
#define IDS_MSG_NOTSAVE     2055   // file not saved msg
#define IDS_MSG_FILEERR     2056   // could not save file
#define IDS_MSG_FILEWRT     2057   // write error
#define IDS_MSG_EDITQUIT    2058   // want to quit msg
#define IDS_MSG_EDIT        2059   // quit header
#define IDS_EDIT            2060   // app id
...
```

There are no significant changes to the application class. The frame window class, FrameWin, which constructs the tool bar and manages the menu, now has two additional command handlers for the file operations as shown in the FrameWin.hpp file. Let's examine the excerpts from the FrameWin implementation to see the modification needed to launch the two edit children.

13.3.7 Listing for File: FrameWin.h—Pgm13a—Excerpts

```
...
/**************************************************************************/
/*                                                                        */
/* FrameWin Class Definition                                              */
/*                                                                        */
/**************************************************************************/
```

```
class FrameWin : public CMDIFrameWnd {
...
afx_msg void  CmFileNew ();                // start new text file
afx_msg void  CmFileOpen ();               // open existing text file
...
```

13.3.8 Listing for File: FrameWin.cpp—Pgm13a—Excerpts

```
...
/***************************************************************************/
/*                                                                       */
/* Control bar buttons and Status bar buttons                            */
/*                                                                       */
/* control bar buttons - IDs are command buttons                         */
/* same order as in the bitmap 'toolbar.bmp'                             */
/*                                                                       */
/***************************************************************************/
static UINT BASED_CODE buttons[] = {

  CM_EXIT,
  CM_FILENEW,
  CM_FILEOPEN,
  CM_FILESAVE,
  CM_FILESAVEAS,
  CM_EDITCUT,
  CM_EDITCOPY,
  CM_EDITPASTE,
  CM_DRAW,
};
...

/***************************************************************************/
/*                                                                       */
/* FrameWin Events Response Table                                        */
/*                                                                       */
/***************************************************************************/
BEGIN_MESSAGE_MAP(FrameWin, CMDIFrameWnd)
 ON_WM_CREATE ()
 ON_WM_CLOSE ()
 ON_COMMAND(CM_EXIT,            CmExit)
 ON_COMMAND(CM_FILENEW,         CmFileNew)
 ON_COMMAND(CM_FILEOPEN,        CmFileOpen)
 ON_COMMAND(CM_DRAW,            CmDraw)
 ON_COMMAND(CM_HELPABOUT,       CmHelpAbout)
 ON_COMMAND(CM_CASCADECHILDREN, CmCascadeChildren)
 ON_COMMAND(CM_TILECHILDRENH,   CmTileChildrenH)
 ON_COMMAND(CM_TILECHILDRENV,   CmTileChildrenV)
 ON_COMMAND(CM_ARRANGEICONS,    CmArrangeIcons)
 ON_COMMAND(CM_CLOSECHILDREN,   CmCloseChildren)
END_MESSAGE_MAP()

/***************************************************************************/
/*                                                                       */
/* Framewin: Construct the window object                                 */
```

```
/*                                                                      */
/***********************************************************************/

        FrameWin::FrameWin (const char* title) {
// create the MDI frame window
Create (NULL, title, WS_OVERLAPPEDWINDOW, rectDefault, NULL, "MAINMENU");
fastclose      = FALSE; // set no express close in operation
numberchildren = 0;     // set number of children to 0 for title additions
}
...

/***********************************************************************/
/*                                                                      */
/* CmFileOpen: open an existent file                                    */
/*                                                                      */
/***********************************************************************/

void      FrameWin::CmFileOpen () {
// create new transfer buffer
CFileDialog filedlg (TRUE,     // use Open dialog
                     "*.CPP", // default extension
                     "*.*",   // current file name
                     OFN_FILEMUSTEXIST | OFN_PATHMUSTEXIST | OFN_LONGNAMES,
                     "All Files (*.*)|*.*|CPP Files (*.CPP)|*.CPP|C Files "
                     "(*.C)|*.C|Header Files (*.H*)|*.H*||",
                     this);
// get user's filename choice
if (filedlg.DoModal () == IDOK) {              // user has chosen a file, so
 char filename[MAX_PATH];
 strcpy (filename, filedlg.GetPathName ()); // extract its filename
 char title[MAX_PATH + 80];
 LoadString (AfxGetApp()->m_hInstance, IDS_EDIT, title, sizeof(title));
 strcat (title, filename);
 // now launch the EditWin child
 EditWin *ptrwin = new EditWin (filename);  // allocate a child edit window
 if (!ptrwin->Create (NULL, title)) {
  delete ptrwin;
  return;
  }
 ptrwin->ShowWindow (SW_SHOW);
 numberchildren++;
 }
}
/***********************************************************************/
/*                                                                      */
/* CmFileNew: new file to edit                                          */
/*                                                                      */
/***********************************************************************/

void      FrameWin::CmFileNew () {
 char title[80];
 LoadString (AfxGetApp()->m_hInstance, IDS_EDIT, title, sizeof(title));
 strcat (title, "(Untitled)");
```

```
EditWin *ptrwin = new EditWin (""); // allocate a child edit window
if (!ptrwin->Create (NULL, title)) {
 delete ptrwin;
 return;
}
ptrwin->ShowWindow (SW_SHOW);
numberchildren++;
}
...
```

Both versions of EditWin are launched similarly. In the case of File | New, a NULL string is passed for the filename, while, with File | Open, the actual filename returned from the common File Open dialog is passed. The coding for this class is straightforward and modeled on sample program Pgm10b's FrameWin class. Notice how the earlier example has been converted into a MDI child. Classes derived from **CFrameWnd** are fairly easy to convert to **CMDIChildWnd**. I have added a helper function, **SetNoFileErr**, to help reduce the long file load sequence in **OnCreate**.

13.3.9 Listing for File: EditWin.h—Pgm13a—Excerpts

```
...
/*****************************************************************************/
/*                                                                         */
/* EditWin Class Definition                                                */
/*                                                                         */
/*****************************************************************************/

class EditWin : public CMDIChildWnd {

/*****************************************************************************/
/*                                                                         */
/* Class Data Members                                                      */
/*                                                                         */
/*****************************************************************************/

protected:

CEdit      *ptreditwin;        // pointer to our CEdit main window
char       filename[MAX_PATH]; // full path file spec

/*****************************************************************************/
/*                                                                         */
/* Class Functions:                                                        */
/*                                                                         */
/*****************************************************************************/

public:
            EditWin (char *);          // constructor
            ~EditWin () {}             // destructor

protected:

afx_msg int   OnCreate (LPCREATESTRUCT);   // load in file - make CEdit ctl
afx_msg void  OnDestroy ();                // paint the window - WM_PAINT
afx_msg void  OnClose ();                  // determines if app can quit yet
```

```
afx_msg void   OnSize (UINT, int, int);          // process window resize

               // utility functions
       void    SaveCheck ();                      // query user about saving file
       void    GetAvgCharDims ();                 // get average char dims for font
       void    SaveFile ();                       // save the file
       int     DisplayMsg (int, int, UINT);       // displays a message box
       void    SetNoFileErr (int, UINT);          // set for no file with open error

               // command processors
afx_msg void   CmFileSave ();                     // save the file with same name
afx_msg void   CmFileSaveAs ();                   // save with new name
afx_msg void   CmEditUndo ();                     // undo last change
afx_msg void   CmEditCut ();                      // cut to clipboard
afx_msg void   CmEditCopy ();                     // copy to clipboard
afx_msg void   CmEditPaste ();                    // paste from the clipboard

               // command enablers
afx_msg void   CmEnableFileSave (CCmdUI*);        // enable/disable FileSave
afx_msg void   CmEnableFileSaveAs (CCmdUI*);      // enable/disable FileSaveAs
afx_msg void   CmEnableEditUndo (CCmdUI*);        // enable/disable Edit Undo
afx_msg void   CmEnableEditCut  (CCmdUI*);        // enable/disable Edit Cut
afx_msg void   CmEnableEditCopy (CCmdUI*);        // enable/disable Edit Copy
afx_msg void   CmEnableEditPaste (CCmdUI*);       // enable/disable Edit Paste
...
```

The MDI conversion removes most of the coding from the constructor of EditWin which now has only to save the passed filename to be opened and to set the pointer to the **CEdit** window to NULL. The **Create** function is now handled when the MDI child is launched. In the function **OnDestroy** first check to see if the data in the **CEdit** control has been modified; if so, invoke **SaveCheck** to see if the user wishes to save the text. Then delete the **CEdit** control and the EditWin proper.

```
if (ptreditwin->GetModify ()) SaveCheck ();
if (ptreditwin) delete ptreditwin;
CMDIChildWnd::OnDestroy ();
```

OnCreate parallels the earlier FrameWin from Pgm10b. Notice that the use of the helper function **SetNoFileErr** lessens the amount of duplicated coding, providing the common code to display an error message, set the filename to NULL, and load NULL text into the **CEdit** control and reset the control's key status indicators.

```
DisplayMsg (IDS_MSG_ERROR, id2, flags);
filename[0]  = 0;
ptreditwin->SetWindowText (NULL);
ptreditwin->SetModify (FALSE);
ptreditwin->EmptyUndoBuffer ();
```

How is the Edit | Undo process handled? First, a command enabler, **CmEnable-EditUndo**, is set up to enable the menu item only when the edit control has an operation that could be undone. The **CEdit** member function **CanUndo** returns TRUE when there is something that could be undone. The enabler coding becomes

```
ptrenabler->Enable (ptreditwin->CanUndo());
```

Then, to actually undo the action, the command response function **CmEditUndo** invokes the **CEdit** member **Undo**.

```
ptreditwin->Undo ();
```

All of the other new command handlers and enablers are as simple as those we have already discussed. In fact, in a real application, all of these one-line functions would likely be coded in-line in the header file similar to the following:

```
afx_msg void  CmEditUndo ()   {ptreditwin->Undo ();}
afx_msg void  CmEditCut ()    {ptreditwin->Cut ();}
afx_msg void  CmEditCopy ()   {ptreditwin->Copy ();}
afx_msg void  CmEditPaste () {if (IsClipboardFormatAvailable (CF_TEXT))
                                  ptreditwin->Paste ();}
afx_msg void  CmEnableFileSave   (CCmdUI *p) {p->Enable (1);}
afx_msg void  CmEnableFileSaveAs (CCmdUI *p) {p->Enable (1);}
afx_msg void  CmEnableEditUndo   (CCmdUI *p) {
                        p->Enable (ptreditwin->CanUndo());}
afx_msg void  CmEnableEditCut   (CCmdUI *p) {
                        p->Enable (ptreditwin->GetSel()>0? 1: 0);}
afx_msg void  CmEnableEditCopy (CCmdUI *p) {
                        p->Enable (ptreditwin->GetSel()>0? 1: 0);}
afx_msg void  CmEnableEditPaste (CCmdUI *p) {
                     p->Enable (IsClipboardFormatAvailable (CF_TEXT));}
```

13.3.10 Listing for File: EditWin.cpp—Pgm13a—Excerpts

```
...
/************************************************************************/
/*                                                                      */
/* EditWin Events Response Table                                        */
/*                                                                      */
/************************************************************************/

BEGIN_MESSAGE_MAP(EditWin, CMDIChildWnd)
 ON_WM_CREATE ()
 ON_WM_DESTROY ()
 ON_WM_CLOSE()
 ON_WM_SIZE()
 ON_COMMAND(CM_FILESAVE,          CmFileSave)
 ON_COMMAND(CM_FILESAVEAS,        CmFileSaveAs)
 ON_COMMAND(CM_EDITUNDO,          CmEditUndo)
 ON_COMMAND(CM_EDITCUT,           CmEditCut)
 ON_COMMAND(CM_EDITCOPY,          CmEditCopy)
 ON_COMMAND(CM_EDITPASTE,         CmEditPaste)
 ON_UPDATE_COMMAND_UI(CM_FILESAVE,    CmEnableFileSave)
 ON_UPDATE_COMMAND_UI(CM_FILESAVEAS,  CmEnableFileSaveAs)
 ON_UPDATE_COMMAND_UI(CM_EDITUNDO,    CmEnableEditUndo)
 ON_UPDATE_COMMAND_UI(CM_EDITCUT,     CmEnableEditCut)
 ON_UPDATE_COMMAND_UI(CM_EDITCOPY,    CmEnableEditCopy)
 ON_UPDATE_COMMAND_UI(CM_EDITPASTE,   CmEnableEditPaste)
END_MESSAGE_MAP()

/************************************************************************/
/*                                                                      */
```

```
/* EditWin: Construct the window object - save file name                */
/*                                                                       */
/*************************************************************************/

          EditWin::EditWin (char *filenm) : CMDIChildWnd () {

 strcpy (filename, filenm); // save the filename
 ptreditwin = NULL;         // set no edit control as yet
}

/*************************************************************************/
/*                                                                       */
/* OnDestroy: delete inited items                                        */
/*                                                                       */
/*************************************************************************/

void     EditWin::OnDestroy () {

 if (ptreditwin->GetModify ()) SaveCheck (); // save file if needed
 if (ptreditwin) delete ptreditwin;          // remove the edit window

 // and destroy this child
 CMDIChildWnd::OnDestroy ();
}

/*************************************************************************/
/*                                                                       */
/* OnCreate: load in the file or new file and alloc a CEdit control      */
/*                                                                       */
/*************************************************************************/

int      EditWin::OnCreate (LPCREATESTRUCT lpCS) {

 int retcd = CMDIChildWnd::OnCreate (lpCS); // pass along to base class

 CRect rect;
 GetClientRect (&rect);

 // allocate a CEdit control as a client window to handle the file editing
 ptreditwin = new CEdit;
 ptreditwin->Create (WS_CHILD | WS_VISIBLE | ES_AUTOHSCROLL | ES_AUTOVSCROLL |
                     ES_MULTILINE | ES_WANTRETURN, rect, this, EDITWINDOW);

 // if not able to build CEdit, display error
 if (!ptreditwin) {
  DisplayMsg (IDS_MSG_ERROR, IDS_MSG_NOMEM, MB_OK);
  return -1;
 }

 // load a null file or load the real file into the CEdit control
 if (filename[0] == 0) {
  ptreditwin->SetWindowText (NULL);    // send new text to CEdit window
  ptreditwin->SetModify (FALSE);       // set CEdit not modified yet
  ptreditwin->EmptyUndoBuffer ();      // clear CEdit's undo buffer
  return retcd;
 }

 // attempt to open the file
 HANDLE hfile = CreateFile (filename, GENERIC_READ, 0, NULL, OPEN_EXISTING,
                           FILE_ATTRIBUTE_NORMAL, NULL);
```

```
 if (hfile == INVALID_HANDLE_VALUE) {
  // file create failed, so show err and install null file
  SetNoFileErr (IDS_MSG_FILEOPEN , MB_OK | MB_ICONSTOP);
  return -1;
 }
 // get file size
 DWORD filesize = SetFilePointer (hfile, 0L, NULL, FILE_END);
 SetFilePointer (hfile, 0L, NULL, FILE_BEGIN); // reset back to start

 // CEdit can handle upto 64K absolute maximum - so we must check filesize
 if (filesize > 65535L) {
  // show err and install null file
  SetNoFileErr (IDS_MSG_FILEBIG, MB_OK);
  CloseHandle (hfile);
  return -1;
 }
 // allocate a file input buffer
 HANDLE  hbuffer = GlobalAlloc (GMEM_MOVEABLE, filesize+1); // for null term
 if (hbuffer==NULL) {  // error, not enough memory for buffer
  // show err and install null file
  SetNoFileErr (IDS_MSG_NOMEM, MB_OK | MB_ICONSTOP);
  CloseHandle (hfile);
  return -1;
 }
 char *ptrbuf = (char*) GlobalLock (hbuffer);// get locked ptr to global buffer
 // input the whole file
 DWORD actsz;
 ReadFile (hfile, ptrbuf, filesize, &actsz, NULL);
 CloseHandle (hfile);                    // close the file

 if (actsz != filesize) {                // input read error
  // show err and install null file
  SetNoFileErr (IDS_MSG_FILEREAD, MB_OK | MB_ICONSTOP);
  GlobalUnlock (hbuffer);                // remove the global memory
  GlobalFree   (hbuffer);
  return -1;
 }
 // install the text file into the CEdit control
 ptrbuf [filesize] = 0;                  // insert null terminator for CEdit
 ptreditwin->SetWindowText (ptrbuf); // set CEdit to new text
 ptreditwin->SetModify (FALSE);         // set CEdit to unmodified
 ptreditwin->EmptyUndoBuffer ();        // clear CEdit's undo buffer
 GlobalUnlock (hbuffer);                // unlock file buffer
 GlobalFree   (hbuffer);                // and free global memory
 return retcd;
}
/***************************************************************************/
/*                                                                         */
/* SetNoFileErr: display file open error and install null file in CEdit   */
/*                                                                         */
/***************************************************************************/
void     EditWin::SetNoFileErr (int id2, UINT flags) {
 DisplayMsg (IDS_MSG_ERROR, id2, flags); // display the error msg
```

```
  filename[0]  = 0;                       // install untitled new file
  ptreditwin->SetWindowText (NULL);       // send null text to CEdit window
  ptreditwin->SetModify (FALSE);          // set CEdit not modified yet
  ptreditwin->EmptyUndoBuffer ();         // clear CEdit's undo buffer
}
...
/***************************************************************************/
/*                                                                         */
/* SaveCheck: query user about needed file save                           */
/*                                                                         */
/***************************************************************************/
void      EditWin::SaveCheck () {

 // based on user request and whether or not file has a name, send save msgs
 if (DisplayMsg (IDS_MSG_NOTSAVE,
                 IDS_MSG_QUERY, MB_YESNO | MB_ICONQUESTION) == IDYES) {
  if (filename[0] == 0)
     SendMessage (WM_COMMAND, CM_FILESAVEAS, 0L);
  else
     SendMessage (WM_COMMAND, CM_FILESAVE, 0L);
 }
}

/***************************************************************************/
/*                                                                         */
/* CmFileSave: save an existent file                                      */
/*                                                                         */
/***************************************************************************/
void      EditWin::CmFileSave () {

 // if no name, use SaveAs otherwise use SaveFile
 if (filename[0]==0)  SendMessage (WM_COMMAND, CM_FILESAVEAS, 0L);
 else SaveFile();
}

/***************************************************************************/
/*                                                                         */
/* SaveFile: write the file                                               */
/*                                                                         */
/***************************************************************************/
void      EditWin::SaveFile () {

 // allocate a file buffer based upon current size in the CEdit control
 long filesize = ptreditwin->GetWindowTextLength ();
 HANDLE hbuffer = GlobalAlloc (GMEM_MOVEABLE, filesize);
 if (hbuffer==NULL) {   // error, not enough memory for buffer
  DisplayMsg (IDS_MSG_ERROR, IDS_MSG_NOMEM, MB_OK | MB_ICONSTOP);
  return;
 }
 char *ptrbuf = (char*) GlobalLock (hbuffer);  // get locked ptr to glbl buffer

 // transfer the updated text from CEdit control into global memory
 ptreditwin->GetWindowText (ptrbuf, ptreditwin->GetWindowTextLength ());

 // open the file, replacing any existing file
```

```
HANDLE hfile = CreateFile (filename, GENERIC_WRITE, 0, NULL, CREATE_ALWAYS,
                           FILE_ATTRIBUTE_NORMAL, NULL);
if (hfile == INVALID_HANDLE_VALUE) { // file create failed, so display error
 DisplayMsg (IDS_MSG_ERROR,IDS_MSG_FILEERR , MB_OK | MB_ICONSTOP);
 GlobalUnlock (hbuffer);                   // unlock buffer
 GlobalFree (hbuffer);                     // and free the global memory
 return;
}

// write the whole file
DWORD actsz;
WriteFile (hfile, ptrbuf, filesize, &actsz, NULL);
CloseHandle (hfile);                                  // close file and
GlobalUnlock (hbuffer);                               // unlock buffer
GlobalFree   (hbuffer);                               // and remove global memory

if (actsz != (DWORD) filesize)                    // if write fails, show error
 DisplayMsg (IDS_MSG_ERROR, IDS_MSG_FILEWRT, MB_OK | MB_ICONSTOP);
else ptreditwin->SetModify (FALSE);               // set CEdit to unmodified
}
/***************************************************************************/
/*                                                                         */
/* CmFileSaveAs: Save an existent file with a new name                     */
/*                                                                         */
/***************************************************************************/
void      EditWin::CmFileSaveAs () {
 // set up transfer buffer
 CFileDialog filedlg (FALSE,    // use SaveAs dialog
                      "*.CPP", // default extension
                      "*.*",   // current file name
                      OFN_HIDEREADONLY | OFN_OVERWRITEPROMPT | OFN_LONGNAMES,
                      "All Files (*.*)|*.*|CPP Files (*.CPP)|*.CPP|C Files"
                      " (*.C)|*.C|Header Files (*.H*)|*.H*||",
                      this);
 strcpy (filedlg.m_ofn.lpstrFile, filename); // install current name
 if (filedlg.DoModal () == IDOK) {               // user has chosen a file, so
  strcpy (filename, filedlg.GetPathName ()); // extract its filename
  SaveFile ();                               // save the file
  char title[MAX_PATH + 80];                 // construct window title
  LoadString (AfxGetApp()->m_hInstance, IDS_EDIT, title, sizeof(title));
  strcat (title, filename);
  SetWindowText (title);                     // install new concatenated title
 }
}
/***************************************************************************/
/*                                                                         */
/* CmEnableEditUndo: enables/disables edit undo menu item                  */
/*                                                                         */
/***************************************************************************/
void      EditWin::CmEnableEditUndo (CCmdUI *ptrenabler) {
 ptrenabler->Enable (ptreditwin->CanUndo());
}
```

```
/***************************************************************************/
/*                                                                       */
/* CmEnableEditCut:  enables/disables edit cut  menu item                */
/*                                                                       */
/***************************************************************************/
void     EditWin::CmEnableEditCut (CCmdUI *ptrenabler) {

 ptrenabler->Enable (ptreditwin->GetSel()>0? 1: 0);
}
/***************************************************************************/
/*                                                                       */
/* CmEnableEditCopy: enables/disables edit copy menu item                */
/*                                                                       */
/***************************************************************************/
void     EditWin::CmEnableEditCopy (CCmdUI *ptrenabler) {

 ptrenabler->Enable (ptreditwin->GetSel()>0? 1: 0);
}
/***************************************************************************/
/*                                                                       */
/* CmEnableEditPaste: enables/disables edit paste menu item              */
/*                                                                       */
/***************************************************************************/
void     EditWin::CmEnableEditPaste (CCmdUI *ptrenabler) {

 ptrenabler->Enable (IsClipboardFormatAvailable (CF_TEXT));
}
/***************************************************************************/
/*                                                                       */
/* CmEnableFileSave: enables/disables file save menu item                */
/*                                                                       */
/***************************************************************************/
void     EditWin::CmEnableFileSave (CCmdUI *ptrenabler) {

 ptrenabler->Enable (1);
}
/***************************************************************************/
/*                                                                       */
/* CmEnableFileSaveAs: enables/disables file save menu item              */
/*                                                                       */
/***************************************************************************/
void     EditWin::CmEnableFileSaveAs (CCmdUI *ptrenabler) {

 ptrenabler->Enable (1);
}
/***************************************************************************/
/*                                                                       */
/* OnClose:  query user if we can terminate this drawing                 */
/*                                                                       */
/***************************************************************************/
void     EditWin::OnClose () {
```

```
 if (ptreditwin->GetModify ()) SaveCheck (); //save file if needed
 if (((FrameWin*) GetParentFrame())->fastclose == FALSE)
   if (DisplayMsg(IDS_MSG_EDITQUIT, IDS_MSG_QUERY, MB_YESNO | MB_ICONQUESTION) ==
       IDYES) MDIDestroy ();
}
...
/**************************************************************************/
/*                                                                      */
/* CmEditCut: Remove text data and place on clipboard                   */
/*                                                                      */
/**************************************************************************/

void       EditWin::CmEditCut () {

 ptreditwin->Cut (); // cut it to clipboard
}
/**************************************************************************/
/*                                                                      */
/* CmEditCopy: copy text to clipboard                                   */
/*                                                                      */
/**************************************************************************/

void       EditWin::CmEditCopy () {

 ptreditwin->Copy (); // copy it to clipboard
}
/**************************************************************************/
/*                                                                      */
/* CmEditPaste: Paste text from the clipboard                           */
/*                                                                      */
/**************************************************************************/

void       EditWin::CmEditPaste () {

 if (IsClipboardFormatAvailable (CF_TEXT))
   ptreditwin->Paste (); // paste from clipboard
}
/**************************************************************************/
/*                                                                      */
/* CmEditUndo: Undo last change                                         */
/*                                                                      */
/**************************************************************************/

void       EditWin::CmEditUndo () {

 ptreditwin->Undo ();
}
```

13.4 HANDLING BITMAPS ON THE CLIPBOARD

Transferring bitmaps to and from the clipboard requires much more effort on our part
because there is no automatic selection process for us to use. Therefore, I begin by discussing exactly how the process should occur from the user's perspective. My model is
the Paintbrush program.

Paintbrush has a bitmap button on its tool box to select Cut/Copy operations. Rather than add that complexity, I use a common alternative method—right mouse button presses. The standard Windows 95 method for selection of a graphical area for Cut/Paste operations involves pressing the right button at the upper-left corner and dragging to the lower-right corner. As the mouse is being dragged, a dotted frame or rectangle appears around the selected portion of the image. When the button is released, one sees the dotted frame outlining the selected area.

If the button is re-pressed, then that original selection is replaced by the beginning of a new one, repeated until the user is satisfied, at which point the menu item Cut or Copy is selected. Note that these menu items are enabled whenever a selection has been made and is outlined by the dotted frame rectangle. After Cut/Copy is selected, that portion of the image is copied onto the clipboard. The dotted frame then disappears. If a cut was requested, the dotted rectangle is filled with the background color (white here).

When a bitmap image is on the clipboard, the Edit | Paste menu item becomes enabled with Cut and Copy disabled. After the Paste menu item is selected, we must remind the user that he/she must go on to select the point at which to paste the image. Here I use a simple change of mouse cursor from the arrow to the cross. The user is expected to position the mouse cursor to the desired insertion point and press the left button. The bitmap is copied onto the current window, using that point as the origin point for the upper-left corner of the clipboard bitmap. Once the paste is done, the cursor is changed back to the normal arrow. As long as the bitmap remains on the clipboard, the Paste menu item remains enabled.

Drawing the dotted frame or rectangle is quite easy using the **DrawFocusRect** function

```
ourdc.DrawFocusRect (&select_rect); // draw dotted frame
```

where **select_rect** is a **CRect** containing the current dimensions of the frame. The actual drawing is done by the Windows 95 API function of the same name—**DrawFocusRect**—using XOR logic to plot the dotted lines. XOR logic is a commonly used graphical trick. If an image is plotted by XORing the pixel colors, then, if the same image is plotted at the same location a second time using XOR, the original colors reappear and the image disappears. For example, using the simpler four-color mode

	pixel color bits	
screen:	01	blue
object:	XOR 10	green
	-------------	
new obj:	11	red<--- the new object appears red
object:	XOR 10	green

	01	blue <--- the original blue is back

Some texts actually set the ROP2 value to XOR before the invocation of the **DrawFrameRect** function similar to

```
dc->SetROP2 (R2_XORPEN);
```

However, this is not needed because the Windows 95 API **DrawFocusRect** function that the MFC invokes in-line always sets this just before drawing the focus rectangle.

Thus, the selection sequence consists of initially drawing the dotted frame. If the user moves the mouse, first redraw the original frame and then the new frame modified by the mouse cursor's position. Tight control over operations is needed, since the left button press can mean three different things: paste here, deselect current selected area, or draw. Therefore, four control BOOLs are used.

```
BOOL lbuttondown, rbuttondown, paste, selected;
```

paste is TRUE only when the user has selected Edit l Paste.

selected is TRUE only while an image area is currently selected, which is that time between releasing the right button and either the next left button press to deselect, another right button press to deselect and reselect a new area, or the Cut/Copy menu item selection.

rbuttondown is TRUE only while the right button is down and we're not in paste mode.

lbuttondown is TRUE only during a Draw operation.

The coding sequence in the **OnLButtonDown** function must check for Paste operations first. If Not Paste is not in effect, then check if any area is selected to determine if a deselection action is required. Finally, if the left button is not down, the Draw operation can commence.

Beyond the **CmEditCut**, **CmEditCopy**, and **CmEditPaste** functions, three command enablers must be used to properly enable these menu items. For the Cut/Copy operations, the selected BOOL member is all that is required. The Paste enabler must check the current contents of the clipboard to see if a bitmap is present.

By checking the clipboard every time, the enabler solves another communication problem for us. If the user task switches to another application, such as Paintbrush and copies, say, LEAVES.BMP to the clipboard, when the user task switches back to our Draw window, our application needs to know that there is now a bitmap currently on the clipboard. Therefore, by continual checking, the enabler correctly notifies our application of the bitmap's presence.

13.5 DRAWWIN—GRAPHICAL CUT/COPY/PASTE

The data members and functions that are highlighted in the class definition are those that are involved in the graphical Cut and Paste operations.

13.5.1 Listing for File: DrawWin.h—Pgm13a—Excerpts

```
...
class DrawWin : public CMDIChildWnd {
...
protected:
```

```
static int        numdraw;           // total number of draw children now active

COLORREF          colors[6];         // the possible colors array
COLORREF          linecolor;         // current drawing pen color
int               colnum;            // current pen color array index
int               linewidth;         // current pen width
CToolBox          toolbox;           // client window's tool box

BOOL              buttondown;        // TRUE when left button is down for drawing
CPen              *ptrpen;           // the current drawing pen
CClientDC         *ptrdc;            // the current drawing DC

CClientDC         *ptrselectdc;      // the current selection DC
CRect             select_rect;       // the selection rectangle for cut/paste

BOOL              hideshow;          // TRUE when tool box is visible
BOOL              lbuttondown;       // TRUE when in drawing mode
BOOL              rbuttondown;       // TRUE when in select mode
BOOL              selected;          // TRUE when image is selected
BOOL              paste;             // TRUE when pasting from the clipboard
...
public:
                  DrawWin ();                       // constructor
afx_msg void      OnPaint ();                       // paint backgrd white

protected:

afx_msg void      OnSize (UINT, int, int);          // remove tool box when minimized
afx_msg BOOL      OnQueryOpen ();                   // reshow tool box when restoring
afx_msg void      OnMove (int, int);                // reposition tool box as win moves
afx_msg void      OnClose ();                       // check if we can close down
afx_msg int       OnCreate(LPCREATESTRUCT);         // construct tool box
afx_msg void      OnDestroy ();                     // remove allocated menus
afx_msg void      OnLButtonDown (UINT, CPoint);     // begin drawing
afx_msg void      OnLButtonUp (UINT, CPoint);       // end drawing
afx_msg void      OnRButtonDown (UINT, CPoint);     // begin drawing
afx_msg void      OnRButtonUp (UINT, CPoint);       // end selection
afx_msg void      OnMouseMove (UINT, CPoint);       // continue drawing

        int       DisplayMsg (int, int, UINT);      // display a message
        void      UpdateStatusBar ();               // display msg on status bar
        void      ShowFocusRect (BOOL);             // fix up focus rect and show it

        void      ToClipboard (BOOL);               // copy to clipboard
afx_msg void      CmEditCut ();                     // cut selected image to clpbd
afx_msg void      CmEditCopy ();                    // copy selected image to clpbd
afx_msg void      CmEditPaste ();                   // paste from clipboard
afx_msg void      CmEnableEditCut  (CCmdUI*);       // enable/disable FileSave
afx_msg void      CmEnableEditCopy (CCmdUI*);       // enable/disable FileSaveAs
afx_msg void      CmEnableEditPaste (CCmdUI*);      // enable/disable FilePrint

afx_msg void      OnUpdateViewToolBox (CCmdUI*);    // checkmark hide/show tool box
afx_msg void      CmLines (UINT);                   // process all line width btns
afx_msg void      CmColors (UINT);                  // process all color btns presses
afx_msg void      OnUpdateToolBoxLines (CCmdUI*);   // enable all line width buttons
afx_msg void      OnUpdateToolBoxColors (CCmdUI*);  // enable all color buttons
...
```

Let's begin our examination of the revised DrawWin class with the three enablers. The Cut/Copy enablers (**CmEnableEditCut** and **CmEnableEditCopy**) simply return the status of the selected BOOL.

```
ptrcmd->Enable (selected);
```

The **CmEnableEditPaste** checks the current contents of the clipboard.

```
ptrcmd->Enable (::IsClipboardFormatAvailable (CF_BITMAP));
```

Next let's look at the selection process involving the right button. **OnRButton-Down** activates only when there is not a right button press in progress and when Paste is chosen. Obtain a DC to our client window. If there is a currently selected area on-screen indicated by **selected** being TRUE, it must be removed by using **DrawFocusRect** with the current **select_rect** values—this makes the frame disappear. Then the new beginning upper-left position is calculated and installed into the **select_rect**, and the mouse events are captured. The new CRect function **SetRect** conveniently resets a new value into the rectangle object.

```
if (!rbuttondown && !paste) {
 rbuttondown = TRUE;
 ptrselectdc = new CClientDC (this);
 if (selected) ptrselectdc->DrawFocusRect (&select_rect);
 select_rect.SetRect (point.x, point.y, point.x, point.y);
 SetCapture ();
}
```

Next, the user drags the mouse to the desired ending lower-right corner. **OnMouseMove** handles the successive removal of the previous dotted frame and the display of the new frame. Again, I use the **SetRect** function to reset new values into the rectangle object.

```
if (lbuttondown) ptrdc->LineTo (point);
else if (rbuttondown) {
 ShowFocusRect (FALSE);
 select_rect.SetRect (select_rect.left, select_rect.top,
                       point.x, point.y);
 ShowFocusRect (FALSE);
}
```

Finally, the right button is released and **OnRButtonUp** is invoked to finish the selection process by setting **rbuttondown** back to FALSE. This removes the DC, releases the mouse, calls **ShowFocusRect** (request permanent fix of coordinates), calculates the image width and height, and—if the dimensions are not zero—sets **selected** to TRUE.

```
if (rbuttondown) {
 rbuttondown = FALSE;
 delete ptrselectdc;
 ReleaseCapture ();
 ShowFocusRect (TRUE);
 int height = select_rect.bottom - select_rect.top;
 int width  = select_rect.right - select_rect.left;
```

```
    if (width == 0 && height == 0) return;
    selected = TRUE;
}
```

Did you notice the new function in both **OnMouseMove** and **OnRButtonUp** called **ShowFocusRect**? This function provides a final nice touch on the selection process. Often the user drags backwards or from the right to the left or even upside down. Our calculated dimensions based upon right-left coordinates are negative. **DrawFocusRect** fails when the coordinates are backwards! Rather than the negative widths and heights being rejected, the **select_rect** coordinates should be reversed and the focus rectangle drawn. If the reversed coordinates are not re-reversed, the user is not able to select more than one pixel dimension. Thus, while moving, **Show-FocusRect** must reverse, show, and re-reverse the coordinates. However, when the Right Button Up message comes, the coordinates must be permanently reversed. The **ShowFocusRect** function is as follows:

```
void        DrawWin::ShowFocusRect (BOOL fixit) {
 BOOL fixleft = FALSE, fixtop = FALSE;
 int temp;
 // since the selection image could be reversed, normalize reversed dims
 if (select_rect.right - select_rect.left < 0) {
  temp = select_rect.right;
  select_rect.right = select_rect.left;
  select_rect.left = temp;
  fixleft = TRUE;
 }
 if (select_rect.bottom - select_rect.top < 0) {
  temp = select_rect.bottom;
  select_rect.bottom = select_rect.top;
  select_rect.top = temp;
  fixtop = TRUE;
 }
 if (fixit) return;  // final fix up, but do not show rectangle
 ptrselectdc->DrawFocusRect (&select_rect); // draw new selection frame
 // now unfix it so user can continue upside down
 if (fixleft) {
  temp = select_rect.right;
  select_rect.right = select_rect.left;
  select_rect.left = temp;
 }
 if (fixtop) {
  temp = select_rect.bottom;
  select_rect.bottom = select_rect.top;
  select_rect.top = temp;
 }
}
```

Now let us examine the Cut and Copy operation via the menu items. **CmEdit-Cut** and **CmEditCopy** are nearly identical except for the removal of the image when Cut is chosen. Therefore, I replaced the common coding with a helper function—**ToClipboard**.

In **CmEditCopy** if **selected** is TRUE, then I must make a bitmap copy of the selected area of our window stored in an HBITMAP object. This bitmap object, which Windows 95 places on the clipboard, is constructed by a **BitBlt** onto a memory DC. Therefore, I get a client DC and a memory DC based upon our client DC. Once the current selected rectangle dimensions are converted into a width and height, the dotted frame that shows the selected area must be removed.

```
void        DrawWin::CmEditCopy () {
  if (selected) {          // when image is selected, select_rect holds dims
   ToClipboard (FALSE);// send image to clipboard, say is not a cut
   selected = FALSE;     // indicate image is no longer selected
  }
}

void        DrawWin::ToClipboard (BOOL /*iscut*/) {
  int height = select_rect.bottom - select_rect.top;
  int width  = select_rect.right - select_rect.left;
  // remove selection dotted frame
  HDC hourdc = ::GetDC(m_hWnd);                    // get a hdc to model
  ::DrawFocusRect (hourdc, &select_rect);     // remove dotted frame
```

Then the bitmap is allocated based upon the current dimensions and inserted into the memory DC

```
HDC hmemdc = ::CreateCompatibleDC (hourdc); // the compatible memory dc
HBITMAP bm = ::CreateCompatibleBitmap (hourdc, width, height);
HBITMAP obm;
obm = (HBITMAP)::SelectObject (hmemdc, bm); // install new bitmap
```

The copy is made using **BitBlt**.

```
::BitBlt (hmemdc,0, 0, width, height, hourdc, select_rect.left,
          select_rect.top, SRCCOPY); // copy our image to memory copy
::SelectObject (hmemdc, obm);        // remove our copy bitmap
::DeleteDC (hmemdc);                 // delete the compatible dc
::ReleaseDC (m_hWnd, hourde);        // remove the model dc
```

The actual transfer to the clipboard is done using the C API clipboard functions.

```
// now copy it to the clipboard
VERIFY(OpenClipboard ());
VERIFY(::EmptyClipboard ());
VERIFY(::SetClipboardData (CF_BITMAP, bm));
VERIFY(::CloseClipboard ());
}
```

If the Cut menu item is selected, the cut is done by using **PatBlt** to replace the **select_rect** area with the background

```
CClientDC newdc (this);
newdc.PatBlt (select_rect, WHITENESS);

// now copy it to the clipboard
VERIFY(OpenClipboard ());
VERIFY(::EmptyClipboard ());
VERIFY(::SetClipboardData (CF_BITMAP, bm));
```

```
        VERIFY(::CloseClipboard ());
      }
```

To implement the Cut operation, after copying the image to the clipboard using **ToClipboard**, use a **PatBlt** to remove the selected area.

```
void       DrawWin::CmEditCut () {
  if (selected) {      // when image is selected, select_rect holds dims
    ToClipboard (TRUE);// send image to clipboard, say is a cut
    // perform cut => set image rectangle to background color
    HDC hourdc = ::GetDC(m_hWnd);      // get a hdc to model
    ::PatBlt (hourdc, select_rect.left, select_rect.top,
            select_rect.Width(), select_rect.Height() , WHITENESS);
    ::ReleaseDC (m_hWnd, hourdc);      // release the dc
    selected = FALSE; // indicate image is no longer selected
  }
}
```

When the **CmEditPaste** function is invoked by selecting the Edit | Paste menu item, if the clipboard contains bitmap data, **paste** is set to TRUE. Some means must be provided to ensure that the user realizes that he/she is to select the desired point upon which to paste the image. Changing the cursor should alert the user to a Paste operation. I change the arrow cursor into the cross cursor. However, since the cursor must remain as the cross across messages and potential task switches, the safest approach is to install the cross cursor in the window's WNDCLASS, using **SetClass-Long**. Thus, the coding of the **CmEditPaste** is only the short sequence

```
if (::IsClipboardFormatAvailable (CF_BITMAP)) {
  paste = TRUE;
  HCURSOR hcross = LoadCursor (NULL, IDC_CROSS);
  SetClassLong (m_hWnd, GCL_HCURSOR, (long) hcross);
}
```

The actual copy from the clipboard and insertion onto the window is done when the left button is pressed. **OnLButtonDown** now has the added responsibility of signaling where to paste and must be handled before checking for deselection and normal drawing. In **OnLButtonDown**, first check for Paste operation in effect; then check for a deselection request; if it is neither, it must be a draw request. To handle the paste action, a **BitBlt** is used to copy from the clipboard copy onto our DC. This means that I need to place the bitmap into a memory DC and **BitBlt** from the memory DC onto our client window DC. (Do not forget to close the clipboard.) The Paste operation is now complete. Cleanup involves setting Paste back to FALSE and restoring the normal cursor.

```
  if (paste) {                       // must handle Paste first
    if (OpenClipboard ()==0) return;   // someone else using clipboard
    HBITMAP hbm = (HBITMAP) GetClipboardData (CF_BITMAP);
    ASSERT (hbm);                    // verify exists
    HDC hourdc = ::GetDC(m_hWnd);       // get a hdc to model
    HDC hmemdc = ::CreateCompatibleDC (hourdc);// a compatible memory dc
    HBITMAP obm = (HBITMAP)::SelectObject (hmemdc, hbm);
    BITMAP bm;
```

```
     ::GetObject(hbm, sizeof(bm), &bm); // retrieve bm section
     int width = bm.bmWidth;            // set bitmap's dimensions
     int height = bm.bmHeight;
     // copy our image to memory copy
     ::BitBlt (hourdc, point.x, point.y, width, height, hmemdc, 0, 0,
             SRCCOPY);
     ::SelectObject (hmemdc, obm);      // remove clipboard's bitmap
     ::DeleteDC (hmemdc);                        // delete the compatible dc
     ::ReleaseDC (m_hWnd, hourdc);              // release the model dc
     CloseClipboard ();
     paste = FALSE;                     // indicate no longer pasting
     HCURSOR harrow = LoadCursor (NULL, IDC_ARROW); // reinstall main arrow
     SetClassLong (m_hWnd, GCL_HCURSOR, (long) harrow);
   }
```

OnLButtonDown then handles any deselect request that is occurring if **selected** is currently TRUE. To deselect, the **DrawFocusRect** function must XOR the current **select_rect** to remove the dotted frame.

```
   // deselect process requested
   else if (selected) {              // if an image is selected, deselect it
    CClientDC ourdc (this);          // acquire a dc to our window
    ourdc.DrawFocusRect (&select_rect); // remove the dotted rectangle
    selected = FALSE;                // indicate image is no longer selected
   }
```

Finally, **OnLButtonDown** can then go on with the normal Draw process.

```
   // draw operation requested
   else if (!lbuttondown) {           // avoid multiple invocations by dblclick
    lbuttondown = TRUE;              // signal drawing
    ptrdc   = new CClientDC (this);// get new draw DC
    linecolor = colors[colnum];     // install current color
    ptrpen = new CPen (PS_SOLID, linenum, linecolor); // create the pen
    ptrdc->SelectObject (ptrpen);  // install pen in DC

    SetCapture ();                  // capture mouse movements for draw
    ptrdc->MoveTo (point);          // set pen to starting point
   }
  }
```

The full DrawWin class coding is not shown here because the remainder of the MDI child coding is the same as that in Pgm12a from chapter 12. All coding for the tool box and floating frame window is unchanged. Consult the full coding on the CD.

Next, let's look at several fancy effects that we can use to polish our applications, in particular, initial splash screens and sound files.

Sound, Animation Effects, Splash Screens, and Animated Presentations

14.1 SOUND

Sound generation is an extensive topic on which we could spend many chapters. Instead, we will cover only the minimal basics so that you can at least play sound files as part of the application. The fancier multimedia applications open with a splash screen and intro music. After you have studied this section and the later one on splash screens, I invite you to add sound effects during the opening logos in Pgm14c. Sounds can be played from the PC's tiny speaker or through sound cards such as Sound-Blaster and compatibles. Sound through the PC speaker is extremely limited not only in fidelity but also in notes. Only one note at a time can be sounded through the PC speaker. With sound cards, many voices or notes can be sounded simultaneously, creating chords. Rather than dwell on the obsolete PC speaker, I am assuming that you have a sound card and have installed the proper Windows 95 sound drivers. You can verify that your sound system is functioning properly by using "Accessories | Multimedia | Media Player" to play the supplied Windows 95 wav short sound sequences.

Windows 95 provides three methods of programming sound operations through the Multimedia API, MMSYSTEM, which provides a media control interface (MCI). The MCI provides a very high-level method to play back recorded sound files known as wav or wave sound files via either **MessageBeep** or **sndPlaySound** functions. For more control, the middle level consists of many MCI driver functions as command strings. For exacting, detailed control, the low-level MIDI API can be accessed. MCI can support MIDI devices, waveform devices, and CD devices.

A note has a specific pitch and duration. A series of notes, such as the melody to "Twinkle, Twinkle, Little Star," becomes a voice. A chord is often made up of three or more separate voices. Several voices are required to emulate the sound quality of certain instruments so that the notes sound like an organ or regal. The PC speaker can play only one voice, while a sound card can play many, often 20 or so, yielding a quality hi-fi sound. In a wav file, all of the voices have been merged into one combined sound. The resulting collected sound waves are recorded in one group or package. It is this packaged collection that is played back when one "plays" a wav file.

The sound recording process consists of two parts: recording and playback. When recording, a microphone picks up the sounds to be recorded. The output of a microphone is an analog signal, fluctuating electric voltage, rather like sine waves. This analog signal is input to the analog-to-digital (A/D) converter section of the sound card that periodically measures the voltage and digitizes that value either as a byte (8-bit sampling) or as a word (16-bit sampling). Obviously, the 8-bit sampling has a much narrower range of fluctuations (0–255 versus 0–65,535). The frequency at which the incoming sound waves are sampled is known as the sampling rate, a variable quantity.

If you are recording voice only, you could use a low sampling rate of, say, 4 kilohertz (kHz) because voice sounds vary over a narrow range. Music-quality sounds, on the other hand, vary in frequency across the entire audible spectrum, requiring a high sampling rate to reproduce fidelity, possibly 44kHz. The music industry standard guideline is to use a sampling rate that is two times the highest frequency in the mix. Thus, if full fidelity up to 20,000 hertz is required, the sampling rate is 44kHz.

The sampling rate affects disk storage. If you are sampling with 8-bit sampling at 44kHz for excellent quality, 1 second of sound requires 44,000 bytes. If you are at 16-bit sampling, 1 second requires 88,000 bytes. Say you want to record a song that lasts for 4 minutes. Using 16-bit sampling at 44kHz, you may need 21 megabytes! If you wish to be able to edit each instrument and adjust the final mix as a sound recording engineer might do, assuming you need eight tracks or voices, you need about 170M of free disk space! If you get into the digital sound recording arena, be sure to have dedicated gigabyte disk drives! On playback, the disk digital data is fed to the sound card's digital-to-audio converter (DAC), which produces a weak analog signal that is then amplified and sent to speakers.

Windows 95 MCI then provides a layered approach. At the highest level, Sound Recorder and **sndPlaySound** create and play back wave files with minimal coding (1 line!). The MCI or string interface permits much more direct control over the entire operation—the coding of this is best encapsulated into C++ classes. Additionally, the low-level API permits total control with a maximal amount of user coding. There is an excellent MCI strings class design presented in William Roetzheim's *Uncharted Windows Programming.*[*] In this chapter, I present only the highest level of the API, using the **sndPlaySound** function. The **sndPlaySound** function accepts the wav file name and the play options flag.

---

[*] Published by Sams, Indianapolis, IN, 1993.

```
sndPlaySound (filename, flags);
```

The commonly used flags are

SND_SYNC	returns after finishing play
SND_ASYNC	starts playing the file asynchronously and returns to application
SND_LOOP	endlessly repeats the sound file
SND_NOSTOP	if a sound is currently playing, returns without playing

If you want to hear only the wave file, the flag would likely be SND_ASYNC. This would allow your application to go on to other processing actions while the sound is playing in the background. If you use SND_LOOP, then, to terminate the endless playing loop, invoke **sndPlaySound** with NULL as the filename.

Pgm14a illustrates the endless loop style, playing the requested wave file for 3 seconds. Since some means for obtaining filenames is required, an Open File dialog box is used. Further, this sample has no visible main window; only the common File Open dialog box is shown. Figure 14.1 shows Pgm14a in operation.

To use the MCI sound API, use the following include: **#include <mmsystem.h>**. Under MFC you also must link using the WINMM.LIB to pick up the **sndPlaySound** function itself. To link properly, use Build I Settings I Link I Category I Input I Obj Mod, and enter WINMM.LIB.

 Windows 3.1 Porting Tip: Under Windows 3.1, the file that contained the function was MMSYSTEM.DLL. Under Windows 95, this file is replaced by WINMM.DLL and we must link to the import lib, WINMM.LIB.

14.1.1 Pgm14a—Playing wav Files—Using a Dialog Box as the Main Window

Examine Pgm14aApp's implementation. It is so short that all coding is contained within the **InitInstance** function. The first action is to construct a File Open dialog box to permit the user to select the desired wav file.

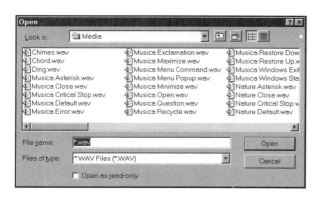

Fig. 14.1 Pgm14a in Operation—Open Dialog Box Is the Main Window

```
CFileDialog filedlg (TRUE,      // use Open dialog
                     "*.WAV",   // default extension
                     "*.WAV",   // current file name
                 OFN_FILEMUSTEXIST | OFN_PATHMUSTEXIST | OFN_LONGNAMES,
                     "*.WAV Files (*.WAV)||",
                     NULL);     // no parent pointer
char filename[MAX_PATH] = "*.wav";   // set initial values for .WAV files
char filter[MAX_PATH] = "*.wav";

filedlg.m_ofn.lpstrFile = filename;
filedlg.m_ofn.lpstrInitialDir = "\\WINDOWS\\MEDIA"; // set the default dir
```

Notice that, for convenience, the **filename** and **filter** data members contain the resultant data so that we can remember the folder last used. I also initially set the directory for the new Windows 95 MEDIA folder that contains numerous wave files. The main loop continues to process requests until the user selects any button other than OK.

```
int retcd = IDOK;               // prime the play sound loop
while (retcd == IDOK) {

 strcpy (filename, filter);     // install *.wav for the filename
 // get user's file choice
 retcd = filedlg.DoModal ();

 // if .wav selected, play the sound file for 3 seconds
 if (retcd == IDOK) {
  strcpy (filename, filedlg.GetPathName ()); // extract its filename
  sndPlaySound (filename, SND_ASYNC | SND_LOOP); // endless play of file
  beginticks = ticks = GetTickCount ();      // set start tick counts
  // delay 3 seconds
  while (ticks < beginticks + 3000) ticks = GetTickCount ();
  sndPlaySound (NULL, SND_ASYNC);            // abruptly terminate play
 }
```

If you have recorded some music, you could install Continuous Background Play and Halt Play menu items. When the Play Music item is selected, invoke the **snd-PlaySound** in the continuous play mode. When the Halt Music option is selected, send the NULL file to terminate. You could even use menu item replacement, like the Hide/Show tool box.

The major difference is that there is no main window at all! The MFC recommends using some form of a main window because the dialog box uses the pointer to the parent window. However, it runs fine without one.

14.1.2 Listing for File: Pgm14aAp.cpp—Pgm14a—Excerpts

```
...
/***********************************************************************/
/*                                                                     */
/* InitInstance: allocate and run the main open dialog box to play sounds */
/*                                                                     */
/***********************************************************************/
```

```
BOOL   Pgm14AApp::InitInstance () {

  DWORD ticks, beginticks;         // for tick delay on endless play

  // create new transfer buffer
  CFileDialog filedlg (TRUE,       // use Open dialog
                       "*.WAV",    // default extension
                       "*.WAV",    // current file name
                       OFN_FILEMUSTEXIST | OFN_PATHMUSTEXIST | OFN_LONGNAMES,
                       "*.WAV Files (*.WAV)||",
                       NULL);      // no parent pointer
  char filename[MAX_PATH] = "*.wav";    // set initial values for .WAV files
  char filter[MAX_PATH] = "*.wav";

  filedlg.m_ofn.lpstrFile = filename;
  filedlg.m_ofn.lpstrInitialDir = "\\WINDOWS\\MEDIA"; // set the default dir

  int retcd = IDOK;                // prime the play sound loop
  while (retcd == IDOK) {

    strcpy (filename, filter);     // install *.wav for the filename

    // get user's file choice
    retcd = filedlg.DoModal ();

    // if .wav selected, play the sound file for 3 seconds
    if (retcd == IDOK) {
      strcpy (filename, filedlg.GetPathName ());    // extract its filename
      sndPlaySound (filename, SND_ASYNC | SND_LOOP); // endless play of file
      beginticks = ticks = GetTickCount ();         // set start tick counts
      while (ticks < beginticks + 3000) ticks = GetTickCount (); // delay 3 sec
      sndPlaySound (NULL, SND_ASYNC);               // abruptly terminate play
    }
  }

  m_pMainWnd = &filedlg;           // avoids assertion failure for NULL main win
  PostQuitMessage(0);              // terminate application
  return TRUE;
}
```

14.2 ANIMATION

We could spend many chapters on this topic, especially if we wish to write games! There are several forms that animation can take. Traditional cartoons use the painstaking cel animation or frame animation approach. Here the action sequence is broken down into frames that are presented or shown at about 20–30 frames per second, yielding a uniform motion. (See *The Animation Studio* or other books listed in the bibliography.) If you are serious about game development, please take a close look at the new Microsoft Games Development Kit (GDK).

The most straightforward approach to displaying graphical animation is to use XOR logic, plotting the previous image for removal and then plotting the new image. The drawback of this approach is flicker. A small amount of flicker is seen as the old image abruptly disappears and the new one appears. Keeping the amount of movement down to one pixel at a time greatly decreases the visual impact of the flicker effect.

If you are lucky enough to have a video card that supports two or more graphics video pages (generally at least 2M is required on the video card for higher resolutions), then, while the user watches the current image, you draw the next scene on the other page and then do an "instantaneous" page swap. This is a nice approach if you have the hardware for it, but most of us do not have the hardware except in low resolution.

Modern games hardware introduces the concept of a **sprite**. A sprite is a small action object that moves about a background image. The background can consist of a series of sprite tiles.

Under Windows 95, the approach that works well is to **simulate** the video page switch by using an off-screen bitmap for drawing. While the user is viewing the current screen, in the memory DC, redraw the scene with the next position of the moving object and then **BitBlt** the altered portion on to the screen, avoiding the flicker. Obviously, we could and should create a fully functional Sprite-Animate class system. However, because of space and time constraints, a simpler example illustrates the basic effect. (See the bibliography for a number of books on this topic.)

Pgm14b illustrates the basic principles of animation via both the XOR and the off-screen bitmap approach. The sample program has been kept very simplistic so that the difference between the two methods can be readily observed. The animation is a spaceship that circles the planet or "tank pong" with a ship. (I have a penchant for the old Tank Pong arcade game.) Figure 14.2 shows Pgm14b in operation. The earth forms the background, and the small spaceship moves about the screen.

The user controls the speed by using the up or down arrow. A beep sounds to let the user know when the slowest timer value (1 ms) has been reached. The program then switches over to fast action. Again the up and down arrows can adjust the speed. When the absolute fastest speed is achieved, any attempts to further decrease the rate also sound the beep. (The ship appears then more like a ray gun!) To switch over to the smooth-move mode, the user can at any time press the right arrow key. The program then resets back to using the timer at a 10-ms delay. Again, the speed is adjusted by

Fig. 14.2 Pgm14b Animation Action—Spaceship Moving Around the Earth

the up and down arrows. When a decrease below the fastest possible timer is requested, the program again shifts into fast action that is similarly controlled by the user. The beep sounds as the change is made and sounds again whenever there is a request to go faster than the fastest possible speed.

The program requires minimal resources: two bitmaps. The earth bitmap serves as the background and is stored as a DIB in BACK.BMP. SAUCER.BMP is a small bitmap that was created with the Resource Editor and is supposed to represent a flying saucer. I load in the larger BACK.BMP as a DIB but include the SAUCER.BMP and its mask SAUCERM.BMP as DDBs in the resource file.

14.2.1 XOR Images and Transparent Backgrounds

Before we begin to examine the application coding, let's discuss how the program operates and see the need for some new functions. The program begins using the fast XOR logic to paint the ship. The cycle of action begins by drawing the ship at position 1 by XORing the ship's color bits with the background's color bits. Pause for the requisite time. Then erase the ship by redrawing it at the original position 1 again XORing the bits. Move the ship to position 2 and repeat the cycle from the beginning. Remember that doing two XOR operations on the same objects results in the original color returning.

background color	0 0 0 1
ship color	0 1 0 0 XOR
	-----------
new resultant color	0 1 0 1
ship color	0 1 0 0 XOR
	-----------
original background color	0 0 0 1

While quite fast, this XOR method has one major drawback—the resultant color is neither that of the ship nor the background. Thus, as the ship moves over the earth, it is rendered in unusual colors. Likewise, continual direct updating of the screen will cause the image to flicker.

By using a smooth-move approach, we can remove the flicker. Smooth moving utilizes off-screen memory DCs to construct the final image which is then **BitBlt**ed once onto the screen. I could have removed the XOR flicker by using a memory DC to construct the final images, but the objectionable resultant color problem made it seem hardly worth the effort. Another AND-OR logic can be combined to render the object's true colors onto the background image. The key to the whole operation is to have the ship's background color become transparent. If you just **BitBlt** (SRCCOPY) the ship's image onto the background, that area of the rectangular ship bitmap (here black) overlays the background (here the earth)—a completely useless result. How do you make the ship's background color transparent over the earth's image?

Make the background around the ship in the ship bitmap black. Then construct a copy of the ship bitmap and make the black background white and make all colors of the ship black—this becomes the mask. The monochrome mask with the white background and black ship image is then ANDed onto the background image, producing a "hole" in the background, silhouetting the ship. AND logic permits any background image colors to remain wherever there is white in the mask. But because the ship proper is black, or color 0, AND logic results in a color 0 appearing, masking out the background image color.

	pel 1	pel 2	
background colors	0001	0001	
ship mask	1111	0000	white & black pels ANDed SCRAND
	-----	-----	
resultant background	0001	0000	
ship proper	0000	1100	black & yellow pels ORed SCRPAINT
	-----	-----	
final image result	0001	1100	

Here pel 1 of the real background image, which is going to be overlain by the background of the ship's image, retains the real background image's color. Pel 2, which is to become part of the actual ship, has its original background image's color removed and the ship's color inserted.

Thus it is quite simple to overlay one background image with another image whose background becomes transparent. Paint the background of the overlaying image black; copy the image and paint the background white and change all colors to white; this becomes the mask. AND the mask onto the background image and then OR the overlay image.

Finally, recall from chapter 9 that there are two methods for converting a DIB into a device-dependent bitmap. Using **CreateDIBitmap** can handle the conversion, maintaining the DIB's color palette. However, in this case, I have chosen a DIB that uses only the normal Windows 95 basic color palette. As a result, I have used Method 1 in chapter 9 to handle the conversion from a DIB into a DDB. This results in a slight simplification of the coding.

14.2.2 Creating Faster Action—Beyond Windows 95 Timers

The sample program begins in the XOR mode using the Windows 95 timer. When the timer goes off, the saucer is moved 1 pixel in both the x and y direction for smooth animation. (You can experiment with the basic values of **dx** and **dy**, the incremental values, and observe the increasing jerkiness of the animation.) Since the timer has at best a 1-ms response, only slow-motion effects can be displayed. The program begins with a 10-ms delay.

The speed of the delay can be controlled by the user through an elementary user interface. By pressing the down arrow, the timing rate is decreased 1 ms. By pressing the up arrow, the rate is increased by 1 ms. As you will see when you run the program, using the timer is acceptable only for slower-motion effects.

To gain a higher motion level or faster movement, the built-in timer is bypassed.

The fastest possible motion for a specific image setup under Windows 95 could be represented by the following loop:

```
while (TRUE) {
 get new position
 show at new position
}
```

Of course there is one fatal flaw in such an implementation—it is endless. Under Windows 95, it is even worse. In such a loop, all other Windows 95 messages begin to pile up in the queue, since the routine never ends. The user may be quite frustrated since the only way to stop the program loop would be to use Ctl-Alt-Del and have Windows 95 abort the program.

This situation or a related one is actually encountered fairly often in Windows 95 programming—the program enters a long sequence that requires a good deal of time to accomplish. How can we avoid locking up the machine or backlogging the message queue while the work is being done? We need a method to yield some CPU time back to Windows 95 and the user as well as a way to have the user halt operations.

While in our endless loop in **OnPaint**, replace the normal message processing loop with C-style code.

```
while (::PeekMessage (&msg, NULL, 0, 0, PM_REMOVE)) {
 if (msg.message == WM_QUIT) {
  ::PostQuitMessage (0);
  ok = FALSE;
  break;
 }
 if (!AfxGetApp()->PreTranslateMessage (&msg)) {
  ::TranslateMessage (&msg);
  ::DispatchMessage (&msg);
 }
}
```

Essentially look for the WM_QUIT message signaling that the application is to be shut down and, if so, post the Quit message. If the message is any other message, such as the user's down arrow key press, the **CWinApp**'s **PreTranslateMessage** function is invoked. If all is OK, the message is then translated and dispatched in the C-style manner from chapter 1. **PreTranslateMessage** translates any accelerator key presses and, if it returns TRUE, no further message processing must be done for it has already handled the hot key. In this example, the command is likely the user attempting to increase or decrease the ship's speed.

14.2.3 Pgm14b: Timer and Fast Animation

Since the background is a large bmp file, a DIB, I once more reuse the CDib class from Pgm09b. Recall that this class handles the inputting of bmp files into a memory DIB structure. Once in memory, use **SetDIBBits** to convert the DIB into a DDB for fast display. The required resources are minimal—a window caption, the folder that contains the files, and the bmp files.

14.2.4 Listing for File: Pgm14b.rc—Pgm14b—Excerpts

```
...
IDB_SHIP      BITMAP "saucer.bmp"
IDB_SHIPMASK BITMAP "saucerm.bmp"

STRINGTABLE
{
 IDS_MAINTITLE, "XOR Animation - Up/Down Arrow adjust speed - Right => Smooth Move"
 IDS_BACK,      "\\learnwin\\bmp\\back.bmp"
}
...
```

14.2.5 Listing for File: resource.h—Pgm14b—Excerpts

```
...
#define   IDS_MAINTITLE 100
#define   IDS_BACK      101
#define   IDB_SHIP      102
#define   IDB_SHIPMASK  103
...
```

14.2.6 Listing for File: MainWin.h—Pgm14b—Excerpts

```
...
/****************************************************************************/
/*                                                                        */
/* MainWin Class Definition: Animate Spaceship XOR style                  */
/*                                                                        */
/****************************************************************************/

class MainWin : public CFrameWnd {

/****************************************************************************/
/*                                                                        */
/* Data Members                                                           */
/*                                                                        */
/****************************************************************************/

protected:
BOOL       first;
CDib       *ptrdib;                 // the dib for the .BMP file background
HDC        hdc;                     // handle to client dc compatible dc
CClientDC  *ptrclientdc;            // client dc for displaying action
CDC        *ptrbackmemdc;           // memory device context for drawing bkground
CDC        *ptrshipmemdc;           // memory device context for drawing ship
CDC        *ptrshipmaskmemdc;       // memory device context for drawing shipmask
CDC        *ptrmovememdc;           // memory device context for drawing bkground
CBitmap    *ptrbackbitmap;          // bitmap of background
CBitmap    *ptrshipbitmap;          // bitmap of ship
CBitmap    *ptrmovebitmap;          // work bitmap for smooth move
CBitmap    *ptrshipmaskbitmap;      // bitmap of ship in mask format

CRect      dimrect, shiprect;       // position / location of ship
int        dx, dy;                  // amount to move the ship each time
```

```
int          rate;               // controls the speed rate of action
BOOL         usetimer;           // TRUE when timer is being used
BOOL         smoothmove;         // TRUE when smooth move is in effect
int          shipheight;         // ship bitmap dimensions
int          shipwidth;
/****************************************************************************/
/*                                                                         */
/* Functions:                                                              */
/*                                                                         */
/****************************************************************************/
public:
             MainWin (const char*);      // constructor
afx_msg void OnPaint ();                  // also handles fast move requests
virtual BOOL DestroyWindow ();            // remove GDI objects
protected:

afx_msg void OnTimer (UINT);              // process slow move requests
afx_msg void OnSize (UINT, int, int);     // sets init ship pos based on size
afx_msg void OnKeyDown (UINT, UINT, UINT); // process user controls
afx_msg void OnClose ();                  // shut down

        void CheckDims ();                // moves ship and handles collisions
        void SmoothMove ();               // perform smooth movement of ship
        void XORMove ();                  // perform XOR movement of ship
        void BuildBitmaps ();             // load bitmaps and start the action
...
```

The MainWin class definition defines several GDI member objects. The **ptrclientdc** provides access to the main client window upon which the animation is seen. The animation uses a memory DC for the background bitmap and for the ship's bitmap. Additionally, the smooth-move operation needs a scratch DC upon which to make needed changes, copying the alterations to the **ptrclientdc**. Each memory DC also must have a corresponding bitmap. To construct the memory DCs to be compatible to the client DC, the **CreateCompatibleDC** function is required. The member **hdc** is used to contain this compatible DC for use in construction of the other three memory DCs. When the program is finished, the **hdc** can be deleted. Failure to do so results in a memory leak.

The current ship's location is contained in the **shiprect**. I assume that the center of the ship bitmap is the current position. To avoid having half of the ship go off the edge of the screen while the remainder is visible, the rectangle **dimrect** contains the altered dimensions of the screen. For example, if the upper-left client area coordinate is 0 pixels and the ship is 20 pixels wide, then the **dimrect**'s upper-left coordinate would be set to 10. To get the correct client area dimensions, **OnSize** is used.

The members **dx** and **dy** hold the current number of pixels to move the ship. Whenever there is a collision with a border, the offending rate is negated, pong style. I have set **dx** and **dy** to 1 pixel for the smoothest effect. You should alter these to larger values to really see the differences between the XOR and smooth-move methods.

When **usetimer** is TRUE, the Windows 95 timer is in use; when FALSE, our faster method is in use. When **smoothmove** is TRUE, the final image is constructed in the move DC and the altered area is copied back onto the screen.

14.2.7 Listing for File: MainWin.cpp—Pgm14b—Excerpts

```
...

BEGIN_MESSAGE_MAP(MainWin, CFrameWnd)
 ON_WM_KEYDOWN()
 ON_WM_SIZE ()
 ON_WM_TIMER()
 ON_WM_PAINT()
 ON_WM_CLOSE()
END_MESSAGE_MAP()

#define TIMERID 1
/***************************************************************************/
/*                                                                         */
/* MainWin: init all GDI objects                                           */
/*                                                                         */
/***************************************************************************/

          MainWin::MainWin (const char far* title) {

 Create ( ...
 ptrdib        = NULL;
 ptrbackbitmap = NULL;
 ptrmovebitmap = NULL;
 ptrshipbitmap = NULL;
 ptrbackmemdc  = NULL;
 ptrshipmemdc  = NULL;
 ptrshipmaskbitmap = NULL;
 ptrshipmaskmemdc  = NULL;

 rate         = 10;     // set for 10 millisec delay
 usetimer     = TRUE;   // begin using timer
 smoothmove   = FALSE;  // begin using XOR logic
 first        = TRUE;   // set no GDI setup yet
 shipheight   = 0;      // and no ship setup yet
 canclose     = TRUE;   // indicate can close - not in fast action
 }

/***************************************************************************/
/*                                                                         */
/* BuildBitmaps: loads, constructs, and set initial bitmaps - starts timer */
/*                                                                         */
/***************************************************************************/

void      MainWin::BuildBitmaps () {

 // create DCs for client, backgrnd, ship, and smooth move
 // construct the bitmaps of the background, smooth move work, flying saucer
 // construct the background dib from BACK.BMP
 CRect r;
```

```
GetClientRect (&r);
char filename[MAX_PATH];
CRect dibrect;
LoadString (AfxGetApp()->m_hInstance, IDS_BACK, filename, sizeof(filename));
ptrdib = new CDib (filename);          // attempt to load the file into a dib
if (!ptrdib) {
 MessageBox("Cannot load in BACK.BMP file", "Error In Construction", MB_OK);
 PostMessage (WM_QUIT); // failure so quit
}
dibrect.left = dibrect.top = 0;        // set up the dib size in a rectangle
dibrect.right = ptrdib->GetDibWidth();
dibrect.bottom = ptrdib->GetDibHeight();
CClientDC dc (this);                         // dc to copy

// copy to back memory set
ptrbackmemdc = new CDC;                       // the memory dc
ptrbackmemdc->CreateCompatibleDC (&dc);  // copy client dc
ptrbackbitmap = new CBitmap ();               // create the bitmap for memdc
ptrbackbitmap->CreateCompatibleBitmap (&dc, dibrect.Width(),
                                     dibrect.Height());
SetDIBits (ptrbackmemdc->m_hDC, (HBITMAP) (ptrbackbitmap->m_hObject), 0,
           dibrect.Height(), ptrdib->GetDibBitsAddr (),
           ptrdib->GetBitmapInfo (), DIB_RGB_COLORS); // copy dib bits into bm

// copy to smooth move memory set
ptrmovememdc = new CDC;
ptrmovememdc->CreateCompatibleDC (&dc);  // copy client dc
ptrmovebitmap = new CBitmap ();               // create the bitmap for memdc
ptrmovebitmap->CreateCompatibleBitmap (&dc, dibrect.Width(),
                                     dibrect.Height());
SetDIBits (ptrmovememdc->m_hDC, (HBITMAP) (ptrmovebitmap->m_hObject), 0,
           dibrect.Height(), ptrdib->GetDibBitsAddr (),
           ptrdib->GetBitmapInfo (), DIB_RGB_COLORS); // copy dib bits into bm

// load in the ship memory set
ptrshipmemdc = new CDC;
ptrshipmemdc->CreateCompatibleDC (&dc);  // copy client dc
ptrshipbitmap = new CBitmap ();
ptrshipbitmap->LoadBitmap (IDB_SHIP);
BITMAP bm;
::GetObject (ptrshipbitmap->m_hObject, sizeof(bm), &bm);
shipheight = bm.bmHeight;
shipwidth = bm.bmWidth;

// load in the ship mask memory set
ptrshipmaskmemdc = new CDC;
ptrshipmaskmemdc->CreateCompatibleDC (&dc);  // copy client dc
ptrshipmaskbitmap = new CBitmap ();
ptrshipmaskbitmap->LoadBitmap (IDB_SHIPMASK);

// ship's position is measured from center of ship's bitmap, so adjust
// real border of screen, dimrect, to account for the ship
dimrect.top    = shipheight / 2;
dimrect.bottom = r.bottom - shipheight / 2;
dimrect.left   = shipwidth / 2;
dimrect.right  = r.right - shipwidth / 2;
```

```
// set ship to initial position - location is actually centered at 110,110
shiprect.top    = 100;
shiprect.left   = 100;
shiprect.bottom = shiprect.top + shipheight;
shiprect.right  = shiprect.left + shipwidth;

// set both incremental values to 1 pixel per move
dx = dy = 1;

ptrclientdc = new CClientDC (this);
if (!ptrbackmemdc     || !ptrbackbitmap ||
    !ptrmovememdc     || !ptrmovebitmap ||
    !ptrshipmemdc     || !ptrshipbitmap ||
    !ptrshipmaskmemdc || !ptrshipmaskbitmap) {
 MessageBox("Cannot create MemoryDCs and Bitmaps", "Error In Construction",
          MB_OK);
 PostMessage (WM_QUIT);
}

ptrbackmemdc->SelectObject (ptrbackbitmap); // install background in back dc
ptrmovememdc->SelectObject (ptrmovebitmap); // install background in move dc
ptrshipmemdc->SelectObject (ptrshipbitmap); // install ship image in ship dc
ptrshipmaskmemdc->SelectObject (ptrshipmaskbitmap); // install ship mask

delete ptrdib;
ptrdib = NULL;

// display ship at the starting point
// copy background to screen
ptrclientdc->BitBlt (0, 0, r.right, r.bottom, ptrbackmemdc, 0, 0, SRCCOPY);

// place ship on screen
ptrclientdc->BitBlt (shiprect.left, shiprect.top, shiprect.right,
                      shiprect.bottom, ptrshipmemdc, 0, 0, SRCINVERT);
SetTimer (TIMERID, rate, NULL); // turn on timer for XOR action
first = FALSE;
return;
}
/***************************************************************************/
/*                                                                         */
/* DestroyWindow: remove all GDI Objects                                   */
/*                                                                         */
/***************************************************************************/

BOOL        MainWin::DestroyWindow () {

 if (usetimer)      KillTimer (TIMERID); // if timer still operating, kill it
 if (ptrdib)        delete ptrdib;
 ...
 return CFrameWnd::DestroyWindow ();
}
/***************************************************************************/
/*                                                                         */
/* OnSize: determine client rect size and adjust border endpoints          */
/*         and initially display the ship at its starting position         */
/*                                                                         */
/***************************************************************************/
```

```
void        MainWin::OnSize (UINT, int cx, int cy) {

 if ((cx==0 && cy==0) || first) return; // avoid if it is the first time
 if (shipheight == 0) return;            // avoid if not setup

 // ship's position is measured from center of ship's bitmap, so adjust
 // real border of screen, dimrect, to account for the ship
 dimrect.top    = shipheight / 2;
 dimrect.bottom = cy - shipheight / 2;
 dimrect.left   = shipwidth / 2;
 dimrect.right  = cx - shipwidth / 2;

 // here the window really has been resized, so start at beginning position
 // display ship at the starting point
 // copy background to screen
 ptrclientdc->BitBlt (0, 0, cx, cy, ptrbackmemdc, 0, 0, SRCCOPY);

 // place ship on screen
 ptrclientdc->BitBlt (shiprect.left, shiprect.top, shiprect.right,
                      shiprect.bottom, ptrshipmemdc, 0, 0, SRCINVERT);
}

/**************************************************************************/
/*                                                                      */
/* OnTimer: plot next position and show                                 */
/*                                                                      */
/**************************************************************************/

void        MainWin::OnTimer (UINT) {

 if (id == TIMERCLOSEID) {        // if we are closing down during fast action,
  KillTimer (TIMERCLOSEID);       // kill the timer
  canclose = TRUE;               // indicate it is now safe to close down
  PostMessage (WM_CLOSE, 0, 0); // and post another close down message
  return;
 }

 // normal action timer event
 if (first) return;
 if (!smoothmove) XORMove (); // process XOR movement of ship
 else SmoothMove ();          // process smooth movement of ship
}

/**************************************************************************/
/*                                                                      */
/* XORMove: using XOR, move the ship one pixel                          */
/*                                                                      */
/**************************************************************************/

void        MainWin::XORMove () {
 // remove old ship
 ptrclientdc->BitBlt (shiprect.left, shiprect.top, shiprect.right,
                      shiprect.bottom, ptrshipmemdc, 0, 0, SRCINVERT);
 // move ship to new position
 CheckDims ();

 // display ship at new position
 ptrclientdc->BitBlt (shiprect.left, shiprect.top, shiprect.right,
```

```
                              shiprect.bottom, ptrshipmemdc, 0, 0, SRCINVERT);
}
/**************************************************************************/
/*                                                                      */
/* SmoothMove: move ship one pixel by off-screen drawing                */
/*                                                                      */
/**************************************************************************/
void      MainWin::SmoothMove () {
 // set offset of ship in backgrnd
 // replace the ship with the original background
 ptrmovememdc->BitBlt (shiprect.left, shiprect.top, shiprect.right,
                       shiprect.bottom, ptrbackmemdc, shiprect.left,
                       shiprect.top, SRCCOPY);
 // move the ship
 CheckDims ();

 // AND a hole in the move bm then OR in the new ship image
 ptrmovememdc->BitBlt (shiprect.left, shiprect.top, shiprect.right,
                       shiprect.bottom, ptrshipmaskmemdc, 0, 0, SRCAND);
 ptrmovememdc->BitBlt (shiprect.left, shiprect.top, shiprect.right,
                       shiprect.bottom, ptrshipmemdc, 0, 0, SRCPAINT);

 // calculate maximum possible affected area to replace on screen
 CRect newrect;
 newrect = shiprect;
 newrect.InflateRect (abs(dx), abs(dy));

 // set offset of affected area in move bitmap
 // copy affected area to screen
 ptrclientdc->BitBlt (newrect.left, newrect.top, newrect.right,
                      newrect.bottom, ptrmovememdc, newrect.left,
                      newrect.top, SRCCOPY);
}
/**************************************************************************/
/*                                                                      */
/* CheckDims: increments ship position by dx,dy - check & handle collisions*/
/*                                                                      */
/**************************************************************************/
void      MainWin::CheckDims () {
 // get new position by offsetting the rectangle by dx,dy values
 shiprect.OffsetRect (dx, dy);

 // check for collision with the top and bottom
 if (shiprect.top <= dimrect.top) { // hit top
  shiprect.top = dimrect.top;
  shiprect.bottom = shiprect.top + shipheight;
  dy = -dy; // reverse direction
 }
 else if (shiprect.bottom >= dimrect.bottom) { // hit bottom
  shiprect.bottom = dimrect.bottom;
  shiprect.top = shiprect.bottom - shipheight;
  dy = -dy; // reverse direction
```

```
  }
  // check for collisions with the left and right sides
  if (shiprect.left <= dimrect.left) { // hit left
    shiprect.left = dimrect.left;
    shiprect.right = shiprect.left + shipwidth;
    dx = -dx; // reverse direction
  }
  else if (shiprect.right >= dimrect.right) { // hit right
    shiprect.right = dimrect.right;
    shiprect.left = shiprect.right - shipwidth;
    dx = -dx; // reverse direction
  }
}
/***************************************************************************/
/*                                                                         */
/* OnKeyDown: handle user requests for speed up/down - smooth move         */
/*                                                                         */
/***************************************************************************/
void       MainWin::OnKeyDown (UINT key, UINT, UINT) {
  if (first) return;

  if (key == VK_RIGHT && !smoothmove) { // check for go onto smooth move mode
    if (usetimer) KillTimer (TIMERID);    // if timer in operating, kill it
    else usetimer = TRUE;                 // if not, enable timer
    smoothmove = TRUE;                    // enable smooth move
    canclose = TRUE;                      // normal action, so can close anytime
    rate = 10;                            // reset rate to initial starting value

    // copy the ship's initial position onto the initial move bitmap
    ptrmovememdc->BitBlt (shiprect.left, shiprect.top, shiprect.right,
                          shiprect.bottom, ptrshipmemdc, 0, 0, SRCPAINT);

    // copy the move image onto the screen
    ptrclientdc->BitBlt (shiprect.left, shiprect.top, shiprect.right,
                         shiprect.bottom, ptrmovememdc, shiprect.left,
                         shiprect.top, SRCCOPY);

    SetTimer (TIMERID, rate, NULL);       // reactivate the timer
    return;
  }

  // process user speed up or slow down requests
  if (key == VK_UP)              // speed up
    if (usetimer) {              // and timer in effect
      KillTimer (TIMERID);       // remove old timer
      SetTimer (TIMERID, ++rate, NULL); // install new timer with increased rate
      canclose = TRUE;           // normal action, so can close
    }
    else {
      rate += 10;                // and timer not in effect, increase by 10
      canclose = FALSE;          // now cannot close at once
    }
  else if (key == VK_DOWN) {     // slow down
```

```
   if (usetimer) {                  // and timer in effect
    rate--;                         // lower time
    if (rate == 0) {                // and if rate now hits 0,
     KillTimer (TIMERID);           // kill timer
     MessageBeep (0);               // warning so we know then fast action begins
     rate = 500;                    // fast loop rate
     usetimer = FALSE;              // signal timer not in use
     canclose = FALSE;              // fast action, so cannot close at once
     Invalidate(FALSE);             // trigger Paint's fast action loop
    }
    else {                          // slow down the timer
     KillTimer (TIMERID);           // remove old timer
     SetTimer (TIMERID, rate, NULL);  // install new timer
    }
   }
   else {                           // slow down and fast action in effect
    rate -= 10;                     // lower by 10
    if (rate<0) {                   // do not let rate go below 1
     rate = 1;
     MessageBeep (0);               // sound warning so we know when going fastest
    }
   }
  }
}

/*****************************************************************************/
/*                                                                         */
/* OnPaint: draw once for XOR - handle non-timer fast action               */
/*                                                                         */
/*****************************************************************************/
void     MainWin::OnPaint () {

 CPaintDC dc (this);                // create a paint dc

 if (!ptrbackbitmap) BuildBitmaps ();  // load and start action

 DWORD x;     // work fields for the delay action
 int i;
 MSG msg;

 // if timer is not operating, then this will handle the faster action scenario
 if (!usetimer) {
  BOOL ok = TRUE;
  while (ok) { // terminated by user keybd or mouse events

   // delay a small amount based upon rate
   i = 0; x = 1;
   while (i<rate) {x *= 2; i++;}

   if (!smoothmove) XORMove (); // process new XOR position
   else SmoothMove ();          // process new smooth move

   // now check for any messages in the queue - break out and handle
   // Pump processes and dispatches all waiting messages
   while (::PeekMessage (&msg, NULL, 0, 0, PM_REMOVE)) {
    if (msg.message == WM_QUIT) {
     ::PostQuitMessage (0);
```

```
      ok = FALSE;
      break;
    }
    if (!AfxGetApp()->PreTranslateMessage (&msg)) {
      ::TranslateMessage (&msg);
      ::DispatchMessage (&msg);
    }
  }
  AfxGetApp()->OnIdle (1); // frees temp objects

  if (usetimer) ok = FALSE; // reset if XOR fast changes to smooth move
  }
 }
}

/***********************************************************************/
/*                                                                     */
/* OnClose: gracefully shut down                                       */
/*                                                                     */
/***********************************************************************/
void     MainWin::OnClose () {

 if (usetimer) KillTimer (TIMERID);          // kill any user timer
 usetimer = TRUE;

 // if coming from fast action Paint, give the system time to finish
 // the paint processing before closing down
 if (canclose) CFrameWnd::OnClose ();        // if it's safe to close, close
 else SetTimer (TIMERCLOSEID, 100, NULL); // if it's not, wait a moment
}
```

After the MainWin constructor creates the window, it initializes all the GDI object pointers to NULL. It then sets the initial situation: use the built-in timer at 10 ms in XOR mode (**smoothmove** is FALSE). Since the bitmaps have not been loaded yet, the **shipheight** is set to 0. The member **canclose** is used to help close the application down while it is in the fast-move mode; when it is TRUE, the application can shut down normally in response to WM_CLOSE.

All objects and any active timer are removed in **DestroyWindow**. **OnSize** is invoked twice as the application launches, once with zero dimensions and then, as the window is set up, with the correct dimensions. Since the bitmaps are not loaded until the first **OnPaint** call, the size function returns if the dimensions are zero or if the ship height is still zero. Any other calls to **OnSize** represent real resize operations while the action is ongoing. These must be handled by recalculating the overall **dimrect**, the action dimensions rectangle, and then BitBlting the background image and the ship onto the resized client area.

As the window is coming up, the first action occurs in the first call to **OnPaint** which then calls **BuildBitmaps** to load the images. **BuildBitmaps** is a rather long sequence. First it loads the main background bitmap into an instance of CDib and initializes the **dibrect** rectangle to contain the DIB's dimensions. Next a pair of memory DCs are created to hold the background image and the smooth-move image, both of which must contain a copy of the background DIB. The image is copied using **SetDIBits**. The memory DC for the ship is built and the ship image is loaded. Notice that I stored the ship as a DDB in the resource file because it is very small and also to illustrate the differences between loading a DIB and a DDB. The ship is actually two images—the ship and its monochrome mask. With the ship image loaded and its size known, the **dimrect**—dimensions rectangle representing the actual range of motion—can be calculated. The full window area cannot be used; the ship would appear to leave the screen before it "bounced" back. I reduce the dimensions rectangle from full client area by one-half of the height and width of the ship. The ship's initial position is then set in **shiprect** and the amount to increment x,y motion—**dx** and **dy**—are set to 1 pixel. Notice that this gives the best motion effect. Try altering these to larger values and observe the jerkier motion. If all has gone well, the four bitmaps are then inserted into their respective memory DCs, and the background is blited to the screen followed by the ship at its initial position. Notice that the background blit uses SRCCOPY while the ship blit uses SRCINVERT, which is the XOR mode. The timer is then set and the action commences.

In **OnTimer** either **XORMove** or **SmoothMove** is called to process the motion. Initially, XOR logic is used. The **XORMove** procedure is quite simple. First a **BitBlt** is used displaying the ship at the same location as before, using SRCINVERT or XOR; the ship disappears. Then **CheckDims** moves the ship and checks for and processes any collisions with the window border. Finally, the ship is again **BitBlt**ed using XOR so that it appears at its new position. **CheckDims** moves the ship. How? **shiprect** contains the position and size of the ship. The increments **dx** and **dy** are added to all four rectangle members by using the new **CRect** function, **OffsetRect**—a convenient method to add values to the rectangle's members. **OffsetRect** adds the **dx** and **dy** values to all rectangle coordinates, effectively moving the center position. Next, collisions with the four screen edges are checked for and handled by reversing direction.

For **SmoothMove**, the move DC and bitmap contain the ship at its current position. First, **BitBlt** with SRCCOPY copies the original background over that portion of the image occupied by the ship, removing the ship. **CheckDims** moves the ship, handling any collisions. **BitBlt** copies the ship onto the move DC and bitmap. Using the procedure described above, the ship mask is ANDed with the background, producing a black hole where the ship will be. Then the ship is ORed onto the background, filling in the hole with the ship's colors. SRCAND is the raster operation (ROP) for AND while SRCPAINT is the ROP for an OR.

Since we do not necessarily know which direction the ship has moved, the on-screen rectangle is set up to be the size of the ship rectangle plus the absolute values of the **dx** and **dy** members. The **InflatedRect** function of the **CRect** class extends the bounds of the rectangle by adding/subtracting the **dx** and **dy** amounts from the current bounds. So **newrect** covers all possible movement directions. Lastly, a **BitBlt** copies the **newrect** area from the move DC onto the screen, producing the illusion of smooth movement.

The **OnKeyDown** user interface is the most complicated portion. If the right arrow is pressed and it has not yet been pressed, then it is safe to switch into smooth-move mode. Any current timer must be halted, and, if no timer was in use, **usetimer** must be reset along with the rate of the initial speed of 10 ms. The move DC can now be initialized by drawing the current ship's position on it and then it can be copied onto the client DC or screen. Once the timer is set, smooth moving automatically commences.

When the up or down arrow is pressed, the timer must be slowed or speeded up. When no timer is in use, fast action—a different rate increment—is used. When the timer rate hits 0 ms, the program switches automatically into fast-action mode. Note that the **Invalidate (FALSE);** both signals **OnPaint** to begin fast-action movement and tells **OnPaint** *not* to erase the background. If only **Invalidate();** were used, then a white background would appear and slowly the ship would paint all of the background. (It's a nice effect—try it.)

The **OnPaint** function processes the fast-action requests. Since **ok** is TRUE, the fast-action process continues. After a small delay based upon the current value of **rate**, either **XORMove** or **SmoothMove** is invoked to move the ship.

When the fast-action sequence is in effect (not the normal timer), **OnPaint** is entered and, from within the function, repeated calls are made to the display routines. In essence the **OnPaint** function is never left! So no more messages get processed by Windows 95. Hence, revert back to the C-style message processing loop—get message, translate message, dispatch message—except that we really do not want to get the message and remove it from the queue; rather we want just a look at the message, letting the message remain in the queue. This is done with the Windows 95 API function **PeekMessage** as we discussed earlier. If it is the Quit message, then, no matter what we do, the application is shutting down. We now have a problem. If we ignore it or if we try to exit out of **OnPaint**, failed assertions result because, when MFC tries to clean up the stack, our whole application and windows are gone! The fix is simple. First, **ok** is set to FALSE to end the **OnPaint** while loop. **OnClose** is called by MFC in response to the WM_CLOSE message. All that must be done when in the fast-action mode is to have **OnClose** pause a few milliseconds to let the **OnPaint** function terminate. Recall back in the constructor, I set a BOOL **canclose** to TRUE. In **OnClose**, as long as **canclose** is TRUE, we can shut down by invoking the base class **OnClose**. Whenever we enter the fast-action processing, set the **canclose** to FALSE.

Whenever **OnClose** is invoked by the framework and **canclose** is FALSE, set or activate another timer, of ID TIMERCLOSEID, and use a small interval, say, 100 ms.

```
if (usetimer) KillTimer (TIMERID);      // kill any user timer
usetimer = TRUE;
// if coming from fast action Paint, give the system time to finish
// the paint processing before closing down
if (canclose) CFrameWnd::OnClose ();     // if it's safe to close, close
else SetTimer (TIMERCLOSEID, 100, NULL); // if it's not, wait a moment
```

Now back in **OnTimer**, check the timer ID that has just gone off. If it is the TIMERCLOSEID, then kill the timer, set **canclose** to TRUE, and post another WM_QUIT message.

```
if (id == TIMERCLOSEID) {       // if we are closing down during fast action,
  KillTimer (TIMERCLOSEID);     // kill the timer
  canclose = TRUE;             // indicate it is now safe to close down
  PostMessage (WM_CLOSE, 0, 0); // and post another close down message
  return;
}
```

This time, **OnClose** terminates the application. This process requires a slight adjustment in **OnKeyDown**. Whenever we switch from normal timer processing into the fast action or vice versa, we must toggle **canclose** appropriately.

Now experiment with the **dx** and **dy** members. Try a value of 4 pixels and see the effect on XOR and smooth move. Experiment with the two methods. While XOR requires less GDI, memory, and coding, the motion is jerkier. With the basics of animation understood, you should examine actual OOP implementations as given in the bibliography.

14.3 SPLASH SCREENS

A splash screen is an initial bitmap that is displayed just at the moment an application is launched and before its main window is displayed. Whenever you click on the Developer Studio icon to launch the IDE, a small splash screen—the colorful logo image—appears in the center of the screen. A splash screen often is displayed when an application takes a rather long time to load and initialize itself. Its purpose is to give the user some idea that something is occurring or to display copyright information, for example. Once the main window is set up, the main window display writes over the area where the bitmap was.

In a C-style application, splash screens can be displayed from the **WinMain** procedure either just before or just after the main **CreateWindow** function. Under MFC, the best point to insert the splash display is in the **CWindApp**'s **InitApplication** overridden function because this function is invoked only once per application and before **InitInstance** is called. Once the splash screen is displayed, the application continues with normal program initialization in **InitInstance**. The splash images are usually centered on the screen and are overlaid by the normal application window when it is finally displayed.

Pgm14c illustrates splash screens. I have designed a simple **ShowSplashScreen** function that can be inserted into any program to display the startup logo. The function requires only three parameters: an hinstance, the string name of the bitmap resource, and the number of seconds delay wanted. **ShowSplashScreen** loads the bitmap and then delays its return for the requested number of seconds. Why the delay? Our applications come up almost at once, so we'd never get the opportunity to view the splash—it would be gone in a blink. The delay can be zero seconds, in which case **ShowSplashScreen** would return at once. Figure 14.3 shows Pgm14c just after the three splash screens have been displayed.

For the bitmaps, I have used three images representing fictitious company logos: ACME.BMP, BUILDER.BMP, and CANDLES.BMP. The sample program uses the shell from Pgm04b that displayed simply a "Hello" screen. Pgm14cAp.cpp illustrates how the splash function can be inserted.

The splash header file must be included to pick up the function prototype. Notice that **ShowSplashScreen** is *not* a class member function, but rather a simple C function. Therefore, it can be invoked by nearly anyone. This means that, if the program had to do a lengthy subsection switch later, another splash could be used. Here it is

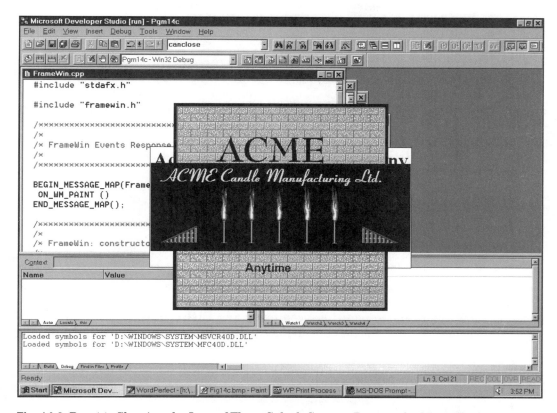

Fig. 14.3 Pgm14c Showing the Last of Three Splash Screens Prior to the Main Window Appearing

invoked three times just for fun. The MFC **InitApplication** function returns TRUE if the application can continue launching.

```
BOOL  Pgm14CApp::InitApplication () {
  ShowSplashScreen (m_hInstance, 2, "IMAGE1");
  ShowSplashScreen (m_hInstance, 2, "IMAGE2");
  ShowSplashScreen (m_hInstance, 2, "IMAGE3");
  return TRUE;
  return CWinApp::InitApplication ();
}
```

These three bitmaps have been included into the resource file.

14.3.1 Listing for File: Pgm14c.rc—Pgm14c—Excerpts

```
...
IMAGE1   BITMAP   "\\learnwin\\bmp\\acme.bmp"
IMAGE2   BITMAP   "\\learnwin\\bmp\\builder.bmp"
IMAGE3   BITMAP   "\\learnwin\\bmp\\candles.bmp"
...
```

The header file Splash.h defines the function as

```
void   ShowSplashScreen (HINSTANCE hinst, int seconds, char *name);
```

The splash function is a C-style function to increase its flexibility. It can be invoked from many places as it really requires only the application's hinstance. It does not require any handles to windows. The basic method is to **BitBlt** from a DC containing the loaded bitmap onto a screen DC. Since the splash screen should appear on top of everything else that is on the whole screen, this DC is the desktop DC. Another DC is created that is compatible with this desktop DC, and the bitmap is inserted into the compatible DC. The **BitBlt** then transfers the bitmap from the compatible DC onto the desktop DC. Since we are dealing with C style, the DCs are of data type HDC. A DC for the whole screen can be gotten by using a **CreateDC** using the name of the screen, "DISPLAY".

```
desktopdc = CreateDC ("DISPLAY", NULL, NULL, NULL); // get screenDC
```

The bitmap is loaded from the resource file using the argument string resource name.

```
hbitmap    = LoadBitmap (hinst, name); // load the bitmap
```

Note that this is the only place where the application's hinstance is needed. You could redesign the splash function to accept a handle to the splash bitmap and remove the hinstance and the resource name. For centering and **BitBlt** purposes, I need the bitmap's dimensions. We can get them by using the **GetObject** function to fill the bitmap information structure.

```
GetObject (hbitmap, sizeof(bm), &bm); // get bitmap info
```

The following calculates the x,y coordinates for the upper-left corner of the bitmap so that it is centered on the screen.

```
int x = (GetSystemMetrics (SM_CXSCREEN)/2) - (bm.bmWidth/2);
int y = (GetSystemMetrics (SM_CYSCREEN)/2) - (bm.bmHeight/2);
```

Next, a compatible DC to the desktop is created and the bitmap inserted into it. However, the original bitmap contents of the compatible DC must be preserved so that the DC can be deleted. Remember, you cannot delete DCs with new objects currently selected in them—memory leaks. The handle of the old bitmap, **holdbitmap**, is used to deselect our splash bitmap before deleting the compatible DC.

```
hcompatdc = CreateCompatibleDC (desktopdc); // get compat DC bitmap
holdbitmap = (HBITMAP) SelectObject (hcompatdc, hbitmap);
```

Next, the bitmap is displayed.

```
BitBlt (desktopdc, x, y, bm.bmWidth, bm.bmHeight, hcompatdc, 0, 0,
        SRCCOPY);
```

The splash screen now appears nicely centered on the whole screen, independent of the resolution in use. However, you may notice that the color palette is wrong. One could improve the splash function by loading and realizing the proper color palette for the bitmap. The cleanup section is straightforward—delete all objects allocated. But remember to deselect objects first.

```
SelectObject (hcompatdc, holdbitmap); // install original bitmap
DeleteDC (hcompatdc);                  // remove compatible dc
DeleteObject (hbitmap);                // remove splash bitmap
DeleteDC (desktopdc);                  // remove screen dc
```

The final action is to delay the requested number of seconds. If the application really had some work to perform, it would have passed in 0 seconds. Further, when the splash function returned, the application most likely would have replaced the arrow cursor with the hourglass wait cursor. Windows 95 provides a function to detect large-scale elapsed times. The unit of resolution is 1 ms, or 1/1000 of a second. This is a large unit compared to the internal clock speed that is in nanoseconds. On the faster machines, this millisecond time may represent nearly one-half million instructions!

The Windows 95 clock maintains a count of the total number of milliseconds that Windows 95 has been up and running. In other words, the clock started from 0 when the DOS command WIN was entered. The count is stored in a DWORD or unsigned long, and the clock rolls over after some 49 hours of continuous operation. The time is retrieved by the Windows 95 function **GetTickCount**. The following represents a simple method to delay the requested number of seconds without using a Windows 95 built-in timer.

```
DWORD beginticks = GetTickCount ();   // the beginning time
DWORD ticks = beginticks;             // the current time

// delay the requested number of seconds
while (ticks < beginticks + 1000*seconds) ticks = GetTickCount ();
```

If 0 seconds is passed, the while loop ends almost at once. When you run Pgm14c and watch the three splash images, realize that the next step would be the construction of your real company or program logo bitmap.

14.3.2 Listing for File: Splash.cpp—Pgm14c—Excerpts

```
...
/*****************************************************************************/
/*                                                                          */
/* ShowSplashScreen: displays start up screen for n seconds                 */
/*                                                                          */
/*****************************************************************************/
void       ShowSplashScreen (HINSTANCE hinst, int seconds, char *name) {

HDC      desktopdc;  // DC for whole screen
HBITMAP  hbitmap;    // handle for the bitmap of the splash .bmp
BITMAP   bm;         // the actual splash bit map
HDC      hcompatdc;  // compatible DC to hold the bitmap for copying
HBITMAP  holdbitmap; // the original screen bitmap

desktopdc = CreateDC ("DISPLAY", NULL, NULL, NULL); // get the screen DC
hbitmap   = LoadBitmap (hinst, name);               // load the bitmap
GetObject (hbitmap, sizeof(bm), &bm);               // get bitmap info

// calculate the center position of screen and back off to upper left corner
int x = (GetSystemMetrics (SM_CXSCREEN)/2) - (bm.bmWidth/2);
```

```
int y = (GetSystemMetrics (SM_CYSCREEN)/2) - (bm.bmHeight/2);
hcompatdc = CreateCompatibleDC (desktopdc);  // get compatible DC for BitBlt

//insert bitmap into the compatible dc, saving the original bitmap present
holdbitmap = (HBITMAP) SelectObject (hcompatdc, hbitmap);

// display the bitmap
BitBlt (desktopdc, x, y, bm.bmWidth, bm.bmHeight, hcompatdc, 0, 0, SRCCOPY);

// clean up section
SelectObject (hcompatdc, holdbitmap);  // install original bitmap
DeleteDC (hcompatdc);                  // remove compatible dc
DeleteObject (hbitmap);                // remove splash bitmap
DeleteDC (desktopdc);                  // remove screen dc

// pause section - ticks are total milliseconds since Windows was started
DWORD beginticks = GetTickCount ();    // the beginning time
DWORD ticks = beginticks;              // the current time

// delay the requested number of seconds
while (ticks < beginticks + 1000*seconds) ticks = GetTickCount ();
}
```

14.4 ANIMATED PRESENTATIONS

The principles of splash screens and animation can be combined into a form for animated business presentations. First, display the basic background image. Second, using a series of drop-in bitmap files, "smooth move" these bitmap overlays from their initial drop-in positions to their ending locations on the final image. Figure 14.4 shows the initial background image, and Figure 14.5 shows the final screen image in the main window after all 11 images have been dropped onto the background.

This example also illustrates another type of window design that is useful not only in business presentation applications but also in writing games. Did you notice anything unusual about the main application window in Figure 14.5? Look again. There is *no* menu bar, title bar, control bar, or status bar! The application main window occupies the entire screen. Gone are all of the normal window's controls. This application definitely does not fit the Windows 95 look-and-feel which is just what might be desired in a game or animated business presentation. In such circumstances, unless otherwise overridden, Alt-F4 and the usual keyboard task switching still operate. It even overlays the Windows 95 task bar across the bottom of the screen. Now the user interface is up to you. Keystrokes, mouse clicks, and pop-up menus are used to create the user interface. In Pgm14d, both Alt-F4 and a right mouse button click terminate the application via the usual **OnClose** message box, while a left mouse click repeats the presentation.

Again, I have chosen DIBs that use only the standard Windows 95 color palette. Therefore, once more, I have used Method 1 given in Chapter 9 for conversion of a DIB into a memory DC, avoiding the use of **CreateDIBitmap**. Its use, however, would speed up the slow display.

The animated drop-in bitmaps can be dropped into the main image from any of the four sides. If a bitmap is dropped in from the top, it smooth moves downward until reaching its predefined location in the final image. Once there, that bitmap is permanently fixed on the main bitmap image. Then, the cycle repeats for the next drop-in bitmap. If dropped in on the bottom, it moves up to its ending place; if dropped in on the right side, it moves left; if dropped in on the left, it moves right. Perhaps the two most useful motions for presentations are top-down and right-left. Once all drop-in bitmaps have been placed on the main image bitmap, that bitmap becomes available to the main window's **OnPaint** which, in response to a WM_PAINT message, **BitBlts** the final image onto the screen. If a left button click requests a repeat presentation, the main bitmap is replaced by the original background bitmap and the drop-in process continues.

You could add a couple of other details that I did not implement in Pgm14d. For real presentations, you could add a "pause before doing the next drop-in" interval to give the presenter, say, 15 seconds to discuss the last drop-in. And an option would be useful that manually controls when the next drop-in starts.

The bitmap construction to smooth move the drop-in bitmaps follows the previous flying ship example, Pgm14c. First, a main background bitmap and an identical smooth-move bitmap are constructed in memory DCs from the same original DIB or

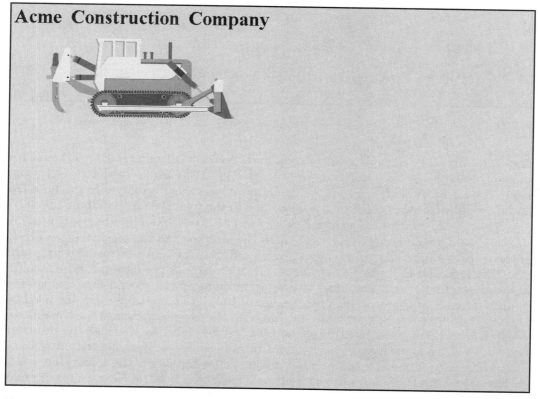

Fig. 14.4 Pgm14d Showing the Initial Background Image

Fig. 14.5 Pgm14d after 11 Images Have Been Dropped Forming the Final Screen

bmp file. Likewise, each drop-in bitmap and its mask bitmap (DIB) are housed in memory DCs. Each time the drop-in is to "move," AND a hole in the move bitmap using the mask version; then OR the drop-in bitmap image's colors into the hole. (All of the bmp files for this program are contained in the folder \learnwin\bmp\demo.)

In order to control the process, some form of "user control text script" must be invented so that the user can construct both the bitmaps and the script independently of the display engine. Examine the listing for DEMO.TXT that controls this presentation. The information that the user must provide includes the background image file name on the first line, the number of drop-in bitmaps on the second line, and specific details for each of the drop-ins on subsequent lines. Two or three lines are used for each drop-in bitmap. The first line begins with the string identifier for the side on which it is to be initially placed: top, bottom, left, or right. Next comes the insertion point x,y coordinates relative to the main bitmap image. I have started all of these drop-in bitmaps 5 pixels into the main image. So for top-down, the y coordinate is 5; for bottom-up, it is 763; for left, x is 5 pixels; for right, x is 1019. Next comes the ending point for that drop-in. The last character on the drop-in line is Y or N indicating the presence of a mask bitmap (Y) or not (N). This allows for static drop-ins in which the insertion point is the ending point. The last line(s) for each drop-in contains the file name of the drop-in bitmap and its mask bitmap if present.

14.4.1 Listing for File: Demo.txt—Pgm14d

```
\learnwin\bmp\demo\demobkgd.bmp
11
Top 380 5 150 Y
\learnwin\bmp\demo\dropit0.bmp
\learnwin\bmp\demo\dropit0M.bmp
Top 530 5 150 Y
\learnwin\bmp\demo\dropit1.bmp
\learnwin\bmp\demo\dropit1M.bmp
Top 730 5 150 Y
\learnwin\bmp\demo\dropit2.bmp
\learnwin\bmp\demo\dropit2M.bmp
Top 880 5 150 Y
\learnwin\bmp\demo\dropit3.bmp
\learnwin\bmp\demo\dropit3M.bmp
Top 050 5 310 Y
\learnwin\bmp\demo\dropit4.bmp
\learnwin\bmp\demo\dropit4M.bmp
Bottom 35 763 310 Y
\learnwin\bmp\demo\dropit5.bmp
\learnwin\bmp\demo\dropit5M.bmp
Right 1019 380 40 Y
\learnwin\bmp\demo\dropit6.bmp
\learnwin\bmp\demo\dropit6M.bmp
Left 5 470 50 Y
\learnwin\bmp\demo\dropit7.bmp
\learnwin\bmp\demo\dropit7M.bmp
Right 1019 550 60 Y
\learnwin\bmp\demo\dropit8.bmp
\learnwin\bmp\demo\dropit8M.bmp
Left 5 610 50 Y
\learnwin\bmp\demo\dropit9.bmp
\learnwin\bmp\demo\dropit9M.bmp
Top 55 5 750 Y
\learnwin\bmp\demo\dropita.bmp
\learnwin\bmp\demo\dropitaM.bmp
```

So now we have an elementary presentation script that could be used for any presentation, not just this one. To actually input the variable data, I use the C++ io-streams, specifically an instance of the **ifstream**, so you can see how to use iostreams in a Windows 95 application. The variable number of sets of drop-in bitmap data is handled by dynamically allocating an array of OBJECTS structure that contains the definition data.

```
struct OBJECTS {
  char filenameobj[MAX_PATH];
  char filenamemask[MAX_PATH];
  TPoint insert;
```

```
    int     end;
  DropType type;
  };
```

Provision is made for two filenames. If no mask file is present, the filename is a NULL string. The insertion coordinates are encapsulated into a **CPoint** object. The drop-in location is encapsulated into an **enum** data type—DropType—that is defined as

```
  enum DropType { TopDown, BottomUp, RightLeft, LeftRight };
```

Additionally, since the user is constructing the text file of directions, some bulletproofing should be done. I performed some basic error checking, but feel free to add much more.

The application design includes two main classes, DisplayObject and Presentation. DisplayObject encapsulates all of the actual bitmap operations including performing the initial loading, the smooth-move drop-ins, and all **BitBlt** operations. The background, smooth-move, and all drop-in sets are instances of the DisplayObject class. While the instances for the move bitmap and all drop-in bitmaps are transitory, kept only as long as needed to perform the actual animated sequence, the instance of the main background, which also holds the resultant image, is kept to service the main window's Paint function. The Presentation class loads the user's text script file and runs the presentation.

Although this presentation assumes a resolution of 1024x768—the size of the main image—smaller-than-full-screen main bitmaps can be used. I assume that smaller main images are going to be centered. Centering adds a final coordinate adjustment when bliting the main window onto the screen.

What may not be clear is exactly how the drop-in process actually operates. If an image is dropped in from 5 pixels from the top edge of the main window, for example, only a tiny portion of the drop-in bitmap is visible. As it moves downward, more and more of the image becomes visible on the main image, until the entire drop-in bitmap is shown. From now on, the size of the drop-in window does not vary, but its position can. Figure 14.6 shows these two situations using the variable names I assigned to them in the program.

When copying from the background image to the screen, the **screenoffset** point is used to offset the destination rectangle for the **BitBlt**. All other coordinates are relative to the start of the background bitmap. The lower-left corner of the drop-in image is initially placed at **insertpt** at Position 1 in the figure and is to be moved until that point reaches the ending y coordinate indicated by the "X" in the figure. Initially, the **dropin** rectangle may be small (even nonexistent if the drop-in point is not on the initial bitmap). As the image is moved downward, the **dropin** rectangle expands until the full size of the drop-in image is reached. In Position 2, the **dropin** rectangle is at its maximum size.

Notice that, until the **dropin** rectangle becomes full size—given by the dimensions of the drop-in bitmap—to move downward, only the **dropin** rectangle's **bottom** member is incremented. Upon reaching full size, thereafter, both the **dropin** rectangle's **top** and **bottom** members are incremented. The **dropin** rectangle is used as the

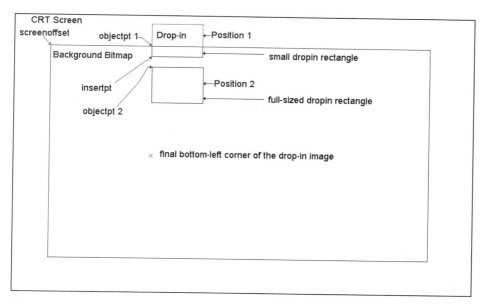

Fig. 14.6 The Drop-in Top-Down Method

destination in **BitBlt** operations. The source point for the **BitBlt** functions is that point within the drop-in bitmap itself from which pixels can be copied, here called **objectpt**. **objectpt**'s x coordinate is fixed at the value of the **insertpt**'s x coordinate. Its y coordinate must be adjusted. Initially, **objectpt**'s y coordinate is the height of the drop-in bitmap less the **insertpt**'s y amount. As the image moves downward, the **objectpt**'s y coordinate must be decremented until it reaches 0 when the **dropin** rectangle is full size. It remains at 0 thereafter.

The bottom-up action is basically the reverse of the top-down. The sideways movements are done similarly, holding the y coordinate fixed at the insertion point while varying the x coordinates of the **objectpt** and **dropin** rectangle. Make a sketch similar to Figure 14.6 and satisfy yourself as to the needed settings. With these preliminaries understood, let's examine the coding for Pgm14d.

14.4.2 Pgm14d—Presentations

The resource file includes the **OnClose** strings and a string that identifies the demo.txt file.

14.4.3 Listings for Files: Pgm14d.rc and resource.h—Excerpts

```
...
STRINGTABLE {
  IDS_DEMO,       "\\learnwin\\pgm14d\\demo.txt"
  IDS_MSG_QUERY,  "Query?"
```

```
IDS_MSG_QUIT,    "Do you want to quit the demo presentation?"
}
...
#define  IDS_DEMO       2250
#define  IDS_MSG_QUERY  2251
#define  IDS_MSG_QUIT   2252
```

The application's **InitInstance** has a couple of changes. The special FrameWin class uses a constructor similar to **CFrameWnd**—that is, it has no parameters. This window is to have no title bar, menu bar, or system controls. To force the frame window to be maximized, I pass SW_SHOWMAXIMIZED to **ShowWindow**.

```
BOOL  Pgm14DApp::InitInstance () {
 FrameWin *ptrframe = new FrameWin ();
 // install the frame window as the main app window and show that window
 m_pMainWnd = ptrframe;
 m_pMainWnd->ShowWindow (SW_SHOWMAXIMIZED); // install show as maximized
 m_pMainWnd->UpdateWindow ();
 return TRUE;
}
```

This special FrameWin class does not appear significantly different from any other FrameWin. Look over the class definition. Notice there is a pointer to the current presentation object which is allocated in the constructor and used in the **OnPaint** function to perform the presentations and later for repainting the main window as needed. The BOOL **shown** controls whether a presentation is required or not. Initially, **shown** is set to FALSE in the constructor. In **OnPaint**, whenever **shown** is FALSE, the Presentation member function **Present** is invoked to carry out another action presentation.

14.4.4 Listing for File: FrameWin.h—Pgm14d—Excerpts

```
...
protected:

 BOOL            shown;     // FALSE when presentation must be made
 Presentation   *ptrpresent; // the presentation object
...
public:
            FrameWin ();      // make spcl window and presentobj
            ~FrameWin ();     // removes the presentation object
protected:

afx_msg void  OnPaint ();                        // requests the presentation
afx_msg void  OnClose ();                        // determines if app can quit yet
afx_msg void  OnRButtonDown (UINT, CPoint);      // quit the application
afx_msg void  OnLButtonDown (UINT, CPoint);      // requests new presentation
...
```

14.4.5 Listing for File: FrameWin.cpp—Pgm14d—Excerpts

```
...
BEGIN_MESSAGE_MAP(FrameWin, CFrameWnd)
```

```
  ON_WM_PAINT ()
  ON_WM_CREATE ()
  ON_WM_CLOSE ()
  ON_WM_RBUTTONDOWN ()
  ON_WM_LBUTTONDOWN ()
END_MESSAGE_MAP ()
/*****************************************************************************/
/*                                                                           */
/* Framewin: Construct the window object                                     */
/*                                                                           */
/*****************************************************************************/

          FrameWin::FrameWin () : CFrameWnd () {

  DWORD style = WS_POPUP;
  // the following rect is an alternative to ShowWindow (SM_SHOWMAXIMIZED)
  // and using rectDefault to get a full screen window
  CRect rect (0, 0, GetSystemMetrics (SM_CXSCREEN),
                    GetSystemMetrics (SM_CYSCREEN));

  Create ( AfxRegisterWndClass (
              NULL,
              AfxGetApp()->LoadStandardCursor (IDC_ARROW),
              (HBRUSH) GetStockObject (LTGRAY_BRUSH),
              AfxGetApp()->LoadStandardIcon (IDI_APPLICATION)),
          NULL,                 // set no window caption
          style,                // wndclass DWORD style
          rect,                 // set initial window position
          NULL,                 // the parent window, here none
          NULL);                // set no menu

  shown = FALSE; // set presentation not yet shown
  ptrpresent = new Presentation (this, IDS_DEMO); // load this presentation
}

/*****************************************************************************/
/*                                                                           */
/* ~FrameWin: remove the presentation object                                 */
/*                                                                           */
/*****************************************************************************/

          FrameWin::~FrameWin () {

  if (ptrpresent) delete ptrpresent;
}
...

/*****************************************************************************/
/*                                                                           */
/* OnRButtonDown: pop up edit menu as a floating menu                        */
/*                                                                           */
/*****************************************************************************/

void      FrameWin::OnRButtonDown (UINT, CPoint) {

  PostMessage (WM_CLOSE);
}
```

```
/************************************************************************/
/*                                                                      */
/* OnLButtonDown: request another presentation run                      */
/*                                                                      */
/************************************************************************/

void       FrameWin::OnLButtonDown (UINT, CPoint) {

 shown = FALSE; // set for repeat presentation
 Invalidate (); // force Paint to repeat the presentation
 }

/************************************************************************/
/*                                                                      */
/* OnPaint: displays presentations or copies final image to screen      */
/*                                                                      */
/************************************************************************/

void       FrameWin::OnPaint () {

 CPaintDC   dc(this);

 if (!shown) {
  ptrpresent->Present (dc);
  shown = TRUE;
 }
 ptrpresent->Copy (dc);
}
```

Examine the constructor to see that the most unusual frame window is constructed. The key is the parameters to the **Create** function. The window style is limited to only WS_POPUP. NULL is passed for the title, for the menu, and for the parent window.

The destructor removes the Presentation object. The buttons provide our rudimentary user interface. **OnRButtonDown** posts the WM_CLOSE message, while **OnLButtonDown** repeats the presentation. In **OnPaint** the status of **shown** controls whether or not the **Present** function is called. In all cases the screen repaint is done by the **BitBlt** of the final completed image via the Presentation class **Copy** function.

14.4.6 Listing for File: Present.h—Pgm14d—Excerpts

```
...
/************************************************************************/
/*                                                                      */
/* DropType: enum to aid in identifying the four directions of motion   */
/*                                                                      */
/************************************************************************/

enum DropType { TopDown, BottomUp, RightLeft, LeftRight };

/************************************************************************/
/*                                                                      */
/* OBJECTS: allocated as an array of the individual objects to move     */
/*          specifying bmp and mask bmp files, insertion pt, end pt, type */
```

```
/*                                                                      */
/**********************************************************************/
struct OBJECTS {
 char filenameobj[MAX_PATH];
 char filenamemask[MAX_PATH];
 CPoint insert;
 int     end;
 DropType type;
};

/**********************************************************************/
/*                                                                    */
/* Presentation: class definition - Performs a graphic presentation   */
/*                                                                    */
/**********************************************************************/

class Presentation {

/**********************************************************************/
/*                                                                    */
/* Class Data:                                                        */
/*                                                                    */
/**********************************************************************/

protected:

BOOL            isvalid;            // TRUE when this is a valid object -no errors
OBJECTS         *objects;           // array of objects to move onto the display
int             numobjs;            // number of objects in the array to move
char            filename[MAX_PATH]; // filename of the main bmp background

DisplayObject *ptrmain;             // the main bmp object, holds final images
int             hmain;              // main bmp's height
int             wmain;              // main bmp's width
DisplayObject *ptrmove;             // smooth move copy of original background

CRect           screenrect;         // rect defining area on screen to BitBlt to
CPoint          screenoffset;       // screen offset of main bmp image
CRect           screendropin;       // corresponding screen are to fill from main

DisplayObject *ptrobj;              // current object to drop in
int             hobject;            // current object's height
int             wobject;            // current object's width

CRect           dropin;             // current main bmp area filled by an object
CPoint          insertpt;           // current insertion point of an object
DropType        type;               // current DropType of this object
int             endat;              // current ending coord for this drop in obj
CPoint          objectpt;           // current offset of the object to dropin
int             xnext;              // incremental value to get to next dropin pt
int             ynext;              // incremental value to get to next dropin pt

/**********************************************************************/
/*                                                                    */
/* Class Functions:                                                   */
/*                                                                    */
/**********************************************************************/
```

```
public:

        Presentation (CWnd*, UINT);     // construct the presentation object
      ~Presentation ();                 // removed allocate items
void    Present (CDC&);                 // perform the presentation
void    Copy (CDC&);                    // copy final image for parent's Paint
BOOL    IsValid () {return isvalid;}    // returns TRUE when all is OK

protected:

void    DropInBitmap (CDC&);            // does the actual drop in of this object
void    AdjustDropInRects ();           // adjusts for the next dropin increment
...
```

Next, look over the Presentation class definition. The Presentation class maintains a number of protected fields. Since numerous bitmaps, memory DCs, and CDibs are going to be constructed, there are many opportunities for a GDI failure or for a "low on memory" failure. Hence, I maintain an **isvalid** BOOL which is set to TRUE only if things go right. If there are any failures, the **isvalid** is set to FALSE. Hence, by checking the **IsValid** function return, I can avoid actually using a presentation that is improperly set up.

The member **objects** contains the dynamically allocated array of OBJECTS structures that define each drop-in bitmap event. **numobjs** conveniently contains the number in the array, while **filename** contains the name of the background bitmap that must be reloaded into both the main and move memory DCs with each presentation. The OBJECTS structure contains the basic information input from the script file, including the pair of filenames (for the image and its mask) and the insertion point. For convenience, in reference to the four locations that a bitmap may be dropped onto the screen, I defined a DropType enum.

```
enum DropType { TopDown, BottomUp, RightLeft, LeftRight };
struct OBJECTS {
 char filenameobj[MAX_PATH];
 char filenamemask[MAX_PATH];
 CPoint insert;
 int    end;
 DropType type;
};
```

The DisplayObject class encapsulates the memory DCs, the bitmaps, and the actual bliting functions. The **ptrmain** DisplayObject instance is permanently kept once the action sequence is complete. It is used for later screen repaints. For convenience, I store its bitmap's height and width. The **ptrmove** DisplayObject instance is allocated at the start of each presentation and deleted when it is finished. Similarly, the **ptrobj** DisplayObject member and its **hobject** and **wobject** height and widths are used to hold the temporary allocation of each drop-in image and its dimensions while it is being dropped in.

Since the final image in the main bitmap must be blited onto the screen and since it could be smaller than the full-screen dimensions, the member **screenrect** holds the current screen destination rectangle, and **screenoffset** contains the upper-left point of the main bitmap on the screen. The rectangle **screendropin** contains the current drop-in rectangle in screen coordinates. Note that, if an image is full screen to begin with, **screenoffset** contains the point (0,0) and **screenrect** matches the screen dimensions.

The rectangle **dropin** coupled with **objectpt** play a crucial role in the actual bliting operations. Again refer to Figure 14.6 for the details. Since I wanted one routine that would perform all four types of drop-ins, I use the members **xnext** and **ynext** to hold the current increment values with which to expand the drop-in rectangle. The members **type**, **endat**, and **insertpt** are copied values from the current OBJECTS structure and are included for convenience.

The member functions include the Presentation constructor that streams in the user's demo.txt presentation commands, verifying their validity to some small extent and storing them in the OBJECTS array. The destructor removes the main background bitmap DisplayObject. **Present** actually runs the action sequence following the commands in the OBJECTS array. **Copy** provides a means of bliting the final resultant image to the screen as requested by the main window's **OnPaint** routine. **DropInBitmap** performs the actual movement of one object from its initial insertion point to its final destination. After each movement, **AdjustDropInRects** handles the calculations to determine the next drop-in position.

14.4.7 Listing for File: Present.cpp—Pgm14d—Excerpts

```
...
#include <fstream.h>
...
/*****************************************************************************/
/*                                                                         */
/* Presentation: construct the presentation object                         */
/*                                                                         */
/*****************************************************************************/

        Presentation::Presentation (CWnd *ptrparnt, UINT presentid) {

objects = NULL;  // the array of objects
ptrmain = NULL;  // the main final image bmp object
isvalid = FALSE; // assume bad, if all is OK reset to good

int x, y;
char mask;
CString mainfile;
char typ[10];

// load in the filename that will define this presentation
mainfile.LoadString (presentid);

// construct an iostream to input the presentation definition
ifstream is (mainfile, ios::in);
if (is.bad ()) {        // trap bad file - and abort
 ptrparnt->MessageBox (mainfile, "Presentation Error - Bad Input File", MB_OK);
 return;
}

// stream in the presentation definition file
```

```
is >> filename >> numobjs;                      // bring in the main bmp filename
ptrmain = new DisplayObject (filename, NULL, TRUE);// construct main image obj
if (!ptrmain->IsValid ()) return;               // abort if bad main image
hmain = ptrmain->Height ();                      // and set its dimensions
wmain = ptrmain->Width  ();

// attempt to allocate the OBJECTS array to store drop in object sets
try {
 objects = (OBJECTS*) malloc (sizeof(OBJECTS) * numobjs);
}
catch (...) {  // if out of memory, abort
 ptrparnt->MessageBox ("Out of Memory", "Presentation Error", MB_OK);
 return;
}

// load in each object's definition
for (int i=0; i<numobjs; i++) {
 is >> typ;             // get the type and convert to DropType enum format
 if (stricmp (typ, "Top") == 0) objects[i].type = TopDown;
 else if (stricmp (typ, "Bottom") == 0) objects[i].type = BottomUp;
 else if (stricmp (typ, "Right") == 0) objects[i].type = RightLeft;
 else if (stricmp (typ, "Left") == 0) objects[i].type = LeftRight;
 else {                        // catch invalid Drop In Types
  ptrparnt->MessageBox (typ,"Presentation Error - Object's DropinType Invalid",
                     MB_OK);
  return;
 }
 is >> x >> y;                           // construct the insertion point
 objects[i].insert = CPoint (x, y);
 is >> objects[i].end >> mask;           // get the Y/N presence of a mask file
 is >> objects[i].filenameobj;           // load object's filename
 if (toupper (mask) == 'Y') is >> objects[i].filenamemask; // load its maskname
 else objects[i].filenamemask[0] = 0;
}
is.close ();
isvalid = TRUE;                             // set successful construction
}
/********************************************************************************/
/*                                                                            */
/* ~Presentation: remove all objects                                          */
/*                                                                            */
/********************************************************************************/
          Presentation::~Presentation () {
 if (ptrmain) delete ptrmain;
 if (objects) free (objects);
}
/********************************************************************************/
/*                                                                            */
/* Copy: BitBlt a final image onto the screen when parent's Paint needs it */
/*                                                                            */
/********************************************************************************/
void      Presentation::Copy (CDC &screendc) {
```

```
  if (IsValid () && ptrmain && ptrmain->IsValid ()) {
   if (ptrmain->GetPalette ()) {    // if there is a color palette
    screendc.SelectPalette (ptrmain->GetPalette (), FALSE); // insert dib's color pal
    screendc.RealizePalette();              // cause palette to be set up & ready
   }
   ptrmain->Copy (screendc, screenrect, CPoint (0, 0));// copy main to screen
  }
}
/***************************************************************************/
/*                                                                         */
/* Present: perform the actual presentation display                        */
/*                                                                         */
/***************************************************************************/
void        Presentation::Present (CDC &screendc) {
  CPoint pt (0, 0);

  if (!IsValid ()) return; // avoid actions if not properly setup

  if (ptrmain->GetPalette ()) {    // if there is a color palette
   screendc.SelectPalette (ptrmain->GetPalette (), FALSE); // insert dib's color pal
   screendc.RealizePalette();               // cause palette to be set up & ready
  }

  // construct a smooth move copy of the main background image
  ptrmove = new DisplayObject (filename, NULL, FALSE);
  if (!ptrmove || !ptrmove->IsValid ()) return; // abort if bad move dc

  // calculate the center position of screen and back off to upper left corner
  screenoffset.x = GetSystemMetrics (SM_CXSCREEN)/2 - wmain/2;
  screenoffset.y = GetSystemMetrics (SM_CYSCREEN)/2 - hmain/2;

  // construct main on-screen full display rectangle and rect for all of main bmp
  screenrect.SetRect (screenoffset.x, screenoffset.y,
                      screenoffset.x + wmain, screenoffset.y + hmain);
  CRect mainrect (0, 0, wmain, hmain);

  // erase any previous showing of this presentation in main and on screen
  ptrmove->Copy (ptrmain, mainrect, pt);    // copy blank move bmp onto main
  ptrmain->Copy (screendc, screenrect, pt); // copy main to screen

  for (int i=0; i<numobjs; i++) { // drop each object into place
   // construct next object to drop in
   ptrobj  = new DisplayObject (objects[i].filenameobj, objects[i].filenamemask,
                               FALSE); // with no palette required
   if (!ptrobj || !ptrobj->IsValid ()) continue; // bad one, skip it, try another
   hobject = ptrobj->Height (); // set its dimensions
   wobject = ptrobj->Width  ();
   insertpt= objects[i].insert; // save its insertion point, end coord, and type
   endat   = objects[i].end;
   type    = objects[i].type;
   DropInBitmap (screendc);      // and go drop this object into place on main bmp
   delete ptrobj;
  }
  delete ptrmove;
}
```

```
/***************************************************************************/
/*                                                                         */
/* DropInBitmap: smooth moves a bitmap object onto the screen and mainmemDC*/
/*                                                                         */
/* when done, the main memory object now has the bitmap copied onto it     */
/* so that when finally done, the main bitmap can be kept and used as the   */
/* completed presentation screen                                           */
/*                                                                         */
/***************************************************************************/

void      Presentation::DropInBitmap (CDC &screenDC) {
 // always does a one pixel movement
 // construct first dropin rectangle which is the initial area occupied on the
 // move and main images - then set the corresponding source point on the
 // objects bmp - last set the incremental values to get to the next drop in pt
 switch (type) {
  case TopDown:    // top-down motion
   dropin.SetRect (insertpt.x, 0, insertpt.x + wobject, insertpt.y);
   objectpt = CPoint (0, hobject - insertpt.y);
   xnext = 0;
   ynext = 1;
   break;

  case BottomUp:   // bottom-up motion
   dropin.SetRect (insertpt.x, insertpt.y, insertpt.x + wobject, hmain);
   objectpt = CPoint (0,0);
   xnext = 0;
   ynext = -1;
   break;

  case RightLeft: // right to left motion
   dropin.SetRect (insertpt.x, insertpt.y, wmain, insertpt.y + hobject);
   objectpt = CPoint (0,0);
   xnext = -1;
   ynext = 0;
   break;

  case LeftRight: // left to right motion
   dropin.SetRect (0, insertpt.y, insertpt.x, insertpt.y + hobject);
   objectpt = CPoint (wobject - insertpt.x, 0);
   xnext = 1;
   ynext = 0;
   break;
 };

 // screenin is screen dc's corresponding area to dropin
 screendropin.SetRect (dropin.left   + screenoffset.x,
                       dropin.top    + screenoffset.y,
                       dropin.right  + screenoffset.x,
                       dropin.bottom + screenoffset.y);

 // display drop in object at its initial position
 ptrobj->TransparentCopy (ptrmove, dropin, objectpt);  // copy object to move
 ptrmove->Copy (screenDC, screendropin, dropin.TopLeft());// copy move to screen
 ptrmain->Copy (ptrmove, dropin, dropin.TopLeft ());   // erase object from move

 // based upon drop in type, move it to its final ending position
```

```
  while (type == TopDown   ? dropin.bottom < endat :
         type == BottomUp  ? dropin.top    > endat :
         type == RightLeft ? dropin.left   > endat : dropin.left < endat) {
    AdjustDropInRects ();  // calc its next position
    ptrobj->TransparentCopy (ptrmove, dropin, objectpt); // copy object to move dc
    screendropin.top--;      // remove from the screen the top piece from last image
    screendropin.bottom++; // and remove the bottom piece,then copy move to screen
    ptrmove->Copy (screenDC, screendropin, CPoint (dropin.left,dropin.top-1));
    screendropin.top++;      // set screen coords back after the removal of the top
    screendropin.bottom--; // and bottom pieces
    ptrmain->Copy (ptrmove, dropin, dropin.TopLeft ()); // erase object from move
  }

  // copy logo object final position to the main & work images, and to the screen
  ptrobj->TransparentCopy (ptrmain, dropin, objectpt);
  ptrobj->TransparentCopy (ptrmove, dropin, objectpt);
  ptrmove->Copy (screenDC, screendropin, CPoint (dropin.TopLeft ()));
}

/***************************************************************************/
/*                                                                         */
/* AdjustDropInRects: adjust all rects and pts for next movement           */
/*                                                                         */
/***************************************************************************/
void       Presentation::AdjustDropInRects () {
 if (type < RightLeft) {
  if (dropin.Height() < hobject) { // reached full object's dimensions yet?
   if (type == TopDown) {            // if top-down motion
    objectpt.y -= ynext;   // inc height, so move source obj's y up one more pel
    dropin.bottom += ynext;// expand the destination area down by one pixel
    screendropin.bottom += ynext;  // expand the screen area down by one pel
   }
   else {                      // if bottom-up motion
    dropin.top += ynext;       // inc height, so move destination area up one pel
    screendropin.top += ynext;// and move screen area up one pel
   }
  }
  else {                       // have hit full object height, so move whole area
   dropin.OffsetRect (xnext, ynext);   // dropin area down one pixel
   screendropin.OffsetRect (xnext, ynext); // and move screen area down one pixel
  }
 }
 else {
  if (dropin.Width () < wobject) { // reached full object dimensions yet?
   if (type == RightLeft) {          // no, so if right-left motion
    dropin.left += xnext;            // inc dropin width
    screendropin.left += xnext;      // and corresponding screen position
   }
   else if (type == LeftRight) {  // no, so if left-right motion
    objectpt.x -= xnext;          // expand object's source point one pel
    dropin.right += xnext;        // inc dropin width
    screendropin.right += xnext;  // and screen width
   }
  }
```

```
else {                        // have hit full object width, so move whole area
  dropin.OffsetRect (xnext, ynext);   // dropin area left/right one pixel
  screendropin.OffsetRect (xnext, ynext); // and move screen area l/r one pixel
}
}
}
```

Now let's see how the user definition text file is streamed in the constructor in the Present.cpp file. The main and object pointers are set to NULL, and **isvalid** set to FALSE. Only if all goes well are these reset to proper values. The filename of the user's commands is retrieved from the resource file. I then attempt to open an **ifstream** using that filename.

```
mainfile.LoadString (presentid);

ifstream is (mainfile, ios::in);
if (is.bad ()) {        // trap bad file - and abort
  ...
  return;

}
```

If the stream cannot be constructed, I display an error message and return. Although no objects have been allocated, the member function **IsValid** when checked returns FALSE, preventing erroneous actions. Then I stream in the background filename and the number of objects. I attempt to construct a DisplayObject using the background filename. By checking the DisplayObject's **IsValid** function, I can tell if the action was successful. Again, if not, I return leaving **isvalid** FALSE so no other actions except destructors can be used.

```
is >> filename >> numobjs;
ptrmain = new DisplayObject (filename, NULL, TRUE);
if (!ptrmain->IsValid ()) return;
hmain = ptrmain->Height ();
wmain = ptrmain->Width  ();
```

Then I allocate the array of OBJECTS which could fail and is therefore a good candidate for try-catch error handling. I wrap a Try block around allocation and catch any errors, displaying an error message and returning. Once more, **isvalid** is still FALSE, so no use can be made of this failed instantiation.

```
try {
  objects = (OBJECTS*) malloc (sizeof(OBJECTS) * numobjs);
}
catch (...) {  // if out of memory, abort
  ...
  return;
}
```

We'll discuss more on the try-catch logic shortly. But next I stream in each set of data for each of the drop-in requests. The only action that is not obvious is the conversion of the user type into the proper instance of the DropType enum. By using a **stricmp**, case-insensitive compare, I can assign the OBJECTS's type member the correct DropType. With the array loaded, I close the stream and finally set **isvalid** to TRUE. Note that I have not checked for any positions that are illogical, nor have I checked for the existence or validity of the drop-in bitmaps or mask bitmaps. If you wish to completely bulletproof at this point in the sequence, you can go ahead and attempt to instantiate each of the drop-in objects. Once allocated, check their **IsValid** functions and then delete the instance. If any return FALSE, then you cannot set **isvalid** to TRUE. It is not necessary to delete the array nor the main DisplayObject at this point because the Presentation class destructor handles this.

```
for (int i=0; i<numobjs; i++) {
 is >> typ;
 if (stricmp (typ, "Top") == 0) objects[i].type = TopDown;
 else if (stricmp (typ, "Bottom") == 0) objects[i].type = BottomUp;
 else if (stricmp (typ, "Right") == 0) objects[i].type = RightLeft;
 else if (stricmp (typ, "Left") == 0) objects[i].type = LeftRight;
 else {
  ...
  return;
 }
 is >> x >> y;
 objects[i].insert = CPoint (x, y);
 is >> objects[i].end >> mask;
 is >> objects[i].filenameobj;
 if (toupper (mask) == 'Y') is >> objects[i].filenamemask;
 else objects[i].filenamemask[0] = 0;
}
is.close ();
isvalid = TRUE;
```

Now turn your attention to the **Copy** function that is invoked by the main window's **OnPaint** routine after a presentation is complete and the screen needs to be repainted. Here the fail-safe actions handle possible invalid conditions. First, I check the Presentation class for validity; then I check for the existence of the main Display-Object; finally I check the main's validity. Nothing is done if any are not valid. If all is OK, I then attempt to acquire the main DisplayObject's color palette using **GetPalette** of DisplayObject.

```
if (IsValid () && ptrmain && ptrmain->IsValid ()) {
 if (ptrmain->GetPalette ()) {
  screendc.SelectPalette (ptrmain->GetPalette (), FALSE);
  screendc.RealizePalette();
 }
 ptrmain->Copy (screendc, screenrect, CPoint (0, 0));
}
```

The color palette insertion is important. If you do not realize the DIB's color palette, then the image is displayed in the wrong color scheme. Try this out. Comment out the Realize Palette function call in the **Present** function and rebuild the program. Next, launch the Paintbrush application which installs its own palette. Then launch the revised Pgm14d. You will see the animation, but it will be done in strange colors. The actual color palette is constructed and owned by the DisplayObject class.

The **Present** function runs the animation sequence. Look over its coding and the function that it calls—**AdjustDropInRects**. From our previous discussions, the sequences should be understandable and followable from the instruction comments.

14.4.8 Listing for File: DsplyObj.h—Pgm14d—Excerpts

```
...
/*************************************************************************/
/*                                                                       */
/* DisplayObject: class definition                                       */
/*                                                                       */
/*************************************************************************/

class DisplayObject {
/*************************************************************************/
/*                                                                       */
/* Class Data:                                                           */
/*                                                                       */
/*************************************************************************/

public:

CPalette   *ptrpalette; // main color palette if requested

protected:

CDC        *ptrobjdc;   // memory dc for the object's image
CDC        *ptrmaskdc;  // memory dc for the object's mask image
CBitmap    *ptrobjbm;   // object's bitmap
CBitmap    *ptrmaskbm;  // mask's bitmap
int        height;      // image's height
int        width;       // image's width
BOOL       hasmask;     // TRUE when object has a mask
BOOL       isvalid;     // TRUE when object is valid

/*************************************************************************/
/*                                                                       */
/* Class Functions:                                                      */
/*                                                                       */
/*************************************************************************/

public:

      DisplayObject (char*, char*, BOOL); // construct the object
      ~DisplayObject ();                  // removes allocated items

BOOL  IsValid () {return isvalid;}                   // returns TRUE when all OK
int   Height () {return IsValid () ? height : 0;} // returns image height
int   Width  () {return IsValid () ? width  : 0;} // returns image width

                      // provide access to the palette if any
CPalette* GetPalette () {return IsValid () && ptrpalette ? ptrpalette : NULL;}

//    transparent copy functions where background color is invisible
void  TransparentCopy (CDC*, CRect&, CPoint&);
```

```
void  TransparentCopy (DisplayObject*, CRect&, CPoint&);

//    normal copy functions which place full image onto destination
void  Copy (CDC*, CRect&, CPoint&);
void  Copy (DisplayObject*, CRect&, CPoint&);
void  Copy (CDC&, CRect&, CPoint&);
...
```

The DisplayObject class encapsulates the construction and low-level manipulations of the drop-in bitmaps and their masks, if present. A memory DC and its corresponding **CBitmap** are constructed for both the drop-in DIB and any mask DIB. If successful, the width and height of the drop-in bitmap are retrieved and saved in protected members, again for convenience. If all is successful, **isvalid** is set to TRUE. The constructor provides for three cases. When constructing the main background DisplayObject, there is no mask file; the second filename is therefore NULL. However, for the main bitmap, I need the color palette constructed and maintained. The assumption I have made is that all the bitmaps use the same color palette. The allocated objects are deleted in the class destructor. There are two key member functions that are overloaded, servicing several combinations of bliting.

```
      void   TransparentCopy (CDC*, CRect&, CPoint&);
      void   TransparentCopy (DisplayObject*, CRect&, CPoint&);

      void   Copy (CDC*, CRect&, CPoint&);
      void   Copy (DisplayObject*, CRect&, CPoint&);
      void   Copy (CDC&, CRect&, CPoint&);
```

TransparentCopy can copy an image onto either another DisplayObject or onto a memory DC. It first ANDs the mask bitmap and then ORs the drop-in bitmap, allowing the background of this object to become transparent. The **Copy** member copies this DisplayObject to another DisplayObject, to a memory DC, or to a real DC—in this case the screen from the main window's **Paint** function.

14.4.9 Listing for File: DsplyObj.cpp—Pgm14d—Excerpts

```
...
/**********************************************************************/
/*                                                                    */
/* DisplayObject: construct the object(s) to be shown                 */
/*                                                                    */
/**********************************************************************/
      DisplayObject::DisplayObject (char *filename, char *maskfilename,
                                    BOOL makepalette) {
isvalid     = FALSE;              // initialize to unsuccessful, then if ok, reset
hasmask     = FALSE;
ptrobjdc    = ptrmaskdc = NULL;
ptrobjbm    = ptrmaskbm = NULL;
ptrpalette  = NULL;

CDib     *ptrdib;
CDC dc;
```

```
if (!filename) return;                    // must have at least one filename
dc.CreateDC ("DISPLAY", NULL, NULL, NULL);
try {
 ptrdib    = new CDib (filename);         // construct a DIB from file
 if (!ptrdib || !ptrdib->IsValid ()) {    // try-catch misses our class
  MessageBox (NULL, filename,
             "Present Display Object Error - bad main filename", MB_OK);
  return;
 }
 height     = ptrdib->GetDibHeight ();     // install bitmap's dimensions
 width      = ptrdib->GetDibWidth ();

 if (makepalette) {
  ptrpalette = new CPalette ();            // construct a new palette
  ptrdib->MakePalette (ptrpalette);        // create new palette from dib
 }

 ptrobjdc  = new CDC();                    // the memory dc
 ptrobjdc->CreateCompatibleDC (&dc);       // copy client dc
 ptrobjbm = new CBitmap ();                // create the bitmap for memdc
 ptrobjbm->CreateCompatibleBitmap (&dc, width, height);
 if ((makepalette && !ptrpalette) || !ptrobjdc || !ptrobjbm) {
  MessageBox (NULL, filename,"Present Display Object Error - bad main filename",
             MB_OK);
  return;
 }
}
catch (CException* e) {
 MessageBox (NULL, filename,"Present Display Object Error - bad main filename",
            MB_OK);
 return;
 e->Delete ();
}
ptrobjdc->SelectObject (ptrobjbm);  // insert bitmap into memdc
// one time conversion of the DIB color bits to the compatible DC display
SetDIBits (ptrobjdc->m_hDC, HBITMAP (ptrobjbm->m_hObject), 0, height,
          ptrdib->GetDibBitsAddr (), ptrdib->GetBitmapInfo (),
          DIB_RGB_COLORS);                 // copy dib bits into bitmap
delete ptrdib;

if (maskfilename) {                        // see if there is a mask .BMP file
 hasmask = TRUE;                           // set yes there is and load it
 try {
  ptrdib  = new CDib (maskfilename);       // construct a DIB from file
  if (!ptrdib || !ptrdib->IsValid ()) {
   MessageBox (NULL, filename,"Present Display Object Error - bad mask filename",
              MB_OK);
   return;
  }

  ptrmaskdc  = new CDC();                  // the memory dc
  ptrmaskdc->CreateCompatibleDC (&dc);     // copy client dc
  ptrmaskbm = new CBitmap ();              // create the bitmap for memdc
  ptrmaskbm->CreateCompatibleBitmap (&dc, width, height);
```

```
    if (!ptrmaskdc || !ptrmaskbm) {
    MessageBox (NULL, maskfilename,"Present Display Object Error - bad mask filename",
              MB_OK);
     return;
    }
   }
   catch (CException* e) {
    MessageBox (NULL, maskfilename,"Present Display Object Error - bad main filename",
              MB_OK);
    return;
    e->Delete ();
    }

   ptrmaskdc->SelectObject (ptrmaskbm);   // insert bitmap into memdc
   // one time conversion of the DIB color bits to the compatible DC display
   SetDIBits (ptrmaskdc->m_hDC, HBITMAP (ptrmaskbm->m_hObject), 0, height,
              ptrdib->GetDibBitsAddr (), ptrdib->GetBitmapInfo (),
              DIB_RGB_COLORS);                  // copy dib bits into bitmap
   delete ptrdib;
   }
  isvalid = TRUE;                             // set this Display Object as valid
  dc.DeleteDC ();
}
/****************************************************************************/
/*                                                                        */
/* ~DisplayObject: delete all GDI objects                                 */
/*                                                                        */
/****************************************************************************/

         DisplayObject::~DisplayObject () {
 if (ptrobjdc)   delete ptrobjdc;
 ...
}
/****************************************************************************/
/*                                                                        */
/* TransparentCopy: use the mask to perform a transparent background copy */
/*                                                                        */
/****************************************************************************/

void     DisplayObject::TransparentCopy (CDC *ptrdest, CRect &dropin,
                                          CPoint &srcpt) {

 if (!IsValid () || !hasmask) return;
 // use mask with AND operation to make hole in destination bitmap
 ptrdest->BitBlt (dropin.left, dropin.top, dropin.right, dropin.bottom,
                  ptrmaskdc, srcpt.x, srcpt.y, SRCAND);
 // use main object image and PAINT over hole in destination bitmap
 ptrdest->BitBlt (dropin.left, dropin.top, dropin.right, dropin.bottom,
                  ptrobjdc, srcpt.x, srcpt.y, SRCPAINT);
}
/****************************************************************************/
/*                                                                        */
/* TransparentCopy: use the mask to perform a transparent background copy */
/*                 Destination is another DisplayObject                   */
```

```
/*                                                                       */
/***********************************************************************/
void     DisplayObject::TransparentCopy (DisplayObject *ptrdest, CRect &dropin,
                                          CPoint &srcpt) {

  if (!IsValid () || !hasmask || !ptrdest->IsValid ()) return;
  // use mask with AND operation to make hole in destination bitmap
  ptrdest->ptrobjdc->BitBlt (dropin.left, dropin.top,
                             dropin.right, dropin.bottom,
                             ptrmaskdc, srcpt.x, srcpt.y, SRCAND);
  // use main object image and PAINT over hole in destination bitmap
  ptrdest->ptrobjdc->BitBlt (dropin.left, dropin.top,
                             dropin.right, dropin.bottom,
                             ptrobjdc,  srcpt.x, srcpt.y, SRCPAINT);
}

/***********************************************************************/
/*                                                                    */
/* Copy: copy as is the actual display object onto the passed memory dc  */
/*                                                                    */
/***********************************************************************/
void      DisplayObject::Copy (CDC *ptrdest, CRect &dropin,
                               CPoint &srcpt) {

  if (!IsValid ()) return;
  ptrdest->BitBlt (dropin.left, dropin.top, dropin.right, dropin.bottom,
                   ptrobjdc, srcpt.x, srcpt.y, SRCCOPY);
}

/***********************************************************************/
/*                                                                    */
/* Copy: copy as is the actual display object onto another object       */
/*                                                                    */
/***********************************************************************/
void      DisplayObject::Copy (DisplayObject *ptrdest, CRect &dropin,
                               CPoint &srcpt) {

  if (!IsValid () || !ptrdest->IsValid ()) return;
  ptrdest->ptrobjdc->BitBlt (dropin.left, dropin.top,
                             dropin.right, dropin.bottom,
                             ptrobjdc, srcpt.x, srcpt.y, SRCCOPY);
}

/***********************************************************************/
/*                                                                    */
/* Copy: copy as is the actual display object onto another TDC          */
/*                                                                    */
/***********************************************************************/
void      DisplayObject::Copy (CDC &destdc, CRect &dropin, CPoint &srcpt) {
  if (!IsValid ()) return;
  destdc.BitBlt (dropin.left, dropin.top, dropin.right, dropin.bottom,
                 ptrobjdc, srcpt.x, srcpt.y, SRCCOPY);
}
```

In the DisplayObject implementation, the coding to construct memory DCs closely parallels that of Pgm09b—loading the fancy DIBs. In the class constructor, to obtain a DC for the entire screen, use the **CDC** function **CreateDC** passing it the key string "DISPLAY" and NULL for all of the other parameters.

```
dc.CreateDC ("DISPLAY", NULL, NULL, NULL);
```

The DisplayObject constructor follows the same pattern as Presentation by setting all pointers to NULL and **isvalid** to FALSE. Only if all objects are successfully constructed is it reset to TRUE. Since a large number of graphical objects are to be constructed, there is a fair chance that something could go wrong. So I wrapped this group in another **try-catch** block.

```
try {
 ptrdib     = new CDib (filename);        // construct a DIB from file
 if (!ptrdib || !ptrdib->IsValid ()) {  // try-catch misses our class
  ...
  return;
 }
 height     = ptrdib->GetDibHeight ();    // install bitmap's dimensions
 width      = ptrdib->GetDibWidth ();

 if (makepalette) {
  ptrpalette = new CPalette ();           // construct a new palette
  ptrdib->MakePalette (ptrpalette);       // create new palette from dib
 }

 ptrobjdc  = new CDC();                    // the memory dc
 ptrobjdc->CreateCompatibleDC (&dc);      // copy client dc
 ptrobjbm = new CBitmap ();               // create the bitmap for memdc
 ptrobjbm->CreateCompatibleBitmap (&dc, width, height);
 if ((makepalette && !ptrpalette) || !ptrobjdc || !ptrobjbm) {
  ...
  return;
 }
}
catch (CException* e) {
 ...
 return;
 e->Delete ();
}
ptrobjdc->SelectObject (ptrobjbm);  // insert bitmap into memdc
// one time conversion of the DIB color bits to the compatible DC display
SetDIBits (ptrobjdc->m_hDC, HBITMAP (ptrobjbm->m_hObject), 0, height,
           ptrdib->GetDibBitsAddr (), ptrdib->GetBitmapInfo (),
           DIB_RGB_COLORS);          // copy dib bits into bitmap
delete ptrdib;
```

Rather than spell out exactly what exceptions I am looking for in the Catch statements, I catch the base class for all exceptions—**CException**. Shortly the various possibilities are presented. Next the sequence is repeated for any mask image file.

The two **TransparentCopy** functions differ only in the destination object. Once more the bliting occurs only if this DisplayObject is valid and the destination is valid. For transparent bliting, this object must have a mask.

```
if (!IsValid () || !hasmask) return;
ptrdest->BitBlt (dropin.left, dropin.top, dropin.right, dropin.bottom,
                 ptrmaskdc, srcpt.x, srcpt.y, SRCAND);
ptrdest->BitBlt (dropin.left, dropin.top, dropin.right, dropin.bottom,
                 ptrobjdc, srcpt.x, srcpt.y, SRCPAINT);
```

Finally, the **Copy** functions, which only really differ in the destination object, perform a SRCCOPY **BitBlt** if the objects are valid.

```
ptrdest->ptrobjdc->BitBlt (dropin.left, dropin.top,
                           dropin.right, dropin.bottom,
                           ptrobjdc, srcpt.x, srcpt.y, SRCCOPY);
```

14.5 THE TRY-CATCH AND TRY-CATCH LOGIC FOR MFC

Originally, the MFC used macros to handle run-time error trapping using TRY, CATCH, AND_CATCH, and END_CATCH. With Version 4.0, these have been replaced with the standard C++ "try and catch."

The try-catch sequence catches the general **CException** class which IDs the base class for a number of possible MFC exceptions that could be thrown.

```
try {
 ...
}
catch (CException* e) {
 MessageBox ...
 e->Delete ();
 return;
}
```

Under MFC, the base class is **CException** which can be used to catch all errors. The list of exceptions thrown include

CMemoryException	thrown if out of memory on an allocation
CFileException	thrown if a file error occurs using the CFile class
CArchiveException	thrown if an error occurs during serialization or archiving (see chapter 15)
CResourceException	thrown if a resource allocation fails
CNotSupportedException	thrown if an action is not yet or no longer supported
CUserException	thrown under programmer-defined circumstances

A sequence that would catch specifically **CFile** errors and Out of Memory, yet pick up any other errors could be

```
try {
 ...
}
catch (CFileException* e) {
 MessageBox ...
 // here e is not deleted and the error passed on up the line to another handler
 throw;
}
catch (CMemoryException* e) {
 MessageBox ...
 // here e is deleted and a new exception is thrown
 e->Delete ();
 throw new AnotherException;
}
catch (CException* e) {
 MessageBox ...
 // here e is deleted and the return says that we have handled the exception
 e->Delete ();
 return;
}
```

You should also consider using the ASSERT, TRACE, and WARN macros to assist in debugging. I have not done so in this book in order to keep the coding at a simpler level.

After looking over this example and running it, I think that you can see many possibilities for similar coding. All manner of presentation screens can be handled. It can be extended to create scrolling marquis. If nothing else, the method of creating a non-Windows 95 main window has its utility, especially in games and business applications.

The Document-View Architecture

15.1 INTRODUCTION

Consider a file of sales data consisting of pairs of year and sales amounts. Likely the data would be displayed in columnar form similar to a spreadsheet for ease in updating. However, management often prefers graphical presentations, and in this case a bar chart graph would ideally illustrate the annual sales variations. How could this example be implemented? The main window can display the columnar report with scroll bars as needed. A menu option or tool bar button could be added to display the bar chart graph in a child window. However, when the user wishes both views on-screen simultaneously, complexity enters with regard to window placement and movement, communication between the main and child windows, and so on. A far better implementation approach is to use the Document-View architecture which supports multiple views.

The document may be thought of as a container for the data itself. It does not have an associated window for display purposes. The document class encapsulates the data, providing services to input and output the data along with prompting the user to save the data when it has been modified. One or more view classes actually display the document's data on-screen and handle printing when requested. In this example, one view class could be written to display the data in columnar fashion, to handle scrolling as needed, and to handle requests for updating the data. More than one instance of this view class can be on-screen simultaneously. For example, in one instance, the user positions the file near the beginning of the data and, in another instance, positions the file near the end so that visual comparisons can be made. These multiple instances of the same view class are often positioned side by side. Additionally, another view class can be constructed to display the bar chart. Probably the user would like a small-width columnar version on the left and the bar chart on the right occupying most of the screen real estate.

Using a *splitter window* greatly simplifies the multiple views' window management. A splitter window can divide a window into multiple sections placing a user-dragable divider border between the views. When the user drags the divider, the splitter window internally adjusts the size and placement of all the view windows with *no* effort on our part!

In this chapter, I illustrate how to implement the Document-View architecture using two different view classes of the same document by utilizing splitter windows. I also discuss and implement more details on the printing process, including print preview. We shall see how the class libraries handle dynamic creation of documents and views in both an SDI and MDI implementation. A powerful feature of any class is the ability to re-create itself from a data file at run time; this is known as *serialization*— I discuss several approaches to the serialization process. Last, the actual sales data is encapsulated into a SalesData object that is also capable of serializing itself. A container class is used to maintain the array of sales objects.

Program Pgm15a is the SDI version and Pgm15b is the MDI version. Again you can see how easy it is to convert a properly designed application to MDI.

15.2 THE APPLICATION DESIGN

Suppose that our company is called the Acme Better Construction Company. Our task is to design a yearly sales application. Begin by examining the main screen of Pgm15a immediately after the application has been launched (see Figure 15.1). Note that I have done nothing except launch the application—it has automatically loaded in the default document and constructed the complex display.

The title bar contains the actual filename—acme.dat—and the document title— ACME Sales Data. The tool bar buttons represent, from left to right, File | New, File | Open, File | Save, File | SaveAs, Add New Record, Update Selected Record, Delete Selected Record, Print, Print Preview, Choose Fonts, and Help—About. The left gray narrow window contains the columnar view with column headings displayed upon a raised rectangle. The large white window on the right is the plot view with a crude title that overlaps the bars themselves (you can alter the design so the title does not overlap if desired). Across the bottom under each bar is the year of that sales amount. (No provision is made for a vertical scale.) Separating the two views is a thick border—the splitter window edge. If the user drags horizontally on this border, both windows resize together—they are coupled.

Next look over Figure 15.2 after I chose to open another much larger file.

Notice that the columnar view window now has scroll bars because the data ranges from 1935 through 1995. The plot view looks quite different. The plot operation

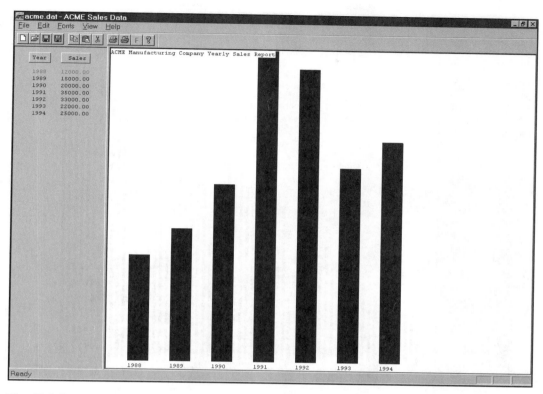

Fig. 15.1 Pgm15a upon Initial Launch Using ACME.DAT

must establish a uniform width for the bars and for the spaces between the bars. In Figure 15.1, the bars are constrained to a maximum width leaving a gap on the graph's right side. In Figure 15.2, in order to display the much larger number of bars, each bar's width must be reduced. But, if the bar's width becomes too narrow, the year's text cannot fit below the bar. One way around this is to display only the last two digits of each year. On printouts, if the widths are still too small to show even the last two digits, merely construct a smaller font to squeeze the two digits into the width at hand.

Printing can be done vertically (portrait style) or horizontally (landscape style). The graphs in our figures are often shown in landscape form. The application must be able to deal with the two different page layouts. The graph printout emulates the screen display; no user fonts are used. However, when printing the columnar report, the user can choose the font and point size to be used. Note that this user font is not used in the on-screen display, which remains a small fixed font. When printing the columnar report, the company title is at the top of every page, along with column headings above the data. On the last line of each page is a footer stating "Prepared by Broquard Consultants." Thus, you can see how to handle headings and footers and, by emulation, setting left, right, top, and bottom margins.

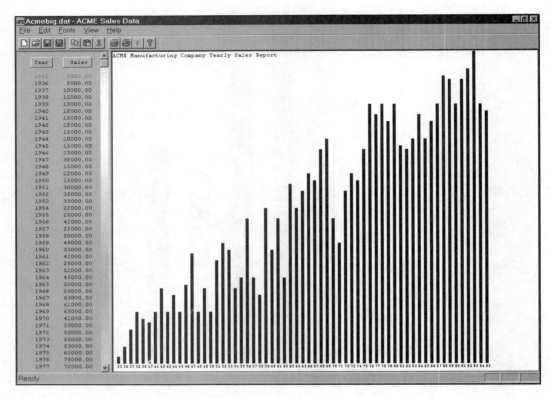

Fig. 15.2 Pgm15a Using the Large File acmebig.dat

Print I Preview is implemented as well. Figure 15.3 shows the preview window from Pgm15a.

The sales data files are in binary format—the year is a long and the sales, a double. When a class serializes itself to a file for later automatic restoration, the serialization process also adds some additional data fields to the binary stream—often the class name, for example, and a version number. If a container array class serializes itself, it appends the index of the next sales data object so that, on input, the container knows where to store that data. Additionally, some run-time class information is added so that it can verify that it is reading in its own data. So how does the data initially get input so that it can build the binary file for the next run? Often the initial data is inputted by a combination of a text file plus user data entry. On the CD you will find both a txt and dat file for the small data case (acme.dat and txt) and for the larger file (acmebig.dat and txt). Serialization and the MFC **CFile** class use a binary format. Therefore, I provide two File menu options to load a document from a txt file and to save a document into a txt file.

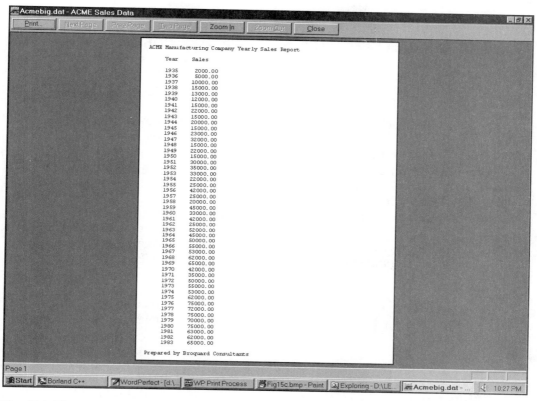

Fig. 15.3 The Print Preview Window from Pgm15a

15.3 THE DOC-VIEW IMPLEMENTATION OF PGM15A

15.3.1 Designing a Serializable SalesData Class

Ignoring the serialization process for a moment and keeping the complexity down, what would a class to encapsulate the sales data look like? We might begin with something like the following:

```
class SalesData {
public:
 long    year;   // year of sales
 double sales;   // sales
        SalesData () {}         // constructor
        SalesData (long, double); // copy constructor
};
```

Always provide a copy constructor. With this simple beginning, let's examine the MFC serialization process. Under MFC, for the environment to support dynamic class serialization, a class must be derived from the MFC class **CObject**. Nearly all MFC classes, like **CWnd** for example, are ultimately derived from **CObject**, which has a virtual function for serialization whose prototype is

```
virtual void Serialize (CArchive &);
```

For a class derived from **CObject** to read or write itself to permanent storage, it must override this function. The function can throw three run-time exceptions: **CMemoryException**, **CArchiveException**, and **CFileException**. Our overridden version handles reading or writing this class instance data to the file. However, the function is not passed a file directly; rather it is passed a reference to an instance of the **CArchive** class which encapsulates the file I/O.

Note that we do not create instances of **CArchive**; instead we use the reference that is passed to us by the MFC system. Normally, our use of **CArchive** involves using one of its member functions and two operators. The **CArchive** function **IsStoring** returns TRUE if the instance is to output itself; it returns FALSE for input.

```
BOOL IsStoring ();
```

The **CArchive** class provides normal C++ stream extraction operators, << and >>, which are used for the I/O to the binary file. The following data types can be streamed.

```
CObject, BYTE, WORD, LONG, DWORD, float, double
```

Notice that an **int** is *not* on the list! Assuming that our SalesData class is derived from **CObject**, the overridden **Serialize** function first calls the base class and then uses the extraction operators on the long and double as follows:

```
void      SalesData::Serialize (CArchive &ar) {
 CObject::Serialize (ar);
 if (ar.IsStoring ()) ar << year << sales;
 else ar >> year >> sales;
}
```

> ***Design Rule 48 Serialization:*** **For a class to be able to use the MFC serialization process, the class must include the DECLARE_SERIAL macro and, in its implementation file, include the IMPLEMENT_SERIAL macro.**

```
DECLARE_SERIAL (class name);
IMPLEMENT_SERIAL (class name, base class, UINT version number)
```

The version number is user defined and is encoded into the stream. In this manner you can keep track of multiple revisions of your classes. The version number cannot be -1. For our SalesData class the coding would be

```
DECLARE_SERIAL (SalesData); // in the header file
IMPLEMENT_SERIAL (SalesData, CObject, 0) // in the .cpp file
```

The **DECLARE_SERIAL/IMPLEMENT_SERIAL** macros implicitly include the **DECLARE_DYNAMIC/IMPLEMENT_DYNAMIC** macros which are used to make a class capable of accessing run-time class information.

> ***Design Rule 49 Serialization:*** **For a class to be able to be serialized, it must have a constructor with *no* arguments—that is a default constructor.**

Often copy constructors are included. Now you can see why the vast majority of MFC classes' constructors take no arguments—they use **CObject** as their ultimate base class and are serializable.

Combining all of these points, our **SalesData** class would now be as shown in the two files SalesDat.h and SalesDat.cpp.

15.3.2 Listing for File: SalesDat.h—Pgm15a—Excerpts

```
...
/**************************************************************************/
/*                                                                        */
/* SalesData & SalesDataArray:the sales data object and array of sales data*/
/*                                                                        */
/**************************************************************************/
class SalesData : public CObject {

DECLARE_SERIAL (SalesData);

/**************************************************************************/
/*                                                                        */
/* Class Data:                                                            */
/*                                                                        */
/**************************************************************************/

public:

long      year;   // year of sales
double    sales;  // sales

/**************************************************************************/
/*                                                                        */
/* Class Functions:                                                       */
/*                                                                        */
/**************************************************************************/

public:
      SalesData () {}            // constructor for serialization
      SalesData (long, double); // copy constructor
 void Serialize (CArchive&);    // handles I/O for sales data object
};

/**************************************************************************/
/*                                                                        */
/* SalesDataArray: array container for sales data objects                 */
```

```
/*                                                                      */
/*********************************************************************/
class SalesDataArray : public CObArray {

DECLARE_SERIAL (SalesDataArray);
/*********************************************************************/
/*                                                                      */
/* Class Functions:                                                     */
/*                                                                      */
/*********************************************************************/
public:
        SalesDataArray () {}            // constructor for serialization
};
...
```

15.3.3 Listing for File: SalesDat.cpp—Pgm15a—Excerpts

```
...
IMPLEMENT_SERIAL (SalesData, CObject, 0)
IMPLEMENT_SERIAL (SalesDataArray, CObArray, 0)
/*********************************************************************/
/*                                                                      */
/* SalesData: copy constructor                                          */
/*                                                                      */
/*********************************************************************/
        SalesData::SalesData (long yr, double sale) {

 year  = yr;
 sales = sale;
}
/*********************************************************************/
/*                                                                      */
/* Serialize: input or output a sales data object                       */
/*                                                                      */
/*********************************************************************/
void     SalesData::Serialize (CArchive &ar) {

 CObject::Serialize (ar);

 if (ar.IsStoring ()) ar << year << sales;
 else ar >> year >> sales;
}
```

The next design factor is: how does one store the array of SalesData objects? Using C style, one could simply code

```
    SalesData sales_array[MAX_LIMIT];
```

However, the array would not be dynamic and would force us to keep track of the current number of objects in the array. Of course, you could add further functions to expand and contract the array as records are added and deleted. But there is a far simpler way—use an MFC object container. The MFC provides some containers that are derived from **CObject**. For our use here, two key possibilities include

CObArray   supporting arrays of CObjects

CObList   supporting ordered linked lists of CObjects

Here, either class could be used. Since I am ignoring all interrelationships between sets of sales data, a simple array container works well. If you desire to maintain sorted lists, try using **InsertAt** or try changing to a **CObList**. Both array classes operate in a similar manner. They maintain an array of pointers to the **CObjects** themselves. Thus, I define a container class, SalesDataArray, to hold all of our Sales-Data objects.

```
class SalesDataArray : public CObArray {
DECLARE_SERIAL (SalesDataArray);
public:
        SalesDataArray () {}        // constructor for serialization
};
```

No other functions are necessary because the base class, **CObArray**, provides all the access methods needed. However, I must include the corresponding **IMPLEMENT_SERIAL** macro in an implementation file. Examine the SalesDat.h and cpp files once more to see our container class definition.

The key member functions of **CObArray** include the following:

```
int      GetSize ();        // rets size of the array
CObject* GetAt (int index); // rets CObject* at this index or NULL
int      Add (CObject*);    // adds new object, rets its index
void     InsertAt (int index, CObject*, int count);
                            // inserts count objs beginning at index
void     RemoveAll ();      // deletes all ptrs in the array
void     RemoveAt (int index, int count);
                            // removes count ptrs beginning at index
```

Note that both Remove functions delete only the container's pointer to the objects. We must delete the actual objects manually. To use our new container class in the appropriate class (derived from **CDocument**), define the array as follows:

```
SalesDataArray sales_array;    // container for list of sales data
```

Notice that the typecast **(SalesData*)** is nearly always required when working with the container classes. To delete the contents of the sales array, code a sequence as follows:

```
if (sales_array.GetSize () ==0) return; // is already empty
for (i=0; i<sales_array.GetSize (); i++)
 delete (SalesData*) sales_array.GetAt (i);
sales_array.RemoveAll ();
```

Next, to serialize the entire array of sales data, just invoke the **Serialize** base class function of **CObArray**. The container serializes itself, inputting or outputting all objects it contains by invoking the **Serialize** function of each object in the array.

```
void        someclass::Serialize (CArchive &ar) {
 if (ar.IsStoring ()) {
  if (sales_array.GetSize () == 0) return; // none to save
  sales_array.Serialize (ar);
 }
 else sales_array.Serialize (ar);
}
```

One could display all sales objects by iterating through the array. Assuming that **ptrarray** contains the address of the sales array, one would code something like this:

```
SalesDataArray *ptrarray;
SalesData       *ptrdata;
for (int i=0; i<ptrarray->GetSize (); i++) {
 ptrdata = (SalesData*) ptrarray->GetAt (i);
 sprintf (msg, "%4ld", ptrdata->year);
 dc.TextOut (avg_char_width*5, avg_char_height*i, msg);
 sprintf (msg, "%8.2f", ptrdata->sales);
 dc.TextOut (avg_char_width*13, avg_char_height*i, msg);
}
```

15.4 MFC FILE HANDLING: THE CFILE CLASS

The **CFile** MFC class is the base class for MFC file-handling operations, from which **CArchive** is derived. Let's examine some of the more commonly used functions and identifiers. There is a default constructor with no arguments that constructs the basic **CFile** object; one would next invoke the **Open** member function. The second constructor is passed the filename to open and some flags that define how the file is to be opened.

```
CFile ();
CFile (const char* filename, UINT flags);
```

The flags most frequently used are

CFile::modeCreate	if file exists, it's set to 0 length
CFile::modeRead	set for read-only operations
CFile::modeReadWrite	set for both read and write operations
CFile::modeWrite	set for write-only operations

Note that **modeCreate** can be ORed with one of the others. To explicitly open the file, use

```
BOOL Open (char* filename, UINT flags, CFileException *ptrexcept);
```

It returns TRUE if the open was successful. The flags are the same as for the constructor version.

The third parameter is a pointer to your instance of the **CFileException** class, which maintains error status and debugging aids should file operations fail. It can also be used to assist in detecting the EOF condition. If the pointer is NULL, then no error information is made available for our use. Other functions include

```
void   Close ();
UINT   Read (void *ptrbuffer, UINT bytecount);
void   Write (void *ptrbuffer, UINT bytecount);
LONG   Seek (LONG offset, UINT flags);
void   SeekToBegin ();
DWORD  SeekToEnd ();
DWORD  GetPosition ();
```

The seek flags are

CFile::begin, CFile::current, CFile::end

Notice the added convenience of the Seek functions. In our sales application, I intend to provide support for loading the sales array container from a text file and for saving in a text file. Both operations use **CFile** operations. If you treat the text file as a binary object, then the basic unit of I/O is likely a BYTE. Single bytes are input and inserted into a string until the CRLF codes are read, at which point the NULL terminator is inserted. One line or set of data has been input, assuming the format of the text line is such that one line contains both the year and its corresponding sales amount, which is the most likely layout. Given a line, **sscanf** can be used to convert the string data into the long and double format. Next a new instance of the SalesData class is allocated and passed the long and double. The sales array base class function **Add** is used to add the new object into the array at the end. The tricky part is detecting EOF. A **try-catch** pair is wrapped around the byte **Read** invocation. If EOF occurs, the **catch** traps the error situation in our **CArchiveException** instance that was passed to the file **Open** function. To detect EOF, check its member **m_cause** for the EOF flag, **CArchiveException::endOfFile**. The Load Text File coding is similar to the following sequence:

```
void LoadTextDocument (const char* filename) {
 int i;         // will index the input buffer during byte reads
 char buf[80]; // the input buffer
 int count;     // 0 at EOF
 long yr;       // conversion field for years
 double sls;    // conversion field for sales
 CFile file;
 CFileException file_err;
 SalesData *ptrdata; // new SalesData object to be inserted
 file.Open (filename, CFile::modeRead, &file_err);
 i = 0;
 while (TRUE) { // read all file bytes, checking for new line codes
  try {
   count = file.Read (&buf[i], 1);   // reads one byte
  }
  catch (CArchiveException *ptrex) { // check for EOF
   if (ptrex->m_cause == CArchiveException::endOfFile)
     ptrex->Delete ();
   else {              // here some other error occurred
    // you could also display a message box
    throw;                         // abort the program
   }
```

```
  break;                          // for EOF, end the main loop
 }
 if (buf[i] == '\n') { // check for CRLF ending one set of data
   buf[i]=0;                // insert NULL terminator
   sscanf (buf, "%ld %lf", &yr, &sls);
   ptrdata = new SalesData (yr, sls); // allocate a new SalesData
   sales_array.Add (ptrdata);      // and add it to the array
   i=0;                            // set count back to 0
 }
 else if (count==0) break; // also end when no more bytes
 else i++;                       // get next byte in the line of data
}
// since last line could be followed by ^Z and not CRLF^Z, check
if (i>0) { // at EOF, see if there is another line
  buf[i+1]=0;
  sscanf (buf, "%ld %lf", &yr, &sls);
  ptrdata = new SalesData (yr, sls);  // allocate new SalesData

  sales_array.Add (ptrdata);      // and add it to the array
}
file.Close ();
}
```

The Text File Save operation is much simpler. After opening the file, iterate through all SalesData objects and convert the long and double into a single string and write out the string.

```
void SaveTextDocument (const char* filename) {
int i;
char buf[80];
CFile file;
CFileException file_err;
SalesData *ptrdata;
file.Open (filename, CFile::modeWrite | CFile::modeCreate,
           &file_err);
for (i=0; i<sales_array.GetSize (); i++) {
  ptrdata = (SalesData*) sales_array.GetAt (i);
  sprintf (buf, " %ld %10.2f\n", ptrdata->year, ptrdata->sales);
  file.Write (buf, strlen (buf));
}
}
```

Actually, no use is made of the file exception. A more robust application would display error messages to the user.

15.5 THE MFC DOCUMENT-VIEW IMPLEMENTATION

With these basic building blocks understood, let's see how to construct a Document-View application. Derive the document class from **CDocument**; its purpose is to house the SalesData, providing facilities for its I/O, both by serialization and by specific text I/O, and to support communications among the possible views. The view's function is to display the document on-screen as well as to render it on the printer. Views may also handle user modifications to the data in that view. MFC provides several different view classes from which we may derive our views. The basic view class is called **CView**. Other view classes include **CScrollView, CFormView, CRecordView**, and **CEditView**. In the sample programs, I use the simplest case, **CView**, from which to derive the two view classes.

The application's document class derived from **CDocument** is often quite small for simpler applications. As expected, there must be a default constructor that takes no arguments and a serializer function that streams the document in or out to the **CArchive** stream when the framework requests it. If the class stores the data in container classes or in a form that is not destroyed automatically on the stack, then the member function **DeleteContents** must be overridden to provide the specific coding necessary to remove the data objects. The framework and the **CDocument** base class handle all other details. In this application, however, methods to I/O a text form of the document are provided. Examine the document header file, AcmeDoc.h.

15.5.1 Listing for File: AcmeDoc.h—Pgm15a—Excerpts

```
. . .
class AcmeDoc : public CDocument {

DECLARE_DYNCREATE (AcmeDoc)

public:

SalesDataArray sales_array;     // container for list of sales data objects
. . .
public:
             AcmeDoc () {};                 // no parms if serializing
        int  GetNumSales ();                // gets number of sales data objs
        void Serialize (CArchive&);         // document I/O - binary version
        BOOL OnNewDocument ();              // construct new document
        BOOL OnOpenDocument (const char*);  // opens existing document
        void DeleteContents ();             // removes SalesData objects
        void LoadTextDocument (const char*); // load text file of data
        void SaveTextDocument (const char*); // saves as a text file
afx_msg void OnFileTextLoad ();             // respond to menu Open As Text
afx_msg void OnFileTextSave ();             // respond to menu Save As Text
. . .
```

The document class defines our sales array as an instance of the SalesDataArray just discussed. The **DeleteContents** function deletes each SalesData object in the array container, then removes all of the container's pointers. Typically with document classes, the constructor does nothing. All of the action occurs in response to the framework's requests for opening a new or existing document—the functions **OnNewDocument** and **OnOpenDocument**, both of which return nonzero values if the action is successful. The sole argument to the **OnOpenDocument** is the filename. Normally, these two functions do not need to be overridden, but I have to show you the places where you can customize the loading of documents.

Since the document does not contain a member that holds the current number of sales objects, I include a user function, **GetNumSales**, that the views may invoke to obtain the current number. The **OnFileTextLoad** and **OnFileTextSave** respond to the menu choices for document loading and saving in text format. Both functions use the common File Open Save dialogs to obtain the user's filename and then invoke either **LoadTextDocument** or **SaveTextDocument** to actually handle the I/O. Did you notice the new macro in the class header?

```
DECLARE_DYNCREATE (AcmeDoc)
```

The entire Document-View system is launched dynamically at run time. In other words, specific instances of the document and view classes are going to be constructed and streamed from disk. In fact, the user can drag the document file and drop it on the icon representing this application (Pgm15a.exe) and Windows 95 launches this application instructing it to open the indicated document file! Try it—open Explorer or File Manager, drag ACME.DAT and drop it on the Pgm15a.exe file, and watch the action.

Specifically, this dynamic creation from disk can be done for objects derived from **CObject**, but the classes must notify the framework that they can be so created in order for the MFC to install proper coding to do so. This is done by using the macros

```
DECLARE_DYNCREATE (classname)
IMPLEMENT_DYNCREATE (classname, baseclassname)
```

There are three vital rules for using macros.

1. The declaration macro must be in the class definition in the header file.
2. The class *must* have a default constructor (one with no arguments).
3. The implement macro must appear in the class implementation file.

Examining the AcmeDoc.cpp implementation file, notice that the first line after the includes is the implement macro. Next comes the message map. The document class responds to the two special menu choices for loading and saving text files. **Get-NumSales** and **DeleteContents** contain the coding discussed previously with the container class, **CObArray**. If you wish to customize the opening of documents process, override **OnNewDocument** and **OnOpenDocument**. First invoke the base class and save the return code or else manually return TRUE or FALSE. After the base class has done its actions, you can insert additional customization code. Additionally, you could alter the filename before passing it to **CDocument**'s **OnOpenDocument**.

Next notice how simple the serialization coding is. Based upon the archiver's **IsStoring** function, invoke the serializer for the SalesDataArray class which in turn invokes the base class **CObArray**'s serializer. **CObArray**'s serializer I/Os each object in the array by invoking our **SalesData**'s serializer, which actually streams the long and double fields.

```
if (ar.IsStoring ()) {
 if (sales_array.GetSize () == 0) return;
 sales_array.Serialize (ar);
 }
else sales_array.Serialize (ar);
```

When the user opts to load or save in text format, **OnFileTextLoad** and **OnFile-TextSave** are invoked. Both use the common dialog box to get the user's choice, but there is one serious problem with the filenames. While I am registering the documents as having the DAT extension, text files should have the txt extension. In the load function, after the user's filename is returned from the Open dialog box and after the file is loaded into memory, the document's name and filename must be altered to the new file that was just loaded. The extension txt must be stripped off and dat installed. Then the **CDocument** member function **SetPathName** can be invoked to install the new file and document name that appears in the title bar.

```
SetPathName (newfilename, TRUE);
```

where the BOOL indicates that this file is to be added to the most recently used listing on the File menu. The reverse must be done when saving a document to a text file. The current document name must have the dat removed and txt installed and the new filename passed into the Save dialog box as the initial file name. The document name can be retrieved using the function **GetPathName**.

```
CString* GetPathName ();
```

With short filenames, the 8.3 version, this is not a problem. However, with Windows 95's long filenames, the rules for filenames have changed. Specifically, blanks and periods can be part of the long filename. For example, one could have a name like "Acme.Dat Main .DAT data file.DAT." Parsing long filenames becomes quite tricky. Rather than make the example coding longer, I have taken an oversimplified approach, upon which you may improve. I convert the filename to uppercase and look for the first occurrence of dat or txt and replace the first two characters with tx or da. For production work, you should examine the complete long filename rules in the documentation and code accordingly. The coding I have used to alter the load text filename is as follows (a similar replacement is done when saving a text file):

```
CString filename (filedlg.GetPathName ());
filename.MakeUpper ();
int i = filename.Find (".TXT");
if (i>-1) {
 filename.SetAt (i+1, 'D');
 filename.SetAt (i+2, 'A');
}
CDocument::SetPathName (filename, TRUE);
```

The actual coding to load and save the document in a text file is exactly the same we discussed before with the SalesDataArray class.

Finally, there are several useful member functions of **CDocument** that are used frequently, especially by view classes that can modify the document's data.

```
UpdateAllViews (CView* ptrsender, LPARAM hint, CObject *ptrhint);
BOOL IsModified ();
SetModifiedFlag (BOOL modified);
```

When a view modifies the document's data, it invokes the document's **UpdateAll-Views** function which sends notification (paint) messages to all views associated with this document so that they can correctly display the altered values. Usually NULLs are passed for the three arguments. However, for customization, the first parameter is a pointer to the sender view, the second is a user-defined long value, and the third is a pointer to the base **CObject** class of the changed data. Additionally, the view that alters the document's data *must* invoke the **SetModifiedFlag** document function. The **CDocument** class maintains a modified flag that is initially set to FALSE. When the document is to be destroyed, either by opening a new document or by the frame window closing, the **CanCloseFrame** member function is called. If the data has been modified, the **CDocument** displays a message to the user and saves the data if so requested by the user. Typical coding in our view class that modifies the data would be

```
ptrdocument->SetModifiedFlag (TRUE);
ptrdocument->UpdateAllViews (NULL);
```

15.5.2 Listing for File: AcmeDoc.cpp—Pgm15a—Excerpts

```
...
IMPLEMENT_DYNCREATE(AcmeDoc, CDocument)
...
BEGIN_MESSAGE_MAP(AcmeDoc, CDocument)
 ON_COMMAND(CM_FILE_LOAD_TEXT,  OnFileTextLoad)
 ON_COMMAND(CM_FILE_SAVE_TEXT,  OnFileTextSave)
END_MESSAGE_MAP()
/****************************************************************************/
/*                                                                        */
/* GetNumSales: returns the number of sales data objects in the collection */
/*                                                                        */
/****************************************************************************/

int      AcmeDoc::GetNumSales () {
 return sales_array.GetSize ();
}
/****************************************************************************/
/*                                                                      */
/* DeleteContents: remove the sales array of Sales objects              */
/*                                                                      */
/****************************************************************************/

void     AcmeDoc::DeleteContents () {
 int i;
 if (sales_array.GetSize () ==0) return;       // return if none to remove
 for (i=0; i<sales_array.GetSize (); i++)      // for each SalesData object
  delete (SalesData*) sales_array.GetAt (i); // get at it and delete it
 sales_array.RemoveAll ();                      // now empty the array container
}
/****************************************************************************/
/*                                                                      */
/* OnNewDocument: launch a new document                                 */
/*                                                                      */
/****************************************************************************/
```

```
BOOL      AcmeDoc::OnNewDocument () {

 if (!CDocument::OnNewDocument ()) return FALSE;
 return TRUE;
}
/**************************************************************************/
/*                                                                      */
/* OnOpenDocument: open existing document                               */
/*                                                                      */
/**************************************************************************/
BOOL      AcmeDoc::OnOpenDocument (const char *filename) {
 BOOL retcd = CDocument::OnOpenDocument (filename);
 return retcd;
}
/**************************************************************************/
/*                                                                      */
/* Serialize: input or output the whole document - I/O binary data only */
/*                                                                      */
/**************************************************************************/
void      AcmeDoc::Serialize (CArchive &ar) {

 if (ar.IsStoring ()) {                    // save to .DAT file
  if (sales_array.GetSize () == 0) return; // none to save
  sales_array.Serialize (ar);              // invoke container's serializer
 }
 else sales_array.Serialize (ar);          // input, ask container to serialize
}
/**************************************************************************/
/*                                                                      */
/* LoadTextDocument: removes this document and loads in a text document  */
/*                                                                      */
/**************************************************************************/
void      AcmeDoc::LoadTextDocument (const char* filename) {

 int i;                     // will index the input buffer during byte reads
 char buf[80];              // the input buffer
 int count;                 // 0 at EOF
 long yr;                   // conversion field for years
 double sls;                // conversion field for sales
 CFile file;                // the file, will be binary I/O still
 CFileException file_err;   // used if more info on errors is desired
 SalesData *ptrdata;        // the new SalesData object to be inserted in array

 // remove the current document's sales array of SalesData objects
 DeleteContents ();

 file.Open (filename, CFile::modeRead, &file_err);
 i = 0;
 while (TRUE) { // read all file bytes, checking for new line codes
  try {
   count = file.Read (&buf[i], 1);   // reads one byte
  }
```

```
 catch (CArchiveException *ptrex) { // check for EOF
  if (ptrex->m_cause == CArchiveException::endOfFile) ptrex->Delete ();
  else {                              // here some other error occurred
   TRACE0 ("Error loading file\n"); // you could also display a message box
   throw;                            // abort the program
  }
  break;                             // for EOF, end the main loop
 }
 if (buf[i] == '\n') {               // check for CRLF ending one set of data
  buf[i]=0;                          // insert NULL terminator
  sscanf (buf, "%ld %lf", &yr, &sls); // convert into proper data types
  ptrdata = new SalesData (yr, sls); // allocate a new SalesData object
  sales_array.Add (ptrdata);         // and add it to the array
  i=0;                               // set count back to 0, and continue
 }
 else if (count==0) break;           // also end when no more bytes
 else i++;                           // get next byte in the line of data
 }
 // since last line could be followed by ^Z and not CRLF^Z, check further
 if (i>0) {                          // at EOF, see if there is another line
  buf[i+1]=0;                        // yes, so add it as well
  sscanf (buf, "%ld %lf", &yr, &sls); // convert data
  ptrdata = new SalesData (yr, sls);  // allocate new SalesData object
  sales_array.Add (ptrdata);         // and add it to the array
 }
 file.Close ();
}
/***************************************************************************/
/*                                                                         */
/* SaveTextDocument: saves this document as a text file                    */
/*                                                                         */
/***************************************************************************/
void       AcmeDoc::SaveTextDocument (const char* filename) {
 int i;
 char buf[80];
 CFile file;
 CFileException file_err;
 SalesData *ptrdata;

 file.Open (filename, CFile::modeWrite | CFile::modeCreate, &file_err);
 for (i=0; i<sales_array.GetSize (); i++) {
  ptrdata = (SalesData*) sales_array.GetAt (i);
  sprintf (buf, " %ld %10.2f\n", ptrdata->year, ptrdata->sales);
  file.Write (buf, strlen (buf));
 }
}
/***************************************************************************/
/*                                                                         */
/* OnFileTextLoad: load a new document from a text file                    */
/*                                                                         */
/***************************************************************************/
```

```
void       AcmeDoc::OnFileTextLoad () {

  // get user's file choice by creating a new File Open Dialog Box
  CFileDialog filedlg (TRUE,     // use Open dialog
                       "*.TXT", // default extension
                       "*.TXT",   // current file name
                       OFN_FILEMUSTEXIST | OFN_PATHMUSTEXIST | OFN_LONGNAMES,
                       "Text Files (*.TXT)|All Files (*.*)|*.*||",
                       NULL);

  // invoke the Open dialog box to get the user's choice
  if (filedlg.DoModal () == IDOK) {            // user has chosen a file, so
   LoadTextDocument(filedlg.GetPathName ());  // pass filename to loader
   // now convert the filename into a proper document name by removing
   // the .TXT extension and substituting .DAT - if possible
   // this is a fairly crude conversion process
   CString filename (filedlg.GetPathName ()); // copy current filename
   filename.MakeUpper ();            // convert to upper case for convenience
   int i = filename.Find (".TXT"); // locate first .TXT - with long filenames
                                   // this very well could be a bad assumption
   if (i>-1) {                       // if found, replace it
    filename.SetAt (i+1, 'D');
    filename.SetAt (i+2, 'A');
   }
   UpdateAllViews (NULL, 0, NULL); // cause all views to be updated with newdata
   // install the new document name and put it in the most "recent list"
   CDocument::SetPathName (filename, TRUE);
  }
}

/******************************************************************************/
/*                                                                          */
/* OnFileTextSave: save a new document to a text file                       */
/*                                                                          */
/******************************************************************************/
void       AcmeDoc::OnFileTextSave () {

  // get user's filename choice by allocating a new File Save dialog box
  CFileDialog filedlg (FALSE,    // use SaveAs dialog
                       "*.TXT", // default extension
                       "*.*",    // current file name
                       OFN_HIDEREADONLY | OFN_OVERWRITEPROMPT | OFN_LONGNAMES,
                       "Text Files (*.TXT)|All Files (*.*)|*.*||",
                       NULL);
  // install an attempt at converting the document name into a .TXT file name
  CString filename (filedlg.GetPathName ()); // copy the document name
  filename.MakeUpper ();          // convert to upper case for convenience
  int i = filename.Find (".DAT"); // look for first .DAT
  if (i>-1) {                     // if one is found, replace with .TXT
   filename.SetAt (i+1, 'T');
   filename.SetAt (i+2, 'X');
  }
  // and copy suggestion of filename into the dialog box
  strcpy (filedlg.m_ofn.lpstrFile, filename);
```

```
// invoke the Save dialog and get user's choice
if (filedlg.DoModal () == IDOK)               // user has chosen a file, so
    SaveTextDocument (filedlg.GetPathName ()); // save it with that name
}
```

15.6 THE RESOURCE FILE FOR PGM15a AND THE APPLICATION AND FRAME WINDOWS

Before we get into the complex coding of the view, let's examine the overall application setup and look at exactly how the document is installed in the framework. Begin by looking at the resource file and its header. There are several new items and many new identifiers. Since I am now using the MFC framework for almost all of the default Document-View implementation, I must use the AppWizard-defined ID values so the framework can invoke the correct member functions. To assist you in spotting which IDs are ours and which are the MFC internal IDs, I use the CM_ prefix for user-defined menu items. All those that begin with ID_ are MFC internal IDs.

In the File pop-up menu File | Print Preview has been added to provide Print Preview support. Also note the special menu item "Recent File." Up to the last four data files that have been opened are inserted into the File menu at this point. The menu ID that corresponds to the most recently used file is **ID_FILE_MRU_FILE1**. Although there is only one menu item reserved, as you open other documents, the framework inserts up to four filenames here. If you select any of these, the current document is closed and the selected one is opened—all without any special coding on our part! In the application class implementation, merely include one line of coding to tell the framework to use this feature.

```
LoadStdProfileSettings ();        // activates Most Recent File menu
```

I use one dialog box to process both Add and Update Records requests. Finally, the identifier IDR_MAINFRAME is used to ID the application icon, the main menu, the accelerator table, and a very special string table entry.

```
IDR_MAINFRAME "ACME Sales Data\n\nACME\nACME Files (*.dat)\n.DAT\nACME\nACME
    Document"
```

(Note that this string can be very long and can never be broken into two lines, in spite of the word processor.) This application string table entry is *vital* for Document-View operations. It has a special syntax that defines seven separate strings, separated by the new-line code (\n). They are as follows:

```
string #  here coded              meaning
   1      ACME Sales Data\n        the application window caption
   2      \n                       constructs the doc name for file new
                                   default is "Untitled"
   3      ACME\n                   the file new name provides a type name
                                   like "DataBase"
   4      ACME Files (*.dat)\n     filter name specifies a description
                                   for the "List File of Type" combo box
   5      .DAT\n                   file extension associated with this
                                   document type
```

| 6 | ACME\n | if using the Registration Database, provides the file type ID to be registered so that Explorer/File Mgr can automatically launch the app |
| 7 | ACME Document | if using the Registration Database, provides a meaningful name for the registered files |

If you are not going to register the document files with Windows 95, the last two strings (6 and 7) can be omitted. Here I register the acme.dat document with Windows 95 the very first time that you run the application. After you have run Pgm15a one time, try launching the Explorer and double-clicking on the acme.dat icon. The Windows 95 registration database is searched for applications that can be launched to view this file. The extension dat is a poor choice because many other commercial packages also use dat. Specifically on my system, WordPerfect for Windows gets first crack at opening the dat files.

15.6.1 Listing for File: Pgm15a.rc—Pgm15a—Excerpts

```
...
IDR_MAINFRAME       ICON      DISCARDABLE      "pgm15a.ico"
IDR_ACMETYPE        ICON      DISCARDABLE      "acmedoc.ico"
IDR_MAINFRAME       BITMAP    MOVEABLE         "toolbar.bmp"
IDR_MAINFRAME MENU PRELOAD DISCARDABLE
BEGIN
  POPUP "&File"
  BEGIN
    MENUITEM "&New\tCtrl+N",              ID_FILE_NEW
    MENUITEM "&Open...\tCtrl+O",          ID_FILE_OPEN
    MENUITEM "&Save\tCtrl+S",             ID_FILE_SAVE
    MENUITEM "Save &As...",               ID_FILE_SAVE_AS
    MENUITEM  SEPARATOR
    MENUITEM "File &Load from .TXT",      CM_FILE_LOAD_TEXT
    MENUITEM "File Sa&ve to .TXT",        CM_FILE_SAVE_TEXT
    MENUITEM  SEPARATOR
    MENUITEM "&Print...\tCtrl+P",         ID_FILE_PRINT
    MENUITEM "Print Pre&view",            ID_FILE_PRINT_PREVIEW
    MENUITEM "P&rint Setup...",           ID_FILE_PRINT_SETUP
    MENUITEM  SEPARATOR
    MENUITEM "Recent File",               ID_FILE_MRU_FILE1,GRAYED
    MENUITEM  SEPARATOR
    MENUITEM "E&xit",                     ID_APP_EXIT
  END

  POPUP "&Edit"
  BEGIN
    MENUITEM "&Add Record...",            CM_ADD
    MENUITEM "&Update Current Record",    CM_UPDATE
    MENUITEM "&Delete Current Record",    CM_DELETE
  END
  MENUITEM "&Fonts",                      CM_FONTS
  POPUP "&View"
```

```
    BEGIN
      MENUITEM "&Toolbar",                    ID_VIEW_TOOLBAR
      MENUITEM "&Status Bar",                 ID_VIEW_STATUS_BAR
    END
    POPUP "&Help"
    BEGIN
      MENUITEM "&About Pgm15a...",            ID_APP_ABOUT
    END
END

IDR_MAINFRAME ACCELERATORS PRELOAD MOVEABLE
BEGIN
    "N",            ID_FILE_NEW,             VIRTKEY,CONTROL
    "O",            ID_FILE_OPEN,            VIRTKEY,CONTROL
    "S",            ID_FILE_SAVE,            VIRTKEY,CONTROL
    "P",            ID_FILE_PRINT,           VIRTKEY,CONTROL
    VK_F6,          ID_NEXT_PANE,            VIRTKEY
    VK_F6,          ID_PREV_PANE,            VIRTKEY,SHIFT
END

IDD_ADD_UPDATE DIALOG DISCARDABLE  0, 0, 146, 77
STYLE DS_MODALFRAME | WS_POPUP | WS_VISIBLE | WS_CAPTION | WS_SYSMENU
CAPTION "Add New Sales Data"
FONT 8, "MS Sans Serif"
BEGIN
    EDITTEXT        IDC_EDIT_YEAR,12,22,40,14,ES_AUTOHSCROLL
    EDITTEXT        IDC_EDIT_SALES,69,22,62,14,ES_AUTOHSCROLL
    DEFPUSHBUTTON   "OK",IDOK,11,47,50,14
    PUSHBUTTON      "Cancel",IDCANCEL,78,46,50,14
    LTEXT           "Year",IDC_YEAR,12,11,37,7,NOT WS_GROUP
    LTEXT           "Sales",IDC_SALES,70,11,52,7,NOT WS_GROUP
END

IDD_ABOUT DIALOG DISCARDABLE  34, 22, 217, 55
CAPTION "Help - About Pgm15"
STYLE DS_MODALFRAME | WS_POPUP | WS_CAPTION | WS_SYSMENU
FONT 8, "MS Sans Serif"
BEGIN
    ICON            IDR_MAINFRAME,IDC_STATIC,11,17,20,20
    LTEXT           "Pgm15a by Vic Broquard",IDC_STATIC,40,10,119,8
    LTEXT           "Illustrates Doc-View",IDC_STATIC,40,25,119,8
    DEFPUSHBUTTON   "OK",IDOK,176,6,32,14,WS_GROUP
END

STRINGTABLE PRELOAD DISCARDABLE
BEGIN
    IDR_MAINFRAME "ACME Sales Data\n\nACME\nACME Files (*.dat)\n.DAT\nACME\nACME
                  Document"
END

STRINGTABLE PRELOAD DISCARDABLE
BEGIN
    AFX_IDS_APP_TITLE        "Pgm15a"
    AFX_IDS_IDLEMESSAGE      "Ready"
END
```

```
STRINGTABLE DISCARDABLE
BEGIN
  ID_INDICATOR_EXT          "EXT"
  ID_INDICATOR_CAPS         "CAP"
  ID_INDICATOR_NUM          "NUM"
  ID_INDICATOR_SCRL         "SCRL"
  ID_INDICATOR_OVR          "OVR"
  ID_INDICATOR_REC          "REC"
END

STRINGTABLE DISCARDABLE
BEGIN
  ID_FILE_NEW               "Create a new sales document\nNew Sales Doc"
  ID_FILE_OPEN              "Open an existing sales document\nOpen Existing Doc"
  ID_FILE_CLOSE             "Close the active sales document\nClose"
  ID_FILE_SAVE              "Save the active sales document\nSave"
  ID_FILE_SAVE_AS           "Save the active sales document with a new name\nSave As"
  ID_FILE_PAGE_SETUP        "Change the printing options\nPage Setup"
  ID_FILE_PRINT_SETUP       "Change the printer and printing options\nPrint Setup"
  ID_FILE_PRINT             "Print the active sales document\nPrint"
  ID_FILE_PRINT_PREVIEW     "Display full pages\nPrint Preview"
  ID_APP_ABOUT              "Display program information\nAbout"
  ID_APP_EXIT             "Quit the application; prompts to save sales documents\nExit"
  ID_FILE_MRU_FILE1         "Open this sales document"
  ID_FILE_MRU_FILE2         "Open this sales document"
  ID_FILE_MRU_FILE3         "Open this sales document"
  ID_FILE_MRU_FILE4         "Open this sales document"
  ID_NEXT_PANE              "Switch to the next window pane\nNext Pane"
  ID_PREV_PANE              "Switch back to the previous window pane\nPrevious Pane"
  ID_WINDOW_SPLIT           "Split the active window into panes\nSplit"
  ID_VIEW_TOOLBAR           "Show or hide the toolbar\nToggle Control Bar"
  ID_VIEW_STATUS_BAR        "Show or hide the status bar\nToggle Status Bar"
  CM_FILE_LOAD_TEXT         "Load document from a text file\nLoad from .TXT"
  CM_FILE_SAVE_TEXT         "Save document to a .TXT file\nSave to .TXT"
  CM_FONTS                  "Choose Fonts\nChoose Fonts"
  CM_ADD                    "Add a new sales data record to the end\nAdd Record"
  CM_UPDATE                 "Update the current record\nUpdate Red Record"
  CM_DELETE                 "Delete the current record\nDelete Red Record"
END

STRINGTABLE DISCARDABLE
BEGIN
  AFX_IDS_SCSIZE            "Change the window size"
  AFX_IDS_SCMOVE            "Change the window position"
  AFX_IDS_SCMINIMIZE        "Reduce the window to an icon"
  AFX_IDS_SCMAXIMIZE        "Enlarge the window to full size"
  AFX_IDS_SCNEXTWINDOW      "Switch to the next document window"
  AFX_IDS_SCPREVWINDOW      "Switch to the previous document window"
  AFX_IDS_SCCLOSE         "Close the active window and prompt to save the documents"
  AFX_IDS_SCRESTORE         "Restore the window to normal size"
  AFX_IDS_SCTASKLIST        "Activate Task List"
  AFX_ID_PREVIEW_PRINT      "Print the document\nPrint Doc"
  AFX_ID_PREVIEW_NEXT       "Preview the next page\nNext Page"
  AFX_ID_PREVIEW_PREV       "Preview the previous page\nPrevious Page"
  AFX_ID_PREVIEW_NUMPAGE    "Change number of preview pages\nChange Number Pages"
```

```
    AFX_ID_PREVIEW_ZOOMIN     "Zoom in, increase magnification\nZoom In"
    AFX_ID_PREVIEW_ZOOMOUT    "Zoom out, decrease magnification\nZoom Out"
    AFX_ID_PREVIEW_CLOSE      "Close preview window\nClose Preview"
    AFX_IDS_PREVIEW_CLOSE     "Close print preview mode\nCancel Preview"
END

STRINGTABLE  // our apps
{
  IDS_MSG_QUIT,      "Do you want to quit the application?"
  IDS_MSG_QUERY,     "Query?"
  IDS_YEARS,         "Year"
  IDS_SALES,         "Sales"
  IDS_ACMETITLE,     "ACME Manufacturing Company Yearly Sales Report"
  IDS_FOOTER,        "Prepared by Broquard Consultants"
  IDS_CONFIRM1,      "Confirm Deletion of the Current Record (in Red)"
  IDS_CONFIRM2,      "Press Yes to confirm deletion"
}
...
```

15.6.2 Listing for File: Pgm15a.RH—Pgm15a—Excerpts

```
...
#define IDR_MAINFRAME       128
#define IDR_ACMETYPE        129
#define IDD_ADD_UPDATE      130
#define IDC_EDIT_YEAR       140
#define IDC_EDIT_SALES      141
#define IDC_SALES           142
#define IDC_YEAR            143

#define CM_FILE_LOAD_TEXT   (WM_USER + 100) // load in a text file
#define CM_FILE_SAVE_TEXT   (WM_USER + 101) // save as text file
#define CM_FONTS            (WM_USER + 102) // choose fonts
#define CM_ADD              (WM_USER + 103) // add a new sales set of data
#define CM_UPDATE           (WM_USER + 104) // update existing sales set
#define CM_DELETE           (WM_USER + 105) // delete a sales set of data

#define IDS_MSG_QUIT        2001  // quit application query msg
#define IDS_MSG_QUERY       2002  // title of quit query messagebox
#define IDS_YEARS           2003  // id for the report title line years
#define IDS_SALES           2004  // id for the report title line sales
#define IDS_ACMETITLE       2005  // id for printed report company logo
#define IDS_FOOTER          2006  // id for printed page's footer
#define IDS_CONFIRM1        2007  // id for delete record confirmation
#define IDS_CONFIRM2        2008  // id for delete record confirmation
...
```

15.7 THE APPLICATION CLASS: PGM15AAPP

While no changes are required in the application class definition, the **InitInstance**
and message map have numerous changes to support Document-View. The **CWinApp**
class handles launching documents as well as main windows. The base class handles

the menu items File | New and File | Open as well as picking one of the most recently used files from the File menu. It also handles the File | Print and File | Preview operations. The message map simply routes these menu requests on down to the base class handler functions.

With Document-View, **InitInstance** is more complex. The first action defines a new instance of the SDI Document-View template. The template ties all of the parts together. The first UINT is the ID for the main menu, icon, accelerator table, and string resource for this document. The string resource, as we have just seen, contains vital information on the filenames and types for this document. The next trio defines the document class that is to be created, the main window that is to be launched to support the document, and the specific view class that is to be instantiated to display the document. Since I am going to have two different view classes, I am using two templates.

```
CSingleDocTemplate *ptrdoctemplate1;
ptrdoctemplate1 = new CSingleDocTemplate (IDR_MAINFRAME,
                                    RUNTIME_CLASS (AcmeDoc),
                                    RUNTIME_CLASS (FrameWin),
                                    RUNTIME_CLASS (AcmeView));
CSingleDocTemplate *ptrdoctemplate2;
ptrdoctemplate2 = new CSingleDocTemplate (IDR_MAINFRAME,
                                    RUNTIME_CLASS (AcmeDoc),
                                    RUNTIME_CLASS (FrameWin),
                                    RUNTIME_CLASS (AcmeView));
AddDocTemplate (ptrdoctemplate1);
AddDocTemplate (ptrdoctemplate2);
```

Both templates are added to the **CWinApp** instance, using the member function **AddDocTemplate**, so that it can dynamically construct the document and views when requested by File | New and File | Open commands. This function takes a pointer to the SDI template instance.

Next, a series of **CWinApp** member functions activates several key features. **EnableShellOpen** and **RegisterShellFileTypes** combine to provide Dynamic Data Exchange (DDE) support. Also, by invoking the frame window's **DragAcceptFiles** member function, the user can drop any of the dat files on the Pgm15a.EXE icon, and Windows 95 launches the application with that document. By invoking the **CWinApp** member function **LoadStdProfileSettings**, we activate the most recently used lists, making them fully functional, all handled by the framework.

```
EnableShellOpen ();              // enable DDE Execute open
RegisterShellFileTypes ();       // register .DAT types for DDE open
LoadStdProfileSettings ();       // activates Most Recent File menu
if (m_lpCmdLine[0] == 0) // none on cmd line, so use default
 OpenDocumentFile ("\\learnwin\\vc\\pgm15a\\acme.dat");
                         // or use: OnFileNew (); for a new file
else OpenDocumentFile (m_lpCmdLine); // open file on cmd line

m_pMainWnd->DragAcceptFiles (); // enable drag and drop open
```

If there is a filename on the command line, it is passed to the member function **OpenDocumentFile** to open the document file and launch the associated frame window and the views. On the other hand, if the command line is NULL, then you have your choice. Here, I chose to open the default small document, acme.dat. If you wish to present the user with an empty new document, use the function **OnFileNew** instead. These functions are the same ones that respond to the File menu commands.

I took the liberty of setting the option for the main window to be maximized when it is created. This makes good sense because most of the screen area is to contain the bar chart.

```
m_nCmdShow = SW_SHOWMAXIMIZED;
```

Have you noticed any "missing" coding? No instance of the FrameWin—main window class—is created! Instead, when the **CWinApp** opens or creates a new document, it examines the installed templates to see what main window class is to be dynamically constructed to support that document.

15.7.1 Listing for File: Pgm15aAp.cpp—Pgm15a—Excerpts

```
...
/**************************************************************************/
/*                                                                        */
/*  Pgm15AApp: message map                                                */
/*                                                                        */
/**************************************************************************/
BEGIN_MESSAGE_MAP(Pgm15AApp,      CWinApp)
 ON_COMMAND(ID_FILE_NEW,         CWinApp::OnFileNew)
 ON_COMMAND(ID_FILE_OPEN,        CWinApp::OnFileOpen)
 ON_COMMAND(ID_FILE_PRINT_SETUP, CWinApp::OnFilePrintSetup)
 ON_COMMAND(ID_APP_ABOUT,        OnHelpAbout)
END_MESSAGE_MAP()

/**************************************************************************/
/*                                                                        */
/*  InitInstance: allocate instance of our frame main window              */
/*                                                                        */
/**************************************************************************/
BOOL  Pgm15AApp::InitInstance () {

 // construct two document templates, one for each view

 CSingleDocTemplate *ptrdoctemplate1;
 ptrdoctemplate1 = new CSingleDocTemplate (IDR_MAINFRAME,
                                           RUNTIME_CLASS (AcmeDoc),
                                           RUNTIME_CLASS (FrameWin),
                                           RUNTIME_CLASS (AcmeView));
 CSingleDocTemplate *ptrdoctemplate2;
 ptrdoctemplate2 = new CSingleDocTemplate (IDR_MAINFRAME,
                                           RUNTIME_CLASS (AcmeDoc),
                                           RUNTIME_CLASS (FrameWin),
                                           RUNTIME_CLASS (AcmeView));

 // install both templates
 AddDocTemplate (ptrdoctemplate1);
```

```
AddDocTemplate (ptrdoctemplate2);

m_nCmdShow = SW_SHOWMAXIMIZED;   // set for mainwindow to be maximized

EnableShellOpen ();              // enable DDE Execute open
RegisterShellFileTypes ();       // register .DAT types for DDE open
LoadStdProfileSettings ();       // activates Most Recent File menu

// determine which document file to open first
if (m_lpCmdLine[0] == 0) // none on cmd line, so use default
 OpenDocumentFile ("\\learnwin\\vc\\pgm15a\\acme.dat");
                         // or use: OnFileNew (); for a new file
else OpenDocumentFile (m_lpCmdLine); // open file on cmd line

m_pMainWnd->DragAcceptFiles (); // enable drag and drop open
return TRUE;
}
...
```

15.8 The Main Frame Window Class—FrameWin

The main window class, FrameWin—derived as usual from **CFrameWnd**, becomes very streamlined. However, since it is being dynamically created during the Document Open process, it must also use the **DECLARE_DYNCREATE** and **IMPLEMENT_DYNCREATE** macros. As expected, the frame window owns the tool bar and the status bar. It also owns the new object, the **CSplitterWnd**, that manages the two views side by side. **OnCreate** as always constructs the tool bar and status bar. In many previous examples, there was no client window attached to the frame, or else I launched a **CWnd**-derived class, such as the DrawWin or ScrollWin, to be the client window. To use a splitter window, the frame window's instance of the **CSplitter-Wnd** must be constructed instead of the normal default client window. This is why **OnCreateClient** is overridden; here I construct the splitter window, telling it exactly what views I want and how they are to be positioned initially. If the user drags on the divider line, the two windows' widths can be adjusted as desired. Although we have not had any need to override the function **PreCreateWindow** that is invoked at the beginning of the window creation process, now it can be used to set the WNDCLASS style flags to best support the Document-View system.

15.8.1 Listing for File: FrameWin.h—Pgm15a—Excerpts

```
...
class FrameWin : public CFrameWnd {

DECLARE_DYNCREATE (FrameWin)
...
protected:

CToolBar     toolbar;    // the control bar
CStatusBar   statusbar;  // the status bar
CSplitterWnd splitterwin; // our splitter window with two views side by side
...
```

```
public:
                 FrameWin () {}    // constructor
protected:

        BOOL    PreCreateWindow(CREATESTRUCT&);        // set wndclass style bits
afx_msg int    OnCreate(LPCREATESTRUCT);        // make control bar, status bar
virtual BOOL  OnCreateClient (LPCREATESTRUCT, CCreateContext*); // and splitter windows

DECLARE_MESSAGE_MAP()
...
```

In the FrameWin.cpp file, the tool bar buttons were mostly AppStudio built-in images. I used the Edit I Cut scissors for the Delete Record, the Edit I Copy image for the Add Record, and the Edit I Paste image for the Update Record. I took the File I Print image and overlaid a red "P" for Print-Preview.

In **PreCreateWindow**, OR in the **FWS_ADDTOTITLE** style which tells the framework to append the document name to the main title automatically during File I New or File I Open or File I SaveAs operations. The coding to construct the tool and status bars has no changes for Document-View.

It is in the **OnCreateClient** that the splitter window construction takes place. The first parameter, the LPCREATESTRUCT, is not needed. However, the second—a pointer to the **CCreateContext** structure—is. When this function is called, the structure has been filled with pointers to the document, the document template, and the current frame, as well as a **CRuntimeClass** pointer to the new view to create. Our use is to simply pass this pointer on to other member functions that require it. The first step in construction of splitter windows that are to appear when the views are initially launched is to construct an instance of a static splitter window by invoking **CreateStatic**, saving the return code to return later when the function ends.

```
BOOL retcd = splitterwin.CreateStatic (this, 1, 2);
```

The first **int** is the number of rows, and the second int is the number of columns. Here I want one row of two columns. This results in space for two side-by-side views. Next, the views that are to be in each pane must be created. The order of creation does not determine into which split window pane the view is placed. Rather the first two parameters to **CreateView** determine the pane to be used. I want the narrow columnar view to be in the left pane, so it is in row 0, column 0.

```
retcd |= splitterwin.CreateView (0, 0, RUNTIME_CLASS (AcmeView),
                                 CSize (180, 100), ptrc);
retcd |= splitterwin.CreateView (0, 1, RUNTIME_CLASS (AcmePlot),
                                 CSize (100, 100), ptrc);
```

The first parameter is the row and the second is the column, both zero-based. The third parameter is the view class to be created and installed in this pane, while the fourth is a **CSize** indicating an initial width and height of the view. After some experimentation, I chose 180 pixels as the initial width of the normal view. When the splitter window is actually displayed, the views are resized to match the client area of the frame window, here maximized. Thus, both views' heights are going to be greatly increased to fill the large maximized window. However, the splitter window respects our initial width for the first window, allowing the last window to expand its width. It maintains the proportions between the windows. If there were three side-by-side windows, then only the last rightmost window would be expanded; the other two would retain their initial widths. The last parameter is the passed pointer to the **CCreate-Context**. Note that I OR into the return code the return code from the **CreateView** function calls. I can then return one combined success or fail return code.

15.8.2 Listing for File: FrameWin.cpp—Pgm15a—Excerpts

```
...
IMPLEMENT_DYNCREATE(FrameWin, CFrameWnd)

// control bar buttons - IDs are command buttons
static UINT BASED_CODE buttons[] =
{
  // same order as in the bitmap 'toolbar.bmp'
  ID_FILE_NEW,
  ID_FILE_OPEN,
  ID_FILE_SAVE,
  ID_FILE_SAVE_AS,
  ID_SEPARATOR,
  CM_ADD,
  CM_UPDATE,
  CM_DELETE,
  ID_SEPARATOR,
  ID_FILE_PRINT,
  ID_FILE_PRINT_PREVIEW,
  CM_FONTS,
  ID_APP_ABOUT,
};

static UINT BASED_CODE indicators[] =
{
  ID_SEPARATOR,              // status line indicator
  ID_INDICATOR_CAPS,
  ID_INDICATOR_NUM,
  ID_INDICATOR_SCRL,
};
/****************************************************************************/
/*                                                                        */
/* FrameWin Events Response Table                                         */
/*                                                                        */
/****************************************************************************/

BEGIN_MESSAGE_MAP(FrameWin, CFrameWnd)
 ON_WM_CREATE ()
END_MESSAGE_MAP()
/****************************************************************************/
/*                                                                        */
/* PreCreateWindow: assign style options                                  */
/*                                                                        */
/****************************************************************************/
BOOL      FrameWin::PreCreateWindow(CREATESTRUCT& cs) {
```

```
    cs.style = WS_OVERLAPPED | WS_CAPTION | FWS_ADDTOTITLE
      | WS_THICKFRAME | WS_SYSMENU | WS_MINIMIZEBOX | WS_MAXIMIZEBOX | WS_MAXIMIZE;

    return CFrameWnd::PreCreateWindow(cs);
}
/************************************************************************/
/*                                                                    */
/* OnCreate: construct status and control bars                        */
/*                                                                    */
/************************************************************************/

int      FrameWin::OnCreate (LPCREATESTRUCT lpCS) {

  if (CFrameWnd::OnCreate (lpCS) == 0)
   if (toolbar.Create (this) && toolbar.LoadBitmap (IDR_MAINFRAME) &&
        toolbar.SetButtons (buttons, sizeof(buttons)/sizeof(UINT)))
    if (statusbar.Create (this) && statusbar.SetIndicators (indicators,
        sizeof(indicators)/sizeof(UINT)));
    else return -1;
   else return -1;
  else return -1;

  toolbar.EnableDocking (CBRS_ALIGN_ANY);
  EnableDocking (CBRS_ALIGN_ANY);
  DockControlBar (&toolbar);
  toolbar.SetBarStyle (toolbar.GetBarStyle() | CBRS_TOOLTIPS | CBRS_FLYBY);
  return 0;
}

/************************************************************************/
/*                                                                    */
/* OnCreateClient: construct splitter window static style             */
/*                                                                    */
/************************************************************************/

BOOL     FrameWin::OnCreateClient (LPCREATESTRUCT, CCreateContext *ptrc) {

  // construct the basic splitter window
  BOOL retcd = splitterwin.CreateStatic (this, 1, 2);
  // construct two views side by side - same row with two columns
  // make a guess at the width needed by the first - the AcmeView - 180 pels
  // let plot have all remaining window width - if short, user can adjust it
  retcd |= splitterwin.CreateView (0, 0, RUNTIME_CLASS (AcmeView),
                            CSize (180, 100), ptrc);
  retcd |= splitterwin.CreateView (0, 1, RUNTIME_CLASS (AcmePlot),
                            CSize (100, 100), ptrc);
  return retcd;
}
```

Splitter windows can also be dynamically created by selecting a menu item or by dragging a splitter box. In an SDI application, splitter windows can hold different views as we have done here, or they can display multiple views of the same view class. Using multiple views from the same view class, we can position one view to the start of the data and position another view to the end for comparison purposes. When using the static splitter windows, the user can drag the separation borders only to alter the respective sizes of the panes. They cannot be unsplit or resplit. On the other hand, dynamic splitter windows can be unsplit and resplit as the user chooses; menu items are added to facilitate the actions.

To construct dynamic splitter windows, alter the coding in the **OnCreateClient** function to use only the **Create** member function.

```
return splitterwin.Create (this, 2, 2, CSize (1,1), ptrc);
```

Then add a menu item Split Window giving it the ID of ID_WINDOW_SPLIT. The framework recognizes this ID to mean "start the splitting process." The user can then adjust the bars to split the client area into a maximum of four panes, all showing the same view class, each of which can be scrolled to a different portion of the data.

15.9 THE CVIEW CLASSES: ACMEVIEW AND ACMEPLOT

Last come the lengthy **CView**-derived classes. AcmeView displays the SalesData objects in a scrollable columnar view, while AcmePlot draws a bar chart. Let's begin with a walk-through of the function sequences involved in launching a document's view. Dynamically the framework allocates a new instance of the **CView**-based class. After invoking **OnCreate** as expected, this first-time allocation sequence then invokes **OnInitialUpdate** to allow the new view to perform beginning actions, such as obtaining the number of sales data in the set of data. As the view window is resized to fit in the client area and in the splitter pane, **OnSize** is invoked and then **OnUpdate**. Every time the document's **UpdateAllViews** is executed, it invokes each view window's **OnUpdate** function to permit that view instance to adapt itself to the changed data, typically reacquiring the current number of sets of sales data. **OnUpdate** ultimately sends a paint message. **OnPaint** in a view class is quite different. First the **OnPaint** function calls **OnPrepareDC** to get the paint DC set up, and then it calls **OnDraw**, passing it the DC. It is **OnDraw**'s responsibility to actually paint the screen.

When the user selects File I Print, the framework first calls **OnPreparePrinting** whose task it is to set the number of pages and other values that are to be shown in the Print dialog box. If the user clicks OK, **OnBeginPrinting** is invoked, starting the lengthy printing cycle. Here one typically saves any needed values that are later tested when the process is ended by a call to **OnEndPrinting**. Additionally, the font is created that will be used while printing. The framework then invokes **OnPrepareDC** followed by **OnPrint** for each page to be printed. **OnPrint** handles the page setup operations, such as printing headings, column headings, and footers. Once these are printed, **OnPrint** invokes **OnDraw** to render the body of the page. **OnPrepareDC** has the added responsibility of notifying the framework when the last page has been printed, at which point the framework then terminates the printing process by calling **OnEndPrinting**.

Did you notice the two dual-duty functions? **OnPrepareDC** and **OnDraw** are used to render the image both on-screen and on the printer! **OnPrepareDC** generally installs the correct font for the device at hand, gets the average character dimensions, and, if printing, determines when the last page has been printed. **OnDraw** can be fairly ignorant of whether it is displaying on a screen DC or a printer DC. It just paints the text. However, you can override **OnPrint** and not invoke the base class which in turn invokes **OnDraw**, substituting instead your own render to the printer function. However, Print or Preview is going to use this same sequence to render the sneak preview, passing a preview DC to this pair of functions. So if you use this dual-duty combo, then you can implement Print Preview with no extra coding!

For our example, more complication enters because I wish to keep track of the current user-selected record so that it can be updated or deleted. (Add records are always placed at the end of the array. You could alter this and place the added data into year-sorted order, if desired; use the **InsertAt** function instead of **Add**.) In addition, the view must be scrollable. I could have derived the class from the **CScrollView** class. However, I chose to use the more basic class **CView** for this first exposure to Document-View. Thus, functions are needed to handle scrolling; they are basically the same functions that have been used throughout all of these examples.

Look over the AcmeView class member functions. Since this class is to be dynamically created, it must have a default constructor (no arguments). This time a destructor is required to delete the fonts used for the display and for printing. **OnDraw** renders the screen display with fancy raised column headings or renders the body of a printed page.

```
void OnDraw (CDC *ptrdc);
```

One task that is constantly needed is obtaining a pointer to the document class. Hence, I define a utility routine, **GetDocument**, that returns a pointer to the document. Similarly, I define a **SetupPrinterFont** that constructs a correctly scaled printer font based upon the user's font choice, if any. The prototypes for the usual printing functions of **CView** that are overridden are

```
BOOL   OnPreparePrinting (CPrintInfo*);
void   OnBeginPrinting (CDC*, CPrintInfo*);
void   OnEndPrinting (CDC*, CPrintInfo*);
void   OnPrepareDC (CDC*, CPrintInfo*);
void   OnPrint (CDC*, CPrintInfo*);
```

The **CPrintInfo** contains several key members.

m_bPreview	a BOOL flag set by the framework indicating if Print Preview is in effect
m_bContinuePrinting	BOOL when TRUE continues the print loop; OnPrepareDC should set this to FALSE after the last page has been printed
m_nCurPage	the number of the current page to print
m_nNumPreviewPages	indicates whether 1 or 2 pages are shown in Preview window
m_rectDraw	rectangle specifying the current usable page area and can be used on OnPrint

In **OnInitialUpdate** the current selected record and the top line for scrolling purposes are both set to the first set of data—the first line. In **OnUpdate**, the scroll range is reset based upon the new number of sales data objects. In addition to the familiar **SetOurScrollRange** utility function to adjust the range and thumb position, **CalcCurrentSelection** maintains the integrity of the user's current record selection. **OnVScroll** responds to scroll bar messages, while **OnKeyDown** provides a keyboard scrolling interface. **OnSize** also must adjust the scroll bar range based upon the new size.

The user may select a specific set of data by clicking the left mouse button on its line. **OnLButtonDown** obtains the new user's current record selection, which is then displayed in a red font. **OnFont** responds to the menu item to choose fonts. Note that the fonts chosen are not going to be used on-screen, just for printing and Print Preview. Finally **OnAdd**, **OnUpdate**, and **OnDelete** provide an elementary interface for altering the sales data.

Now examine the data members that coordinate all of this action. The average character dimensions trio holds the current dimensions of the font currently in use, whether it is the screen or printer font. When printing is requested the screen values are saved in the "old" set along with the window's height and width. The field **topline** contains the index of the SalesData object that appears at the top of the screen or the current page being printed. The screen's value is also saved so that the screen can be restored after printing. **selrecnum** contains the index into the sales array of the current user selection, while **sellinenum** contains the corresponding line on which it is currently displayed in red.

The last group of fields is used during printing. **prlogfont** contains the user's font in a LOGFONT structure, while **ptrlogfont** points to the scaled version of that font. The pair of **CSize** objects—**clsize** and **pagesize**—contain the size values for viewport scaling during printing.

15.9.1 Listing for File: AcmeView.h—Pgm15a—Excerpts

```
...
class AcmeView : public CView {

DECLARE_DYNCREATE(AcmeView)

protected:

int avg_caps_width;     // average capital letter width
int avg_char_width;     // average character width
int avg_char_height;    // average character height
int height;             // window height
int width;              // window width
int topline;            // current top line for scrolling
int selrecnum;          // current record number selected in Red font
int sellinenum;         // corresponding screen line number of selected record

int num_sales;          // current number of SalesData objects

int num_lines_per_page; // the number of lines per page
int max_vscroll_lines;  // maximum number of vertical lines to scroll
```

```
int old_width;          // saved screen char width when printing
int old_height;         // saved screen char height when printing
int old_selrec;         // old selected record number when printing
int old_selline;        // old selected record line number
int old_topline;        // old top line when printing
int old_num_lines;      // old number of lines

CRect    rect_print;    // working area of the printed page
int      footer_y;      // location of footer on a page
LOGFONT  prlogfont;     // printer version of user selected font
LOGFONT *ptrlogfont;    // scaled copy of the user font
CFont   *ptrfont;       // the display font in use
CFont   *ptrprfont;     // the corresponding printer font in use scaled
CSize    clsize;        // holds the size of the screen for scaling
CSize    pagesize;      // holds the size of the printed page for scaling

public:
            AcmeView ();        // no parms required for serialization
            ~AcmeView ();       // removes any fonts
    AcmeDoc* GetDocument ();    // returns the doc associated with this view
        void OnDraw (CDC*);     // displays a screen of printer page

protected:
        BOOL OnPreparePrinting (CPrintInfo*);       // sets values in dlg box
        void OnBeginPrinting (CDC*, CPrintInfo*);   // save screen data values
        void OnEndPrinting (CDC*, CPrintInfo*);     // restore screen values
        void SetupPrinterFont (CDC*, CPrintInfo*);  // make the printer font
        void OnPrepareDC (CDC*, CPrintInfo*);       // install font-get char dims
        void OnPrint (CDC*, CPrintInfo*);           // print heading and footer
        void OnInitialUpdate ();                    // initialize settings
        void OnUpdate (CView*, LPARAM, CObject*);   // reset settings/scroll val
        void SetOurScrollRange ();                  // reset scroll range
        void CalcCurrentSelection ();               // maintains cur. selection

afx_msg int  OnCreate (LPCREATESTRUCT);            // make gray brush and font
afx_msg void OnKeyDown (UINT, UINT, UINT);         // scroller keybd interface
afx_msg void OnVScroll (UINT, UINT, CScrollBar*);  // scroll screen display
afx_msg void OnSize (UINT, int, int);              // set window height/width
afx_msg void OnLButtonDown (UINT, CPoint);         // get new current record
afx_msg void OnFonts ();                           // get new user font
afx_msg void OnAdd ();                             // adds new record at end
afx_msg void OnUpdate ();                          // updates current record
afx_msg void OnDelete ();                          // deletes current record
...
```

Notice that the class implements dynamic creation as expected. The constructor sets the initial user-selected record as the top line or index 0 and sets the pointer to the user fonts to NULL. If the user does not select a font, I use a fixed font from the Courier New group in **OnCreate**. I used a height of 14, which is arbitrary—it works well on my system in 1024×768 resolution. This font is the main display font. If the user does not select a printing font, this font is scaled to the printer.

In this example, **OnInitialUpdate** does not really need to be overridden since the constructor has already set these values and **OnUpdate** is invoked before the initial display occurs anyway. In **OnUpdate** the scroll range may need to be reset after obtaining the current number of sales objects.

Next let's look at the **OnPrepareDC** and **OnDraw** pair from the viewpoint of screen display only. When **OnPrepareDC** is invoked, the window is at last completely constructed with the final dimensions, and, at this point, the average character dimensions are finally correct. After the current font is installed and character dimensions obtained, the scroll range can now be properly adjusted as required. The framework then passes the prepared DC to **OnDraw** to paint the screen. Since the document and the sales array are going to be referenced several times, **OnDraw** first makes a local copy of the pointer to the document and also a pointer to the sales array. The integer **line** is used in the **TextOut** functions to determine the y coordinate; it is initialized to the second line, 1, so that the column headings are not immediately touching the top border. To avoid repetitive function calls, the BOOL **isprinting** is set to the BOOL returned from the **CDC** member function **IsPrinting** which returns TRUE if this is a printer DC.

```
BOOL IsPrinting (); // a handy CDC member function
```

If the current DC is not a printer, then the column headings are drawn on a raised area. To construct a raised box, draw the top and left edges in white and the bottom and right edges in black. To create a depressed box, reverse these, drawing the top and left edges in black and the bottom and right in white.

Next, **OnDraw** must display the correct screenful of sales data objects. Recall that **topline** contains the index of the SalesData object to be displayed on the first line of this page. If the entire set of data can be displayed on one screen, then **topline** will always be zero. It is nonzero if the user has scrolled down. The number of lines that can fit on this DC is the lesser of the maximum number of lines that can potentially be on this screen and the number of remaining sales data objects, given by the **num_sales** minus **topline**. If **topline** is then added to this, the result is the index of the last sales object to be displayed this time. The display loop begins by getting a pointer to the current SalesData object in the array.

```
int num_to_do = min (num_sales - topline, num_lines_per_page) +
                    topline;
for (int i=topline; i<num_to_do; i++) {
ptrdata = (SalesData*) ptrarray->GetAt (i);
```

Next, I handle the current record situation. The application must indicate which record being displayed is the current record (which could be updated or deleted by the user). I choose to display that record in red. The extra field, **sellinenum**, contains the line number of that selection (the value is kept in synch with the actual sales array index, **selrecnum**, in the **CalcCurrentSelection** function). Thus, if printing is not ongoing and the current line matches the selected line number, I insert a red pen. Otherwise the default black pen is used to display the data.

```
if (!isprinting && line == sellinenum)
  ptrdc->SetTextColor (RGB (255,0,0));
sprintf (msg, "%4ld", ptrdata->year);
ptrdc->TextOut (avg_char_width*5, avg_char_height*line, msg);
```

```
    sprintf (msg, "%8.2f", ptrdata->sales);
    ptrdc->TextOut (avg_char_width*13, avg_char_height*line++, msg);
    if (!isprinting && line-1 == sellinenum)
      ptrdc->SetTextColor (RGB (0,0,0));
  }
```

Remember that this very same loop must also render a full printed page. The key items are the correct font with its corresponding average character dimensions already installed in the **CDC** by **OnPrepareDC** and the fields **topline** and **num_lines_per_page**. So when printing, if these last two values are set correctly, **OnDraw** can print a page. Notice that, to get to the next printed page, we just add **num_lines_per_page** to **topline**. For the screen display, **num_lines_per_page** gets assigned in **SetOurScrollRange**, once the current pane in the splitter window's height and width are found.

```
GetClientRect (&rect);
height = rect.Height();
width  = rect.Width();
num_lines_per_page = height / avg_char_height
                    - (HEAD_LINE+HEAD_SPACE);
if (num_lines_per_page <1) num_lines_per_page = 1;
```

Next, the maximum number of lines to scroll is calculated. At this point, **topline** may need to be reset. Remember that the index of the topmost line must be less than the maximum number of lines to scroll or else you can scroll a lot of blank lines as you near the end of the data.

```
    max_vscroll_lines = max (0, num_sales - num_lines_per_page );
    topline = min (topline, max_vscroll_lines);
    SetScrollRange (SB_VERT, 0, max_vscroll_lines, FALSE);
    SetScrollPos (SB_VERT, topline, TRUE);
  }
```

Once the scrolling factors are adjusted, the effect, if any, on the user's current record selection must be examined. For example, if record 0 shown on the top line is the selected record and if the user scrolls down one line, the current record must be moved down one. This adjustment is done in **CalcCurrentSelection**. In order to simplify the **OnDraw**, which must know which line is the current selection to be shown in red, I maintain **sellinenum**, which is the screen line number of the selected record. This complicates the adjustment process. If the selected record is now less than **topline**, the user's choice has been scrolled off-screen; make the selection be the top record. If the selected record is off the bottom of the screen—that is, greater than **topline** plus the number of lines per page—then force the selected record to be the last line on-screen.

```
    int num_to_eof = num_sales - topline;
    if (selrecnum < topline) {
      selrecnum = topline;
      sellinenum = HEAD_LINE + HEAD_SPACE;
    }
    else if (selrecnum >= topline + num_lines_per_page) {
      selrecnum = topline + num_lines_per_page;
```

```
 if (selrecnum >= num_sales) {
  selrecnum = num_sales -1;
  sellinenum = (selrecnum - topline) + HEAD_LINE + HEAD_SPACE;
 }
 else sellinenum = HEAD_LINE + HEAD_SPACE + selrecnum - topline;
 }
 else sellinenum = (selrecnum - topline) + HEAD_LINE + HEAD_SPACE;
```

Finally, user selections are made by pressing the left mouse button on the desired line. In **OnLButtonDown**, hit testing is done to determine first which line is selected and then what record number or SalesData object that line represents. You must avoid bogus selections.

```
// calculate the line number clicked upon
int line = point.y / avg_char_height - HEAD_LINE - HEAD_SPACE;
// select that line if it is within range
if (line < 0 || line > num_lines_per_page) return;
if (line <= num_sales - topline -1) {
 selrecnum = topline + line;
 sellinenum = line + HEAD_LINE + HEAD_SPACE;
 Invalidate ();
}
```

Most of the rest of the scrolling code is the same as in all previous examples. However, I made one slight alteration in the keyboard interface to accommodate user selection of the current record. Suppose that the current record is the top line and the user wishes to make the second line be the selected line. It is likely that the user may press the down arrow to do so. Hence, in **OnKeyDown** the up arrow and down arrow key pressed must consider this effect in addition to normal scrolling requests.

```
case VK_UP:
 if (selrecnum <= topline) SendMessage (WM_VSCROLL, SB_LINEUP, OL);
 else {
  if (selrecnum -1 <0) break;
  selrecnum--;
  sellinenum--;
  Invalidate ();
 }
 break;

case VK_DOWN:
 if (selrecnum + 1 < num_sales) {
 selrecnum++;
 sellinenum++;
 Invalidate ();
 }
 SendMessage (WM_VSCROLL, SB_LINEDOWN, OL); break;
```

Alterations to the document's data are done through the functions **OnAdd**, **OnUpdate**, and **OnDelete**, with the last two using the current record in red. In this example, since the dialogs are executed by the view class and the new or modified data gathered, I had the view class go ahead and update the data directly in the document's array. Assuming **ptrdata** is an instance of the SalesData class that is filled with the new data to be added, **OnAdd** then inserts the data into the document.

```
        ptrarray->Add (ptrdata);
        ptrdoc->SetModifiedFlag (TRUE);
        ptrdoc->UpdateAllViews (NULL, 0, NULL);
```

The document's modified flag is set and all views are notified of the change so that
they can repaint their screens. Personally, I would prefer that the document class
actually handle all modifications to its data.

15.9.2 Listing for File: AcmeView.cpp—Pgm15a—Excerpts

```
...
IMPLEMENT_DYNCREATE(AcmeView, CView)

#define  HEAD_LINE      1  // line number on which to display header line
#define  HEAD_SPACE     2  // number of blank lines after header
#define  MAX_LINE_LEN  20  // max line width in characters
/****************************************************************************/
/*                                                                        */
/* AcmeView Events Response Table                                         */
/*                                                                        */
/****************************************************************************/
BEGIN_MESSAGE_MAP(AcmeView, CView)
 ON_WM_VSCROLL ()
 ON_WM_KEYDOWN ()
 ON_WM_LBUTTONDOWN ()
 ON_WM_SIZE ()
 ON_WM_CREATE ()
 ON_COMMAND(ID_FILE_PRINT,         CView::OnFilePrint)
 ON_COMMAND(ID_FILE_PRINT_PREVIEW, CView::OnFilePrintPreview)
 ON_COMMAND(CM_FONTS,              OnFonts)
 ON_COMMAND(CM_ADD,                OnAdd)
 ON_COMMAND(CM_UPDATE,             OnUpdate)
 ON_COMMAND(CM_DELETE,             OnDelete)
END_MESSAGE_MAP()
/****************************************************************************/
/*                                                                        */
/* AcmeView: Construct the view object                                    */
/*                                                                        */
/****************************************************************************/
         AcmeView::AcmeView () {

 topline = 0;                       // sales array index of top line on scrn
 selrecnum = 0;                     // sales array index of current selection
 sellinenum = HEAD_LINE + HEAD_SPACE; // the screen line number of cur select
 ptrprfont = NULL;                  // set for no printer font
 ptrlogfont = NULL;
 }
/****************************************************************************/
/*                                                                        */
/* OnCreate: build the window with gray brush & make display font         */
/*                                                                        */
```

```
/**************************************************************************/

int      AcmeView::OnCreate (LPCREATESTRUCT lpCS) {

 int retcd = CView::OnCreate (lpCS); // pass along to base class

 // install new background color
 ::DeleteObject ((HBRUSH)::SetClassLong (m_hWnd, GCL_HBRBACKGROUND,
                  (long) (HBRUSH) ::GetStockObject (LTGRAY_BRUSH)));
 ptrfont = new CFont ();
 ptrfont->CreateFont (14, 0, 0, 0, FW_NORMAL, FALSE, FALSE, FALSE,
                  ANSI_CHARSET, OUT_TT_PRECIS, CLIP_TT_ALWAYS,
                  DEFAULT_QUALITY, DEFAULT_PITCH, "Courier New");
 return retcd;
}

/**************************************************************************/
/*                                                                      */
/* ~AcmeView: remove all fonts that were used                          */
/*                                                                      */
/**************************************************************************/

         AcmeView::~AcmeView () {

 delete ptrfont;
 if (ptrlogfont) delete ptrlogfont;
}

/**************************************************************************/
/*                                                                      */
/* GetDocument: retrieve a pointer to the main document                */
/*                                                                      */
/**************************************************************************/

AcmeDoc*  AcmeView::GetDocument () {

 return (AcmeDoc*) m_pDocument;
}

/**************************************************************************/
/*                                                                      */
/* OnInitialUpdate: update num_sales and set index into sales array on scrn*/
/*                                                                      */
/**************************************************************************/

void      AcmeView::OnInitialUpdate () {

 num_sales = GetDocument ()->GetNumSales ();
 topline = selrecnum = 0;
 CView::OnInitialUpdate ();
}

/**************************************************************************/
/*                                                                      */
/* OnUpdate: reset num_sales, avg char dims, scroll range, cur selection */
/*                                                                      */
/**************************************************************************/

void      AcmeView::OnUpdate (CView *ptrsender, LPARAM hint, CObject *ptrdata) {
```

```
// re obtain the current number of entries in the sales array
num_sales = GetDocument ()->GetNumSales ();

SetOurScrollRange ();      // set scroll range based on num recs and char dims
CalcCurrentSelection (); // update current user selected record
CView::OnUpdate (ptrsender, hint, ptrdata); // pass on to base class
}
/****************************************************************************/
/*                                                                        */
/* OnPrepareDC: setup printer or screen DC - insert the fixed font and mode*/
/*                                                                        */
/****************************************************************************/
void      AcmeView::OnPrepareDC (CDC *ptrdc, CPrintInfo *ptrinfo) {

TEXTMETRIC  tm;

CView::OnPrepareDC (ptrdc, ptrinfo); // let base class get the DCs

if (ptrinfo != NULL) {                    // is printer this time
  // Option 1: use mode and extents
  ptrdc->SetMapMode (MM_ANISOTROPIC); // set for scaling on x and y axis
  ptrdc->SetWindowExt (clsize);        // set window size to screen
  ptrdc->SetViewportExt (pagesize);   // set viewport size to printer page
  // Option 2: no mode and extents - use scaling factors in setup print font
  // so remove Option 1 above three lines
  ptrdc->SelectObject (ptrprfont);    // install printer font
  // set the continue printing flag if there are more lines to print
  if (topline < num_sales) ptrinfo->m_bContinuePrinting = TRUE;
  else ptrinfo->m_bContinuePrinting = FALSE;
  ptrdc->GetTextMetrics (&tm);         // get the font information
  // calculate average character parameters
  avg_char_width  = tm.tmAveCharWidth;
  avg_char_height = tm.tmHeight + tm.tmExternalLeading;
  avg_caps_width  = (tm.tmPitchAndFamily & 1 ? 3 : 2) * avg_char_width / 2;
}
else {                              // paint screen dc this time
  ptrdc->SelectObject (ptrfont);     // install fixed font
  ptrdc->GetTextMetrics (&tm);       // get the font information
  // calculate average character parameters
  avg_char_width  = tm.tmAveCharWidth;
  avg_char_height = tm.tmHeight + tm.tmExternalLeading;
  avg_caps_width  = (tm.tmPitchAndFamily & 1 ? 3 : 2) * avg_char_width / 2;
  SetOurScrollRange ();              // reset scroll bar range using real font
  CalcCurrentSelection ();           // update current user selected record
}
}
/****************************************************************************/
/*                                                                        */
/* OnDraw: display the document as a table on screen or on the printer    */
/*                                                                        */
/****************************************************************************/
void      AcmeView::OnDraw (CDC *ptrdc) {

char msg[80];
```

```
AcmeDoc *ptrdoc = GetDocument ();              // acquire access to the doc
SalesDataArray *ptrarray = &ptrdoc->sales_array; // get ptr to the sales array
SalesData      *ptrdata;                       // will point to a SalesData
int line = HEAD_LINE;                          // current line to show
BOOL isprinting = ptrdc->IsPrinting();         // get printing/screen flag
ptrdc->SetBkMode (TRANSPARENT);                // set transparent dsply mode

if (!isprinting) {  // if on screen display,  display column headings
  // as raised areas above columns of data
  CString yrs, sls;
  yrs.LoadString (IDS_YEARS);
  sls.LoadString (IDS_SALES);
  ptrdc->SelectStockObject (WHITE_PEN);

  // draw years box and show "Year" in it
  CRect ryr (4*avg_char_width, line*avg_char_height-3, 10*avg_char_width,
             (line+1)*avg_char_height+3);
  ptrdc->MoveTo (ryr.right, ryr.top);
  ptrdc->LineTo (ryr.left,  ryr.top);
  ptrdc->LineTo (ryr.left,  ryr.bottom);
  ptrdc->SelectStockObject (BLACK_PEN);
  ptrdc->LineTo (ryr.right, ryr.bottom);
  ptrdc->LineTo (ryr.right, ryr.top);
  ptrdc->TextOut (5*avg_char_width, avg_char_height, yrs);

  // draw sales box and show "Sales" in it
  CRect rsl (13*avg_char_width, line*avg_char_height-3, 21*avg_char_width,
             (line+1)*avg_char_height+3);
  ptrdc->SelectStockObject (WHITE_PEN);
  ptrdc->MoveTo (rsl.right, rsl.top);
  ptrdc->LineTo (rsl.left,  rsl.top);
  ptrdc->LineTo (rsl.left,  rsl.bottom);
  ptrdc->SelectStockObject (BLACK_PEN);
  ptrdc->LineTo (rsl.right, rsl.bottom);
  ptrdc->LineTo (rsl.right, rsl.top);
  ptrdc->TextOut (15*avg_char_width, avg_char_height*line, sls);
}

// display each sales entry
line += HEAD_SPACE;         // set line to first data line
if (isprinting) line++;  // if printing add one line for readability
// set the number of lines to do on this screen/page
int num_to_do = min (num_sales - topline, num_lines_per_page) + topline;
// for each line beginning at topline offset in the array, show sales data
for (int i=topline; i<num_to_do; i++) {
  ptrdata = (SalesData*) ptrarray->GetAt (i); // get a ptr to the SalesData obj
  // if not printing, if this is the selected record, then use Red as the color
  if (!isprinting && line == sellinenum) ptrdc->SetTextColor (RGB (255,0,0));
  sprintf (msg, "%4ld", ptrdata->year);
  ptrdc->TextOut (avg_char_width*5, avg_char_height*line, msg);
  sprintf (msg, "%8.2f", ptrdata->sales);
  ptrdc->TextOut (avg_char_width*13, avg_char_height*line++, msg);
  if (!isprinting && line-1 == sellinenum) ptrdc->SetTextColor (RGB (0,0,0));
}
}
```

```
/*****************************************************************************/
/*                                                                         */
/* OnPreparePrinting: set the number of pages to 1 for the Print dialog    */
/*                                                                         */
/*****************************************************************************/

BOOL      AcmeView::OnPreparePrinting (CPrintInfo *ptrinfo) {

 if (ptrinfo->m_bPreview) {
  ptrinfo->m_nNumPreviewPages = 1;
  ptrinfo->SetMaxPage (1);
 }
 return CView::DoPreparePrinting (ptrinfo);
}

/*****************************************************************************/
/*                                                                         */
/* OnBeginPrinting: save display values, install print values & print font */
/*                  `                                                      */
/*****************************************************************************/

void      AcmeView::OnBeginPrinting (CDC *ptrdc, CPrintInfo *ptrinfo) {
  old_width     = avg_char_width;      // save old display values
  old_height    = avg_char_height;
  old_topline   = topline;
  old_selline   = sellinenum;
  old_selrec    = selrecnum;
  old_num_lines = num_lines_per_page;

  topline = 0;                         // set for whole document
  selrecnum = 0;
  sellinenum = HEAD_LINE + HEAD_SPACE;
  SetupPrinterFont (ptrdc, ptrinfo);   // make up the printer font
}

/*****************************************************************************/
/*                                                                         */
/* OnEndPrinting: ending printing cycles                                   */
/*                                                                         */
/*****************************************************************************/

void      AcmeView::OnEndPrinting (CDC* /*ptrdc*/, CPrintInfo* /*ptrinfo*/) {
  avg_char_width      = old_width;     // restore display values
  avg_char_height     = old_height;
  topline             = old_topline;
  sellinenum          = old_selline;
  selrecnum           = old_selrec;
  num_lines_per_page  = old_num_lines;
  delete ptrprfont;                    // and remove the print font
}

/*****************************************************************************/
/*                                                                         */
/* SetupPrinterFont: setup the printer font and get new avg char dims      */
/*                                                                         */
/*****************************************************************************/
```

```
void        AcmeView::SetupPrinterFont (CDC *ptrdc, CPrintInfo* /*ptrinfo*/) {

 int savedc = ptrdc->SaveDC ();  // save the DC

 // load user's chosen font, if any, and scale TrueType fonts
 if (!ptrlogfont) {               // no user font, so use the default font
  ptrdc->SelectObject (ptrfont); // and extract the LOGFONT object for scaling
  ptrfont->GetObject (sizeof(LOGFONT), &prlogfont);
 }
 else prlogfont = *ptrlogfont; // assign the user's font

 // Begin Option 1 coding - use mode and extents
 // set screen size to that of a full screen
 CRect clrect (0, 0, GetSystemMetrics (SM_CXSCREEN),
                    GetSystemMetrics (SM_CYSCREEN));
 clsize = clrect.Size();  // will hold the size of the screen for window extent
 // set the printer page size for viewport extent
 pagesize = CSize (ptrdc->GetDeviceCaps (HORZRES),
                   ptrdc->GetDeviceCaps (VERTRES));

 // install mode and scaling effects
 ptrdc->SetMapMode (MM_ANISOTROPIC);
 ptrdc->SetWindowExt (clsize);
 ptrdc->SetViewportExt (pagesize);
 // end Option 1 coding

 // begin Option 2 coding
 /*
 HDC hdc = CreateDC ("DISPLAY",NULL,NULL,NULL); // get a screen DC for scaling
 // calculate both x and y scale dimensions between the screen and the printer
 float xscale = ptrdc->GetDeviceCaps (LOGPIXELSX) /
                (float) GetDeviceCaps(hdc, LOGPIXELSX);
 float yscale = ptrdc->GetDeviceCaps (LOGPIXELSY) /
                (float) GetDeviceCaps(hdc, LOGPIXELSY);
 // or scale by true size
 CRect clrect (0, 0, GetSystemMetrics (SM_CXSCREEN),
                    GetSystemMetrics (SM_CYSCREEN));
 CSize clsize = clrect.Size();
 pagesize = CSize (ptrdc->GetDeviceCaps (HORZRES),
                   ptrdc->GetDeviceCaps (VERTRES));

 float xx = pagesize.cx/(float)clsize.cx;
 float yy = pagesize.cy/(float)clsize.cy;
 DeleteDC (hdc);

 // install scaled dimensions
 // scale choice 1:
 // prlogfont.lfHeight = (long) (prlogfont.lfHeight * yscale);
 // prlogfont.lfWidth = (long) (prlogfont.lfWidth * xscale);
 // scale choice 2:
 prlogfont.lfHeight = (long) (prlogfont.lfHeight * yy);
 prlogfont.lfWidth = (long) (prlogfont.lfWidth * xx);
 */
 // end Option 2 coding

 // construct the true printer font from the logfont
 ptrprfont = new CFont ();
```

```
ptrprfont->CreateFontIndirect (&prlogfont);  // create the font from LOGFONT
ptrdc->SelectObject (ptrprfont);             // install font

ptrdc->RestoreDC (savedc);                   // restore the DC
}
/************************************************************************/
/*                                                                    */
/* OnPrint: handle headings and footers                               */
/*                                                                    */
/************************************************************************/
void     AcmeView::OnPrint (CDC *ptrdc, CPrintInfo *ptrinfo) {

// calculate y location for the footer
footer_y = ptrinfo->m_rectDraw.Height () - avg_char_height -1;
// adjust the printer info drawing rectangle to exclude header/footers
ptrinfo->m_rectDraw.top += 4*avg_char_height;
ptrinfo->m_rectDraw.bottom -= avg_char_height + 1;
rect_print = ptrinfo->m_rectDraw;
// calc the number of data lines that fit on a printed page inside margins
num_lines_per_page = rect_print.Height () / avg_char_height;

// print the title and column headings
CString s;
s.LoadString (IDS_ACMETITLE);
ptrdc->TextOut (0, 0, s);
s.Empty ();
s.LoadString (IDS_YEARS);
ptrdc->TextOut (avg_char_width*5, 2*avg_char_height, s);
s.Empty ();
s.LoadString (IDS_SALES);
ptrdc->TextOut (avg_char_width*13, 2*avg_char_height, s);
// print the main SalesData objects
CView::OnPrint (ptrdc, ptrinfo);

// print the footers
s.Empty ();
s.LoadString (IDS_FOOTER);
ptrdc->TextOut (0, footer_y, s);

// in case of multiple pages, increment the current position within the data
topline += num_lines_per_page;
}
/************************************************************************/
/*                                                                    */
/* OnFonts: get the user's font choice for printing NOT for display   */
/*                                                                    */
/************************************************************************/
void     AcmeView::OnFonts () {

CFontDialog  *ptrdlg;
static char   printer[80];
char          *device, *driver, * output;
CDC           *ptrprinterDC = new CDC;

// get access to a printer DC from the ini file installed printer
```

```
  GetProfileString ("windows", "device", "...", printer, 80);
  if (NULL != (device = strtok (printer, ",")) &&
      NULL != (driver = strtok (NULL,    ",")) &&
      NULL != (output = strtok (NULL,    ","))) {
   // a default printer exists, so get a DC for it
   ptrprinterDC->CreateDC (driver, device, output, NULL);
   // if the user has already chosen a font, use that one as the initial font
   if (ptrlogfont) ptrdlg = new CFontDialog (ptrlogfont, CF_EFFECTS |
                   CF_PRINTERFONTS | CF_FORCEFONTEXIST, ptrprinterDC, this);
   else ptrdlg = new CFontDialog (NULL, CF_EFFECTS |
                   CF_PRINTERFONTS | CF_FORCEFONTEXIST, ptrprinterDC, this);
  }
  else {
   // cannot find the default printer, so use printer only fonts instead, if
   // user has already chosen a font, use it as the initial font in the dialog
   if (ptrlogfont) ptrdlg = new CFontDialog (ptrlogfont, CF_EFFECTS |
                   CF_PRINTERFONTS | CF_FORCEFONTEXIST, NULL, this);
   else ptrdlg = new CFontDialog (NULL, CF_EFFECTS |
                   CF_PRINTERFONTS | CF_FORCEFONTEXIST, NULL, this);
  }

  if (ptrdlg->DoModal () == IDOK) {      // get user font choice
   if (!ptrlogfont) ptrlogfont = new LOGFONT; // 1st time, create LOGFONT
   memcpy (ptrlogfont, &(ptrdlg->m_lf), sizeof (LOGFONT)); // copy user choice
   // here I notify user that chosen font is only used for printing
   MessageBox ("Use Print Preview to see results", "Font Chosen For Printing",
           MB_OK); // you could display a msg on status bar
  }
  delete ptrprinterDC;
  delete ptrdlg;
}

/***************************************************************************/
/*                                                                         */
/* OnSize: gets window dims and sets new scroll bar range                  */
/*                                                                         */
/***************************************************************************/

void      AcmeView::OnSize (UINT a, int b, int c) {
 CView::OnSize    (a, b, c);
 SetOurScrollRange ();        // reset scroll bars ranges
 CalcCurrentSelection ();     // recalc the current selected record position
 Invalidate();                // force repainting of window
}

/***************************************************************************/
/*                                                                         */
/* SetOurScrollRange: sets up the new scroll range                         */
/*                                                                         */
/***************************************************************************/

void AcmeView::SetOurScrollRange () {

 CRect rect;
 GetClientRect (&rect);       // get the size of the client window
 height = rect.Height();      // calc and save current height
```

```
width  = rect.Width();      // calc and save current width
// calc the number of SalesData objects per page
num_lines_per_page = height/avg_char_height - (HEAD_LINE+HEAD_SPACE);
if (num_lines_per_page <1) num_lines_per_page = 1; // force at least one
// set max number of scrolling lines for the range to scroll
max_vscroll_lines = max (0, num_sales - num_lines_per_page );
// adjust current top of page index into the Sales array
topline = min (topline, max_vscroll_lines);
// then set the scroll range and current thumb bar position
SetScrollRange (SB_VERT, 0, max_vscroll_lines, FALSE);
SetScrollPos (SB_VERT, topline, TRUE);
}
/*****************************************************************************/
/*                                                                         */
/* CalcCurrentSelection: set the current selection if it's on-screen       */
/*                                                                         */
/*****************************************************************************/
void     AcmeView::CalcCurrentSelection () {

 int num_to_eof = num_sales - topline;  // calc number records from top to end
 if (selrecnum < topline) {              // if selection is no longer on screen,
  selrecnum = topline;                   // reset cur selection to be top line
  sellinenum = HEAD_LINE + HEAD_SPACE;   // and set its screen line number
 }
 else if (selrecnum >= topline + num_lines_per_page) { // here it's off screen
  selrecnum = topline + num_lines_per_page; // so force cur sel to be last line
  if (selrecnum >= num_sales) {           // check this goes off end of array
   selrecnum = num_sales -1;              // yes, so make last array item it
   sellinenum = (selrecnum - topline) + HEAD_LINE + HEAD_SPACE;
  }
  else sellinenum = HEAD_LINE + HEAD_SPACE + selrecnum - topline;
 }
 else sellinenum = (selrecnum - topline) + HEAD_LINE + HEAD_SPACE;
}
/*****************************************************************************/
/*                                                                         */
/* OnLButtonDown: get current record selection                             */
/*                                                                         */
/*****************************************************************************/
void     AcmeView::OnLButtonDown (UINT, CPoint point) {

 // calculate the line number clicked upon
 int line = point.y / avg_char_height - HEAD_LINE - HEAD_SPACE;

 // select that line if it is within range
 if (line < 0 || line > num_lines_per_page) return; // ignore out of range
 if (line <= num_sales - topline -1) {              // in range, so select it
  selrecnum = topline + line;
  sellinenum = line + HEAD_LINE + HEAD_SPACE;
  Invalidate ();
 }
}
/*****************************************************************************/
```

```
/*                                                                      */
/* OnKeyDown: provides a keyboard scroller interface                    */
/*            and allows user to up/down arrow for current record select */
/*                                                                      */
/***********************************************************************/

void      AcmeView::OnKeyDown (UINT key, UINT, UINT) {

 // check for and handle any possible keyboard scroll request

 switch (key) {

  case VK_UP:                    // requests scroll up 1 line
   if (selrecnum <= topline)     // if cur rec is off screen, scroll
    SendMessage (WM_VSCROLL, SB_LINEUP, 0L);
   else {                        // cur record is on screen, so no scroll
    if (selrecnum -1 <0) break;  // quit if already at the top
    selrecnum--;                 // back cur rec selection up by one line
    sellinenum--;
    Invalidate ();
    }
   break;

  case VK_DOWN:                  // requests scroll down 1 line
   if (selrecnum + 1 < num_sales) { // can do down one line, so
    selrecnum++;                 // set cur record selection down one line
    sellinenum++;
    Invalidate ();
    }
   SendMessage (WM_VSCROLL, SB_LINEDOWN, 0L); break;

  case VK_LEFT:  // requests scroll left 1 col
   SendMessage (WM_HSCROLL, SB_LINEUP, 0L); break;

  case VK_RIGHT: // requests scroll right 1 col
   SendMessage (WM_HSCROLL, SB_LINEDOWN, 0L); break;

  case VK_PRIOR: // request scroll 1 page up
   SendMessage (WM_VSCROLL, SB_PAGEUP, 0L); break;

  case VK_NEXT:  // request scroll 1 page down
   SendMessage (WM_VSCROLL, SB_PAGEDOWN, 0L); break;

  case VK_END:   // request goto the bottom
   SendMessage (WM_HSCROLL, SB_PAGEDOWN, 0L); break;

  case VK_HOME:  // request goto the top
   SendMessage (WM_HSCROLL, SB_PAGEUP, 0L);  break;
 }
}

/***********************************************************************/
/*                                                                      */
/* OnVScroll: scroll window vertically                                  */
/*                                                                      */
/***********************************************************************/

void      AcmeView::OnVScroll (UINT type, UINT pos, CScrollBar *ptrsb) {

 int num_lines_to_scroll;
```

```
  switch (type) {

   case SB_LINEUP:      // scroll up 1 line
    num_lines_to_scroll = -1; break;

   case SB_LINEDOWN:    // scroll 1 line down
    num_lines_to_scroll = 1; break;

   case SB_PAGEUP:      // scroll 1 page up
    num_lines_to_scroll = min (-1, -num_lines_per_page); break;

   case SB_PAGEDOWN:    // scroll 1 page down
    num_lines_to_scroll = max (1, num_lines_per_page); break;

   case SB_THUMBTRACK:  // follow thumb bar
    num_lines_to_scroll = pos - topline; break;

   default:
    num_lines_to_scroll = 0;
  }

  num_lines_to_scroll = max (-topline,
                        min (num_lines_to_scroll,
                              max_vscroll_lines - topline));

  if (num_lines_to_scroll !=0) {          // if there are any lines to scroll,
   topline +=num_lines_to_scroll;         // add to top line index
   SetScrollPos (SB_VERT, topline, TRUE); // set new scroll position
   CalcCurrentSelection ();               // do any cur record select adjustment
   Invalidate (TRUE);
  }
  CView::OnVScroll (type, pos, ptrsb);
}
/***********************************************************************************/
/*                                                                              */
/* OnAdd: add a new sales data record at the end of the set                     */
/*                                                                              */
/***********************************************************************************/

void      AcmeView::OnAdd () {

 TRANSFER_SALES  xfer_sls;  // transfer buffer for sales

 xfer_sls.yr[0] = 0;        // install NULL strings in the xfer buffer
 xfer_sls.sls[0] = 0;

 CAddUpdateDlg add (this, &xfer_sls); // construct dialog instance
 if (add.DoModal () == IDOK) {        // execute dlg, if ok get new name
  AcmeDoc *ptrdoc = GetDocument ();   // get access to the document
  SalesDataArray *ptrarray = &ptrdoc->sales_array; // and the array of sales
  // allocate a new SalesData object with user entered values from dialog box
  SalesData *ptrdata = new SalesData (atol (xfer_sls.yr), atof (xfer_sls.sls));
  ptrarray->Add (ptrdata);            // add the new object to the array
  ptrdoc->SetModifiedFlag (TRUE);     // tell document it has been modified
  ptrdoc->UpdateAllViews (NULL, 0, NULL); // tell document to update all views
 }
}

/***********************************************************************************/
/*                                                                              */
```

```
/* OnUpdate: alter the current record in red                              */
/*                                                                        */
/**************************************************************************/

void       AcmeView::OnUpdate () {

 TRANSFER_SALES xfer_sls;          // transfer buffer for sales
 AcmeDoc *ptrdoc = GetDocument (); // get access to the document
 // get access to the current record to be updated
 SalesData *ptrdata = (SalesData*) ptrdoc->sales_array.GetAt (selrecnum);

 // install current SalesData values into the xfer buffer
 sprintf (xfer_sls.yr, "%ld", ptrdata->year);
 sprintf (xfer_sls.sls, "%9.2f", ptrdata->sales);

 CAddUpdateDlg update (this, &xfer_sls); // construct dialog instance
 if (update.DoModal () == IDOK) {        // execute dlg, if ok get new name
  ptrdata->year  = atol (xfer_sls.yr);   // copy into the SalesData object
  ptrdata->sales = atof (xfer_sls.sls);  // the new updated values
  ptrdoc->SetModifiedFlag (TRUE);        // tell document that it is modified
  ptrdoc->UpdateAllViews (NULL, 0, NULL); // tell document to update all views
 }
}

/**************************************************************************/
/*                                                                        */
/* OnDelete: remove the current record in red                            */
/*                                                                        */
/**************************************************************************/

void       AcmeView::OnDelete () {
 // confirm the deletion request
 CString msg1, msg2;
 msg1.LoadString (IDS_CONFIRM1);
 msg2.LoadString (IDS_CONFIRM2);
 if (MessageBox (msg2, msg1, MB_YESNO) == IDYES) { // user confirms, so delete
  AcmeDoc *ptrdoc = GetDocument ();                 // get access to document
  SalesDataArray *ptrarray = &ptrdoc->sales_array;  // get access to array
  if (ptrarray->GetSize () > selrecnum) {           // verify record is there
   SalesData *ptrdata = (SalesData*) ptrarray->GetAt (selrecnum); // get record
   ptrarray->RemoveAt (selrecnum, 1);               // remove ptr from array
   delete ptrdata;                                  // delete the Sales object
   selrecnum--;                                      // dec current record number
   ptrdoc->SetModifiedFlag (TRUE);                  // tell doc it's changed
   ptrdoc->UpdateAllViews (NULL, 0, NULL);          // tell doc to update views
  }
 }
}
```

15.10 THE PRINTING AND PRINT PREVIEW PROCESSES OF ACMEVIEW

At last we come to the details of the printing process. First examine the font situation. In **OnCreate** a default screen font—14-point Courier New fixed font—is constructed. If the user does not choose another font, then the LOGFONT structure of this font is extracted and used as the base for the printer font. In **OnFonts**, should the user choose another font for printing (the rest of the coding is the standard "choose fonts" coding used in the chapter 10 examples), I allocate and copy the LOGFONT structure that defines the user's selected font.

```
if (ptrdlg->DoModal () == IDOK) {
 if (!ptrlogfont) ptrlogfont = new LOGFONT;
 memcpy (ptrlogfont, &(ptrdlg->m_lf), sizeof (LOGFONT));
```

So either way I have a LOGFONT to be utilized for printing. Now look over Chart 15.1. In **OnPreparePrinting** the number of pages and potential page range values

Chart 15.1 The Flow of Control During the Printing Process

File Print is chosen by user:

OnPreparePrinting—No printer DC as yet

    Set the Print dialog box values, such as the number of pages.

    Base Class -> displays Print dialog box and gets the user's choices such as Landscape.

    Here user's choices are available.

OnBeginPrinting

    Save screen values for later restoration.

    Set up printing values, such as beginning page number, current line.

    Construct the printer font to be used.

For each page to be printed:

OnPrepareDC

    Base Class -> construct the DC.

    Install the font.

    Get character dimensions.

    Set window and viewport extents and the mapping mode.

    Determine if there are any more pages to be printed.

OnPrint—only called if there is another page to be printed

    Adjust main print rectangle, if desired, to allow for headings, footers, and margins.

    Print headings, footers, and page numbers, as required.

    Could install a clipping rectangle to force **OnDraw** to stay within margins.

    Base Class -> calls **OnDraw**.

OnDraw

    Paints one page

    If margins are desired, use the main print rectangle to assist **TextOut** positions.

OnEndPrinting

    Restore screen settings and delete printer font.

may be transferred into the Print dialog box. The problem, of course, is that there is no printer DC as yet upon which to base page calculations. The expedient solution is to ignore the settings or install only All Pages as the user-selectable options. If you wish a more complete handling, you must manually acquire the printer DC similar to the coding in **OnFonts**. Then, for an accurate page count, you could perform a dummy run fake-printing all pages, handling line wrap. Then, with the accurate page count and therefore page number range, set the dialog values. The base class invocation actually invokes the Print dialog. When the base class returns, the user selections are available, if needed.

In **OnBeginPrinting**, I save the screen values, such as the current record number and the current top line index. Then the printer font is constructed. Notice there is no base class invocation required here; it does nothing. Next the framework begins the printing process by repetitive calls to **OnPrepareDC** followed by **OnPrint**. Notice that **OnPrint** is called only *if* **OnPrepareDC** determines that there is another page to be printed.

The framework saves the printer DC context, then calls **OnPrepareDC** and **OnPrint**, and then restores the DC. Thus, whatever alterations are made to the printer DC in **OnPrepareDC** remain in effect through the **OnPrint** process. The changes made always include installing the printer font and setting the average character dimensions. However, there are two different methods you may use for printing that handle proper scaling of the font. Option 1 involves setting the mapping mode to MM_ANISOTROPIC and then setting the window and viewport extents to the size of the screen and the size of the printer page, respectively. Here the mapping mode handles all scaling effects. Using this method, every time **OnPrepareDC** is called for printing, the mode and extents must be reset. Option 2 involves manually scaling the LOGFONT's height and width before the font is actually created and installed. Once multiplied by the scaling factor (often a factor of around 4 or 5) and created, the font only needs to be selected into the printer DC. No changes to the mapping mode or extents are done. Option 2 is perhaps a little faster in execution if text only is printed on a large number of pages. Option 1 also permits the occasional graphic bitmap or drawing to be correctly scaled as well.

How are we going to determine in **OnPrepareDC** whether or not there are more pages to be printed? The member **topline** is used. The total number of SalesData objects in the array is known. When the printing process begins, **topline** is set to 0. The last line of code in **OnPrint** adds the number of lines per page to **topline**. Hence, **OnPrepareDC** can simply check **topline** to determine if there are more pages.

In **OnPrint** one can adjust for margins, headers, and the like. Here headings and footers are printed. If you desire margins, set up a rectangle with the extents allowed for **OnDraw** to use. Although not done here, you could install a clipping rectangle or region so that **OnDraw** could not draw outside the margins. If you desire margins, then you must make **OnDraw** aware of the available area. The passed **CPrintInfo** structure contains just such a member for this communication—**m_rectDraw**. In **OnPaint** adjust the rectangle to account for your margins and headings and footers. Then let **OnDraw** use that information in its **TextOut** function calls.

If you have set up the printing process as shown, then the framework can also use these same routines to support the Print Preview process! With Print Preview, often two pages are shown side by side. However, in this case, I wish to have only one page shown, with the button for page two disabled. In **OnPreparePrinting**, the **CPrintInfo** member **m_bPreview** is TRUE if Print Preview is in effect. You can impact the Preview setup at this point. I set the number of pages to be shown to 1 by using other **CPrintInfo** members: **m_nNumPreviewPages** is set to either 1 or 2 pages, and the function **SetMaxPage** installs the number of pages to be shown in the preview. Notice that the values are set before the base class is invoked.

```
BOOL      AcmeView::OnPreparePrinting (CPrintInfo *ptrinfo) {
  if (ptrinfo->m_bPreview) {
    ptrinfo->m_nNumPreviewPages = 1;
    ptrinfo->SetMaxPage (1);
  }
  return CView::DoPreparePrinting (ptrinfo);
}
```

Now look over the implementation of these printing functions in AcmeView.cpp. **OnBeginPrinting** and **OnEndPrinting** should be self-explanatory at this point. In **SetupPrinterFont** several options are available. Since several changes are going to be made to the DC, rather than saving and restoring each GDI object, I use the **SaveDC/RestoreDC** pair. If there is no user font, I extract the LOGFONT from the default display font (from Courier New). Otherwise, I use the user-selected LOG-FONT. If you are using Option 1, setting the mapping mode and extents, then the screen size and printer size must be calculated; these two values are used to set the window and viewport extents, respectively.

```
int savedc = ptrdc->SaveDC ();
if (!ptrlogfont) {
  ptrdc->SelectObject (ptrfont);
  ptrfont->GetObject (sizeof(LOGFONT), &prlogfont);
}
else prlogfont = *ptrlogfont;

// Begin Option 1 coding - use mode and extents
  CRect clrect (0, 0, GetSystemMetrics (SM_CXSCREEN),
                     GetSystemMetrics (SM_CYSCREEN));
  clsize = clrect.Size ();
  pagesize = CSize (ptrdc->GetDeviceCaps (HORZRES),
                    ptrdc->GetDeviceCaps (VERTRES));

  ptrdc->SetMapMode (MM_ANISOTROPIC);
  ptrdc->SetWindowExt (clsize);
  ptrdc->SetViewportExt (pagesize);
// end Option 1 coding

ptrprfont = new CFont ();
ptrprfont->CreateFontIndirect (&prlogfont);
ptrdc->SelectObject (ptrprfont);
ptrdc->RestoreDC (savedc);
```

If you wish to use Option 2, manually scaling the font size, the basic principle is to multiply the LOGFONT's height and width by a proper scaling factor. Here there are two ways of determining the desired scaling factor. One way is to divide the logical pixels per inch of the screen by the logical pixels per inch of the printer. The other way is to divide the total full-screen number of pixels by the total number of pixels of the printed page. The difference is that the logical pixels per inch on-screen have been adjusted for better visibility and are slightly larger than a true point size. I chose the second method, but you can switch to the other quickly.

```
// begin Option 2 coding
HDC hdc = CreateDC ("DISPLAY",NULL,NULL,NULL);
float xscale = ptrdc->GetDeviceCaps (LOGPIXELSX) /
                (float) GetDeviceCaps(hdc, LOGPIXELSX);
float yscale = ptrdc->GetDeviceCaps (LOGPIXELSY) /
                (float) GetDeviceCaps(hdc, LOGPIXELSY);
CRect clrect (0, 0, GetSystemMetrics (SM_CXSCREEN),
                GetSystemMetrics (SM_CYSCREEN));
CSize clsize = clrect.Size();
pagesize = CSize (ptrdc->GetDeviceCaps (HORZRES),
                ptrdc->GetDeviceCaps (VERTRES));
float xx = pagesize.cx/(float)clsize.cx;
float yy = pagesize.cy/(float)clsize.cy;
DeleteDC (hdc);
// install scaled dimensions
// scale choice 1:
// prlogfont.lfHeight = (long) (prlogfont.lfHeight * yscale);
// prlogfont.lfWidth = (long) (prlogfont.lfWidth * xscale);
// scale choice 2:
prlogfont.lfHeight = (long) (prlogfont.lfHeight * yy);
prlogfont.lfWidth = (long) (prlogfont.lfWidth * xx);
// end Option 2 coding
```

As you look over the coding sequences, the only other one that is not obvious is **OnPrepareDC**. How can this routine determine whether or not the DC is for a printer? The framework passes a NULL **CPrintInfo** pointer when the DC is not for the printer. Thus, when printing the first actions depend upon which option you are using. Always invoke the base class first to get the real printer DC created by the framework. Then make your additions or changes to that DC. If Option 1 is in effect, the mapping mode and extents are set (MM_ANISOTROPIC lets both dimensions be scaled); if Option 2 is used, nothing is coded.

```
CView::OnPrepareDC (ptrdc, ptrinfo);
if (ptrinfo != NULL) {
// Option 1: use mode and extents
ptrdc->SetMapMode (MM_ANISOTROPIC);
ptrdc->SetWindowExt (clsize);
ptrdc->SetViewportExt (pagesize);
// Option 2: no mode and extents, so remove Option 1's three lines
```

Next install the font and determine if printing is to continue. **CPrintInfo**'s **m_bContinuePrinting** member is set to TRUE to continue or FALSE to quit.

```
ptrdc->SelectObject (ptrprfont);
if (topline < num_sales) ptrinfo->m_bContinuePrinting = TRUE;
else ptrinfo->m_bContinuePrinting = FALSE;
```

```
    ptrdc->GetTextMetrics (&tm);
    avg_char_width  = tm.tmAveCharWidth;
    avg_char_height = tm.tmHeight + tm.tmExternalLeading;
    avg_caps_width  = (tm.tmPitchAndFamily & 1 ? 3 : 2) *
                      avg_char_width / 2;
}
```

15.11 THE ACMEPLOT VIEW CLASS

The plot view presents different challenges. Reexamine Figures 15.1 and 15.2 where the short file and the larger file are displayed on-screen. The static splitter window expands the width of the last view to the unused remainder of the frame window's client area so that there is the maximum space available to display a graph. Design criteria must include how the width and uniform spacing between the bars is determined. For this I divide the window width by two times the number of SalesData objects plus 1 so that there can be both left and right margins. However, if there are only a few objects, monster widths would result. If that is the case, I force the bar width to be less than the window's width divided by 20 pixels. To cover all bases you should also decide what to do when there are too many bars for the given space. In this example I ignored that situation. To see the effect, run the application and drag the splitter bar to the left, expanding the columnar view while shrinking the plot view, and watch what happens. What impact does this design have on the implementation? It simplifies **OnDraw**. As long as the current width and height associated with the passed DC are used for the bar scaling, the drawing function does not need to know anything else. Specifically, this means that the mapping mode and window/viewport extents do not need to be used. Instead, the font can be scaled as indicated in Option 2 in AcmeView.

The corresponding year is displayed beneath each bar. As we discussed earlier in this chapter, when the bar's width becomes so narrow that there is not enough room to fit the four-digit year, I display only the last two digits. Should the bars become even smaller, then I attempt to create a smaller font to squeeze the two digits into the space.

Since no user fonts apply to the plot view and since there is no mechanism for user modifications to the data in this view, the class definition becomes much smaller, with most member functions dealing with the printing process. When you run the application, watch the tool bar buttons. When you click in the plot view, the Font, Add, Update, and Delete buttons become grayed. If you then click in the columnar view, these buttons become active once more. Examine the AcmePlot definition file, and notice that it likewise must use the **DECLARE_DYNCREATE** and **IMPLEMENT_DYNCREATE** macros so that the framework can dynamically construct instances of the plot class. The member variables parallel those of the Acme-View class, storing the average character dimensions and the window's height and width with other save areas defined to save these screen values while printing. The usual printer members are present, including the fonts for screen and printer displays and the copied screen's LOGFONT used for scaling during construction of the printer font. The only really new item is the BOOL **pagedone** which I set to TRUE when the graph has printed out.

15.11.1 Listing for File: AcmePlot.h—Pgm15a—Excerpts

```
...
class AcmePlot : public CView {

DECLARE_DYNCREATE(AcmePlot)

protected:

int avg_caps_width;        // average capital letter width
int avg_char_width;        // average character width
int avg_char_height;       // average character height
int old_width;             // save screen char width while printing
int old_height;            // save screen char height while printing
int height;                // window's height
int width;                 // window's width

int print_height;          // printer's display height
int print_width;           // printer's display width
BOOL pagedone;             // TRUE when a page has been printed
LOGFONT  prlogfont;        // printer version of user selected font
CFont *ptrfont;            // main font for screen display
CFont *ptrprfont;          // main font for printing
float savescale;           // font scaling factor for printing

int num_sales;             // number of SalesData objects in document
/****************************************************************************/
/*                                                                          */
/* Class Functions:                                                         */
/*                                                                          */
/****************************************************************************/
public:
            AcmePlot ();     // constructor
            ~AcmePlot ();    // destructor - removes fonts
    AcmeDoc* GetDocument (); // returns the doc associated with this view
        void OnDraw (CDC*);  // the paint function to display or print graph

protected:

        BOOL OnPreparePrinting (CPrintInfo*);        // set Print dlg values
        void OnBeginPrinting (CDC*, CPrintInfo*);    // save display settings
        void OnEndPrinting (CDC*, CPrintInfo*);      // restore settings
        void OnPrepareDC (CDC*, CPrintInfo*);        // get char dims/ctrl print
        void OnPrint (CDC*, CPrintInfo*);            // print the chart
        void OnInitialUpdate ();                     // not really needed here
        void OnUpdate (CView*, LPARAM, CObject*);    // redisplay the data
        void SetupPrinterFont (CDC*, CPrintInfo*);   // make a printer font

afx_msg int  OnCreate (LPCREATESTRUCT);      // construct the display font
afx_msg void OnSize (UINT, int, int);        // set height/width for display
...
```

Much of the implementation of AcmePlot is similar to AcmeView. The constructor sets **pagedone** to FALSE and the pointer to the printer font to NULL, indicating none is yet created. The destructor removes any allocated fonts. AcmePlot responds to only a few messages: the Print and Print View pair along with Create and Size messages. In **OnCreate** the sole display font is created just as it was in AcmeView. **GetDocument** returns a pointer to the actual document so that the sales array can be accessed. **OnInitialUpdate** and **OnUpdate** do not need to be overridden; I did so in order that you might have a more complete framework for your modifications.

Most of the coding lies in the **OnPrepareDC** and **OnDraw** functions. Let's examine the screen display first and then the printing section. **OnPrepareDC** now becomes quite streamlined. Based on whether this is a printer or screen DC, it selects into the passed DC the correct font and acquires the average character dimensions that **OnDraw** is going to require. The real work lies in **OnDraw**. After gaining local access to the document and to the sales array, based upon whether the function is printing or not, the local copy of the height and width (**h** and **w**) are set. This is a crucial action, because if all scaling is done based on the local height and width, the drawing becomes independent of the device characteristics. Once these are set, I draw a black border around the entire graph, framing it nicely on the printed page.

```
void        AcmePlot::OnDraw (CDC *ptrdc) {
  AcmeDoc *ptrdoc = GetDocument ();
  SalesDataArray *ptrarray = &ptrdoc->sales_array;
  SalesData       *ptrdata;
  num_sales = ptrdoc->GetNumSales ();
  BOOL isprinting = ptrdc->IsPrinting();
  char msg[10];
  int  h, w;
  if (isprinting) {
   h = print_height;
   w = print_width;
  }
  else {
   h = height;
   w = width;
  }
  ptrdc->SelectStockObject (WHITE_BRUSH);
  ptrdc->SelectStockObject (BLACK_PEN);
  ptrdc->Rectangle (0, 0, w, h);
  ptrdc->SelectStockObject (BLACK_BRUSH);
```

Next, if there are no sales data to plot, I print the title and return. If there are data, the range of sales amounts must be determined to construct the vertical scale. Hence, a pass through all SalesData objects is made, storing the largest value.

```
int spacing   = num_sales*2 + 1;
double mx = ((SalesData*) ptrarray->GetAt (0))->sales;
int i = 1;
while (i < num_sales) {
 ptrdata = (SalesData*) ptrarray->GetAt (i);
 if (mx< ptrdata->sales) mx = ptrdata->sales;
 i++;
}
```

Now the scaling factors can be determined. Note that the vertical pixels per sales dollar, **vpels_per_val**, must be a double.

```
double vpels_per_val = (h - 5 - avg_char_height) / mx;
```

From the device height total pixels, I removed one character height for the year display across the bottom, and I removed 5 additional pixels to account for the top/bottom border line, another 2 for a 1-pixel gap between the edge of the bar and the border, plus a 1-pixel gap above the year display. Similarly, the horizontal uniform spacing allowing for both a left and right margin is given by

```
int    hpels_per_val = (w - 4) / spacing;
if (hpels_per_val > w/20) hpels_per_val = w/20;
```

The "4" accounts for the left/right border and a 1-pixel gap. Again, I avoided monster-width bars. You could at this point check for a 0 width and force it to at least a 1-pixel width. Now the actual plotting of the bars can begin. It is convenient to fix the bottom coordinates—they do not vary from bar to bar—and calculate the height based on the current sales amount. Since the y-axis is positive downward, it looks as if I am plotting backwards.

```
int x, y, yobj;
x = hpels_per_val + 2;
y = h - 3 - avg_char_height;
for (i=0; i<num_sales; i++) {
  ptrdata = (SalesData*) ptrarray->GetAt (i);
  yobj = y - (int)( vpels_per_val * ptrdata->sales);
  ptrdc->Rectangle (x, yobj, x+hpels_per_val, y);
  x += 2*hpels_per_val;
}
```

Notice how easy it is to draw the bars once the scaling details are calculated.

Next the title is printed across the top. You could avoid having a title print through the top of a tall sales bar by subtracting another average character height when determining the vertical pixels per dollar.

Now for the tricky part—displaying the years beneath the bars—an action that can be complicated by narrow bars. The new x,y position for the start of the year display is calculated, once more allowing for the single-line border and a 1-pixel gap on all sides. The display action uses two local variables to help sort out the exact situation. If only the last two digits of the year are to be displayed, the BOOL **which** is set to TRUE. Then, if the bars are still too narrow, a tiny font is constructed and selected into the DC. The old font is saved in **ptrold**.

```
x = hpels_per_val + 2;
y = h - avg_char_height -1;
CFont *ptrold = NULL;
BOOL which = FALSE;
if (avg_char_width*4 > hpels_per_val) {
  if (avg_char_width*2 > hpels_per_val) {
    CFont smallfont;
    if (isprinting) smallfont.CreateFont ((int)(-8*savescale), 0, 0,
            0, FW_NORMAL, FALSE, FALSE, FALSE,
```

```
                      ANSI_CHARSET, OUT_TT_PRECIS, CLIP_TT_ALWAYS,
                      DEFAULT_QUALITY, DEFAULT_PITCH, "Courier New");
      else smallfont.CreateFont (8, 0, 0, 0, FW_NORMAL,
                      FALSE, FALSE, FALSE,
                      ANSI_CHARSET, OUT_TT_PRECIS, CLIP_TT_ALWAYS,
                      DEFAULT_QUALITY, DEFAULT_PITCH, "Courier New");
      ptrold = ptrdc->SelectObject (&smallfont);
      which = TRUE;
      }
      else which = TRUE;
```

If the average character width times the four digits exceeds the bar width
(**hpels_per_value**), **which** is set to TRUE. Additionally, if the character width times
two digits exceeds the bar width, make a smaller font. At this point, one must know
whether it is a printer font or screen font that must be made, because the printer font
must be scaled properly. I arbitrarily chose a smaller font of height 8. As the new font
is selected into the DC, the old font is saved in **ptrold** so that it can be reinstalled and
the small font deleted. Remember: do not delete GDI objects that are selected into an
active DC. At last, iterate through the SalesData object's years and display them
underneath the bars. What happens if the bar width is still too small for the small
font? Overprinting of the year digits occurs.

```
      for (i=0; i<num_sales; i++) {
       ptrdata = (SalesData*) ptrarray->GetAt (i);
       wsprintf (msg, "%d", ptrdata->year);
       if (which) ptrdc->TextOut (x, y, &msg[2]);
       else ptrdc->TextOut (x, y, msg);
       x += 2*hpels_per_val;
      }
      if (ptrold) ptrdc->SelectObject (ptrold);
      }
```

The printing process is much simpler in AcmePlot than in AcmeView primarily
because the printing requirements are stripped down to the basics. A few values must
be saved and restored; the font is created and destroyed as it was in AcmeView.
OnPrint merely has to get the printed page dimensions and invoke the base class's
OnPrint, which in turn invokes **OnDraw** to perform the work. Upon its return,
OnPrint sets **pagedone** to TRUE since there is only one page. Follow through with
the printing sequence. Notice that it is the same sequence used should Print Preview
be selected.

15.11.2 Listing for File: AcmePlot.cpp—Pgm15a—Excerpts

```
IMPLEMENT_DYNCREATE(AcmePlot, CView)

/************************************************************************/
/*                                                                      */
/* AcmePlot Events Response Table                                       */
/*                                                                      */
/************************************************************************/

BEGIN_MESSAGE_MAP(AcmePlot, CView)
```

```
 ON_WM_SIZE ()
 ON_WM_CREATE ()
 ON_COMMAND(ID_FILE_PRINT,         CView::OnFilePrint)
 ON_COMMAND(ID_FILE_PRINT_PREVIEW, CView::OnFilePrintPreview)
END_MESSAGE_MAP()
/*************************************************************************/
/*                                                                     */
/* AcmePlot: Construct the view object                                 */
/*                                                                     */
/*************************************************************************/

        AcmePlot::AcmePlot () {

 pagedone  = FALSE;
 ptrprfont = NULL;
}

/*************************************************************************/
/*                                                                     */
/* OnCreate: build the window and construct initial display font       */
/*                                                                     */
/*************************************************************************/

int     AcmePlot::OnCreate (LPCREATESTRUCT lpCS) {

 int retcd = CView::OnCreate (lpCS); // construct the window

 // make a fixed font for display
 ptrfont = new CFont ();
 ptrfont->CreateFont (14, 0, 0, 0, FW_NORMAL, FALSE, FALSE, FALSE,
                      ANSI_CHARSET, OUT_TT_PRECIS, CLIP_TT_ALWAYS,
                      DEFAULT_QUALITY, DEFAULT_PITCH, "Courier New");
 return retcd;
}

/*************************************************************************/
/*                                                                     */
/* ~AcmePlot: remove all fonts that were used                          */
/*                                                                     */
/*************************************************************************/

        AcmePlot::~AcmePlot () {

 delete ptrfont;
}

/*************************************************************************/
/*                                                                     */
/* GetDocument: retrieve a pointer to the main document                */
/*                                                                     */
/*************************************************************************/

AcmeDoc* AcmePlot::GetDocument () {

 return (AcmeDoc*) m_pDocument;
}

/*************************************************************************/
/*                                                                     */
```

```
/* OnInitialUpdate: does not really need to be overridden in this case    */
/*                                                                         */
/**************************************************************************/

void      AcmePlot::OnInitialUpdate () {

 CView::OnInitialUpdate ();
}
/**************************************************************************/
/*                                                                         */
/* OnUpdate: redisplay graph - not really needed to be overridden          */
/*                                                                         */
/**************************************************************************/

void      AcmePlot::OnUpdate (CView *a, LPARAM b, CObject *c) {

 CView::OnUpdate (a, b, c);
}
/**************************************************************************/
/*                                                                         */
/* OnPrepareDC: insert the fixed font and get char dims                    */
/*                                                                         */
/**************************************************************************/

void      AcmePlot::OnPrepareDC (CDC *ptrdc, CPrintInfo *ptrinfo) {

 CView::OnPrepareDC (ptrdc, ptrinfo); // invoke base class first
 TEXTMETRIC  tm;

 // separate printing from display cases
 if (ptrinfo != NULL) {               // here we are printing
  ptrdc->SelectObject (ptrprfont); // install printing font
  // set the continue printing flag
  if (!pagedone) ptrinfo->m_bContinuePrinting = TRUE;
  else ptrinfo->m_bContinuePrinting = FALSE;
 }
 else ptrdc->SelectObject (ptrfont); // install fixed font for screen display

 // and get the text dimensions for this case
 ptrdc->GetTextMetrics (&tm);
 avg_char_width  = tm.tmAveCharWidth;
 avg_char_height = tm.tmHeight + tm.tmExternalLeading;
 avg_caps_width  = (tm.tmPitchAndFamily & 1 ? 3 : 2) * avg_char_width / 2;
}
/**************************************************************************/
/*                                                                         */
/* OnDraw: display the document as a bar chart                             */
/*                                                                         */
/**************************************************************************/

void      AcmePlot::OnDraw (CDC *ptrdc) {

 AcmeDoc *ptrdoc = GetDocument ();                    // get access to the document
 SalesDataArray *ptrarray = &ptrdoc->sales_array;// get access to the array
 SalesData       *ptrdata;
 num_sales = ptrdoc->GetNumSales ();                 // get the number in the array
 BOOL isprinting = ptrdc->IsPrinting();              // get printing flag
```

```
char msg[10];
int  h, w;

// set the height and width based upon screen or printing size
if (isprinting) {
 h = print_height;
 w = print_width;
}
else {
 h = height;
 w = width;
}

// draw an outline around the graph
ptrdc->SelectStockObject (WHITE_BRUSH);
ptrdc->SelectStockObject (BLACK_PEN);
ptrdc->Rectangle (0, 0, w, h);

ptrdc->SelectStockObject (BLACK_BRUSH); // install the display pen color

// handle the null case by just printing a title and leaving
if (num_sales == 0) {
 CString s;
 s.LoadString (IDS_ACMETITLE);
 ptrdc->TextOut (1, 1, s);
 return;
}

// calculate uniform spacing between bars - left and right margins included
int spacing  = num_sales*2 + 1; // number of equi-distant bars and gaps

// calculate the maximum range of sales values to plot
double mx = ((SalesData*) ptrarray->GetAt (0))->sales; // set first value
int i = 1;
while (i < num_sales) {                     // for all sales objects
 ptrdata = (SalesData*) ptrarray->GetAt (i);  // get access to object in array
 if (mx< ptrdata->sales) mx = ptrdata->sales; // replace if it's bigger
 i++;
}

// calc plot parameters: vertical and horizontal number pixels per unit
// leaving margins at the top and bottom
double vpels_per_val = (h - 5 - avg_char_height) / mx;
int    hpels_per_val = (w - 4) / spacing;
// for few bars, avoid monster bar widths
if (hpels_per_val > w/20) hpels_per_val = w/20;

// set up the plotting coordinates
int x, y, yobj;
x = hpels_per_val + 2;        // set initial x position of first value
y = h - 3 - avg_char_height; // set bottom y position of all values

// now plot all sales bars
for (i=0; i<num_sales; i++) {
 ptrdata = (SalesData*) ptrarray->GetAt (i);            // get access to SalesData
 yobj = y - (int)( vpels_per_val * ptrdata->sales); // get top y position
 ptrdc->Rectangle (x, yobj, x+hpels_per_val, y);   // plot this value
 x += 2*hpels_per_val;                              // set x for next value
```

```
          }

          // print title
          CString s;
          s.LoadString (IDS_ACMETITLE);
          ptrdc->TextOut (1, 1, s);

          // print captions
          x = hpels_per_val + 2;          // set x for first caption
          y = h - avg_char_height -1;     // set y for all captions

          // if bars are tiny, use last two digits of the year
          // if that is still too big, try a smaller font size
          CFont *ptrold = NULL;           // non-NULL when using smaller font
          BOOL which = FALSE;             // TRUE when using only 2 digits

          if (avg_char_width*4 > hpels_per_val) {  // is there room for whole year?
           if (avg_char_width*2 > hpels_per_val) { // is there room for 2 digits?
            CFont smallfont;
            // construct a smaller font based upon display or printer dimensions
            if (isprinting) smallfont.CreateFont ((int)(-8*savescale), 0, 0, 0, FW_NORMAL,
                          FALSE, FALSE, FALSE,
                          ANSI_CHARSET, OUT_TT_PRECIS, CLIP_TT_ALWAYS,
                          DEFAULT_QUALITY, DEFAULT_PITCH, "Courier New");
            else smallfont.CreateFont (8, 0, 0, 0, FW_NORMAL,
                          FALSE, FALSE, FALSE,
                          ANSI_CHARSET, OUT_TT_PRECIS, CLIP_TT_ALWAYS,
                          DEFAULT_QUALITY, DEFAULT_PITCH, "Courier New");
            ptrold = ptrdc->SelectObject (&smallfont);
            which = TRUE;       // set using 2 digits only
           }
           else which = TRUE; // set using 2 digits only
          }

          // now display the year values
          for (i=0; i<num_sales; i++) {                    // for each year
           ptrdata = (SalesData*) ptrarray->GetAt (i); // get access to the SalesData
           wsprintf (msg, "%d", ptrdata->year);          // convert to caption string
           if (which) ptrdc->TextOut (x, y, &msg[2]);    // display caption 2 digits only
           else ptrdc->TextOut (x, y, msg);              // display full year caption
           x += 2*hpels_per_val;                          // advance x for next caption
          }
          if (ptrold) ptrdc->SelectObject (ptrold);      // remove any small font
      }

/********************************************************************************/
/*                                                                              */
/* OnPreparePrinting: prepare doc for printing                                  */
/*                                                                              */
/********************************************************************************/

BOOL        AcmePlot::OnPreparePrinting (CPrintInfo *ptrinfo) {

 if (ptrinfo->m_bPreview) {
  ptrinfo->m_nNumPreviewPages = 1;  // set only one page to print
  ptrinfo->SetMaxPage (1);
 }
```

```
    return CView::DoPreparePrinting (ptrinfo);
}
/**************************************************************************/
/*                                                                      */
/* OnBeginPrinting: start of printing process                           */
/*                                                                      */
/**************************************************************************/
void       AcmePlot::OnBeginPrinting (CDC *ptrdc, CPrintInfo *ptrinfo) {
 old_width  = avg_char_width;          // save the screen char values
 old_height = avg_char_height;
 pagedone   = FALSE;                   // set not yet printed
 SetupPrinterFont (ptrdc, ptrinfo);   // construct a printer font
}
/**************************************************************************/
/*                                                                      */
/* OnEndPrinting: ending printing cycles                                */
/*                                                                      */
/**************************************************************************/
void       AcmePlot::OnEndPrinting (CDC* /*ptrdc*/, CPrintInfo* /*ptrinfo*/) {
 avg_char_width  = old_width;          // restore character dimensions
 avg_char_height = old_height;
 delete ptrprfont;                     // remove the printer font
}
/**************************************************************************/
/*                                                                      */
/* SetupPrinterFont: setup the printer font scaled to the printer       */
/*                                                                      */
/**************************************************************************/
void       AcmePlot::SetupPrinterFont (CDC *ptrdc, CPrintInfo* /*ptrinfo*/) {
 int savedc = ptrdc->SaveDC ();  // save the DC

 ptrdc->SelectObject (ptrfont);  // install the default font
 // retrieve the LOGFONT object for the fixed font in use
 ptrfont->GetObject (sizeof(LOGFONT), &prlogfont);

 HDC hdc = CreateDC ("DISPLAY",NULL,NULL,NULL); // get a screen DC for scaling
 // calculate both x and y scale dimensions between the screen and the printer
 // option 1 - based on the logical pixels per inch
 float xscale = ptrdc->GetDeviceCaps (LOGPIXELSX) /
               (float) GetDeviceCaps(hdc, LOGPIXELSX);
 float yscale = ptrdc->GetDeviceCaps (LOGPIXELSY) /
               (float) GetDeviceCaps(hdc, LOGPIXELSY);

 // option 2 - based upon the device max dimensions
 CRect clrect (0,0, GetSystemMetrics(SM_CXSCREEN),
                    GetSystemMetrics(SM_CYSCREEN));
 CSize clsize = clrect.Size();
 CSize pagesize = CSize (ptrdc->GetDeviceCaps (HORZRES),
                         ptrdc->GetDeviceCaps (VERTRES));
 float xx = pagesize.cx/(float)clsize.cx;
```

```
float yy = pagesize.cy/(float)clsize.cy;
DeleteDC (hdc);

// install scaled dimensions
// Option 1:
// prlogfont.lfHeight = (long) (prlogfont.lfHeight * yscale);
// prlogfont.lfWidth = (long) (prlogfont.lfWidth * xscale);
// Option 2:
prlogfont.lfHeight = (long) (prlogfont.lfHeight * yy);
prlogfont.lfWidth = (long) (prlogfont.lfWidth * xx);

savescale = yy; // save for later use, if needed

// install scaled dimensions
ptrprfont = new CFont ();
ptrprfont->CreateFontIndirect (&prlogfont);  // create the font from LOGFONT
ptrdc->RestoreDC (savedc);
}
/*****************************************************************************/
/*                                                                         */
/* OnPrint: control printing the page                                      */
/*                                                                         */
/*****************************************************************************/

void      AcmePlot::OnPrint (CDC *ptrdc, CPrintInfo *ptrinfo) {

// set the printed page dimensions
print_height = ptrinfo->m_rectDraw.bottom;
print_width  = ptrinfo->m_rectDraw.right;

CView::OnPrint (ptrdc, ptrinfo);  // print the chart
pagedone = TRUE;                  // signal no more pages
}

/*****************************************************************************/
/*                                                                         */
/* OnSize: gets window dimensions                                          */
/*                                                                         */
/*****************************************************************************/

void      AcmePlot::OnSize (UINT a, int b, int c) {

CView::OnSize    (a, b, c);
CRect rect;
GetClientRect (&rect);        // get the size of the client window
height = rect.Height();       // calc and save current height
width  = rect.Width();        // calc and save current width
Invalidate();                 // force repainting of window
}
```

15.12 USING THE DOCUMENT-VIEW IN THE MULTIPLE DOCUMENT INTERFACE: PGM15b

The last step is to wrap the MDI around the Document-View architecture so that multiple documents can be viewed simultaneously. In Figure 15.4 I have launched Pgm15b, opened the larger file, and tiled the two MDI child splitter windows. The user

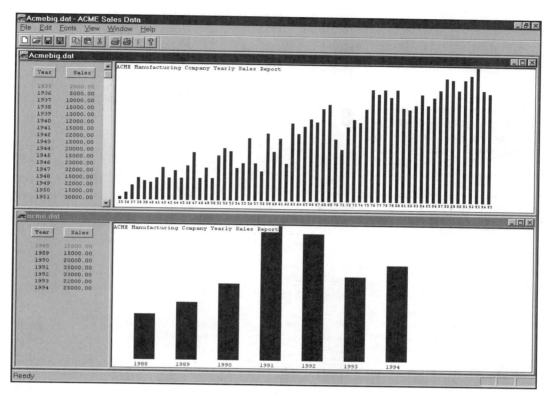

Fig. 15.4 Pgm15b—the MDI Version with Two Child Views

can easily compare documents in this manner. You may be pleased to know that no changes are required to any of the Document-View files from Pgm15a to port them into MDI in Pgm15b!

All changes from SDI to MDI lie at the application and frame window level. The Pgm15bApp class changes occur in the **InitInstance** function which now launches a MDI frame with MDI documents. Specifically, the document templates are now instances of the **CMultiDocTemplate** class; one set is allocated for each view class on the document and then added as before. Then a MDI frame window is allocated and launched. The other **CWinApp** function calls are the same as in the SDI example.

15.12.1 Listing for File: Pgm15bApp.cpp—Pgm15b—Excerpts

```
...
BOOL   Pgm15BApp::InitInstance () {

  // set up both view templates
  CMultiDocTemplate *ptrdoctemplate1;
  ptrdoctemplate1 = new CMultiDocTemplate(IDR_MAINFRAME,
                                  RUNTIME_CLASS (AcmeDoc),
```

```
                                        RUNTIME_CLASS (ChildWin),
                                        RUNTIME_CLASS (AcmeView));
CMultiDocTemplate *ptrdoctemplate2;
ptrdoctemplate2 = new CMultiDocTemplate(IDR_MAINFRAME,
                                        RUNTIME_CLASS (AcmeDoc),
                                        RUNTIME_CLASS (ChildWin),
                                        RUNTIME_CLASS (AcmePlot));
// install both view templates
AddDocTemplate (ptrdoctemplate1);
AddDocTemplate (ptrdoctemplate2);
EnableShellOpen ();              // enable DDE Execute open
RegisterShellFileTypes ();       // register .DAT types for DDE open
LoadStdProfileSettings ();       // activates Most Recent File menu

// create main MDI Frame window
FrameWin* ptrframe = new FrameWin ();
if (!ptrframe->LoadFrame (IDR_MAINFRAME)) return FALSE;
m_pMainWnd = ptrframe;
m_pMainWnd->DragAcceptFiles (); // enable drag and drop open

// The main window has been initialized, so show and update it.
ptrframe->ShowWindow (SW_SHOWMAXIMIZED);
ptrframe->UpdateWindow ();

// create a new (empty) document
if (m_lpCmdLine[0] != 0) OpenDocumentFile (m_lpCmdLine);
else OpenDocumentFile ("\\learnwin\\vc\\pgm15b\\acme.dat");
// or use:  OnFileNew();

return TRUE;
}
```

The frame window is derived from **CMDIFrameWnd**. Its basic function is to construct and maintain the tool and status bars. All splitter window coding has been moved from the frame down to the MDI child windows.

15.12.2 Listing for File: FrameWin.h—Pgm15b—Excerpts

```
...
class FrameWin : public CMDIFrameWnd {

DECLARE_DYNCREATE (FrameWin)
...
protected:

CToolBar      toolbar;   // the control bar
CStatusBar    statusbar; // the status bar
...
public:
              FrameWin () {}    // constructor

virtual BOOL  PreCreateWindow(CREATESTRUCT&); // set wndclass style bits

protected:

afx_msg int   OnCreate(LPCREATESTRUCT); // construct toolbar and statusbar
...
```

15.12.3 Listing for File: FrameWin.cpp—Pgm15b—Excerpts

```
...
IMPLEMENT_DYNCREATE(FrameWin, CMDIFrameWnd)
// control bar buttons - IDs are command buttons
static UINT BASED_CODE buttons[] =
{
  // same order as in the bitmap 'toolbar.bmp'
  ID_FILE_NEW,
  ...
  ID_APP_ABOUT,
};
...
/****************************************************************************/
/*                                                                        */
/* PreCreateWindow: install window style flags                            */
/*                                                                        */
/****************************************************************************/
BOOL      FrameWin::PreCreateWindow(CREATESTRUCT& cs) {
 cs.style = WS_OVERLAPPED | WS_CAPTION | FWS_ADDTOTITLE
  | WS_THICKFRAME | WS_SYSMENU | WS_MINIMIZEBOX | WS_MAXIMIZEBOX | WS_MAXIMIZE;
 return CMDIFrameWnd::PreCreateWindow(cs);
}
```

The coding to create the splitter windows is moved into the **OnCreate** of the ChildWin MDI child class.

15.12.4 Listing for File: ChildWin.h—Pgm15b—Excerpts

```
...
class ChildWin : public CMDIChildWnd {

DECLARE_DYNCREATE (ChildWin)
...
protected:

CSplitterWnd splitterwin; // our splitter window
...
public:
            ChildWin () {}   // constructor
virtual BOOL  PreCreateWindow(CREATESTRUCT&); // install wndclass style bits
virtual BOOL  OnCreateClient(LPCREATESTRUCT, CCreateContext*); // make splitwnd
...
```

15.12.5 Listing for File: ChildWin.cpp—Pgm15b—Excerpts

```
...
IMPLEMENT_DYNCREATE(ChildWin, CMDIChildWnd)
...
/****************************************************************************/
/*                                                                        */
```

```
/* OnCreateClient: construct client window                                   */
/*                                                                           */
/***************************************************************************/

BOOL      ChildWin::OnCreateClient (LPCREATESTRUCT, CCreateContext* ptrc) {

  // construct the splitter window itself asking for two side by side views
  BOOL retcd = splitterwin.CreateStatic (this, 1, 2);

  // set AcmeView as left window - use width of 180 pixels - let user adjust
  retcd |= splitterwin.CreateView (0, 0, RUNTIME_CLASS (AcmeView),
                                   CSize (180, 100), ptrc);
  retcd |= splitterwin.CreateView (0, 1, RUNTIME_CLASS (AcmePlot),
                                   CSize (100, 100), ptrc);
  return retcd;
}

/***************************************************************************/
/*                                                                         */
/* PreCreateWindow: set the window style bits                              */
/*                                                                         */
/***************************************************************************/

BOOL      ChildWin::PreCreateWindow (CREATESTRUCT& cs) {

  cs.style = WS_CHILD | WS_VISIBLE | WS_OVERLAPPED | WS_CAPTION | WS_SYSMENU
           | FWS_ADDTOTITLE | WS_THICKFRAME | WS_MINIMIZEBOX | WS_MAXIMIZEBOX
           | WS_MAXIMIZE;

  return CMDIChildWnd::PreCreateWindow(cs);
}
```

The resource file has an added pop-up Windows menu for child window operations. Note the framework-defined IDs.

15.12.6 Listing for File: Pgm15b.rc—Pgm15b—Excerpts

```
...
IDR_MAINFRAME    ICON    DISCARDABLE      "pgm15b.ico"
IDR_ACMETYPE     ICON    DISCARDABLE      "acmedoc.ico"
IDR_MDITYPE      ICON    DISCARDABLE      "mdidoc.ico"
IDR_MAINFRAME    BITMAP  MOVEABLE         "toolbar.bmp"

IDR_MAINFRAME MENU PRELOAD DISCARDABLE
BEGIN
...
  POPUP "&Window"
  BEGIN
    MENUITEM "&New Window",             ID_WINDOW_NEW
    MENUITEM "&Cascade",                ID_WINDOW_CASCADE
    MENUITEM "&Tile",                   ID_WINDOW_TILE_HORZ
    MENUITEM "&Arrange Icons",          ID_WINDOW_ARRANGE
    MENUITEM "S&plit",                  ID_WINDOW_SPLIT
  END
...
  ID_WINDOW_NEW          "Open another window for the active document\nNew Window"
```

```
ID_WINDOW_ARRANGE        "Arrange icons at the bottom of the window\nArrange Icons"
ID_WINDOW_CASCADE        "Arrange windows so they overlap\nCascade Windows"
ID_WINDOW_TILE_HORZ      "Arrange windows as non-overlapping tiles\nTile Windows"
ID_WINDOW_TILE_VERT      "Arrange windows as non-overlapping tiles\nTile Windows"
ID_WINDOW_SPLIT          "Split the active window into panes\nSplit"
ID_VIEW_TOOLBAR          "Show or hide the control bar\nToggle Control Bar"
ID_VIEW_STATUS_BAR       "Show or hide the status bar\nToggle Status Bar"
...
```

15.13 YOUR NEXT STEP

At this point, you should experiment with the App Wizard, generating basic shells and investigating the resultant code. Then try out the Class Wizard to add additional functionality.

Bibliography

This is a short review of other available Windows 3.1, Windows 95, and C++ books that you might find useful, depending upon your needs and pocketbook. If your C++ is weak or shaky, you will find that some provide an excellent review. Some cover earlier releases of Visual C++ as well as Windows 3.1.

C-Style

Heller, M., *Advanced Windows Programming*, New York: John Wiley & Sons, 1992. *C-style coverage of graphics format, DIBs, DDE, and OLE.* ISBN 0-471-55172-4

Petzold, C., *Programming Windows 3.1*, Redmond, WA: Microsoft Press, 1992. *This is* the C-style interface book for Windows 3.1—a must have. ISBN 1-55615-395-3

Petzold, C., and P. Yao, *Programming Windows 95*, Redmond, WA: Microsoft Press, 1996. *This is* the C-style interface book for Windows 95. Updated from 3.1, this too is a must have! ISBN 1-55615-676-6

Visual C++

Ezzell, B., *Visual C++*, Chicago: WROX Press, 1994. *Beginning Windows programming using Visual C++ and the App Wizard.* ISBN 1-874416-22-2

Gurewich, O., and N. Gurewich, *Master Visual C++ 1.5*, Indianapolis, IN: Sams, 1994. *Extensive coverage of all MFC topics, including multimedia; all coding is done using the App Wizard.* ISBN 0-672-30468-6

Hipson, P., *What Every Visual C++ 2 Programmer Should Know*, Indianapolis, IN: Sams, 1994. *Newer features discussed plus extensive coverage of both OLE and ODBC.* ISBN 0-672-30493-7

Holzner, S., *Microsoft Foundation Class Library Programming*, New York: Brady, 1993. *Broad coverage of the MFC using the App Wizard.* ISBN 1-56686-102-0

Kruglinski, D., *Inside Visual C++ 4*, Redmond, WA: Microsoft Press, 1996. *Wide coverage of the MFC; all coding is done using the App Wizard.* ISBN 1-55615-661-8

Perry, P., et al., *Using Visual C++ 2 Special Edition*, Indianapolis, IN: Que, 1994. *New features plus broad coverage of OLE 2, exception handling, and ODBC.* ISBN 1-56529-810-1

Shammas, N., *Using Visual C++*, Indianapolis, IN: Que, 1994. *Extensive coverage of dialogs and controls.*

Create Your Own Class Library

Porter, A., *C++ Programming for Windows*, Berkeley, CA: Osborne/McGraw-Hill, 1993. *Shows how to create your own classes and gives on disk a small, easy-to-use class library.* ISBN 0-07-881881-8

Advanced Topics

Aitken, P., and S. Jarol, *Visual C++ Multimedia*, Scottsdale, AZ: Coriolis, 1995. *Extensive Visual C++ App Wizard examination of multimedia topics including sound and animation.* ISBN 1-883577-19-5

Brockschmidt, K., *Inside OLE 2*, Redmond, WA: Microsoft Press, 1994. *Extensive coverage of the new OLE 2 specification, uses Visual C++.* ISBN 1-55615-618-9

Clark, J., *Windows Programmer's Guide To OLE/DDE*, Indianapolis, IN: Sams, 1992. *Covers OLE 1, not the latest OLE 2.* ISBN 0-672-30226-3

Gryphon, R., et al., *Special Edition Using ODBC 2*, Indianapolis, IN: Que, 1995. *Comprehensive coverage of ODBC 2 and the MFC.*

Holzner, S., *Heavy Metal OLE 2.0 Programming*, San Mateo, CA: IDG Books, 1994. *Uses MFC to illustrate OLE 2.0; large percentage of the book is code listings.* ISBN 1-56884-301-1

Jennings, R., and P. Hipson, *Database Developer's Guide with Visual C++*, Indianapolis, IN: Sams, 1995. *Covers Visual C++ 2.0 classes for databases.*

Klein, M., *Windows Programmer's Guide to DLLs and Memory Management*, Indianapolis, IN: Sams, 1992. *Covers DLLs and Windows 3.1 memory management.* ISBN 0-672-30236-5

Roetzheim, W. *Uncharted Windows Programming*, Indianapolis, IN: Sams, 1993. *DLL, custom controls, interfacing with Paradox, sound, video, and screen savers.* ISBN 0-672-30299-3

Toohey, J., and E. Toupin. *Building OCXs*, Indianapolis, IN: Que, 1995. *Good coverage of OLE and the MFC classes.*

Williams, A., *OLE 2.0 and DDE Distilled*, Reading, MA: Addison Wesley, 1994. *Good introduction and can use either compiler.* ISBN 0-201-40639-X

Windows 95 and WIN32

Andrews, M., *C++ Windows NT Programming*, New York: M&T Books, 1994. *Covers many advanced topics using MFC and Win32.* ISBN 1-55828-300-5

Blaszczak, M., *WIN32 Programming Using Visual C++*, Chicago: WROX Press, 1995. *Good coverage of OLE, database, and doc-view.* ISBN 1-874416-47-8

Chen, S., *Windows 95: A Programmer's Case Book*, New York: M&T Press, 1995. *A book of coding in the C style covering numerous "how-tos" with little textual discussion.* ISBN 1-55851-411-2

Cilwa, P., and J. Duntemann, *Windows Programming Power with Custom Controls*, Scottsdale, AZ: Coriolis Group, 1994. *How to create Windows 3.1 custom controls that can provide the basic starting point for creating custom controls under Windows 95 in C-style.* ISBN 1-883577-00-4

Cluts, N., *Programming the Windows 95 User Interface*, Redmond, WA: Microsoft Press, 1995. *Broad C-style coverage of the new Windows 95 controls.* ISBN 1-55615-884-x

Heller, M., *Advanced WIN32 Programming*, New York: John Wiley & Sons, 1993. *Short coverage of a wide range of 32-bit topics including sockets, pipes, DDE, security; major emphasis on the GDI.* ISBN 0-471-59245

Ladd, S., *WIN32 API Programmer's Reference*, New York: M&T Press, 1995. *Complete listings of the API functions and parameters.* ISBN 1-55851-427-9

Mischel, J., *The Developer's Guide to WINHELP.EXE*, New York: John Wiley & Sons, 1994. *Guide to creating Windows Help facilities.* ISBN 0-471-30325-9

Richter, J., *Advanced Windows, Developer's Guide to the Win32 API for Windows NT 3.5 and Windows 95*, Redmond, WA: Microsoft Press, 1995. *Excellent coverage of many advanced topics with many key features using C-style.* ISBN 1-55615-677-4

Schildt, H., *Windows 95 Programming in C and C++*, Berkley, CA: Osborne/McGraw-Hill, 1995. *Extensive C-style coverage of the new Windows 95 features.* ISBN 0-07-882081-2

Schulman, A., *Unauthorized Windows 95 Developer's Resource Kit*, San Mateo, CA: IDG, 1994. *Advanced Windows 95 internals topics.* ISBN 1-56884-305-4

Taylor, P., *3D Graphics Programming in Windows*, Reading, MA: Addison-Wesley, 1994. *Extensive coverage of many basics done under Windows 3.1.* ISBN 0-201-60882-0

Thompson, N., *Animation Techniques in Win32*, Redmond, WA: Microsoft Press, 1995. *Covers all the basics of animation using MFC; good introduction.* ISBN 1-55615-669-3

Special C++ Topics

Heller, S., *Efficient C/C++ Programming*, Boston: Academic Press, 1995.

Hughes, C., T. Hamilton, and T. Hughes, *Object-Oriented I/O Using C++ Iostreams*, New York: John Wiley & Sons, 1995. *Extensive coverage of iostreams.* ISBN 0-471-11809-5

Ladd, S., *C++ Templates and Tools*, New York: M&T Books, 1995. *In-depth coverage of templates.* ISBN 1-55851-437-6

Microsoft Press, *The Windows Interface—An Application Design Guide*, Redmond, WA: Microsoft Press, 1992. *An extensive discussion of what and how a Windows program's interface should be designed to stay compatible with the Windows look-and-feel updated to Windows 95.* ISBN 1-55615-439-9

Magazines

Microsoft Systems Journal. Timely topics on all aspects of Windows programming.

PC Techniques. Some Windows topics discussed in each issue; programmer oriented.

Windows/DOS Developer's Guide. Extremely good for hot Windows tips, coding, and sample coding for special effects.

Windows Tech Journal. Many Windows tips, sample coding, timely topics.

LICENSE AGREEMENT AND LIMITED WARRANTY

READ THE FOLLOWING TERMS AND CONDITIONS CAREFULLY BEFORE OPENING THIS DISK PACKAGE. THIS LEGAL DOCUMENT IS AN AGREEMENT BETWEEN YOU AND PRENTICE-HALL, INC. (THE "COMPANY"). BY OPENING THIS SEALED DISK PACKAGE, YOU ARE AGREEING TO BE BOUND BY THESE TERMS AND CONDITIONS. IF YOU DO NOT AGREE WITH THESE TERMS AND CONDITIONS, DO NOT OPEN THE DISK PACKAGE. PROMPTLY RETURN THE UNOPENED DISK PACKAGE AND ALL ACCOMPANYING ITEMS TO THE PLACE YOU OBTAINED THEM FOR A FULL REFUND OF ANY SUMS YOU HAVE PAID.

1. **GRANT OF LICENSE:** In consideration of your payment of the license fee, which is part of the price you paid for this product, and your agreement to abide by the terms and conditions of this Agreement, the Company grants to you a nonexclusive right to use and display the copy of the enclosed software program (hereinafter the "SOFTWARE") on a single computer (i.e., with a single CPU) at a single location so long as you comply with the terms of this Agreement. The Company reserves all rights not expressly granted to you under this Agreement.

2. **OWNERSHIP OF SOFTWARE:** You own only the magnetic or physical media (the enclosed disks) on which the SOFTWARE is recorded or fixed, but the Company retains all the rights, title, and ownership to the SOFTWARE recorded on the original disk copy(ies) and all subsequent copies of the SOFTWARE, regardless of the form or media on which the original or other copies may exist. This license is not a sale of the original SOFTWARE or any copy to you.

3. **COPY RESTRICTIONS:** This SOFTWARE and the accompanying printed materials and user manual (the "Documentation") are the subject of copyright. You may not copy the Documentation or the SOFT-WARE, except that you may make a single copy of the SOFTWARE for backup or archival purposes only. You may be held legally responsible for any copying or copyright infringement which is caused or encouraged by your failure to abide by the terms of this restriction.

4. **USE RESTRICTIONS:** You may not network the SOFTWARE or otherwise use it on more than one computer or computer terminal at the same time. You may physically transfer the SOFTWARE from one computer to another provided that the SOFTWARE is used on only one computer at a time. You may not distribute copies of the SOFTWARE or Documentation to others. You may not reverse engineer, disassemble, decompile, modify, adapt, translate, or create derivative works based on the SOFTWARE or the Documentation without the prior written consent of the Company.

5. **TRANSFER RESTRICTIONS:** The enclosed SOFTWARE is licensed only to you and may not be transferred to any one else without the prior written consent of the Company. Any unauthorized transfer of the SOFTWARE shall result in the immediate termination of this Agreement.

6. **TERMINATION:** This license is effective until terminated. This license will terminate automatically without notice from the Company and become null and void if you fail to comply with any provisions or limitations of this license. Upon termination, you shall destroy the Documentation and all copies of the SOFT-WARE. All provisions of this Agreement as to warranties, limitation of liability, remedies or damages, and our ownership rights shall survive termination.

7. **MISCELLANEOUS:** This Agreement shall be construed in accordance with the laws of the United States of America and the State of New York and shall benefit the Company, its affiliates, and assignees.

8. **LIMITED WARRANTY AND DISCLAIMER OF WARRANTY:** The Company warrants that the SOFTWARE, when properly used in accordance with the Documentation, will operate in substantial conformity with the description of the SOFTWARE set forth in the Documentation. The Company does not warrant that the SOFTWARE will meet your requirements or that the operation of the SOFTWARE will be uninterrupted or error-free. The Company warrants that the media on which the SOFTWARE is delivered shall be free from defects in materials and workmanship under normal use for a period of thirty (30) days from the date of your purchase. Your only remedy and the Company's only obligation under these limited warranties is, at the Company's option, return of the warranted item for a refund of any amounts paid by you or replacement of the item. Any replacement of SOFTWARE or media under the warranties shall not extend the original warranty period. The limited warranty set forth above shall not apply to any SOFTWARE which the Company determines in good faith has been subject to misuse, neglect, improper installation, repair, alteration, or damage by you. EXCEPT FOR THE EXPRESSED WARRANTIES SET FORTH ABOVE, THE COMPANY DISCLAIMS ALL WARRANTIES, EXPRESS OR IMPLIED, INCLUDING WITHOUT LIMITATION, THE IMPLIED WARRANTIES OF MERCHANTABILITY AND FITNESS FOR A PARTICULAR PURPOSE. EXCEPT FOR THE EXPRESS WARRANTY SET FORTH ABOVE, THE COMPANY DOES NOT WARRANT, GUARANTEE, OR MAKE ANY REPRESENTATION REGARDING THE USE OR THE RESULTS OF THE USE OF THE SOFTWARE IN TERMS OF ITS CORRECTNESS, ACCURACY, RELIABILITY, CURRENTNESS, OR OTHERWISE.

IN NO EVENT, SHALL THE COMPANY OR ITS EMPLOYEES, AGENTS, SUPPLIERS, OR CONTRACTORS BE LIABLE FOR ANY INCIDENTAL, INDIRECT, SPECIAL, OR CONSEQUENTIAL DAMAGES ARISING OUT OF OR IN CONNECTION WITH THE LICENSE GRANTED UNDER THIS AGREEMENT, OR FOR LOSS OF USE, LOSS OF DATA, LOSS OF INCOME OR PROFIT, OR OTHER LOSSES, SUSTAINED AS A RESULT OF INJURY TO ANY PERSON, OR LOSS OF OR DAMAGE TO PROPERTY, OR CLAIMS OF THIRD PARTIES, EVEN IF THE COMPANY OR AN AUTHORIZED REPRESENTATIVE OF THE COMPANY HAS BEEN ADVISED OF THE POSSIBILITY OF SUCH DAMAGES. IN NO EVENT SHALL LIABILITY OF THE COMPANY FOR DAMAGES WITH RESPECT TO THE SOFTWARE EXCEED THE AMOUNTS ACTUALLY PAID BY YOU, IF ANY, FOR THE SOFTWARE.

SOME JURISDICTIONS DO NOT ALLOW THE LIMITATION OF IMPLIED WARRANTIES OR LIABILITY FOR INCIDENTAL, INDIRECT, SPECIAL, OR CONSEQUENTIAL DAMAGES, SO THE ABOVE LIMITATIONS MAY NOT ALWAYS APPLY. THE WARRANTIES IN THIS AGREEMENT GIVE YOU SPECIFIC LEGAL RIGHTS AND YOU MAY ALSO HAVE OTHER RIGHTS WHICH VARY IN ACCORDANCE WITH LOCAL LAW.

ACKNOWLEDGMENT

YOU ACKNOWLEDGE THAT YOU HAVE READ THIS AGREEMENT, UNDERSTAND IT, AND AGREE TO BE BOUND BY ITS TERMS AND CONDITIONS. YOU ALSO AGREE THAT THIS AGREEMENT IS THE COMPLETE AND EXCLUSIVE STATEMENT OF THE AGREEMENT BETWEEN YOU AND THE COMPANY AND SUPERSEDES ALL PROPOSALS OR PRIOR AGREEMENTS, ORAL, OR WRITTEN, AND ANY OTHER COMMUNICATIONS BETWEEN YOU AND THE COMPANY OR ANY REPRESENTATIVE OF THE COMPANY RELATING TO THE SUBJECT MATTER OF THIS AGREEMENT.

Should you have any questions concerning this Agreement or if you wish to contact the Company for any reason, please contact in writing at the address below.

Robin Short
Prentice Hall PTR
One Lake Street
Upper Saddle River, New Jersey 07458